# ENCYCLOPEDIA OF
# PLANTING COMBINATIONS

# ENCYCLOPEDIA OF

# PLANTING
# COMBINATIONS

## FIREFLY BOOKS

# A FIREFLY BOOK

Published by Firefly Books Ltd. 2012

Copyright © Octopus Publishing Group Ltd 2008
Text © Tony Lord 2008

All rights reserved. No part of this publication may be reproduced, stored in a retrieval system, or transmitted in any form or by any means, electronic, mechanical, photocopying, recording or otherwise, without the prior written permission of the Publisher.

First printing

**Publisher Cataloging-in-Publication Data (U.S.)**

A CIP record of this book is available from Library of Congress

**Library and Archives Canada Cataloguing in Publication**

Lord, Tony
    Encyclopedia of planting combinations / Tony Lord.
Includes index.
Co-published by: Octopus Publishing.
ISBN 978-1-55407-997-1
    1. Plants, Ornamental. 2. Companion planting. 3. Color in gardening. 4. Gardens—Design. I. Title.
SB454.3.C64L67 2012          635.9          C2011-906523-1

Published in the United States by
Firefly Books (U.S.) Inc.
P.O. Box 1338, Ellicott Station
Buffalo, New York 14205

Published in Canada by
Firefly Books Ltd.
66 Leek Crescent
Richmond Hill, Ontario L4B 1H1

Printed in China

First published in 2003 by Mitchell Beazley, an imprint of Octopus Publishing Group Ltd, Endeavour House, 189 Shaftesbury Avenue, London WC2H 8JY www.octopusbooks.co.uk
New edition published in 2008 in association with the Royal Horticultural Society.

Art Director: Tim Foster
Senior Art Editor: Juliette Norsworthy
Commissioning Editor: Helen Griffin
Project Editor: Ruth Patrick
Design: Lizzie Ballantyne
Editor: Joanna Chisholm
Contributing Editors: Rae Spencer-Jones, Chris Young
Production Controller: Peter Hunt
Picture Researcher: Juliet Duff, Giulia Hetherington
Indexer: Joanna Chisholm

**Tony Lord** is an author, photographer and horticultural consultant. He edits the Royal Horticultural Society's annually published *RHS Plant Finder*. His books include *Best Borders* – winner of the Garden Writers' Guild "Best General Gardening Book" award for 1994 – *Gardening at Sissinghurst* and *Designing with Roses*, winner of the Literary Award of the World Federation of Rose Societies in 2006. He holds the Royal Horticultural Society's Victoria Medal of Honour and chairs its Floral Trials Subcommittee.

Leading garden photographer **Andrew Lawson** is a frequent contributor to magazines such as *Gardens Illustrated* and *House & Garden*, and he was a major contributor to the book *Highgrove, Portrait of an Estate* by HRH The Prince of Wales. As author and photographer, he has published *Performance Plants*, *Plants for All Seasons* and *The Gardener's Book of Colour*, winner of a Garden Writers' Guild Award in 1996. Andrew Lawson was honoured with the Royal Horticultural Society's Gold Medal for photography and has twice been named "Garden Photographer of the Year" by the Garden Writers' Guild. He also played an instrumental role in establishing the Garden Photographers Association in 1999.

# CONTENTS

# How to use this book

This book is not meant to be a series of recipes for perfect planting but rather a menu of suggestions from which readers can choose, revise or augment combinations to suit their own tastes and conditions. Some combinations are bright to the point of garishness; others delicate to the point of blandness, depending on one's own viewpoint. An inspirational section on planting ideas and styles is featured in the new edition, including case studies on groundbreaking gardeners. As the book does not discuss the culture, propagation or a wide range of varieties in the detail found in a planting encyclopedia, such a work would be invaluable used in conjunction with this book, both to supply such detail, and to show similar but different varieties that could be used to refine combinations suggested here, or to rework them in different colors.

## Key to symbols

These indicate the main characteristics of the plant and its cultural requirements.

| | |
|---|---|
| **H & S** (Height & Spread) | These are given at reasonable maturity, although shrubs and small trees can exceed stated figures in old age or hot climates. For tender perennials used for summer bedding or containers, they represent the dimensions reached by a plant overwintered from cuttings taken the previous year. |
| ✾ | The flower symbol indicates the typical flowering season, and can vary a little from that stated, especially in extreme climates. Accurate matching of flowering season is essential for successful combined floral effect, and can be judged from plants that flower together in your own locality. |
| ▭▬▬▬ | The colored bar represents the full range of light levels from full, day-long sun on the left, via partial shade to dense leaf-canopy shade on the right. The white and black bar beneath represents the featured plant's preferred part of this range (black) and the part of the range it will tolerate (white). |
| ◊◊◊ | The raindrop symbols show the plant's preferred soil water content. One raindrop indicates dry conditions; two raindrops, soil that is always moist, never waterlogged, or dry; while three indicates plenty of moisture throughout the year, suited, for example, to marginal (waterside) plants. |
| ▯▮▮▮ | The colored squares show the plant's preferred soil conditions. From left to right, these are: light, well-drained, e.g., chalky or sandy; medium with adequate drainage, e.g., silty loam; heavy soil, usually based on clay; humus-rich, for instance, peaty soils or leaf mold, preferred by e.g., ericaceous plants. |
| **Z3 pH** | The hardiness zone on the left is explained on pp.8–9. The pH range shows the soil acidity or alkalinity the plant will tolerate, pH7 being neutral, lower values acidic, and higher ones alkaline. Acid-loving species, such as rhododendrons, generally prefer pH6.5 or below. |

**RUNNING HEADS**
On the left, the page number, chapter title and name of the first plant covered are given; opposite, the plant named in the running head is the last entry on that page.

**PHOTOGRAPHIC CROSS-REFERENCES**
The letter here will be found in cross-references from plant combinations given under featured plants elsewhere in the book.

**PLANT ENTRY HEADINGS**
The full botanical name of the featured plant is given for each plant. The genus is followed by the species and, where appropriate, the variety.

**COMMON NAME**
The plant's common name, if it has one, follows the botanical name and is given in small capitals, with large capitals for those letters that are conventionally always capitalized, e.g., Madonna lily, Siberian squill. If the plant itself has no common name but belongs to a species or genus that does, this common name appears in the first sentence of the text; e.g., yarrow appears in all the entries for Achillea.

**INDIVIDUAL PLANT ENTRY**
An analysis of the characteristics of the featured plant, mentioning also any unusual cultural requirements, leads to discussion of combinations that could be created with plants suited to the same conditions and, in the case of floral effects, having the same flowering season.

**FLOWERING SEASON**
This symbol indicates the plant's typical flowering season. Where the season appears in parentheses the flowers are insignificant, or not the plant's main feature. See Key to Symbols.

**LIGHT LEVELS**
This symbol indicates the full range of light levels and the featured plant's preferred part of this range. See Key to Symbols.

**SOIL WATER CONTENT**
This symbol shows the plant's preferred soil water content. See Key to Symbols.

300   PERENNIALS – *Iris pallida*

## PLANT PORTRAITS
These are chosen to show the featured plant in an effective combination, whether a harmony or a contrast, with one or more other plants. A second photograph is sometimes used, for instance, if there is more than one season of interest, or to show both a harmony and a contrast.

## AWARD OF GARDEN MERIT
This symbol is for those plants that have the Royal Horticultural Society's Award of Garden Merit because of their outstanding excellence and easy culture.

### *Iris pseudacorus* 'Variegata' ♔
VARIEGATED YELLOW FLAG

Like *I. pseudacorus* itself, this is a moisture-loving plant that also thrives in ordinary border soil that is not too dry. Its leaves emerge boldly variegated with yellow, but become greener in summer; the flowers are yellow with brown markings. It makes a strong accent in waterside plantings, especially when grown through darker leaved plants such as purple bugles or heucheras, and mixes well with warm or hot colors, yellow-green foliage and flowers, and white flowers. Good partners include Candelabra primulas, euphorbias, ligularias, calthas and *Trollius*

In late spring, *Iris pseudacorus* 'Variegata' contrasts effectively with purple bugle (*Ajuga reptans* 'Atropurpurea').

cultivars. It makes an inspired contrast with meconopsis, and also with the markedly different foliage of ferns.

**Perfect partners:** *Caltha palustris* p.199 **A**, *Hosta sieboldiana* var. *elegans* p.246 **C**, *Hydrangea arborescens* p.58 **B**, *Lysichiton americanus* p.262 **A**, *Primula florindae*

**H: 4 ft. (1.2 m)  S: 30 in. (75 cm)**
❀ Early to midsummer
◊◊-◊◊◊   ■-■   Z5 pH4–7.5

## HEIGHT AND SPREAD
This symbol indicates the approximate height and spread of each feature plant. See Key to Symbols.

## SOIL CONDITIONS
These symbols indicate the plant's preferred soil conditions. In this example, the preferred soil is either light, well-drained conditions or medium conditions. See Key to Symbols.

## HARDINESS ZONES
This symbol shows the hardiness zone for each featured plant, while the pH indicates the amount of soil acidity or alkalinity the plant will tolerate. See Key to Symbols.

### *Iris* 'Rocket'

The profuse apricot-colored flowers of this Tall Bearded iris blend particularly well with warm colors such as peach, apricot, soft yellow or soft scarlet, and with bronze foliage and yellow-green foliage or flowers. Plants can be combined with early yellow roses, euphorbias, columbines in warm colors, geums and dark-leaved heucheras, as well as with shrubs such as brooms, helianthemums, halimiums, halimiocistus, phlomis and santolinas. 'Supreme Sultan' is butterscotch-yellow with crimson-brown falls; and 'Beyond' is creamy apricot-yellow.

**Perfect partners:** *Aquilegia chrysantha* 'Yellow Queen', *Berberis thunbergii* f. *atropurpurea*, *Cytisus* × *praecox* 'Warminster', *Helianthemum* 'Ben Hope'

**H: 30 in. (75 cm)  S: 24 in. (60 cm)**
❀ Late spring to early summer
◊-◊◊   □-■   Z4 pH5.5–8

## PLANT COMBINATIONS
At the end of each plant entry are further suggestions for effective planting partners. A plant name, followed by a page number and a letter (A, B, etc.) denotes an illustrated entry elsewhere in the book, showing the featured plant in a successful combination. Where only a page number and a letter are given, this denotes a photograph in which the featured plant appears but not as one of the main players of the planting scheme. Where only a page number and a letter are given, following the symbol ❑, this denotes a photograph in which the featured plant appears but not as one of the main players of the planting scheme.

## CAPTIONS
Captions give detailed information on the color and form of the plants shown in combination, with prominence given to the featured plant. They also give suggestions for varying the planting schemes.

In late spring, the warm amber tints of *Iris* 'Rocket' blend perfectly with a bicolored columbine (a hybrid of *Aquilegia canadensis*), while providing a contrast of floral form.

# Hardiness zones

The hardiness zone for each plant according to the system devised by the United States Department of Agriculture (USDA) is given towards the end of each entry. The letter "Z" is followed by a number relating to the minimum winter temperature a plant will tolerate according to the chart below. Comparing this with a zoned map of average winter minimum temperatures gives a helpful indication of where the plant should survive the winter without protection. However, zones can only be a rough guide. The hardiness of a plant depends on a great many factors, including the depth of its roots, its water content at the onset of frost, the duration of cold weather, and, especially for evergreens, the force of the wind. For woody plants, hardiness can depend on light- and heat-induced summer ripening of the wood; where summers are hot and long, trees and shrubs can often with-

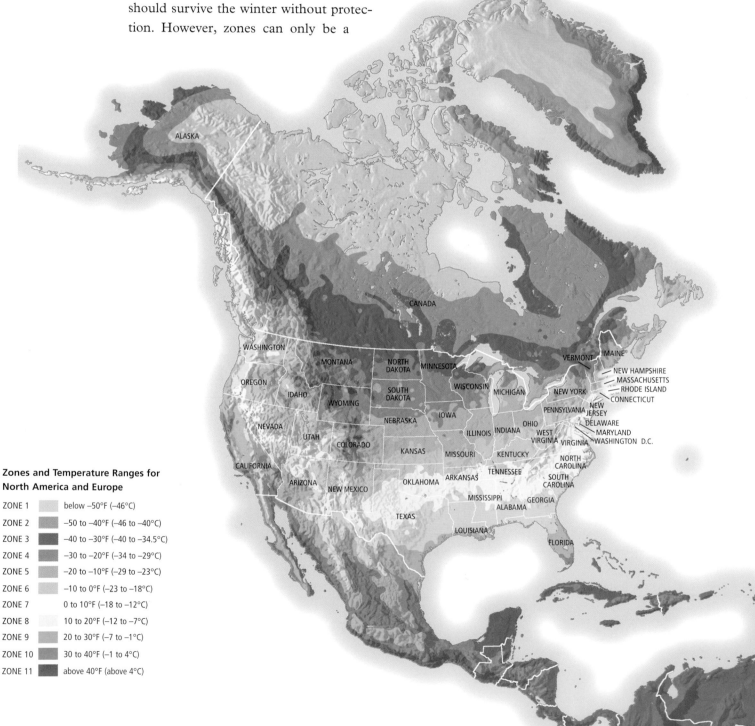

**Zones and Temperature Ranges for North America and Europe**

| ZONE 1 | below −50°F (−46°C) |
| --- | --- |
| ZONE 2 | −50 to −40°F (−46 to −40°C) |
| ZONE 3 | −40 to −30°F (−40 to −34.5°C) |
| ZONE 4 | −30 to −20°F (−34 to −29°C) |
| ZONE 5 | −20 to −10°F (−29 to −23°C) |
| ZONE 6 | −10 to 0°F (−23 to −18°C) |
| ZONE 7 | 0 to 10°F (−18 to −12°C) |
| ZONE 8 | 10 to 20°F (−12 to −7°C) |
| ZONE 9 | 20 to 30°F (−7 to −1°C) |
| ZONE 10 | 30 to 40°F (−1 to 4°C) |
| ZONE 11 | above 40°F (above 4°C) |

stand colder winter temperatures. The zone ratings also assume that the plants have no winter protection; a blanket of snow could insulate them, allowing them to grow in colder climates than their hardiness ratings suggest. In addition, it is not uncommon for, say, a Zone 8 area, such as the British Isles, to experience a Zone 7 winter, and Zone 6 winters occur perhaps every 10–30 years. Inevitably, severe winters kill some plants but this then gives opportunities for new combinations.

Within each zone and even within every garden, there are likely to be areas that are especially sheltered or unusually exposed, where the effective zone rating is one more or less than the maps suggest. Using sheltered areas, such as sunny walls or slopes, for plants that need one zone warmer than the local norm can extend the range of plants that will survive and hence increase the possible combinations.

Zone ratings are allocated to plants according to their tolerance of winter cold in cool temperate areas (latitudes 50–60°). In climates with hotter and/or drier summers, as in the southern United States, some plants will survive colder temperatures: their hardiness in these areas will occasionally be one or, rarely, two zones lower than that quoted. Because Australasia is, on average, hotter than North America, an alternative system, shown below, is used there, with

seven zones covering the range of average winter minimum temperatures experienced throughout the continent.

**Zones and Temperature Ranges for North America, Europe, Australia and New Zealand**

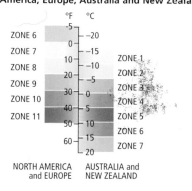

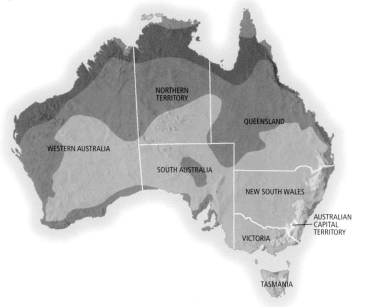

# THE ART OF COMBINING PLANTS

For most people, a garden's beauty comes
from the plants it contains, the way they
work together and the overall effect the
plants produce. A successful garden also
fits comfortably into its surroundings
yet has its own distinctive character.

## Assessing the site

Making a successful garden is a question of balancing what is already there with what is required of the plot. Most gardens take several years to create and there are bound to be mistakes along the way; however, careful planning can greatly accelerate the emergence of something satisfying.

In the first place, analysis of the site – its structures, existing planting, soil and climate – is important. Taking aspect and microclimates into consideration will help ensure that suitable plants are selected for each part of the garden. Where buildings cast shade for most of the day, the growing conditions will be cool and usually damp to the west, dry to the east, while walls or fences that face the sun will have dry, warm soil at their feet. Even on a small scale, high ground will be drier than its surroundings, and hollows wetter. Under trees the soil will be shaded and full of roots, making it dry and low in nutrients. Aspect can be important in unexpected ways: many flowers, especially daisylike ones, face towards the sun, so they should be planted with care, otherwise only their backs might be visible. Conversely, plants such as busy Lizzies whose flowers face in every direction, irrespective of the position of the sun, can be very useful, especially in shade.

It is essential to take time before making any long-lasting decisions. For example, the first impression of an old apple tree may be that it fills invaluable space with useless branches. With careful pruning, however, it could frame a view, provide welcome shade and retain the garden's sense of maturity, as well as yield apples once again. Alternatively, a suitable companion plant, such as a clematis or Rambler rose, might revive its beauty in a different way. Time will also give seasonal plants such as bulbs a chance to show and may reveal patches of invasive weeds that need to be dealt with.

It is useful to look beyond the garden's boundaries. By doing this, gardeners will get an indication of what plants thrive in local conditions (a soil-testing kit will confirm the nature of the soil) and may reveal views that could be emphasized through structures such as paths, trellis or pergolas, or by careful positioning of trees and shrubs.

## Choosing plants

Once any hard landscaping is in place, selection of the plants can begin. An important first consideration is the overall effect required: options include bright and cheerful, or cool and restrained; neat and tidy, or informal and naturalistic. It also makes sense to match plant selection to the energy of the person who is to tend the plot: a keen gardener may enjoy some more challenging plants, whereas someone who likes to relax outdoors would probably prefer low-maintenance varieties.

To ensure a wide and effective choice, it is helpful to make lists of plants that look good together and are suitable for the various sites around the garden. This book provides plenty of ideas for plant associations. Gardens – whether open to the public or privately owned – are also a good source of inspiration. When out visiting them, it is always worth noting information such as height, season, color and other useful plant characteristics, so when a particular combination of features is required a selection of suitable candidates is readily accessible. Photographic reminders are also useful.

Walled gardens, such as this one designed by Pamela Woods, provide good shelter, making it easier to grow tender Mediterranean plants. This patio area has been planted with an evergreen foundation structure including boxwood topiary that is softened by summer flowering annuals and perennials in terracotta containers.

Many gardeners, including perhaps the majority of professionals, adopt an historic style of planting. This may be an unwitting decision – a subconscious desire to recreate the gardens of a golden past or of their grandparents – or it may be deliberate. Gardeners working in parks or the gardens of old houses often try to create a period feel by using plants that reflect a bygone age. This might be achieved by selecting only varieties introduced by a certain date, such as before 1680 or after 1920 or, less rigidly, by using those that look like ones of that period. Conversely, gardeners might choose to avoid anything that smacks of the historical and instead try to achieve a modern look, perhaps by selecting exotic plants and tender species – that is, exactly those plants that were least likely to have been found in gardens of the past.

## Planning priorities

When designing an entire garden, structural plants (comprising trees, major shrubs and hedges) and those required for specific purposes (for example, screens or windbreaks) should be decided on first. These will establish the overall character of the site and provide its basic structure. For an individual border, it is the taller plants, the chief focal points, and any major tone-setters that should top the agenda and especially any evergreen shrubs needed to give year-round structure.

Flowers are important, but foliage, with its variations in form and texture, also makes an invaluable contribution and should always be taken into account. For year-round interest, planting lists should include a reasonable proportion of evergreens of all types and sizes according to the climate, to give structure and substance to the garden. Even in predominantly herbaceous borders, strategically sited groups of bergenias and liriopes, winter-green plants such as arums and cyclamens, and small shrubs such as daphnes might provide color during the winter months.

In addition, it makes sense to combine plants of different growth habits. By carpeting the ground beneath a deciduous shrub with bulbs, for example, there will be at least two seasons of interest, and the permanence of the shrub will accentuate the fleeting charm of the bulb flowers. Similar long-lasting displays can be achieved with climbers grown through and over shrubs with a compatible growth rate, or roses planted with herbaceous perennials.

**Above Left:** Vermilion crocosmias and daylilies plus bronze foliage provide warm tones in Darren Clement's courtyard garden in Staffordshire, England. In a restricted space, it helps to have upright rather than spreading plants.

**Above Right:** Grasses have outstanding design potential, as focal points, in intimate contrasting partnerships or as a lively and extended community of species and cultivars — all of similar form and habitat but with infinite subtle variations in color and texture.

## Scale and size

Every garden needs plants of varied sizes to prevent monotony, even to provide excitement. A tiny plot filled with miniatures will serve only to emphasize the garden's smallness, while numerous small plants in a large area will make it seem flat and desolate. The inclusion of a towering bamboo, a tall grass or a giant gunnera will draw attention away from the tight confines of a small garden, but could become oppressive. Some gardeners love the thrill of an extended planting of gigantic plants, even, perhaps especially, when in a relatively small space. Those who have the room could add to the drama by contrasting areas of such planting with others where the scale is conventional or miniature.

## Plant habit

In making successful plant combinations, it is essential to consider the entire plant – the habit of the plant as a whole and the form and texture of its component parts – the flowers, stems and foliage. With most plants, these are the most durable attributes, so a planting scheme that makes good use of all of them will be much more satisfying than one based solely on flowers.

Habit is generally what separates this book into separate chapters, so to discuss every sort of habit here, such as trees, shrubs or herbaceous perennials, would be superfluous. However, the distinction between shrubs, shrubby wall plants, climbers, scandent plants and groundcover plants is not clear-cut and merits some discussion if some of the plants that might fit into either of two categories are to be used in the most effective combinations.

Plants to grow on a wall may be divided into two habit types: those that are rigid ("wall shrubs" and some small trees, including trained fruit trees) and climbers. Rigid types can grow out from the wall if not pruned and tied hard against it and thus can be used to disguise its flatness or the rectangularity of a walled

**Below right:** Judy Pearce's New Perennial style planting at Lady Farm, in Somerset, U.K., emphasizes late summer and autumn display. The flowers of *Rudbeckia fulgida* var. *sullivantii* 'Goldsturm' effectively contrast with the diffuse grasses *Stipa tenuissima* and strongly vertical *Calamagrostis* x *acutiflora* 'Stricta'.

**Below left:** Repeated vertical stems of *Digitalis grandiflora*, *Phlomis russeliana* and salvias provide unity in this scheme by the renowned designer Tom Stuart-Smith. The Irish yew (*Taxus baccata* 'Fastigiata') adds emphasis and draws the eye to the horizon.

enclosure. Climbers are generally lax and, unless they are self-clinging (for example, ivy or Boston ivy), they need to be manually attached to wires on the wall.

Climbers may be woody (in which case they usually have a perennial structure that can reach to the top of their wall), or they may be herbaceous (in which case they have to start from ground level each year and will usually need light at the base each spring and so should not be hemmed in with bulky evergreens). Many can be used as a veil or curtain, perhaps most easily grown up the back of the wall and allowed to tumble down the front. For dwarf walls or retaining walls, shorter climbers or groundcover plants can be introduced.

### Habit within a planting scheme

The surface of a wall can be used to assemble a variety of planting combinations. Climbers will generally intermingle more intimately than other sorts of plants, so that a section of wall can have two or three different sorts, sizes and colors of flower thoroughly mixed.

The habit of a climber allows it to be used in still more ways, for instance to cover banks: herbaceous plants or bulbs growing in the bank can push through the covering of climber to produce a charming composition. Climbers can be combined up a brushwood tepee, over a pergola or draping a large shrub or small tree, though the most vigorous sorts such as *Rosa filipes* 'Kiftsgate' can swamp even quite large trees and in such sites are impractical to prune.

Lax plants that are shorter than full-scale climbers are also invaluable, and some – whether herbaceous or woody – are scandent. These might be thought of as plants that have half-heartedly not quite decided whether to climb or not: they might climb a bit, but if they can manage without climbing they will not bother. Such plants can be trained up brushwood supports or onto shrubs. Many aconitums, including the well-known 'Spark's Variety', grow this way and can be supported or allowed to grow onto a neighboring shrub with

contrasting or harmonious foliage or flowers. Others plants show not the least inclination to climb but make excellent ground cover, while in some cases, for instance *Geranium* 'Ann Folkard', the plant can be treated as ground cover or be supported with stakes and used as a conventional border plant.

### The effects of different habits

Plants of softly rounded habit are gentle in their effect and make excellent companions for extravagant focal points or other visually demanding specimens, such as plants with a vertical habit. One tall and thin plant, such as a columnar conifer, draws the eye to it, perhaps

In some circumstances, a single fastigiate plant can seem too insistent and a group of them will look more natural, as here, where three *Juniperus communis* 'Gold Cone' provide a welcome contrast of form to the surrounding plant shapes.

Purple-flowered *Aconitum* 'Spark's Variety' contrasts well here with *Heliopsis helianthoides* var. *scabra* 'Incomparabilis'. When used as a border perennial, this aconite tends to sprawl and needs support. Here, its stakes have been well hidden beneath its foliage.

*Rubus squarrosus* and *Muehlenbeckia* species, and they can be used as a foil through which to grow, for instance, thin-textured bulbs.

## Plant form

The form of foliage and flowers derives from the shape of its component parts. For foliage, the form may be: broadly linear, strappy or grassy; compound (usually pinnate or palmate) or simple; lobed, deeply cut or entire. Too much of the same sort of foliage form, particularly if the scale and/or color is the same, can seem dull, though it is possible to produce a subtly modulated scheme with grasses alone. Marginal variegation helps to emphasize foliar form, but mottled variegation tends to obscure it.

Flowers come in a variety of forms: vertical spikes or horizontal plates, fluffs of tiny flowers like *Thalictrum* or *Gypsophila*, or globes like *Echinops* or *Allium*. Even flowers whose outline is more or less round can be of different sorts, for instance stars, daisies or trumpets like morning glory. As with foliage, using all the same flower shape can appear dull unless there is a marked variation in size. Herbaceous perennials with flat flowerheads or upright spires provide useful architectural weight in a crowded setting: for example, the flattened heads of some achilleas are very effective among less formal shapes in mixed borders. The most exciting use of floral form comes from contrasting different shapes – for instance spikes, plates and globes – perhaps using a froth of tiny flowers as a foil or to modulate the color relationships between the component plants.

## Plant texture

A plant's texture is determined by the scale of its parts, usually its leaves and flowers, and by their direction, whether they be horizontal, vertical, radiating or random. A large, entire glossy leaf is coarser in effect than a small, matte one. The texture could be coarse, medium, fine or amorphous. For example, an ash tree has a fine-textured appearance because of its small

emphasizing a long vista; two upright plants draw attention to the space between them and are good for framing a view. By using identical plants of graduated height at a diminishing spacing, it is possible to exaggerate perspective.

Shrubs and trees of strongly horizontal growth, such as *Cornus controversa* 'Variegata', need space to display their beauty. Some such plants just have too much character to be equal associates with others and so must be allowed a starring role within a bed or border.

Like those with a rounded habit, weeping or arching plants are useful for softening strong foliage shapes or rigidly upright habits. Grasses with fountain-like leaves make good partners for hostas or rodgersias, while the flowing branches of a Japanese maple can be stunning beside an upright yew, their colors as well as their forms creating an attractive contrast. Again, this habit needs ample room all around for the shape to express itself gracefully.

Diffuseness is usually a characteristic of the inflorescence alone, and then can often be used to great effect. However, there are a few plants in which the entire habit, both foliage and flowers, seems diffuse so that the plant presents a hazy, structureless appearance between plants of more definite shape. Some grasses possess this quality, for instance the grass *Stipa tenuissima* and some sprawling plants such as leaflets, while with its large glossy leaves a low-growing *Bergenia* seems much coarser. The same principle applies to flowers, but the form of the inflorescence also plays a part. Although the individual flowers of a *Kniphofia* are small, the spiky flowerhead has strong presence.

The surface finish of foliage, whether glossy, matte or downy, affects the perception of texture and also influences what combinations will work. Very glossy foliage is glittery, sometimes appearing near black with highlights of bright white light in sun. This can be attractive, for instance giving the sparkle to holly foliage, but in some situations can seem restless. A matte surface is less prone to appearing black and white in full sun and reveals its true foliage color in a more restful way. Downy foliage tends to be whitish or grayish, thus useful for relieving large expanses of ordinary green, and can often be appealingly tactile, as in deeply felted *Sideritis candicans*, making it a good choice for planting beside sitting areas. It is sometimes sumptuosly satin-sheened as in *Convolvulus cneorum* or *Plectranthus argentatus*.

Many planting displays can be lifted out of the ordinary by careful positioning of textures. For example, *Lonicera nitida* 'Baggesen's Gold' has tiny bright leaves that provide a gentle but contrasting background for a large-flowered clematis; a small-flowered climber or shrub would simply appear fussy with the lonicera.

## RHS Award of Garden Merit

A considerable part of the work of the Royal Horticultural Society revolves around plantsmanship, not solely through having planting of the highest quality in its gardens but also through its very considerable commitment to trials. It has been a great privilege and an education to have been a member of the Floral Trials Subcommittee since 1990 and its chairman since 1995. This subcommittee deals with hardy herbaceous perennials, annuals, bedding plants (including tender plants for outdoor summer display) and ornamental plants for use under glass. (There are several other trials subcommittees: for example, for alpines, woody plants and some individual genera such as *Dahlia* and *Delphinium*.)

The Floral Trials Subcommittee meets every two weeks from late spring to autumn (occasionally but less frequently through winter and early spring) and assesses about a thousand plants a year to identify those that are of excellence and easy culture, thus deserving the Society's Award of Garden Merit (AGM). Members come from a variety of backgrounds, including nurseries, major retailers, planting design, private and public gardens, and the gardening press. Representatives from the major seedhouses are essential, covering the rapidly changing world of seed-raised plants

**Below left:** The upright, strappy leaves of *Phormium tenax* 'Veitchianum' provide a bold accent and a color contrast to *Canna* 'Roi Humbert'.

**Below center:** *Clematis* 'Ruby', an Atragene Group cultivar, harmonizes closely with the flowers of *Malus* × *Zumi* var. *calocarpa* while providing a subtly different form of flower.

**Below right:** In this knot garden at Little Hill, Sussex, U.K., the paving gives structure and emphasis to the rounded forms of *Berberis thunbergii* 'Atropurpurea Nana' and *Lavandula angustifolia* 'Hidcote', which by themselves could seem amorphous and dull.

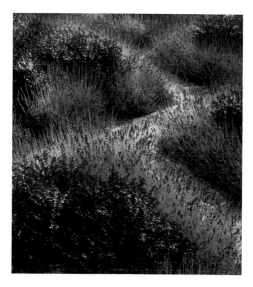

newer varieties, the old AGMs have to be rescinded. Conversely, committee members are frequently delighted to find a plant almost none of them knew that is excellent and seems to have been overlooked.

Often, the difference in performance between an AGM plant and a popular but non-AGM cultivar of the same genus is very marked: it is quite common for some popular varieties to flower for half the time and with only half the intensity of an AGM cultivar. This highlights the crucial importance of carefully selecting the very best plants if combinations are to be fully effective for as long a period as possible. There are elements of the assessment of an AGM plant that apply universally, though the award is a particularly useful indicator of plant quality for climates similar to those of most of northern Europe.

## Plant mixtures

Particularly in the case of annuals, plants are often sold as mixtures. These form a large part of the AGM assessments, but – except in the case of "designer mixes" in a planned and restricted range of colors – they are generally of little use in plant combinations: flowers in every color of the rainbow plus white might provide a jolly jumble but cannot be expected to enhance a planned combination. Individual plants can often clash uncomfortably with others in the mixture, and the overall effect can be jarring and untidy. This is difficult for the gardener because many retail outlets and garden centers sell mostly mixtures, though it has been heartening to have seen a trend towards single-color cultivars in recent years.

(particularly bedding plants) and clonally propagated ornamentals of the sort used for bedding and containers.

Generally a significant fault such as susceptibility to disease or a demand for staking in a genus that does not usually need it would preclude a plant from the AGM. Some aspects of trialed plants, such as floriferousness and length of flowering, are easily assessed and quantifiable. Others, such as the quality of the flowers, the poise with which they are borne or the beauty of the foliage, are matters of opinion. These vary greatly: an exquisite bloom in delicate pink might be admired by many of the subcommittee while others consider its color "not definite enough"; some members might greatly relish a flower in gold, orange or magenta while others would think it too brash to be generally useful. The subcommittee is large enough and diverse enough, and its members' opinions sufficiently independent, not to be diverted from recognizing a good plant. When old favorites with AGMs of long-standing have been greatly superseded by

Another trend in bedding plant production that the Wisley trials have identified is the production of ever shorter cultivars with disproportionately large flowers. Such plants are also a mainstay of major retail outlets, being suited to pack-production and transport, but their awkward proportions make them difficult to use in combinations in a bed or border.

# Color in the garden

As with all other aspects of garden design, color choice is very personal. A riot of different shades, a serene scene of white or blue, or simply a variety of greens – all these are acceptable if the gardener likes them. However, too much of one color could become bland, so some points of contrasting color in any planting are useful to enliven the scene. In the words of Gertrude Jekyll, "a blue garden, for beauty's sake, may be hungering for a group of white Lilies, or for something of palest lemon-yellow, but it is not allowed to have it because it is called the blue garden, and there must be no flowers in it but blue flowers. I can see no sense in this; it seems to me like fetters foolishly self-imposed. Surely the business of the blue garden is to be beautiful as well as to be blue."

Most single colors have some limitations if they are to be used as the basis for an extended planting. For blue, this is the unusualness of pure blues; using purple as a substitute is rarely satisfactory and diminishes the impact of the flowers that really are the primary color. Yellow, though the basis of well-known color-themed gardens, for instance at Crathes Castle in Scotland, is a component of green; expert gardeners including Graham Stuart Thomas thought yellow was not sufficiently distinct to use on its own. Purple does not glow in full sun and can look leaden, being more pleasing and sumptuous on a cloudy day or at twilight.

## The "hot" colors

Red and orange are thrilling, especially when used in a transitional part of the garden, as in the Red Borders at Hidcote Manor, in Gloucestershire, United Kingdom. A rare color in Old World plants, red and orange are often found in New World species and in many of the tender perennials that are the mainstay of late summer and autumn planting. The magical effect of red or orange blooms lit from behind by the sun makes them especially effective in planting that runs along an east–west orientation, where the *contre-jour* effect works best. It is

important therefore to suit the colors not only to personal preference but also to the times of day when the garden will be used most often.

The relationship between colors is often described using the color wheel. This is divided into six main segments in which the primary colors (red, yellow and blue) alternate with the secondary colors (orange, green and purple). Orange is a combination of red and yellow so is positioned between them. For the same reason, green is between yellow and blue, and purple

Flowers of bold shape can be effectively set against a cloud of much smaller flowers in a contrasting color, as here with *Osteospermum* 'Pink Whirls' and *Veronica austriaca* subsp. *teucrium* 'Crater Lake Blue'.

between red and blue. The spectrum is increased by variations in the amounts of each primary color in each secondary color. For example, brick-red contains more red than yellow, and lime-green contains more yellow than blue.

The color wheel is helpful in garden design in that it indicates the effect a combination of colors might produce. For example, unrelated colors, such as yellow and purple or orange and blue, contrast most strongly with each other, while related colors, such as yellow and orange or red and purple, are more harmonious. However, in gardens the fact that colors are never seen in isolation complicates the theory: flowers, which are rarely a single color

Wallflowers (*Erysimum cheiri*) and tulips are a classic combination. For the superlative shape of the tulips to be appreciated, either they or the wallflowers need to be of a single color. Mixed colors of both would seem jumbled and ineffective to many gardeners.

themselves, always have a background of foliage, which can be various shades of green, gray, bronze, purple, yellow or a combination. Despite this, it is still possible to predict that some color mixtures will be gentle, while others will be exciting or dazzling. Pinks, lavender-blues and similar soft colors are relaxing. Blue with pink, particularly soft tones of both, is normally a safe choice, producing gentle, cool combinations – roses in warm mauve-pink with lilac clematis, for instance.

Reds, oranges and strong yellows (the "hot" colors) are exciting, so when they are combined the effect is exhilarating: red roses paired with orange crocosmias; or scarlet tulips with orange wallflowers, for example. The majority of reds have impact when grouped with most other colors, but particularly with deep greens, bronze and blues – scarlet poppies with blue delphiniums, for example, can be quite startling. Although invigorating, this type of contrast should be used with care. If the required effect is of a woodland glade, then the choice of shrubs such as rhododendrons should be restricted mainly to those in cooler colors, with just a few brighter hues interspersed. Many of the azaleas are best left out of such an arrangement because they cover themselves too thickly with flowers, making strong, solid blankets of color, which do not suit such naturalistic planting, particularly not those in carmine, shocking pink, orange or scarlet.

## Color density

The strength of the colors involved will influence the effect of a grouping. For example, soft yellow with almost any shade of blue, such as wild primroses with muscari or hyacinths, will be soothing, but if the yellow is stronger – a golden yellow goldenrod with a blue or purple heliotrope, for instance – the overall result is much more demanding. Generally the paler a color, the less is its power to produce fierce contrasts. Conversely, very dark colors such as blood red or holly green are less disputatious than bright scarlet or dayglo green. Both yellow and blue flowers are common in spring, making this a popular choice for a refreshing contrast; the color theme for the same area can be quite different for summer and autumn.

For those who find color schemes in a restricted range of colors dull or contrived, a pleasing and more varied style can be achieved simply by leaving some colors out. A gentle, unforced effect can be created by omitting strong yellow, scarlet and orange, the remaining colors being leavened by a dash of light lemon.

In this white border, set against *Hosta undulata* var. *albomarginata*, *Bellis perennis* and a froth of forget-me-not or Cerastium are three different tulips: Single Late 'Snowpeak' (closed), Triumph 'White Dream' (open) and Double Late 'Mount Tacoma'. This might be more variety than is needed, though it can be useful to include different cultivars of the same height and color but with different flowering dates to get an extended display. The singles have great purity of shape, while the doubles remain more open in dull or cool weather.

If a scheme is intended to be rich and sumptuous, the presence of any pastel tones or white would make the ensemble seem jarring and muddled; the diverse golds, purples, reds and blues that remain might be augmented and unified by purple foliage. Again, a touch of lemon might be needed here and there to prevent the whole from seeming too dull.

Where richness is not the main intention, colors containing some white (soft silvers or creamy shades) or those with warming tones (blood red, salmon, apricot or peach) can be used to tone down a number of stronger colors, although the flowers or foliage concerned need a pronounced form to avoid losing their identity. A butter-yellow rose can hold its own against red valerian because the rose has a more defined flower shape than the valerian, while the loose beige-brown flowerheads of a tall grass will mitigate any heavy effect created by, say, orange-red gallardias, but its stature ensures it is in no danger of being overwhelmed.

A curious effect occurs when mixing colors across a primary one: it is well known that hues to the orange side of red clash with those to the purple side. Gardeners are not helped by reference works that describe flowers as red or pink without distinguishing to which side of the primary the colors lie: sensitive souls would find some of the resulting clashes unbearable. However, just such a clash can be immensely exhilarating if well managed: a shimmer of tiny vermilion flowers set above larger magenta ones would be electrifying. The same effect occurs with other primaries: kingfisher blue would work with a bright, strong violet or lavender. There are some flowers that captivate a gardener because of just such combinations within a single floret, for instance chorizemas in vermilion and magenta or *Tweedia caerulea* in kingfisher blue and lavender. Orange and yellow-green are an altogether more piquant combination than orange and yellow, though yellow-green might be taken for granted because so many foliage plants are that color.

The trick of superimposing small flowers over larger ones in a contrasting color has long been known as the "shot silk effect." It is popularly used in flowerbeds, for instance casting a veil of flowers of *Verbena rigida* over vermilion pelargoniums. There is no reason why it should be restricted to bedding schemes – it could work equally with herbaceous plants – but a suffcient area of intermingled plants is needed to pull off the trick, not just one or two of each. It can equally be used for harmonies, though the two colors need to be distinct.

### White plants

In carefully chosen situations, white flowers and foliage in chalky white and gray – silvery elaeagnus, variegated grasses or white-flowered campion – create Mediterranean warmth, while translucent greenish white blooms among light or bright green foliage will provide a sense of a cool woodland area – pale hellebores or white foxgloves with ferns and hostas, for instance. In a "white garden" care needs to be taken with different tones of white: though some flowers that are not necessarily pure white – perhaps tinted with blue or yellow – will flatter each other, some shades of white can look distinctly dirty next to purer neighbors. In mixed plantings, white needs to be used in moderation to avoid overpowering any more subdued or softer colors, and it should not be scattered around in small groups because it draws too much attention to itself. In combination with hot colors, white is useful in emphasizing the richness of red and brightening yellows and oranges, though the starkest white can be too severe, and white containing a touch of cream is usually more pleasing. White is also good for injecting sparkle into combinations of more muted shades. For example, two clematis in vinous red and lavender-blue benefit from the addition of a companion with small white flowers to brighten their luxurious effect. Without the white, they would be in danger of receding into the background.

Vita Sackville-West created the White Garden at Sissinghurst, in Kent, United Kingdom, because of the unearthly glow of white flowers at twilight. Pastel colors, particularly those in the cool part of the spectrum, will also glow marvelously in twilight, especially if lit by the setting sun, and are generally more successful in shade than more saturated hues.

Once the garden is planted, it helps to watch the varying distribution of color throughout the year: the best effects are achieved where plants that flower over a similar period are grouped together, rather than sprinkled all over the garden. This ensures that the strong areas of color and interesting combinations will draw the eye to them, while nonflowering areas will merge into a fine green backdrop. When flowers are scattered, the surrounding nonperformers dilute their effect.

For any color scheme to "read," at least one-third, and preferably one-half, of the component groups need to perform at any and every time throughout the border's season. For planting that has to work from spring to autumn, this is a tall order unless the spring flowers, for instance bulbs, make way for other plants in the same space to provide a later display. Colored foliage is useful in that it contributes to the essential quotient for as long as it is in leaf. Variegation can also play its part in adding to the display throughout the seasons, though too much can seem restless.

## Timing the season

Because of the one-third performance rule, it is hard, though not impossible, to make the same area of planting function from spring to autumn. If it is to last for only a part of the year, the task of creating an interplay of shapes, colors and textures becomes easier. Most people have only the one garden area, so they tend to make it work for as much of the year as possible. However, the delights of single-season gardening are many and worth considering if the space and the resources are available.

Getting the individual plants of a combination to coincide in their display is not

easy. It helps always to choose varieties that have a long season and to eschew any that perform for only a few weeks, leaving an area of green that adds nothing to the combination for the rest of the year. Flowering dates need to be carefully checked, especially since those quoted in many reference works have been passed down from author to author over the centuries without question but now do not tally with those found in the current climate with its earlier springs. The actual modern flowering dates very often differ by one, sometimes even two months. It is wisest to check seasons with actual flowering dates, either from personal observation or from accounts on reputable horticultural websites.

**Below:** The Top Border at the Priory, Kemerton, Worcestershire, U.K., was planted by Elizabeth and Peter Healing and contains a complete spectrum of colors. Such a feast is not planned to be consumed all at once but one course at a time: the hot-colored section of the border is the main course for late summer and autumn, when color is provided by *Rudbeckia fulgida* var. *deamii* and *Monarda* 'Mrs. Perry', with bold vertical accents from *Kniphofia uvaria* 'Nobilis'.

**Following pages:** The Fellows' border at Clare College, Cambridge, U.K., boasts a classic late spring combination with tulips. It is in primary colors and includes *Tulipa* 'West Point'. The forget-me-nots are an attractive alternative to more conventional wallflowers, and they offer a completely different set of options, with flowers in rich rose-pink, pure white or blue – colors wallflowers lack.

## Planting beds and borders

Before putting any plants into the garden, it is a good idea to make some sort of planting plan. This can be detailed or just an overall aim, and it can be adapted as ideas change or plants different from those originally envisaged are chosen. It is much easier to alter planting plans than to move plants around once they are in the soil, and the plan will provide a sound basis from which to lay out a border.

Almost every gardener tries to cram in too many groups at too close a spacing when making a plan. The result sometimes looks pleasant enough during the first season, but thereafter plants become overcrowded and something has to be removed. At this stage, adjustments to the plan are difficult without marring the interplay of colors and textures. Furthermore, too many plants make the planting much more expensive than it needs to be. The general rule for spacing plants is to follow the recommended spacing given in standard reference works, allowing rather more space between adjacent groups of different plants: thus if Plant A is spaced at 16 in. (40 cm) apart and Plant B at 24 in. (60 cm) apart within its own group, the general rule is to allow 75 percent of the sum of the spacings, that is 30 in. (75 cm) in this case, between adjacent groups; rather more would usually do no harm.

Thorough preparation of the ground is necessary for a successful and healthy display. This will enable new plants, fresh from luxurious conditions in the nursery, to adapt quickly to the hard life in the garden. All plants will make a better start if the soil is deeply dug, and plenty of manure, compost or other organic material is incorporated. The addition of organic material will enrich the soil without providing too many nutrients; it will also improve its moisture-retaining properties as well as the drainage of water and help to ensure that air reaches plant roots, which will avoid stagnation and encourage growth.

Where shrubs or trees are to be planted at wide intervals, it is more sensible and less time-

### A border in spring

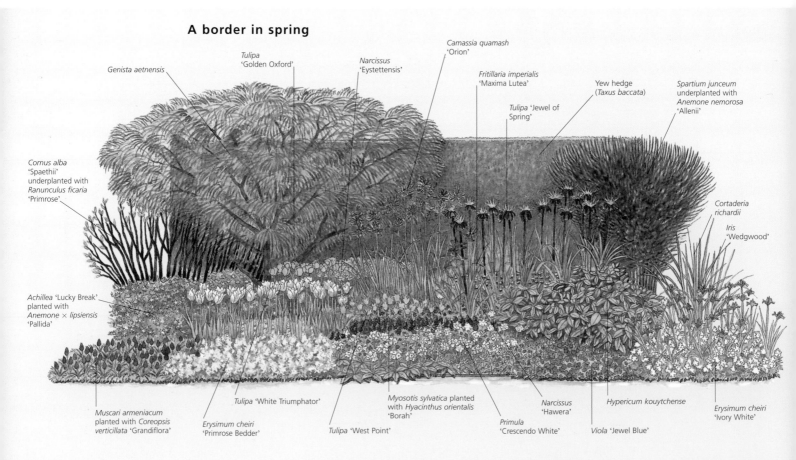

Genista aetnensis

Tulipa 'Golden Oxford'

Narcissus 'Eystettensis'

Camassia quamash 'Orion'

Fritillaria imperialis 'Maxima Lutea'

Tulipa 'Jewel of Spring'

Yew hedge (Taxus baccata)

Spartium junceum underplanted with Anemone nemorosa 'Allenii'

Cornus alba 'Spaethii' underplanted with Ranunculus ficaria 'Primrose'

Cortaderia richardii

Iris 'Wedgwood'

Achillea 'Lucky Break' planted with Anemone × lipsiensis 'Pallida'

Muscari armeniacum planted with Coreopsis verticillata 'Grandiflora'

Erysimum cheiri 'Primrose Bedder'

Tulipa 'White Triumphator'

Tulipa 'West Point'

Myosotis sylvatica planted with Hyacinthus orientalis 'Borah'

Primula 'Crescendo White'

Narcissus 'Hawera'

Viola 'Jewel Blue'

Hypericum kouytchense

Erysimum cheiri 'Ivory White'

consuming to prepare individual planting holes; these should be generously sized and well dug. Whole beds or sections of beds for replanting are best fully dug over. Existing plants that are to be retained in the new design can be left in place or dug up and divided before replanting to give them a new lease on life.

## Eradicating weeds

Although expert advice generally stresses the importance of eradicating perennial weeds before planting, no one admits that this is virtually impossible. Nettles, docks and many other tough weeds may be dug out without too much difficulty. Dandelions and thistles are more persistent but can be eliminated in time. The great villains are couch grass, bindweed, horsetail and ground elder. The easiest way to deal with them is to spray with a suitable herbicide. Follow the timing guidelines on the label, as they are generally temperature specific. The area then needs to be left for the amount of time suggested so that the herbicide acts on the roots, then the

soil should be cultivated and resprayed as regrowth appears; after a further wait, it can be cultivated again. If there is no regrowth after a significant wait time (this might mean waiting until the following year in some cases), the area is ready for planting. Such treatment is not always enough to kill horsetail or ground elder, which may need extra persistence.

Hand-digging is an organic alternative but can take several years before complete eradication and is not likely to be successful if weeds continually reinvade from neighbors' gardens, as the worst can – entering either beneath foundations or through old mortar. Covering the affected area with a membrane impenetrable to weeds, such as heavy-duty polyethylene or old carpet is another alternative, but this can be unsightly even when covered with mulch.

Where weed infestation was very heavy, planting annuals in the first summer will allow any weed fragments still remaining to emerge, and they can be treated again when the annuals have died off at the end of the growing season.

## The same border in midsummer/autumn

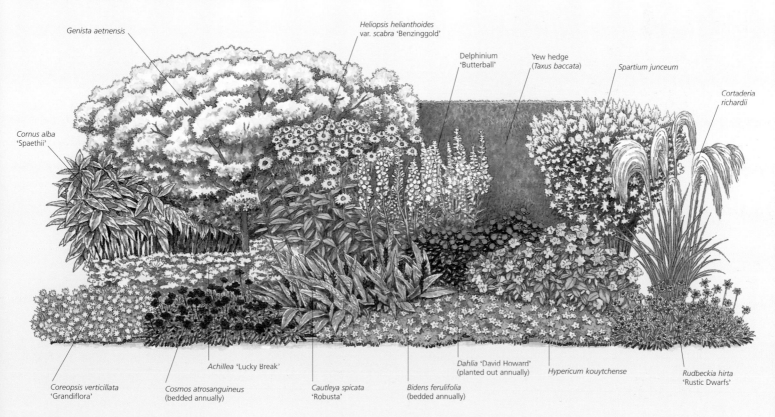

Genista aetnensis

Heliopsis helianthoides var. scabra 'Benzinggold'

Delphinium 'Butterball'

Yew hedge (Taxus baccata)

Spartium junceum

Cortaderia richardii

Cornus alba 'Spaethii'

Coreopsis verticillata 'Grandiflora'

Cosmos atrosanguineus (bedded annually)

Achillea 'Lucky Break'

Cautleya spicata 'Robusta'

Bidens ferulifolia (bedded annually)

Dahlia 'David Howard' (planted out annually)

Hypericum kouytchense

Rudbeckia hirta 'Rustic Dwarfs'

Cucurbits such as pumpkins or zucchini are good because of their allelopathic effect of suppressing weed growth (see p.31). A crop of potatoes can also be useful for smothering annual weeds. There is always a risk of reinfection from deep in the soil or from beneath nearby shrubs, hedges or paving, so it is wise to avoid planting ground covers or clump-forming perennials for a year or two. Spot treatment of isolated weeds is not difficult if it is done regularly, but ground ivy and bindweed can easily regain a foothold, meaning the whole border will need to be cleaned and replanted once more.

Late-spring planting from container-grown plants already in leaf enables the gardener to get a better idea of the likely look of the mature planting and the interplay of shapes and colors. It also allows plants to settle quickly with minimal disturbance. Adequate spacing is especially important for the key long-term plants such as shrubs and trees, and for invasive plants such as some bamboos.

Deciding on the best way to plant a complete border all at the same time can be difficult. While it is possible to buy plants in sufficient quantities, it is cheaper and perhaps more satisfying to purchase a few and propagate them, or to lift and divide plants that are already in the garden. Species and botanical variants can often be cheaply raised from seed, but few perennial or woody cultivars come true to type from seed. Unfortunately, many major retailers raise their stock of cultivars from seed, producing just such inferior plants and not the cultivar whose name appears on the label: any

sign of variation within a garden center or nursery batch of, for example, lavenders or achilleas is a likely sign of mediocre seed-raised plants that will not give uniformity within the group and will not achieve the standard of the cultivar they are purported to be.

Where large areas are to be planted, a combination of propagating and buying is probably most sensible. If speed is important, it is worth remembering that many mail-order nurseries will sell plants in batches of five and 10, as well as hundreds, if the total order is of a reasonable size. Buying in this way can be up to 75 percent cheaper than going to the local garden center, especially with herbaceous perennials. Small plants are considerably less expensive than larger ones, too, and will usually adapt more quickly to their new situation, soon catching up with larger pot-raised neighbors.

## Useful planting techniques

Once the soil is prepared and the plants obtained, or earmarked to be moved from other parts of the garden, the next step is to transfer the planting plan to the ground. The easiest way to do this is to divide the area into sections and then to use silver sand to indicate the position of each group of plants. If there is a general planting strategy but no specific plan, it is advisable to start by positioning key elements and then the secondary groups before filling in with the rest. Trying out ideas with the still potted plants, with branches or stems cut from shrubs and other plants that are to be moved into the area, and with canes and other objects, will make sure that everything works before anything is installed in the ground.

Planting systematically, from the middle to the edge of an island border or from one end to another of a long border, will ensure there is no chance of treading on new plants. Generous holes make it easy to position plants without damaging the roots. To encourage roots to grow outward, specimens that have been grown in pots should have their rootball teased out a little at the edges.

Sand can be used to mark out the likely spread of each group and will help the gardener see quite clearly when plants have been placed much too close together, as they have here.

The perfect planting conditions are when the temperature is cool, and the plants are put into moist but not wet soil; after planting, a gentle downfall of rain is ideal to settle everything in. However, where this situation cannot be arranged, planting can still be done successfully as long as exposed roots are protected from drying out and all newly planted specimens are watered well immediately afterward. Generally, autumn planting is best for evergreens, early-flowering plants and members of the Saxifragaceae such as heucheras, bergenias and astilbes. Spring planting is preferable for plants that are intolerant of winter wet such as silver foliage plants.

One of the keys to successful planting of beds and borders is to ensure that the front of the planting area is well furnished. It is preferable not to leave areas of bare soil there, but how close the plants should be to the front will depend on the surface adjacent to the bed or border. If it is against sod, the plants should not smother the grass. If the bed or border adjoins paving, some plant overhang is both practical and attractive, often helping to soften a hard line. The plants at the front should generally have stems and leaves down to ground level and should not have tattered or dying leaves at the bottom, nor should they have a habit that might reveal any untidy, debris-strewn soil.

Mulches should be applied after planting to retain moisture, suppress weeds and reduce the work required to establish the plants. Annual mulching (and other seasonal jobs such as pruning and replanting) should be tackled in autumn if there is an underplanting of spring flowers. Whether the mulch is shredded bark or other materials such as garden compost or gravel, it should be spread thickly and evenly over the whole area. It is important to ensure that it does not smother the crowns of dormant or emerging herbaceous perennials.

## Allelopathy

Allelopathy is the suppression by some plants of their neighbors by means of naturally exuded chemical substances. This mechanism can give a plant an advantage over its neighbors in a competitive environment and is a characteristic of some weeds such as couch grass, creeping thistle, chickweed, wild garlic (*Allium ursinum*) and garlic mustard (*Alliaria petiolata*). Allelopathy can affect growth or germination and, though not usually fatal to other plants, it can determine whether or not plants in a grouping will thrive together. It might reduce vigor, hence relative heights, and so sometimes throw a plant association out of kilter. The effect can be passed on through composted foliage or wood chippings, though small quantities are unlikely to cause noticeable harm.

Known since Greek and Roman times and first studied scientifically in the mid-19th century, it is only in recent decades that interest and research have widened, led by the possibility that some of the chemicals involved or their analogs could be used as herbicides or germination inhibitors. Even so, there is no comprehensive source on the relevance of allelopathy to gardeners, nor is it easy to find which ornamental or edible plants are involved.

Some of the best-known trees that exhibit the effect include *Acer negundo*, *A. rubrum*, black walnut (*Juglans nigra*), tree of heaven (*Ailanthus altissima*), *Magnolia grandiflora*, western red cedar (*Thuja plicata*), plane (*Platanus*) and *Eucalyptus*: it should be expected that some, though not all, other plants will not thrive if grown close to these. Other plants known to exhibit allelopathy include *Artemisia*, *Bassia*, *Callistemon*, *Casuarina*, *Centaurea*, *Cistus*, Cucurbitaceae, *Ephedra*, *Helianthus annuus*, *Lantana*, *Phalaris*, *Salvia* (some), *Tanacetum*, *Verbena* and *Vitex*.

Though a single shrub or group of a smaller plant is unlikely to kill its neighbors by allelopathy, gardeners may well find difficulty growing some other plants where allelopathic plants dominate, for instance in an extensive planting of *Cistus* or in a bed of *Verbena* or *Lantana*. When seed sown *in situ* does not germinate, or where self-sowing does not occur, allelopathy may also be to blame, though seedlings transplanted into the same ground may still thrive.

## Aftercare

As the plants grow and flower, it is almost inevitable that unexpected associations will reveal themselves. These might be pleasant, or they may mar the overall effect. It is best to remove or resite any plants that are unattractive as soon as possible. There is no point in spoiling

the border for any longer than is necessary. Photographs taken of the garden through the seasons will serve as reminders of any other necessary alterations, and will enable plans to be made for sowing seed or taking cuttings in readiness for the following year.

Routine tasks such as pruning of shrubs and trees and dividing perennials should be done as necessary, before the balance of the planting becomes affected. Because of the tendency by many gardeners to plant too many groups of too many plants at too close a spacing, it is likely that some plant groups will need to be removed and what remains be adjusted. When doing this, take care to retain the main interplays of form, texture and color in the design.

**Above:** When pruning with secateurs, the anvil blade is positioned above the cutting blade so that any bruising is on the discarded stem (here of a cotoneaster). The cut is made just above the node.

**Opposite:** In Les Jardins de Bellevue, Martine Lemonnier's garden in Normandy, France, *Magnolia* 'Heaven Scent' coexists happily with spring flowers such as *Helleborus* × *hybridus* and *Narcissus* 'Jenny' without any sign of suppression of their growth through allelopathy.

# GREAT PLANTING STYLES

Whether clashing colors or tonal harmony,
naturalistic style or modern simplicity
are used, successful planting combinations
can truly inspire and connect people
to gardens. With a little knowledge,
enthusiasm and trial and error, great
planting styles can create just about
any effect a gardener wants them to.

# About planting styles

Although the way people have gardened has developed over time, in essence two core beliefs stay true to this day: a garden can be both productive and beautiful. Often these two aims occur at the same time. Many gardeners – no matter where in the world they may be – thrill at the simple joy of plants. For the novice it may be the fact that they have grown a plant from seed; for the professional the enjoyment may be in discovering a specific plant as yet unknown in cultivation. But what unites all types of gardeners is the sheer pleasure, and challenge, of nuturing that plant.

As horticultural techniques and identification have become more refined, plant selection and placement have developed similarly. People have experimented with combinations, colors, leaf shapes, flower sizes, planting times, densities, seasonal interest, wildlife benefits … the list is endless. The naming of plants has also

Foliage combinations can make for stunning displays in the garden, such as here where the large leaves of gunnera, hostas, ferns and the slate-gray leaves of *Rosa glauca* set off the vertical shards of iris.

developed, with family name, genera, species and cultivar being the generally agreed breakdown. The classification of trees, shrubs, herbaceous perennials, bulbs, annuals, aquatics and so on also allows for clearer understanding of plants, as does their role in medicines, herbology, building materials and cooking. In so

doing, all of these refinements have allowed collective knowledge to grow.

The result, as found in this book, is that home gardeners, professional plantspeople and landscape designers have tried selecting and growing a huge variety of plants – probably in the order of 70,000, but that is a rough figure. What is more certain is that this diversity has triggered different styles of planting. These styles are not prescriptive, of course, but they do allow people who want to emulate a particular effect to understand that style's theoretical and practical application.

Many such names, for example cottage gardening, bedding or minimalism, may be thrown around, and there is a general understanding as to their intent or outcome. This may be subconscious or learned, but it permits a common language for those who want to speak it. It enables people with shared interests to exchange information or thoughts, therein also developing and refining that style still further. For nations that enjoy gardens, gardening or both, such as the United States, Canada and the United Kingdom, that means constant inspiration, backed by a thirst for knowledge and experimentation. Thankfully, over many hundreds of years, our forebears have put a considerable amount of time and effort into this interest, so gardeners are fortunate to be surrounded by such learning, while at the same time recognizing there is still much they do not fully understand.

## Basic considerations

Every gardener has his or her desires, which are reflected in their garden. Yet each person must also be sure they know the basic dynamics of their garden; for example what type of soil there is, the aspect of the site and the amount of rainfall each year. This is especially important not only for those trying to grow fruits and vegetables but also for those balancing different planting requirements such as trees, alpines and acid-loving plants. Such information is crucial for enabling the most to be got from a plot – especially if a gardener is trying to achieve a consistent planting style.

How, where and why a certain look fits into the garden are important considerations, as are cost, levels of maintenance and longevity. In addition, how a gardener manages or develops that chosen aesthetic with its differing needs, interests or demands is other major factor. For example, if young children are likely to use the garden, a large, grassed open space may be useful for them to run around in; but as they mature, some of that grass may be reclaimed for more decorative plants.

A specific type of planting is chosen because that gardener has a connection – whether emotional, practical or intellectual – with the desired effect. By studying the style, and comprehending the subtleties, a truly remarkable outcome can be achieved. Such exploration should not be arduous but rather should inform an innate reaction as to why that planting combination is worth pursuing.

Whether a first-time gardener or experienced botanist, perhaps the biggest success of any planting scheme should be its ability to render the gardener unable to describe what that style really means to them. Then they really know they are onto something special.

**Bottom left:** Some of the most successful schemes balance not only plant choice but also location, using the available natural light to enhance the spectacle, as here at Lady Farm, in Somerset, U.K.

**Bottom right:** Color, form, structure and texture are essential components of a strong planting association, which here combines soft grasses, red hot *Kniphofia* and dahlias with luxuriant canna leaves.

# Bedding

Over the years, the enthusiasm for bedding schemes has peaked and troughed. From public park displays of the most vivid combinations to more domestic window boxes or patio containers, the activity of "bedding out" is for many gardeners the epitome of summer. Colorful blooms, a wide range of leaf shapes and bountiful growth in just one season mean that bedding has a place in many gardens.

In its simplest form, summer bedding is the range of tender and semi-tender plants that are grown early in the year for planting out after the first frosts. Usually easy to cultivate – or bought young from a garden center – the range of plants is as wide as the designs made from them. Pelargoniums, snapdragons, marigolds, lobelia, ageratum, tradescantia and nicotiana are just a tiny selection of some of the staples of modern bedding plants.

It is not only summer bedding that has to be considered. Spring bedding, which comprises biennials and bulbs planted in autumn for a mid-spring display, ensures that more color can be added to any garden. Wallflowers, forget-me-nots, pansies and *Bellis perennis* valiantly brave the cold of winter while the bulbs of tulips and daffodils slowly emerge.

## Early history

It was in the first few decades of the 19th century that bedding plants started to gain popularity in Great Britain. As with so much to do with recent history, it was the exuberance of Victorian gardeners that pushed the boundaries on color combinations, planting densities and plant choice. Then, as gardening became increasingly democratized in post–Second World War Great Britain, more home and professional gardeners saw bedding schemes as part of their gardening calendar. They believed such plants not only showed prowess among their peers but also added cultural value to towns and front yards where they were on display.

### Current fashions

The imagination with which bedding plants are used is evolving. Instead of beds and pots dedicated to bedding, many gardeners intermingle existing shrubs, grasses or even sculpture with their summer or spring display. Bedding is often dotted into large borders, to fill awkward holes or unexpected plant casualties; some may even use vegetables (such as lettuce).

Gardeners are becoming more adventurous too, with taller, climbing or scrambling climbers growing against an ugly wall or awkward fence. Planters such as Alan Gray and Graham Robeson (owners of the East Ruston Old Vicarage garden in Norfolk, United Kingdom) create stunning displays using well-known and recently introduced combinations. Countless local park departments consider the value of such planting socially important and so they still fight to have some bedding – as can be seen throughout the Britain in Bloom campaign and those entering the RHS Flower Show at Tatton Park National Flower Bed Competition, United Kingdom.

### Future bedding

But these are more climate-conscious times, and summer bedding is especially greedy for water, and schemes often need regular feeding for truly strong displays. As a result, bedding schemes may change – with drought-tolerant plants (such as sempervivums or low-growing sedums) used instead of more thirsty ones, and those that remain in hanging baskets or pots are being grown in moisture-retentive growing media. Yet none of this will see the demise of bedding displays.

Raising bedding plants is cheap and fun: just one packet of seed, sown and grown correctly, can quickly bring color to any garden. Style and taste may have changed, but the principle of growing plants for one big seasonal hit is very much a part of gardening seasonality – and many a gardener's psyche.

Annual bedding schemes can make a significant floral contribution to a garden, as can be seen at Hampton Court Palace, in Surrey, U.K. The effect of color, repetition and balance is clear for all to appreciate.

# Herbaceous borders

From the mid-1800s onward, herbaceous borders were at their prime. Used as a way to show off the grandeur of the property owner, combined with the unquestioning skill of the gardener, this element of garden design is probably one of the most difficult to get right. Herbaceous borders take exactitude, timing, patience, knowledge, and skill. They are labor intensive and need endless care and attention. But – and it is a big but – when successful the scene that they conjure is truly unforgettable. They inspire the visitor to view them in awe, and the gardener/owner to look on in pride.

Their concept is really quite simple. Take a long border, usually on both sides of a wide grass path, and ensure that there is a fence, wall or a hedge at the back of the beds. Then plant the available soil with summer-flowering perennials. Cram in as many plants as possible and, with some regular maintenance, stand back and enjoy the rewards.

For many rich garden owners, such a border was that simple, because they had the gardeners and resources to make it happen. Thanks to the skill and ability of so many hands-on owners and head- and under-gardeners over the past many decades, good herbaceous borders have shown horticultural practice at its best. Historical proponents such as Gertrude Jeykll or Vita Sackville-West also demonstrated just how well they could be done.

### Experimenting with plants

At the heart of a successful border is the desired effect that combining certain plants can make. Whether it be a repeated color dotted throughout the scheme, or a crescendo of color going from soft grays and whites to searing pinks and reds, such a floral association can dazzle as much as it can calm. For some gardeners, these borders are an opportunity to mix plants that complement each other in color but may contrast in form; for others, it is a lesson in mass and void, with plants breathing and growing next to blocks or spires of planting en masse. Musical rhythm can be interpreted through a border with highs, lows, periods of calm and utter exuberance. As growth changes over the season, the nature of the border changes, with, later in the summer, increasing height and dominance creating a very different feel from that in early spring.

### Pinacles of excellence

Historically, herbaceous borders were really about plant vigor and floral splendor for three to four months a year – roughly early summer

**Above:** Planting of summer stalwarts such as red-flowered *Crocosmia* 'Lucifer', *Geranium* 'Gerwat' and *Heliopsis* 'Lorraine Sunshine' create a passionate color scheme.

**Top:** The late-summer border drama in this herbaceous border at Fudlers Hall, in Essex, U.K., is provided by dahlias, hostas and heleniums among other plants.

These swathes of tall and mid-height herbaceous perennials were in a summer border at Bressingham Gardens, in Norfolk, U.K. The mass planting of just a few plant types in such a large space reinforces the feeling of movement and freedom.

through to early autumn. Over time, eager gardeners have added bulbs, obelisks, woody shrubs, annuals in pots and dividing "screens" (in-bed hedges or trellis work), to complete the effect and extend the bed's attraction to more like 10 months of the year. In so doing, they have made the display more interesting and pushed out the boundaries with their plant and color combinations and their fundamental structural compositions.

One of the oldest herbaceous borders still in cultivation – at Arley Hall gardens in Cheshire,

United Kingdom – uses a brick wall on one side and a perfectly trained yew hedge on the other to control the cool, late-spring colors, which then develop into hotter hues by the end of summer. Hidcote Manor Garden, in Gloucestershire, United Kingdom, created by Lawrence Johnston in the 1920s and possibly one of the most famous gardens in the world, has an entire red border that uses perennials, bulbs, annuals and foliage plants to convey a scene of cohesion and interest. In Powys, Wales, Powis Castle and Garden boasts a hugely long border at the foot of the castle

In this more traditional country garden scene, at Frith Lodge, in Sussex, U.K., the gravel path is edged with *Lavandula angustifolia* 'Hidcote' and backed by white-flowered *Sisyrinchium striatum* and roses. The solid clipped hedges in the distance provide an end to the scheme.

tempo, but the overall planting is about consistency. At the back of borders *Macleaya, Anenome, Eupatorium,* roses, *Buddleja, Phormium, Rudbeckia* and others give height and structure; in the middle, salvias, *Coreopsis, Acanthus, Allium, Dahlia, Veronicastrum, Delphinium* and *Helenium* add full-blown color; and toward the front, lower growing sage, geraniums, *Alchemilla mollis, Dianthus* and *Phlox* lend visual detail.

The contents of a herbaceous border is not prescriptive, and a truly memorable one will mix and match many of these elements. To bring planting up to date, many such schemes now welcome grasses, exotics such as cannas or bananas, and Mediterranean types such as *Agave,* maybe in containers placed into the border, to show they are still places of creativity and relevance.

A successful border is one that has space to mature – in terms of the depth of the border itself and how far the plants can grow out and up. Therefore when planning a herbaceous border, it is important to allow as much space as possible, if – once the plants get established – the gardener is not to wish he or she had been more generous with the border size.

In order to keep a herbaceous border looking good, it is necessary to work really hard with the plants, which will flourish if tended with care. Ensure the ground is fertile and healthy; stake and support plants as they grow; bring order to the more aggressive types while leaving space for the less pushy. Remember the effect to be created and be ruthless in placing the right plants in the right place; and keep trying new combinations until fully satisfied. Some may call it tinkering; others would deem it artisanry.

It is because of this required skill that herbaceous borders are less common in gardens today. But once a gardener really gets a grip on good planting combinations, herbaceous borders are the horticultural holy grail. The possibilities are endless, and the effect can be one of planting heaven.

(itself encased by amazing yew hedges), which shows color and texture throughout the season, even though it is surrounded by a dominant building and endless countryside.

### Basic structure

It is the plants that make the show. As a rule, herbaceous borders require the lower growing plants to be at the front, with medium-sized and larger subjects toward the back; every now and then, for interest if nothing else, a tall spire of *Verbascum, Lilium* or *Kniphofia* may change the

## GREAT PLANTING DESIGNERS CASE STUDY

# NORI AND SANDRA POPE

In the 1990s, Canadian gardeners Nori and Sandra Pope took the English gardening scene by storm with their spectacular herbaceous and mixed borders at Hadspen House in Somerset, United Kingdom. What excited gardeners most was the grand scale on which the Popes demonstrated the theory behind the monochrome border. By planting the majority of each border largely using shades of one color, they showed that concentrating on shapes and texture, rather than on a range of colors, was very effective.

At Hadspen, one of the Popes' most spectacular examples of this theory was the yellow border, in which yellow and yellow-variegated foliage were given as important a profile as yellow flowers. The leaves of lacy cut-leaved elder (*Sambucus racemosa* 'Plumosa Aurea') acted as a foil to the ramrod vertical flower spikes of yellow lupins, which in turn were softened by and appeared to rise out of a cloud of feathery fennel (*Foeniculum vulgare*). In similar fashion the red border comprised shades of red, orange and the deep plum-based colors for which the Popes became known.

The success of the monochrome border rested not only on an artful arrangement of similar-colored plants but also on an element of scientific know-how. Importantly, Nori Pope noted that if the eye is saturated by too much of one color it suffers from "fatigue." To relieve this, each border was planted with a small percentage of a complementary color to rest the eye. For example, in the yellow border, the Popes injected a small amount of blue; in the red border, the dramatic tones and shades of alliums, nasturtiums and lupins were alleviated by hints of silver foliage courtesy of plants such as *Artemisia* 'Powis Castle'.

In the mixed border the Popes also demonstrated their brilliant touch at combining plants of every kind. Traditional cottage garden plants such as deep pink hollyhocks (*Alcea rosea*) were placed against dark purple foliage, while exotics such as *Phormium tenax* were unexpectedly but happily married with traditional herbaceous plants: perennial poppies and astrantias. Thus a perfect balance was struck between height, form and texture.

Nori and Sandra designed the borders at Hadspen to flower for the longest possible season. In so doing they became modern exponents of successional planting. Bulbs, particularly tulips, provided a burst of color and form from spring until early summer when annuals, which had been sown in situ earlier, took over to keep gaps to a minimum until perennials had established around them. By late summer and early autumn dahlias bloomed as the perennials started to fade.

The yellow border at Hadspen House is a riot of form and texture where exuberant grasses contrast with buttonlike blooms of santolina, and sulfur-yellow lupins rise above mounds of feathery foliage.

# Mixed borders

More than any other, this style of planting has most resonance and understanding with gardeners. While some may aspire to the traditional herbaceous border, and others might yearn for a naturally inspired meadow, in reality most people have (or have had) an element of a mixed border somewhere in their garden.

For many, the memory of a mixed border is the type that their parents or grandparents gardened. It comprised a sprinkling of shrubs, herbaceous perennials, spring-flowering bulbs, roses and possibly a small tree or climber, planted together on one side of the garden. And it is that basic understanding that has recently made the mixed border a curiously unfashionable yet emotionally dependable addition to a new garden.

## Wise choice

People gardened this way because it provided a balanced garden – something for all seasons. As a general rule, a mixed border normally sits in front of a hedge or fence; it is longer than it is deep; and its success depends on the balance of plants. Generally, the tree or larger shrubs (often but not always evergreen) grow along the back or at given points along the bed, affording height, structure and screening. Herbaceous perennials inject seasonal growth and color; bulbs fill gaps at less colorful times of year; and climbers scrabble around mature plants or structures such as an obelisk or along the fence panel.

Nowadays, a very wide selection of genera and cultivars is available, and grasses (such as *Stipa*, *Miscanthus* and *Calamagrostis*) can be added to the mix, with sublime results. Pot-filled, heat-loving agaves or exotic types can be brought out in summer and placed at strategic points; and sculpture can enhance movement and add visual interest to the planting design.

To succeed, a mixed border needs little attention – except at the planning phase – and an eye for effective combinations. Although relatively easy to achieve, there are some initial questions to consider. How big is the area for planting? At what rates do the different species and cultivars grow? How much time should be allowed for growth? Is there interest in each season, and how can a succession be encouraged through the border? Does the mix enjoy the same soil and aspect requirements?

Although these considerations sound daunting, they are not. They are practical questions that gardeners ask themselves constantly (often without thinking). In a mixed border, however, they are especially important. The reason: with this style, some of the contenders – small trees, shrubs, climbers – are in for the long run, giving continuity and balance throughout the year, for years to come. They do

not like being moved. Faster growing, sometimes more floriferous herbaceous plants, bulbs and annuals fill in the gaps, bringing the effect together, and are easier to chop and change.

Maintenance demands are generally quite low in a mixed border, but they do entirely depend on the effect and range of plants being grown. But, if the nature, habit and choice of foliar and floral interest are considered carefully, seasonal splendor, reliable interest and beautiful combinations can be achieved. Long live the mixed border.

**Above:** Many gardeners retain elements of mixed borders because they give consistency throughout the year, by using conifers, shrubs, herbaceous perennials and annuals.

**Opposite:** A mixed autumnal border with *Aster novi-belgii* 'Chequers', red-leaved ornamental cabbages, *Heuchera* 'Amethyst Myst' and grasses gives a timely and cohesive display.

# Woodland planting

Woodlands are almost universally popular. There is something that gardeners inherently relate to when walking through a wood – whether it be the apparent security of the canopy overhead; the relative cool in summer; an unexpected clearing here or there; or the endless silhouettes of trees.

In terms of planting design, woodlands offer opportunities and constraints. The key is to make sure that any horticultural intervention appears to be in keeping with the natural order of things. It is an essential rule. The minute a gardener makes something look too busy, too gardenesque or too unnatural, the illusion is shattered and any sense of enjoyment endangered.

The word illusion is important, for gardening under a small canopy of trees, or in a wood, is on the whole unnatural. Woods by their very nature are not concerned with offering a stable environment for fussy herbaceous perennials, deep-rooting bulbs or moisture-hungry shrubs. Whatever grows on the surface under an oak wood, beech forest or ash planting has to contend with a lack of light, low moisture levels and impoverished soil.

## Under the trees

Once their habitat is understood, however, woodland gardens are a hugely exciting planting opportunity. If there is already a collection of trees in the garden, then a garden can be made there by improving the soil (lots of compost and well-rotted manure), by removing some of the lower tree branches (to let in more light) and by careful plant selection.

Remember to keep designs simple, and plant en masse. When you are competing with 40 ft. (12 m) high tree trunks one of each plant will not do; plant in threes, fives or sevens. It may be limiting at first, but the result will be infinitely more rewarding. In addition, pick and choose your planting sites: there is no point in wanting to locate your most treasured plants right at the base of a large oak, where the surface roots from

the tree will always win out for nutrients and water. Dig where there is most soil, and work accordingly around opportunities. A little planning, especially in such a challenging environment, will help you no end.

## Right place right plant

Beth Chatto, the principal exponent of "right place right plant" at her gardens in Colchester, Essex, United Kingdom, proves these principles beyond doubt. She has been able to bring color, texture, seasonality and change into her oak

**Above:** The fern *Dryopteris*, claret-flowered *Aquilegia* and white *Paeonia* 'Late Windflower' all flourish in this ground-cover planting in the shady Woodland Garden at Beth Chatto's.

**Top:** Large-leaved *Hosta sieboldiana* backed by pink-flowered *Hyacinthoides* makes for a bold display in this delightful woodland glade.

Above left: Pink and white candelabra primroses in the foreground give color to this woodland scene on a sloped part of a garden.

Above right: A path runs through a woodland-style garden designed by Ulf Nordfjell in Sweden, bringing together grass, wildflowers and stone outcrops.

Woodland Garden. The list of suitable plants is endless: from early flowering winter aconites and snowdrops, through hellebores, *Narcissus*, *Erythronium* and unraveling ferns, to autumn-flowering colchicum and cyclamen.

For more open woodland areas, try shrubs such as mahonia, choisyas, euonymus and hydrangeas; those that like full or dappled shade are all candidates. When combined with the actual color of the trunk, branches and leaves of the trees themselves, woodland gardens can be truly spectacular.

The final consideration with this style, however, is just how closely the gardener is drawn to nature, and his or her awareness of even the smallest changes enhanced. When light levels are low, for example, woodland gardens add further depth to the scene; when summer heat gets too much, the plants show visible (and often speedy) signs of stress; as autumn leaves fall, noises never heard elsewhere in the garden can be deafening. Such elemental senses remind gardeners of the power of the woodland, and that they are mere gardeners within it.

GREAT PLANTING DESIGNERS CASE STUDY

# BETH CHATTO

For more than 40 years, Beth Chatto has been regarded as an icon among gardeners. One of Great Britain's most influential planters, she happily admits to perfecting the art of turning problem garden areas into horticultural havens.

Her success is not only borne out of an encyclopedic knowledge of plants and her talent as an artist but is also suckered by a staunch belief that plants with similar needs and habits should be combined together and placed in the habitats for which they are naturally adapted. She has famously said that she "follows, not

A thorough understanding of the conditions that her plants require has allowed Beth Chatto to tame her garden wasteland and create inspirational naturalistic plantings.

copies, Nature," and her innate ability to combine color, texture, and form has allowed her to take ecological planting to new heights. When she began her gardening career, this was a brand-new and ground-breaking approach to planting.

In 1960 Beth Chatto took up the challenge of transforming the overgrown wasteland at her home in Elmstead Market in Essex, and it has since become one of the most famous gardens in England. On a site of extreme conditions where impoverished gravel soil contrasts sharply with waterlogged soil and natural ponds, and where patches of shade meet full sun, she learned to work with the site, turning its problems to her advantage by selecting and combining the right plants for the right place.

None of Beth Chatto's garden areas – among them a Water Garden and Woodland Garden – demonstrates this more effectively than the much-admired Gravel Garden, which was begun in the early 1990s. Built on what was a driveway in full sun, she used evergreen and "evergray" plants such as artemisia, cistus and bergenias to lend structure to the garden. Grasses supply movement, transparency, texture and year-long interest, while bulbs (including species of allium and tulip) and herbaceous plants (such as fleshy sedums) are the fluid elements in the design and they come and go as the season dictates, injecting form, color and texture into the scene.

Despite being located in an area where rainfall is minimal, her Dry Garden is never watered, allowing plants to flourish and behave as they would in their natural environment.

Beth Chatto has been quoted as saying, "Choose plants adapted by nature to the conditions you have and they will repay you by flourishing, harmonizing with each other, and requiring little attention because they are in the right environment." To visit her own garden is to appreciate that she knows exactly what she is talking about.

# Exotic planting styles

This style of planting is perhaps the one that divides gardening opinion most. Some see it as brash and vulgar; others perceive it as yet another way for those who love plants and gardens to express themselves. However, it cannot be denied that, when exotic style planting really works, it can be like nothing else in the garden.

The linchpins of this type of planting are those of foliar contrast and floral cohesion. The aim is for dense, colorful planting to give a flavor of faraway lands: to impart some of the drama, the unruliness and the bewildering scales so associated with those natural habitats, yet not to recreate them. Dramatic foliage from cannas, bananas, gingers and bamboos can be set against each other complementarily or aggressively. Colors can collide, pushing the boundaries of taste (for some) to the utmost and challenging convention.

## Plant selection

Bananas (*Musa basjoo*) and cannas are probably the plants most commonly associated with the exotic style, and are rightly used frequently. Yet other garden favorites – dahlias, *Verbena bonariensis*, irises, phormiums, sempervivums, agaves, echiums – can be thrown into the brash mix as well. Some species and cultivars are tender, many are annuals, while others are fully hardy; each type will grow at different rates. Due to this range, exotic planting can be seen as another form of bedding schemes – the height of the effect will run from end of late summer to autumn.

This exuberant display of color and foliage at Overbecks in Devon, U.K., features yellow daylilies, a banana plant, hedychium and canna set against a backdrop of palm trees.

**Above left:** A lush planting at Teasdale, in Gloucestershire, U.K., reveals contrasting foliage sizes, colors and textures.

**Above right:** A veritable fireworks of color can be created by combining *Kniphofia uvaria* 'Nobilis', *Canna* 'King Humbert' and (red-leaved) 'Wyoming', red-flowered *Crocosmia* 'Lucifer' and *Echinacea purpurea*.

It is not only plant selection that defines a successful scheme, but also location. More often that not, exotic plants work best where there is a backdrop (a building or hedge, for example) on more than one side. This allows the sheer exuberance to be contained and absorbed by the garden visitor, rather than cause an interruption to other elements of the garden.

Perhaps the greatest exponent of this style was the late Christopher Lloyd, of Great Dixter, in East Sussex, United Kingdom, who famously ripped out Edwin Lutyens' rose garden in favor of exotic drama. The resulting design is one of balanced scale, color and contrast.

### Other considerations

As an exotic display depends on myriad combinations, there are no steadfast rules for when to plan and start your plants off. But, if using a lot of tender material, be sure to get it off to a good start in a greenhouse, and always plant in the ground only once all frosts have gone. Conversely, if you are aiming to keep exotic plants for a similar display next year, bring them into shelter prior to the first frosts.

During the growing season, remember that some plants may require a lot of feeding, while others are in need of more practical support such as staking or tying in. Whatever the planting scheme, a little consideration of each plant's growing needs can only be of benefit for that truly stunning display.

In truth, exotic style planting is not so much about a set list of plants to use (as in, for example, a cottage garden or traditional herbaceous border) but more about a mindset, a spirit in the creator's brain. If the overall look is achieved, then who is to argue whether it is "exotic" enough? The designer will be able to tell that by the reaction on other people's faces.

# CHRISTOPHER LLOYD AND FERGUS GARRETT

The essence of the energetic gardening partnership between the late Christopher Lloyd and his head gardener Fergus Garrett at Great Dixter in Sussex, United Kingdom, was experimentation, an unfettered delight in ignoring the rules, and above all fun. As Fergus Garrett said, "We were playmates in this incredible garden and, with such a strong creative link between us, we got a kick from each other's company and from working together."

In the 16 years that they worked side by side, the result was and remains a garden that burgeons with original and fresh planting ideas all year long. Together the pair blazed a trail in exploding the traditional conventions of color combining. "I take it as a challenge to combine every sort of color effectively," explained Christopher Lloyd. Thus shocking pink phlox is in an unlikely partnership with yellow mullein, or a clump of red poppies vibrates against a planting of deep purple delphiniums behind. He would regularly find inspiration in happy accidents where plants self-seeded to produce unexpected combinations.

All the borders at Great Dixter are mixed. Christopher Lloyd wrote, "I see no point in segregating plants of differing habits. They can all help one another." The result is a series of complex tapestries throughout the garden where all kinds of plants – herbaceous, shrubs and grasses – are woven together. Among the carefully constructed mêlée, which was often the result of long evenings when the pair discussed nothing but planting combinations, annuals and bedding plants are replanted two or three times a year to hide the bare earth exposed by emerging or fading perennials or the gaps created after the leaf fall of deciduous shrubs. This practice, despite the intensive maintenance that it requires, also fulfilled one of Christopher Lloyd's and Fergus Garrett's main priorities for the garden: that the garden should maintain interest throughout the year.

Quite often they would revel in resurrecting plants that were out of favor. In the Exotic Garden, an

exuberant display of dahlias in startling shades of red, orange, yellow and pink was supported by canna lilies, grasses and perennials, such as *Verbena bonariensis* with its airy purple blooms. This caused vigorous debate among the gardening establishment. Needless to say, such was the influence of this much-respected and much-loved gardening duo that it was not long before dahlias came back into fashion.

Whether upright, sulphur-yellow verbascum against sprays of scarlet crocosmia (top) or the sword-shaped leaves of a yucca among *Rheum palmatum* (above) the planting combinations at Great Dixter are carefully planned and constructed yet exuberant and joyful, reflecting the close partnership between Christopher Lloyd and Fergus Garrett.

# Meadow planting

Within this broad gardening style, planting combinations range from the controlled order of a gardener's desire to the seemingly wild, where plants roam at will; from mixed borders to the semi-control of prairie style. In among all of these is meadow planting: it may seem wild, natural and totally "as by nature," but there is as much rigor and consideration as any other planting style.

Meadow-style planting can be split into two: naturally occurring meadows; and those in which cultivated plants have been introduced.

### Natural meadows

A wide range of flowers and grasses grow in this type of meadow, whether it is a 2-acre (0.8 ha) field or a strip of long grass at the back of the garden. Different locations will sustain different mixes – from clay or wet soils through to chalk downland or cornfield annuals. As a general rule, meadows prefer impoverished soil. The choice of meadow plants ranges from annuals to some perennials, biennials, grasses and, in some cases, some deeper rooting plants.

From a gardener's point of view, the objective is to maintain the natural balance; allowing one species to dominate will upset the whole. In a practical sense, this type of meadow needs the gardener to keep a check on what can and cannot be allowed to grow. Cutting the meadow back, at the appropriate time of the year, is also key to ensuring the life cycle is continued. The introduction of bulbs, plug plants, or seeds can broaden the range of what occurs in that location. The benefit of such a meadow to native flora, and wildlife as a whole, should not be underestimated.

### Humanmade meadows

In a more gardenesque sense, meadow planting is about taking certain elements and recreating them with cultivated plants (although wild flowers can be used too, if desired). A naturalized meadow has: seasonal highs – red poppies in early summer, for example – and dots of flowers; grasses at differing levels swaying in the wind; and seasonal longevity where specimens can be left in place for the benefit of insects and increasing biodiversity. Many of the plants found in a naturalistic planting style can be used in a cultivated one, but not en masse. Meadow planting should be more subtle, with finer details intermingling. Herbaceous perennial species of *Achillea*, *Echinops*, *Erigeron*, *Salvia* and *Euphorbia* can grow easily with grasses such as *Pennisteum*, *Stipa*, *Miscanthus* and *Molinia* and biennials such as hollyhocks and *Verbascum*. Proponents such as landscape designer Dan Pearson, and some of Julie Toll's work, include strong elements of meadow combinations.

Meadow styles are everlastingly popular, whether there is space to allow grasses and flowers to grow "wild" in the garden, or a more cultivated-plant approach is preferable; indeed it is possible to have an element of both types somewhere in the garden.

**Opposite:** Bright red *Papaver rhoeas* grows seamlessly in the Wildflower Meadow at Knoll Gardens, in Dorset, U.K.

**Below:** Growing happily in the front meadow at Great Dixter, in East Sussex, U.K., are *Camassia quamash* bulbs, which bring blue delight in late spring.

GREAT PLANTING DESIGNERS CASE STUDY

# DAN PEARSON

translates this knowledge into his planting designs, choosing plants that are appropriate for the variety of conditions found in any given domestic environment and that have an ability to form self-supporting communities. He is a great admirer of Beth Chatto and her principles of ecological planting, and in many of his gardens he seeks to generate the sense of wildness that is a by-product of the ecological philosophy.

Color, texture, form, foliage and scent are all treated with the same importance, and his palette of plants is wide ranging – from trees and shrubs to herbaceous perennials, grasses, annuals and bulbs. "The combining of plants can instill a garden with a mood that is particular and specific to that place and the conditions that prevail there. A combination should always provide for every month of the year but also have the potential to sing at one or more given moments," Dan Pearson explained.

He is passionate about color – his mother is a textile and fashion designer and his father is a painter so his artistic skill in combining plants is inherent. His earlier approach focused on harmonious plantings where he wove together similar tones and shades of colors such as deep rich plum, chocolate and burgundy. These days Dan Pearson favors clear, pure colors such as magenta, yellow, red, green, blue, orange and white. His combinations are energetic and occasionally shocking, and are always interpretations of how color and color combinations appear in nature. "I like to use strong colors to invite vibrancy into the garden," he stated. However, in his plantings, strong color is invariably interrupted by another to prevent it from becoming too heavy or distracting.

Dan Pearson is respected worldwide for his thoughtful approach to garden and planting design, the core of which is a sound knowledge of plants and horticulture coupled with a deeply felt emotional response toward his subject matter.

Having traveled the world over, his planting schemes are embedded in a plant's origins. When choosing plants he refers back to the conditions that they inhabit in the wild, how they relate visually to their natural surroundings and how they perform in nature. He then

Dan Pearson never stops experimenting from one year to the next, and his planting designs are not only about appealing to the perceptible senses; by virtue of his ingenuity they almost always strike a deeper chord and imbue his gardens with an intangible but profoundly felt spirit.

In this elegant yet dramatic planting, *Iris* 'Deep Black', *Anchusa* 'Loddon Royalist' and French lavender (*Lavandula stoechas*) against a golden grass show Dan Pearson's inherent skill at marrying color, form and texture.

# Naturalistic gardens

Many gardeners may claim that they take their cue from nature, and the truly informed or talented undoubtedly do so. When dealing with life cycles, microclimates, weather dependency and intricate organism relationships (that is, gardening) there should be no other way. Nature should not only guide and inform but also inspire learning.

But there is a style of planting that takes its lead from the colors, tones and styling of natural plant associations. For the gardener, naturalistic planting should mean "inspired by nature"; it does not mean "as found exactly in nature" (though some of the leading proponents do use some such harmonies). The gardening combinations are endless, as are the cues for aspiration.

This style is a recreation of tonal, visual and seasonal balance, replicated in a garden, all of which is drawn from nature. Think of swathes of herbaceous perennials and grasses; colors, textures, leaf and flower shapes, and seedheads; peaks and troughs of seasonal interest; the orchestral harmony that is a hard-fought link between land, atmosphere and light. All these qualities are at the essence of this style.

## Shared elements

There is a common theme between some of the best examples of a naturalistic garden. The majority of plants are herbaceous perennials (plants that die down in winter and come up again in spring); grasses and sedges add texture and movement; planting in sets of three, five or more is essential; and color and planting rhythms are crucial, as is the sense of scale. Together, each element needs careful consideration to make sure it does not over-dominate the other.

A naturalistic planting, however, often needs a fairly large space in order to work. If a path can be sited through the scheme, then all the better: the sensation of approach, envelopment and exit can make for a special experience. But if space is very restricted, then

no matter: work out where the best views will be and use every available inch. Exact flowering times, color hues and changes, and leaf shape and pattern should be studied, as should continuity over time.

Even though some of the best schemes are bigger in scale, the charm of a sublime floral combination up close can be equally stimulating. The wildlife benefits that such a range of plants can bring are considerable, too: in summer they are nectar sources and in winter seed repositories and places of shelter. Thus a naturalistic planting scheme can add a sense of worth to any garden.

Spires of *Verbascum* and *Kniphofia* add vertical accent to the lower growing *Coreopsis* and *Stipa tenuissima* in this planting at Lady Farm, in Somerset, U.K.

## Plant choice

Species and cultivar selection is crucial to ensure success. This is where it is worth learning from those who have already tried endless combinations, such as leading Dutch planter Piet Oudolf.

Suitable perennials for a naturalistic garden should include spires of *Salvia*, *Veronicastrum*, and *Digitalis*; the more rounded flowerheads of *Eupatorium*, *Sedum* and *Angelica*; the showers of *Miscanthus* and *Molinia* grasses; the dots and spots of *Sanguisorba*, *Helenium*, *Echinacea* and *Aster*; and the plumes of *Thalictrum* and *Persicaria*. These may read like a daunting list, but just pick a few favorites, then a good start will have been made to the design.

For many gardeners, there are still questions over how sensible it is to commit a whole garden to the naturalistic style. To be successful, these gardens require a good, cold winter to ensure straggly, weak growth is curtailed, so gardens that are experiencing warmer winters may need to adopt such a scheme only in part. And maybe that is where the possibilities lie: Piet Oudolf, for example, often creates naturalistic planting enclosed by formal hedging, or with trees to act as boundaries amid the swell of grasses, flowers and different planting forms. The marrying of nature-inspired combinations, with human-considered planting intervention, can be just what many people want from their garden. Given a careful selection of plants, why not?

By combining different flower shapes, such as the tall, thin, red *Kniphofia uvaria* and rounded balls of *Echinops ritro* 'Veitch's Blue', the contrast in visual interest can be heightened.

GREAT PLANTING DESIGNERS CASE STUDY
# PIET OUDOLF

Credit for catapulting the New Wave Perennial Planting into the public domaine belongs to Dutchman Piet Oudolf. In the last 20 years he has taken naturalistic planting to ever greater heights and succeeded in popularizing many plants by redefining their role in the garden bed or border.

A love of native American meadow perennials, and his desire to design and plant spaces that "give you the feeling that you are walking in nature," have led Piet Oudolf to create some of the most admired gardens and borders of recent times, in both the United States and Europe. These include the spectacular Glasshouse

borders at RHS Wisley in Surrey, United Kingdom, the Millennium Garden in Chicago and the garden at Pensthorpe Waterfowl Trust in Norfolk, United Kingdom. "The vision I have developed on gardening and especially in my work with perennials is based not only out of respect for nature but also the power, energy, emotions, beauty and aesthetics it gives," he commented.

In all of Piet Oudolf's planting schemes, structure, texture and shape take precedence over color or height. Piet Oudolf's use of tall plants such as the diaphanous *Stipa tenuissima* or wiry *Verbena bonariensis* at the front of a border breaks all the rules of conventional border planting – their transparent qualities allowing views through to the plants behind. To Piet Oudolf, composition is infinitely more important than simply following the rules.

Many of the plants that he uses are wild species or varieties of those species chosen deliberately for their greater proportion of leaves to flowers. Burnets, knotweeds, filipendula, astrantia, echinacea and grasses are among his favorites with this characteristic. Plants

are also chosen for their interest throughout the season and are just as much included for their seedheads, spent flowerheads or their stems as they are for their flowers and foliage.

The overall scenes that Piet Oudolf creates are airy yet often dramatic. He uses large quantities of plants in ribbons or blocks of bold color combinations such as red *Knautia macedonica* together with yellow *Digitalis ferruginea*, or wine-red yarrow alongside vibrant purple *Salvia* × *superba*. Yet, on close examination, the devil is in the detail and the detail is shape and form: spires contrast with umbels or plumes, while tiny buttons are a foil for more substantial forms. Each combination is an exquisite vignette in its own right, yet Piet Oudolf has proved repeatedly that he is also a master in threading the detail together to create a powerful and breathtaking spectacle.

The combination of form and texture supplied by *Phlomis russeliana*, *Monarda* 'Aquarius' and *Echinacea* weaves a striking floral tapestry in this border designed by Piet Oudolf at Scampston Hall, in North Yorkshire, U.K.

# Country style

It may be a sweeping generalization, but there is an element of a "country garden" within most gardens. Such a concept is difficult to describe fully, because it is more about an atmosphere than a prescribed planting plan. There is, however, something about the combination of informal planting positioned alongside an old brick path, with a neatly clipped hedge backdrop or balanced by a tree or sculpture, that hints at this style.

A country garden is often, but not exclusively, one that is found in rural areas – by its nature it benefits from more space, usually found in the country and with views to neighboring fields beyond. Yet its appeal certainly straddles both city and country. There is a homeliness to this style that seems to sit with those who appreciate the creation of a garden in a setting that is both gardenesque but also interesting. It is not cottage gardening (which has overtones of a time gone by) because the effect is more honest and possibly evolutionary. Here the garden has seemingly evolved over time, growing as its owner has, mixing maturity with youthful endeavor, splendor with reality and color associations (of both plants and hard landscaping material) that are complementary rather than lurid. In a really good example of a country garden, there should be a very real feel of the owners living in the space, using and working with the garden.

So what are the hallmarks of this style? In an overall garden plan sense, it is about how spaces and "rooms" relate to each other; how garden users will move from one area to the next; and whether hedges, trellis, screens or walls are used as dividing lines. Pergolas and arches may be introduced to link spaces or frame a view. Once in those areas, the linearity of the dividers is softened with planting mixtures, of herbaceous perennials and woody shrubs, annual bulbs under trees, "messy" summer growth flopping over evergreen dependents. Color coding can take place (as in the White Garden, at Sissinghurst Castle Garden, in Kent, United

Kingdom, where plants with whites, grays and greens calmly live together). Topiary formality can create structure and seasonal continuity, while interconnecting views in and out of garden rooms can make the garden feel bigger than it really is.

## Scale and proportion

The relationship between space and void – grass to border for example – is key. Proportion and scale of paths, beds or planting associations are also crucial to retain a balanced experience,

A medley of color and form give a quintessential country-style feel to these gardens. This can be seen (top) in the reds of *Centranthus ruber* and the rose, the spire of yellow *Verbascum* and blue-purple of *Salvia*. The use of lawn and a focal conifer (above) give balance and scale, with the luxury of a countryside view beyond.

ensuring that both gardener and garden know there is an implied harmony. A quality of skillfulness and materials, gluing the possibly different areas together, is another subtle but important addition. Yet, as with other styles, techniques such as floral and foliar repetition, the use of focal points, harmonious/contrasting textures and shapes, and a mixed palette of plant groups are all welcome.

Country gardens may have the association of well-off landowners wandering around in their garden, but the reality is that they have a deep resonance of appeal to a wide range of gardeners. Their strength lies in the fact that they can be used throughout the year; clever structure of hedges or evergreen shrubs ensures there is interest even in deep winter that can then retire to the background once summer's splendor performs.

By making sure that planting combinations are thought through, spatial dividers kept in good order and there is a consistency of color, a country-style garden proves an atmospheric and invaluable asset.

**Above right:** The cutting garden at planter Sarah Raven's Perch Hill Farm, in East Sussex, U.K., includes *Hesperis matronalis* and *Anchusa azurea* 'Dropmore' in the foreground. These reinforce the link that beautiful spaces can also be productive.

**Above left:** Using clipped box balls gives structure to this space, as does the obelisk strewn with *Clematis* 'Alionushka'. The brick path also adds to the overall country-style feel of the scene.

GREAT PLANTING DESIGNERS CASE STUDY

# ROSEMARY VEREY

The late Rosemary Verey remains one of the great doyennes of the gardening world. Images of her famous garden at Barnsley House in Gloucestershire, United Kingdom, particularly the laburnum walk underplanted with purple alliums, are instantly recognizable, and despite her death in 2001 her planting philosophies are as valid today as they were in her heyday. Her iconic book *Good Planting* encapsulated theories that centered around companion planting in which she perfected the art of combining color, texture and form while all the time acknowledging and accommodating each plant's characteristics and habitat needs. Like her counterpart

Beth Chatto, Rosemary Verey was always concerned with selecting the right plants for the right place.

An accessible and inspirational analysis of planting combinations, *Good Planting* not only captured gardeners' imaginations but also gave them the confidence to aspire to the kind of planting combinations that Rosemary Verey practiced at Barnsley and which previously they might have thought were beyond their reach. She was also one of the most high-profile writers to galvanize gardeners into thinking beyond spring and summer, encouraging them to plant trees and shrubs with strong shapes that come into their own when denuded of leaves in winter. She also liked to incorporate evergreen plants – whether as topiary or left to their own devices – as well as autumn-flowering bulbs and plants with colorful stems.

Color was of great importance to Rosemary Verey, and her schemes were always well mannered, following the rules set by the color wheel, where color pairings should consist of harmonious complementary colors. Planting combinations of blue and yellow became her signature, and such was her influence that much of her color theory was replicated in many country gardens. Texture and form, however, were just as important, and she was as successful at creating monochrome borders of nothing but foliage – feathery or leathery, variegated, purple or silver. This allowed her to experiment with contrasting forms and textures without the distraction of the floral color and shapes.

Rosemary Verey applied her planting principles to every kind of plant. Whether it was the neatly arranged vegetables in her potager, autumnal plantings of trees and shrubs, or romantic partnerships of bulbs and perennials, each combination was touched by her impeccable taste and always seemed to succeed.

Whether they were vegetables or perennials, Rosemary Verey cast an artistic eye over every kind of planting in her garden at Barnsley House.

# Cottage gardens

Perhaps universally recognized, cottage-style gardens have a charm and simplicity about them that makes them clearly identifiable – and still so popular today. Just watch the crowds swelling around a cottage-style garden at a flower show, or see how many books are sold on this topic, to realize how true this is.

Historically associated with an old, timber-framed or red-brick cottage, this style has evolved into a garden that people emotionally relate to – one that links back to the mid- to late 19th century, when life was slower, pride was taken in the flowers and crops grown and floral combinations seemed to happen as if by chance.

Of course, this idealized view of cottage gardens was far removed from the reality of those times. The harsher truth is that these small properties, providing accommodation for

workers, had to sustain the occupants. Emphasis in the garden was therefore on vegetable and fruit growing, and the addition of a tree, such as pear or apple. Because money was limited, ornamental flowers were used to encourage pollinating insects into the garden and get to work on the crops being grown. Life was hard, so every bit of the garden had to be used; time would not have been wasted on caring for lawns or growing flowers for the sake of it. Hence species were allowed to self-seed or grow among each other in any leftover space.

The main plant palette of a cottage garden was species of, for example, hollyhocks, pinks and carnations, pansies, delphiniums, herbs, lupins, foxgloves and roses. Primarily herbaceous perennials and biennials, the combinations swell in color and height from late spring to summer; hollyhocks and foxgloves

*Mysotis* and *Aquilegia* help create this tumbledown but charming effect in a spring border at Eastgrove Cottage, Worcestershire, U.K.

race skyward, scattering their seed across the garden after their floral finale, so as to perpetuate their blooms in coming years.

## Gradual evolution

Over time, arbors or pergolas were introduced to cottage gardens in order to accommodate climbing ornamentals or crops; topiary was used to bring form and interest throughout the year; and garden statuary, such as stone sundials, included to beautify the scene. Such aesthetics started to change the cottage gardener's outlook, but never so as to diminish the original role of the actual garden itself.

So how does this type of garden sit in today's society – and with its range of buildings and plant choice? The answer is quite well. Cottage gardening is a way of life; it should never be contrived and must happen by default – an unconsciously conscious way of gardening. What this means is that the principles of relaxed planting, intermingling ornamentals and crops, a less fussy or strict maintenance regime, and a closer adherence to the seasons or weather,

links owner to garden, climate and seasonality. In today's society of wanting to reconnect people to land, the cottage garden may therefore seem unusually timely.

To modern gardeners, the other benefit of cottage gardening is its association with wildlife. These gardens have always been a balance of people working with nature to benefit each other; but this sentiment alone has been lost in so many gardens today with recent horticultural developments such as double flowers, which are often sterile and therefore produce no nectar for insects. With continued pressure on wildlife spaces across the globe, if a garden can act as a resource for both nature and its animals, then all the better.

This style of gardening does not have to remain the preserve of the cottage owner; it can be applied anywhere. Whether around a newly built house in the middle of a city or a rambling old country house, its approach of using informal, seasonally appropriate planting and a balance of crops and ornamentals is suitable for any garden anywhere.

**Below left:** At RHS Garden Wisley, in Surrey, U.K., seasons have a strong effect on planting combinations. In summer, *Penstemon* 'Alice Hindley', *Perovskia*, lavender and *Nepeta* all mix attractively together with their color and foliage tone.

# PENELOPE HOBHOUSE

Like her mentor Rosemary Verey, Penelope Hobhouse has made the seemingly complex art of flower gardening accessible to gardeners worldwide. Through her books, international lecture tours and garden designs both at home and in the United States, Penelope Hobhouse has inspired a fiercely loyal following of plantspeople who appreciate her traditional English approach to combining all kinds of plants within the formal garden structure. Her association with Tintinhull House and earlier restoration of the gardens at Hadspen House in Somerset, both in the United Kingdom, caused them to become garden icons for those who aspired to create billowing and romantic plantings of shrubs, herbaceous perennials and annuals.

Penelope Hobhouse is a great exponent of combining color using conventional color theory as her basis. Influenced by Chevreul's work on 19th-century color theory and Gertrude Jekyll's harmonious planting associations, she believes that gardens are the result of a collaboration between art and nature. She has also been heavily affected by the ways in which French Impressionist painters such as Monet approached the use of color in their work.

Consequently, Penelope Hobhouse's planting associations are almost always characterized by layers of vibrant color often separated by and contained within a formal structure – whether it be evergreen hedges or hard landscaping that provide the constant – while a rich palette of herbaceous plants and bulbs ebb and flow with the changing seasons.

In her Country Garden, at RHS Garden Wisley in Surrey, United Kingdom, the herbaceous planting is contained within a typically formal rectilinear layout of paths. Based on the 19th-century plant expert William Robinson's theory of combining hardy plants in suitable situations, the plants are allowed a certain amount of freedom to blend with each other. Repetition, however, in the form of evergreen shrubs, the ornamental grass *Stipa gigantea* and *Nepeta* 'Six Hills Giant' lends the garden rhythm and cohesion and is a reminder that there is nothing random despite the naturalistic appearance. In spring bulbous plants such as scilla and chionodoxa provide some interest, while in summer the garden is in full swing with repeat-flowering roses, verbena, cosmos, salvia, clematis, and annual bedding taking it through until early autumn.

Rightly regarded as one of the most influential and outstanding gardeners of the 20th century, Penelope Hobhouse is noted for her prowess as a combiner of plants and just as much for her energy and enthusiasm in sharing her knowledge with gardeners the world over.

Carefully contrived but exuding freedom, Penelope Hobhouse's exuberant herbaceous borders in the Country Garden at RHS Garden Wisley contain a rich blend of *Angelica gigas*, *Achillea filipendulina* 'Gold Plate' and *Verbena bonariensis*.

## Grasses

Of all the horticultural developments over the last 20 years or so, it is possibly the inclusion of grasses into professional and private planting schemes that has made the most difference. In their simplest form, and with their natural habit, they bring a new type of texture, color and accent to a planting scheme. And at their most successful they add movement, sound and a depth of light that many other types of plant cannot readily achieve. By repeating specific cultivars or by planting different species together, it is possible to create many desirable effects with grasses.

**Above:** Among the striped splendor at Pensthorpe Millennium Garden, in Norfolk, U.K., are (at the back) *Eupatorium*, swaying grasses and some *Echinacea* seedheads.

**Opposite:** Grasses can mix well in a border as can be seen in this planting of *Pennisetum setaceum*, *Agastache rugosa* hybrid, *Canna* 'Mystique', *Miscanthus sinensis* 'Kaskade', *Sambucus nigra* f. *porphyrophylla* 'Black Beauty' and a *Penstemon* cultivar.

In common garden parlance, the term "grasses" is used when referring to (botanically speaking) grasses, sedges, grasslike plants and even bamboos. Though technically wrong, the terminology does, however, imply the visual qualities that so many gardeners and designers desire. These include spires or mounds of plants that range in seasonal interest and habit as well as in the effects of screening or transparency that change the entire atmosphere of a scheme. One additional benefit is the striking color combinations that can be achieved between grasses and other plants, which demonstrate clever planting skills.

The joy of using grasses in any garden is their ability to fill the available space, and their flexibility in achieving the desired look. For smaller spaces, species of *Pennisetum*, *Hakonechloa*, *Carex* and *Stipa* are perfect; for grander statements, taller *Stipa*, *Molinia*, *Miscanthus* and *Calamagrostis* species and cultivars should be used. For a really bold effect, pampas grass such as *Cortaderia selloana* or bamboos such *Sasa palmata* f. *nebulosa* can be used to add height and structure where room allows. The combinations are as endless as the affects their planting can create – and, with ever increasing cultivars being introduced, this choice is set to continue still further.

Grasses can be included in any sort of planting style. For instance, there could be a whole border full of grasses (such as at RHS Garden Wisley, Surrey, or at the Royal Botanic Gardens, Kew, Surrey, both in the United Kingdom). In these, the combination of foliage shape and color, seedheads, habit of plant and repeated rhythms make for a dramatic display – especially in winter when there may be little other interest in a garden. Alternatively, grasses can be used in meadow- or prairie-style combinations, mimicking the grasses found in nature but living happily alongside the gamut of herbaceous perennials. Yet another approach may be to intersperse some species within a mixed border, where the shrubs, perennials and bulbs work with the grass species to ensure seasonal change. Finally, grasses also have their place in more exotic or Mediterranean-style gardens, adding flavor and drama to bold expressions of planting.

For some gardeners, grasses have been over-used in recent times and this may well be true. But like all fashions, there is a natural leveling out of the good and not-so-good, resulting in many species and cultivars being truly garden-worthy plants, of value to any gardener. Until a gardener has tried growing grasses, he or she will not know what they can truly bring to the garden; and, once a gardener has, it will be difficult to stop growing them.

GREAT PLANTING DESIGNERS CASE STUDY

# OEHME AND VAN SWEDEN

The powerful design partnership of Wolfgang Oehme and James van Sweden has been reinvigorating the American gardening scene since the mid-1970s. When they began, their approach to planting in particular was seen as a revolution in a continent that had hitherto largely failed to recognize the garden-worthiness of its extraordinary native flora.

The pair made such a profound impression that their work led a brand-new movement in gardening. Labeled the "New American Garden style," it was summed up

Succulent sedum with its ever-changing flowerheads, *Miscanthus sinensis* and *Pennisetum alopecuroides* are plants typically used by Oehme and van Sweden in the free-flowing plantings of their New American Garden style.

by Professor Darrel Morrison, Fellow of the American Society of Landscape Architecture, as "exposing a wide audience to the importance of layered landscapes where flowing herbaceous vegetation patterns enrich a strong spatial framework made up of trees, shrubs and structural elements."

Although the inspiration for their planting associations is drawn from the American meadow and the Midwestern prairie, Oehme and van Sweden seek only to imitate nature rather than to copy it. James van Sweden described their approach to planting as being "vigorous and audacious, and it vividly blends the natural and the cultivated."

The basis for these layered landscapes is the exuberant use of ornamental grasses and a mix of herbaceous perennials, many of them American natives, all planted on a grand scale among trees and shrubs for structure. Chosen for their changing form throughout the season, grasses and perennials are woven together to create a harmonious and relaxed tapestry of color and texture. James van Sweden explained, "Good planting design does not follow a formula. At best, it allows you to experiment with nature and through nature to make an original statement."

Signature plants include grasses of every kind from the low-growing hummocky *Festuca glauca* to *Pennisetum alopecuroides*, *Miscanthus sinensis* and *Calamagrostis plumbaginoides*. Stems, leaves and seedheads are always left untouched to provide winter interest. The perennials, such as rudbeckia, sedum and astilbes, are partnered with some evergreens (including hypericum and *Liriope muscari*), and are also left to fulfil their seasonal promise.

Despite the scale and complexity of their planting associations, Oehme and van Sweden are great advocates of low-maintenance gardens. Grasses are cut back once a year, while the perennials and shrubs must tolerate drought and flourish without cosseting. The result is maximum impact with a minimum of fuss.

# Mediterranean style

The Mediterranean style of planting includes not only that area in Europe but also parts of Australia, central Chile, coastal California and the Western Cape in South Africa, according to the Mediterranean Garden Society.

When Mediterranean-style gardens are mentioned, people either roll their eyes and switch off or they lean closer for an intelligent conversation. The reason is that this style has been a victim of its own success: as people have started using their outside space more, they have wanted brighter colors, bolder planting and less maintenance. Mediterranean-inspired planting was the perfect answer. Seemingly easy to create and at a low cost, such gardens appeared to be a quick-fix, repeatedly suggested as a fast route to the instant lifestyle.

Because this style stems from how plant associations and gardens have evolved across the world, all gardeners can learn from its principles. Water conservation, mulching, planting according to microclimate and an eye for flamboyancy and drama set out this style as one for any garden. Whether in San Diego, California, or Bogotá, Columbia, these core blocks of understanding underpin a Mediterranean-style planting scheme.

So why are these factors so important? It is all to do with the natural growing conditions. Most Mediterranean plants only really awaken in autumn, after the intense heat of the summer; with cooler weather imminent, the plant takes every opportunity to grow, flower and set seed. Over winter and into spring, growth continues provided there is sporadic but, usually, acceptable rainfall. It is for this reason that springtime in these regions can be so special, with local flora in abundance. But once the energy is spent, and the heat of summer starts again, the garden quietens down into a season of relative dormancy.

For home gardeners, there is much to copy. The seasonality may differ from place to place – for example the heat of U.K. summers is still relatively tolerable – but by choosing plants that can survive extremes of heat, poor soil and sporadic rainfall, gardeners can save themselves a lot of time. As climate change challenges gardening habits, the Mediterranean garden holds many answers.

This does not mean that it will be necessary to have just gravel gardens or rocky banks, although such elements can be seen successfully employed at Denmans Garden, West Sussex, or the Dry Garden at RHS Garden Hyde Hall, Essex, both in the United Kingdom. But it is

**Bottom:** This planting, which includes *Lavandula stoechas* and *L. dentata*, *Salvia officinalis* and white-flowered *Thymus vulgaris*, produces a wonderful aroma and provides useful culinary herbs.

**Below:** The Mediterranean-style planting in the Dry Garden at RHS Garden Hyde Hall, in Essex, U.K., shows just how successful it can be at combining plants such as *Eryngium*, *Verbascum*, *Cistus*, *Phlomis* and *Ballota*.

**Above left:** Here at La Casella, in Alpes Maritimes, France, *Echium candicans* in the foreground complements the lawn, steps, fastigiate conifers and *Olea europaea* beyond in this Mediterranean garden.

**Above right:** Blending a range of plant groups, such as dark green columnar yew, white flowering yucca and pink-flowering *Armeria maritima*, is a different approach to gardening with plants that need little water.

useful to include certain features of them. Growing lavenders, sages, myrtle, *Eucomis* and echiums through beds mulched with gravel makes a visual spectacle as well as practically ensuring maintenance is low. Cultivating agaves, sempervivums, or other succulents in pots adds to the Mediterranean feel, while requiring much less watering than conventional outdoor pot plants. Also, using roses, grape vines, bougainvillea and campsis to create shade for a sunny terrace gives a practical answer to a real-life problem of intense summer heat.

The thought of a Mediterranean-style planting may be unfairly offputting for some people, compared to the reality of what it actually entails. For those gardeners who see the inevitability of climate change, however, and the need to reduce inputs (such as watering or staking) and to make the most of available microclimates, this style can easily be incorporated into an existing garden. It just takes some imagination and a little bit of conviction – and free-draining soil if there is a heavy rainfall.

# TOM STUART-SMITH

Since the 1980s Tom Stuart-Smith has carved a reputation for his elegant and subtle approach to planting design. Yet it was not until 1998, when he won the first of six Gold Medals at the Chelsea Flower Show in the United Kingdom, that he began to receive the international recognition that he deserved.

An educational grounding in ecology is the basis for Tom Stuart-Smith's planting designs. His skill is not simply in using the right plants for the right conditions but also in how he analyses a plant's behavior in nature and translates that to his planting schemes: for example, whether a species is solitary or grows in colonies. Factors such as these then determine how he uses plants in combination.

"I tend to base each idea on a natural model: a dry prairie, or a hazel coppice, then use a much wider range of plant species than would occur in nature to create a supernormal effect," explained Tom Stuart-Smith. Some are simple blocks of planting. In others he aims for plantings that he describes as intermeshed, complex, but ecologically stable. "I look to combine plants that possess the same degree of aggression so no one plant outdoes the other." A combination that demonstrates this technique most successfully is a grouping of *Eryngium* x *zebellia*, which is planted to grow through *Festuca amethystina* along with sedums, *Allium sphaerocephalon* and *Alchemilla erythropoda*.

Tom Stuart-Smith prefers plantings that incorporate several levels of naturalness. In his garden around the Bicentenary Glasshouse at RHS Garden Wisley, U.K., one side is composed of large beds planted with the grass *Hakonechloa macra* and studded with columns of

clipped beech. This contrasts with more complex planting, which as it radiates around the garden becomes more intermingled. Most of his plantings are compositions that can be viewed from many different sides. They are not borders in the traditional sense — more extracts of a larger idealized planting.

In general Tom Stuart-Smith's designs comprise 15–25 percent grasses; shrubs are interplanted with herbaceous plants to add a greater dynamic. While the herbaceous plants come and go throughout the season, the shrubs are in a process of change but still provide an element of continuity and structure. Like Piet Oudolf, texture and form are considered before color. Yet Tom Stuart-Smith is respected for his artistic color combinations, which are often harmonious mixes of several colors and tend to follow a traditional English approach similar to that of Penelope Hobhouse.

Intermeshed combinations of herbaceous perennials and grasses characterize many of Tom Stuart-Smith's planting schemes and are often offset against less complex monocultures.

The clean, cool lines of a low wall supporting a simple bench, fronted by a black-lined pond, shows minimalism at its best. It is all the richer for the frothy planting in the foreground.

# Minimalist styles

This style is a fine example of something having to be done really well in order to succeed. All too often, poor, cheap or ill thought-out examples are shown in the vain hope that they be considered a minimalist garden. But the reality is that even though they may be minimal (in other words have a limited color, material or plant palette), they are certainly not a good exponent of what is a deeply considered and articulate way to create a garden.

Minimalist gardens stem from modernism – the Western artistic and cultural movement from the first few decades of the 20th century. In a garden sense, minimalism and modernism are (wrongly) colloquially intertwined, with a "modern" garden not necessarily being "minimal." Modernism was a movement of questioning, exploration, re-evaluation and redefinition, while minimalism pared those concepts back still further. The result is a style of garden that is seemingly light-years away from the traditional herbaceous border, although, with greater understanding, it can be argued that traditional herbaceous borders actually share certain values with minimalistic ones – for example fluidity, context and pace.

## Less is more

A gardener goes about making such a garden by taking time out to define exactly what he or she wants the garden to do. They need to detach some of their built-in emotions, to specify materials on their own merit and to be focused.

Minimalist gardens are not spaces for people wanting to collect one of every plant. Instead, they are spaces that have an intelligent response to the location; the creator knows exactly what is wanted from the space and how to achieve it. Often in urban areas (where there is a higher

propensity of differing architectural and societal influences), minimalist gardens are spaces of calm and intent. For example, a back wall may be painted or rendered into a color that will harmonize, or completely contrast, with other colors within the space. Plants are often used in repetition – maybe a set of sculptural agaves in matching pots at equal distances from each other; the same species of tree used in one space, with the detail of the trunk at eye level; or riots of mixed herbaceous perennials tightly regimented into a defined space. Minimalism does not have to mean plantless, but it does mean every plant has an important job to do.

It is perhaps this notion that challenges most gardeners into making a minimalist garden – the concept that with more than 70,000 plants available, why be limited to just four or five? The answer is that the minimalism style is not about the plants, it is about the garden space itself.

Plants, stone, wood, water, space/void – they are elements of equal importance to achieve the desired look. It is the rigorous and academic skill to refine these into a usable garden that fails many gardeners. The other consideration is that, because there are a lot less materials in the space, the work of seating, planting, paving, water features and so on, has to be of the highest quality – something many home gardeners might not be able to achieve.

Minimalist gardens, when they work, are special places – there is something intangible about them. When a landscape designer such as Christopher Bradley-Hole (the leading British exponent) creates such spaces, the quality of craft and clarity of thought are self-evident. It is this rarity that makes minimalist gardens so exciting and challenging. Even if gardeners are not willing to try it, they could just try to understand it. They will be the richer for it.

**Above right:** The repetition of hedging, planting and quality hard materials look good under the dappled shade of bamboo, in Christopher Bradley-Hole's gold medal winning show garden at RHS Chelsea Flower Show 2005.

**Above left:** In the Kotoske Garden, Phoenix, Arizona, cacti are planted in line among a pebble mulch, while farther back succulents in pots are given a rendered and painted wall backdrop.

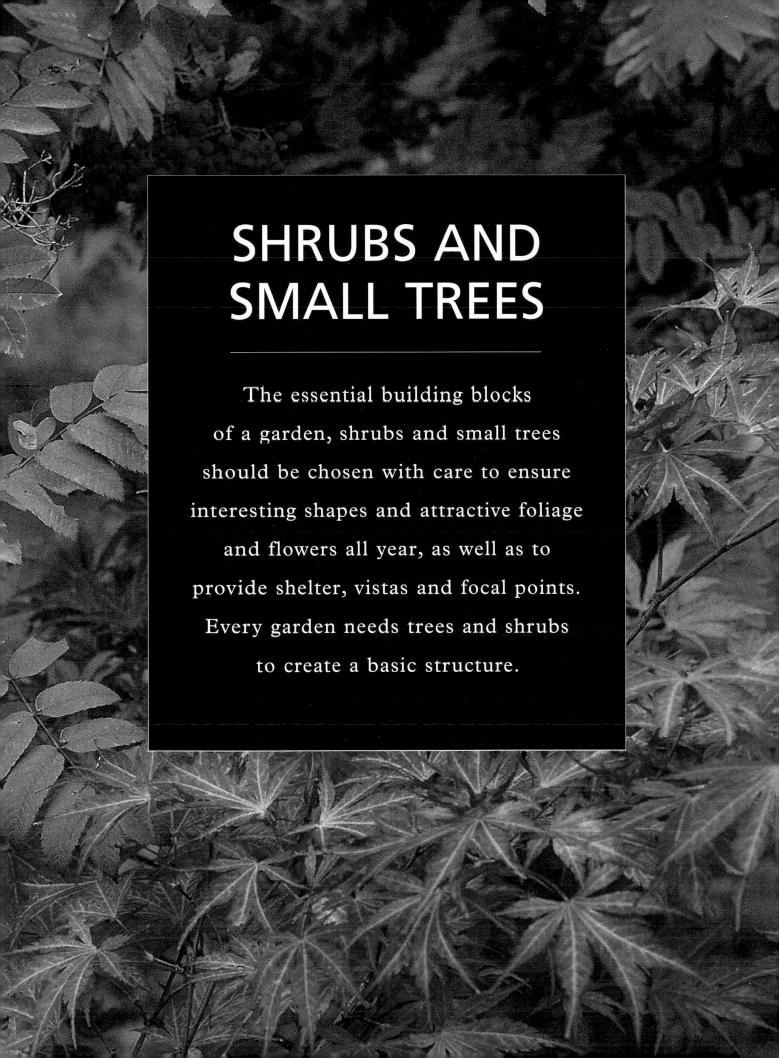

# SHRUBS AND SMALL TREES

The essential building blocks
of a garden, shrubs and small trees
should be chosen with care to ensure
interesting shapes and attractive foliage
and flowers all year, as well as to
provide shelter, vistas and focal points.
Every garden needs trees and shrubs
to create a basic structure.

**In most garden plantings** a proportion of shrubs and a small selection of trees are essential to provide height, bulk, structure and, with the inclusion of some evergreens, year-round interest.

There is a wide choice of shrubs, varying from low ground-covering potentillas to towering abutilons, from fine-textured genistas to giant-leaved rhododendrons, from those with fleeting flowers such as amelanchiers to those that are nonstop performers such as hydrangeas, their dried flowerheads persisting through the winter months. Some shrubs are deciduous, perhaps with colorful autumn foliage, others are evergreen.

The boundary between shrubs and small trees is a blurred one. Pittosporums, lilacs, philadelphus and many others start their life as shrubs but develop treelike proportions and, with help from the gardener, eventually make picturesque small trees. Trees display all the attributes of shrubs, but higher above ground level, often on trunks that have their own merits of elegant outline or attractive bark.

## Making a selection

Trees and shrubs contribute to both the structure and the decoration of the garden, and it is important to bear these two aspects in mind when selecting and arranging them. In most situations, it is best to avoid thinking in terms of the "shrub border" and to plan instead to use trees and shrubs to enhance the whole garden. Selecting only those species that will grow well in the particular soil and situation will ensure that they thrive with minimum effort and will also create a strong sense of unity in the garden.

Small trees and the taller shrubs can be used to create height and as focal points. Birches with their pale trunks, lilacs with their spring blossom, or the very elegant paperbark maple, in groups or as single specimens, will draw the eye, frame views and create a canopy to capture views of the sky. In large enough groups – even a well-placed trio in a small garden – the atmosphere of a wood or wild garden can be created: viewed

from the rest of the garden, the trees form attractive masses, while under their canopy is a scene of vertical trunks and cool green shade with a rich woodland ground flora.

Once the high points have been decided on, the major shrubs can be distributed to form bold accents at a lower level: witch hazels for their spidery winter flowers, magnolias and rhododendrons for their blooms in spring and early summer, along with bright green-yellow or gold-leaved specimens such as euphorbias and *Philadelphus coronarius* 'Aureus'. Hydrangeas are ideal for autumn interest. Mahonias and many

In this intimate partnership between neighboring shrubs the solid yellow-green spikes of *Pinus mugo* 'Winter Gold' are enlivened by the airy soft yellow flower sprays of broom (*Cytisus × praecox*). The reddish purple foliage of purple sage (*Salvia officinalis* 'Purpurascens') introduces a note of restraint and is linked to the main display by a ribbon of vivid blue *Lithodora diffusa* 'Grace Ward'.

of the conifers are good for texture and greenery all year round, playing an especially important role in maintaining structure and interest through the winter. The shrubs at this level should not be crowded together to grow into shapeless masses but, instead, are best placed where they will display themselves most effectively: those with autumn color where the sun will shine through them; those with bright winter stems where the low winter light falls; fragrant plants near enough to the edge of the planting to be smelled and in sheltered situations so the scent will be concentrated.

When the star cast of trees and specimen shrubs has been assembled, attention can be turned to the chorus, the less dramatic but no less important plants that will enclose and shelter the garden, guide people through it, subdivide larger plots into smaller and more comfortable spaces, and conceal any undesirable views. For these purposes there is a great army of well-behaved but less exciting (and usually much less expensive) shrubs.

Finally, having established the structure of the garden with shrubs growing from waist height (where they will obstruct physical movement) to eye level and above (as visual barriers), attention can be turned to the ground plane. Here low plants can be woven together: lavenders, cistus and rosemaries do well on dry soils, while the heathers, leucothoes, smaller rhododendrons and many others are ideal for moist, acidic situations. Knee-high shrubs will cover the ground to reduce the necessity for weeding; they will also soften the transition between lawns and paving and fences, walls, and trees, and will create their own tapestry of foliage, flowers and form.

## Designing shrub borders

Where a shrub border is what is required, it should not be thought of as a form of herbaceous border – a series of more-or-less equally sized blocks or drifts with a different plant in each. While occasionally helpful in a herbaceous border, in a shrub border this

approach can be disastrous because the basic building unit, the shrub, is much larger and usually less colorful than the individual herbaceous plant. Therefore, each shrub group will be too large to relate effectively to its neighbors. What is needed in shrub planting is much greater variation in grouping, from individual specimen plants to substantial masses of 10, 20, or more lower groundcovers. The outlines of the larger groups should be irregular, like pieces in a jigsaw puzzle, so that they are linked together more firmly. The spacing between specimens in a group should also be varied, unless formality is intended. Lessons can be learned from natural groupings of trees, rocks, or even animals in a field, and it is worth spending time playing with circles on paper to achieve the right effect.

Shrubs can act as highlights in a complex composition, as above, where yellow robinia and philadelphus are framed by the reds and blues of anchusas, alliums and cranesbills, or they can blend into a monochrome canvas like the yellow azaleas and laburnum below.

## Finishing touches and care

Woody plants usually start off much too small for their situation but then grow inexorably, often eventually becoming much too large. Thinness in the early stages can be compensated for by interplanting the permanent selection with short-lived and quick-growing shrubs (brooms and lavateras, for example), herbaceous perennials or annuals. Care must be taken to avoid smothering the long-term plants with their temporary companions, but this type of planting is much better than crowding together the permanent plants for instant effect, and paying the penalties of overcrowding forever after.

In fact, useful though trees and shrubs are in a garden, it is neither necessary nor desirable to grow them to the exclusion of other plants. Spring bulbs provide an intensity of color and freshness of new life unrivaled by any shrub, and they will clothe the ground beneath deciduous shrubs and trees with an early and beautiful carpet. Lilies will push through the lower shrubs to flower in late summer. Herbaceous plants extend the flowering season and break the monotony of an overreliance on shrubs. Stout clumps of peonies, arching sheaves of daylilies and tall branching heads of Japanese anemones will all create a greater sense of seasonal change and welcome lightness among the woody permanence of the shrubs. For an even lighter effect, proportions can be shifted from a mainly shrubby border, relieved by occasional marginal groups of other plants, to a thoroughly "mixed" border in which shrubs, herbaceous plants, annuals, bulbs and climbers are assembled in a balanced community.

Once the permanent shrubs and trees have reached the desired size, it may be necessary to restrict their growth to prevent the garden deteriorating into a tangle of the more thuggish species. If time is available, rule-book pruning can be adopted. This is an art in itself and very satisfying. On a larger scale it is often simpler to coppice plants periodically, cutting one in five – or perhaps one group in five – to ground level and allowing them to regrow.

**Opposite:** In a mid-spring display of foliage in green and yellow-green, the bulky forms of evergreens such as euonymus and *Ozothamnus ledifolius* perfectly balance a foreground of smaller shrubs and lush herbaceous plants such as salvias and euphorbias.

**Below:** The star of this border is a young *Cornus controversa* 'Variegata', whose fresh spring foliage shines in a lively but not overcrowded scheme that includes Exbury azaleas and varied herbaceous plants.

The gold-variegated foliage of *Abelia* × *grandiflora* 'Francis Mason' contrasts effectively with the blue flowers of *Caryopteris* × *clandonensis* 'Ferndown'. This partnership is perhaps seen at its best before the abelia's pink flowers and bronze calyces appear.

Crowded spikes of white foxgloves (*Digitalis purpurea* f. *albiflora*) lift themselves high enough to offer a contrast of floral form with *Abutilon vitifolium* var. *album*, while providing a quiet color harmony.

## *Abelia* × *grandiflora* 'Francis Mason'

Most often grown as a foliage plant, this vigorous semi-evergreen shrub has bright gold-edged leaves, which rather overwhelm its pale blush-pink flowers and reddish bronze stems, calyces and young shoots. It is most effective with warm and hot colors, gold-variegated foliage, red- or orange-leaved shrubs like photinias and yellow-green foliage and flowers. Its slightly amorphous form benefits from association with plants of contrasting habit, such as bamboos, grasses, Japanese maples and pyracanthas. 'Sunrise' is similar, less than 3¼ ft. (1 m) high and wide, and makes excellent ground cover – as do 'Prostrata' and cream-variegated Confetti ('Conti'), both 20 in. (50 cm) by 5 ft. (1.5 m). *A.* × *grandiflora* ♀ is more vigorous than the cultivars and is useful for its late flowers.

**Perfect partners:** *Aralia elata* 'Aureovariegata', *Berberis temolaica*, *B. thunbergii* 'Red Chief', *Delphinium* Belladonna Group, *Fargesia murielae* 'Bimbo', *Pyracantha* 'Golden Dome'

**H: 5 ft.** (1.5 m) **S: 6½ ft.** (2 m)
❀ **Mid- to late summer**
◊◊ ▢-■ **Z6 pH6–8**

## *Abies koreana* 'Silberlocke' ♀

A slow-growing fir with glaucous silver-backed needles and deep purplish blue upright cones, 'Silberlocke' produces its best colors in full sun and relatively poor soil. It deserves prominence as a single specimen in a heather garden, island bed or large rockery, surrounded by shorter plants such as heaths and heathers, dwarf rhododendrons, prostrate vacciniums, cassiopes and smaller grasses like fescues. This ground cover may be underplanted with smaller spring bulbs, especially blue-flowered kinds such as scillas and muscari, and soft yellow or white narcissi. 'Silberlocke' is not suitable for borders, where adjacent plants can suppress growth, spoiling its attractive symmetry.

**Perfect partners:** *Calluna vulgaris* 'Gold Haze', *Cassiope* 'Edinburgh', *Narcissus* 'April Tears', *N.* 'Ice Wings', *Rhododendron* 'Sarled', *Scilla siberica*, *Vaccinium vitis-idaea* 'Koralle'

**H: 12–15 ft.** (3.6–4.5 m) **S: 4 ft.** (1.2 m) ❀ **(Spring)**
◊◊ ▢-■ **Z5 pH5–6.5**

The bold form of *Abies koreana* 'Silberlocke', its glaucous leaves twisted to reveal their showy white undersides, presents a telling focus in a mixed bed of winter heaths, including the rich pink *Erica carnea* 'Myretoun Ruby' (bottom) and the slightly paler *E.c.* 'R.B. Cooke' (top). Planting small grasses such as stipas and blue fescues around the abies would provide interest in summer.

## *Abutilon vitifolium* var. *album*

This large, upright deciduous shrub, quick-growing but short-lived, has gray-white woolly stems, vine-shaped leaves and large, translucent white flowers with a central golden boss. It benefits from a sunny site, particularly in areas with cool summers, and looks effective against a dark evergreen background, or in a shrub border if isolated to emphasize its habit. It mixes well with tall herbaceous plants, such as white foxgloves or delphiniums and silvery Scotch thistles, while its flowering season suits combinations with early flowering buddleias and larger Shrub roses. It is outstanding with pale flowers and silver or glaucous foliage, and may be used to support clematis or honeysuckles flowering in late spring or early summer. 'Tennant's White' ♀ is a particularly choice selection.

**Perfect partners:** *Buddleja alternifolia* 'Argentea', *Clematis* 'Bees Jubilee', *Delphinium* Galahad Group, *Eremurus robustus*, *Onopordum nervosum*, *Rosa* 'Fantin-Latour'

**H: 16 ft.** (5 m) **S: 8 ft.** (2.5 m)
❀ **Late spring to midsummer**
◊◊ ▢-■ **Z8 pH5.5–7**

The rich brown bark of the paperbark maple (*Acer griseum*) glows orange where lit from behind by the sun, allowing it to harmonize with *Crocosmia* 'Lucifer'. Bold rodgersia leaves provide a foil without masking the maple's stem.

## *Acer griseum* ♀
PAPERBARK MAPLE

The trifoliate leaves of this small deciduous tree turn orange-yellow in autumn, but its most attractive feature is its orange-brown peeling bark, especially striking when lit by the sun. As with silver-barked birches, a single plant can look unsatisfactory unless made to fork into three to five branches, with a length of exposed stem below its canopy of leaves; where there is room, a small, loosely spaced grove, perhaps with a path between the trees, is enchanting. This maple blends well with bronze and red-flushed foliage plants, including some Japanese maples, and also with other autumn-coloring shrubs, small trees, herbaceous plants and some of the deciduous azaleas. Surplus shoots arising from main stems should be removed to reveal as much of the bark as possible.

**Perfect partners:** *Berberis thunbergii* 'Atropurpurea Nana', *B. wilsoniae*, *Ceratostigma plumbaginoides*, *Euphorbia amygdaloides* 'Purpurea', *Stephanandra tanakae*

H: 33 ft. (10 m)   S: 23 ft. (7 m) ( ❀ Mid-spring)
▨▨▨ ◊◊ ▧-▨ Z5 pH5.5–7

## *Acer palmatum*

This elegant deciduous shrub or small tree is the commonest Japanese maple, with several hundred cultivars notable for their habit and autumn tints. The species is suitable for a woodland garden, underplanted with azaleas and rhododendrons. 'Aoyagi' turns from bright green to golden yellow in autumn; 'Arakawa' has red autumn tints; and the tall 'Asahizuru' bears leaves splashed pinkish white. *A.p.* f. *atropurpureum* and 'Atropurpureum Superbum' are purplish red, turning bright red; deep blackish purple 'Bloodgood' ♀ is crimson in autumn. Cultivars of var. *dissectum* ♀ are the smallest, with deeply cut leaves, and include reddish purple 'Crimson Queen' ♀. Japanese maple looks very effective near water, with Japanese irises in warm or hot colors.

**Perfect partners:** Green-leaved: *Fothergilla major* Monticola Group p.100 **C**, *Hosta fortunei* var. *hyacinthina* p.293 **A** ❏p.81 **C**
Purple-leaved: *Erysimum cheiri* (red-flowered), *Fuchsia* 'Checkerboard' p.101 **A**, *Nandina domestica* p.117 **B**, *Rhododendron* Blinklicht Group p.129 **B**, *R.* 'Fandango' p.130 **C**, *Sambucus nigra* f. *laciniata* p.139 **A** ❏p.363 **B**

H: 3¼–33 ft. (1–10 m)   S: 5–26 ft. (1.5–8 m)
( ❀ Mid-spring)
▨▨▨ ◊◊ ▧-▨ ■ Z6 pH5.5–7

The delicate, feathery leaves of *Acer palmatum* Dissectum Atropurpureum Group contrast subtly with those of black mondo grass (*Ophiopogon planiscapus* 'Nigrescens') while dusky purple, before turning a dramatic scarlet in autumn.

Grown through a carpet of *Gaultheria mucronata*, the fiery coral stems of *Acer pensylvanicum* 'Erythrocladum' clash agreeably with rich pink *Camellia* × *williamsii* 'E.T.R. Carlyon'. A scarlet or blood-red camellia would be a harmonious alternative to flatter the maple.

## *Acer pensylvanicum* 'Erythrocladum'

This deciduous large shrub or small tree has twigs that are bright coral when young, turning golden yellow in autumn. They lose this yellow coloration in their second season, but the branches and trunk remain attractively striped and marked, most effectively in winter if lit by the sun against a dark evergreen background. It can be used as a specimen or planted in a border with dogwoods, witch hazels and other shrubs with warm winter colors, or surrounded by herbaceous perennials or ground-cover plants that do not compete with its upright shape. Good companions include scarlet camellias, gold-variegated evergreens, stephanandras, and rubus or willows with colored stems.

**Perfect partners:** *Camellia japonica* 'Bob Hope', *Cornus sanguinea* 'Anny', *Hamamelis* × *intermedia* 'Jelena', *Ilex aquifolium* 'Pyramidalis', *Rubus thibetanus*

**H: 40 ft.** (12 m) **S: 33 ft.** (10 m) (✳ Mid-spring)
◊◊ ▢-▦ Z4 pH5.5–7

## *Acer shirasawanum* 'Aureum' ♕

This deciduous Japanese maple has the brightest yellow-green foliage of its genus. Slow-growing, it makes a dense, upright shrub that, except in areas with cool summers, benefits from some shade. It is best planted through a carpet of shorter companions, so that its elegant vase-shaped habit is not impaired. In autumn the leaves may take on scarlet tints, or change to golden brown. It can be combined with yellow, cream, or white deciduous azaleas, lilies, hostas, gold-variegated hollies, bamboos and other autumn-coloring shrubs.

**Perfect partners:** *Brunnera macrophylla*, *Hosta* 'Blue Vision', *Iris* 'Cambridge', *Lilium martagon* var. *album*, *Lindera obtusiloba*, *Meconopsis grandis*, *Miscanthus sinensis* 'Zebrinus', *Pleioblastus viridistriatus*, *Rhododendron* 'Persil'

**H: 20 ft.** (6 m) **S: 16 ft.** (5 m) (✳ Mid-spring)
◊◊ ▢-▦ ■ Z5 pH5.5–7

The fan-shaped leaves of *Acer shirasawanum* 'Aureum', almost pure yellow on unfurling, contrast with the bold glaucous foliage of *Hosta* 'Krossa Regal'. White, blue or pale yellow flowers could be added to extend the planting.

Showy leaves of *Amelanchier lamarckii* and bright berries of *Cotoneaster frigidus* 'Cornubia', borne at the same height, make a classic autumn combination that could be topped by a sorbus and woven through by a colorful vine.

## Amelanchier lamarckii ♈

This is perhaps the most satisfactory June berry or snowy mespilus for a sunny garden, where it offers two seasons of interest, first when the bronze foliage emerges with the white spring flowers, and again in autumn, when its leaves turn fiery red. It is a dainty tree, suited to a wild garden or a sunny woodland glade with spring bulbs. Trees such as ornamental cherries and crab apples are good partners, as are magnolias, early roses, kolkwitzias, flowering dogwoods, hawthorns, whitebeams and more delicately colored deciduous azaleas. Larger plants can support a spring climber or a purple vine. White and pale-colored lilacs combine well in spring, while Japanese maples, aronias and cotoneasters add autumn harmonies.

**Perfect partners:** *Anthriscus sylvestris* 'Ravenswing', *Clematis* 'Gothenburg', *Exochorda giraldii* var. *wilsonii*, *Magnolia* × *loebneri* 'Merrill', *Malus hupehensis*, *Narcissus* 'Geranium', *N. poeticus* var. *recurvus*, *Pieris* 'Forest Flame', *Prunus* 'Shirotae', *Pyrus communis* 'Beech Hill'

**H: 33 ft. (10 m)  S: 23 ft. (7 m)** ❁ **Mid-spring**
◊◊ ▢-▉ Z4 pH5–7

## Aralia elata 'Aureovariegata'

In late summer this deciduous shrub bears attractive clouds of creamy white flowers on branching panicles, but the foliage is its most eye-catching feature. The leaves, up to 5 ft. (1.5 m) long and almost as wide, are edged with yellow when young, fading to cream. With its bright color and complexity, it makes a magnificent specimen plant, or striking focal points along a border, planted among shorter subjects that tolerate partial shade, so that the aralias ultimately provide a canopy of leaves above the underplanting. It combines well with warm or hot colors, cream flowers, glaucous foliage and yellow-green foliage and flowers, and can be contrasted with blue, most dramatically while its foliage is young. White-marked 'Variegata' ♈ is also impressive.

**Perfect partners:** *Agapanthus* 'Loch Hope', *Crocosmia* 'Vulcan', *Dahlia* 'Autumn Lustre', *D.* 'Glorie van Heemstede', *Hibiscus syriacus* 'Oiseau Bleu', *Ipomoea tricolor* 'Heavenly Blue', *Miscanthus sinensis* 'Strictus', *Nepeta sibirica*, *Philadelphus coronarius* 'Aureus'

**H & S: 16 ft. (5 m)** ❁ **Late summer**
◊◊-◊◊◊ ▢-▉ Z5 pH5.5–7.5

The dramatic foliage of *Aralia elata* 'Aureovariegata' harmonizes with the warm apricot-yellow of *Crocosmia* × *crocosmiiflora* 'Lady Hamilton'. Agapanthus would give a similar foliage effect with a contrasting flower color.

A filigree cushion of *Artemisia* 'Powis Castle' nestles beneath gracefully arching stems of *Fuchsia magellanica* 'Versicolor', with its elegant, pendent flowers and grayish leaves flushed red and edged with white – an association that is especially charming at close range. The slender fuchsia flowers set off the silvery artemisia, while the foliage colors blend agreeably.

## Artemisia 'Powis Castle' ♈

This relatively hardy, semi-evergreen sub-shrub is an outstanding foliage plant, its filigree silver-gray leaves developing into dense, mounded hummocks that look good at the front of a border or in pots. It tolerates poor soils and dry conditions, helping it to thrive with Mediterranean plants such as lavenders and cistus. It is very effective with other silver-leaved plants, glaucous foliage, and plants with contrasting leaf form and texture, especially grasses such as fescues, and it is an essential component of a white garden. It combines well with flowers in cool colors and looks satisfying growing in front of roses, including old shrub roses. The bush benefits from cutting back in mid-spring.

**Perfect partners:** *Ballota pseudodictamnus* p.244 **C**, *Cistus* × *argenteus* 'Silver Pink', *Convolvulus cneorum*, *Cosmos bipinnatus* 'Sonata White', *Euphorbia dulcis* 'Chameleon' p.267 **A**, *Lavandula* 'Sawyers', *Rosa* **Surrey** p.219 **C** ▢p.424 **A**

**H: 24 in. (60 cm)  S: 36 in. (90 cm)** ❁ **Summer**
◊-◊◊ ▢-▉ Z6 pH5.5–7.5

Evergreen *Berberis darwinii* supplies a pleasing backdrop for the bright spring flowers of *Forsythia × intermedia*, its stems yet to be furnished by foliage. The soft orange flowers of the berberis, here just starting to open, will also dazzle before the forsythia fades.

## *Berberis darwinii* ♀

One of the best evergreen, spring-flowering shrubs, this is invaluable for contributing structure and solidity to the garden early in the year. The lobes and prickles on its leaves add sparkle to the shiny surfaces. Plants may be grown as specimen shrubs or as a hedge, combined with white or hot-colored flowers or with gold-variegated, evergreen foliage. They also associate well with bamboos, forsythias, white or deep red camellias, winter jasmine, narcissi and gold-variegated hollies or elaeagnus. Any surplus growth should be cut back immediately after flowering. Very large specimens may be cut hard back to 4–6 in. (10–15 cm) above ground to maintain the elegant, arching habit of the stems.

**Perfect partners:** *Chaenomeles × superba* 'Rowallane', *Euphorbia griffithii* 'Dixter', *Narcissus* 'Ambergate', *Rosa* 'Helen Knight', *Syringa vulgaris* 'Primrose'

**H & S: 10 ft. (3 m)** ❀ **Mid- to late spring**
◊-◊◊◊ ▢-▦ **Z7 pH5–7.5**

## *Berberis thunbergii* ♀

The most striking feature of this deciduous shrub is its autumn display of fiery orange and red tints and red, elliptical fruits, but it suits a wild garden and other subdued plantings. Useful cultivars include f. *atropurpurea*, often rich deep purple turning rich red in autumn; 'Atropurpurea Nana' ♀ (24 in./60 cm) and 'Bagatelle' ♀ (12 in./30 cm); and the columnar 'Helmond Pillar' (5 ft./1.5 m). The leaves of 'Golden Ring' ♀ have narrow yellow-green edges, while those of 'Harlequin' and 'Rose Glow' ♀ are pale-pink splashed. Yellow-green 'Aurea' contrasts well with pure

**Perfect partners:** Purple-leaved: *Agastache* 'Firebird' p.229 **B**, *Clematis* 'Prince Charles' p.165 **A**, *Euphorbia myrsinites* p.268 **A**, *Phalaris arundinacea* var. *picta* 'Picta' p.320 **B**, *Phygelius × rectus* p.121 **C**, *Rosa* Evelyn Fison p.212 **A**, *R.* 'Madame Pierre Oger' p.197 **A** ▢pp.94 **B**, 106 **C**, 147 **A**, 147 **C**, 232 **C**, 241 **C**, 242 **C**, 264 **B**, 355 **C**
Yellow-green leaved: *Eryngium giganteum* p.426 **A**

**H: 5 ft. (1.5 m)  S: 6½ ft. (2 m)** ❀ **Late spring**
◊-◊◊ ▢-▦ **Z5 pH5–7.5**

**Above:** *Berberis thunbergii* 'Atropurpurea Nana' is the key player in this combination of smoky purple foliage and flowers. The other purples, of dark-leaved *Rosa* 'Rosemary Rose' and *Tulipa* 'Queen of Night', are joined by gently contrasting hybrid bluebells and the soft yellow berberis flowers. Adding another taller berberis farther back in the border would provide a unifying theme.

**Below:** Nodding wands of dark-leaved *Berberis thunbergii* f. *atropurpurea*, carrying pale yellow flowers tinged with red, contrast dramatically with the yellow-green foliage of *Philadelphus coronarius* 'Aureus'. Although the outer flowers of the berberis are camouflaged by the philadelphus, most show well against the dusky berberis leaves.

A carpet of low foliage provides a soft foil for a multi-stemmed *Betula utilis* var. *jacquemontii*, grown in moist semi-shade. In the foreground, the bronze-flushed leaves of Japanese shield fern (*Dryopteris erythrosora*) tone with the biscuit-tinted white stems of the birch and its brown twigs, while the creamy white flowers of *Astilbe* 'Deutschland' harmonize with the birch's base.

## *Betula utilis* var. *jacquemontii*

Birches are elegant, fast-growing trees that cast dappled shade and offer good deciduous cover for woodland plants, including rhododendrons, in medium-sized to large gardens. This variety is a variant of Himalayan birch with strikingly white-barked stems, dramatic when placed where the tree catches the winter sun against a dark background of evergreens such as yew and holly. Cultivars with particularly white bark include 'Doorenbos' ♥, 'Jermyns' ♥, and 'Silver Shadow' ♥. In smaller gardens, create a multi-branched birch by cutting back a young tree or by planting several in one hole. Surround the birch with ferns, dicentras, epimediums, spring bulbs such as cyclamens and snowdrops, or other woodland plants.

**Perfect partners:** *Dicentra* 'Pearl Drops', *Epimedium* × *versicolor* 'Sulphureum', *Fatsia japonica*, *Ilex aquifolium* 'Pyramidalis', *Narcissus* 'Actaea', *Polystichum setiferum*, *Rubus cockburnianus*, *Stephanandra tanakae*

**H: 60 ft. (18 m)  S: 33 ft. (10 m) ( ❀ Mid-spring)**
◌◌  ▢-◼  Z6  pH4.5–7

The broad panicles of *Buddleja davidii* 'Dartmoor' form a magnificent lilac backdrop for a planting in which the curious sunflower *Helianthus salicifolius*, grown principally for its bold bottle-brush columns of foliage, is the other main attraction, partnered by the bamboo *Phyllostachys nigra* f. *punctata*. A pretty pale blue covering of *Clematis* 'Praecox' fills the foreground.

## *Buddleja alternifolia* ♥

This deciduous, large shrub or small tree bears long, drooping wands of lilac blooms. Silver-leaved 'Argentea' is even prettier and slightly less vigorous than the species, but not as free-flowering in areas with cool summers. Both are superb when combined with purple, white, blue, mauve, carmine or lime green flowers, and with purple or silver foliage. Good companions include delphiniums, old roses, lupins, purple sloe and purple smoke bush. These buddleias need pruning annually straight after flowering. Unpruned plants develop short, tangled flowering stems, so it is best to limit the number of stems to five or six, stopping these 40 in. (1 m) below the height ultimately required, or to train a single main stem to form a standard.

**Perfect partners:** *Allium* 'Gladiator', *Campanula lactiflora*, *Delphinium* 'Bruce', *Elaeagnus* 'Quicksilver', *Geranium psilostemon*, *Philadelphus* 'Belle Etoile', *Rosa* 'Cerise Bouquet'

**H & S: 13 ft. (4 m) ❀ Early summer**
◌-◌◌  ▢-◼  Z6  pH5.5–7.5

The slightly unruly habit of *Buddleja alternifolia* turns to one of exuberance as its lilac pompons of flowers appear, strung together to make continuous garlands. Purple sage (*Salvia officinalis* 'Purpurascens') furnishes beneath, while in front matching pompons of chives and *Allium hollandicum* 'Purple Sensation' chime in close harmony.

## *Buddleja davidii* 'Dartmoor' ♥

This dramatic cultivar of the common buddleia or butterfly bush is distinguished by its immensely wide panicles of lilac flowers. It forms a broad, spreading deciduous bush at first, becoming narrower and more upright. Each arching stem flowers for several months, even longer if panicles are pruned as their blooms fade. It is superb planted behind old roses or harmonizing in a mixed or shrub border with mauve, purple, lilac and blue flowers, or with silver, purple or glaucous foliage. It contrasts well with soft yellow flowers, and with yellow-green foliage or flowers. Most *B. davidii* cultivars are pruned like *B. alternifolia* (left), as a standard or a bush with a few main stems; if they originate close together the annual stems of 'Dartmoor' fall apart after heavy rain, so the bush should be hard pruned to encourage basal growth.

**Perfect partners:** *Cotinus coggygria* 'Royal Purple', *Elaeagnus commutata*, *Euphorbia schillingii*, *Lilium* 'Casa Blanca', *L.* Imperial Gold Group, *Rosa* 'Felicia', *R. glauca*

**H & S: 10 ft. (3 m) ❀ Midsummer to early autumn**
◌-◌◌  ▢-◼  Z5  pH5–7.5

## *Buxus sempervirens* ♔
COMMON BOX

The great virtue of this versatile evergreen is its fine-textured, fairly amorphous foliage, which provides a superb background for plants of more definite form or leaf color. It is a handsome shrub for a woodland garden, and can help to define a space, screen a boundary or give a backbone to a mixed border. Cultivars such as cream-splashed 'Elegantissima' ♔ and yellow-variegated 'Latifolia Maculata' ♔ are attractive supports for flowering climbers. Box is excellent as a hedge or topiary piece; the best cultivar for this is 'Suffruticosa' ♔. (In cold climates, a hardier plant such as *B*. 'Green Mountain' or a cultivar of *B. sinica* var. *insularis* is more successful.) Foliage color varies between blue- and gray-green and yellow-green. For informal plantings in a woodland garden, seedling box has a pleasing, natural-looking variation in color and habit. Upright cultivars can be less satisfactory as taller hedges, because their branches cannot withstand a heavy fall of snow.

**Perfect partners:** *Aruncus dioicus* p.239 **A**, *Aucuba japonica*, *Camellia japonica* 'Lovelight', *Euonymus japonicus* 'Ovatus Aureus', *Fatsia japonica* p.99 **C**, *Hedera colchica*, *Helleborus* × *hybridus*, *Ilex* × *altaclerensis* 'Golden King', *Polystichum setiferum*, *Rhododendron* 'Dora Amateis', *Sarcococca confusa*, *Taxus baccata* 'Fastigiata'

**H & S: 16 ft. (5 m) (❀ Spring)**
◊◊ ▢-◼ Z5 pH5.5–8

**Right:** Box does not have to be clipped to be attractive, although its size may have to be limited by pruning, taking care not to impair its natural habit. Here, the tiny, neatly cream-edged leaves of *Buxus sempervirens* 'Marginata' lend themselves to a small scale and close inspection, partnered by a Lenten rose (*Helleborus* × *hybridus*) and spring bulbs.

**Below:** Dwarf box (*Buxus sempervirens* 'Suffruticosa') is an ideal parterre plant, clipped into bold patterns of crisp compartments and filled with more informal planting. Its fine texture and geometric shape can provide a perfect foil for a froth of spring flowers followed by summer annuals. Here, each compartment is simply planted with herbs – common and purple sage (*Salvia officinalis* and *S.o.* 'Purpurascens') and curry plant (*Helichrysum italicum*).

Colored-leaved heathers are immensely valuable ground-cover plants for the winter garden. Combining *Calluna vulgaris* 'Ariadne', whose leaves are tipped with orange and cream, with the Darley Dale heath *Erica* × *darleyensis* 'White Perfection' avoids the often seen clash between orange-, gold- or bronze-leaved sorts and those with mauve-pink flowers.

Camellias (here, *Camellia japonica* 'Latifolia') and early narcissi are well suited to informal planting in deciduous woodland. Scarlet camellias could equally be paired with white narcissi, perhaps with a red-rimmed cup or salmon trumpet, or where a jazzier effect is acceptable, with a rich orange sort such as *N.* 'Ambergate'.

## Calluna vulgaris
HEATHER, LING

The foliage of these acid-loving evergreens can be green, gray, gold, orange, bronze or brick-red, sometimes tipped gold or cream, and often changing with the seasons; the flowers are pink, mauve, crimson, burgundy, magenta or white. Heathers make excellent ground cover among other heathland plants such as smaller rhododendrons. Varieties with orange or reddish foliage go well with tinted dogwoods or willows and early bulbs. Among the most useful are burgundy 'Allegro' ♥; double pink 'Annemarie' ♥; white 'Anthony Davis' ♥, with gray-green leaves; crimson 'Dark Star' ♥; white 'Gold Haze' ♥, with yellow-green foliage; white 'Mair's Variety' ♥; white 'Spring Cream' ♥, with spring foliage tipped cream; double magenta 'Tib' ♥; and prostrate 'White Lawn' ♥.

**Perfect partners:** *Abies koreana* 'Silberlocke', *Cornus alba* 'Sibirica', *Gaultheria mucronata*, *Juniperus horizontalis* 'Wiltonii', *Molinia caerulea* 'Variegata', *Pinus mugo* 'Ophir', *Salix daphnoides* 'Aglaia', *Vaccinium vitis-idaea* 'Koralle' ❏ pp.158 **C**, 218 **A**

**H: 4–24 in.** (10–60 cm)  **S: 12–30 in.** (30–75 cm)
❀ **Midsummer to late autumn**

◖◗ ◌◌ ▨ ■ **Z4  pH4–6**

## Camellia 'Cornish Snow' ♥

This evergreen hybrid between *C. cuspidata* and *C. saluenensis* has masses of small, single white flowers, delicately flushed with pink. Although a fairly hardy plant, the blooms are sometimes damaged in cold weather, so it is best grown in areas that seldom experience frost. Its graceful, open habit and simple flowers suit a woodland garden. It looks best in subtly colored schemes, especially with shrubs of similar natural grace, such as other camellias and early rhododendrons with soft coloring and loose habit. Other companions include winter honeysuckles, evergreen shrubs such as osmanthus and early bulbs – pale crocuses or cyclamens for example.

**Perfect partners:** *Camellia* 'Winton', *Galanthus* 'Straffan', *Lonicera* × *purpusii*, *Osmanthus delavayi*, *Prunus pendula* 'Pendula Rosea', *Rhododendron lutescens* 'Bagshot Sands'

**H: 10 ft.** (3 m)  **S: 5 ft.** (1.5 m)
❀ **Midwinter to late spring**

◖◗ ◌◌ ▨ ■ **Z8  pH4.5–6.5**

*Camellia* 'Cornish Snow' with one of several valuable early rhododendrons, *R.* Cilpinense Group. An intervening evergreen with contrasting foliage, for instance a bamboo, and a carpet of early bulbs could enhance the planting.

## Camellia japonica
COMMON CAMELLIA

Cultivars of this superlative evergreen shrub vary in flower color from white to deep red, and in floral form from single to very formal double; some blooms are anemone-centered or have prominent anthers. Plants should ideally face west in frost-prone regions to protect the flowers. Cultivars with formal double flowers and rich colors have a sophistication that may seem unnatural in outer parts of the garden, but they are excellent near the house, perhaps combined with early rhododendrons and spring bulbs such as narcissi. Their solid form benefits from association with shrubs of lighter, more open habit, such as bamboos, *Prunus mume* cultivars and early-flowering deciduous trees, which provide beneficial overhead shade.

**Perfect partners:** *Fargesia murielae*, *Fatsia japonica*, *Galanthus elwesii*, *Magnolia* × *loebneri*, *Narcissus* 'Mount Hood', *N.* 'Thalia', *Prunus* 'Accolade', *P. mume* 'Omoi-no-mama', *P. pendula* 'Pendula Rubra', *Rhododendron augustinii*, *R.* 'Christmas Cheer', *R. schlippenbachii*

**H: 30 ft.** (9 m)  **S: 26 ft.** (8 m)  ❀ **Early to late spring**

◖◗ ◌◌ ▨ ■ **Z7  pH4.5–6.5**

The rich blue flowers of *Ceanothus* 'Cascade' contrast strikingly with the acid yellow-green foliage of *Hedera helix* 'Buttercup'. Although here the ivy is in its shrubby phase, this combination would more normally be seen with the ivy clinging to a wall and the ceanothus loosely trained in front of it.

## Ceanothus 'Cascade' ♛

Evergreen Californian lilacs or ceanothus are quick-growing shrubs that are relatively short-lived, particularly in frosty gardens, where they prefer a sheltered sunny wall. 'Cascade' has an open, arching habit and rich blue flowers in long, airy clusters. It is tall enough to interact with large shrubs and small trees, especially laburnums, brooms and early-flowering Climbing and Shrub roses. Its color combines well with yellow, white, yellow-green or pale blue flowers, and with silver, glaucous or yellow-green foliage –

a wall clothed with yellow-green or gold-variegated ivies makes a stunning backdrop. It should not be allowed to grow too large.

**Perfect partners:** *Cytisus* × *praecox* 'Warminster', *Euphorbia characias* subsp. *wulfenii* 'John Tomlinson', *Laburnum* × *watereri* 'Vossii', *Rosa banksiae* 'Lutea', *R.* × *fortuneana*, *R. xanthina* f. *hugonis*, *Syringa vulgaris* 'Madame Lemoine', *S.v.* 'Primrose', *Viburnum opulus* 'Roseum'

**H & S: 13 ft. (4 m)** ❀ **Late spring to early summer**
◇-◇◇ ◻-◼ **Z8 pH5.5–7**

Usually a sprawling shrub, *Ceanothus foliosus* can be trained upward, for instance against a wall, allowing it to achieve double its usual height. This means it can be combined with a range of different plants, among them the broom *Cytisus nigricans*, with its graceful, arching sprays of yellow flowers.

## Ceanothus × delileanus 'Gloire de Versailles' ♛

This deciduous ceanothus with airy clusters of powder-blue flowers is hardier than the evergreen kinds, and thrives in an open site as well as against a wall. Its soft texture and subtle coloring make it suitable for combinations with bold foliage and plants of more definite floral form. The flower color complements cool shades such as deep blue, lavender or mauve, and looks effective with white, cream or very pale yellow. It associates well with silver or glaucous foliage. On a wall it goes well with repeat-flowering Climbing roses, while in a border it looks charming planted with repeat-flowering bush roses.

**Perfect partners:** *Aconitum* 'Spark's Variety', *Clematis* 'Huldine', *Elaeagnus* 'Quicksilver', *Euphorbia schillingii*, *Hydrangea macrophylla* Libelle, *H. paniculata* 'Grandiflora', *Lilium* Imperial Gold Group, *Miscanthus sinensis* 'Morning Light', *Rosa* 'Climbing Iceberg', *R.* 'Mermaid'

**H & S: 5 ft. (1.5 m)** ❀ **Midsummer to mid-autumn**
◇-◇◇ ◻-◼ **Z7 pH5.5–7**

The powder-blue flowers of *Ceanothus* × *delileanus* 'Gloire de Versailles' provide a delicate haze of bloom alongside the bold flowerheads and handsome foliage of *Hydrangea quercifolia*. The height of the ceanothus is usually kept to 5 ft. (1.5 m) by annual pruning to a low framework, but by building up a taller framework of perennial branches, the ceanothus can be made to overtop the hydrangea.

## Ceanothus foliosus

This spreading, semi-prostrate evergreen shrub bears numerous long-stalked, round clusters of dark blue flowers, with paler filaments. It is best placed toward the front of a border because it is furnished with foliage down to the ground. It looks particularly attractive with silver or glaucous foliage; with white, cream, yellow and pale blue flowers; and with yellow-green foliage and flowers. Suitable companions include smaller Shrub or bush roses, early-flowering annuals or biennials, white-flowered cistus and any halimiocistus or halimiums.

**Perfect partners:** *Camassia leichtlinii*, *Choisya ternata* Sundance, *Cytisus* 'Moonlight', *Euonymus fortunei* 'Silver Queen', *Exochorda* × *macrantha* 'The Bride', *Rosa* × *harisonii* 'Harison's Yellow', *R.* 'Madame Alfred Carrière', *Spiraea* 'Arguta', *Tulipa* 'Spring Green', *T.* 'White Triumphator'

**H: 3 ft. (90 cm) S: 4 ft. (1.2 m)**
❀ **Late spring to early summer**
◇-◇◇ ◻-◼ **Z8 pH5.5–7**

## *Ceanothus impressus*

This is one of the hardier evergreen ceanothus species, which may be grown as a freestanding bush or trained against a wall, where it will reach a height of 10 ft. (3 m). It produces billowing masses of solid blue flowers that look most impressive contrasted with yellow, white and the very palest or deepest pure blue flowers, silver or glaucous foliage, and yellow-green foliage or flowers. Early yellow roses are satisfying companions, as are low-branching laburnums. Other fine deep blue ceanothus include *C.* 'Concha' ♀, 'Dark Star' ♀ and 'Puget Blue' ♀, which has sumptuous coloring.

**Perfect partners:** *Clematis* 'Moonlight' p.116 A, *Cytisus* × *praecox* 'Warminster', *Euphorbia characias*, *Fritillaria imperialis* 'Maxima Lutea', *Rosa spinosissma* 'Grandiflora', *R.* × *xanthina* f. *hugonis*, *Sambucus nigra* 'Aurea', *Tulipa* 'Maja', *T.* 'Sweet Harmony'

**H: 5 ft.** (1.5 m)   **S: 8 ft.** (2.5 m)
✹ **Mid- to late spring**
⬛▬▭▯   ◊-◊◊   ▯-▮   **Z8   pH5.5–7**

*Laburnum anagyroides* is here made to branch, and thus produce blooms, lower down than usual, allowing it to contrast spectacularly with the much lower growing *Ceanothus impressus*. *L.* × *watereri* 'Vossii' has longer racemes and might be even more dramatic, while a little shade would subdue flowering for a more subtle effect.

Trained low across a wall, flowering quinces such as *Chaenomeles* × *superba* 'Knap Hill Scarlet' will produce plentiful bloom at a height that allows them to combine effectively with spring bulbs such as narcissi, as well as with relatively short plants such as wallflowers, euphorbias and geums.

## *Chaenomeles* × *superba* 'Knap Hill Scarlet' ♀

The rounded vermilion blooms of this deciduous flowering quince are followed in autumn by amber-yellow fruits. It can be grown as a rather sprawling shrub near the front of a border, but it is even more effective trained on a wall or trellis and pruned in midsummer. Its brilliant coloring is good with orange, or warm shades like salmon-pink; it also contrasts well with light apple-green and yellow-green flowers or foliage. The flowers coincide with most of the spring bulbs and look outstanding with tulips, crown imperials and narcissi, while their season lasts long enough to interact with the red-flushed growth of shrubs such as photinias, spiraeas and bush roses. Hellebores make equally congenial partners.

**Perfect partners:** *Cytisus* 'Lena', *Fritillaria imperialis* 'Aurora', *Helleborus* × *sternii*, *Narcissus* 'Ambergate', *Spiraea japonica* 'Goldflame', *Tulipa* 'Orange Favourite'

**H: 5 ft.** (1.5 m)   **S: 6½ ft.** (2 m)   ✹ **Mid- to late spring**
⬛▬▭▯   ◊-◊◊   ▯-▮   **Z5   pH5–6.5**

## *Chamaecyparis lawsoniana* 'Winston Churchill'

The Lawson cypress (*C. lawsoniana*) is a fairly hardy, evergreen conifer, useful as a specimen tree or for hedges. 'Winston Churchill', one of its brightest yellow cultivars, grows fairly slowly to produce a small to medium-sized tree. As a hedging plant, its brightness may be a disadvantage, distracting attention from the plants growing in front, but it makes a superb specimen tree of regular conical habit, useful both in isolation and as a punctuation mark among other planting. It combines easily with other conifers, contrasting particularly well with the darkest kinds and those with glaucous foliage, and it looks appropriate planted among ericaceous shrubs such as rhododendrons, pieris and kalmias, especially cultivars with yellow, white or contrasting lavender-blue flowers.

C.l. 'Lutea' ♀, up to 50 ft. (15 m) high, is another fine yellow cultivar for specimen planting, broadly columnar but less formal in habit, with large, flattened feathery sprays of foliage and a slim, drooping top.

*Chamaecyparis lawsoniana* 'Winston Churchill' and *Picea pungens* Glauca Group have been juxtaposed for the foliage contrast of the feathery cypress with the layered spruce.

**Perfect partners:** *Abies concolor* Violacea Group, *Rhododendron* 'Albatross Townhill White', *R. maccabeanum*, *Sequoia sempervirens* 'Cantab', *Thuja plicata* 'Atrovirens'

**H: 33 ft.** (10 m)   **S: 13 ft.** (4 m)   (✹ **Spring)**
⬛▬▭▯   ◊◊   ▮   **Z6   pH5.5–6.5**

## *Cistus* × *cyprius* ♀

One of the hardiest of the rock roses, this upright, fairly open shrub usually has white flowers, with a central boss of golden anthers and a deep maroon blotch at the base of each petal. With its preference for hot, sunny sites and good drainage, it is well suited to a gravel garden or sunny border or shrubbery, especially with other Mediterranean shrubs such as helianthemums, lavenders and sages. Its color allows associations with almost any other, and it combines well with shrubby helichrysums, artemisias, catmints, phlomis, alstroemerias and summer-flowering bulbs such as smaller species gladioli. Plain white 'Albiflorus' looks good with blue flowers, including nigellas, glaucous or silver foliage, and yellow-green foliage and flowers.

**Perfect partners:** *Ceanothus* 'Blue Mound', *Dianthus* 'Paisley Gem', *Euphorbia seguieriana* subsp. *niciciana*, *Lavandula stoechas* subsp. *pedunculata*, *Salvia lavandulifolia*

**H & S: 5 ft. (1.5 m)** ❀ **Early to late summer**
◊-◊◊ ☐-■ **Z8 pH6–7.5**

The stark white blooms of *Cistus* × *cyprius* are tempered by *Alstroemeria ligtu* hybrids in warm shades of salmon. The yellow in the center of the cistus flowers is echoed by golden flashes on the alstroemeria's upper petals.

## *Choisya ternata* ♀
### MEXICAN ORANGE BLOSSOM

With its solid shape, glistening foliage and fragrant, white spring blooms, this evergreen shrub is useful for the front of a shrub or mixed border, as foundation planting, or as a hedge. Some shade is acceptable, especially where summers are hot, but in areas with cool summers it needs full sun and protection from cold winds. It makes an excellent background for winter and spring flowers, or it can be combined with more open plants and lighter foliage, such as ceanothus, ozothamnus, pyracanthas or cistus. Larger specimens can be draped with a spring-flowering climber such as a small clematis. *C. ternata* Sundance ('Lich') ♀ has bright

Swags of a pale pink *Clematis montana* var. *rubens* here drape themselves prettily across *Choisya ternata*. The vigor of the clematis makes this an effect most easily achieved if the choisya is large and planted toward the limit of the spread of the clematis, although a less rampant Alpina clematis could be substituted. A cultivar with flowers of a more definite pink might be even more effective.

yellow-green foliage and makes a spectacular contrast with blue flowers. Like the species, in areas with hot summers it tends to scorch.

**Perfect partners:** *Camassia cusickii* 'Zwanenburg', *Ceanothus* 'Blue Jeans', *Cistus* × *hybridus*, *Cytisus* × *praecox* 'Albus', *Pyracantha* 'Navaho', *Rosa* 'Maigold' ❏ pp.137 **C**, 157 **A**

**H & S: 8 ft. (2.5 m)** ❀ **Late spring**
◊◊ ☐-■ **Z8 pH5–7**

The large crinkled blooms of *Cistus* × *purpureus* are perfectly complemented by the small crimson flowers and loosely branched habit of *Leptospermum scoparium*. Both plants are suited to sunny, well-drained conditions.

## *Cistus* × *purpureus*

This is a rounded evergreen rock rose with dark green leaves and carmine flowers enlivened with a central boss of golden anthers and a maroon blotch at the base of each petal. Thriving in well-drained sunny sites, it is a choice plant for combining with helianthemums, lavenders, phlomis and sages in a gravel garden, scree bed, large rock garden or sunny border. Its vivid pink coloring suits associations with other cool colors, crimsons and reddish purples, and with silver- or glaucous-leaved plants. Good companions include leptospermums, pinks, eryngiums, earlier gypsophilas, summer-flowering alliums, smaller gladioli and convolvulus, and annuals such as alyssums, nigellas or annual lupin species.

**Perfect partners:** *Allium* 'Globemaster', *Convolvulus cneorum*, *Dianthus* 'Haytor White', *D.* 'Old Velvet', *Eryngium bourgatii* 'Picos Blue', *Gypsophila* 'Rosenschleier'

**H & S: 40 in.** (1 m) **Early to late summer**
**Z9 pH6–7.5**

## *Clerodendrum bungei*

The heart-shaped leaves of this deciduous suckering shrub are bold and handsome, but its chief glory is the tightly bunched, domed heads of vivid pink blooms, borne from late summer into autumn. Its upright habit makes a strong impact in large borders, where its flower color combines successfully with cool tints and purple, silver or gray foliage, using late partners such as Japanese anemones, large fuchsias, hydrangeas, indigoferas, lespedezas, Rugosa roses and late-flowering hostas. Seasonal companions include *Cosmos bipinnatus* cultivars, chrysanthemums, cleomes and asters. A larger specimen can be draped with a late-flowering climber or an autumn-coloring vine to contrast with its own strong green foliage.

**Perfect partners:** *Anemone* × *hybrida* 'Elegans', *Clematis* 'Minuet', *Cotinus* 'Grace', *Fuchsia* 'Riccartonii', *Hibiscus syriacus* 'Red Heart', *Hydrangea macrophylla* 'Veitchii'

**H & S: 6½ ft.** (2 m) **Late summer to mid-autumn**
**Z8 pH5.5–7**

*Clerodendrum bungei*, grown against a sunny wall for protection and to encourage production of its vibrant pink blooms, mingles easily with the sumptuous purple foliage of the claret vine (*Vitis vinifera* 'Purpurea').

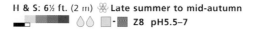

Growing through the outer branches of the soft blue *Ceanothus thyrsiflorus* var. *repens*, the white flowers and silvery foliage of *Convolvulus cneorum* combine charmingly, enhanced by other plants that thrive in Mediterranean climates, including the perennial wallflower *Erysimum* 'Bowles Mauve'. Both the convolvulus and the wallflower will continue to bloom long after the ceanothus.

## *Convolvulus cneorum*

This small evergreen shrub forms a mound of silky silver leaves, with funnel-shaped white flowers, yellow at their base and pink on the reverse, appearing mainly in late spring. In areas with cool summers it needs a warm, sunny, sheltered site with good drainage, and will then thrive in a gravel or rock garden, or scree bed, at the front of a border, and even in walls that do not become bone-dry for long. Its flower color allows combinations with any other, while its foliage works well with other silver- or glaucous-leaved plants, and with contrasting foliage such as that of fescues. It associates well with Mediterranean plants like cistus, lavenders, phlomis and sages, and can also be used with perennial wallflowers, ceanothus, daphnes and hebes.

**Perfect partners:** *Ceanothus* 'Southmead', *Cistus* 'Silver Pink', *Dianthus* 'Inchmery', *Festuca glauca* 'Blaufuchs', *Lavandula stoechas*, *Nigella damascena* 'Miss Jekyll'

**H: 24 in.** (60 cm) **S: 36 in.** (90 cm)
**Late spring to late summer**
**Z8 pH5.5–7.5**

## *Cornus alba* and *Cornus sericea*

These deciduous dogwoods, with winter stems in red, yellow or black, look best when sited to catch the low rays of the sun and given contrasting underplanting. Some also have gold or variegated leaves and color well in autumn. *C. alba*, the red-barked dogwood, quickly develops into a thicket of upright stems with conspicuous red bark, especially when young, and foliage that assumes orange and red tints in autumn. Older stems bear flattened heads of white flowers, sometimes followed by creamy white or light blue berries. *C. sericea* (syn. *C. stolonifera*), the red osier dogwood, is even more vigorous, suckering freely, especially in moist soils, to produce dense thickets of tall stems with deep red bark. It flowers, fruits and colors in autumn like *C. alba*. Both species are taller and more rampant than their many cultivars, most of which have been selected for improved stem color or variegated foliage.

All these dogwoods grow well near water, where reflections can double the display of their stems. Regular pruning gives the brightest stem color. Stooling the clumps to 4–6 in. (10–15 cm) each year in late winter or early spring results in stems about 3¼ ft. (1 m) tall the following season, although the slower growing *C. alba* 'Kesselringii' is best stooled every two to three years. Pruning on a two-year cycle, cutting half the stems to the base each year, gives a looser, more natural appearance, although a little brightness is sacrificed. If grown as foliage plants in a mixed border, pruning will be determined by the size of companion plants, which might include Tall Bearded irises, dieramas, red or green smoke bush, and purple *Cercis canadensis*. In wilder situations, they combine well with elders, wild roses, willows and viburnums. For winter display, the bright red stems look spectacular rising from a green and gold bed of foliage, such as variegated euonymus, or partnering the parchment seedheads of grasses like pennisetums.

*C.a.* 'Sibirica' ♀, the Westonbirt dogwood, is great for rich red stems. Among those with white-edged leaves, the compact 'Sibirica Variegata' is held to be superior to the more common 'Elegantissima' ♀ and to the taller and coarser 'Variegata'. Gold-variegated 'Spaethii' ♀ has the showiest foliage of all the cultivars; 'Gouchaultii' has leaves edged with soft yellow and tinged pink; and 'Aurea' ♀ has golden leaves; all have good autumn

**Above:** The creamy variegation and bold leaf shape of *Cornus alba* 'Elegantissima' set off the dissected foliage and blue, early summer flowers of *Geranium* × *magnificum*.

**Left:.** The apple-green flowers of stinking hellebore (*Helleborus foetidus*) contrast with the bright stems of *Cornus alba* 'Sibirica'. White-flowered heaths or golden heathers could be used instead of the mauve heaths *Erica carnea* 'King George' and *E.* × *darleyensis* 'Darley Dale'.

**Below:** With its yellow-green stems, *Cornus sericea* 'Flaviramea' makes a subtle partner for the white-variegated *Euonymus fortunei* 'Variegatus'. This is a combination that works most effectively when viewed at close range.

color. 'Buds Yellow' has very yellow stems, and the black-stemmed 'Kesselringii' has red and purple autumn leaf color. The shoots of *C. sericea* 'Flaviramea' ♀ have a yellowish green tinge, not quite as buttery as 'Buds Yellow', while *C.s.* 'White Gold' ♀ has stems like 'Flaviramea' and white-edged leaves.

**Perfect partners:** Black-stemmed: *Carex oshimensis* 'Evergold'
Red-stemmed: *Rubus thibetanus* ❑p.95 **B**
Yellow-stemmed: *Phyllostachys nigra* ❑p.93 **B**
Yellow-green/yellow-edged foliage: *Alchemilla*

*mollis* p.230 **C**, *Astilbe* 'Red Sentinel' p.242 **B**, *Eryngium bourgatii* 'Picos Blue' p.264 **C**, *Helianthus* 'Monarch' p.283 **A**, *Rudbeckia aciniata* 'Herbstsonne' p.330 **A**
White-edged foliage: *Dahlia* 'Grenadier' p.421 **B**, *Zinnia* 'Chippendale' p.455 **B**
Autumn color: *Deschampsia cespitosa*, *Juniperus virginiana* 'Grey Owl', *Miscanthus sinensis* 'Silberturm'

**H: 6½–10 ft. (2–3 m) S: 10–13 ft. (3–4 m)**
❀ **Late spring to early summer**

 ◊◊-◊◊◊ ■-■ **Z2 pH4.5–7.5**

## *Cornus controversa* 'Variegata' ♀

This dogwood – a large, upright, deciduous shrub or small tree – has spreading side-branches arranged in table-like layers, giving it a dramatic horizontal structure. This makes a particularly telling contrast to columnar shrubs and small trees and to herbaceous plants with flowers borne in tall spikes. The bold leaves are emphasized by neat white margins, giving the whole plant a pale tone that contrasts with dark foliage and harmonizes with silver leaves or white flowers. Its creamy white blooms are largely camouflaged by the young leaves.

The plant can be used as a focal point, perhaps with a carpet of woodland flowers in white or blue beneath, but is difficult to use in quantity without the risk of overstatement. Sited in a border, it needs space to display its structure and should not be hemmed in: other shrubs or tall herbaceous plants of comparable size should be kept at one remove, although shorter plants can provide a foil beneath its spread. *C. alternifolia* 'Argentea' ♀ is similar but has smaller leaves, suiting it to schemes on a smaller scale.

**Perfect partners:** *Fatsia japonica, Hedera colchica, Hesperis matronalis, Hosta ventricosa, Lilium martagon* var. *album, Phlox divaricata, Stephanandra tanakae* ❑ p.303 **C**

**H & S: 26 ft. (8 m)** ❀ **Early summer**
▬▬▬ ◊◊ ▨-▨ **Z6  pH5–7**

The layered habit and cream-edged leaves of *Cornus controversa* 'Variegata' combine well with the looser form and colored leaves of *Philadelphus coronarius* 'Aureus'.

## *Cornus florida*
FLOWERING DOGWOOD

Flowering dogwoods are deciduous large shrubs or small trees of conical habit with clusters of tiny green florets surrounded by showy, white or pink bracts. Their leaves turn rich red or purple in autumn. There are many cultivars selected for their large bracts (such as 'Cherokee Princess' and 'Cloud Nine', both white), rich bract color (deep carmine 'Cherokee Chief' ♀), plentiful flowers ('White Cloud') or variegated foliage ('Hohmann's Gold' and 'Welchii'). Their habit is less striking than that of *C. controversa* 'Variegata' (left) so they are more amenable to grouping; however, they still need space and all-round light to flower evenly and profusely. Although relatively hardy, they can be damaged by late spring frosts and do not flower well in areas with cool summers. Attractive plants for a sunny glade in a woodland garden, they associate well with kalmias and deciduous azaleas, and with late spring flowers such as violets, sweet rocket and cranesbills.

**Perfect partners:** *Dicentra* 'Bacchanal', *Hesperis matronalis* var. *albiflora, Hyacinthoides hispanica, Lunaria annua, Rhododendron austrinum, Tiarella wherryi*

**H & S: 20 ft. (6 m)** ❀ **Late spring**
▬▬▬ ◊◊ ▨ **Z6  pH5–6.5**

This charmingly simple combination of *Cornus florida* underplanted with *Phlox divaricata* is made more pleasing by the pervasive fragrance of the phlox.

In a subtle essay in color and form, the glaucous cream-edged leaves and yellow flowers of *Coronilla valentina* subsp. *glauca* 'Variegata' are joined by silver-leaved *Teucrium fruticans*, backed by golden hop (*Humulus lupulus* 'Aureus'). The coronilla and the hop both have compound leaves, while those of the teucrium are simple and lance-shaped; the teucrium's small blue flowers present a delicate contrast.

## *Coronilla valentina* subsp. *glauca* 'Variegata'

With its tiny cream-edged glaucous leaflets and small fragrant yellow flowers, this pretty semi-evergreen shrub is best appreciated at close range. Its main flowering is from late winter into spring, but it produces some bloom all year round. A charming plant for the front of a border, a sunny bank or a gravel garden, it associates well with yellow, white or blue flowers, yellow-green foliage and flowers, and glaucous foliage. It mixes well with smaller ceanothus, brooms, choisyas, helianthemums, genistas, *Aurinia saxatilis* cultivars, smaller narcissi and white, yellow or yellow-green daphnes, and benefits from association with plants of more definite form – celmisias, for example.

**Perfect partners:** *Brunnera macrophylla*, *Ceanothus* × *delileanus* 'Gloire de Versailles', *Choisya* Goldfingers, *Narcissus* 'Charity May', *Rosmarinus officinalis*, *Scilla siberica*

**H & S: 31 in. (80 cm)** ❀ **Late winter to mid-spring**
◊-◊◊ ☐-■ Z9 pH5.5–7

## *Cotinus coggygria* 'Royal Purple' ♕

The reddish purple leaves of this smoke bush have a fiery red glow when backlit by the sun. This shrub forms rosettes of leaves toward the shoot tips and flowers profusely when mature, covering the foliage with cloudlike inflorescences. Its ultimate size may be too large for many situations, but it can be pruned to 6½–10 ft. (2–3 m) high, when it will support herbaceous or annual climbers such as morning glories or perennial peas; larger plants can be draped with climbers such as Viticella or Texensis clematis. Its coloring blends well with purple, blue, crimson and carmine-pink flowers, or with scarlet, coral, orange or flame. Specimen plants can be underplanted with harmonious flowers such as dark-leaved heucheras laced with *Lilium speciosum* cultivars. Other variants include 'Notcutt's Variety'; Purpureus Group, with green leaves and purplish flowers; and Rubrifolius Group, plum-purple, turning red.

**Perfect partners:** *Agastache* 'Firebird', *Alonsoa warscewiczii* p.410 **C**, *Dahlia* 'David Howard', *Hemerocallis* 'Stafford' p.287 **B**, *Ipomoea lobata*, *Knautia macedonica* p.302 **A**, *Ligularia dentata* 'Desdemona' p.306 **A**, *Lilium* 'Journey's End', *Lonicera caprifolium* p.174 **B** ❏pp.120 **C**, 143 **C**, 278 **B**

**H & S: 16 ft. (5 m)** ❀ **Midsummer**
◊◊ ☐-■ Z5 pH5.5–7.5

By keeping this smoke bush (*Cotinus coggygria* 'Royal Purple') well furnished with branches to ground level, sprawling and scrambling plants can be encouraged to weave themselves through its stems, creating an attractive tapestry of foliage and flowers. The vigorous cranesbill *Geranium* × *oxonianum* 'Claridge Druce' here provides contrasting leaves and harmonious mauve-pink flowers.

A subdued combination of the gray-green leaves of *Cotoneaster conspicuus* 'Decorus' and silvery *Brachyglottis* (Dunedin Group) 'Sunshine' is saved from monotony by the elegantly arching sprays of the cotoneaster's pink-tinged blooms. The brachyglottis flowers will be bright yellow when they open and might upstage the quiet charm of the cotoneaster; they can be pruned away before they develop fully.

Herringbone sprays of *Cotoneaster horizontalis* laden with scarlet fruits and the amber leaves of *Aronia arbutifolia* about to be shed supply satisfyingly warm autumnal tints. The ground beneath is carpeted with the fan-shaped leaves of lady's mantle (*Alchemilla mollis*).

## *Cotoneaster conspicuus* 'Decorus' ♛

Pinkish white, early summer flowers and scarlet autumn fruits emphasize the arching branches of this low evergreen shrub. It is useful for the front of a shrub border or for ground cover, and it blends well in wild and woodland gardens. For maximum flower and fruit production, it is best in a sunny site, where it combines easily with deutzias, small-flowered roses, kolkwitzias, kerrias, later-flowering rhododendrons and lilacs, spiraeas, potentillas, and plants like columbines, geums, cranesbills and foxgloves. It is good with martagon lilies, and with foliage of more definite form, such as bergenias or hostas. Draping its dusty gray-green foliage with a scrambling plant, such as a small-flowered clematis, can enhance its appearance.

**Perfect partners:** *Bergenia* 'Sunningdale', *Philadelphus* 'Natchez', *Rosa elegantula* 'Persetosa', *R.* 'Manning's Blush', *Syringa meyeri* var. *spontanea* 'Palibin'

H: 5 ft. (1.5 m)  S: 8 ft. (2.5 m)  ✳ **Early summer**
◌◌ ☐-■ **Z6 pH5–7.5**

## *Cotoneaster frigidus* 'Cornubia' ♛

This tall, elegant deciduous shrub produces long, arching stems, weighed down through autumn and winter with glistening red fruits. It can be used to provide a light canopy over other shrubs and plants, especially those coloring well in autumn and winter. The fairly open branch structure casts little shade, allowing a wide range of plants to be grown beneath its spread. These include aronias, deciduous azaleas and euonymus, nandinas, Chinese lanterns, berrying or variegated hollies, dogwoods and berberis. Bamboos, fruiting crab apples and amelanchiers make good companions, while the strong stems will happily support a wispy vine.

**Perfect partners:** *Acer palmatum* 'Crimson Queen', *Amelanchier lamarckii* p.31 **A**, *Euonymus alatus*, *Miscanthus sinensis* 'Zebrinus', *Nandina domestica* 'Umpqua Chief', *Parthenocissus tricuspidata* 'Lowii'

H & S: 20 ft. (6 m)  ✳ **Early summer**
◌◌ ☐-■ **Z6 pH5–7.5**

The tiny yellow-green leaves of *Lonicera nitida* 'Baggesen's Gold' contrast in size with those of *Cotoneaster frigidus* 'Cornubia' while harmonizing with those cotoneaster leaves that have turned yellow before being shed; they also act as a foil for the cotoneaster's bright scarlet fruits.

## *Cotoneaster horizontalis* ♛

A versatile semi-evergreen fruiting shrub, this makes excellent ground or wall cover, each branch forming a flat spray of branchlets arranged like a fishbone. Its tiny glistening leaves often remain until late winter, turning vivid scarlet before they fall and making a colorful combination with the dusky red fruits; even when bare, its branchlets form a pleasing pattern. It fruits best in sun, but will tolerate a shady wall, behind plants of contrasting form, including hostas, ferns, willow gentians and smaller scrambling plants. On a bank or at the front of a border, it again goes well with smaller scramblers and plants of contrasting foliage; here it may be backed by taller perennials and small shrubs, especially those grown for autumn color, such as aronias, berberis and smaller maples.

**Perfect partners:** *Codonopsis grey-wilsonii*, *Geranium kishtvariense*, *G.* × *riversleaianum*, *Hosta* 'Buckshaw Blue', *Nandina domestica* 'Fire Power', *Polystichum setiferum*, *Schizostylis coccinea* 'Major' p.332 **C**

H: 40 in. (1 m)  S: 10 ft. (3 m)  ✳ **Late spring**
◌◌ ☐-■ **Z5 pH5–7.5**

The tiny flowers and warm tints of *Cytisus* 'Zeelandia' perfectly complement the boldly shaped, orange and vermilion tulip 'Queen of Sheba', although the broom would normally overtop the tulip. Both are set off effectively by the immature yellowish green flowerheads of the snowball tree (*Viburnum opulus* 'Roseum').

## Cytisus hybrid cultivars

The numerous broom hybrids raised by crossing *C. multiflorus* with *C. scoparius* and *C. purgans* are among the most useful of late spring flowers. They vary from yellow to red, white, pink or peach, including bicolors, which gives them the potential to mix pleasingly with spring bulbs and biennial bedding plants, while their diffuse structure provides a foil for plants of more definite form. Cultivars include cream to deep pink 'Hollandia' ♀ and pale creamy yellow and pink 'Zeelandia' ♀. They are outstanding companions for late narcissi, tulips and wallflowers; yellow cultivars contrast well with forget-me-nots, and rich scarlet ones with euphorbias. These deciduous shrubs will last longer and flower more lavishly if most of the flowered wood is removed after flowering.

**Perfect partners:** *Aquilegia formosa*, *Euphorbia characias*, *E. griffithii* 'Dixter', *Exochorda* × *macrantha* 'The Bride', *Geranium phaeum* 'Album', *Narcissus poeticus* 'Plenus', *Rosa* 'Roseriae de l'Haÿ' p.208 **A**, *Tulipa* 'Spring Green'

**H & S: 5 ft.** (1.5 m) ❀ **Late spring to early summer**
◌-◌◌ ▢-▧ **Z6 pH5–7**

Delicate sprays of *Cytisus* × *praecox* 'Warminster', its flowers sulfur-yellow on dark green stems, are set against the acid yellow-green leaves of *Philadelphus coronarius* 'Aureus'. This bright combination will have an impact in any border, but the philadelphus may scorch in hot sites.

## Cytisus nigricans

This late summer broom produces its flowers in a solid spike, creating a structured effect. An erect, deciduous shrub, it is attractive with hot colors, cream or yellow-green foliage or flowers, and glaucous or yellow-variegated foliage, and makes an effective partner for grasses, cranesbills and *Buddleja* × *weyeriana* cultivars. It contrasts memorably with blue flowers such as late aconites and *Ceanothus* × *delileanus* cultivars, and purple-leaved shrubs such as *Prunus* × *cistena* and smoke bush. 'Cyni' is 40 in. (1 m) tall and across, and better suited to the front of a border. Prune plants in early spring.

**Perfect partners:** *Aconitum* 'Spark's Variety', *Ceanothus* × *delileanus* 'Gloire de Versailles', *Crocosmia* 'Vulcan', *Dahlia* 'Moonfire', *Hemerocallis* 'Marion Vaughn', *Lilium* Imperial Gold Group, *Miscanthus sinensis* 'Pünktchen', *Nicotiana* 'Lime Green'

**H: 5 ft.** (1.5 m) **S: 40 in.** (1 m)
❀ **Late summer to early autumn**
◌-◌◌ ▢-▧ **Z6 pH5–7.5**

The sharp yellow flowers of *Cytisus nigricans* harmonize with the yellow-green leaves of *Geranium* 'Ann Folkard' while contrasting strikingly with its magenta flowers.

## Cytisus × praecox 'Warminster' ♀
WARMINSTER BROOM

This airy deciduous shrub is particularly useful for combining with late spring flowers such as tulips, narcissi, forget-me-nots, wallflowers, brunneras, crown imperials, and euphorbias, as well as with yellow-green foliage. Its soft yellow coloring mixes well with warm colors such as peach and apricot, but is also strong enough to contrast with blues. In a border, its gently arching shoots can be used to show off the contrasting habit of *C.* × *kewensis* ♀, a prostrate broom. *C.* × *praecox* 'Allgold' ♀ has rich gold flowers.

**Perfect partners:** *Aquilegia canadensis*, *Brunnera macrophylla*, *Choisya ternata* Sundance, *Euphorbia polychroma* 'Major', *Geranium sylvaticum* 'Mayflower', *Narcissus poeticus* 'Plenus', *Rosa primula*, *Syringa* × *persica* 'Alba', *Tulipa* 'Golden Artist', *T.* 'Queen of Sheba'

**H: 4 ft.** (1.2 m) **S: 5 ft.** (1.5 m)
❀ **Mid- to late spring**
◌-◌◌ ▢-▧ **Z6 pH5–7**

Daphne cneorum 'Eximia' and the perennial candytuft *Iberis sempervirens* are of similar height and habit, allowing them to interweave to create a harmonious late spring carpet of pink and white flowers.

## Daphne cneorum 'Eximia' �

This particularly showy, large-flowered daphne, with evergreen foliage and heavily fragrant rose-pink blooms opening from crimson buds, requires good soil, with efficient drainage and enough moisture never to become dry at the roots. As long as it is given these exacting conditions, the shrub will create an enchanting carpet of bloom in a rock garden or at the front of a border. It is an excellent choice for a prominent position near a sitting area or alongside a path. It blends well with cool colors, especially white or apple-green flowers, and purple-flushed or glaucous foliage. Good partners include other daphnes, aubrietas, rock cress, saxifrages and smaller spring bulbs, even tulips if larger cultivars in hot colors are avoided.

**Perfect partners:** *Arabis alpina* subsp. *caucasica* 'Schneehaube', *Dicentra* 'Stuart Boothman', *Helleborus* × *sternii*, *Omphalodes cappadocica* 'Lilac Mist', *Ornithogalum nutans*, *Tulipa saxatilis*

**H: 8 in. (20 cm) S: 5 ft. (1.5 m)** ❀ **Late spring**
━━ ◊◊ ▢ ■ **Z5 pH6–7.5**

## Daphne mezereum
MEZEREON

This invaluable early-flowering deciduous shrub has flowers varying in color from mauve-pink to burgundy, followed by scarlet fruits in summer. The white form, f. *alba*, has yellow fruits. Both enjoy limy soils and cool positions, and prefer an open site; they can also be used near the front of a border, although they may become misshapen if hemmed in by herbaceous plants. They are successful with winter heaths and flowers in cool colors, including bulbs such as crocuses, snowdrops, white or palest yellow early narcissi, and *Cyclamen coum* variants, as well as pale green hellebores. Plants can suffer from root-rock if planted when pot-bound, so unwind the roots before planting.

**Perfect partners:** *Bergenia cordifolia* 'Purpurea', *Galanthus* 'S Arnott', *Helleborus* × *nigercors*, *H.* × *sternii*, *Heuchera* 'Purple Petticoats', *Narcissus* 'Dove Wings'

**H: 4 ft. (1.2 m) S: 3¼ ft. (1 m)**
❀ **Late winter to early spring**
━━ ◊◊ ■ **Z5 pH6–8**

*Daphne mezereum*, here growing through a carpet of white Darley Dale heath (*Erica* × *darleyensis* 'Silberschmelze'), harmonizes in habit with the stems of *Cornus alba* 'Flaviramea' while contrasting effectively with their yellow-green color. Heaths with pale mauve or rich ruby flowers could be added to the carpet, avoiding colors too close to that of the daphne.

## Deutzia longifolia 'Vilmoriniae'

In full sun this deciduous shrub makes a billowing mass of growth almost completely smothered by a froth of white blooms. It is a superlative plant for a white garden or a mixed or shrub border, especially partnered by old roses. It combines successfully with almost any other color, and can be used as a host for late-flowering clematis such as Viticella cultivars. Immediately after flowering, its stems need to be pruned back to a framework of branches, which will stimulate production of the next year's flowering wood. 'Veitchii' ♀ is another fine cultivar of *D. longifolia*, producing mauve-pink blooms that have white margins to the petals.

**Perfect partners:** *Campanula lactiflora*, *Hebe* 'Midsummer Beauty', *Iris* 'Cambridge', *I. orientalis*, *Lupinus arboreus*, *Potentilla fruticosa* 'Vilmoriniana', *Rosa* 'Fantin-Latour'

**H: 6½ ft. (2 m) S: 10 ft. (3 m)**
❀ **Early to midsummer**
━━ ◊◊ ▢-■ **Z6 pH5–7.5**

Contrasting red valerian (*Centranthus ruber*) and yellow-green *Euphorbia polychroma* provide a foil for *Deutzia longifolia* 'Vilmoriniae'. The deutzia leavens the color scheme and adds height, while occasional foxgloves supply punctuation and help unify the scheme, white harmonizing with the deutzia and magenta with the valerian.

Brightly variegated *Elaeagnus × ebbingei* 'Gilt Edge' harmonizes with *Rubus cockburnianus* 'Goldenvale'. In winter the bramble's white stems make a striking contrast.

In a colorful foliage scheme *Elaeagnus pungens* 'Maculata' combines with harmonious *Lonicera nitida* 'Baggesen's Gold' and contrasting *Berberis thunbergii* f. *atropurpurea*.

## *Elaeagnus pungens* 'Maculata'

This large, variegated evergreen elaeagnus (syn. 'Aureovariegata') makes a fine spreading bush for the middle of a border or the front of a shrubbery. It is less upright than *E. × ebbingei* 'Gilt Edge' (left) but the foliage is of similar coloring. It is striking as a partner for blue ceanothus cultivars or as a support for climbers such as white perennial peas, or a restrained clematis or honeysuckle. Other *E. pungens* for these roles cultivars include 'Frederici', which has narrow, creamy leaves with green margins; 'Variegata', with narrow white leaf edges; and the fairly slow-growing 'Dicksonii', with broad gold leaf margins. Stems that revert to green should be cut out while still small.

**Perfect partners:** *Ceanothus arboreus, Cytisus × praecox, Dahlia* 'Klankstad Kerkrade', *Euphorbia characias, Iris* 'Cambridge', *Lilium* Imperial Gold Group, *Mahonia × media, Miscanthus sinensis* 'Strictus', *Rosa* Elina

**H: 10 ft. (3 m) S: 16 ft. (5 m)** ✹ **Mid-autumn**
◊◊ ■ **Z7 pH5–7.5**

## *Elaeagnus × ebbingei* 'Gilt Edge' ♆

Variegated cultivars of evergreen *E. × ebbingei* are dependable foliage plants for mixed borders and shrubberies on most soils except chalk. 'Gilt Edge' is one of the most colorful, with brilliant yellow leaf margins and fragrant, creamy white flowers in autumn. Plants harmonize successfully in yellow and cream schemes, and make a lively contrast to pure blue flowers; they also blend with other evergreens in hedges and screens. The coloration is vivid in sun or light shade. 'Limelight' is less strident, with yellow-green splashes on its green-edged leaves. Any stems that revert to green should be pruned out. Grafted specimens are best avoided because they usually have shorter lives than plants on their own roots.

**Perfect partners:** *Aconitum* 'Ivorine', *Berberis julianae, Euphorbia sikkimensis, Forsythia ovata* 'Tetragold', *Kerria japonica* 'Golden Guinea', *Physocarpus opulifolius* 'Dart's Gold', *Rosa* 'Chinatown', *Syringa vulgaris* 'Primrose'

**H & S: 13 ft. (4 m)** ✹ **Mid-autumn**
◊◊ ■ **Z7 pH5–7.5**

## *Elaeagnus* 'Quicksilver' ♆

The middle of a border is the best place for this outstanding, fairly tall deciduous shrub (syn. *E. angustifolia* Caspica Group). Grown mainly for its dainty silvery foliage, it also has small, sweet-scented creamy flowers in early summer. Its soft coloring, especially when young, mixes wonderfully with old-fashioned roses, blue-flowered shrubs and Viticella or Texensis clematis. Annual climbers such as morning glories are also excellent partners. If pruned low down to encourage production of basal sideshoots, 'Quicksilver' may be grown among herbaceous plants, which then mingle with the lower branches. This shrub enjoys plenty of sun and a well-drained sandy site, but will tolerate most soils and drier conditions than other elaeagnus.

**Perfect partners:** *Aconitum hemsleyanum, Clematis* 'Huldine', *C.* 'Prince Charles', *Delphinium* Summer Skies Group, *Ipomoea tricolor* 'Heavenly Blue', *Rosa* 'Sander's White Rambler' ❑ pp.99 **B**, 127 **B**, 153 **B**, 313 **C**

**H & S: 13 ft. (4 m)** ✹ **Early summer**
◊-◊◊ ■-■ **Z3 pH5–7.5**

Leaving the lower stems on *Elaeagnus* 'Quicksilver' allows its softly silver foliage to blend attractively with herbaceous plants such as *Symphytum caucasicum*.

## *Erica carnea*
WINTER HEATH

Among the hundreds of heath and heather cultivars some of the most popular are those of *E. carnea*, a low-growing, shrubby heath that flowers in late winter and early spring. The wiry, branching plants spread to form hummocks of evergreen ground cover on most well-drained soils. The flowers, tiny and tightly packed in long, slender spikes, have a wide range of colors, from white through lilac-pink to purplish red. There are also richly colored gold- and bronze-leaved forms, many with deeper red and orange foliar tints in very cold weather.

Winter heaths are effective when massed in beds, although care should be taken to avoid any color clash between flowers and foliage. They look especially fine when underplanted with late winter and early spring bulbs, such as snowdrops, hardy cyclamens and *Crocus tommasinianus,* and are very much at home with other ericaceous shrubs such as dwarf rhododendrons, gaultherias, vacciniums or the prostrate *Leiophyllum buxifolium.* Daphnes and prostrate brooms are also congenial partners; bergenias offer dramatic contrasts of leaf shape and texture; and dwarf junipers make natural heathland associations. Taller forms of *Juniperus communis* can provide startling accents among the heaths.

All heaths benefit from an overall trim after flowering to prevent straggly growth. However, since plants are naturally rounded, each one should be clipped individually to avoid producing a flat carpet. Hot, impoverished sites may lead to fungal ailments; plants will tolerate some shade but not the gloom beneath trees.

**Perfect partners:** Bronze-leaved: *Cornus alba* 'Sibirica', *Crocus* 'Gipsy Girl', *Heuchera* 'Amber Waves', *H.* 'Sashay'
Mauve/purple-flowered: *Bergenia stracheyi, Cyclamen coum, Pulmonaria* 'Lewis Palmer' p.327 **B** ❑ p.88 **B**
White-flowered: *Bergenia ciliata, Galanthus* 'S. Arnott', *Heuchera* 'Green Spice', *Ipheion uniflorum*
Yellow-green leaved: *Cornus sericea* 'Flaviramea', *Narcissus* 'Little Witch', *Scilla siberica*

**H: 8–10 in.** (20–25 cm) **S: 20 in.** (50 cm)
❀ **Late winter to early spring**
▬▭▬ ◊◊ ▢-▆ ▆ Z5 pH4.5–7

Winter heaths such as *Erica carnea* 'Springwood White' are delightful partners for early bulbs such as *Narcissus* 'Tête-à-tête' and the persistently perennial *Tulipa turkestanica.* Even fairly small bulbs such as these are vigorous enough to grow beneath the spread of the heaths.

## *Erica × darleyensis*
DARLEY DALE HEATH

This is a natural hybrid between *E. carnea* (above) and the tree heath *E. erigena* (syn. *E. mediterranea*). It forms a vigorous, bushy shrub with textured plumes of young growth, and it likes similar sites in sun or light shade with moist but well-drained soil. The cultivars include the original hybrid 'Darley Dale', which produces pale pink flowers over many weeks. Flower color ranges from the purity of 'White Perfection' ♀ and 'Silberschmelze', through pink to the deep rose-red of 'Jack H. Brummage'. This neat form has yellow foliage darkening to reddish gold in winter, and cream and pink young growth in spring. *E. × darleyensis* cultivars are natural companions for *E. carnea*, their greater height and bulk making them most effective as a backdrop to their more compact relatives. They combine equally well with the associates recommended for *E. carnea*, and with smaller gorses.

**Perfect partners:** *Calluna vulgaris* p.83 **A**, *Crocus sieberi, Daphne mezereum* p.93 **B**, *Galanthus elwesii, Hedera colchica* p.169 **A**, *Heuchera* 'Can-can', *Picea pungens* Pendula Group p.122 **C**, *Rhododendron* 'Praecox' ❑ pp.88 **B**, 138 **A**

**H: 12–24 in.** (30–60 cm) **S: 12–30 in.** (30–75 cm)
❀ **Late winter to early spring**
▬▭▬ ◊◊ ▢-▆ ▆ Z6 pH4.5–7

Pink *Erica × darleyensis* 'Darley Dale' and *Euonymus fortunei* 'Variegatus' provide a carpet for bright-stemmed dogwoods *Cornus alba* 'Sibirica' and *C. sericea* 'Flaviramea'.
*E. × d.* 'White Perfection' would also be effective here.

Subdued mauves, purples and pinks, together with gray-green foliage, make up this carpet of late spring flowers in which *Erysimum* 'Bowles Mauve' is the prominent plant, with *E. cheiri* 'Purple Queen' and *Skimmia japonica* 'Rubella'. *Allium hollandicum* and tulips will follow shortly.

## *Erysimum* 'Bowles Mauve' 🏆

This wallflower is a short-lived sub-shrub that forms a domed bush with slightly grayish leaves. Its purplish mauve flowers appear continually through much of the year, most profusely in late spring and early summer. An excellent candidate for the front of a border, it also thrives in rock gardens and gravel gardens, and even grows well in walls. The distinctive flower color can be combined with cool shades and with purple, silver or glaucous foliage, and contrasts effectively with yellow-green foliage and flowers. It associates well with euphorbias, catmints, artemisias, pinks and alliums, and looks particularly attractive when grown in front of old roses. Plants must be propagated from cuttings, which should not be allowed to become pot-bound because they are then difficult to establish. As a general rule, windy sites are unsuitable for this plant.

**Perfect partners:** *Artemisia alba* 'Canescens', *Convolvulus cneorum* p.87 **C**, *Dianthus* 'Musgrave's Pink', *Euphorbia characias*, *Tulipa* 'Angélique' p.391 **B** ❑ pp.173 **B**, 308 **B**

**H & S: 24 in. (60 cm)** ❀ **Late winter to late summer**
▬▬▭▭▭▬ ◊-◊◊ ▢-▇ Z7 pH5.5–8

## *Erysimum* 'Wenlock Beauty'

A charming plant for the front of a border or for a rock garden, this perennial wallflower has a more prostrate habit than 'Bowles Mauve' (left) and is less prone to wind-rock. The florets open buff and then develop shadings of tawny-red before aging to dusky mauve-purple, a slightly subdued color scheme that is flattered by dusky pink, deep crimson, wine-purple and dusky mauve. Plants combine well with cream flowers and purple foliage, and make satisfying blends with apple-green and yellow-green. Another perennial wallflower for similar planting schemes is *E. mutabile*, a spreading plant with flowers in a blend of rose-madder and purple that can be used to echo dusky shades, including those of 'Wenlock Beauty'.

**Perfect partners:** *Artemisia caucasica*, *Aubrieta* 'Joy', *Euphorbia polychroma* 'Major', *Helleborus* × *sternii*, *Heuchera* 'Purple Petticoats', *Narcissus* 'Hawera'

**H & S: 18 in. (45 cm)** ❀ **Early to late spring**
▬▬▭▭▭▬ ◊-◊◊ ▢-▇ Z7 pH5.5–8

*Erysimum* 'Wenlock Beauty' mixes with soft yellow, double-flowered *Narcissus* 'Yellow Cheerfulness' – the wallflower's amber young florets harmonize while its purple mature florets contrast. Both plants are overtopped by the sharp yellow-green heads of *Euphorbia characias* subsp. *wulfenii*.

The weeping crab apple *Malus* 'Butterball', its abundant yellow fruits flushed with warm orange, cascades in a curtain, forming a backdrop for the dazzling autumn tints of *Euonymus alatus* var. *apterus* as it changes color from warm mahogany to blazing red.

## *Euonymus alatus* var. *apterus*

The prime attraction of this deciduous spindle is its fine display of brilliant tints in autumn, especially in full sun, when the leaves assume shades of pink, crimson and scarlet, making a flamboyant accompaniment to the purplish fruits as they split open to reveal scarlet seeds. The flowers are relatively insignificant, and neither foliage nor growth habit offers great interest in spring and summer, although the shrub can be draped with a flowering climber. It is an outstanding companion for large grasses such as pampas grass, sorbus, deciduous hollies and other autumn-coloring plants. *E. alatus* ♀ itself has corky wings growing from its stems. *E.a.* 'Compactus' ♀ is no more than 40 in. (1 m) high, with very dense foliage that withstands clipping, making it good for dwarf hedging.

**Perfect partners:** *Acer palmatum* f. *atropurpureum*, *Berberis wilsoniae*, *Cortaderia selloana* 'Pink Feather', *Cotinus* 'Grace', *Ilex verticillata* 'Winter Red', *Miscanthus sinensis* 'China', *Rhododendron quinquefolium*, *Rhus typhina*

**H: 6½ ft. (2 m) S: 10 ft. (3 m)** (✼ **Early summer)**
◊◊ ▢-▨ **Z4 pH5.5–8**

## *Euonymus fortunei* 'Silver Queen'

The dark green leaves of this bushy evergreen spindle have butter-yellow margins in spring, turning white by summer. This variegation is attractive at close range, while at a distance the foliage has a paler tone useful for contrasts with darker-leaved plants or for illuminating a shady corner. The yellow spring coloring harmonizes with other yellows, yellow-greens and cream, and contrasts with pure blue flowers such as forget-me-nots and omphalodes. Other good variegated cultivars are 'Emerald Gaiety' ♀, with white leaf margins that assume pink tints in winter, and 'Emerald 'n' Gold' ♀, with bright gold leaf margins flushed red in winter. All three tolerate sun or shade, grow in quite poor soil, and are invaluable for edging beds, as ground cover and for growing up a wall.

**Perfect partners:** *Brunnera macrophylla*, *Helleborus argutifolius*, *H.* × *hybridus*, *Meconopsis grandis*, *Milium effusum* 'Aureum', *Muscari armeniacum*, *Narcissus* 'Pipit', *Omphalodes cappadocica*, *Tulipa* 'Monte Carlo'

**H: 8 ft. (2.5 m) S: 5 ft. (1.5 m)** (✼ **Early summer)**
▬▬▭ ◊◊ ▢-▨ **Z5 pH5.5–7.5**

The yellowish cream variegation of *Euonymus fortunei* 'Silver Queen' contrasts effectively with the sky-blue flowers of Spanish bluebells (*Hyacinthoides hispanica*). Other spring bulbs with blue, soft yellow or white flowers could be added to enhance the scheme.

The curious rose-pink fruits of *Euonymus hamiltonianus* subsp. *sieboldianus*, opening to reveal clashing orange seeds, are borne on a spreading and unstructured bush that benefits from companion plants of more definite form, such as dwarf pampas grass (*Cortaderia selloana* 'Pumila').

## *Euonymus hamiltonianus* subsp. *sieboldianus*

This deciduous spindle makes a spreading bush and is suitable for planting schemes on a large scale. Its most appealing feature is the autumn coloring of its foliage, the leaves turning various shades of peach, pink and red, and providing a warm background for the ripening fruit capsules that display orange seeds on splitting. The autumn leaf tints may vary according to climate, situation and the clone. Like *E. alatus* var. *apterus* (left) it has few charms in spring and summer, but makes an excellent host for flowering climbers, and succeeds in the same plant combinations.

**Perfect partners:** *Celastrus orbiculatus*, *Clematis* 'Abundance', *C. rehderiana*, *Miscanthus sinensis* 'China', *Sorbus* 'Eastern Promise', *Xanthorhiza simplicissima*

**H & S: 20 ft. (6 m)** (✼ **Early summer)**
▬▬▭ ◊◊ ▢-▨ **Z5 pH5.5–7.5**

## *Euphorbia characias* subsp. *wulfenii*

This upright, evergreen sub-shrub has yellow-green nectaries at the center of each floret. Its flower stems are formed in summer and start to bloom the following spring, when they look very effective with late bulbs such as narcissi and the daintier tulips. Plants sometimes appear a little stalky at the base, and benefit from screening with shorter, cushion-forming plants. Impressive harmonies can be made with yellow-green or cream flowers and hot colors like orange, while bronze foliage and blue flowers such as brunneras and omphalodes contrast well. Good companions include crown imperials and Mediterranean shrubs such as white-flowered cistus and phlomis. Plants enjoy well-drained soil and tolerate some drought, although the foliage can lose its handsome appearance in prolonged dry spells.

**Perfect partners:** *Aquilegia* 'Hensol Harebell', *Camassia leichtlinii*, *Ceanothus* 'Cascade', *Erysimum cheiri* 'Primrose Bedder', *Euphorbia griffithii* 'Dixter', *Fritillaria imperialis* 'The Premier', × *Halimiocistus wintonensis*, *Lupinus* 'Thundercloud' p.308 **B**, *Phlomis chrysophylla*, *Rosa spinosissima* 'Grandiflora' ◻ pp.96 **B**, 428 **C**

**H: 40 in. (1 m) S: 4 ft. (1.2 m)**
❋ **Early spring to early summer**

◐-◐◐  ◼-◻  **Z8 pH5.5–7.5**

**Right:** *Euphorbia characias* subsp. *wulfenii* 'Lambrook Gold' and *E. polychroma* 'Major' match exactly in color but differ sufficiently in form to make an attractive combination.

**Below:** A large-scale planting of *Euphorbia characias* subsp. *wulfenii* 'Lambrook Gold' and *E. polychroma* 'Major' with *Physocarpus opulifolius* 'Luteus', *Smilacina racemosa* and *Kirengeshoma palmata*, creates a symphony in chartreuse.

## *Euphorbia* × *martini* ♈

A hybrid derived from *Euphorbia characias* crossed with wood spurge (*E. amygdaloides*), this evergreen sub-shrub has yellowish green flowers with reddish nectaries, together with red stems and dark green leaves. It makes an altogether very impressive clump for a woodland garden or a sunny or lightly shaded border. The flowers lose some of their yellow coloring as they age, turning a dull green that is lighter than the foliage and very effective as a contrast with rich deep red flowers, which will harmonize with the euphorbia's stem and nectary coloring. It works well with bronze or yellow-green foliage, and looks pleasing when associated with flowers in shades of yellow, light yellow-green, cream and orange.

**Perfect partners:** *Epimedium* × *youngianum* 'Niveum' p.263 **B**, *Geum* 'Beech House Apricot', *Helleborus argutifolius*, *H.* × *hybridus*, *Primula* Cowichan Venetian Group

**H & S: 40 in. (1 m)** ❀ **Mid-spring to midsummer**
⬛ ◊-◊◊ ⬜-⬛ **Z7 pH5–7.5**

The sumptuously colored, shade-tolerant *Primula* 'Tawny Port' has flowers that harmonize with the stems of *Euphorbia* × *martini* but contrast with its blooms.

## *Fagus sylvatica* 'Purpurea Pendula'

This deciduous, dwarf weeping beech makes an excellent specimen but is also small enough to include in large borders. It is usually top-grafted as a standard onto a 5–6½ ft. (1.5–2 m) stock, and grows slowly into a mushroom-shaped mound of foliage, spreading as it ages. As a border specimen it needs planting forward from neighbors that might obscure its round, even shape. It tends to form a visual block to views along the length of a border, but it will not compromise distant views from an angle. It suits dusky schemes with dark foliage and blue, purple or dark red flowers, and makes effective contrasts with silver or yellow-green foliage, or as a background for pale flowers such as white or apricot foxgloves.

**Perfect partners:** *Angelica gigas*, *Digitalis purpurea* 'Sutton's Apricot', *Lilium* 'Ariadne', *Lonicera sempervirens* 'Cedar Lane', *Phormium tenax* Purpureum Group

**H: 80 ft. (25 m) S: 50 ft. (15 m)** (❀ **Mid-spring**)
⬛ ◊-◊◊ ⬜-⬛ **Z5 pH5–8**

The dwarf weeping beech *Fagus sylvatica* 'Purpurea Pendula' acts as a full stop in this deep border, where it is combined with other purple-leaved plants, such as *Berberis* × *ottawensis* f. *purpurea*, and contrasting *Elaeagnus* 'Quicksilver' and yellow asphodel (*Asphodeline lutea*). The beech will need careful pruning to keep it within bounds without impairing its natural habit.

## *Fatsia japonica* ♈

Both sun and shade are acceptable to this immensely handsome evergreen shrub, which is an excellent plant for shady city courtyard gardens. It bears imposing panicles of spherical, creamy white flowerheads in autumn and broad, glossy, dark green leaves whose size can be increased by keeping plants moist and removing the clusters of black fruits that form after flowering. This results in an almost tropical luxuriance, which qualifies it for inclusion in plantings with exotic foliage such as that of tetrapanax, stooled paulownias or catalpas, bananas, hedychiums and cannas (with the exception of brash canna cultivars). It is also a superb candidate for Japanese themes, combined for example with bamboos, hostas and Japanese maples.

**Perfect partners:** *Hedychium coccineum* 'Tara', *Hosta* 'Sum and Substance', *Lilium auratum*, *Musa basjoo* 'Sakhalin', *Nandina domestica*, *Pleioblastus viridistriatus* ❑p.171 **C**

**H & S: 6½ ft. (2 m)** ❀ **Mid- to late autumn**
⬛ ◊◊-⬜-⬛ **Z6 pH5–7.5**

Used in a relatively narrow border, this pairing of *Fatsia japonica* with contrasting *Phormium tenax* 'Variegatum' has an almost tropical air. The fatsia's dramatic white-stemmed inflorescences contribute to the effect above a carpet of fine-textured dwarf box (*Buxus sempervirens* 'Suffruticosa').

## *Forsythia × intermedia*

Renowned for its yellow spring display, this deciduous shrub mixes well with white flowers, hot-colored tulips (Fosteriana and Darwinhybrid Groups), and yellow-green foliage and flowers, and contrasts effectively with blue flowers such as forget-me-nots. Good companion plants include white flowering currants, early-flowering euphorbias, white and pale yellow narcissi, blue hyacinths and plants with gold-variegated foliage, such as evergreen

elaeagnus cultivars. *F. × i.* 'Spectabilis' has a slightly untidy appearance, improved in 'Lynwood' ♀; Week-End ('Courtalyn') ♀ is shorter, at 6½ ft. (2 m), with neater, erect stems, while 'Minigold', at 5 ft. (1.5 m), is a useful size for combining with spring bulbs. Most of these tend to be amorphous and uninteresting in summer unless draped with summer-flowering climbers; larger specimens, especially grouped together, look impressive supporting an early-flowering white clematis.

**Perfect partners:** *Aucuba japonica*, *Berberis darwinii* p.80 **A**, *Corylopsis pauciflora*, *Daphne mezereum* f. *alba*, *Helleborus hybridus*, *Ilex aquifolium* 'Silver Queen', *Narcissus* 'February Silver', *Ribes sanguineum* 'Tydeman's White', *Salix aegyptiaca*, *Tulipa* Fosteriana Group

**H & S: 5–8 ft.** (1.5–2.5 m) ✽ **Early spring**
◊◊ ☐-■ **Z5 pH5.5–7.5**

Left: The handsome foliage of tender evergreen *Mahonia napaulensis* provides a foil for the bright flowers of *Forsythia × intermedia*, furnished in front with *Symphytum* 'Goldsmith', its leaves margined yellowish cream.

Below: When grown large, perhaps trained against a wall, *Forsythia × intermedia* may be draped lightly with an early-flowering clematis such as *C. armandii*, preferably in a white-flowered selection rather than pale pink.

The gold, orange and red autumn tints of *Fothergilla major* Monticola Group perfectly complement the seasonal colors of Japanese maples such as *Acer palmatum* 'Ōsakazuki' while providing a contrast of leaf shape.

## *Fothergilla major* Monticola Group

*Fothergilla major* ♀ is a deciduous 10 ft. (3 m) relative of witch hazel, bearing creamy white bottle-brush flowers before the leaves unfurl, and with yellow, orange or scarlet leaf tints in autumn. Monticola Group is smaller, with brilliant orange or scarlet autumn color. Its spring flowers are effective with bluebells, yellow or warm-tinted deciduous azaleas, and the yellow-green of smyrniums. Later in the year it associates well with other autumn-coloring shrubs, such as linderas, berberis, dogwoods, deciduous euonymus, vacciniums, sumachs, maples and clethras. It can also be used with Chinese lanterns, and Rubellum or Korean chrysanthemums in autumn colors.

**Perfect partners:** *Acer palmatum* f. *atropurpureum*, *Berberis wilsoniae*, *Lindera obtusiloba*, *Physalis alkekengi*, *Rhododendron luteum*, *R.* 'May Day' p.132 **B**, *Rhus typhina*

**H: 8 ft.** (2.5 m) **S: 6½ ft.** (2 m) ✽ **Late spring**
◊◊-◊◊◊ ☐-■ **Z5 pH4.5–6.5**

The nodding flowers of *Fuchsia* 'Checkerboard', their red tubes and corollas harmonizing with the reddish purple foliage of *Acer palmatum* Dissectum Atropurpureum Group, are enlivened by their white sepals. The male fern cultivar *Dryopteris affinis* 'Cristata' provides a pleasing contrast of foliage form.

## *Fuchsia* 'Checkerboard' ♆

The dramatic red and white flowers help this relatively hardy, deciduous fuchsia show up in situations where cultivars with purple and red flowers might be less visible. It is most successful with cooler colors and with the purple or red foliage of plants like Japanese maples and dark-leaved dahlias or berberis. Plants need full sun where summers are cool, but tolerate partial shade in hotter climates. In frost-free areas, growth survives winter without injury, allowing earlier flowering and taller stems to combine with old shrub roses and other large neighbors. It mixes well with contrasting foliage – that of watsonias, ferns, grasses and bronze sedges, for example – or with tender perennials, such as argyranthemums and osteospermums.

**Perfect partners:** *Anemone* × *hybrida* 'Elegans', *Berberis thunbergii* 'Red Chief', *Rosa* 'Mevrouw Nathalie Nypels', *Schizostylis* 'Sunrise', *Watsonia* 'Stanford Scarlet'

**H: 36 in.** (90 cm)  **S: 30 in.** (75 cm)
❁ **Early summer to mid-autumn**

▬▬▭▬ ◊◊ ▭-▪ **Z8  pH5–7.5**

## *Fuchsia magellanica* var. *gracilis* ♆

This fairly hardy fuchsia is particularly showy from midsummer to the frosts, with small, dainty, red and deep violet-purple flowers. It has a spreading habit, and slender arching growth that suits positions near the front of a border, behind a low wall or within a carpet of short, shade-tolerant groundcover plants such as ivies or bugles, together with spring bulbs or early-flowering annuals or biennials. Its flowers, best at close range, blend equally well with salmons, carmines or mauves, and with red or purple-flushed foliage, and red, deep pink or purple flowers; yellow-green foliage or flowers make pleasing contrasts. Good companions include late-flowering heucheras, smaller Japanese anemones, nicotianas, prostrate verbenas, nerines, asters and Korean, Rubellum or Charm chrysanthemums. It prefers partial shade in hot climates, but in cooler regions needs full sun to flower well. A deciduous shrub, its spreading stems are cut back to the ground in winter in frost-prone areas.

The dainty flowers of *Fuchsia magellanica* var. *gracilis* give the shrub a diffuse covering of red.

**Perfect partners:** *Aster amellus* 'Jacqueline Genebrier', *Chrysanthemum* 'Emperor of China', *Heuchera* 'Purple Petticoats', *Nerine* 'Zeal Giant', *Pennisetum setaceum* 'Rubrum'

**H & S: 6½ ft.** (2 m)  ❁ **Midsummer to late autumn**
▬▬▭▬ ◊◊ ▭-▪ **Z8  pH5–7.5**

The flowers of *Fuchsia* 'Tom Thumb', borne on a plant short enough for the very front of a border, are to the blue side of primary red in color, making them clash gently but not disagreeably with the orange-red berries of *Arum italicum* 'Marmoratum', whose marbled leaves occupy the fuchsia's space before it emerges in late spring. A polypody fern provides foliage contrast.

## *Fuchsia* 'Tom Thumb' ♆

More dwarf than many hardy fuchsias, 'Tom Thumb', which is deciduous, is suitable for the front of a border, and can be used as an edging or to fill a parterre. Its light red and lilac flowers mix prettily with most of the companions recommended for *F. magellanica* var. *gracilis* (above), and with short, dark-leaved dahlias, *Begonia* Semperflorens Cultorum Group, impatiens, pelargoniums and petunias. It is also effective with softer yellow-green foliage and lime green flowers. Used en masse, it can be underplanted with spring flowers such as scillas, muscari and blue or pink wood anemones, and with bronze foliage. This rather amorphous shrub is best combined with plants of more definite structure and form.

**Perfect partners:** *Artemisia alba* 'Canescens', *Brassica oleracea* (Acephala Group) 'Redbor', *Festuca glauca* 'Blaufuchs', *Geranium* × *antipodeum* 'Chocolate Candy', *Nerine bowdenii*, *Nicotiana* Domino Series, *Sedum* 'Bertram Anderson'

**H & S: 8 in.** (20 cm)  ❁ **Midsummer to late autumn**
▬▬▭▬ ◊◊ ▭-▪ **Z8  pH5–7.5**

The small, evenly spaced flowerheads of *Genista hispanica* create a fine-textured effect, contrasting with the large heads and layered habit of *Viburnum plicatum* 'Mariesii'.

## Genista hispanica
SPANISH GORSE

This cheerful, robust Mediterranean shrub forms a dense mound of evergreen twigs and spines, with tiny, deciduous leaves only on the flowering stems. Yellow pea-shaped flowers smother the neat bush, making a strong block of color in a dry border or gravel bed. The even mounds look more natural in irregular groups, with neighboring plants infiltrating their fringes. Good companions include other Mediterranean plants such as sages, cistus and halimiums, and most other drought-tolerant plants from hot, dry regions. The dense habit and bright coloring complement silver-leaved plants and those with a looser, more open form, and make striking contrasts with purple and blue shades.

**Perfect partners:** *Convolvulus cneorum, C. sabatius, × Halimiocistus wintonensis, Phlomis chrysophylla, Rosmarinus officinalis* 'Aureus', *Salvia officinalis* 'Icterina'

**H: 30 in. (75 cm) S: 5 ft. (1.5 m)** ❀ **Early summer**
◊ ▢ **Z7 pH5.5–7.5**

## Halimium ocymoides ♀

This slightly lax, spreading bush is evergreen, with small grayish leaves. These make a perfect background for the delicate-looking, purple-centered, golden yellow blooms in summer. The flowers resemble those of cistus and helianthemums, to which the halimium is closely related; like them, it prefers hot, dry, well-drained sites. It associates well with more formal shrubs such as lavenders and sages, and with white and mid-blue flowers.

## Hamamelis × intermedia

Witch hazels are an indispensable genus of moisture-loving, deciduous shrubs and small trees. They are appreciated for their attractive vaselike shape and their spidery flowers with curiously strap-shaped petals, borne on leafless stems in winter. Cultivars of this popular hybrid range from the pale yellow of 'Moonlight', through gold and orange, to the rich tawny brown of 'Jelena' ♀ and 'Ruby Glow'; lemon-yellow 'Pallida' ♀ has the

**Perfect partners:** *Cistus × hybridus, Helianthemum* 'Boughton Double Primrose', *Lavandula angustifolia* 'Nana Alba', *Phlomis fruticosa, Potentilla fruticosa* 'Maanelys', *Rosa* 'Golden Wings', *Spartium junceum, Stachys citrina*

**H: 24 in. (60 cm) S: 40 in. (1 m)** ❀ **Early to midsummer**
◊ ▢ **Z8 pH6–7.5**

In this combination of plants favoring a Mediterranean climate, all of them of comparable stature and growth rate, *Halimium ocymoides* provides plentiful golden flowers, matched by the yellow-edged foliage of *Salvia officinalis* 'Icterina'. The gray leaves of *Lotus hirsutus* and its near-white flowers harmonize with the scheme.

The silvery leaves of *Brachyglottis* (Dunedin Group) 'Sunshine' provide an effective foil for the mahogany-red flowers of a young witch hazel, *Hamamelis × intermedia* 'Diane'. When mature, the witch hazel flowers will be borne too high to interact with such a companion, and its shade will prevent the brachyglottis from growing.

largest flowers. In autumn, cultivars such as 'Diane' ♀ and 'Arnold Promise' ♀ assume opulent red leaf tints. Some cultivars, such as 'Moonlight' and 'Vesna', are also spicily fragrant, making them welcome cut flowers for winter vases. The elegant shape of these shrubs needs its own personal space, ideally where it will be lit by the winter sun and set against a dark background, perhaps of evergreen hollies or yew, to emphasize the fragile beauty of the flowers. Witch hazels can be combined with colored-stemmed dogwoods for maximum winter effect, and carpeted with spring bulbs and bergenias, with hardy cranesbills for summer interest.

**Perfect partners:** *Camellia* 'Cornish Snow', *Eranthis hyemalis, Erica × darleyensis* 'White Perfection', *Galanthus* 'Atkinsii', *Hedera colchica* 'Sulphur Heart', *Mahonia japonica*

**H & S: 13 ft. (4 m)** ❀ **Mid- to late winter**
◊◊ ▢ **Z5 pH5.5–7.5**

## *Hebe* 'Midsummer Beauty' 🏆

Taller hebes are outstandingly showy evergreen shrubs, although some of the most eye-catching are the least hardy. 'Midsummer Beauty' is a reliable cultivar for gardens with fairly mild winters and cool summers, where its flowers are less likely to be bleached by bright sunlight; it is ideal for windy, exposed sites near the sea. The flowering season lasts for much of the summer and autumn, and sometimes even into winter. In full bloom this rounded bush has a two-tone effect, varying from the rich lilac of the younger flowers and buds to the much paler lilac of older blooms. It is effective in the middle of a mixed border, among pink, purple, red or white flowers, although strong yellow can overwhelm its subtle coloring. It is good, too, with purple and silver foliage, and can be combined with restrained climbers such as clematis or perennial peas that will not smother this neat, domed bush.

**Perfect partners:** *Buddleja* 'Pink Delight', *Lavandula stoechas* subsp. *pedunculata*, *Lavatera* × *clementii* 'Barnsley', *Penstemon* 'Burgundy', *P.* 'Evelyn', *Perovskia* 'Blue Spire', *Rosa* Iceberg

**H & S:** 6½ ft. (2 m) **Midsummer to late autumn**
**Z8 pH5–7.5**

A mature plant of *Hebe* 'Midsummer Beauty' is large enough to be draped with a late-flowering Texensis or Viticella clematis. Here, the harmonious but much deeper color of Viticella 'Etoile Violette' and its contrasting floral shape make a successful combination.

This combination of *Hebe* 'Nicola's Blush' and *Euonymus fortunei* 'Emerald 'n' Gold' would work equally well with a rich lavender-blue hebe or a white-variegated euonymus.

## *Hebe* 'Nicola's Blush' 🏆

This is one of the most popular smaller hebes, hardier than larger cultivars and easy to grow in an open site. The younger blooms are a clear soft pink, fading to white with age. It makes effective ground cover or a slightly formal edging to a border, on its own or combined with pinks, carnations, dwarf lavenders and grasses of similar stature. Its quiet coloring blends charmingly with blue, mauve, crimson and white flowers, and with silver foliage plants. Other fine small hebes include white-flowered *H.* 'Pewter Dome' 🏆, 'Red Edge' 🏆, with red margins to its gray-green leaves, and the prostrate, glaucous *H. pinguifolia* 'Pagei' 🏆.

**Perfect partners:** *Artemisia* 'Powis Castle', *Festuca glauca* 'Blaufuchs', *Lavandula angustifolia* 'Hidcote', *Salvia officinalis* 'Purpurascens', *Sedum* 'Vera Jameson', *Senecio viravira*

**H & S: 30 in.** (75 cm)
**Late summer to late autumn**
**Z8 pH5–7.5**

*Hebe ochracea* combines with other hummock-forming plants that have leaves of contrasting shapes and sizes to create a subtle patchwork at the front of a border. The white flowers of the hebe echo the pale-edged leaves of *Astrantia major* 'Sunningdale Variegated', while purple sage (*Salvia officinalis* 'Purpurascens') and heucheras add to the display.

## Hebe ochracea

This whipcord hebe has tiny evergreen leaves borne on sprays of arching branchlets that slowly form a domed shrub, and white flowers when five or six years old. Its perfect shape needs space to develop – it will star in an island bed or large rock garden, with good drainage, full sun and a surround of shorter plants such as heaths, heathers with colored leaves and prostrate junipers. It is effective with bronze or yellow-green foliage and with warm-colored flowers such as heleniums, helianthemums and smaller hypericums, and with white flowers like smaller cistus. 'James Stirling' ♀ is brighter and more compact.

**Perfect partners:** *Celmisia semicordata, Euphorbia rigida, Helianthemum* 'Wisley White', *Hypericum cerastioides, Juniperus communis* 'Depressa Aurea', *Salvia officinalis* 'Icterina'

H: 40 in. (1 m)  S: 30 in. (75 cm)
❉ Late spring to early summer
◊◊ ▣-■ Z7 pH5–7.5

The success of this pretty combination with *Hebe* 'Watson's Pink' depends on a contrast of foliage, rather than of flower form or color. The silvery, slightly invasive *Artemisia ludoviciana* lingers at the outer fringes of the hebe rather than scrambling into it.

## Hebe stenophylla

This bushy evergreen (syn. *H. parviflora* var. *angustifolia*) forms a loose dome of light green upright shoots that look effective in borders and can support a scrambling plant such as codonopsis, *Helichrysum petiolare*, or cranesbill. Its spikes of lilac-tinted white flowers excel with mauve, lilac, pink and white flowers, and with silver foliage. Good companions are larger lavenders, olearias, tree poppies, silver-leaved alstroemerias, philadelphus, early-flowering hydrangeas and smaller deutzias, buddleias and weigelas. Its second flowering in autumn coincides with late asters and nerines, abelias, fuchsias, lespedezas and early-flowering winter heaths.

**Perfect partners:** *Artemisia ludoviciana, Buddleja davidii* 'Nanho Petite Indigo', *Geranium* 'Brookside', *Lavandula lanata, Penstemon* 'Sour Grapes', *Phygelius aequalis* Sensation

H & S: 40 in. (1 m) ❉ Mid- to late summer
◊◊ ▣-■ Z8 pH5–7.5

*Hebe stenophylla*, like other hebes that are not too dense and remain furnished to the ground, is an attractive host for plants of contrasting floral form or color. Here, *Geranium × oxonianum* scrambles through its lower branches.

## Hebe 'Watson's Pink'

This showy, broad-leaved evergreen shrub prefers mild winters and relatively cool summers, in a border where the soil does not dry out. It works well with silver or purple foliage, and with flowers in white, deep pink, crimson, mauve, lilac or campanula-blue. It mixes congenially with veronicas, smaller old-fashioned roses and scrambling convolvulus, together with feathery silver-leaved plants like artemisias and grasses such as blue fescues. Tender perennials such as argyranthemums and early-flowering annuals such as nigellas are other good partners. It has a second flush of flowers in mid- to late autumn, when it can be used with asters, Japanese anemones and later-flowering annuals such as cosmos.

**Perfect partners:** *Argyranthemum* 'Summer Melody', *Campanula* 'Van-Houttei', *Helictotrichon sempervirens, Lavandula angustifolia* 'Bowles Early', *Penstemon* 'Cherry'

H & S: 40 in. (1 m) ❉ Early to midsummer
◊◊ ▣-■ Z8 pH5–7.5

**Above:** Helianthemums are spreading plants that can scramble into other open and low-growing shrubs. Here, 'Mrs C.W. Earle' ♀ pushes its way through *Juniperus communis* 'Depressa Aurea', resulting in a striking contrast of scarlet flowers and yellow-green plumes of foliage.

**Below:** Two helianthemums, coral 'Fire Dragon' ♀ and scarlet 'Ben Hope', interplanted with dramatically contrasting and gently invasive *Euphorbia cyparissias*, combine to create a tapestry of flowers in varied colors. Seedling *Eryngium giganteum* is poised to continue the display.

## *Helianthemum* cultivars
SUN ROSES

These are low, spreading, evergreen or semi-evergreen shrubs, with flowers of yellow through orange to scarlet, or pale yellow through apricot to rose-pink, and mid- to deep green or silvery foliage. They like full sun and well-drained soil, at the front of a border or in a rock, scree or gravel garden. Some are single-flowered, opening fully only in sunlight and lasting through the morning, with a charming simplicity enlivened by a central boss of golden anthers. Double forms stay open even in dull weather, and last longer into the afternoon. The strong yellows, oranges and scarlets can be combined with other hot colors, and with bronze, red or yellow-green foliage, and associate well with smaller poppies, *Rosa persica* hybrids, bronze sedges, halimiums and halimiocistus, Bearded irises and yellow-green prostrate junipers. Paler colors such as peaches, apricots and pale yellows look outstanding with bronze foliage and white flowers, while rose, salmon-pink, scarlet and white cultivars blend with alpine pinks and glaucous foliage. Yellow cultivars make good contrasts with blue flax.

**Perfect partners:** *Acaena caesiiglauca*, *Anthemis* 'Beauty of Grallagh', *Briza maxima* p.414 **B**, *Carex comans* (bronze), *Euphorbia seguieriana* subsp. *niciciana* p.269 **B**

**H: 12 in. (30 cm) S: 18 in. (45 cm)** ❀ **Early summer**
◊-◊◊ ▢-▮ **Z5 pH6–7.5**

The soft lavender flowers of *Hibiscus syriacus* 'Oiseau Bleu', enlivened by their red markings and white stamens, are valuable for late-blooming schemes in cool colors.

## *Hibiscus syriacus*

This late-flowering deciduous shrub, equally at home in shrub and mixed borders, has upright growth useful for training into a standard. There are white, pink, mauve and lavender-blue kinds, some with double flowers, others with a crimson blotch near the petal base. Single flowers open more readily than double ones in damp, cool weather. The delicate shading harmonizes with cool-colored flowers such as actaeas, penstemons and asters, and with silver, glaucous or purple foliage, especially purple sloe, berberis and smoke bush, and silver elaeagnus and artemisias. Contrasting foliage such as that of taller grasses (including *Miscanthus sinensis*) adds a dramatic flourish. Good companions include cultivars of *Hydrangea paniculata* and *H. macrophylla*, late-flowering lilies, ceanothus, lespedezas, elsholtzias and fuchsias. Larger hibiscus can be draped with late-flowering climbers such as Viticella or Texensis clematis.

**Perfect partners:** *Aconitum* 'Blue Sceptre', *Agapanthus* 'Loch Hope', *Anemone* × *hybrida* 'Honorine Jobert', *Aster* 'Little Carlow', *A. turbinellus*, *Elaeagnus* 'Quicksilver'

**H: 10 ft. (3 m) S: 6½ ft. (2 m)**
❀ **Late summer to mid-autumn**
 ◊◊ ▢-▮ **Z5 pH6–8**

## *Hippophae rhamnoides* ♔
SEA BUCKTHORN

With its tolerance of poor, dry or wet soils and salt spray, this upright, suckering deciduous shrub is invaluable for seaside sites, gravelly soils and roadside plantings. It has long, slender, silvery gray-green leaves and, in drier sites, it is a good foliage plant for mixed or shrub borders, combined with cool colors and white flowers or draped with climbers such as morning glories. It is also effective in wilder parts of the garden. The flowers are inconspicuous; if pollinated by a male, female plants produce a crop of orange fruits, which can last into spring. One male – such as 'Pollmix' – is needed for every five or six female clones – 'Leikora', for example – to ensure a good display. Their impact is greater with other fruiting or autumn-coloring shrubs, such as pyracanthas, amelanchiers, deciduous euonymus and smoke bush.

**Perfect partners:** *Clematis* 'Blekitny Aniol', *Ipomoea tricolor* 'Heavenly Blue', *Lavatera* × *clementii* 'Barnsley', *Miscanthus sinensis* 'Morning Light', *Pittosporum* 'Garnettii', *Rosa* 'Prosperity'

H & S: 20 ft. (6 m) ( ❀ Mid-spring)
◐–◐◐  ▢–▮  Z4 pH6–7.5

A useful component of a white garden, a large plant or group of sea buckthorn (*Hippophae rhamnoides*) can readily be draped with a Viticella clematis such as *C.* 'Alba Luxurians'. Beneath, a white Shasta daisy (*Leucanthemum* × *superbum* 'Wirral Pride') continues the color theme. An extra rank of herbaceous plants or shrubs of intermediate height could be added between daisy and buckthorn.

## *Hydrangea arborescens*

Lacy white heads of small fertile flowers, with an irregular margin of large sterile flowers, make this deciduous shrub a bold plant for a woodland garden or a mixed or shrub border in light shade (full sun in cooler areas). The showiest cultivars are those with mainly sterile florets, especially 'Annabelle' ♔, with its 12 in. (30 cm) heads, 'Grandiflora' ♔, and subsp. *discolor* 'Sterilis'. All have pale green blooms, maturing to creamy white and aging back to light green. They go well with hostas, lilies, daylilies, larger cranesbills, herbaceous phlox such as *P. paniculata* cultivars, Japanese anemones, holodiscus, *Potentilla fruticosa* cultivars and Rugosa roses. Other hydrangeas associate well with them, as do larger grasses such as miscanthus. They are good shrubs for pots, edged with trailing plants like ivy, and for the front of a border surrounded by low carpeting plants, or further back in a border.

**Perfect partners:** *Aconitum* 'Ivorine', *Cortaderia richardii*, *Hemerocallis* 'Marion Vaughn', *Hosta plantaginea*, *Lilium regale* p.377 **A**, *Phlox maculata* 'Omega' ❑ p.231 **B**

H & S: 8 ft. (2.5 m) ❀ Mid- to late summer
◐◐–◐◐◐  ▢–▮  Z4 pH5.5–7.5

The solid outline of *Hydrangea arborescens* and its bold flowerheads act as full stops at the end of a pair of matching white borders. Beyond, not part of the white-flowered theme, the emphatically vertical variegated yellow flag (*Iris pseudacorus* 'Variegata') terminates the vista, acting equally as a full stop but of contrasting form, flanked by the deep peach-pink plumes of *Filipendula rubra*.

## *Hydrangea aspera* Villosa Group ♔

A very variable deciduous shrub that may be spreading or upright, this has downy leaves and delicate Lacecap heads of flowers, with pink fertile florets ageing to lilac within a ring of sterile lilac or lavender florets. It benefits from the shade of a high canopy of deciduous trees or a wall, ideally facing west, where the soil is moister and there is less risk of rapid thawing after frost. It is useful for late color in woodland gardens and shrub or mixed borders, combined with pink, mauve, lilac, lavender, blue and crimson flowers, including aconites, lilies, Japanese anemones and smaller hydrangeas. Other good companions include holodiscus, late-flowering deutzias, paler *Potentilla fruticosa* cultivars, fuchsias, and plants of contrasting form, such as tree ferns. Larger plants in light shade can be draped with a Texensis, Viticella or other wispy clematis. 'Macrophylla' ♔ is another attractive variant of *H. aspera*, with larger leaves and flowerheads.

Lacy flowerheads of *Hydrangea aspera* Villosa Group contrast with a more solid *Phlox paniculata* cultivar.

**Perfect partners:** *Aconitum* 'Newry Blue', *Clematis* 'Madame Julia Correvon', *C.* 'Prince Charles', *Fargesia nitida*, *Fuchsia* 'Riccartonii', *Lilium* 'Marie North', *Phlox maculata*

H & S: 10 ft. (3 m) ❀ Mid- to late summer
◐◐  ▢–▮  Z7 pH4.5–7.5

**Above:** *Hydrangea macrophylla* 'Générale Vicomtesse de Vibraye', one of the most reliably floriferous Hortensia hydrangeas, contrasts with the Lacecap hydrangea *H. serrata* 'Rosalba'. The boldly striped *Hosta undulata* var. *univittata* furnishes the front of the planting scheme.

**Below:** *Hydrangea macrophylla* 'Mariesii Perfecta', perhaps the most popular of the Lacecap Group, combines attractively with cool colors and silver foliage, such as *Artemisia absinthium* 'Lambrook Silver'.

## *Hydrangea macrophylla*

This late-flowering deciduous shrub is useful in mixed or shrub borders, particularly in maritime climates. Flower colors range from red to blue, with white. Cultivars that are blue in acid soils often turn pink or red in alkaline ones, but can be changed back to blue with aluminum and iron salts. There are two basic types: Hortensias (Mopheads), with large sterile florets, and Lacecaps, with heads of tiny fertile florets ringed by showy sterile ones. Hortensias succeed in formal settings, whereas the Lacecaps are more attractive in a semi-natural situation. Their colors blend with other cool tints such as mauve, crimson, lavender, blue and pink; blue cultivars go with yellow-green foliage and flowers and make telling contrasts with yellow. Contrast them with softer, looser plants – grasses, ferns, bamboos, maples, late-flowering lilies and Japanese anemones, for example.

**Perfect partners:** *Aconitum × cammarum* 'Bicolor', *Astilbe chinensis* var. *taquetii*, *Miscanthus sinensis* 'Gracillimus', *Monarda* 'Beauty of Cobham', *Potentilla fruticosa* 'Maanelys'

**H: 3¼–6½ ft. (1–2 m) S: 4–10 ft. (1.2–3 m)**
**❀ Mid- to late summer**

 ◊◊·◊◊◊ ▢·▩ ■ Z6 pH4.5–7.5

The conical flowerheads of *Hydrangea paniculata* make a boldly emphatic statement here, with the glaucous foliage of the giant reed (*Arundo donax*) providing contrast behind.

## *Hydrangea paniculata*

This elegant, fairly upright deciduous shrub has conical, creamy white, lacy flowerheads of mainly fertile flowers, studded with larger sterile ones. Its color mixes particularly agreeably with pale green, blue or white, and with glaucous or white- or gold-variegated foliage. Good companions are hypericums, agapanthus, later-flowering lilies, Japanese anemones, larger grasses such as miscanthus, buddleias, *Hibiscus syriacus* cultivars and holodiscus; larger plants can be draped with climbers like perennial peas and morning glories. Cultivars with a pronounced lacy shape include 'Floribunda' (creamy white with a pink flush) and 'Kyushu' ♥ (white with green tints later). 'Praecox', with leaves emerging yellow in mid-spring, flowers early with domes of greenish and pure white florets.

**Perfect partners:** *Agapanthus caulescens* subsp. *caulescens*, *Ipomoea tricolor* 'Heavenly Blue', *Lathyrus latifolius* 'Blushing Bride', *Lilium* 'Casa Blanca', *Nicotiana* 'Lime Green'

**H: 10–16 ft. (3–5 m) S: 6½–13 ft. (2–4 m)**
**❀ Mid- to late summer**

 ◊◊ ▢·▩ ■ Z5 pH5–7.5

This contrast in flowerhead shapes, conical *Hydrangea paniculata* 'Grandiflora' set against round agapanthus, is striking and perhaps most appealing when the hydrangea blooms are young, before they assume their eventual pink shading.

## *Hydrangea paniculata* 'Grandiflora' ♖

This vigorous deciduous shrub produces conical flowerheads, packed with large sterile florets that hide the smaller fertile flowers. Initially white tinged with pink, the panicles develop a pronounced pink flush as they age. This hydrangea's bold shape is useful for providing accents along a border, and it looks particularly attractive grouped with pink, crimson or white flowers, or with glaucous, purple-flushed, silver or white-variegated foliage. It combines well with hostas, Japanese anemones, nicotianas, the larger grasses and late-flowering lilies; in autumn its reddish pink tints complement Korean, Rubellum and Charm chrysanthemums.

**Perfect partners:** *Actaea racemosa*, *Buddleja* 'Lochinch', *Ceanothus × delileanus* 'Gloire de Versailles', *Lilium regale*, *L.* 'Sterling Star', *Potentilla fruticosa* 'Tilford Cream'

**H: 10 ft. (3 m)  S: 6½ ft. (2 m)**
❀ **Mid- to late summer**
◊◊ ▢-▨ ▉  Z5  pH5–7.5

## *Hydrangea paniculata* 'Greenspire'

This is a lax deciduous shrub, reaching to 13 ft. (4 m) across unless pruned annually. Its conical panicles are entirely green before the flowers mature, but later the large sterile florets near the base of the panicle become creamy white, with a froth of white fertile flowers higher up; fertile florets toward the tip remain green and often do not open, and the whole panicle ages to green once more. This coloring provides restful combinations with green, blue or white flowers, yellow-green foliage and flowers, and glaucous foliage. Plants are especially effective with white agapanthus, green nicotianas, white or cream lilies, hostas and miscanthus.

**Perfect partners:** *Fuchsia magellanica* 'Versicolor', *Hosta* 'Sum and Substance', *Ilex × altaclerensis* 'Golden King', *Rosa* 'Ballerina', *R.* Iceberg

**H: 6½ ft. (2 m)  S: 13 ft. (4 m)**
❀ **Mid- to late summer**
◊◊ ▢-▨ ▉  Z5  pH5–7.5

Combining one plant with large inflorescences and another with small individual flowers often succeeds, as here with *Hydrangea paniculata* 'Greenspire' and *Nicotiana langsdorffii*, both in subtle shades of green.

*Hydrangea serrata* 'Rosalba', its relatively small Lacecap flowerheads assuming shadings of red as they age, are gracefully draped with the flame flower (*Tropaeolum speciosum*) and studded with its scarlet blooms.

## *Hydrangea serrata* 'Rosalba' ♖

Sometimes called the mountain hydrangea, *H. serrata* (syn. *H. macrophylla* subsp. *serrata*) is a compact deciduous shrub, with Lacecap flowers consisting of tiny fertile florets surrounded by showier sterile ones. It suits the front of a sunny or lightly shaded border, where it starts to flower quite early and continues until the frosts. 'Rosalba' has pink fertile florets and white sterile ones, aging to deep pink in the center (lilac on acidic soils), with a pink-edged border. It is excellent for large-scale schemes and lighter parts of a woodland garden, especially with late summer flowers in cool colors, hostas, smaller bamboos, grasses and Japanese maples.

**Perfect partners:** *Buddleja* 'Pink Delight', *Deutzia setchuenensis* var. *corymbiflora*, *Hydrangea macrophylla* p.107 **A**, *Perovskia* 'Blue Spire', *Rosa* Bonica, *R.* 'Yesterday'

**H & S: 4 ft. (1.2 m)** ❀ **Mid- to late summer**
◊◊-◊◊◊ ▢-▨ ▉  Z6  pH4.5–7.5

## *Hypericum forrestii* ♇

This deciduous shrub (semi-deciduous to evergreen in warm climates) has an elegant, arching habit and large golden yellow flowers. It can be rather tall and spreading for general use in shrub and mixed borders, unless limited to about half its height by annual spring pruning. It combines well with hot colors, yellow-green, yellow-variegated and glaucous foliage, and yellow flowers, and contrasts with blue. Suitable partners include agapanthus and variegated grasses such as hakonechloas and miscanthus. In autumn it has reddish brown seed capsules and red leaf tints. *H.* 'Hidcote' ♇ flowers into mid-autumn.

**Perfect partners:** *Agapanthus* 'Blue Moon', *Crocosmia* × *crocosmiiflora* 'Lady Hamilton', *Hosta* 'August Moon', *Miscanthus sinensis* 'Strictus', *Rosa* Elina, *R.* Graham Thomas

H: 4 ft. (1.2 m)  S: 5 ft. (1.5 m) ❀ **Late summer**
◊◊ ☐-■ **Z6 pH5.5–7**

Hard annual pruning restricts the height of *Hypericum forrestii* to about 24 in. (60 cm), allowing it to be combined with herbaceous plants of similar height – as with the contrasting foliage and flowers of *Crocosmia* × *crocosmiiflora*.

## *Ilex aquifolium* ♇

COMMON HOLLY

One of the most useful evergreen shrubs, holly is available in hundreds of cultivars, some variegated and others with different leaf shapes or growth habits. Leafy to its base, it is invaluable in woodland gardens and shady shrub or mixed borders. If male and female clones are grown together, females produce bright red, occasionally gold berries that color in mid-autumn and remain until spring – one male plant is needed for every six females. Green-leaved hollies provide a marvellous foil for swags of pale flowers such as small-flowered clematis and scrambling forsythias. Among variegated kinds, those with paler marginal coloring are the most effective.

**Perfect partners:** *Clematis potaninii*, *Forsythia suspensa* 'Nymans', *Holodiscus discolor*, *Miscanthus sinensis* 'Strictus', *Parthenocissus tricuspidata* 'Lowii', *Rosa* 'Climbing Paul Lédé' p.188 **B**

H: 6½–65 ft. (2–20 m)  S: 5–26 ft. (1.5–8 m)
( ❀ **Late spring to early summer**)

 ◊◊ ☐-■ **Z6 pH4.5–7.5**

**Right:** The narrow, neat gold edging to the leaves of *Ilex aquifolium* 'Pyramidalis Aureomarginata' emphasizes the shape of its foliage and harmonizes with a hybrid of *Mahonia aquifolium* in spring. This upright, free-fruiting, red-berried holly eventually reaches 20 ft. (6 m) high with a spread of 16 ft. (5 m).

**Below:** Compact *Ilex aquifolium* 'Myrtifolia Aurea Maculata' ♇, its relatively small leaves generously splashed with yellow on a bush well furnished to ground level, provides a support for scrambling *Potentilla* 'Flamenco' in fiery scarlet. This is a non-fruiting holly that ultimately achieves a height of 6½ ft. (2 m) and a spread of 5 ft. (1.5 m).

**Above:** The feathery foliage of *Juniperus squamata* 'Filborna', a vigorous, upright cultivar, harmonizes with the blue flowers of *Brunnera macrophylla* in spring.

**Left:** Glaucous sprays of *Juniperus squamata* 'Blue Carpet' contrast boldly with the fiery autumn foliage of Virginia creeper (*Parthenocissus quinquefolia*). Removing some parthenocissus shoots helps to stop it engulfing the juniper.

## *Juniperus squamata*
FLAKY JUNIPER

This evergreen conifer varies between a spreading prostrate shrub and a small tree. All flaky junipers are characterized by drooping shoot tips, which give a feathery appearance. Many have glaucous foliage that looks attractive with other heathland plants such as dwarf conifers, heaths and heathers. They are suitable for inclusion in large rock gardens or, if more prostrate, toward the front of a border. Useful cultivars include the spreading, glaucous 'Blue Carpet' ♀; 'Blue Star' ♀ (makes a low-growing bush); 'Holger' ♀ (yellowish green foliage that turns sulfur-yellow); and 'Hunnetorp' (glaucous foliage). 'Meyeri' is semi-erect, with ascending angular branches and glaucous foliage.

**Perfect partners:** *Abies koreana* 'Silberlocke', *Calluna vulgaris* 'Beoley Gold', *Erica* × *darleyensis* 'Silberschmelze', *Rhododendron* 'Blue Diamond', *R.* 'Yellow Hammer'

H: 13–20 ft. (4–6 m)  S: 3¼–20 ft. (1–6 m)
(✣ Late summer)

◐-◐◐ ▢-■ Z4 pH4.5–7

## *Juniperus virginiana* 'Grey Owl' ♀

The evergreen pencil cedar (*Juniperus virginiana*) has produced many cultivars, varying in habit from conical or bushy to prostrate. Possibly the most useful is 'Grey Owl', a low, spreading shrub with glaucous, slightly arching branches, capable of forming excellent ground cover. It can be combined with the same heathland plants as *J. squamata* (above), or grouped to make dense ground-cover, perhaps draped with a wispy climber such as a perennial pea or slender clematis. It also looks effective in a large shrub or mixed border, but tends to spread inexorably if planted at the front.

**Perfect partners:** *Clematis* × *cartmanii* 'Avalanche', *C.* 'Edward Prichard', *Daboecia cantabrica* f. *alba*, *Erica arborea* 'Albert's Gold', *Lathyrus latifolius* 'Albus'

H: 6½ ft. (2 m)  S: 10 ft. (3 m) (✣ Late spring)
◐-◐◐ ▢-■ Z3 pH4.5–6.5

A carpet of *Juniperus virginiana* 'Grey Owl' is set off by the amber autumn foliage of *Cornus sanguinea* Winter Flame. The dogwood's bright stems remain showy through winter.

## *Laburnum* × *watereri* 'Vossii' ♀

Probably the commonest cultivar of laburnum, or golden rain, this deciduous tree bears long, lavish racemes of yellow flowers. Its growth habit is suitable for training over an arcade, or it may be allowed to develop as a tree, either freestanding as a specimen or within a very large shrub or mixed border. In more modest borders, a tree that is not top-grafted can be pruned back to encourage low branching, and will then make a bushy plant with flowers that can interact successfully with shrubs of intermediate size, such as early white or cream Shrub roses, snowball tree and ceanothus cultivars. Its color harmonizes splendidly with yellow-green foliage, and with orange flowers such as those of some berberis species. Full-size specimens can be used to host a late summer flowering climber, such as honeysuckle, to maintain color and interest as the leaves begin to lose their freshness.

**Perfect partners:** *Berberis darwinii*, *B.* × *stenophylla* 'Lemon Queen', *Ceanothus* 'Cascade', *Clematis montana* var. *grandiflora*, *Prunus padus* 'Watereri', *Rhododendron* 'Persil', *Rosa* × *fortuneana*, *R. primula*, *Rubus* 'Benenden', *Syringa vulgaris* 'Firmament', *S.v.* 'Primrose', *Wisteria floribunda* 'Alba', *W.f.* 'Multijuga'

**H & S: 26 ft. (8 m)** ❀ **Late spring**
◊-◊◊  ■-■ **Z5 pH5–7.5**

This classic combination features a tunnel of *Laburnum* × *watereri* 'Vossii' woven with wisteria, with *Allium hollandicum*, contrasting in floral form and color, growing from below to frame porthole views to silvery *Brachyglottis* (Dunedin Group) 'Sunshine' in the garden beyond.

*Lavandula angustifolia* 'Hidcote' makes a telling contrast with gold-variegated sage (*Salvia officinalis* 'Icterina'), a popular combination both visually and for its fragrance. The partnership is useful equally in a herb garden, at the front of a border or alongside a path, where passersby will brush against the plants, releasing their aromatic scent.

## *Lavandula angustifolia* 'Hidcote' ♔

*L. angustifolia*, an evergreen Mediterranean sub-shrub 6–36 in. (15–90 cm) tall, has greyish leaves and flowers in pale to deep lavender, occasionally white or mauve-pink. 'Hidcote' is a richly colored dwarf cultivar, suitable for use at the front of a border, or for edging or a dwarf hedge. The true cultivar is difficult to obtain and is propagated by cuttings; seed-raised plants are more common, but tend to be variable and often lack the rich color of 'Hidcote'. It associates with mauve, pink, purple or blue, and with purple or silver foliage, and contrasts well with yellow-green foliage and flowers. Like all lavenders, it can become leggy and die in patches unless pruned annually in early to mid-spring, although some gardeners prefer to prune as the blooms fade.

**Perfect partners:** *Anthemis* Susanna Mitchell, *A. tinctoria* 'E.C. Buxton', *Cistus* 'Grayswood Pink', *Convolvulus cneorum*, *Dianthus* 'Haytor White', *Sedum* 'Vera Jameson'

**H:** 24 in. (60 cm) **S:** 30 in. (75 cm)
❀ **Mid- to late summer**
 Z6 pH5.5–7.5

*Lavandula stoechas* subsp. *pedunculata* combines agreeably with many alliums, whose round flowerheads provide a contrast of form, while their colors are usually harmonious. In this informal patchwork of plants suited to Mediterranean conditions, the dying leaves of *Allium cristophii* are hidden by young shoots of gypsophila, with chives (*Allium schoenoprasum*) in the foreground.

## *Lavandula stoechas* subsp. *pedunculata* ♔

The flowers of this deep purple lavender, almost black and scarcely visible except at close range, sport a showy topknot of mauve bracts. The flowerheads are borne on long stems and are held well above the grayish evergreen foliage. The mauve coloring, useful for echoing similar tints in plants such as alliums, pinks and cranesbills, combines well with cool shades such as lilac or lavender and with carmine, crimson or rich purple. Attractive when partnered with silver or glaucous foliage, or with plants such as cistus and other lavenders, it is excellent for the front of a border or in gravel. 'James Compton' has particularly showy bracts.

**Perfect partners:** *Cistus* 'Grayswood Pink', *Crambe cordifolia*, *Dianthus* 'Becky Robinson', *D.* 'Musgrave's Pink', *Helianthemum* 'Wisley White', *Rosa* Pink Flower Carpet

**H & S:** 24 in. (60 cm)
❀ **Late spring to early summer**
 Z8 pH5.5–7.5

The silvery foliage of *Lavandula lanata* is perhaps never more effective than when set against rich blue. *Ceanothus* 'Puget Blue', kept furnished with branches down to ground level, is a perfect companion in a sunny border backed by a wall.

## *Lavandula lanata* ♔

The appeal of this lavender lies in its purple flowers and the broad, intensely silver foliage. A little more demanding than *L. angustifolia* cultivars (above), it requires good drainage, full sun, and freedom from winter dampness. It is a superlative shrub for the front of a border, especially with gray-leaved plants or cool-colored flowers, and is an asset in rock or gravel gardens, where it may be combined with other Mediterranean plants such as cistus, helianthemums, halimiums and phlomis. It harmonizes well with yellow-green foliage and flowers, and contrasts with yellow flowers. Mid-spring is the best time to prune.

**Perfect partners:** *Anthemis punctata* subsp. *cupaniana*, *Artemisia schmidtiana*, *Halimium* 'Susan', *Phlomis chrysophylla*, *Salvia chamaedryoides*, *S. officinalis* 'Purpurascens'

**H:** 30 in. (75 cm) **S:** 36 in. (90 cm)
❀ **Late summer**
 Z7 pH5.5–7.5

## *Lavatera* × *clementii* 'Barnsley'

This floriferous, long-flowering, deciduous mallow rapidly develops into a medium to large shrub, useful for quickly filling gaps in a border. There it blends with cool colors and purple, silver or glaucous foliage, and makes an excellent partner for old roses or a backdrop of clematis. Its slightly amorphous habit is best combined with architectural plants, or those with flower spikes or plates or other equally contrasting floral forms. As long as it is not severely frosted, it will regenerate from the roots, although it does then tend to revert to the original clone, the deeper colored 'Rosea' ♀. Protecting the base of the plant over winter usually averts this danger. Spare plants can very easily be raised from cuttings.

**Perfect partners:** *Aconitum* × *cammarum* 'Bicolor', *Buddleja davidii* 'Nanho Petite Purple', *Cistus* × *argenteus* 'Blushing Peggy Sammons', *Dahlia* 'Gerrie Hoek' p.420 **B**, *Hebe* 'Midsummer Beauty', *Romneya californica*, *Rosa* Iceberg, *Thalictrum delavayi* 'Hewitt's Double' ❑p.226 **A**

H & S: 6½ ft. (2 m)  ❀ Early to late summer
◊◊ ▪-▪  Z5  pH5.5–7.5

Later clematis such as *C.* 'Perle d'Azur' make an ideal backcloth for *Lavatera* × *clementii* 'Barnsley'. Planted nearby, the odd trail of clematis, perhaps an Early Large-flowered Viticella or Texensis cultivar in carmine, crimson or sumptuous burgundy, can be allowed to weave itself through the lavatera.

With identically shaped foliage in dramatically contrasting colors, *Ligustrum ovalifolium* 'Aureum' and *Prunus* × *cistena* make a striking combination. Pruning will keep both of comparable size, even to below 40 in. (1 m), allowing this partnership to be used in the smallest gardens.

## *Ligustrum ovalifolium* 'Aureum' ♀

GOLDEN PRIVET

The foliage of this bright deciduous shrub can vary between uniform yellow-green and green with a yellow-green margin. In full sun its color approaches yellow, which is especially useful for mixing with hot yellows or oranges and red foliage or flowers, and with blue flowers such as delphiniums. The foliage is less markedly yellow in shade, but very attractive with sulfur-yellow or cream flowers. Plants can be used as specimens or as a repeated accent along a border, and make excellent hedges, both on their own and with other colored-foliage shrubs. They are valuable hosts for climbers whose flowers contrast or harmonize with the creamy white panicles of the privet – a blue clematis or cream honeysuckle, for example.

**Perfect partners:** *Achillea* 'Lucky Break', *Clematis macropetala* p.161 **A**, *Delphinium* 'Butterball', *D.* 'Fenella', *Hemerocallis* 'Golden Chimes', *Kniphofia* 'Sunningdale Yellow', *Miscanthus sinensis* 'Strictus', *Phlomis russeliana*, *Rosa* Graham Thomas, *Tithonia rotundifolia*

H & S: 10 ft. (3 m)  ❀ Midsummer
◊◊ ▪-▪  Z6  pH5–7.5

## *Lonicera nitida* 'Baggesen's Gold' ♡

When grown in full sun, the tiny, glistening leaves of this evergreen shrub are almost pure gold, with bronze tints developing in winter. In shade they are not so brightly colored, but their light green effect is still useful for illuminating dark corners. Tiny cream flowers in spring are followed by translucent purple-blue berries. Plants quickly become shaggy unless trimmed frequently. Annual pruning back to a billowing mound or a geometric shape will encourage attractive feathery shoots to develop. Treated in this way, plants can be used to support elegant and wispy climbers such as tropaeolums and clematis, in contrasting or harmonious colors. Plants can be pruned back to 6 in. (15 cm) high.

The billowing pale foliage of *Lonicera nitida* 'Baggesen's Gold' makes a successful foil for boldly shaped flowers in contrasting colors. Provided the shrub is not kept too small by pruning, it can support a moderately vigorous climber – a perennial pea, for example, or a Viticella clematis, such as *Clematis* 'Venosa Violacea' shown here.

**Perfect partners:** *Achillea* 'Hella Glashoff', *Aconitum hemsleyanum*, *A*. 'Ivorine', *Clematis* × *durandii* p.156 **B**, *Delphinium* 'Lord Butler', *Geranium* 'Johnson's Blue', *Hosta fortunei* var. *aureomarginata*, *Ipomoea tricolor*, *Lathyrus sativus*, *Miscanthus sinensis* 'Zebrinus', *Yucca flaccida* 'Golden Sword' p.341 **A** ❑ pp.91 **B**, 94 **B**, 141 **C**

H & S: 5 ft. (1.5 m) (✿ Late spring)
◌◌ ▢-■ Z6 pH5.5–7.5

## *Lupinus arboreus* ♡
### TREE LUPIN

A sunny, well-drained position best suits this short-lived, semi-evergreen shrub, which looks extremely attractive when mixed with Mediterranean plants such as brooms and cistus. The spires of bloom borne in early summer give it a distinctive structure, highly effective in contrasts with flowers of different shapes such as the plates of achilleas. The yellow form is most common, but named clones such as 'Mauve Queen' and 'Snow Queen' are also available. Other colors, especially blue and cream, are often grown from seed, but these may not come true to type. The tree lupin is excellent with white or orange Oriental poppies, early-flowering annuals or biennials such as poached egg plant and California poppies, and yellow-green or glaucous foliage.

**Perfect partners:** *Anchusa azurea*, *Aquilegia canadensis*, *Cistus* × *hybridus*, *Nigella damascena* 'Miss Jekyll', *Paeonia lactiflora* 'Jan van Leeuwen', *Papaver orientale* 'Black and White', *P.o.* 'May Queen', *Rosa* 'Frühlingsgold', *Thalictrum flavum* subsp. *glaucum* ❑ p.208 **A**

H & S 5 ft. (1.5 m) ✿ **Early summer**
◌-◌◌ ▢-■ Z8 pH5.5–7

Purple smoke bush, dramatically backlit by the sun, presents a striking contrast to the vertical spikes of this soft yellow tree lupin (*Lupinus arboreus*), which is furnished in front with cushions of lady's mantle (*Alchemilla mollis*). A single white-flowered species rose of simple and ethereal beauty provides the background.

A

*Magnolia* × *loebneri* 'Leonard Messel' has blush-pink flowers that are often a deeper mauve-pink on the outside of the petals and in the buds. Here, it is combined with *M.* × *soulangeana* 'Etienne Soulange-Bodin', and overtopped by the evergreen foliage and white bark of the snow gum (*Eucalyptus pauciflora* subsp. *niphophila*).

## *Magnolia* × *loebneri* 'Leonard Messel' ♀

This is a deciduous large shrub or small tree, with upright growth and delicate blush-pink flowers, deeper in color on the reverse of the petals and in the buds, which appear before the leaves in mid-spring. It makes a charming specimen plant and in a prominent position needs only a surrounding carpet of spring flowers such as pulmonarias, cream or white narcissi, chionodoxas, erythroniums or primroses. When grown in a border, it benefits from being placed forward of other plants of similar height, to encourage even flowering on all sides. Like all magnolias, early selection of main branches is essential to establish a well-shaped plant, since pruning larger branches causes internal rotting. Other attractive cultivars include white 'Merrill' ♀ and 'Snowdrift', and pink 'Raspberry Fun'.

**Perfect partners:** *Amelanchier lamarckii*, *Camellia* × *williamsii* 'Donation', *Chionodoxa forbesii*, *Narcissus* 'Thalia', *Pulmonaria* 'Blue Ensign', *Rhododendron williamsianum*

**H & S: 26 ft. (8 m)** ❀ **Mid-spring**

⬛⬜⬛⬜⬛ ◊◊-◊◊◊ ⬜-⬛ ⬛ **Z5 pH5–7**

B

## *Magnolia* × *soulangeana*

The blooms of this small deciduous tree are usually goblet-shaped and vary in color between pure white and wine-red. The first flush appears in mid-spring; a few more flowers are borne later on, with the unfurling leaves, but they are largely hidden. The tree's spreading habit is difficult to accommodate in a border, because the wide canopy usually branches near the ground, but it looks enchanting as a specimen tree underplanted with spring flowers, including small shrubs.

## *Mahonia aquifolium*
OREGON GRAPE

This evergreen, suckering shrub has glossy, rich green, hollylike leaves and yellow flowers borne in terminal panicles. It is happy in sun or shade, and is a good plant for a woodland garden or for positions toward the front of a shrub border. An attractive companion for spring flowers – especially blue, cream, white, palest yellow and orange bulbs – it associates particularly well with bluebells, muscari, smaller narcissi and tulips, and white flowering currants. Plants hybridize freely with related species such as *M. pinnata* and *M. repens* to produce seedlings of varying height, foliage and flower. In most cases, it is preferable to use a named clone such as 'Apollo' ♀, which has large and prolific panicles of flowers.

**Perfect partners:** *Cornus mas*, *Forsythia ovata* 'Tetragold', *Helleborus foetidus*, *Ilex aquifolium* 'Pyramidalis Aureomarginata' p.109 **C**, *Milium effusum* 'Aureum', *Vinca minor*

**H: 40 in. (1 m) S: 5 ft. (1.5 m)** ❀ **Early to mid-spring**

⬛⬜⬛⬜⬛ ◊◊-◊◊◊ ⬜-⬛ ⬛ **Z5 pH5.5–7.5**

The goblet-shaped flowers of *Magnolia* × *soulangeana* 'Rustica Rubra' ♀, elegantly shaded from their pink tips to burgundy bases, harmonize perfectly with *Clematis montana* var. *rubens*. Training the clematis over an adjacent tree, shrub, or structure works best; grown into the magnolia, it could mar the poise and rhythm of the evenly spaced, sumptuous blooms.

Useful cultivars include 'Alexandrina', which is rich pink and has relatively upright growth. 'Lennei' ♀ with wine-red blooms almost pure white inside, and pure white 'Lennei Alba' ♀.

**Perfect partners:** *Camellia* 'Inspiration', *Malus* × *atrosanguinea*, *Narcissus* 'Empress of Ireland', *Primula* 'Iris Mainwaring', *Rhododendron schlippenbachii* ⊐ p.115 **A**

**H: 16–26 ft. (5–8 m) S: 26 ft. (8 m)** ❀ **Mid- to late spring**

⬛⬜⬛⬜⬛ ◊◊-◊◊◊ ⬜-⬛ ⬛ **Z5 pH4.5–6.5**

C

The mahonia cultivar 'Apollo', here contrasting spectacularly with *Muscari armeniacum* 'Blue Spike', has less glossy leaves and many more lateral flower clusters than typical *Mahonia aquifolium*, making it a good choice where uniformity or plentiful color is needed.

**Above:** The flowers of *Mahonia × media* emerge when many shrubs still bear colorful autumn fruits, including the European spindle (*Euonymus europaeus*), its deep pink fruits here split open to reveal vermilion seeds.

**Below:** Autumn foliage as well as fruits may remain as *Mahonia × media* 'Charity' comes into bloom, as here with *Malus* 'Professor Sprenger'. This crab apple's fruits will stay on the tree throughout the flowering of the mahonia.

## Mahonia × media

There are at least a dozen clones of this autumn- to winter-flowering shrub, each varying slightly in flower color, habit and hardiness. All form stiff, erect shrubs, with evergreen hollylike leaflets and intensely yellow flowers that smell like lily-of-the-valley. To appreciate the scent, they may be grown near the house, through a carpet of short evergreens such as variegated hollies, early-flowering winter heaths, evergreen ferns and sedges, and the earliest snowdrops. 'Lionel Fortescue' ♀ has erect, bright yellow racemes; 'Underway' ♀ is more compact, with paler primrose-yellow flowers; and 'Winter Sun' ♀, also compact, is outstandingly fragrant.

**Perfect partners:** *Euonymus fortunei* 'Emerald 'n' Gold', *Galanthus* 'Atkinsii', *Hamamelis × intermedia* 'Pallida', *Hedera helix* 'Buttercup', *Helleborus niger*, *Sarcococca confusa*

**H: 13–16 ft. (4–5 m)   S: 10–13 ft. (3–4 m)**
❀ **Late autumn to late winter**
 ◊◊ ▢-▦ **Z8   pH5–7**

Wall training hides the rather unappealing habit of *Malus × zumi* 'Golden Hornet', also allowing it to be lightly clad with an early-flowering clematis such as *C.* 'Ruby'.

## Malus × zumi 'Golden Hornet' ♀

Although grown principally for its golden yellow fruits, this crab apple also has pretty white flowers, opening from pink buds. It can be grown as a freestanding tree, as an espalier trained on a wall or, if bottom-grafted, as a low, spreading shrub. For spring display it can be draped with an early-flowering clematis. The fruits look particularly effective on the bare branches when sunlit against dark foliage. It goes well with other autumn-coloring trees including maples, nyssas, hickories, cladrastis, parrotias and oaks, along with many larger shrubs, such as Japanese maples, berberis, dogwoods, smoke bush, deciduous euonymus, sumachs, roses, sorbarias and larger deciduous azaleas and viburnums.

**Perfect partners:** *Aucuba japonica* 'Crotonifolia', *Clematis* 'Markham's Pink', *Cotoneaster salicifolius* 'Rothschildianus', *Hamamelis × intermedia* 'Advent', *Ilex aquifolium* 'Amber', *Mahonia × media*, *Pyracantha* 'Soleil d'Or', *Rosa helenae*, *Sorbus* 'Joseph Rock', *Taxus baccata* 'Semperaurea'

**H: 33 ft. (10 m)   S: 26 ft. (8 m)** ❀ **Late spring**
◊◊ ▢-▦ **Z4   pH5.5–7.5**

## *Morus alba* 'Pendula'

The branches of this small deciduous tree fall dramatically to form a dense curtain of glossy foliage, bright yellow in autumn, making a mushroom-shaped backdrop for other plants with light foliage or pale flowers. Its own flowers are insignificant and the fruits are hidden by the foliage, but it is excellent for training over a tunnel or bower, combined with other autumn-coloring plants such as vines, or with celastrus. It may be trained as a standard by tying one of the most vigorous stems to a post 13–20 ft. (4–6 m) high, and then makes a strong visual impact in the very largest shrub or mixed borders; ultimately, however, it forms a very spreading tree. Spring flowers like snowdrops, crocuses, wood anemones and celandines grow happily beneath its canopy. Although very hardy, it needs warm sunlight to ripen the wood, and does not thrive in areas with cool summers.

**Perfect partners:** *Ampelopsis brevipedunculata* var. *maximowiczii*, *Aralia elata* 'Variegata', *Celastrus orbiculatus*, *Rosa* 'Pax', *Rubus cockburnianus* 'Goldenvale', *Vitis* 'Brant'

**H: 10 ft. (3 m) S: 16 ft. (5 m) (✿ Late spring)**
▬▬▭▭ ◊◊ ▭-▬ Z5 pH5.5–7.5

The bold outline and dark foliage of *Morus alba* 'Pendula' act as a punctuation mark at the corner of this box-edged bed. Other plants of striking habit and subdued coloring contribute to the scheme, including *Phormium cookianum* subsp. *hookeri* 'Tricolor', striped green, creamy yellow and red, and the arching white plumes of *Ligustrum quihoui*.

In this combination of Japanese plants designed principally for foliage effect, the mahogany coloring of *Acer palmatum* Dissectum Atropurpureum Group is echoed by the fruits and some bronze-flushed leaves of sacred bamboo (*Nandina domestica*). In winter, the nandina will adopt more bronze coloring, as will the cryptomeria (top right).

## *Nandina domestica* ♔

SACRED BAMBOO

This upright shrub, semi-deciduous to evergreen has dainty compound leaves that often assume bright red or orange tints late in the year, and bears large panicles of white flowers, followed (in warm climates) by red fruits. Its elegant habit warrants a position among plants that do not mask it. The airy foliage harmonizes with Japanese maples and bamboos, and in autumn associates well with smoke bush, clethras, deciduous dogwoods, cotoneasters, deciduous azaleas, witch hazels and stephanandras. Chrysanthemums (Rubellum, Korean or Charm) in sunset colors, Chinese lanterns and hostas are all good herbaceous companions.

**Perfect partners:** *Acer palmatum* 'Seiryû', *Cercidiphyllum japonicum*, *Cornus alba* 'Kesselringii', *Fatsia japonica*, *Miscanthus sinensis* 'Zebrinus', *Physalis alkekengi*, *Pleioblastus viridistriatus*, *Rhus typhina* 'Dissecta', *Sorbus vilmorinii*, *Xanthorhiza simplicissima*

**H: 6 ft. (1.8 m) S: 5 ft. (1.5 m) ✿ Midsummer**
▬▬▭▭ ◊◊ ▭-▬ Z7 pH5–7.5

## *Neillia thibetica*

This gracefully arching, deciduous shrub is very much at home in wilder parts of the garden. Its slender racemes of rose-pink flowers, emerging from rust-red calyces, make a very attractive complement to species roses, philadelphus, deutzias, late azaleas in pastel colors, guelder roses, cranesbills, cow parsley, and pink, white or red columbines.
If left untrimmed for three or four years, the shrub will tend to lose its distinctive arching habit, but this can be avoided by hard pruning occasionally, immediately after flowering. This will also stimulate plenty of young stems, whose bark is a conspicuous bright green in winter, and this could justify neillia's inclusion in a bed of shrubs with colored stems, such as dogwoods, willows and stephanandras.

**Perfect partners:** *Chaerophyllum hirsutum* 'Roseum', *Philadelphus* 'Belle Etoile', *Rhododendron viscosum, Rosa glauca, Spiraea cantoniensis, Viburnum opulus* 'Roseum'

**H & S: 6½ ft. (2 m)** ❀ **Early summer**
 ◊◊  ▢-▪ **Z6  pH5–7.5**

After flowering the rose-pink inflorescences of *Neillia thibetica* take on brickist tints as its seeds ripen, and the same hues are echoed along its leaf veins and margins. The mauve-pink flowers of the vigorous cranesbill *Geranium × oxonianum* 'Claridge Druce' scrambling through its stems clash slightly but not disagreeably.

A

Scrambling among the lower branches and flowers of *Philadelphus* 'Beauclerk', the mauve-pink cranesbill *Geranium* × *oxonianum* 'Claridge Druce' proves itself an agreeable invader. When both plants are in bloom, the effect is pretty and informal, and well suited to the wilder parts of a garden.

## *Philadelphus* 'Beauclerk' ♛

This arching deciduous mock orange has powerfully fragrant white flowers, each with a pinkish stain at its center. Although rather too vigorous for most mixed and shrub borders, it is perfectly suited to large-scale plantings in wilder, less formal parts of the garden. It blends successfully with almost any color, but especially with pink flowers that echo the stain at the base of the petals, and combines well with early species roses, cranesbills, pale columbines, early single peonies and pink cow parsleys. It tends to look rather dull later in the year, and benefits from draping with a wispy climber such as a late-flowering clematis, or a climbing annual. Remove one in four main stems each year after flowering.

**Perfect partners:** *Anthriscus sylvestris* 'Ravenswing', *Aruncus dioicus*, *Campanula latifolia* 'Gloaming', *Chaerophyllum hirsutum* 'Roseum', *Kolkwitzia amabilis*, *Rosa elegantula* 'Persetosa', *R.* 'Nevada', *Syringa* × *prestoniae* 'Elinor', *Thalictrum aquilegiifolium*

**H & S: 6½ ft. (2 m)** ❀ **Early summer**
◌◌ ▣-▪ **Z5 pH5.5–7.5**

## *Philadelphus* 'Belle Etoile' ♛

This mock orange suits smaller-scale designs and more sophisticated plantings. It has a slightly more pronounced pinkish stain at the base of the petals than 'Beauclerk' (above), and excels in harmonies with pink flowers and silver or white-variegated foliage. 'Belle Etoile' mixes well with the same plants as 'Beauclerk', together with some of the more elegant Tall Bearded irises, camassias, semi-double and double peonies, and double roses. It should be pruned in the same way as 'Beauclerk', and can be draped in a similar fashion with climbers. Since it is deciduous, it can be underplanted with spring bulbs that flower early, before the philadelphus leafs up.

**Perfect partners:** *Ammi majus*, *Aquilegia vulgaris* var. *stellata* 'Nora Barlow', *Campanula lactiflora*, *Clematis montana* var. *wilsonii*, *Geranium sylvaticum* 'Baker's Pink', *Hesperis matronalis*, *Paeonia lactiflora* 'White Wings', *Papaver orientale* 'Black and White', *Rosa* 'New Dawn' p.191 **A**

**H & S: 6½ ft. (2 m)** ❀ **Early summer**
◌◌ ▣-▪ **Z5 pH5.5–7.5**

Covered in headily fragrant, pink-stained white flowers in early summer, *Philadelphus* 'Belle Etoile' combines charmingly with *Spiraea canescens*, whose tiny, creamy white florets are massed along arching sprays.

Both contrast and harmony feature in this planting scheme, combining *Philadelphus coronarius* 'Aureus', *Narcissus* 'Hawera' and a pansy (*Viola*). Placing the narcissus irregularly through an extended carpet of the pansy would avoid it being camouflaged by the philadelphus, whose bulk could be broken up by wisps of a blue-flowered Alpina clematis.

## *Philadelphus coronarius* 'Aureus' ♛
### GOLDEN MOCK ORANGE

This philadelphus is grown principally for the brightness of its foliage, rather than for its white flowers. The leaves are vivid yellow-green in spring, and approach full yellow later on when grown in sun, although they can scorch in areas with hot summers. Shade reduces flowering and turns the leaf color more toward green. Pleasing combinations include harmonies with yellow, cream and white flowers, and contrasts with blue, orange or scarlet flowers and bronze foliage. The shrub forms an excellent background for late-flowering spring bulbs such as camassias; and it can be draped with wispy climbers such as clematis, honeysuckles and morning glories.

**Perfect partners:** *Allium hollandicum* p.349 **A**, *Berberis thunbergii* f. *atropurpurea* p.80 **C**, *Clematis* × *durandii*, *Consolida ajacis*, *Cytisus* × *praecox* 'Warminster' p.92 **C**, *Eryngium* × *tripartitum*, *Ipomoea tricolor* 'Heavenly Blue', *Primula veris* p.327 **A** ❏ p.89 **A**

**H: 8 ft. (2.5 m) S: 5 ft. (1.5 m)** ❀ **Early summer**
◌◌ ▣-▪ **Z4 pH5.5–7.5**

## Philadelphus intectus

One of the larger, more vigorous mock oranges, this deciduous shrub has strong, arching stems. The flowers are short-lived but prolific and very fragrant. A freestanding specimen creates a graceful cascade when in bloom but is rather undistinguished in leaf alone. The shrub is most effective scrambling into a crab apple, pear, or birch 30–50 ft. (9–15 m) high. A wild garden is the best site and avoids any need for hard pruning. Alternatively it can be included in a scented floral hedge or walkway, entwined with honeysuckle, eglantine roses and pink early-flowering Rambler roses.

**Perfect partners:** *Lonicera periclymenum* 'Graham Thomas', *Rosa* 'Cerise Bouquet', *R. nutkana* 'Plena', *Styrax japonicus* 'Pink Chimes', *Syringa* × *josiflexa* 'Bellicent'

**H: 20 ft. (6 m)  S: 16 ft. (5 m)** ❀ **Early summer**
◊◊ ■ **Z5 pH5–7.5**

The creamy plumes of handsome *Aruncus dioicus* contrast in form with *Philadelphus intectus*, here unpruned and so remaining furnished to ground level with flowering stems.

## Phillyrea latifolia

Sometimes called mock privets, phillyreas are slow-growing shrubs or small trees closely related to osmanthus. *P. latifolia* resembles a small olive tree, with intriguingly gnarled and twisted branches, bending under their weight of glistening evergreen leaves to produce a softly billowing outline. Although scented white flowers appear in late spring, the strongly sculptural shape of the shrub has always been its irresistible appeal, and it is traditionally planted as an architectural feature. It has particularly dramatic impact when planted to contrast with the formal shape of a box or yew hedge. It is perhaps best underplanted with bulbs, short herbaceous plants, and low shrubs that do not obscure its unique branch structure. In warm gardens, small black fruits sometimes develop during autumn.

**Perfect partners:** *Arctostaphylos uva-ursi*, *Epimedium* × *versicolor* 'Sulphureum', *Euonymus fortunei*, *Shibataea kumasasa*, *Stephanandra incisa*, *Viburnum davidii*

**H & S: 30 ft. (9 m)** ❀ **Late spring**
◊◊ ■-■ **Z7 pH5–8**

Placed toward the corner of a house to divide views from two facades, *Phillyrea latifolia* has here achieved the size of a small tree. Its handsome clouds of evergreen foliage and attractive branch structure provide the perfect foil to the severe lines of the building and to the paler, smooth-surfaced hedge of box (*Buxus sempervirens*).

The mounded habit of *Phlomis fruticosa* makes it useful toward the front of a border, with taller shrubs behind. Here, its bright flowers harmonize with cream-variegated *Ligustrum sinense* 'Variegatum' and are set off by purple smoke bush (*Cotinus coggygria* 'Royal Purple').

## Phlomis fruticosa ♆
JERUSALEM SAGE

Even when out of flower, this popular Mediterranean shrub catches the eye in a gravel bed or at the front of a border, where its spreading mound of felted grayish leaves makes a strong evergreen statement. In summer, whorls of bright yellow flowers are held high above the foliage and appear in huge numbers. It combines naturally with other hot-climate plants such as sages, white cistus and ornamental grasses; it blends well with other yellow or orange flowers; and it makes an effective contrast with blue and mid-purple and with silver or purple foliage. Dwarf *P. italica* is slightly less hardy, and produces soft mauve blooms.

**Perfect partners:** *Artemisia stelleriana* 'Boughton Silver', *Festuca glauca* 'Blaufuchs', *Geranium* 'Johnson's Blue' p.275 **A**, *Hakonechloa macra* 'Aureola', *Iris* 'Jane Phillips', *Nepeta* 'Six Hills Giant' p.315 **B**, *Salvia lavandulifolia*

**H: 40 in. (1 m)  S: 5 ft. (1.5 m)** ❀ **Early summer**
◊ ■ **Z7  pH5.5–7.5**

## *Photinia × fraseri*

This photinia and its cultivars are evergreen shrubs or small trees, primarily used as foliage plants. They are most striking in spring, when their young shoots appear flushed brilliant red, later turning bronze and then green. New red sideshoots continue to form throughout the season, but without the startling impact of the spring flourish. Small white flowers are produced freely in warm, dry areas, less prolifically elsewhere. The plants' rough-and-ready habit suits a wild or informal garden rather than a shrub border, and their open base makes them ideal for underplanting with smaller shrubs and bulbs such as red crown imperials. For maximum effect, they can be combined with other hot colors such as red, vermilion, or scarlet azaleas and rhododendrons. *P. × fraseri* 'Red Robin' ♀, 'Robusta', and 'Rubens' are all popular for their flaming red growth, while 'Birmingham' is a darker coppery red. All can suffer from the bacterial disease fireblight.

**Perfect partners:** *Fritillaria imperialis* 'Aurora', *Geum* 'Beech House Apricot', *G. chiloense*, *Rhododendron* 'Coccineum Speciosum', *Tulipa* 'Prinses Irene' ❑p.392 **A**

**H & S: 16 ft. (5 m)** ❀ **Early summer**
◊◊ ▇ **Z7 pH5–7**

The coppery red spring shoots of *Photinia × fraseri* 'Birmingham' have here lost their initial brilliance but still remain in perfect harmony with *Euphorbia griffithii* 'Dixter'.

## *Phygelius aequalis* 'Yellow Trumpet' ♀

This remarkable phygelius produces creamy yellow-green, trumpet-shaped blooms that nod gently on one side of tall, angular stems. In frost-free gardens, especially in a sheltered site such as the foot of a warm wall, this South African sub-shrub is reliably evergreen or semi-evergreen and forms suckering clumps of upright stems. Elsewhere it may be cut down by frost and so starts flowering later, producing larger flowerheads; hard annual pruning will have the same effect. The soft, magical coloring goes well with hot and cool shades, but it looks particularly breathtaking with magenta, blue, gold or scarlet. More rounded flowers contrast well with the prominent spikes of the phygelius, which is equally at home near the front of a mixed or herbaceous border, or in a shrubbery.

**Perfect partners:** *Argyranthemum maderense*, *Euphorbia seguieriana* subsp. *niciciana*, *Felicia amelloides* 'Santa Anita', *Geranium* 'Ann Folkard', *Nicotiana* 'Lime Green', *Petunia* Surfinia Purple, *Salvia greggii*, *S. patens*

**H: 40 in. (1 m) S: 20 in. (50 cm)**
❀ **Midsummer to early autumn**
◊◊ ▢-▇ **Z8 pH5.5–7.5**

The soft yellow florets of *Phygelius aequalis* 'Yellow Trumpet', borne along one side of the stem, contrast dramatically in color and form with *Geranium psilostemon*.

## *Phygelius × rectus*

Greater vigor and larger size distinguish this evergreen or semi-evergreen hybrid shrub from its parents, *P. aequalis* and *P. capensis*. There are several cultivars in a range of sizes and colors, and some are noted for their large, flared trumpet flowers with attractive markings. Outstanding cultivars include light red 'African Queen' ♀, salmon 'Pink Elf', and 'Moonraker', which is a similar creamy yellow to *P. aequalis* 'Yellow Trumpet' (above) but has blooms all round the stems. Plants look good among bronze or silver shrubs or with herbaceous plants in fairly warm colors.

**Perfect partners:** *Achillea* 'Lachsschönheit', *Argyranthemum* 'Peach Cheeks', *Dianthus* 'Doris', *Diascia barberae* 'Blackthorn Apricot', *Euphorbia seguieriana* subsp. *niciciana*, *Heuchera* 'Smokey Rose', *Kniphofia* 'David'

**H: 30–60 in. (75–150 cm) S: 24 in. (60 cm)**
❀ **Midsummer to early autumn**
◊◊ ▢-▇ **Z8 pH5.5–7.5**

A gentle contrast between two harmonies, silver and blue versus coral-salmon and red-purple, from four plants of markedly differing form: from front to back, *Senecio viravira*, *Phygelius × rectus*, *Eryngium alpinum* 'Amethyst' and *Berberis thunbergii* 'Rose Glow'.

## *Physocarpus opulifolius* 'Dart's Gold' ♥

This deciduous shrub with gracefully arching branches is brightest in spring, with its radiant yellow young foliage, and in early summer, when the stems are packed with dense clusters of tiny white flowers. A surround of low-growing ground-cover plants can emphasize its arching growth. A slender Alpina Group clematis growing through the branches is a good companion, and purple foliage plants nearby produce a dramatic color contrast. 'Dart's Gold' harmonizes well with other yellow-leaved plants such as euphorbias and decorative grasses. 'Luteus' is a more subtle shade of yellow; 'Diabolo' ♥ has leaves flushed dusky purple.

**Perfect partners:** *Agapanthus* 'Loch Hope', *Clematis* 'Frances Rivis', *Cotinus coggygria* 'Royal Purple', *Ipomoea tricolor* 'Heavenly Blue', *Miscanthus sinensis* 'Strictus' ❑ p.98 **B**

H & S: 5 ft. (1.5 m) ❈ Early summer
▬▬▬ ◌◌ ▮ Z3 pH5–6.5

**A**

When in flower, *Physocarpus opulifolius* 'Dart's Gold' has dazzlingly bright yellow-green leaves, here making a striking contrast with purple filbert (*Corylus maxima* 'Purpurea'). The leaves become greener as the season advances.

**B**

The essentially horizontal branches and silvery gray-green foliage of *Picea pungens* 'Globosa' contrast dramatically with weeping, green-leaved *Juniperus recurva* var. *coxii*.

## *Picea pungens* Pendula Group
WEEPING COLORADO SPRUCE

This elegant group has irregular weeping growth, more vigorous than that of *P.p.* 'Globosa' (above) and other small spruces, and with a loose habit. The best forms retain their glaucous coloring well. The group's graceful habit and conical shape are effective as a focal point or vertical accent in larger gardens. Space and light are critical for producing a well-shaped specimen. Prostrate conifers, heathers and low herbaceous plants can be grown around these conifers, but not beneath them. The central stem should be trained vertically to encourage good height early on. Other choice glaucous spruces include 'Procumbens', a dwarf, spreading cultivar with pendulous branches; 'Hoopsii' ♥, brilliant blue and densely conical in shape; and 'Koster' ♥, also conical with silvery blue foliage. Two other conical cultivars are 'Moerheimii', with tight, intensely blue foliage, and 'Montgomery', bright grayish blue and a little more rounded in shape.

**Perfect partners:** *Ajuga genevensis*, *Calluna vulgaris* 'Beoley Gold', *Euonymus fortunei* 'Emerald 'n' Gold', *Hakonechloa macra* 'Aureola', *Rhododendron* 'Sarled'

## *Picea pungens* 'Globosa' ♥

A compact blue-green form of the Colorado spruce, 'Globosa' is often planted as an evergreen focal point in garden schemes. It makes a dense bush, globe-shaped but with a flat top, and can take as long as 15 years to reach 5 ft. (1.5 m) in height and spread. It sits easily with other conifers, especially junipers, and looks particularly good as a specimen in a bed of heathers. Crowding it in a small border or using it to support climbing plants can spoil the satisfying geometrical shape. For this reason it should be sited where sunlight and fresh air reach all sides. It looks good with low-growing herbaceous plants, especially bugles and other blue-flowered plants, or those with soft yellow flowers such as primroses.

**Perfect partners:** *Carex oshimensis* 'Evergold', *Erica carnea* 'Cecilia M. Beale', *Hosta* (Tardiana Group) 'June', *Juniperus horizontalis* 'Mother Lode', *Omphalodes cappadocica*

H & S: 5 ft. (1.5 m) ❈ (Late spring)
▬▬▬ ◌◌ ▮ Z2 pH5–6.5

**C**

Winter-flowering heaths such as *Erica* × *darleyensis* 'Arthur Johnson' make an effective foil for *Picea pungens* Pendula Group, furnished to the ground with glaucous foliage.

H: 33 ft. (10 m) S: 10 ft. (3 m) ❈ (Late spring)
▬▬▬ ◌◌ ▮ Z2 pH5–6.5

*Pieris formosa* is of comparable size and habit to many rhododendrons, making possible some dazzling combinations with its brilliant young shoots – as with the lilac-flowered cultivar here. A rhododendron or perhaps a deciduous azalea with peach, orange, apricot or salmon blooms would make an equally satisfying partner.

The yellow-green foliage of *Pinus mugo* 'Winter Gold' mixes agreeably with the blue flowers of *Lithodora diffusa* 'Grace Ward'. The lithodora prefers neutral to alkaline soil.

## Pieris formosa

Pieris are some of the loveliest evergreen shrubs, with handsome foliage and long trusses of usually white, spring flowers, reminiscent of lily-of-the-valley. The blooms of *P. formosa* are exceptionally beautiful, and its young leaves take on vivid red tints in mid- and late spring. It harmonizes with salmon, peach apricot, cream and yellow flowers or early-leafing bronze foliage, and contrasts with the apple-green of hellebores and with yellow-green leaves. It flowers well in full sun, although light overhead shade provides useful protection from frost. As with all pieris, it needs acid soil or ericaceous compost.

**Perfect partners:** *Amelanchier lamarckii*, *Camellia* 'Black Lace', *Dryopteris erythrosora*, *Embothrium coccineum*, *Euphorbia griffithii*, *E. palustris*, *Helleborus argutifolius*, *Paeonia delavayi*, *Rhododendron* 'Gloria Mundi', *R.* 'Golden Torch' ❑ p.132 **B**

**H: 16 ft. (5 m) S: 13 ft. (4 m)** ❀ **Mid- to late spring** ◊◊-◊◊◊ ■ **Z8 pH4–6**

## Pieris japonica

This compact evergreen shrub has glossy foliage and masses of very sweetly scented white flowers gathered in heavy, branching trusses. The buds form early in autumn and, in a mild season, can open from late winter onward. It is effective in small gardens, in mixed borders or in large containers, and also in woodland or wild garden settings. It can be combined with spring bulbs of all kinds, and other ericaceous shrubs such as heathers or rhododendrons. Acid soil or ericaceous compost is essential, as is plenty of light for flowering. 'Firecrest' ♀ and 'Red Mill' bear flamboyant red new leaves as the flowers open.

**Perfect partners:** *Camellia japonica* 'Hagoromo', *C.* × *williamsii* 'J.C. Williams', *Cryptomeria japonica* Elegans Group, *Erica* × *darleyensis* 'Silberschmelze', *Helleborus* × *hybridus*, *Magnolia kobus*, *Narcissus* 'Mrs. R.O. Backhouse', *Rhododendron arboreum*, *Skimmia japonica* 'Rubella'

**H: 13 ft. (4 m) S: 10 ft. (3 m)** ❀ **Late winter to early spring** ◊◊-◊◊◊ ■ **Z5 pH4–6.5**

Drooping panicles of creamy white flowers on a young *Pieris japonica* are partnered prettily by *Corydalis solida* 'Lahovice'. A mature pieris would need larger companions.

## Pinus mugo 'Winter Gold'

*P. mugo*, the mountain pine, is a very variable conifer from Central Europe with numerous dwarf cultivars ideal for garden use. 'Winter Gold' is particularly useful, with an open arrangement of many low branches. These are thickly leaved and resemble bottle-brushes, upturned at their tips, giving strong textural impact. The foliage is fresh greenish yellow from late spring until early autumn, but it is at its best in winter when the whole conifer turns a brilliant and sunny shade of golden yellow. The spreading plant needs space to achieve its full beauty; annual pruning is recommended if a compact plant is needed. It can be used with low-growing blue, cream, or yellow herbaceous flowers, underplanted with spring bulbs, or combined with foliage plants such as heathers, gaultherias and bergenias.

**Perfect partners:** *Campanula poscharskyana*, *Corydalis ochroleuca*, *Festuca glauca* 'Blaufuchs', *Geranium* Rozanne, *Omphalodes cappadocica*, *Tulipa* 'Spring Green'

**H: 24 in. (60 cm) S: 40 in. (1 m)** ❀ **(Late spring to early summer)** ◊◊ ■ **Z2 pH4.5–7.5**

The small, white-mottled leaves of *Pittosporum tenuifolium* 'Irene Paterson' contrast effectively in both form and color with a dark-leaved phormium – both are New Zealanders with similar hardiness and cultivation requirements.

## *Pittosporum tenuifolium* 'Irene Paterson' ♧

The variegated foliage of this evergreen shrub emerges cream, matures to deep green mottled with white, and becomes flushed with pink in winter. Its pale markings provide a lighter tone that is useful for harmonies with other pale foliage and for contrasts with darker plants. *P. tenuifolium* and its cultivars thrive in maritime climates, where they can be grown with other pittosporums, olearias, hoherias, smaller or stooled eucalyptus, larger hebes, griselinias and atriplex; other good partners include brachyglottis, escallonias, ozothamnus and tamarisks. Larger cultivars look good with small-flowered clematis; shorter, silver-variegated kinds blend well with blue *Hydrangea macrophylla* cultivars.

**Perfect partners:** *Agapanthus inapertus*, *Ceanothus* 'Delight', *Choisya* **Goldfingers**, *Dodonaea viscosa* 'Purpurea', *Maurandya barclayana*, *Pseudopanax lessonii* 'Purpureus'

**H: 5 ft.** (1.5 m) **S: 24 in.** (60 cm)
❀ Late spring to early summer
▬▬□▬■ ◊◊ □-■ Z9 pH5–7

## *Pittosporum tenuifolium* 'Tom Thumb' ♧

This compact evergreen shrub has a neat shape and glistening foliage flushed bronze-purple. It makes dramatic contrasts with pale-leaved plants, and suits sumptuous color schemes of dark-leaved plants such as purple or bronze cannas, sages or dahlias, as well as flowers in hot colors or purple shades. Other good companions are smaller, deep purple or pink *Hydrangea serrata* or *H. macrophylla* cultivars, corokias, crocosmias, and smaller escallonias and phormiums. 'Purpureum' is larger, with very dark purple leaves.

**Perfect partners:** *Celmisia semicordata*, *Dahlia* 'Moonfire', *Diascia barberae* 'Ruby Field', *Hebe speciosa* 'La Séduisante', *Nicotiana* 'Lime Green', *Phormium* 'Maori Sunrise'

**H: 36 in.** (90 cm) **S: 24 in.** (60 cm)
( ❀ Late spring to early summer)
▬▬□▬■ ◊◊ □-■ Z9 pH5–7

*Pittosporum tenuifolium* 'Tom Thumb' and *Corokia* × *virgata* harmonize in leaf color. Their similar textures might benefit from an intervening plant of contrasting form, perhaps with straplike or grassy leaves.

## *Pleioblastus viridistriatus* ♧

Grown for its bright, gold-variegated leaves, this evergreen bamboo spreads slowly to form a large clump that looks effective toward the front of a shrub border or in a woodland garden, mixed with hot colors, blue flowers and glaucous foliage. Its foliage is brightest in late spring and early summer, when it is striking with yellow or orange azaleas, hostas, euphorbias, bluebells and Tibetan poppies; in midsummer it combines well with blue or white hydrangeas, and later with autumn-coloring shrubs. Acanthus and larger ferns, grasses, and bergenias make good contrasts.

At the front of a border, the slightly invasive, brightly variegated *Pleioblastus viridistriatus* provides an attractive contrast to soft orange *Geum* 'Dolly North'.

**Perfect partners:** *Corydalis flexuosa*, *Euphorbia griffithii* 'Dixter', *Helleborus foetidus*, *Hosta* (Tardiana Group) 'Halcyon', *Hydrangea arborescens* subsp. *discolor* 'Sterilis', *H. macrophylla* 'Blue Bonnet', *Meconopsis grandis*, *Ophiopogon planiscapus* 'Nigrescens', *Phormium* 'Dark Delight', *Rhododendron augustinii*, *R*. 'Coccineum Speciosum', *R*. 'Narcissiflorum'

**H: 4 ft.** (1.2 m) **S: 5 ft.** (1.5 m) ( ❀ Summer)
▬▬□▬■ ◊◊-◊◊◊ □-■ ■ Z7 pH5–7

A

The pale yellow-green foliage of annually pruned *Populus alba* 'Richardii' contrasts sharply with a purple *Cleome hassleriana*, the magenta flowers of *Geranium* 'Ann Folkard', and mauve *Allium carinatum* subsp. *pulchellum*.

## Populus alba 'Richardii'

When pollarded or stooled, this deciduous tree or large shrub has particularly large, vivid yellow-green leaves and makes a handsome foliage plant for a mixed or shrub border, especially when ruffled by a breeze to reveal the downy white underside of its foliage. Its bright leaves make striking contrasts with hot colors such as magenta, scarlet or orange, and they also associate well with white, yellow or pure blue flowers and silver, yellow-green or yellow-variegated foliage. It is outstanding with lavender-blue buddleias and yellow or orange *Buddleja* × *weyeriana* cultivars, and it also succeeds as a support for a wispy flowering climber such as a Viticella clematis. Other suitable partners include yellow-green catalpas, honey locust and robinias; silver atriplex, elaeagnus and hippophae; and tall yellow flowers such as helianthus.

**Perfect partners:** *Buddleja* 'Lochinch', *Clematis* 'Rhapsody', *Delphinium* 'Blue Jay', *Euphorbia sikkimensis*, *Ipomoea tricolor* 'Heavenly Blue', *Rosa* 'Golden Wings', *R.* 'Sally Holmes', *Rudbeckia* 'Juligold', *Tithonia rotundifolia*

**H: 50 ft.** (15 m)  **S: 40 ft.** (12 m)  (�֎ **Early spring**)
△△-△△△ ▢-▮ **Z3  pH5–7.5**

## Potentilla fruticosa

SHRUBBY CINQUEFOIL

This variable deciduous shrub may have an erect or prostrate habit, deep green or silvery leaves, and flowers that are white to golden yellow, sometimes orange-red or peach. The flowers and dainty filigree foliage excel at close range, especially with plants of more definite form such as hostas, eryngiums and crocosmias. The flowers suit combinations with warm colors and yellow-green, gold-variegated or glaucous foliage, and they contrast well with blue flowers. Good partners include lavender-blue or white hebes, old Shrub roses, lavenders, buddleias, olearias, hydrangeas and hypericums. 'Beesii' (24 in./60 cm) bears silvery leaves and golden flowers; 'Abbotswood' ♀ (30 in./75 cm), bluish green leaves and white flowers; free-flowering 'Goldfinger' (30 in./75 cm) has large golden flowers; 'Elizabeth' (3¼ ft./1 m) is rich yellow; 'Maanelys' (Moonlight) (4 ft./1.2 m) has soft yellow flowers until late autumn; 'Katherine Dykes' (up to 6½ ft./2 m), is primrose yellow.

**Right:** The silvery leaves of *Potentilla fruticosa* 'Primrose Beauty' and its pale flowers blend with almost any other color. Here, it spreads over edging stones at the front of a border among flowers of varied colors and forms – *Rosa* 'Felicia', purple-leaved *Actaea simplex* Atropurpurea Group, blue *Polemonium foliosissimum*, coral kniphofias, white violas and variegated *Phlox paniculata* 'Norah Leigh'.

**Below:** In a simple but striking combination, *Potentilla fruticosa* 'Tangerine' is draped gracefully with the cream-edged foliage of *Vinca major* 'Variegata'.

**Perfect partners:** *Agapanthus* 'Donau', *Caryopteris* × *clandonensis*, *Eryngium* × *tripartitum*, *Hakonechloa macra* 'Aureola', *Helictotrichon sempervirens*, *Hemerocallis* 'Corky', *Hosta* 'Big Daddy', *Lavandula angustifolia* 'Hidcote', *Nepeta* × *faassenii*, *Perovskia* 'Blue Haze', *Rosa* 'Sally Holmes' p.209 **A**, *Sedum* 'Herbstfreude' p.333 **B**

**H: 1–6½ ft.** (30 cm–2 m)  **S: 40 in.–6½ ft.** (1–2 m)
�֎ **Late spring to mid-autumn**
△△ ▢-▮ **Z3  pH5–7.5**

B

C

The ornamental cherry *Prunus pendula* 'Pendula Rosea', grown as a specimen tree, is underplanted with crocuses in purple, lilac and white. The effect is pleasing for its subtlety – adding golden yellow crocuses here would be too strident.

## *Prunus pendula* 'Pendula Rosea' ♀

The rose-pink flowers of this deciduous ornamental cherry appear before the leaves, in early and mid-spring, coinciding with crocuses, narcissi and early tulips, any of which can be used beneath its spread. With its elegantly weeping habit, it makes a fine specimen tree, but it may also be grown in a large border above shade-tolerant plants and spring flowers, preferably where it is screened from early morning sun to avoid frost injuring the blooms. The flowers blend well with red-flushed evergreen foliage such as that of bergenias, and with other short spring flowers, including wood anemones, *Cyclamen coum* variants and hellebores. This charming tree also associates well with camellias and with *Viburnum tinus* cultivars and early rhododendrons. *Prunus* × *subhirtella* 'Autumnalis' ♀ is a slightly less graceful *P. pendula* hybrid, with white or palest blush flowers through the winter and into spring; the blooms of *P.* × *s.* 'Autumnalis Rosea' ♀ are a more definite pink, while those of *P.* × *s.* 'Fukubana' are dark rose-pink.

**Perfect partners:** *Camellia japonica* 'Hagoromo', *C.* × *williamsii* 'J.C. Williams', *Helleborus* × *hybridus*, *Rhododendron dauricum*, *R. mucronulatum*, *Viburnum* × *bodnantense*

**H & S: 33 ft. (10 m)** ✽ **Early to mid-spring**
◊◊ ▢-▉ **Z5 pH5.5–7.5**

## *Prunus* Sato-zakura Group
JAPANESE FLOWERING CHERRY

These spring-flowering deciduous small trees bear single, semi-double or double flowers in white to deep pink, and green, bronze-flushed, or purple foliage. Upright or columnar cultivars are useful in restricted spaces or formal schemes, whether as focal points or repeated accents. Spreading kinds can be trained high enough to be underplanted with shrubs or to allow a walkway beneath, or they can arch gracefully above their neighbors. Strongly colored cultivars can be used for dramatic partnerships with other small trees and large shrubs such as flowering crab apples, lilacs, hawthorns, magnolias, rhododendrons and *Camellia japonica* or *C.* × *williamsii* cultivars. Specimen trees look particularly fine carpeted beneath with spring flowers such as narcissi, tulips, pulmonarias, brunneras, forget-me-nots, wood anemones, cardamines, corydalis and bluebells.

Attractive white cultivars include 'Shirotae' ♀, with single and semi-double flowers; single 'Taihaku' ♀ (the great white cherry); 'Ukon' ♀, a spreading tree with double flowers that are white-flushed yellow-green; and 'Shirofugen' ♀, whose blush-white flowers open from pink buds. Among pale pink cultivars are semi-double 'Accolade' ♀; narrowly columnar 'Amanogawa' ♀, double; 'Ichiyo' ♀, double; and the late-flowering 'Taoyame', semi-double. The weeping double 'Kiku-shidare-zakura' ♀ (syn. 'Cheal's Weeping'), semi-double 'Chôshû-hizakura' and double 'Pink Perfection' ♀ are all bright pink. Double 'Kanzan' ♀ is outstanding for its abundance of pink flowers, while the similar 'Royal Burgundy' has purple foliage.

**Perfect partners:** *Amelanchier* × *grandiflora* 'Rubescens', *Camellia japonica* 'Alba Simplex', *Crataegus monogyna* 'Biflora', *Magnolia kobus*, *Malus floribunda*, *Rhododendron schlippenbachii*, *Syringa oblata*, *Viburnum* × *burkwoodii*

**H: 20–33 ft. (6–10 m) S: 10–33 ft. (3–10 m)**
✽ **Early to late spring**
◊◊ ▢-▉ **Z5 pH5.5–7.5**

*Prunus* 'Shirotae' makes a widely spreading tree, with pure white, single and semi-double flowers emerging from palest pink buds. It is underplanted here with uneven clumps and drifts of cream *Narcissus* 'February Silver'.

Even without a companion, the potential of *Pyracantha angustifolia* for combining with autumn foliage or fruits is apparent, with its glossy evergreen leaves showing pale undersides and copious berries on arching stems.

## *Pyracantha coccinea*

This large deciduous shrub differs from *P. angustifolia* (above) in having broader leaves, deeper red berries and slightly later, creamy white flowers. Although the species itself is rarely available, there are a few good cultivars. 'Lalandei', a more vigorous, erect plant, has larger berries. 'Red Column', with heavy clusters of early scarlet berries, is dense and erect, and 'Red Cushion' is useful for ground cover. Hybrids include 'Orange Glow' ♥, with plenty of orange-red berries; 'Golden Charmer' ♥, with arching branches; 'Mohave', with orange-red, early ripening berries; and white-edged 'Mohave Silver'.

**Perfect partners:** *Acer palmatum* 'Ōsakazuki', *Buddleja* × *weyeriana*, *Cotoneaster frigidus* 'Cornubia', *Euonymus europaeus* 'Red Cascade', *Juniperus* × *pfitzeriana* Gold Sovereign, *Photinia beauverdiana*, *Rhododendron calendulaceum*, *Rhus typhina*, *Rosa* 'Blanche Double de Coubert'

H & S: 13 ft. (4 m) ✺ Early summer
◌◌ ▪ Z5 pH5.5–7.5

## *Pyracantha angustifolia*

This is a variable evergreen shrub, erect or prostrate, with creamy white flowers followed by orange-yellow to orange-red berries. It can be grown as a freestanding shrub, as a hedge or trained against a wall, perhaps with winter jasmine or ivy. The berries look striking in winter, and are usually still plentiful when spring bulbs such as narcissi and tulips are in bloom. This pyracantha combines well with prostrate junipers, other berrying shrubs such as cotoneasters, white-flowered winter heaths, ground-covering ivies, evergreen euonymus, and dogwoods, willows and other deciduous shrubs with colored stems. For autumn effect it may be combined with late-coloring deciduous shrubs such as Japanese maples, witch hazels, sumachs and azaleas.

**Perfect partners:** *Amelanchier laevis*, *Berberis wilsoniae*, *Cotinus coggygria*, *Cryptomeria japonica* Elegans Group, *Fothergilla major*, *Hedera algeriensis* 'Gloire de Marengo', *H. colchica* 'Sulphur Heart', *Rhododendron luteum*, *Rosa* 'Alchymist', *R.* 'Golden Wings'

H & S: 10 ft. (3 m) ✺ Early summer
◌◌ ▫-▪ Z6 pH5.5–7.5

The arching sprays of blossom of *Pyracantha coccinea*, harmonizing here with *Elaeagnus* 'Quicksilver', are as appealing as its berries, although shorter-lived. The effect is most dramatic on fairly young or recently pruned bushes.

A classic element of the white garden, where it can be combined with foliage in silver, glaucous or plain green and with white flowers, *Pyrus salicifolia* 'Pendula' here harmonizes with the foliage of sea kale (*Crambe maritima*) in front. *Leucojum aestivum* and the contrasting form of ostrich-plume fern (*Matteuccia struthiopteris*) sit to one side.

## *Pyrus salicifolia* 'Pendula'
WEEPING SILVER PEAR

This elegant, weeping deciduous tree has narrow silver-green leaves and white flowers borne as the leaves emerge. Its blooms are slightly camouflaged by the pale foliage, which is this plant's chief attraction. The most commonly sold form has a low mushroom of foliage suitable for smaller gardens, but for larger plantings trees can be trained to a taller stake to allow underplanting with shade-tolerant evergreens and spring flowers such as anemones and celandines. It associates well with cool colors, white flowers and other silver foliage plants, and makes a dramatic contrast with dark green or dark purple foliage. Occasional removal of stems from the crown will provide a more graceful appearance. If a larger, non-weeping tree is needed, the plain species or the similar *P. elaeagnifolia* can be grown.

**Perfect partners:** *Clematis alpina* 'Ruby' p.155 B, *Cosmos bipinnatus* 'Purity', *Crambe cordifolia*, *Delphinium* 'Lilian Basset', *Digitalis purpurea* f. *albiflora*, *Miscanthus sinensis* 'Morning Light', *Onopordum nervosum*, *Rosa* Iceberg, *R.* 'Lavender Lassie' p.205 C

H: 16 ft. (5 m) S: 13 ft. (4 m) ✺ Mid-spring
◌◌ ▫-▪ Z4 pH5.5–7.5

# Rhododendrons including Azaleas

RHODODENDRONS COMPRISE one of the most important genera of garden plants. There are approximately 4,000 sorts available, flowering from late winter to midsummer, in every color except pure blue. They vary greatly in habit, from low, carpeting cultivars suitable for ground-cover to large, treelike species; many have an open, branching habit. Rhododendron foliage is almost always respectable and sometimes exceptionally handsome, as in larger species such as *R. maccabeanum* ♀ and *R. rex*. A few, for instance *R.* Shilsonii Group, have attractive bark. Most rhododendrons in this book fall into three main groups: evergreen hardy hybrids (or "iron clads") and their parent species, deciduous azaleas and evergreen azaleas.

All rhododendrons prefer moist, acidic soil with high humus content and dappled shade, suiting them ideally to a woodland garden. Many evergreen rhododendrons make useful screens or informal hedges, although large expanses of their foliage can look dull through summer and autumn unless leavened by more varied leaf textures. Summer-flowering sorts include selections of some of the North American azaleas and their hybrids, as well as the sweet-scented *R. auriculatum* and its hybrid 'Polar Bear'. Most deciduous azaleas have a rich and pervasive scent; many also have brilliant autumn color, provided they are not grown in dense shade.

In cool climates, rhododendrons described as sun-tolerant can be grown in almost full sun, although this may result in a very tight habit and unnaturally dense flower cover. More shade can help to loosen the habit of excessively spherical sorts: birches provide good quick cover in a rhododendron garden, as do oaks for the longer term (beech should be avoided, as the dense canopy and dry soil it creates are not suitable for rhododendrons).

In an intimate garden, a jumble of deciduous azaleas in harmonious, sugared almond colors can look charming. The true *Allium aflatunense*, with its spherical, pinkish purple heads, almost matches the azaleas in height.

An evergreen windbreak is vital for the more tender evergreen rhododendrons, the large-leaved kinds usually needing the most shelter. Most rhododendrons prefer an acidic soil with a pH of 4.5–5.5 but will tolerate a pH of 4–6. However, some nurseries may offer a new kind of rhododendron, grafted onto lime-resistant rootstocks, and these will grow on even quite alkaline soil.

When planting rhododendrons, it is useful to bear in mind that irregular groups tend to look more natural, and that the scale of the group needs to relate to its setting (in a large area, single plants can create a "spotty" effect). The very brightly colored and most floriferous sorts, particularly if they have a densely spherical habit, can seem out of place in a natural setting such as a woodland garden, and tend to look better near the house. Rules decreeing that azaleas should not be combined with other rhododendrons should be ignored; however, it is worth noting that combinations of flowers in the yellow to scarlet range with those in crimson through magenta to lavender can clash horribly or excitingly, depending on personal preference.

Rhododendrons are surface-rooting, with a spreading, fibrous root plate: even mature specimens can be transplanted without impairing their growth, allowing plants to be eased out when they become congested and colors to be rearranged. Leggy plants, if growing vigorously, can be restored to shape by hard pruning in late winter, although smooth-barked sorts do not regenerate easily and should not be cut back so severely. New strains of rhododendron powdery mildew mean that regular use of fungicides is essential for some species. Deadheading significantly increases the following year's bloom.

## *Rhododendron* 'Amethyst'

The brilliant violet-blue of this sun-tolerant hardy hybrid makes a dazzling contrast with greenish yellow, and a slightly less punchy one with sulfur-yellow flowers. It also goes pleasantly with carmine, campanula-blue, mauve-pink or lilac blooms. Extremely pale colors, such as light blues, mauves and pinks, as well as white, tend to be less successful, since they do not contrast or harmonize as effectively. However, the tiniest of flowers in these colors – cow parsley, for example – can work well. Generally, the fine texture and

The feathery, bright yellow-green new leaves of *Acer palmatum* 'Linearilobum' provide delicate texture and a striking color contrast with *Rhododendron* 'Amethyst'.

relatively amorphous habit of 'Amethyst' demand companions of definite form to avoid an excessively diffuse effect.

**Perfect partners:** *Allium hollandicum,
Anthriscus sylvestris* 'Ravenswing', *Lunaria annua, Meconopsis integrifolia, Milium effusum* 'Aureum', *Smyrnium perfoliatum*

H & S: 5 ft. (1.5 m)  ✽ **Mid- to late spring**
  ◊◊-◊◊◊  ■-■  ■  Z6  pH4–6

## *Rhododendron* Blinklicht Group

Blinklicht Group has a fairly solid habit, bold leaves, large flowerheads and a stronger form than small-leaved rhododendrons with few-flowered inflorescences. Its solidity can be offset by partners with a more elegant, open habit, and its strong color looks best in more formal areas. It contrasts well with soft yellow and yellow-green flowers and leaves, and harmonizes with rich peach, deep salmon-pink, apricot, soft orange and deep rose-pink blooms. Combinations with bronze foliage also need lighter colors to leaven them.

**Perfect partners:** *Aquilegia canadensis,
Euphorbia amygdaloides* 'Purpurea', *Helleborus* × *sternii, Hosta* 'Sum and Substance', *Physocarpus opulifolius* 'Luteus', *Rhododendron* 'Elizabeth Lockhart', *R.* 'Fabia'

H: 8 ft. (2.5 m)  S: 5 ft. (1.5 m)
✽ **Mid- to late spring**
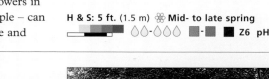  ◊◊-◊◊◊  ■-■  ■  Z6  pH4–6

*Rhododendron* Blinklicht Group, underplanted with *Tiarella cordifolia*, harmonizes with *Acer palmatum* f. *atropurpureum*. *Polygonatum* × *hybridum* gives a graceful contrast of form.

*Hosta fortunei* 'Crowned Imperial' adds bold structure here, its glaucous leaves with yellow-green margins contrasting with the lilac flowerheads of *Rhododendron* 'Blue Peter'.

## *Rhododendron* 'Blue Peter' ♛

Bold lilac flowerheads, with their repeated pattern of dark basal blotches, are almost too sumptuous and sophisticated for the wilder parts of the garden. This is one of the bluest hardy hybrids; it makes attractive contrasts with pale yellow, apricot and yellow-green flowers, and harmonizes with pink, carmine, and campanula-blue. It is especially effective as a quieter foil for some of the intense violet-blue, smaller-flowered species rhododendrons such as *R. fastigiatum, R. impeditum* and *R. russatum* ♛ and their hybrids, including *R.* 'Amethyst' (above left). Combinations with glaucous blue-green, yellow-green, purple and smoky purple-gray foliage also work well. 'Blue Peter' becomes leggy and shy-flowering if deprived of adequate light.

**Perfect partners:** *Camassia leichtlinii,
Euphorbia amygdaloides* var. *robbiae, Heuchera* 'Can-can', *Hyacinthoides non-scripta, Mertensia virginica, Milium effusum* 'Aureum', *Prunus spinosa* 'Purpurea', *Smyrnium perfoliatum*

H & S: 10 ft. (3 m)  ✽ **Late spring**
◊◊-◊◊◊  ■-■  ■  Z5  pH4–6

## Rhododendron campylocarpum

The soft yellow blooms and slightly lax, informal growth habit of this evergreen species suit it to wild gardens, where it can mingle with meadow buttercups, cow parsley and bluebells. It also combines well with gold, apricot, white and chartreuse flowers and yellow, chartreuse and glaucous foliage. Pure blue flowers, such as *Corydalis flexuosa*, contrast well; purplish blue cranesbills and campanulas are also effective. Good drainage helps prevent flower damage from late frosts.

**Perfect partners:** *Brunnera macrophylla, Hosta sieboldiana* var. *elegans, Meconopsis betonicifolia, Milium effusum* 'Aureum', *Myosotis sylvatica, Smyrnium perfoliatum*

**H: 16 ft.** (5 m) **S: 13 ft.** (4 m) �֎ **Mid-spring**
◊◊-◊◊◊ ☐-■ ■ Z6 pH4–6

The ivory-white flowers of *Fothergilla gardenii*, emerging from greenish yellow buds, create a color harmony with *Rhododendron campylocarpum* and a contrast of floral form.

## Rhododendron 'Fandango'

'Fandango' (not to be confused with the hardy hybrid of the same name) makes a spreading, compact plant that is covered by dazzling flowers in spring. Its deep purplish pink can be mixed with other bright flowers and foliage, perhaps to make an impact when seen in passing; however, the intensity of such combinations can pall if the plant is sited where it will be viewed for longer periods of time. The solid sheets of purplish pink can be rendered more digestible by using a scattered group rather than a single block, by combining it with soft bronze or glaucous foliage, or by adding slightly paler, dusky mauve-pink flowers. Clashes with vermilion or chartreuse might appeal to the daring. Although 'Fandango' is a neat shrub, it lacks distinction out of flower; neighbors with a strong habit or textured foliage should be chosen to extend the period of interest.

**Perfect partners:** *Dicentra* 'Stuart Boothman', *Helleborus* × *sternii, Primula* 'Guinevere', *Pulmonaria saccharata* Argentea Group, *P.s.* 'Dora Bielefeld'

**H: 3 ft.** (90 cm) **S: 4 ft.** (1.2 m) ✖ **Late spring**
◊◊-◊◊◊ ☐-■ ■ Z6 pH4–6

The colors and textures of *Acer palmatum* f. *atropurpureum* and *Rhododendron* 'Fandango' mix well. An additional, intermediate shrub would balance the difference in height.

## Rhododendron Cilpinense Group ♔

The pale sugary pink of the floriferous, evergreen Cilpinense Group looks good with darker pink, white or deep crimson flowers and with red-tinted foliage. Harmonies with mauve, lilac, peach and pale apricot also work well. Its color is not strong enough for telling contrasts, except possibly with pale apple-green. Flowering earlier than most hardy hybrids, it blooms before most deciduous or herbaceous foliage unfurls. It can be used successfully with spring bulbs

*Pulmonaria* 'Lewis Palmer' makes superb ground cover beneath the pink bloom of *Rhododendron* Cilpinense Group.

– narcissus cultivars are particularly effective. The young foliage and flower buds are susceptible to damage from late frosts.

**Perfect partners:** *Anemone nemorosa* cultivars, *Helleborus argutifolius, H.* × *hybridus, Narcissus* 'February Silver', *Primula* 'Old Port', *Rhododendron* 'Elizabeth Lockhart' ❑p.83 **B**

**H & S: 3¼ ft.** (1 m) ✖ **Early spring**
◊◊-◊◊◊ ☐-■ ■ Z6 pH4–6

A

*Helleborus × hybridus* is a good companion for *Rhododendron hippophaeoides*. Cultivars in clear pink, plum, soft yellow or white work best with the rhododendron's bright violet.

## Rhododendron hippophaeoides

This sun-tolerant evergreen rhododendron can vary in color between lavender-blue, as seen in the superlative clone 'Habashan' ♀, and mauve-pink. It tends to be upright when young, becoming more spreading with age. Lavender-blue variants form striking contrasts with greenish yellow and sulfur-yellow, and combine attractively with mauve-pink, lilac, carmine and campanula-blue flowers. The pinkish variants combine well with white, purple and darker blue shades, and contrast effectively with light apple-green, but not yellow. Its tolerance of sunnier situations suits it to more open, heathlike planting schemes rather than to a woodland garden, and its neat habit makes it suitable for smaller gardens.

**Perfect partners:** *Allium aflatunense, Corydalis solida, Euphorbia amygdaloides* var. *robbiae, E. polychroma* 'Major', *Helleborus argutifolius, H. × hybridus* (primrose), *Narcissus* 'Liberty Bells', *N.* 'Pipit'

H: 5 ft. (1.5 m)  S: 2½ ft. (75 cm)  ❀ Mid-spring
◊◊-◊◊◊ ▢-■ ■ Z6 pH4–6

## Rhododendron 'Kirin'

This brilliant rich cerise evergreen azalea produces hose-in-hose flowers (with two flower tubes, one inside the other). Its color and uses are similar to those of the lower-growing 'Fandango' (facing page); however, taller 'Kirin' is more suited to grading into borders and shrubberies. The strong colors of both azaleas are their greatest assets and their chief limitations: although their brilliance can be moderated by combining them with more muted, harmonious tones, they can seem brash if used with other strong colors and are more suited to momentary spectacle than to contemplative, wild or woodland gardens.

**Perfect partners:** *Bergenia* 'Bressingham Bountiful', *Dicentra spectabilis, Helleborus argutifolius, Heuchera* 'Can-can', *Prunus × cistena, Pulmonaria* 'Vera May'

H & S: 5 ft. (1.5 m)  ❀ Mid-spring
◊◊-◊◊◊ ▢-■ ■ Z6 pH4–6

B

*Rhododendron* 'Kirin' creates a dazzling combination with *Hosta undulata* var. *undulata*: all panache and pizzazz, it is not for those who seek tranquility in the garden.

C

## Rhododendron 'Linda' ♀

The sumptuous cerise of this hardy hybrid and its tight, compact habit make it effective in more cultivated areas near the house, where it might be combined with Lily-flowered tulips and pink and white forget-me-nots. In a wild or woodland garden, its companion plants should have a looser habit and more delicate or duskier coloring. It combines well with carmine to lavender-blue flowers, but it is perhaps most effective in harmonies with pale pink, mauve or deep

*Rhododendron* 'Linda' and bluebells (*Hyacinthoides non-scripta*) make a lovely pairing for a woodland garden.

crimson blooms and purple-flushed leaves. Pale apple-green flowers or glaucous foliage could also provide a pleasing contrast.

**Perfect partners:** *Anthriscus sylvestris* 'Ravenswing', *Chaerophyllum hirsutum* 'Roseum', *Geranium sylvaticum* var. *wanneri, Helleborus × sternii, Hyacinthoides* 'Rose Queen'

H & S: 4 ft. (1.2 m)  ❀ Mid-spring
◊◊-◊◊◊ ▢-■ ■ Z6 pH4–6

## *Rhododendron luteum* ♑

This is often known by its former name, *Azalea pontica*. Showy, intensely fragrant, easy to grow and not too stiff in habit, it is eminently suitable for a wild or woodland garden. Its flowers are usually golden yellow, although there is some variation in both flower and autumn leaf color when raised from seed. This is an advantage if it is to be used extensively in a large area, the occasional individuals with paler yellow flowers helping to leaven the ensemble. *R. luteum* combines well with palest yellow, cream, peach and apricot flowers, including other deciduous azaleas, and with yellow-green foliage and flowers, blue flowers and yellow-variegated or glaucous foliage. For a more dramatic effect, it can be planted with orange or vermilion flowers and bronze

*Rhododendron luteum* and bluebells (*Hyacinthoides non-scripta*) are effective partners; including another plant of intermediate height for spring and one or more for autumn would provide additional interest.

foliage; yellow-green also works well with this color range. It benefits from neighbors with good autumn color but contrasting leaf shape, such as Japanese maples or some of the larger grasses.

**Perfect partners:** *Camassia quamash* 'Orion', *Euphorbia griffithii* 'Dixter', *Hosta* 'Sum and Substance', *Luzula sylvatica* 'Hohe Tatra', *Miscanthus sinensis* var. *purpurascens*, *Rhododendron* 'Klondyke', *Symphytum caucasicum*

**H & S: 13 ft. (4 m)** ❀ **Late spring**
▢▢▢▢▢ ◊◊-◊◊◊ ▢-▢ ■ Z5 pH4–6

## *Rhododendron* 'May Day' ♑

Tolerant of full sun, this spreading evergreen hybrid has deep scarlet flowers backed by petal-like calyces of the same shade. Its rich color suits it to schemes of unashamed, even unnatural, sumptuousness – either with hot colors such as flame, orange and bronze foliage and sharply contrasting yellow-green leaves and flowers, or in slightly less punchy combinations with warm coral, peach and apricot. Such vibrant hues are suitable in more cultivated schemes, perhaps near the house. 'May Day' is best planted in loose groups, combined with less dense foliage such as that of ferns, sedges, Japanese maples and grasses, including those with a bronze flush. Although its foliage is always respectable, the spring flowers are its chief glory, and it contributes little in other seasons. Spraying with fungicide may be necessary to protect it from rhododendron powdery mildew.

**Perfect partners:** *Acer palmatum* 'Corallinum', *Calluna vulgaris* 'Red Carpet', *Dryopteris erythrosora*, *Leucothoe* Scarletta, *Photinia × fraseri* 'Red Robin', *Rhododendron* 'Fabia'

**H: 4 ft. (1.2 m) S: 5 ft. (1.5 m)**
❀ **Mid- to late spring**
▢▢▢▢▢ ◊◊-◊◊◊ ▢-▢ ■ Z7 pH4–6

Bright new shoots of *Pieris formosa* var. *forrestii* 'Wakehurst' harmonize with *Rhododendron* 'May Day', while the feathery heads of *Fothergilla major* Monticola Group provide contrast.

## *Rhododendron orbiculare* ♔

This sun-tolerant evergreen species has neat, oval leaves and flared pink flowers. It is slow-growing, ultimately becoming a large shrub, with a dense habit and formal, domed shape that make it a good choice for a specimen. If grown in this way, it benefits from sun and air on all sides to ensure even growth and a uniform covering of flowers. It can look charming surrounded by winter heaths, spring bulbs and hellebores. Its flowers harmonize well with those in carmine, cerise, crimson or white, and with purple foliage,

The sugar-pink flowers of *Rhododendron orbiculare* form a close harmony with the deeper pink blooms produced by a shorter-growing hybrid of *R. williamsianum.*

and are sufficiently strongly colored to contrast with light apple-green.

**Perfect partners:** *Bergenia* 'Sunningdale', *Erica erigena* 'Irish Dusk', *Fritillaria verticillata, Helleborus* × *hybridus, H.* × *sternii, Narcissus* 'Thalia', *Pulmonaria* Opal

**H & S: 10 ft.** (3 m) ❀ **Mid-spring**
◊◊·◊◊◊ ☐-■ ■  Z6  pH4–6

The glowing orange flowers of *Rhododendron* 'Spek's Brilliant' clash dazzlingly with the magenta-purple of the evergreen azalea *R.* 'Chanticleer' – an exhilarating effect, but one that is perhaps too stimulating for those areas of the garden intended for repose.

## *Rhododendron* 'Spek's Brilliant'

This vibrant orange deciduous azalea can bring richness to warm schemes with apricot, peach and soft yellow flowers, and bronze foliage. Pacified by such gentle colors, it is good in a woodland garden, where some shade will moderate its flowering. It can also be used for hot schemes with vermilion, scarlet, and gold flowers and bronze foliage, with yellow-green leaves and flowers and gold-variegated leaves added for contrast. Its orange flowers create an explosive combination with magenta blooms – even more daring is the mixture of orange, magenta and yellow-green. Such fiery associations require profuse flowering to look their best, and therefore demand more light than for subdued woodland schemes.

**Perfect partners:** *Acer palmatum* 'Sango-kaku', *Fritillaria imperialis* 'The Premier', *Geum* 'Werner Arends', *Trollius* × *cultorum* 'Orange Princess', *Tulipa* 'Apricot Beauty'

**H & S: 8 ft.** (2.5 m) ❀ **Late spring**
◊◊·◊◊◊ ☐-■ ■  Z7  pH4–6

## *Rhododendron pseudochrysanthum* ♔

Trusses of pale rose-pink or white flowers, lined deep pink on the outside and spotted dark pink within, adorn this sun-tolerant evergreen species. Its chief glory, however, is its handsome foliage, covered with buff down when young, and later becoming deep green. It ultimately forms a medium-sized, dense, dome-shaped bush, which is good as a specimen. Pink-flowered selections harmonize with rose-pink, white, salmon or red flowers, while the white-flowered clone allows harmonics with apricot, peach and pale yellow flowers, and with bronze foliage.

**Perfect partners:** *Acer palmatum* f. *atropurpureum, Carex brunnea, Dryopteris wallichiana, Epimedium* × *warleyense, Geum* 'Beech House Apricot', *Narcissus* 'Geranium'

**H & S: 10 ft.** (3 m) ❀ **Mid-spring**
◊◊·◊◊◊ ☐-■ ■  Z7  pH4–6

The glossy, bright green young leaves of a Japanese shield fern (*Dryopteris erythrosora*) provide an ideal contrast of form and color for *Rhododendron pseudochrysanthum.*

## *Rhus × pulvinata* Autumn Lace Group

The sumachs are most striking in autumn, when their attractively feathered, deciduous leaves assume glorious seasonal tints of rich yellow, orange and red. They are extremely handsome for the rest of the year, the large shrubs or small trees branching freely to produce a widely spaced canopy of decorative foliage. For a really incendiary effect, they can be combined with plants that turn different but complementary colors, for example 'Red Autumn Lace' ♀ with an orange or yellow maple. For maximum color, they should be grown at the back of a border, where they may be left to sucker freely. Plants sometimes appear under other guises: for example, 'Red Autumn Lace' may be sold as *Rhus glabra* 'Laciniata', which is an equally choice cultivar. These plants are related to poison ivy and their sap may cause skin irritation.

**Perfect partners:** *Acer palmatum* 'Sango-kaku', *Cortaderia selloana* 'Sunningdale Silver', *Helianthus* 'Monarch', *Rudbeckia fulgida* var. *sullivantii* 'Goldsturm'

H: 10 ft. (3 m)  S: 16 ft. (5 m)  ❀ Midsummer
○○  Z3  pH5–7.5

The distinctive foliage of *Rhus × pulvinata* Autumn Lace Group provides a backcloth for *Geranium* 'Ann Folkard', *Salvia officinalis* 'Purpurascens' and *Artemisia abrotanum*.

## *Ribes sanguineum*
### FLOWERING CURRANT

This easy, fast-growing deciduous shrub has slightly drooping racemes of flowers, in shades from white to pink and red, which appear with the first tiny leaves. From late spring onward, it will blend satisfactorily into a general planting scheme for the rest of the season, and it may be used to support a honeysuckle or summer-flowering clematis. The species itself can be indifferent, and the best display will be given by a superior cultivar such as 'Pulborough Scarlet' ♀ or 'King Edward VII', planted in full sun with other spring-flowering shrubs and bulbs.

**Perfect partners:** *Forsythia × intermedia* 'Lynwood', *Helleborus foetidus*, *Muscari latifolium*, *Narcissus* 'Ice Follies', *Spiraea* 'Arguta', *Tulipa* 'Golden Oxford'

H & S: 6½ ft. (2 m)  ❀ Mid- to late spring
○○  Z6  pH5–7.5

A mature flowering currant (*Ribes sanguineum*) is large enough to support an Alpina clematis such as *C.* 'White Swan', creating a charming contrast of floral form. Mid- to deep pink cultivars of the currant, or white with a blue or ruby clematis, are perhaps more effective than paler pink ones, emphasizing the different flower shapes.

## *Ribes sanguineum* 'Brocklebankii'

One of the best flowering currants for a long season of color, this compact, relatively slow-growing, deciduous shrub bears bright yellow-green foliage, which is particularly striking in late spring and summer. The contrast with its pink flowers is not to everyone's taste, but growing the shrub in shade will partially suppress flowering and emphasize the yellow foliage, which can in any case scorch in bright sun. It associates well with plants that have purple foliage or purple, blue, yellow or white flowers such as anchusas, bugles or ceanothus. It is smaller than other flowering currants, but it develops a similar shape and requires occasional hard pruning, removing the oldest wood to maintain a high proportion of vigorous young stems.

**Perfect partners:** *Anchusa azurea* 'Loddon Royalist', *Berberis thunbergii* 'Rose Glow', *Camassia leichtlinii* 'Semiplena', *Ceanothus* 'Cascade', *Cotinus coggygria* 'Royal Purple', *Narcissus* 'Irene Copeland', *Tulipa* 'Burgundy'

H & S: 4 ft. (1.2 m)  ❀ Mid- to late spring
○○  Z6  pH5–7.5

The gold leaves of the flowering currant *Ribes sanguineum* 'Brocklebankii' contrast with the lavender-blue flowers and purple calyces of *Ajuga* 'Tottenham'. Using a darker-leaved bugle such as *A. reptans* 'Atropurpurea' would give a more striking foliage contrast after flowering has finished.

## *Robinia pseudoacacia* 'Frisia' ♛

There are several attractive selections of the false acacia (*Robinia pseudoacacia*), a large, rugged tree that suckers freely. Probably the most valuable of these for general garden use is 'Frisia', a much smaller and more versatile deciduous tree with rich yellow-green foliage turning golden yellow in autumn. It has an informal, irregularly branching shape. This dominating tree needs plenty of space to show itself to best effect, and is often planted as a bold punctuation mark in a large border, standing slightly forward of other plants of similar height. Contrasting shrubs with green or purple foliage may be planted beneath, or a summer-flowering rose can be grown through the branches. White, cream or apple-green flowers, together with a late-flowering white clematis or a cream or white Rambler rose, would make perfect partners. Young plants should be staked, the brittle stems sheltered from strong winds, and suckers removed at once. In restricted spaces, *Gleditsia triacanthos* or honey locust will provide a similar effect, especially the golden-leaved 'Sunburst' ♛, which withstands hard pruning.

**Perfect partners:** *Allium hollandicum* p.349 **A**, *Anchusa azurea* 'Loddon Royalist', *Geranium* 'Johnson's Blue', *Rosa* 'Sander's White Rambler', *Sedum telephium* p.334 **A**

**H: 50 ft. (15 m)  S: 26 ft. (8 m)**
❁ **Early to midsummer**
⬛⬜ ⬡ ⬜ **Z4  pH5.5–7.5**

*Robinia pseudoacacia* 'Frisia' can be used to support a contrasting clematis, in this case *C.* 'Etoile Violette', one of the earlier flowering Viticella Group cultivars.

# *Rosmarinus officinalis*
COMMON ROSEMARY

This is an aromatic evergreen shrub that flowers from mid-spring to early summer, continuing in some varieties until late autumn. While most have blue flowers, several sorts are mauve-pink. Rosemary is slightly tender, and proves hardiest in sunny sites in relatively poor, sharply drained soil. Here, whether in a border or in a pot, it can be combined with other Mediterranean shrubs including lavenders, cistus and phlomis, and makes a wonderful addition to a sitting area, where its fragrance can be fully appreciated.

One of the best rich blue kinds is 'Miss Jessopp's Upright' ♀, a relatively hardy, columnar shrub that can grow exceptionally tall if sheltered on a warm wall. Its brittle main branches tend to twist and bend under the weight of foliage, so that it ages to a broad bush; occasional pruning immediately after flowering helps maintain a balanced shape. The rather more tender *R.o.* var. *angustissimus* 'Benenden Blue' ♀ is also rich blue, and similar in habit, with narrow leaves. The upright 'Sissinghurst Blue' ♀ is fairly hardy, whereas the long-flowering 'Severn Sea' ♀ can be rather tender. Prostratus Group is tender but useful for sprawling on a sunny bank or tumbling over a dwarf wall. Gold-variegated 'Aureus' has intricately yellow-banded foliage and suits combinations with other gold-leaved plants, while Silver Spires ('Wolros') recreates the silver-variegated "striped rosemary" popular in the 17th century.

With its long tradition of cultivation, rosemary is an especially appropriate plant for old-fashioned gardens, and hardier kinds can be used for short hedges or knots if clipped once a year after flowering. All blue cultivars make good harmonies with blues, mauves and pinks, and contrast with soft yellow or yellow-green. Sages, teucriums, catmints and Bearded irises are excellent partners.

**Perfect partners: Prostrate:** *Cytisus* × *kewensis*, *Helianthemum lunulatum*, *Iris* 'Curlew', *Nepeta* × *faassenii*
**Upright:** *Genista hispanica*, × *Halimiocistus wintonensis* 'Merrist Wood Cream', *Lavandula stoechas* subsp. *pedunculata* 'James Compton', *Santolina chamaecyparissus* p.140 **A**, *Stipa tenuissima* p.337 **B**

**H:** 6 in.–6½ ft. (15 cm–2 m) **S: 4–6 ft.** (1.2–1.8 m)
❀ Mid-spring to early summer
 ◊◊ ▣-■ Z8 pH5.5–7.5

**Above:** Pink-flowered rosemaries such as *Rosmarinus officinalis* 'Roseus' combine well with other cool-colored flowers and with silver, purple or red foliage – as here with purple sage (*Salvia officinalis* 'Purpurascens'). 'Roseus' is fairly upright in habit, with mauve-pink flowers and short greyish leaves. 'Majorca Pink', another mauve-pink sort, starts upright, sprawling outward with age.

**Top:** Sprawling rosemaries – here *Rosmarinus officinalis* 'McConnell's Blue' with the perennial candytuft *Iberis sempervirens* 'Schneeflocke' – tend to be rather less hardy than more upright sorts but are immensely useful plants for clothing a bank or tumbling over a dwarf wall. They can also be attractive grown in a large pot or container.

**Above:** Blue-flowered rosemaries combine especially well with silver or glaucous leaves and with white or cream flowers, and can contrast with yellow-green, for instance euphorbias – as in this combination of *Rosmarinus officinalis* 'Sissinghurst Blue' with purple wood spurge (*Euphorbia amygdaloides* 'Purpurea'). Only the most floriferous or richest blue sorts contrast well with yellow.

*Rubus cockburnianus* 'Goldenvale' is combined here with lady's mantle (*Alchemilla mollis*) – the leaves of the two plants contrast markedly in shape, while the flowers of the alchemilla harmonize with the rubus foliage. Both are deciduous, allowing underplanting with early bulbs.

## *Rubus cockburnianus* 'Goldenvale' ♥

The yellow-green fernlike foliage of this deciduous shrub (syn. 'Wyego') is brightest in a sunny site. Its arching white stems make a dramatic winter tracery, particularly if set against a dark evergreen background. Its impact is greatest in borders if the bare stems are not hemmed in by other shrubs, but it can be underplanted with evergreen ground-cover or spring bulbs such as snowdrops. In winter it is particularly effective with winter heaths, prostrate dwarf conifers and *Cyclamen coum*, and makes a stark contrast with red or orange dogwoods. From late spring it combines well with blue-flowered plants like aconites, and with glaucous foliage such as that of hostas.

**Perfect partners:** *Ajuga reptans* 'Catlin's Giant', *Bergenia cordifolia* 'Purpurea', *Elaeagnus × ebbingei* 'Gilt Edge' p.94 **A**, *Erica carnea* 'Vivellii', *Galanthus nivalis*, *Gentiana asclepiadea* p.271 **C**, *Hosta sieboldiana* var. *elegans*, *Muscari latifolium*, *Ranunculus ficaria* 'Brazen Hussy', *Viburnum tinus* 'Eve Price'

**H: 6 ft. (1.8 m) S: 4 ft. (1.2 m) ❀ Midsummer**
◊-◊◊ ■-■ Z6 pH5–7.5

The yellow-green flowers of *Ruta graveolens* 'Jackman's Blue' perfectly match the foliage of *Choisya ternata* Sundance, while the rue's foliage provides a gentle and pleasing contrast. To produce so much bloom, the rue should receive only the minimum of pruning. Larger cream flowers would be effective for leavening the scheme, while strong blue could be used for contrast.

## *Ruta graveolens* 'Jackman's Blue'

This is a superlative, compact evergreen rue that enjoys a sunny position on well-drained soil. It may be sited toward the front of a border or in a gravel garden, and mixes well with Mediterranean plants such as sages. Its blue-green foliage makes a good contrast with its yellow-green flowers, which help it to relate to other plants with yellow-green foliage or flowers, such as alchemillas and golden marjorams, and to those in white, yellow or blue. Annual pruning in mid-spring can maintain shapeliness; alternatively, selective pruning after flowering can prevent plants from developing gaps. 'Variegata', with foliage heavily splashed with white, has a more open habit.

**Perfect partners:** *Ajuga reptans* 'Atropurpurea', *Cistus × cyprius*, *Euphorbia myrsinites*, *Halimium ocymoides*, *Iris* 'Joyce' p.369 **C**, *Nepeta* 'Six Hills Giant', *Rosmarinus officinalis* Prostratus Group, *Salvia officinalis* 'Icterina', *Symphytum × uplandicum* 'Variegatum'

**H & S: 24 in. (60 cm) ❀ Midsummer**
◊-◊◊ ■-■ Z5 pH5–7.5

## *Rubus thibetanus* ♥

An erect deciduous shrub with white winter stems and greyish pinnate leaves, this bramble is used and pruned for winter color in the same way as *R. cockburnianus* 'Goldenvale' (above), removing second-year stems to leave only the newest, brightest shoots. The effect of its foliage is less obviously showy, and plants are better suited to more subdued schemes and styles of planting. It succeeds in the same winter combinations as 'Goldenvale', but for summer use it is best associated with white or pale or rich blue flowers and dark green foliage. From a distance its foliage is somewhat amorphous, but at close range is quietly pretty, especially if draped with an annual or perennial white-flowered climber.

**Perfect partners:** *Clematis heracleifolia*, *Cornus alba* 'Sibirica', *C. sanguinea* 'Midwinter Fire', *Crocus tommasinianus*, *Eranthis hyemalis*, *Helleborus atrorubens*, *Juniperus horizontalis* 'Bar Harbor', *Lathyrus latifolius* 'White Pearl', *Lobelia siphilitica*, *Narcissus* 'Actaea'

**H & S: 8 ft. (2.5 m) ❀ Mid- to late summer**
◊-◊◊ ■-■ Z6 pH5–7.5

Striking white stems of *Rubus thibetanus* harmonize with the pale-spotted leaves and white flowers of *Pulmonaria* 'Sissinghurst White'. The combination depends on the stems of the rubus not being pruned away until they start to be hidden by its leaves (usually in mid- to late spring). Later-flowering bulbs can be planted through the pulmonaria to add height while the rubus is laid low.

## *Salix alba* subsp. *vitellina* ♛
GOLDEN WILLOW

Boggy situations and moist soils suit this medium to large deciduous tree, noted for its feathery, fairly pale green foliage and orange-yellow stems. It is usually stooled or regularly pruned to encourage the production of bright new shoots. As a waterside or winter garden plant, it mixes well with dogwoods and other bright-stemmed deciduous shrubs to make a harmonious display of warm colors, and may be underplanted with ground-cover plants such as ivies. Good companions include evergreen *Euonymus fortunei* cultivars, bergenias, winter heaths, heucheras, forsythias and early-flowering bulbs such as narcissi, scillas, snowdrops and winter aconites. 'Britzensis' ♛ is a rich red clone, often sold as 'Chermesina' (a different plant with bright red winter stems).

**Perfect partners:** *Bergenia cordifolia* 'Purpurea', *Cornus stolonifera* 'Flaviramea', *Erica carnea* 'Springwood White', *Hedera colchica* 'Dentata Variegata', *Narcissus* 'February Silver', *Viburnum tinus* 'Eve Price'

H & S: 80 ft. (25 m) ( ❀ **Mid-spring**)
◊◊-◊◊◊ ☐-■ **Z2 pH5.5–7.5**

Stooled plants of *Salix alba* var. *vitellina* 'Britzensis' glow in the low light of the winter sun, their rich red stems, golden yellow at the base, showing up most effectively against the shady side of a cypress. Winter-flowering heaths make an ideal carpet: here *Erica × darleyensis* 'Darley Dale' is used; a white cultivar would be an attractive alternative.

A Spanish clone of the hybrid crack willow *Salix × rubens*, stooled to produce bright winter stems, is here underplanted with the lungwort *Pulmonaria angustifolia* subsp. *azurea* and crocuses. Relatively late pruning makes the most of the combination with the lungwort.

## *Salix × rubens*
HYBRID CRACK WILLOW

This cross between the white willow (*Salix alba*) and the crack willow (*S. fragilis*) occurs naturally wherever the two parents are found together. The best selections belong to *S. × r.* var. *basfordiana*, which has more brightly colored winter twigs, most commonly a glowing yellowish orange; nurseries often offer a female clone with showy, bright red catkins in early spring. The rather slower-growing var. *rubens* has reddish winter twigs.

All variants of *S. × rubens* are suited to the same combinations as *S. alba* var. *vitellina* (above), including evergreen ground-cover plants and early-flowering spring bulbs. They are easily propagated from hardwood cuttings.

**Perfect partners:** *Chionodoxa forbesii*, *Erica × darleyensis* 'Silberschmelze', *Galanthus elwesii* var. *monostictus*, *Helleborus foetidus* Wester Flisk Group, *Rubus thibetanus*

H & S: 80 ft. (25 m) ( ❀ **Mid-spring**)
◊◊-◊◊◊ | ☐-■ **Z5 pH5.5–7.5**

## *Salvia officinalis* 'Purpurascens' ♛
PURPLE SAGE

The common sage (*Salvia officinalis*) is a more or less evergreen sub-shrub for well-drained sunny spots at the front of a border and in gravel or herb gardens, where it forms attractive grayish green mounds that associate well with other Mediterranean plants such as lavenders, cotton lavender, cistus, phlomis and rosemaries. Purple sage is a spreading selection, its leaves lightly flushed with purple and combining happily with other purple-leaved plants, as well as with silver foliage and cool-colored flowers. Its lavender-blue florets, enhanced by reddish purple calyces, look particularly showy with harmonious cool colors, or with a contrasting color such as the pale sulfur-yellow of achilleas or the acid yellow-green of euphorbias.

**Perfect partners:** *Buddleja alternifolia* p.81 **B**, *Geranium × riversleaianum* cultivars, *Hebe ochracea* p.104 **A**, *Limnanthes douglasii* p.432 **C**, *Rhus × pulvinata* Autumn Lace Group p.134 **A**, *Rosmarinus officinalis* 'Roseus' p.136 **B**

H: 31 in. (80 cm) S: 40 in. (1 m)
❀ **Early to midsummer**
◊-◊◊ ☐-■ **Z6 pH5.5–7**

Purple sage (*Salvia officinalis* 'Purpurascens') makes an attractive contrast with variegated periwinkle (*Vinca major* 'Variegata'). Planted close to the sage, the periwinkle's slender stems push through its neighbor, the creamy margins to the leaves emphasizing their simple shape.

## Sambucus nigra
COMMON ELDER

This large deciduous shrub with pinnate leaves bears creamy white flowers in broad, flat heads, followed by nodding bunches of purple-black fruits. Although suitable for a wild garden, where its fruits benefit birds and other wildlife, it is a little coarse for general garden use, except as part of an informal hedge, perhaps mixed with other wildlife hedging species, such as beech, blackthorn or wild roses, and embellished with climbing plants such as honeysuckles. A number of attractive and more refined cultivars have been developed, most notably 'Guincho Purple', which has purple-flushed leaves, darker when grown in sun, and pink flowers. A newer cultivar, also purple-leaved but with deeper foliage and richer pink flowers, is 'Gerda' ♀ ('Black Beauty'), a spreading bush that is useful where more somber foliage or brighter pink flowers are needed. Both can be planted in a mixed border or in a woodland garden, and as regularly coppiced shrubs in larger herb gardens, where the simple species was traditionally grown for its many culinary and medicinal uses. Both dark-leaved cultivars combine well with Japanese maples, species roses, foxgloves and other dark-leaved shrubs like purple berberis or sloe, and can be used to contrast with silver or yellow-green foliage, or to harmonize with flowers in white or pink; the slightly peachy tint in 'Guincho Purple' makes it less satisfactory when used with cool colors such as mauve, purple or blue. For the most spectacular display of foliage, they are best coppiced annually to a framework of branches, or stooled if a lower bush is required. This technique does, however, sacrifice the flowers; if both flowers and bold, well-colored foliage are required, stems can be removed on a two- or three-year cycle – the flowers are borne on two-year-old stems.

Other pleasing cultivars include 'Aurea' ♀, with yellowish green leaves (brightest in sun) that look attractive with blue flowers such as delphiniums, and also with hot colors or contrasted with purple foliage. *S.n.* f. *laciniata* ♀ has narrow leaflets, darker than those of the typical species and very deeply divided if grown in shade, although plants flower more profusely in sun. While variants with purple-flushed or yellow-green leaves generally color better in sun, one of the most valuable features of common elder is its tolerance of dry shade, where some of the variegated cultivars excel:

'Marginata', with white-edged leaves, is outstanding, while white-speckled 'Pulverulenta' works well in shade where a lighter tone of green is needed.

**Perfect partners:** *Acer shirasawanum* 'Aureum', *Ammi majus*, *Berberis* × *ottawensis* f. *purpurea* 'Superba', *Lonicera nitida* 'Baggesen's Gold', *Prunus spinosa* 'Purpurea'

**H & S: 20 ft. (6 m)** ❀ **Early summer**
◊◊ ▢-▩ ▮ Z5 pH4.5–7.5

**Right:** The cut-leaved elder (*Sambucus nigra* f. *laciniata*) has leaflets larger than but otherwise similar to those of this Japanese maple (*Acer palmatum* Dissectum Viride Group), making a perfect harmony but with the bonus of plentiful, flat, creamy white flowerheads borne on a taller bush.

**Below:** Horizontal flowerheads of *Sambucus nigra* 'Guincho Purple' match exactly the color of upright foxgloves *Digitalis purpurea* 'Sutton's Apricot', leavened by white *D.p.* f. *albiflora*. The elder's dark foliage adds sumptuous depth.

## *Santolina chamaecyparissus* ♻

LAVENDER COTTON

An evergreen sub-shrub with intensely silvery foliage, this is a Mediterranean plant that revels in poor and sharply draining soils, whether at the front of a border or gravel garden, clipped in pots, or massed as a filler for parterres. As a foliage plant it blends well with cool colors such as mauves, blues and pinks, and mixes with other silver-leaved or glaucous foliage plants and those with contrasting leaf form such as fescues or phlomis. It is a natural companion for other Mediterranean plants like lavenders, catmints, cistus and helianthemums, and also looks agreeable in front of old-fashioned roses, perhaps partnered by dianthus or euphorbias. Its blooms can limit successful combinations, but it remains effective with blue flowers and glaucous leaves such as those of *Cerinthe* species. *S.c.* 'Lemon Queen' is a cultivar with paler flowers, while 'Lambrook Silver' has particularly silver foliage; var. *nana* ♻ is a compact variety suitable for smaller gardens.

**Perfect partners:** *Cerinthe major* 'Purpurascens', *Cistus* 'Silver Pink', *Dianthus* 'Haytor White', *Euphorbia myrsinites*, *Festuca glauca* 'Blaufuchs', *Helianthemum* 'Rhodanthe Carneum', *Nepeta* × *faassenii*, *Phlomis fruticosa*

**H:** 20 in. (50 cm)  **S:** 36 in. (90 cm)  ✿ **Midsummer**
◐-◐◐ ☐-■ Z7 pH6–7.5

In this Mediterranean planting, santolinas occupy the foreground, contrasting silver *S. chamaecyparissus* with deep green *S. rosmarinifolia*. A pale lavender and an upright rosemary fill the border against the wall. The attractive billowing masses of santolina will need occasional pruning to prevent them becoming gappy.

The neat foliage and pretty flowerheads of *Skimmia japonica* 'Rubella', effective at the front of a border, especially when viewed at close range, are here augmented by the marbled foliage of *Arum italicum* 'Marmoratum'.

## *Sorbus* 'Joseph Rock'

This small deciduous tree stars in autumn when its bunches of small spherical fruits mature from green through white to soft amber-yellow, against a canopy of brilliant crimson, purple and scarlet foliage. It goes well in a large mixed border or a shrubbery, and as a specimen tree to interact with other plants with bright autumn fruits or foliage. Good companion trees include linderas, maples, deciduous hollies, liquidambars, some crab apples, hawthorns and other sorbus, particularly those with soft-colored fruits such as some of the Lombarts hybrids. Among the most suitable shrubs are deciduous berberis and euonymus, sumachs, deciduous azaleas and vacciniums, roses and stephanandras. Larger specimens can be lightly swagged with a vine or parthenocissus.

**Perfect partners:** *Amelanchier lamarckii*, *Cladrastis kentukea*, *Euonymus alatus* var. *apterus*, *Hamamelis* × *intermedia* 'Arnold Promise', *Lindera benzoin*, *Rhododendron luteum*

**H:** 33 ft. (10 m)  **S:** 23 ft. (7 m)  ✿ **Late spring**
◐◐ ☐-■ Z4 pH5–7.5

## *Skimmia japonica* 'Rubella' ♻

This neat, non-fruiting skimmia has rounded heads of rich red buds that color in early winter and remain attractive until spring, when they open to white-petaled flowers borne above reddish stalks. A useful pollinator for fruiting cultivars of skimmia, it is suitable for loose groups in mixed or shrub borders in partial or full shade. It is also a fine specimen plant for large containers, with other evergreens such as ivies and (in milder areas) winter cherries, cinerarias, smaller *Cyclamen persicum* cultivars and variegated hebes. Good companions are other winter- or spring-flowering plants like abeliophyllums, cyclamens, viburnums, snowdrops, evergreens such as heucheras, asarums, hollies and *Euonymus fortunei* and *E. japonicus* cultivars, and contrasting foliage such as of bamboo.

**Perfect partners:** *Bergenia cordifolia* 'Purpurea', *Cyclamen coum*, *Erysimum* 'Bowles Mauve' p.96 **A**, *Hebe* × *franciscana* 'Variegata', *Hedera algeriensis* 'Gloire de Marengo'

**H & S:** 4 ft. (1.2 m)  ✿ **Mid- to late spring**
◐◐ ☐-■ Z7 pH5–7

The rich autumn coloring of *Sorbus* 'Joseph Rock' lends itself to combinations with other large shrubs and small trees with contrasting leaf form, especially if these have foliage color matching the fruits of the sorbus.

A

The grayish leaves and pink fruits of *Sorbus vilmorinii* make it especially suitable for combinations with other large shrubs or small trees that have crimson autumn color and/or white or crimson fruits.

## Sorbus vilmorinii ♀

This deciduous sorbus is a large shrub or small tree with leaves composed of pretty, tiny leaflets that assume autumn tints of orange, scarlet, crimson and deep purple; its deep pink fruits mature to almost pure white, with occasional crimson flecks. It suits a mixed border, shrubbery or woodland garden. It can be used with the same sort of plants as *S.* 'Joseph Rock' (facing page), and may also be surrounded by shorter evergreens such as small hollies, junipers and fruiting skimmias and berberis, or planted in grass with white autumn crocuses and colchicums. In a mixed border it combines well with larger, looser autumn daisies such as *Leucanthemella serotina* and Korean and Rubellum chrysanthemums and with grasses such as miscanthus.

**Perfect partners:** *Berberis* × *carminea* 'Pirate King', *Colchicum speciosum* 'Album', *Helianthus* 'Monarch', *Ilex aquifolium* 'J.C. van Tol', *Juniperus squamata* 'Meyeri'

**H & S: 16 ft. (5 m)** ❄ **Late spring to early summer**
◊◊ ▢-▢ **Z6 pH5–7.5**

## Spartium junceum ♀
SPANISH BROOM

Long flowering and tolerance of poor, dry soils distinguish this shrub, which has erect, cylindrical green stems and vestigial leaves. It bears its golden yellow flowers most profusely in early to midsummer, when it combines successfully with other Mediterranean shrubs such as white cistus, coluteas, brooms, halimiocistus, halimiums, phlomis, genistas and olearias. It works well with yellow-green foliage and flowers, and with blue flowers or glaucous foliage. Its slim stems harmonize with those of larger early-flowering grasses (stipas, for example), and also look good in seaside settings with New Zealand plants such as ozothamnus, or with large whipcord hebes.

**Perfect partners:** *Cistus* × *cyprius, Colutea arborescens, Cytisus multiflorus, Genista hispanica,* × *Halimiocistus wintonensis* 'Merrist Wood Cream', *Hebe cupressoides, Olearia* × *haastii, Ozothamnus ledifolius*

**H & S: 10 ft. (3 m)**
❄ **Early summer to early autumn**
◊-◊◊ ▢-▢ **Z8 pH5.5–7.5**

B

In this relatively narrow border planned to provide color throughout summer and autumn, Spanish broom (*Spartium junceum*) is one of the longest-flowering and most reliable performers. It is overtopped by toetoe grass (*Cortaderia richardii*), and accompanied by yellow *Calceolaria angustifolia* and paler yellow *Achillea* 'Moonshine', together with the dark-leaved orange *Dahlia* 'David Howard'.

C

## Spiraea japonica

With hard pruning in early spring, this deciduous spiraea blooms freely through the summer. Cultivars vary in flower color from white or pink to crimson, and a few have foliage emerging golden yellow flushed with orange and red. All are good near the front of a mixed or shrub border. Those with green leaves and pink flowers ('Bumalda' or dwarf 'Nana' ♀, for example) are effective with cool flowers and purple, glaucous, silver or white-variegated foliage. Golden-leaved 'Goldflame' and 'Gold Mound' are invaluable for spring.

A bright-leaved cultivar of *Spiraea japonica*, its form contrasting with a neat globe of *Lonicera nitida* 'Baggesen's Gold', makes an attractive combination with the lilac pompons of *Allium cristophii*, lavender cranesbills (*Geranium* 'Johnson's Blue' and *G.* × *magnificum*) and a short blue *Anchusa azurea* cultivar. The white in the leaves of *Astrantia major* 'Sunningdale Variegated' leavens the planting.

**Perfect partners:** Green-leaved: *Berberis thunbergii* f. *atropurpurea, Caryopteris* × *clandonensis, Ceratostigma plumbaginoides, Coronilla valentina* subsp. *glauca* 'Variegata' Golden-leaved: *Dicentra eximia* p.259 **B**, *Polemonium caeruleum* p.323 **B**, *Tulipa* 'Jewel of Spring' p.397 **A**

**H: 12–60 in. (30–150 cm) S: 20–60 in. (50–150 cm)**
❄ **Mid- to late summer**
◊◊ ▢-▢ **Z4 pH5.5–7.5**

## *Spiraea nipponica* 'Snowmound' ♀

Sometimes wrongly called *S. nipponica* var. *tosaensis*, this vigorous deciduous shrub makes a moundlike bush with arching branches, very pretty in early summer when smothered with white flowers. It mixes well with other early summer flowering shrubs, including Shrub roses, weigelas, hebes and *Potentilla fruticosa* cultivars, and can be draped with annual or herbaceous climbers, such as perennial peas. Although perhaps a little stark to contrast with hot shades, its color will combine successfully with most others, especially blue flowers and silver or glaucous foliage. Good herbaceous companions include cranesbills, campanulas, later-flowering Tall Bearded irises, achilleas, paler daylilies and most summer-flowering bulbs, particularly lilies. 'Halward's Silver' is more compact and erect, about 3¼ ft. (1 m) high and wide.

**Perfect partners:** *Berberis thunbergii* 'Aurea', *Geranium* 'Mavis Simpson', *Iris* 'Cambridge', *Lathyrus latifolius* 'Rosa Perle', *Lilium pyrenaicum* var. *pyrenaicum*, *Potentilla fruticosa* 'Beesii'

**H & S: 4 ft.** (1.2 m) ✽ **Early summer**
▬▬ ◖◗ ◻-◼ **Z5 pH5.5–7.5**

Grown in a narrow border and crowded with bloom from top to toe, the arching stems of *Spiraea nipponica* 'Snowmound' contrast with billowing masses of *Ceanothus* 'Puget Blue'. The yellow-green foliage beyond contrasts equally effectively with the ceanothus. Given a wider border, adding a shorter, yellow-flowered shrub or another with yellow-green leaves would unify the scheme.

The informal habit of a *Syringa vulgaris* cultivar, massed with conical panicles of bloom, contrasts with neat columns of dark Irish yew (*Taxus baccata* 'Fastigiata'), which effectively counteract the lilac's amorphousness.

## *Syringa vulgaris*
COMMON LILAC

Cultivars of this large deciduous shrub are essential plants for late spring display in a shrub or mixed border, their panicles of fragrant flowers in white, creamy yellow, pink, lavender-blue or plum-purple combining well with ceanothus and the more sun-tolerant rhododendrons. Larger specimens can be lightly draped with white or pink *Clematis montana* cultivars. White or pale yellow lilacs contrast with colors closest to blue, and go well with Banksian roses, brooms, genistas and berberis, yellow-green foliage and flowers, purple foliage and white flowers such as exochordas. They also associate well with small flowering trees such as Japanese cherries, magnolias, osmanthus, daphnes, dipeltas, early species roses, cercis and hawthorns. Gently colored cultivars look charming underplanted with cow parsley, bluebells and pheasant's-eye narcissi.

**Perfect partners:** *Anthriscus sylvestris*, *Ceanothus* 'Cascade', *Clematis montana* var. *rubens* p.162 **C**, *Exochorda* × *macrantha* 'The Bride', *Hyacinthoides non-scripta*, *Laburnum* × *watereri* 'Vossii', *Rosa banksiae* 'Lutea'

**H: 6½–23 ft.** (2–7 m) **S: 5–16 ft.** (1.5–5 m)
✽ **Late spring to early summer**
 ◖◗ ◻-◼ ◼ **Z2 pH5–8**

## *Syringa vulgaris* 'Charles Joly' ♀

With double, rich plum-purple flowers, this large deciduous common lilac suits sumptuous late spring color schemes. It blends well with purple foliage, such as that of purple plums or berberis, although dark combinations may not show up well from a distance unless lifted by pink or mauve flowers. Effective partners are euphorbias, shrubs with yellow-green leaves such as philadelphus, and later-flowering, paler lilacs. It contrasts well with soft yellow – *Rosa xanthina* variants, for example – and with yellow-green foliage and flowers, and may be underplanted with late-flowering tulips, pink umbellifers and early cranesbills.

**Perfect partners:** *Euphorbia characias* subsp. *wulfenii* 'Lambrook Gold', *Physocarpus opulifolius* 'Dart's Gold', *Prunus cerasifera* 'Pissardii', *Rosa* × *fortuneana* p.189 **C**

**H:** 10 ft. (3 m)  **S:** 6½ ft. (2 m)
✿ **Late spring to early summer**
◊◊ ▢-▥ ■ Z4 pH5–8

A

Rich, reddish purple *Syringa vulgaris* 'Charles Joly' is here woven through with Chinese wisteria (*Wisteria. sinensis*). It is hard to prune the wisteria in such situations, so it needs warm or hot summers if it is to flower reliably.

## *Taxus baccata* ♀
COMMON YEW

This evergreen conifer is suited to clipping for hedges and topiary, and to planting beneath other trees and shrubs in a woodland garden, where it tolerates dry, dense shade. With its dark green feathery foliage it is excellent as a foil for other plants at the back of a border or as an architectural specimen. 'Fastigiata' ♀ makes a fine specimen tree, as does the golden 'Fastigiata Aureomarginata' ♀. 'Dovastoniana' ♀ and the gold-variegated 'Dovastonii Aurea' ♀ are large, spreading shrubs with curtains of branchlets, while 'Repandens' ♀ and gold-edged 'Repens Aurea' ♀ are spreading, groundcover shrubs. 'Semperaurea' ♀ is a slow-growing bush with ascending branches. All golden variants contrast well with blue flowers or glaucous foliage, and harmonize with hot colors.

**Perfect partners:** *Amelanchier lamarckii*, *Chamaecyparis lawsoniana* 'Pembury Blue', *Ilex* × *altaclerensis* 'Golden King', *Kniphofia* 'David' p.302 **C**, *Picea pungens* 'Koster', *Syringa vulgaris* p.142 **B**, *Tropaeolum speciosum* p.178 **B**

**H:** 3¼–40 ft. (1–12 m)  **S:** 3¼–33 ft. (1–10 m)
✿ **(Early to mid-spring)**
◊◊ ▢-▥ Z5 pH5–8

In late spring, the new shoots of the low, spreading yew *Taxus baccata* 'Summergold' emerge sulfur-yellow, making a striking contrast with the reddish purple young leaves of a purple smoke bush (*Cotinus coggygria* 'Royal Purple').

C

B

## *Tamarix tetrandra* ♀

Like other tamarisks, this arching deciduous shrub is suited to well-drained soils, maritime sites and gravel gardens. Although slightly ungainly, at flowering time the whole plant is wreathed in blooms. These open rose-pink and age to a brickish color, blending agreeably with plum-purple and partnering other rose-pink or red flowers such as pink umbellifers, astrantias, *Smyrnium perfoliatum*, late tulips and pheasant's-eye narcissi. It is very effective with white flowers and purple or copper foliage, such as that of berberis.

A cloud of sugar-pink *Tamarix tetrandra* is here backed by the short-panicled *Laburnum alpinum*. Pink and yellow can be difficult to combine successfully, but the softness of the tamarisk's color makes this combination a happy one. A laburnum with longer panicles, such as *L. anagyroides* or *L.* × *watereri* 'Vossii', could be used for more flamboyance.

**Perfect partners:** *Anthriscus sylvestris* 'Ravenswing', *Chaerophyllum hirsutum* 'Roseum', *Cistus* × *hybridus*, *Cytisus* × *praecox* 'Allgold', *Hippophae rhamnoides*, *Narcissus poeticus* var. *recurvus*, *Tulipa* 'Queen of Night'

**H & S:** 10 ft. (3 m)  ✿ **Late spring**
◊-◊◊ ▢-▥ Z6 pH5.5–7.5

## *Ulmus minor* 'Dicksonii'

DICKSON'S GOLDEN ELM

This slow-growing deciduous tree seldom reaches sufficient size to be susceptible to Dutch elm disease. It is suitable for growing in a large border or shrubbery. Its bright yellow-green foliage is particularly effective in plantings designed around hot color schemes of yellow, orange or scarlet, and can also be used as a striking contrast for blue flowers or purple foliage. Good companions include plants with silvery foliage, such as willows, and larger herbaceous plants like helianthus or delphiniums; it may also be draped with a clematis such as a Viticella cultivar in dusky red-purple or purplish blue.

**Perfect partners:** *Clematis viticella* 'Mary Rose', *Delphinium* 'Alice Artindale', *Helianthus decapetalus* 'Soleil d'Or', *Pyrus salicifolia* 'Pendula', *Rosa* 'Frensham'

**H: 33 ft. (10 m)   S: 20 ft. (6 m)**
**(❀ Early to mid-spring)**
◊-◊◊  ▣-■  Z4  pH5–8

Adding dramatic height to a deep border, *Ulmus minor* 'Dicksonii' is contrasted with silver willow (*Salix alba* var. *sericea*), pollarded annually to prevent it becoming too large; lavender *Hebe* 'Jewel' furnishes the front. A lavender-blue Viticella clematis could also be included to drape the willow and elm, further unifying the design.

## *Viburnum* × *bodnantense*

This large deciduous shrub has very fragrant blooms in white or pink. Three cultivars are often grown: 'Charles Lamont' ♀, with flowers in pure pink; 'Dawn' ♀, also pink; and 'Deben' ♀, with white flowers opening from pink buds. All are best sited close to an entrance or path. They associate well with other winter-flowering plants such as *Prunus* × *subhirtella* cultivars, *Prunus pendula* cultivars, *Viburnum tinus*, *V. grandiflorum*, winter heaths, early-flowering camellias and sarcococcas, and with handsome evergreens like *Euonymus japonicus* cultivars, white-variegated hollies, fatsias and garryas. Other good partners include *Daphne mezereum* and *D. odora* cultivars, winter-flowering honeysuckles and ground-covering ivies and bergenias. Thinning the branches

*Viburnum* × *bodnantense* 'Dawn' starts flowering in autumn, allowing it to be combined with berrying shrubs such as cotoneasters. Crab apples, euonymus, gaultherias, hollies, pyracanthas, roses, sorbus and snowberries would also make pleasing companions.

helps prevent congestion, and the occasional removal of older branches encourages the growth of vigorous young flowering wood.

**Perfect partners:** *Camellia* 'Cornish Snow', *Erica carnea* 'Springwood White', *Hamamelis* × *intermedia* 'Moonlight', *Ilex aquifolium* 'Silver Queen', *Lonicera fragrantissima*, *Rhododendron mucronulatum*, *Sarcococca confusa*

**H: 10 ft. (3 m)   S: 6½ ft. (2 m)**
❀ Late autumn to mid-spring
◊◊  ▣-■  Z5  pH5–8

## *Viburnum* × *burkwoodii*

This is a useful evergreen or semi-evergreen shrub that produces intensely fragrant white blooms, opening from pink buds from mid- or late winter to late spring. It is a cross between deciduous *V. carlesii* and glossy evergreen *V. utile*, and some of the finest cultivars are the result of back-crossing this hybrid with one of the parents. 'Anne Russell' ♀, back-crossed with *V. carlesii*, is compact and semi-evergreen, with large, very fragrant flowers; fragrant 'Mohawk', another compact back-cross to *V. carlesii*, has bright red buds opening white, and orange-red autumn leaf tints; both are in bloom in mid- to late spring. 'Chenaultii' is typical of *V.* × *burkwoodii*, flowering at the same time, but more compact. Later-blooming 'Park Farm Hybrid' ♀ is vigorous and spreading, with dark pink flowers, fading to white. All but the last can be used like *V.* × *bodnantense* (left), combined with winter-flowering plants, evergreen shrubs and ground cover. 'Park Farm Hybrid' associates well with spring bulbs such as hyacinths, tulips and rock cress.

**Perfect partners:** *Bergenia cordifolia* 'Purpurea', *Camellia* × *williamsii* 'Donation', *Erythronium californicum* 'White Beauty', *Myosotis sylvatica* 'Victoria Rose', *Narcissus* 'Ice Follies', *Rhododendron* × *mucronatum*

**H: 5–8 ft. (1.5–2.5 m)   S: 6½ ft. (2 m)**
❀ Midwinter to late spring
◊◊  ▣-■  Z5  pH5.5–8

**Opposite:** The many-flowered heads of *Viburnum* × *burkwoodii*, here trained as a standard, provide a contrast of floral form with more solid blooms such as tulips.

A

## *Viburnum opulus* 'Roseum'

SNOWBALL TREE

This large, sterile form of the deciduous guelder rose is a classic partner for other late spring flowering shrubs such as kolkwitzias, ornamental cherries and crab apples, larger deciduous azaleas, early species roses, hawthorns and *Kerria japonica* cultivars. Its white flowers permit combinations with any other color of flower or foliage, although they are especially attractive with yellow-green foliage and flowers, with blue flowers such as those of larger ceanothus, or with a draping of a light pink *Clematis montana* var. *rubens* cultivar. The bold shape of its flowerheads provides an effective contrast in form with the flowers of other genera, such as lilacs and dipeltas, as well as ceanothus. It requires a position towards the back of a mixed border or shrubbery and, if used in combinations with herbaceous plants, benefits from an intervening group of smaller shrubs.

**Perfect partners:** *Crataegus laevigata* 'Rosea Flore Pleno', *Kolkwitzia amabilis* 'Pink Cloud', *Malus* 'Royalty', *Rosa* 'Complicata', *Syringa vulgaris* 'Firmament' ❏ p.92 **A**

H: 16 ft. (5 m) S: 13 ft. (4 m)
❀ Late spring to early summer
◊◊ ◻-◼ Z3 pH5–8

A billowing mass of evergreen ceanothus forms a dramatic dusky blue backdrop for the bold flowerheads of *Viburnum opulus* 'Roseum'. Good as this grouping is, adding an early yellow rose would flatter both partners.

## *Viburnum davidii*

Since this low, spreading evergreen shrub bears its flattened heads of white male and female flowers on separate bushes, a pollinator – ideally one male plant to about six females – is necessary if female plants are to produce bright blue berries on reddish stalks. The boldly veined, glossy foliage makes a striking impression towards the front of a border and the fruits, which are produced in autumn, are carried for a long time. It may be grown with evergreens such as *Euonymus fortunei* cultivars, ivies and winter heaths, and it is also invaluable for providing ground-cover, especially when grown through a contrasting cover of yellow-green or white-variegated foliage. However, a large, dense

The boldly structured foliage and domed flowerheads of *Viburnum davidii* allow it to be used in combination with more diffuse and amorphous shrubs such as broom. Rich pink or white flowers are perhaps most flattering for the viburnum's subdued coloring.

expanse can easily mask the individual character of each shrub, and extensive plantings are perhaps most effective with slightly wider spacings between bushes to ensure they do not completely coalesce.

**Perfect partners:** *Bergenia* 'Morgenröte', *Erica* × *darleyensis* 'Silberschmelze', *Euonymus fortunei* 'Emerald Gaiety', *Hedera helix* 'Glacier', *Ilex crenata* 'Golden Gem'

H & S: 4 ft. (1.2 m) ❀ Late spring
◊◊ ◻-◼ Z7 pH5.5–8

The large off-white flowerheads and handsome leaves of *Viburnum rhytidophyllum* benefit from companions in subdued colors and of contrasting scale, as in this *Berberis thunbergii* f. *atropurpurea* in late spring bloom.

## *Viburnum rhytidophyllum*

With its splendid glossy foliage, pale biscuit-colored flowers, and shiny fruits, this statuesque evergreen shrub is a magnificent plant for the back of large shrub or mixed borders, and for sunny glades in a woodland garden. The leaves are long and corrugated, deep green above with thickly felted gray undersides, providing a strong impact in winter. The soft, subdued blooms are effective with subtle tones such as peach, buff-yellow, apricot, cream and pale salmon, and with bronze-flushed foliage. Plants may be combined with gently colored roses such as some of the Hybrid Musks, kolkwitzias, later-flowering rhododendrons including deciduous azaleas, xanthoceras, *Buddleja globosa*, hybrid brooms, deutzias, large species hydrangeas, philadelphus and hybrid lilacs. It also goes well with bronze-flushed hazels, maples, plums and photinias, and with honeysuckles and early clematis on neighboring walls or shrubs.

**Perfect partners:** *Dipelta floribunda*, *Philadelphus coronarius*, *Photinia* × *fraseri* 'Birmingham', *Rhododendron* 'Irene Koster', *Rosa* 'Buff Beauty', *Syringa vulgaris* 'Primrose'

**H: 16 ft. (5 m)   S: 13 ft. (4 m)**
❀ **Late spring to early summer**
�◗◗ ▢-■ **Z6  pH5.5–7.5**

## *Weigela florida* 'Foliis Purpureis' ♛

This compact deciduous shrub has purplish gray-green leaves enhanced at flowering time by soft pink flowers. In partial shade the leaf color is less intense and flowering diminished; a site in full sun is preferable. It is excellent near the front of a shrub or mixed border, where it combines well with pink or crimson flowers and gray, glaucous, or deeper purple foliage. Attractive partners include pinks, old roses, pink convolvulus, cistus, mauve-pink campanulas and mallows, cranesbills, heucheras and plants with contrasting foliage, such as glaucous fescues or Tardiana hostas. Similar weigelas with purple-flushed foliage include 'Red Prince' ♛, with ruby-red flowers, and 'Victoria', more upright, with deep bronze-purple foliage and purplish pink flowers.

**Perfect partners:** *Achillea millefolium* 'Cerise Queen', *Dianthus* 'Doris', *Geranium* × *antipodeum* 'Chocolate Candy', *Hosta* (Tardiana Group) 'Halcyon', *Rosa* 'Tuscany Superb'

**H: 3¼ ft. (1 m)   S: 5 ft. (1.5 m)** ❀ **Early summer**
■■▢◗◗ ▢-■ **Z5  pH5.5–7.5**

## *Weigela* 'Florida Variegata' ♛

Leaves edged in creamy yellow and rose-pink flowers opening from deep pink buds make this small to medium-sized deciduous shrub a handsome candidate for growing in the front or second rank of a shrub or mixed border. It goes well with salmon or cream flowers, and blends with bronze-flushed foliage. In shade, flowering is suppressed, allowing it to be used in plantings intended mainly for foliage effect, combined with yellow-green foliage and flowers, or with cream, white or soft yellow flowers. When used as a foliage plant, it can be pruned in mid-spring rather than at the usual time straight after flowering. 'Praecox Variegata' ♛ has creamy yellow leaf margins, turning white with age, and large fragrant blooms, rich pink with yellow throats, in mid-spring.

**Perfect partners:** *Choisya ternata* Sundance, *Euphorbia* × *martini*, *Geranium albanum* p.273 A, *Potentilla fruticosa* 'Tilford Cream', *Rosa* 'Carmenetta', *Tulipa* 'Elegant Lady'

**H & S: 5 ft. (1.5 m)** ❀ **Early summer**
◗◗ ▢-■ **Z5  pH5.5–7.5**

*Weigela florida* 'Foliis Purpureis' is combined with plants of similar dusky purple leaf color but contrasting form. Purple New Zealand flax (*Phormium tenax* Purpureum Group) provides a dramatic vertical accent, while the cow parsley *Anthriscus sylvestris* 'Ravenswing' contributes lacy white umbels of flowers over feathery foliage.

*Weigela* 'Florida Variegata' is furnished in front with *Berberis thunbergii* 'Atropurpurea Nana', whose reddish purple foliage harmonizes with the weigela's rose-pink flowers, while contrasting strikingly with its leaves.

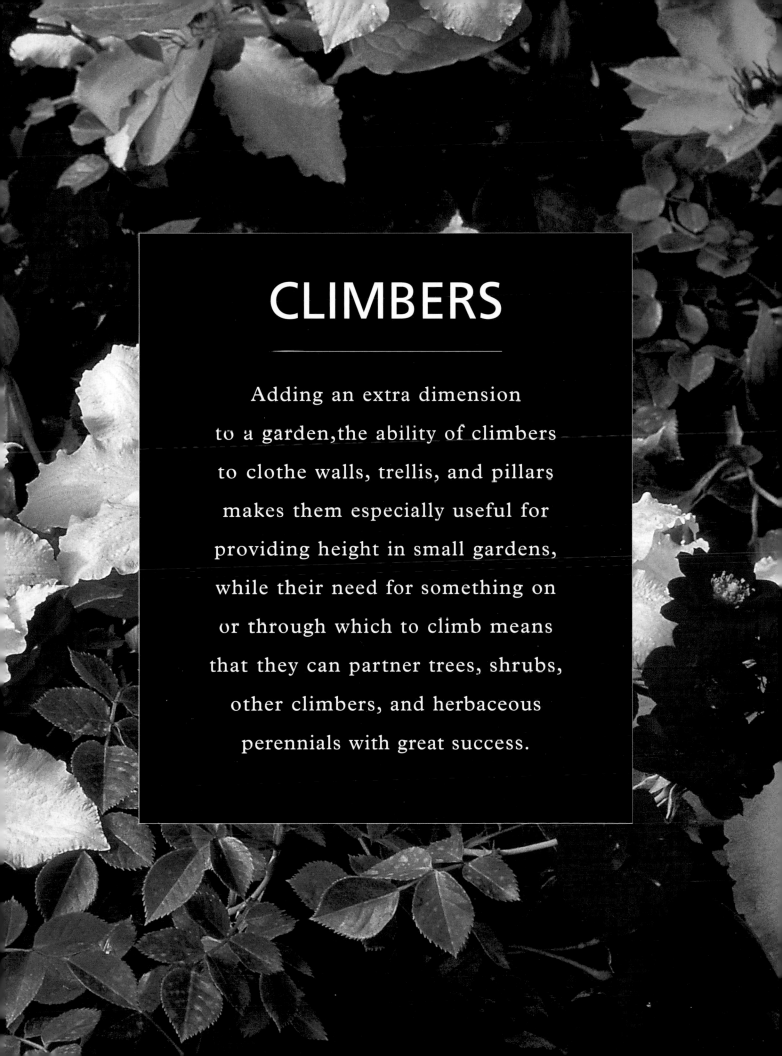

# CLIMBERS

Adding an extra dimension
to a garden, the ability of climbers
to clothe walls, trellis, and pillars
makes them especially useful for
providing height in small gardens,
while their need for something on
or through which to climb means
that they can partner trees, shrubs,
other climbers, and herbaceous
perennials with great success.

**In the wild, climbers** have adapted to scramble through other plants to reach the sun. It is vital to understand how these plants climb if they are to be used successfully in the garden: a wisteria planted at the base of a stout pergola pillar will writhe forever on the ground unless it is given a slimmer support, such as a wire, around which it can wind. It is also very important to match the vigor of the plant to its situation. Eccremocarpus will be satisfied with a bamboo cane 6½–10 ft. (2–3 m) high, while crimson glory vine and wisterias will eventually climb to the top of the tallest tree. Finally, it makes sense to position those climbers that have scented flowers – honeysuckles, jasmines, sweet peas, wisterias – in sheltered situations where both their scent and those who appreciate it will be inclined to linger.

## How climbers climb

Some climbers, such as clematis, sweet peas or vines, climb by tendrils or leaf stalks that curl tightly around any convenient support. Others twine their whole stem spirally around thin supports – wisterias, honeysuckles, morning glories and summer jasmine, for example. A third method of climbing is by aerial roots or suckers that adhere to and sometimes penetrate rough brick, stone, timber or bark. Ivy climbs like this and can cling so tightly that it damages the wall when attempts are made to remove it; campsis, on the other hand, never seems to cling quite tightly enough – unless growth is lightened by regular pruning, whole branches will tear away from the wall in heavy rains or strong winds. If there is any concern about potential damage from this group of climbers, they can be grown on trellis: they will cling to the rough surface of the wood or can be tied in for additional support if needed, and the trellis can be lowered from the wall for painting or other maintenance from time to time. A few plants, roses and bougainvilleas among them, are scramblers rather than climbers, with long stems clothed with sharp thorns to hook on to their supports. Such plants are never secure until their

stems can intertwine and form a self-supporting structure. Lastly, there are those plants – figs, forsythias, flowering quinces and winter jasmine – that are naturally shrubs but which, in cultivation, are often fastened to a wall, either because they are decorative in such a position or because they benefit from the shelter and warmth offered by the wall. They can be held in place on trellis or with wires.

Because they take up very little space, climbers can be used in a variety of ways around even the smallest garden. They will disguise and decorate house walls, garages, sheds, fences and eyesores. They can be trained on purpose-

**Opposite:** Although often grown on its own, Japanese wisteria (*W. floribunda*) associates amicably with many of the other climbers and wall shrubs, such as this ceanothus, that flower in the same season.

**Below:** On walls backing borders, climbers are invaluable for extending planting schemes upwards, whether the grouping is planned for riotous flower color, here for clematis, or for bold foliage effect.

built trellises, arches, pergolas and pillars to provide a lighter and more colorful vertical emphasis than trees or walls. A pergola draped entirely in wisteria, a fragrant tangle of jasmine, billowing masses of ivy on an old stump or a bower of cascading roses – each has a magic of its own. It is also possible to grow plants in combination: dark red clematis through purple-leaved vines; yellow or green vines with blue *Clematis macropetala*, or interwoven strands of early and late honeysuckles. Of course, with such mixtures, great care has to be taken to prevent the plants growing into an unruly mass. This is easier if each year one of the partners can be cut to the ground, as with many clematis, or back to a basic framework of rods, as with vines.

## Climbers in borders and pots

In a border, the wigwams, obelisks or single posts up which many climbers like to grow will add height while occupying minimal ground area, and the lighter-stemmed climbers can be used, without artificial support, to scramble through shrubs or over robust perennials to give a second period of interest. Gertrude Jekyll used to drape the dying stems of delphiniums with white perennial peas, then *Clematis* 'Jackmanii' and, finally, *Clematis flammula* to achieve a very long season. It is easy to think of other combinations: large-flowered clematis over peonies; white-flowered clematis through the gray leaves of Brachyglottis 'Sunshine' or the diminutive pink-flowered *Convolvulus althaeoides* through lavenders, for example.

Annual climbers, especially, are excellent in large pots. A tripod of canes will support sweet peas, eccremocarpus, canary creepers or morning glories. These can also be allowed to trail down over the edge of the pot. Generous feeding of potted climbers will lead to prolific flowering, and the flowering season can often be prolonged by moving the pots into a greenhouse at the end of the summer.

Finally, grown horizontally, many climbers will hide septic tank covers or other ugly features with a blanket of foliage and flowers.

A purplish blue selection of *Aconitum hemsleyanum* contrasts with the pendent yellow flowers of climbing *Dicentra scandens*. Both have the same rate of growth, habit and cultivation requirements, making them ideal partners for clothing a wall (with support), trellis or large shrub.

## Aconitum hemsleyanum

Often wrongly identified as *A. volubile*, this scrambling herbaceous plant has broad, lobed, rich green leaves and racemes of large, hooded flowers that can vary considerably in color between shades of dull greenish gray, grayish lilac, lavender-blue and a rich deep purple-blue. Recent introductions of the species from the wild have brought some more definite flower colors into cultivation, and for this reason it is best to check the catalogue description of the color before buying. The flowers are seldom bright enough to show well from a distance, but plants look charming when scrambling over a shrub with silver or yellow-green foliage, especially yellow-green maples, elders, physocarpus, philadelphus and silver elaeagnus or willows. Although flowering will be diminished if it is planted in the densest shade, *A. hemsleyanum* is fairly shade-tolerant, and makes a good plant for a small town or courtyard garden.

**Perfect partners:** *Acer shirasawanum* 'Aureum', *Clematis* 'Prince Charles', *Elaeagnus* 'Quicksilver', *Ipomoea tricolor* 'Heavenly Blue', *Salix elaeagnos* subsp. *angustifolia*

H: 6½–10 ft. (2–3 m) ❀ Midsummer to early autumn
◊◊ ■ ■ Z5 pH5.5–7.5

## Actinidia kolomikta ♈

Many of the leaves of this vigorous, deciduous twining climber have a white zone tipped with pink. This leaf coloring is most pronounced on male specimens (the white male and female flowers are borne on separate plants) and develops maximum intensity in full sun. Plants with pink, white or crimson flowers and those with purple foliage make excellent associates. In areas with fairly cool summers, actinidia benefits from being grown against a wall. With careful training it is possible to combine it with two or more other climbers quite uniformly, but for this to be effective at long range, the coloring of companion plants should not be too close to that of the actinidia – suitable partners include many roses, clematis and pink or white jasmines. If trained on a wall, it is advisable to prune this actinidia every winter, leaving a framework of branches but shortening sideshoots to one or two buds.

**Perfect partners:** *Clematis florida* var. *sieboldiana* p.158 **B**, *C.* 'Madame Julia Correvon', *Jasminum* × *stephanense*, *Rosa* 'Madame Grégoire Staechelin', *Vitis vinifera* 'Purpurea'

H: 16 ft. (5 m) ❀ Early summer
◊◊ ■ - ■ Z5 pH5.5–7.5

The boldly splashed leaves of *Actinidia kolomikta* harmonize with the pink and red in the flowers of the honeysuckle *Lonicera* × *italica*, both supported by wires against a moderately sunny wall. The actinidia will remain colorful after the honeysuckle has finished flowering.

## *Ampelopsis brevipedunculata* var. *maximowiczii* 'Elegans'

A deciduous tendril climber with foliage irregularly splashed with white and pink, this cultivar has berries that turn a brilliant blue on ripening and look spectacular once the leaves are shed in autumn. Except in climates with hot summers, it usually needs to be grown against a warm wall to encourage fruiting. The filigree effect of its small, three-lobed leaves is best appreciated at close quarters, making it a useful plant for small gardens and patio areas, whether attached to wires or trellis on a wall or allowed to clamber over other wall plants, especially those with an early flowering season or with dark foliage. Suitable companions include dark-leaved ceanothus, smaller evergreen clematis such as some of the Forsteri Group, and climbers of similar vigor, like rhodochitons, pink- or red-flowered jasmines and small-leaved ivies. Combinations with other variegated plants can look muddled from a distance.

**Perfect partners:** *Billardiera longiflora fructu-albo*, *Ceanothus* 'Autumnal Blue', *Clematis* 'Duchess of Albany', *Ipomoea lobata*, *Jasminum beesianum*, *Maurandya barclayana*, *Tropaeolum tricolor*

H: 13 ft. (4 m) ( ❀ Summer)
◌◌ ▢-■ Z9 pH6–7.5

This subtle tapestry of variegated foliage owes much of its charm to the different leaf shapes – palmate in *Ampelopsis brevipedunculata* var. *maximowiczii* 'Elegans', pinnate in *Jasminum officinale* 'Aureum', and peltate in nasturtium. The mottled variegation lightens the color of the leaves without emphasizing their shape as white or gold edges would, making this scheme more effective seen at close range.

## *Campsis radicans*
TRUMPET VINE

This vigorous deciduous climber uses aerial roots to attach itself to supports. It has pinnate leaves, and clusters of flowers that are usually scarlet shading to orange in the throat. Color variants include 'Atrosanguinea', which has deep blood-red blooms, and f. *flava* ♀, in rich yellow; *C.* × *tagliabuana* 'Madame Galen' ♀ is a similar hybrid with more spreading clusters of flowers in a rich salmon-red. All may be grown on walls or allowed to climb into large shrubs or small trees. The flowers blend well with other hot colors and bronze foliage, and continue into autumn to partner seasonally coloring shrubs and climbers such as crimson glory vine. Trumpet vine is also effective with yellow-green foliage, including ivies, golden hops and golden catalpas, and with deep red Viticella or Texensis clematis and purple vines.

**Perfect partners:** *Clematis* 'Kermesina', *Cotinus obovatus*, *Hedera helix* 'Buttercup', *Parthenocissus himalayana* var. *rubrifolia*, *Rosa* Altissimo, *Vitis* 'Brant', *V. vinifera* 'Purpurea'

H: 33 ft. (10 m) ❀ Late summer to mid-autumn
◌◌ ▢-■ Z5 pH5.5–7.5

Trumpet vine (*Campsis radicans*) gracefully clothes the top of a wall, its flowers harmonizing with the brick. From here it can scramble into the adjacent *Elaeagnus* 'Quicksilver', contrasting with its pale leaves. The foliage of the smoke bush (*Cotinus coggygria*) behind will assume autumnal tints that match the color of the vine's late flowers.

# Clematis

THE GENUS *CLEMATIS* is immensely diverse, with flowers, from large to tiny, of almost every color except pure blue, always presented with poise and elegance. Most are moderately vigorous and easy to keep in balance with other plants, producing slender stems that can drape themselves over or through their companions without suppressing them. Along with roses, they are the most useful climbers for plant associations. Yet clematis are often grown in isolation, without any attempt to allow them to interact with their neighbors. It is true that the most vigorous sorts – like *Clematis montana* var. *rubens* – create such large areas of color that any interaction is apparent only around the fringes of the plant; and on a pillar or obelisk, a single clematis of reasonable vigor allows little space for a companion, except for wispy climbers such as morning glories or perennial peas. A clematis "balloon," however, gives scope for two cultivars to be interwoven, perhaps with another slender scrambler.

On a wall, different clematis can be used to carry upward the color scheme of the border beneath, possibly mixed with a bold-leaved vine or *Actinidia kolomikta* to compensate for their lack of good foliage, and enhanced by using clematis with flowers of differing sizes. Small-flowered *C.* × *triternata* 'Rubromarginata' ♀ or *C.* 'Praecox' ♀, for example, can be mixed with medium-sized Viticella and larger Early Large-flowered cultivars.

Clematis may also be draped over shrubs, to contrast with gold or silver foliage or harmonize with purple, or to add interest to shrubs that are dull after flowering. A number of species and almost all clematis in the Tangutica Group have decorative seedheads, some persisting through winter, and these are particularly effective if sited in the open garden, rather than on walls. Texensis cultivars have upward-facing blooms, which are an asset

if grown across a carpet of groundcover. Shorter clematis, such as *C.* × *bonstedtii*, *C.* × *durandii* ♀, *C. heracleifolia* and *C. recta*, can be grown as border plants with the help of brushwood stakes.

Clematis climb by means of their twining leaf-stalks. They may be deciduous or evergreen, although all those described in this book are deciduous. Early-flowering kinds with axillary flowers (for example,

**Above:** Summer-flowering Early Large-flowered and Viticella clematis (purple *C.* 'Jackmanii Superba', crimson 'Ville de Lyon', and pink 'Comtesse de Bouchaud') mingle harmoniously here against a dry stone wall.

**Left:** Combining clematis of different flower size and distinct colors can add sparkle, as here with red Texensis 'Gravetye Beauty', soft lavender Early Large-flowered 'Perle d'Azur' and white Viticella 'Huldine'.

Alpina Group cultivars and *C. montana*) are pruned after flowering, while large- or later small-flowered cultivars are pruned in late winter or early spring. Regular tying in of new shoots, ideally at least once every two weeks, helps to spread out the stems for maximum floral display and prevent them kinking at the base, which encourages clematis wilt disease. If the rootball is set 3 in. (8 cm) or so below the soil surface, the plant will usually regrow after an attack by wilt. Mildew can be a problem for groups such as Early Large-flowered, Texensis and some Viticellas, particularly if grown on a wall. Bare stems at the base of the clematis are best hidden by other plants, casting the roots into the shade they prefer.

## *Clematis* 'Alba Luxurians' ♀

From midsummer onward, *C.* 'Alba Luxurians' produces flowers of the purest white, its sepals often having a leafy green tip and/or central section. These wither and turn brown. As with its parent *C. viticella*, some of its flowers nod gracefully downward: the reverse of the flower is not such a pure white, but the plant is still attractive if grown across the ground. Its vigor is sufficient to smother smaller shrubs and ground cover; if used with these, some thinning of its shoots might be needed. It combines well with pink, mauve, blue or soft yellow flowers and looks pleasing grown through gold foliage. Gentle harmonies with silver-leaved shrubs are also possible, although the overall color tones of clematis and shrub are often so similar that such combinations are best seen at close range. It flowers well in areas where summers are hot, but in cooler regions it may not be so floriferous unless given the sunniest position. Like all other members of the Viticella Group, this clematis should be pruned hard in early spring.

**Perfect partners:** *Buddleja* 'Lochinch', *B.* 'Pink Delight', *Ceanothus* × *delileanus* 'Gloire de Versailles', *Clematis* 'Prince Charles', *Hippophae rhamnoides* p.106 **A**, *Prunus spinosa* 'Purpurea', *Salix elaeagnos* subsp. *angustifolia*

**H: 13 ft. (4 m)** ✿ **Midsummer to early autumn**
⬛⬜ ◊◊ ⬜-⬛ Z5 pH5–8

*Clematis* 'Alba Luxurians' scrambles among pretty blue periwinkle (*Vinca major*) and arching white *Lysimachia clethroides*, with spiky-leaved *Astelia chathamica* behind.

## *Clematis alpina* ♀ and hybrids

*C. alpina* and the other species and hybrids of the Alpina Group, including *C. macropetala* (see p.161), usually have nodding blue flowers, with white petal-like staminodes at the center, although many mauve-pink, light purplish red, purple and white variants also occur. The single bell-shaped blooms of *C. alpina* have a charming simplicity, while those of *C. macropetala* variants and hybrids are more showy, with numerous sepals making them appear double, and staminodes extending beyond these. All Alpina Group clematis produce their flowers in spring, and tend to carry a few more later in the year.

The best blue cultivars are quite bright enough to stand up to combinations with yellow flowers or foliage, particularly soft, light lemons such as in *Forsythia suspensa* f. *atrocaulis*. However, Alpina clematis do not usually bloom profusely. Pinkish, purplish or most white cultivars are not sufficiently pure for shining color combinations, although the best whites, *C.* 'White Columbine' ♀ and *C.* 'White Moth', are excellent with the blue of early ceanothus or the rich pink of the better *Ribes sanguineum* cultivars. The repeat-

The soft, light purplish red of *Clematis* 'Ruby' creates a subdued harmony with the unfurling leaves of weeping silver pear (*Pyrus salicifolia* 'Pendula'). A combination with any strong color would have overwhelmed the delicate tints of the clematis.

flowering white *C.* 'Riga' is sweetly scented, as are other Alpina Group cultivars such as 'Columella' and 'Propertius'.

Alpina Group clematis do not need regular pruning unless intertwined with another plant. Stems that have bloomed should be cut out immediately after flowering.

**Perfect partners: Blue:** *Amelanchier lamarckii*, *Chaenomeles* × *superba* 'Issai White', *Philadelphus coronarius* 'Aureus', *Prunus glandulosa* 'Alba Plena', *Ribes sanguineum* 'Tydeman's White', *Rosa primula*, *Viburnum opulus* 'Roseum'
**Pink/Ruby:** *Berberis thunbergii* 'Rose Glow', *Exochorda* × *macrantha* 'The Bride', *Malus* × *zumi* 'Golden Hornet' p.116 **C**
**White:** *Chaenomeles* × *superba* 'Pink Lady', *Ribes sanguineum* p.134 **B**, *R.s.* 'Poky's Pink', *Rosa xanthina*

**H: 10 ft. (3 m)** ✿ **Mid- to late spring**
⬛⬜ ◊◊ ⬜-⬛ Z4 pH5–8

## *Clematis* 'Comtesse de Bouchaud' ♔

This is a vigorous and justly popular cultivar, whose color tends towards mauve. Good harmonies can be achieved with mauve-pink, crimson or burgundy flowers, especially roses or other clematis; added interest comes by varying the flower size, combining it with a small-flowered Viticella Group cultivar for example. Deep purple, rich blue or white make good contrasts, and it is effective grown over purple foliage. Those who dare mixing pink and yellow might try it with soft sulfur. Like all other Early Large-flowered Group cultivars this needs pruning in early spring.

**Perfect partners:** *Clematis* × *triternata* 'Rubromarginata', *C. viticella* 'Flore Pleno', *Ipomoea batatas* 'Blackie', *Lathyrus rotundifolius* 'Albus', *Maurandya barclayana*, *Prunus cerasifera* 'Nigra', *Rosa* 'Brenda Colvin' p.188 **A**

H: 13 ft. (4 m) ✺ **Early summer to early autumn**
▰▱▱ ◊◊ ▢-◼ Z5 pH5–8

Grown with *Clematis* 'Jackmanii', *C.* 'Comtesse de Bouchaud' gives a good color contrast, while erect stems of white *Actaea cordifolia*, yellow *Thalictrum flavum* subsp. *glaucum* and magenta lythrum provide variety of form.

## *Clematis* × *durandii* ♔

With the exception of some Alpina cultivars, this is one of the bluest clematises, its relative lack of purple providing better contrasts with yellow flowers or foliage. It is also stunning against silver leaves. The deep ridges on its sepals emphasize the shape of the flower. It can be grown in a border, with support, as a herbaceous perennial up to 5 ft. (1.5 m); it may also be trained against a wall or allowed to sprawl over ground cover. It will scramble happily over middle-sized shrubs without smothering them. Hard autumn pruning gives an early to midsummer flush of flowers. For mid- to late summer flowers, it should be pruned in spring.

**Perfect partners:** *Achillea* 'Lucky Break', *Atriplex halimus*, *Berberis temolaica*, *Calluna vulgaris* 'Gold Haze', *Lonicera periclymenum* 'Graham Thomas', *Philadelphus coronarius* 'Aureus', *Rosa* 'Leverkusen', *R. multiflora* p.190 **C**, *Verbascum* 'Gainsborough'

H: 6½ ft. (2 m) ✺ **Early summer to mid-autumn**
▰▱▱ ◊◊ ▢-◼ Z5 pH5–8

**Above:** *Clematis* × *durandii* looks effective trained over gold-leaved shrubs such as *Lonicera nitida* 'Baggesen's Gold'.

**Right:** Grown as a herbaceous perennial on tall brushwood stakes, *Clematis* × *durandii* harmonizes with purplish red *Knautia macedonica*, violet *Nepeta sibirica* and pinkish purple *Stachys macrantha*, with vivid *Rosa* News behind.

## *Clematis* × *diversifolia* 'Blue Boy'

Although this clematis is as near to true blue as *C.* × *durandii* (facing page), it differs from it in its strongly recurved sepals and paler tone, which give it an altogether daintier appearance. This and its smaller flower size make it suitable for smaller-scale groupings to be seen at closer range. Its color combines well with yellow-flushed or silver foliage and soft yellow, white, palest blue or deep blue flowers. 'Blue Boy' shares the herbaceous character of *C.* × *durandii*, and its pruning requirements are identical. If it is allowed to scramble over ground cover or shrubs, its flowers will display themselves elegantly; however, when trained to brushwood or fixed to a wall flowering is slightly hampered.

**Perfect partners:** *Achillea* 'Lucky Break', *Brachyglottis* 'Sunshine', *Calluna vulgaris* 'Gold

Haze', *Crocosmia* 'Honey Angels', *Philadelphus coronarius* 'Aureus', *Rosa* Iceberg

H: 6½ ft. (2 m) ❀ Midsummer to early autumn
◊◊ ☐-■ Z5 pH5–8

*Clematis* × *diversifolia* 'Blue Boy' presents its flowers with poise when allowed to scramble freely over bright yellow-green *Choisya ternata* Sundance. The rich, dark leaves and flowers of *Bupleurum fruticosum* provide an excellent foil, while the whole is leavened by creamy white *Anthemis tinctoria* 'Sauce Hollandaise'.

## *Clematis* 'Etoile Rose'

Most Texensis cultivars have upward-facing blooms, making them ideal for growing across ground-covering plants, but the flowers of 'Etoile Rose' nod downward so that they are perhaps best seen from beneath. The deep rose-pink petals have paler margins. As with *C.* × *diversifolia* 'Blue Boy' (above), the grace with which the flowers are borne can be lost if the plant is trained too tightly against a wall; it is also more prone to mildew here than in an open situation. A much more pleasing effect is obtained if the clematis can arrange itself loosely over a wall plant or a tall, freestanding shrub. 'Etoile Rose' works well with silver or purple foliage, or with mauve, purple, crimson or pale pink flowers, including larger-flowered Viticella clematis. Like all Texensis Group cultivars, it needs hard pruning to about 14 in. (35 cm) in early spring.

**Perfect partners:** *Ceanothus* × *pallidus* 'Marie Simon', *Clematis* 'Hagley Hybrid', *C.* 'Prince Charles', *Cotinus coggygria* 'Royal Purple', *Hibiscus syriacus* 'Hamabo', *H.s.* 'Red Heart', *Prunus spinosa* 'Purpurea', *Rosa* Super Dorothy, *Salix alba* var. *sericea* (pollarded)

H: 8 ft. (2.5 m) ❀ Midsummer to mid-autumn
◊◊ ☐-■ Z5 pH5–8

The mix of *Clematis* 'Etoile Rose' and *Buddleja* 'Lochinch' benefits from the excellent contrast of flower form, size and color as well as from the buddleia's silver foliage.

## *Clematis* 'Etoile Violette' ♛

Creamy anthers enliven the rather somber violet flowers of this Viticella Group cultivar, which have six sepals, unlike *C. viticella* which has four. Its rich color is scarcely visible from a distance, making it more suitable for viewing at close range. It is useful for adding resonant depth to larger-flowered clematis of middling tone such as 'Victoria'. While it can be used for opulent and dusky harmonies, it is perhaps most often seen with lighter colors such as mauve, carmine or blue. The lightest colors can present too stark a contrast: yellow and the palest blues or mauves work best if supplied by flowers much smaller than the clematis itself, such as honeysuckles or smaller species clematis. 'Polish Spirit' ♛ is similar but has red anthers.

**Perfect partners:** *Buddleja davidii* 'Dartmoor', *Ceanothus* × *delileanus* 'Gloire de Versailles', *Clematis* 'Perle d'Azur' p.164 **B**, *Hebe* 'Midsummer Beauty' p.103 **A**, *Hosta* 'August Moon' p.291 **A**, *Lathyrus latifolius*, *Lophospermum erubescens*, *Passiflora caerulea*, *Robinia pseudoacacia* 'Frisia' p.137 **A**

H: 13 ft. (4 m) ❀ Midsummer to early autumn
◊◊ ☐-■ Z5 pH5–8

**A**

The sumptuous but recessive tone of *Clematis* 'Etoile Violette' provides a good foil for honeysuckles such as *Lonicera* × *americana*. Although their flower shape is very different, they have similar foliage texture; contrasting daylily leaves beneath help to prevent monotony.

**B**

*Clematis florida* var. *sieboldii* is flattered here by the bold pink-tipped foliage of *Actinidia kolomikta*. Such a vigorous companion could overwhelm it unless regularly curbed.

**C**

## *Clematis* 'Gravetye Beauty'

With their pinched sepals, the cross-shaped flowers of this crimson Texensis cultivar are extremely effective seen from above but not from below, making it best suited to growing across ground cover. Its slender growth stops it smothering its companions, and it will sprawl elegantly over low shrubs, especially Ground Cover roses such as Grouse. Although the blooms clash with mauve-pink, they harmonize with gold, orange or other rich red flowers, and with bronze foliage.

The combination of *Clematis* 'Gravetye Beauty' with summer-flowering heathers is a classic one – although white or deepest red-purple heathers might be more agreeable than the mauve-pink *Calluna vulgaris* cultivar used here.

**Perfect partners:** *Bergenia* 'Sunningdale', *Calluna vulgaris* 'Beoley Gold', *Clematis* 'Huldine', *C.* 'Perle d'Azur', *Erica carnea* 'Vivellii', *E. cinerea* 'Pentreath', *Juniperus horizontalis* 'Wiltonii', *J. sabina* var. *tamariscifolia*

H: 16 ft. (5 m) ❀ Midsummer to early autumn
◊◊ ☐-■ Z4 pH5.5–7.5

## *Clematis florida* var. *sieboldiana*

This clematis has greenish cream flowers with a central boss of inky purple petaloid stamens, which blend well with almost any color save scarlet or orange. A weak grower, resenting root competition and drought, it is not entirely hardy and in cool gardens is best against a warm wall. In milder climates with hotter summers, it can be used to scramble into shrubs such as roses of moderate size. It can also be grown in a large pot and is good trained into a tall cone or to cover an obelisk, combined with, for example, large fuchsias and good foliage plants such as *Melianthus major*. *C.f.* var. *flore-pleno* is a good double.

**Perfect partners:** *Fuchsia magellanica* var. *gracilis*, *Lathyrus odoratus* 'Matucana', *Rosa* 'Climbing Pompon de Paris', *R.* 'Leverkusen', *R.* 'Reine Victoria'

H: 8 ft. (2.5 m) ❀ Early summer to early autumn
◊◊ ☐-■ Z7 pH5.5–7.5

*Clematis integrifolia* is similar in height to *Rosa gallica* var. *officinalis* and sets off the rich carmine color of its blooms as well as providing a contrast of flower shape.

## Clematis integrifolia

This lax herbaceous plant can be encouraged to scramble into shrubs of similar height or trained on stakes for use as a conventional border plant. Four twisting sepals give the blooms an attractive, lively shape. The dusky blue flowers are best seen at close range. Their gentle shade combines happily with lighter or brighter blues, mauves and pinks. It is especially effective as a foil for soft, light yellows. If it is grown over a gold-leaved shrub, its subtle color may be overwhelmed, but it works well with silver foliage. Where a taller scrambler is needed, *C.* × *diversifolia* cultivars could be substituted. As a border plant, *C. integrifolia* is best supported with hazel twigs inserted through the clump when 20 in. (50 cm) high, the twig tops bent over just above this height.

**Perfect partners:** *Achillea* 'Credo', *Artemisia ludoviciana* 'Silver Queen', *Iris* 'Jane Phillips', *Nepeta sibirica* 'Souvenir d'André Chaudron', *Stachys macrantha* 'Robusta'

H: 27 in. (70 cm) ❁ **Mid- to late summer**
◌◌ ▢-◼ Z3 pH5–8

## Clematis 'Jackmanii' ♛

Each flower of 'Jackmanii' usually has four rhomboid blue-purple sepals, making it seem almost square in outline. 'Jackmanii Superba' is similar, although slightly less blue in color and with a greater number of six-sepaled flowers, in which the more oval sepals overlap slightly. Because of this, the flowers do not provide the same patterned effect as 'Jackmanii'. They may even make integration with another climber or shrub less complete. Both plants are good combined with a bold, grayish-leaved vine, late-flowering Rambler roses in rich pink or other clematis cultivars in lighter shades such as mauve, powder-blue or mid- to deep rose-pink. Startling contrasts can be achieved by partnering 'Jackmanii' with gold *Senecio doria*, strong pink *Phlox paniculata* 'Bright Eyes' or 'Windsor' and white *Hydrangea arborescens* 'Annabelle'.

**Perfect partners:** *Buddleja* 'Lochinch', *Ceanothus* × *pallidus* 'Perle Rose', *Clematis* 'Comtesse de Bouchaud' p.156 **A**, *C.* 'Ville de Lyon' p.166 **B**, *C. viticella* 'Purpurea Plena Elegans' p.167 **A**, *Rosa* 'Lavender Lassie', R. **Super Dorothy**, *Salix alba* var. *sericea*, *Vitis vinifera* 'Incana'

H: 13 ft. (4 m) ❁ **Early summer to early autumn**
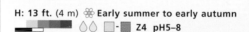 ◌◌ ▢-◼ Z4 pH5–8

**Above:** *Luma apiculata* 'Variegata' makes an effective backdrop for *Clematis* 'Jackmanii Superba', with orange *Lilium pardalinum* adding a touch of brightness.

**Below:** Arching gracefully above a wrought-iron gate, *Clematis* 'Jackmanii' contrasts dramatically with the gold-variegated ivy *Hedera colchica* 'Sulphur Heart'.

## *Clematis* 'Praecox' ♢

The delicate blue of *C.* 'Praecox' might seem indistinct in isolation but can leaven sugary or heavily sumptuous colors without the harsh contrast of pure white. While admirable with mauves, and deep pinks and blues, it is not flattered by yellow, orange or scarlet, and its subtle coloring would be lost against white-variegated or silver leaves. Its small flowers provide a dainty setting for Viticella and Early Large-flowered clematis or morning glories, although several well-grown plants of the latter would be needed to match its volume. A strong-growing, woody-based, semi-herbaceous plant, which needs pruning to about 12 in. (30 cm) in late winter or early

*Clematis* 'Praecox' acts as a foil for *C.* 'Victoria', toning down its possible excess of gorgeousness.

spring, it is too vigorous for draping shrubs, but it can be trained on a wall with other clematis and climbers, or used as a ground-covering carpet through which perennials, shrubs or bedding plants may be grown.

**Perfect partners:** *Buddleja davidii* 'Dartmoor' p.81 **C**, *Caryopteris × clandonensis* 'Pershore', *Ipomoea tricolor* 'Heavenly Blue', *Monarda* 'Beauty of Cobham', *Pulmonaria saccharata* p.327 **C**

H: 20 ft. (6 m) ❀ Midsummer to mid-autumn
◊◊ ☐-■ Z4 pH5–8

## *Clematis* 'Kermesina' ♢

The slightly nodding flowers of this purple-crimson Viticella cultivar, and of the very similar 'Rubra', retain much of the grace and poise of their parent *C. viticella*. Their slender habit of growth allows them to be draped over shrubs, although they will scarcely show against purple foliage and contrast too starkly against silver or gold leaves. They are especially effective with deep to mid-pink or mauve flowers. Partners in light orange are particularly striking; those in pale yellow are less pleasing, but still agreeable. When 'Kermesina' is grown across ground cover, it displays the silver-pink reverse of its flowers rather than their faces. It perhaps looks best if the flowers are at eye level or above, whether grown over shrubs or trained with other climbers against a wall.

**Perfect partners:** *Clematis* 'Victoria' p.166 **A**, *Eccremocarpus scaber*, *Humulus lupus* 'Aureus', *Lathyrus odoratus* 'Noel Sutton', *Rosa* 'Climbing Madame Caroline Testout', *R.* 'Mermaid', *R.* Super Dorothy

H: 13 ft. (4 m) ❀ Midsummer to early autumn
◊◊ ☐-■ Z5 pH5–8

The gently nodding blooms of *Clematis* 'Kermesina' mingle easily with the old, richly scented sweet pea *Lathyrus odoratus* 'Matucana'. The sweet pea has been sown in spring to make its flowering coincide with that of the clematis.

**Above:** A rich blue hybrid of *Clematis macropetala* is needed to balance the brightness of golden privet (*Ligustrum ovalifolium* 'Aureum'). These will not remain in equilibrium without careful management. The easiest method is to clip both after the privet's first flush of growth, but this can reduce the flowering of the clematis. Alternatively, the clematis can be removed from the privet and the latter clipped after its first flush; or individual parts can be pruned out of the privet without disturbing the clematis.

**Right:** *Clematis* 'Markham's Pink' with *C.* 'Blue Bird' is a subtle and charming mixture, best at close range.

## *Clematis macropetala*

This Alpina Group clematis has double flowers, frillier than those of *C. alpina* (p.155). Ideas for combining it with other plants are given under *C. alpina*. Among the best cultivars are *C.m.* 'Maidwell Hall' hort. in rich blue (*C.m.* 'Lagoon' ♀ and *C.m.* 'Pauline' are similar), *C.* 'Markham's Pink' ♀ and *C.* 'Snowbird' in pure white. *C.* 'Ballet Skirt' opens rich pink and becomes paler as the flowers age. Mauve-purple *C.* 'Jan Lindmark' is one of the first into bloom, while *C.* 'Purple Spider' is the richest of its color.

**Perfect partners: Blue:** *Amelanchier lamarckii*, *Chaenomeles* × *superba* 'Issai White', *Philadelphus coronarius* 'Aureus', *Prunus glandulosa* 'Alba Plena', *Ribes sanguineum* 'Tydeman's White', *Rosa primula*, *Viburnum opulus* 'Roseum'
**Pink/Ruby:** *Berberis thunbergii* 'Rose Glow', *Exochorda* × *macrantha* 'The Bride', *Lathyrus odoratus* 'Noel Sutton' p.173 **A**
**White:** *Chaenomeles* × *superba* 'Pink Lady', *Ribes sanguineum* 'Poky's Pink', *Rosa xanthina*

**H: 13 ft. (4 m)** ❀ **Mid to late spring**
◊◊ ▩–▩ **Z4 pH5–8**

## *Clematis* 'Margot Koster'

Unlike most other Viticella clematis, this cultivar has flowers that face outward and slightly upward, suiting it for use below eye level on shrubs and over ground cover as well as at a greater height on a wall. Its bright cerise flowers are light enough to show against a background of purple foliage and make effective contrasts with pale peach roses, light sky-blue clematis, or chartreuse flowers or leaves. 'Madame Julia Correvon' ♀ is a similar Viticella cultivar that blooms even longer and may be used in the same way. Both are invaluable for their color rather than their rather irregular flower shape.

**Perfect partners:** *Ceanothus* × *delileanus* 'Gloire de Versailles', *C.* × *pallidus* 'Perle Rose', *Cercis canadensis* 'Forest Pansy', *Clematis* 'Prince Charles', *Euphorbia schillingii*

**H: 10 ft. (3 m)** ❀ **Midsummer to early autumn**
◊◊ ▩–▩ **Z4 pH5–8**

The contrasting form and soft peach coloring of old glory rose (*R.* 'Gloire de Dijon') make a telling combination with *Clematis* 'Margot Koster'.

## *Clematis montana*

This sweet-scented species typically has white flowers, but most of its cultivars are pink, derived from var. *rubens*. Free-flowering and easy to grow, it is admirably suited to bold planting on the largest scale. It is almost uncontrollably vigorous, tending to form a large sheet of growth that is covered in bloom in late spring; the white var. *wilsonii* flowers about two weeks later, allowing different planting combinations with the first of the summer flowers.

Although *C. montana* can produce the most exquisite late spring partnerships, its vigor is its greatest limitation in achieving them. Stunning combinations are sometimes seen – with wisteria, for example, or when the clematis drapes itself into a small or moderately sized tree. However, the chances of achieving a successful balance without careful management of the clematis and often its partner too are very small; even if such a balance is found, it is not likely to last more than a few years. On a wall or a large pillar, it is possible to spur-prune the clematis as if it were a grape vine, allowing only five to 10 main stems to develop and cutting back all lateral shoots close to these after flowering. In this way a wall can be lightly clad with swags of clematis mixed with another climber that flowers at the same time. If *C. montana* is grown over a large shrub or small tree, pruning can be less draconian, but considerable thinning is advisable after flowering each year.

White variants mix well with pale lilacs, or early yellow or pink roses, as well as mauve wisteria. Light pink cultivars of var. *rubens* are attractive with white wisteria or early white roses, or scrambling across palest or mid-mauve to deep purple lilacs, while rich pink variants are effective trained into purple plums or crab apples.

**Perfect partners: White:** *Ceanothus arboreus* 'Trewithen Blue', *Lonicera* × *americana* p.174 **A**, *Rosa banksiae* 'Lutea', *Syringa vulgaris* 'Madame Antoine Buchner', *Wisteria sinensis* p.179 **B**
**Pink:** *Choisya ternata* p.86 **A**, *Malus* × *zumi* 'Golden Hornet', *Prunus cerasifera* 'Nigra', *P.* 'Shirotae', *P.* 'Shôgetsu', *Rosa* 'Cooperi', *Syringa vulgaris* 'Congo', *S.v.* 'Krasavitsa Moskvy', *Wisteria floribunda* 'Alba'

**H 33 ft. (10 m)** ❀ **Late spring to early summer**
◌◌ ☐-■ **Z6 pH5–8**

**Top:** A harmonious pairing of *Clematis montana* var. *rubens* 'Tetrarose' ♀ and *Spiraea* 'Arguta' needs regular attention to maintain the balance and attractive habit of both plants.

**Above:** *Clematis montana* var. *rubens* drapes itself over *Syringa vulgaris*. The relatively small flowers of the clematis contrast with the bold panicles of the lilac.

**Left:** *Clematis montana* var. *rubens* forms an attractive backdrop to *Allium hollandicum*, white variegated honesty (*Lunaria annua* 'Alba Variegata'), and wood forget-me-nots.

**Opposite:** A fence clothed with a pale selection of *Clematis montana* var. *rubens* provides an effective background for purple and white honesty (*Lunaria annua*).

A

## *Clematis* 'Moonlight'

'Moonlight' has twisted buds opening into large, showy blooms in palest lemon-yellow with yellow stamens. Although full sun encourages flowering, the delicate coloring of this charmingly informal cultivar is liable to fade. The elegance of its gently cupped blooms can be heightened by training it on an open shrub such as a rhododendron, while their pale color is particularly effective with blue or gold flowers. Brighter yellow flowers such as *Acacia pravissima* and softly colored hellebores make good companions.

**Perfect partners:** *Ceanothus* 'Cascade', *Genista tenera* 'Golden Showers', *Kerria japonica* 'Golden Guinea', *Lonicera* × *tellmanniana*, *Rosa* × *odorata* 'Pseudindica'

H: 8 ft. (2.5 m) ❀ **Late spring to early summer**
○○ ☐-■ **Z4 pH5–8**

*Clematis* 'Moonlight' *looks glorious growing with* Ceanothus impressus *and a burnt-orange hybrid* Paeonia delavayi.

## *Clematis* 'Perle d'Azur'

Among the most floriferous and spectacular of the Early Large-flowered clematis, 'Perle d'Azur' is capable of making almost too solid an expanse of bloom. Such indigestible and excessive gorgeousness can be relieved by intermingling it with another climber such as a vine, honeysuckle, perennial pea, rose or small-flowered clematis. It is famously paired with the claret vine (*Vitis vinifera* 'Purpurea') in the Rose Garden at Sissinghurst Castle, using several plants to cover a large curved wall with a sheet of bloom. It looks great with pink, purple and pale or rich lavender-blue flowers, and with soft purple or silver foliage. Its blue is not sufficiently strong or pure to balance golden yellow, although it is effective with pale lemon. Ideal for walls, it can also be allowed to scramble over large shrubs.

**Perfect partners:** *Clematis* 'Ville de Lyon' p.166 **B**, *C.* 'Purpurea Plena Elegans' p.167 **B**, *Hemerocallis* 'Hyperion' p.287 **A**, *Lavatera* × *clementii* 'Barnsley' p.113 **A**, *Lonicera sempervirens* f. *sulphurea*, *Prunus spinosa* 'Purpurea', *Rosa* 'Sander's White Rambler', *Vitis vinifera* 'Purpurea' p.179 **A**

H: 13 ft. (4 m) ❀ **Midsummer to late autumn**
○○ ☐-■ **Z5 pH5–8**

**Above:** *Clematis* 'Perle d'Azur' is used to extend a border's color scheme upward, above the pink-purple spikes of *Stachys macrantha* and the red heads of *Monarda* 'Prärienacht'.

**Left:** *Clematis* 'Etoile Violette' makes a good match for 'Perle d'Azur', although here both are so large that the supporting obelisk is hidden beneath them. With a bigger support, the clematis could produce a more spectacular display.

## *Clematis* 'Prince Charles' ♟

Compared to 'Perle d'Azur' (facing page), this Early Large-flowered cultivar has slightly paler, smaller, more delicate flowers with four or six sepals, making it perhaps more interesting in flower shape, and better suited to smaller-scale plantings seen at closer range. While 'Perle d'Azur' is just strong enough in color to be used in bright harmonies with magenta and cerise and contrasts with lemon, 'Prince Charles' is best in gentler schemes with white, soft pinks, mauves and blues, or with smoky purple or silver foliage.

*Clematis* 'Prince Charles' is shorter than most other Early Large-flowered or Viticella cultivars, allowing it to be draped over shrubs of moderate size, such as *Berberis thunbergii* 'Golden Ring'.

**Perfect partners:** *Buddleja* 'Lochinch', *Ceanothus* × *delileanus* 'Gloire de Versailles', *Clematis* 'Alba Luxurians', *C.* × *triternata* 'Rubromarginata', *Hydrangea aspera*, *Lavatera* × *clementii* 'Barnsley', *Prunus spinosa* 'Purpurea', *Rosa* 'Climbing Iceberg', *Salix elaeagnos* subsp. *angustifolia*

H: 8 ft. (2.5 m) ❀ **Early summer to early autumn**
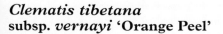 ◊◊ ▢-▧ **Z5  pH5–8**

*Clematis* 'Venosa Violacea' provides a contrast of floral form with *Lonicera tragophylla*. After its spring pruning, the clematis should be trained out into the honeysuckle, with care being taken to maintain a balance between the two, neither plant being allowed to crowd out the other.

## *Clematis tibetana* subsp. *vernayi* 'Orange Peel'

Often sold under the collectors' number LS&E 13342, this Tangutica clematis has finely divided, glaucous leaves and bell-shaped flowers that open chartreuse, are pure yellow in full bloom, and age to orange-brown. Partners in cream, pale yellow or orange will flatter all these color phases. Light pruning in spring results in flowers from early summer to mid-autumn. Its silky white seedheads appear before flowering finishes and last through winter.

**Perfect partners:** *Campsis radicans*, *Eccremocarpus scaber*, *Hedera colchica* 'Sulphur Heart', *Helianthus debilis* subsp. *cucumerifolius* 'Italian White', *Ipomoea lobata*, *Tithonia rotundifolia* 'Torch', *Tropaeolum majus* Gleam Series

H: 20 ft. (6 m) ❀ **Early summer to mid-autumn**
▰▰ ◊◊ ▢-▧ **Z6  pH5–8**

The yellow of *Clematis tibetana* subsp. *vernayi* 'Orange Peel' flatters *C.* 'Perle d'Azur', although its greenish young flowers and orange-brown older ones mix less pleasingly.

## *Clematis* 'Venosa Violacea' ♟

One of the most vigorous Viticella cultivars, 'Venosa Violacea' also has as large a flower as any in its class. The white center to each purple sepal gives a strong accent, although the variable number of sepals (from four to six) fails to establish a pattern across the plant. The flowers look attractive grown over purple-flushed foliage, although if the purple is too solid the darker zone of the flower will almost disappear at middle range. Contrasts with yellow or white are pleasing in detail but may lose their appeal over the large area that this cultivar can fill. Harmonies with deep mauve or dusky carmine are more successful. 'Minuet' ♟ is similar, having flowers with four sepals and of a slightly lighter tone.

**Perfect partners:** *Clematis* × *triternata* 'Rubromarginata', *C.* 'Purpurea Plena Elegans', *Lonicera nitida* 'Baggesen's Gold' p.114 **A**, *Prunus spinosa* 'Purpurea', *Rosa glauca*, *R.* 'Karlsruhe' p.190 **A**, *R.* 'Sophie's Perpetual' p.193 **C**

H: 13 ft. (4 m) ❀ **Midsummer to mid-autumn**
▰▰ ◊◊ ▢-▧ **Z5  pH5–8**

This harmonious mixture of *Clematis* 'Victoria' (right), an unnamed Viticella (center) and *C.* 'Kermesina' (left), also of the Viticella Group, offers blooms of varying size. It is chosen so that all three plants flower together.

## *Clematis* 'Victoria' ♕

The Early Large-flowered cultivar 'Victoria' matches 'Perle d'Azur' (see p.164) in the quality and quantity of its blooms, although it has never gained the same popularity. Its color combines agreeably with pinks, carmines, crimsons, lavender-blues and purples, as well as with purple foliage, although its vigor suits it to draping only larger shrubs or small trees. Like all clematis with regularly shaped flowers, the repeated pattern of its blooms enhances the display. 'Victoria' is superb planted in association with late-flowering Rambler roses and smaller-flowered clematis.

**Perfect partners:** *Clematis* 'Huldine', *C.* 'Praecox' p.160 **A**, *C.* × *triternata* 'Rubromarginata', *C.* 'Venosa Violacea', *Lathyrus grandiflorus*, *L. latifolius*, *L. odoratus* 'Matucana' (spring sown), *Maurandya barclayana*, *Prunus cerasifera* 'Nigra', *P. spinosa* 'Purpurea', *Rosa* Super Dorothy, *R.* Super Excelsa, *Vitis vinifera* 'Purpurea'

**H: 13 ft. (4 m)** ❀ **Midsummer to early autumn**
◊◊ ☐-■ **Z4 pH5–8**

## *Clematis* 'Ville de Lyon'

'Ville de Lyon' is a Early Large-flowered cultivar with six slightly overlapping sepals. The rather solid outline of the flower is alleviated by the color gradation within each sepal, dark at the edge with a bright crimson center, and the contrasting central boss of creamy yellow stamens. Its color is just light enough to show against deep purple foliage and it goes well with pink, mauve or lavender-blue flowers. Acidic contrasts with chartreuse flowers or foliage are good. 'Ville de Lyon' can be trained over shrubs of moderate size, or against a wall with tall herbaceous plants in front. This helps hide the bareness of the lower parts of the stems by late summer. While usually hard-pruned in early spring,

*Clematis* 'Ville de Lyon' with *C.* 'Comtesse de Bouchaud' and *C.* 'Jackmanii Superba' provide an eye-catching combination of sumptuous crimson, pink and purple. Greater variety of flower size might give even more impact.

it can be treated less severely by shortening stems to the uppermost pair of plump buds – it will then produce flowers in early summer.

**Perfect partners:** *Aconitum* 'Newry Blue', *Cercis canadensis* 'Forest Pansy', *Clematis* 'Hagley Hybrid', *C.* 'Minuet', *C.* 'Prince Charles', *C.* 'Victoria', *Eupatorium purpureum*, *Filipendula rubra*, *Foeniculum vulgare*, *Humulus lupulus* 'Aureus', *Prunus cerasifera* 'Nigra'

**H: 10 ft. (3 m)** ❀ **Midsummer to mid-autumn**
◊◊ ☐-■ **Z4 pH5–8**

## *Clematis viticella*, double-flowered derivatives ♈

Although lacking the elegantly nodding flowers of the plain *C. viticella*, 'Purpurea Plena Elegans' ♈ and larger-flowered, deep lavender-blue *C. viticella* 'Flore Pleno' are both plants of considerable charm. Their blooms usually have four larger outer sepals, giving them a roughly square outline, the pale reverse of the unopened sepals providing a contrasting button center. Soft plum-purple 'Purpurea Plena Elegans' is more vigorous, although 'Flore Pleno' has a better color for contrasts with soft yellow or yellow-green.

Both plants carry their flowers with a poise that can be lost if they are trained too tightly against a wall. Their slender habit makes them ideal for growing through shrubs and wall plants and into small trees; they rarely produce a solid canopy of foliage and so do not harm their companions. Their muted colors and complex flowers make them most effective when seen at close range, for example on a pergola. They are excellent with late-blooming Rambler roses or clematis with larger, brighter flowers. Like all Viticella clematis, these plants need pruning in early spring.

**Perfect partners:** *Actinidia kolomikta, Clematis* 'Hagley Hybrid', *C.* 'Little Nell', *C.* 'Prince Charles', *C.* 'Victoria', *Hydrangea aspera* Villosa Group, *Ipomoea purpurea, I. tricolor* 'Crimson Rambler', *Jasminum officinale, Lophospermum erubescens, Mutisia oligodon, Rosa* **Super Dorothy**, *Salix alba* var. *sericea, S. elaeagnos* subsp. *angustifolia, Vitis vinifera* 'Purpurea'

**H: 13 ft. (4 m)** ☼ **Midsummer to early autumn**
◊◊ ■-■ **Z5  pH5–8**

**Right:** A successful blend combines *Clematis* 'Purpurea Plena Elegans' with the bolder, dark purple *C.* 'Jackmanii', grown together on an iron "balloon."

**Below:** The colors, sizes and growth habits of *Clematis* 'Purpurea Plena Elegans' and *C.* 'Perle d'Azur' are ideally suited to each other. After pruning, both cultivars need careful training and tying in to their supports to ensure they are well blended and balanced.

## Eccremocarpus scaber
### CHILEAN GLORY FLOWER

The flowers of this rather tender semi-evergreen climber are usually orange, but several variants exist, including gold f. *aureus*, carmine-red f. *carmineus*, f. *roseus* with deep carmine-pink flowers and an unnamed apricot variant. All produce a cheerful display from late spring through to the autumn frosts. In cold areas the plant may be grown as a half-hardy annual, and where summers are cool it benefits from a warm site against a sunny wall. It climbs by means of leaf tendrils and so needs wires on a wall or trellis; in the open it will climb up a wigwam of poles or drape over a large shrub. It combines well with hot colors, and with yellow-green, purple or bronze foliage, and contrasts with pure blue or blue-green, for example glaucous-leaved shrubs or blue-green painted trellis. If grown in containers, plants can be overwintered in frost-free conditions, and then will flower earlier the following year.

**Perfect partners:** *Ceanothus* × *delileanus* 'Gloire de Versailles', *Clematis* 'Perle d'Azur', *Cotinus coggygria* 'Royal Purple', *Solanum crispum* 'Glasnevin'

**H: 16 ft. (5 m)** ❊ **Late spring to mid-autumn**
◊◊ ▢-◼ **Z9 pH5.5–7.5**

Typical orange-flowered *Eccremocarpus scaber* is matched in vigor by the Tangutica clematis 'Bill MacKenzie', the two mingling together without either being suppressed by the other. The flowers of the eccremocarpus harmonize in color and contrast in form with those of the clematis.

## Hedera algeriensis
### 'Gloire de Marengo' ♛

This evergreen climber has large leaves, shallowly lobed and deep green with gray-green and creamy white variegation. It is one of the least hardy of commonly grown ivies, and its foliage is easily damaged during a cold winter, but plants recover rapidly in spring. Even so, in cold areas it benefits from wall training, perhaps with foliage of a different color such as purple or yellow-green, or as a contrast to bright flowers. In favored localities it is an excellent ground-cover plant, valuable as winter cover through which to grow evergreen shrubs, early-flowering perennials such as hellebores and plants like dogwoods and willows with colorful winter stems. It may also be combined with another climber against a trellis or chain-link fence. Although blending well with any color,

The severity of a house wall is here softened by a covering of pale *Hedera algeriensis* 'Gloire de Marengo', contrasting with the bright berries of a pyracantha. Purple smoke bush (a cultivar of *Cotinus coggygria*) and *Juniperus chinensis* 'Plumosa Aurea' furnish the space in front.

it looks outstanding with cool colors like carmine-pink, and harmonizes with silver foliage and white flowers. Good companions include pyracanthas and plants with large flowers or inflorescences, especially clematis and climbing hydrangeas; it will also contrast effectively with autumn-coloring climbers such as parthenocissus or a vine.

**Perfect partners:** *Fuchsia magellanica* var. *gracilis* p.101 **B**, *Hedera helix* 'Buttercup' p.170 **A**, *Parthenocissus quinquefolia*, *P. tricuspidata*, *Vitis vinifera* 'Purpurea'

**H: 16 ft. (5 m)** ( ❊ **Autumn**)

◊◊ ▢-◼ ◼ **Z8 pH5.5–7.5**

## *Hedera colchica* ♔

PERSIAN IVY

This handsome evergreen climber with deep green, shiny, heart-shaped leaves is a vigorous, relatively hardy plant invaluable for training on wires against a wall and for use as ground-cover over a large area. It is immensely useful for a woodland garden or borders planted for spring or winter, particularly where foliage effect is needed before deciduous plants have come into leaf. When used as ground cover, and kept close to the ground by occasional cutting back in spring, it can be underplanted with bulbs such as lilies or narcissi. Its variegated forms bring welcome light to dark corners, especially if underplanted with colchicums and autumn-flowering crocuses,

their lilac blooms producing a striking effect against the creamy yellow mat of foliage. An effective foil for plants of any color, it is great with pale flowers, and lighter green, yellow-green, silver or variegated foliage.

Among several cultivars are 'Dentata' ♔, which has lobed leaves and less of a tendency to climb; and 'Dentata Variegata' ♔, with yellow-edged leaves dazzlingly variegated with pale green shot with yellow – this can be used in the same way as *H. algeriensis* 'Gloire de Marengo' (facing page), especially with hot colors or for contrasts with purple or blue. In 'Sulphur Heart' ♔, the center of the leaf is greenish yellow. It makes a good backcloth for a richly colored climber, such as a red rose or purple clematis, remaining attractive in winter when its companion is leafless.

**Perfect partners:** *Bergenia cordifolia* 'Purpurea', *Clematis* 'Jackmanii' p.159 **C**, *Cornus stolonifera* 'Flaviramea', *Lonicera* × *tellmanniana* p.175 **C**, *Parthenocissus henryana* p.128 **A**, *P. quinquefolia* p.176 **B**, *Rosa* 'Mermaid' p.190 **B**, *Salix alba* subsp. *vitellina* 'Britzensis'

H: 33 ft. (10 m) ( ❀ Autumn)
△△ ☐-■ ■ Z6 pH5.5–7.5

Grown across a carpet of winter heaths, the bright variegation of *Hedera colchica* 'Sulphur Heart' can add sparkle in winter, especially if the heaths have such richly colored flowers as this *Erica* × *darleyensis* 'Arthur Johnson'. Heathers with colored foliage could also be used.

**Above:** *Hedera helix* 'Buttercup', rather pale through being grown in sun, and white-variegated *H. algeriensis* 'Gloire de Marengo' here show the shrubby or "arborescent" habit characteristic of mature ivies, producing attractively billowing branches. Such a partnership could serve as an effective backdrop for blue flowers or dark foliage.

**Below:** Ivies such as *Hedera helix* 'Manda's Crested' ♀ can provide a carpet of attractive ground-covering foliage, even spreading across paving as here. Used in this way, the ivy acts as a foil for a formal globe of dwarf box (*Buxus sempervirens* 'Suffruticosa') and a loose lime-green mound of lady's mantle (*Alchemilla mollis*).

## *Hedera helix*
COMMON IVY

There are hundreds of cultivars of this evergreen self-clinging climber, including some with variegated foliage in yellow-green, gold or silver, and many with differently shaped leaves. It thrives in sun or shade, although yellow-green cultivars are brightest in full sun. Because it attaches itself permanently to walls, it does not combine easily with other climbers, but different ivies planted near each other can create a tapestry of varied leaf forms, and once these are established other climbers can be trained in – parthenocissus is a particularly striking partner, especially in full autumn color. Ivy also makes an effective ground-covering foil for herbaceous plants and bulbs, although hormones from its roots can suppress and even kill competing shrubs such as yew.

**Perfect partners:** *Anemone blanda, Calluna vulgaris* 'Robert Chapman', *Ceanothus* 'Cascade' p.86 **A**, *Galanthus elwesii* var. *monostictus, Lonicera caprifolium* p.174 **B**, *Parthenocissus quinquefolia* p.177 **A**, *P. tricuspidata* p.176 **C**, *Schizophragma hydrangeoides* 'Roseum', *Solenostemon scutellarioides* (mixed) p.449 **C**

**H: 16 ft. (5 m) (✺ Autumn)**
◊◊ ▢-◾ Z5–7 pH5–8

The bright yellow-green foliage of *Humulus lupulus* 'Aureus' contrasts with a carpet of long-flowering, soundly perennial *Viola* 'Huntercombe Purple'. Another climber with flowers that harmonize with the viola, such as a clematis or morning glory, could be planted a little distance away from the roots of the hop and trained into it, to help break up the mass of hop leaves and unify the scheme.

## *Humulus lupulus* 'Aureus' ♀
GOLDEN HOP

This rampant herbaceous climber has yellow-green leaves and greenish yellow flowers in summer. Although it tolerates some shade, it is most colorful in full sun. It can smother any shrub over which it is grown, so it is most useful as a background to contrasting flowers or foliage – to the tall spikes of aconites, for example, or to late-flowering blue shrubs such as *Ceanothus* × *delileanus* cultivars. It may be trained on wires or trellis on a wall or pillar, perhaps as a foil for dark green evergreens, or behind columns or obelisks of climbers with richly contrasting flowers such as clematis. It tends to grow straight upward on a wall, and it is helpful to train it sideways at frequent intervals from spring onward.

**Perfect partners:** *Aconitum hemsleyanum, Campanula latifolia, Ceratostigma willmottianum, Clematis* 'Kermesina', *Coronilla valentina* subsp. *glauca* 'Variegata' p.90 **A**, *Delphinium* 'Alice Artindale' p.256 **B**, *Lonicera* × *heckrottii* 'Gold Flame' p.174 **C**, *Phormium tenax* 'Veitchianum', *Rosa* 'Frensham', *Tolpis barbata* p.451 **A**

**H: 20 ft. (6 m) (Summer)** ✺
◊◊ ▢-◾ Z5 pH5.5–7.5

Spanish flag (*Ipomoea lobata*) can be used to weave through much shorter herbaceous plants or shrubs, including bush roses. Here, its flowers create a brilliant contrast of color and form with a rich rose-pink cultivar of *Phlox paniculata*. For a more subtle effect, a cream phlox could be used, or a magenta one for even more pizzazz.

## *Ipomoea lobata*
SPANISH FLAG

Although it is strictly a perennial climber, the Spanish flag (syns *I. versicolor, Mina lobata*) is usually treated as an annual. Its flowers are borne in a spike, with florets along one side and becoming smaller toward the tip; these range in color from red through orange and yellow, to soft cream on the mature flowers. This makes an excellent contrast for flowers of larger size and more solid outline. When grown as an annual, the Spanish flag makes a wispy climber, suitable for training into shrubs and over herbaceous plants, or for growing against a wall. It is particularly effective with hot colors, set against bronze, purple or dark red foliage, or contrasted with lime green, carmine-pink or magenta flowers. 'Citronella' is mainly pale yellow, and is useful with rich gold or contrasting blue.

**Perfect partners:** *Atriplex hortensis* var. *rubra, Berberis thunbergii* f. *atropurpurea, Dahlia* 'Bishop of Llandaff', *Lychnis coronaria, Nicotiana* 'Lime Green', *Parthenocissus tricuspidata, Rosa* 'Frensham', *Tropaeolum speciosum*

**H: 10 ft. (3 m)** ❀ **Midsummer to mid-autumn**
◊◊ ■ **Z10 pH6–7.5**

A cascade of *Ipomoea tricolor* 'Heavenly Blue' tumbles through a wall-trained *Plumbago auriculata* in matching azure. Broad-leaved *Fatsia japonica*, gray-green *Brachyglottis* (Dunedin Group) 'Sunshine' and pots of agapanthus provide a contrast of foliage and form to furnish the base.

## *Ipomoea tricolor* 'Heavenly Blue' ♔

A tender perennial often grown as an annual, this is perhaps the best known morning glory, with exquisite sky-blue flowers with a white eye. Like the other ipomoeas on this page, it needs warm summer weather to thrive, but when suited it is a superb climber for draping over shrubs or to intertwine with other wall plants, and also looks outstanding scrambling up an obelisk or pillar, against a contrasting background. It is particularly effective with glaucous, silver or yellow-green foliage and cream or white flowers, and in contrasts with yellow flowers. The most suitable partners are those with flowers of contrasting size or form – the tiny white blooms of *Solanum laxum* or yellow canary creeper, for example, or a small-flowered white clematis.

**Perfect partners:** *Argyranthemum* 'Jamaica Primrose', *Artemisia ludoviciana, Coronilla valentina* subsp. *glauca, Elaeagnus* 'Quicksilver', *Fremontodendron californicum, Hedera helix* 'Buttercup', *Hemerocallis* 'Golden Chimes', *Hippophae rhamnoides, Kniphofia* yellow cultivars, *Lonicera caprifolium, Philadelphus coronarius* 'Aureus'

**H: 10 ft. (3 m)** ❀ **Midsummer to mid-autumn**
◊◊ ■ **Z10 pH6–7.5**

## *Ipomoea tricolor* 'Crimson Rambler'

Although sky-blue morning glories are perhaps the most familiar, purple, red and even light brown cultivars are also available. Despite its name, 'Crimson Rambler' is almost primary red, and mixes well with both hot colors and cool shades such as true crimson, purple and lavender. Like *I. lobata* (above), it is a tender perennial, usually grown from seed as an annual for planting out when temperatures are warm enough for it to grow vigorously (midsummer in cooler regions). It stands out most conspicuously against flowers of significantly different size, form or color, and contrasts well with silver foliage. Good partners are small-flowered clematis, flamboyant climbers including campsis, lophospermums and *I. lobata*, and contrasting yellow-green climbers such as golden hop (facing page).

**Perfect partners:** *Abutilon vitifolium* 'Veronica Tennant', *Artemisia ludoviciana* 'Silver Queen',

Trained tall to be seen against the blue of the sky, red *Ipomoea tricolor* 'Crimson Rambler' and yellow canary creeper (*Tropaeolum peregrinum*), with their contrasting flower shapes and compatible habits, create a striking combination of primary colors.

*Clematis* 'Etoile Violette', *Crocosmia* 'Lucifer', *Lophospermum erubescens, Pyrus salicifolia* 'Pendula'

**H: 10 ft. (3 m)** ❀ **Midsummer to mid-autumn**
◊◊ ■ **Z10 pH6–7.5**

## *Jasminum nudiflorum* ♀
WINTER JASMINE

The green winter stems of this sprawling deciduous shrub provide a satisfying contrast to the bright yellow flowers. Its habit of growth makes it an easy plant to train up against a wall, allow to tumble downward from the top of a wall or bank, or even grow in the mortar of an old wall. It can be used as a flowering backdrop for hellebores, winter irises and snowdrops, and combines well with evergreen wall plants such as ivies, or with berrying plants that retain their fruits over winter, including *Cotoneaster horizontalis*. While the plant itself is relatively hardy, the flowers can be harmed by severe frost – where this may be a problem, a west-facing aspect should be chosen to avoid morning sun damaging frosted buds and flowers.

**Perfect partners:** *Galanthus nivalis*, *Garrya elliptica* 'James Roof', *Hedera colchica*, *Helleborus* × *hybridus*, *Ilex aquifolium* 'J.C. van Tol', *Pyracantha coccinea* 'Lalandei'

**H & S: 10 ft. (3 m)** ✿ **Late autumn to early spring**
〇〇 ■ Z6 pH5.5–8

Trained low across a wall, winter jasmine (*Jasminum nudiflorum*) can interact with even the shortest early-flowering plants such as this winter iris, *I. unguicularis*. Used in this way, the jasmine could equally be combined with snowdrops, hellebores or Reticulata irises.

A

B

The blooms of the white Chilean bellflower (*Lapageria rosea* var. *albiflora*) are strikingly pure in form and color, contrasting well with darker flowers such as *Rhodochiton atrosanguineus*. They need a site with enough sun for the rhodochiton but not too much for the lapageria.

## *Lathyrus latifolius* 'Albus' ♀

The slender growth of this white variant of the broad-leaved everlasting or perennial pea allows it to be draped over other shrubs and climbers such as flowering currant, deutzias or lilac without smothering them. It can also be used to scramble through plants on a wall. The flower color is perhaps most effective with cool-colored flowers, in contrasts with the foliage of dark evergreens, and in subtle or subdued harmonies with silver-leaved plants. It combines well with flowers of contrasting shape and color, such as Viticella clematis cultivars or pure blue morning glories. 'White Pearl' ♀ has larger flowers, while 'Rosa Perle' ♀ bears pale pink blooms.

**Perfect partners:** *Artemisia ludoviciana*, *Clematis* 'Venosa Violacea', *Deutzia scabra*, *Elaeagnus* 'Quicksilver', *Lavandula lanata*, *Paeonia lactiflora* 'Albert Crousse', *Ribes sanguineum*, *Rosa* 'Carmenetta', *R.* 'Cerise Bouquet', *R.* 'Constance Spry', *R.* 'Pink Perpétué', *Santolina chamaecyparissus*, *Syringa vulgaris*

**H: 6 ft. (1.8 m)** ✿ **Early summer to early autumn**
〇〇 ■ Z5 pH5.5–7.5

## *Lapageria rosea* ♀
CHILEAN BELLFLOWER

This evergreen climber is a variable species in the wild, and although its large, bell-shaped flowers are normally rich crimson, color variations include 'Flesh Pink', 'Nash Court', in which the flowers are delicately marbled in pale pink, and the creamy white var. *albiflora*. It needs moisture, a mild climate and preferably some shade, requirements that often make it most suitable for growing in a greenhouse. It may be combined with smilax species with marbled leaves, berberidopsis, billardieras, vinelike plants such as some species of cissus and parthenocissus, mandevillas, sollyas, maurandyas, rhodochitons and silver- or white-variegated foliage.

**Perfect partners:** *Asparagus densiflorus* Sprengeri Group, *Cissus rhombifolia*, *Euonymus fortunei* 'Silver Queen', *Hedera helix* 'Glacier', *Smilax aspera*

**H: 16 ft. (5 m)** ✿ **Early summer to late autumn**
〇〇 ■ ■ Z9 pH5–6.5

C

Herbaceous (or annual) climbers such as *Lathyrus latifolius* 'Albus' are in many respects easier to use for draping shrubs such as *Berberis* × *ottawensis* f. *purpurea* 'Superba' than are woody climbers like clematis or honeysuckle: each can be managed between leaf fall and spring, pruning the shrub or removing some of the pea to maintain balance without the need for fiddly disentanglement. A dark-leaved shrub such as this berberis makes a superb foil for the pea.

**Above:** Sweet peas combine well with clematis flowers or seedheads, as here with *Lathyrus odoratus* 'Noel Sutton' and the silvery heads of *Clematis macropetala*, although the seeds tend to lose their silky sheen before the pea stops blooming.

**Below:** *Lathyrus odoratus* 'Matucana', a sweet pea with relatively small, unruffled but intensely fragrant flowers in maroon and light pinkish violet, here blends perfectly with soft magenta *Geranium psilostemon* 'Bressingham Flair' and *Erysimum* 'Bowles Mauve'. The round seedheads of *Allium hollandicum* repeated throughout add interest and unity.

## *Lathyrus odoratus*
SWEET PEA

Modern sweet peas, all classed as Spencer cultivars, come in a wide range of colors, from white to deep indigo-blue and plum-purple, as well as cream, scarlet and salmon-pink. These climbers, grown as biennials from an autumn sowing to flower in early to midsummer, or as spring-sown annuals to flower from midsummer to early autumn, may be grown on supports such as trellises or wigwams, or be allowed to scramble over shrubs. Some cultivars are strongly scented, and where this is the case, a position near a window or sitting area is ideal to appreciate the fragrance. Partnerships should be with plants that flower at about the same height and time – possibly other annual climbers such as lophospermums and morning glories or, for a contrast, eccremocarpus or perennial peas. Dwarf cultivars can tumble over a low wall or be grown in containers, either trained upward on short supports – for instance a tripod up to about 24 in. (60 cm) high – or allowed to trail over the edge to intermingle with other plants.

**Perfect partners:** *Clematis* 'Kermesina' p.160 **B**, *Crambe maritima*, *Gypsophila paniculata*, *Lathyrus rotundifolius* p.173 **C**, *Lophospermum erubescens*, *Verbena bonariensis*

**H: 2–8 ft.** (60 cm–2.5 m)
✿ **Early summer to early autumn**
◌◌ **Z6 pH5.5–7.5**

The rather small flowers of the Persian everlasting pea (*Lathyrus rotundifolius*) provide subtle variety when scrambling together with those of a sweet pea (*L. odoratus*) cultivar. Beneath, the imposing flowerheads of spider flowers (*Cleome hassleriana*), in a mixture of perfectly harmonious colors, offer a more striking contrast of form.

## *Lathyrus rotundifolius*
PERSIAN EVERLASTING PEA

This is a slender herbaceous perennial pea, useful for planting so that it twines over small or medium shrubs, or covers the base of a wall. The brick coloring of its flowers blends with other warm hues such as dusky red, burnt orange, salmon-pink, peach or apricot, and mixes well with bronze foliage, such as some berberis or cotinus. It will also scramble over Ground Cover or Patio roses, and it is slender enough to be allowed to twine into herbaceous plants with flowers in sympathetic colors, such as achilleas. 'Tillyperone', which is vibrant magenta-pink, combines successfully with purple foliage and cool colours such as mauve, paler pink, crimson, lavender and lilac.

**Perfect partners:** *Achillea* 'Lachsschönheit', *Berberis thunbergii* f. *atropurpurea*, *Cotinus coggygria* 'Royal Purple', *Rosa* 'Buff Beauty', *R.* Sweet Dream

**H: 6 ft.** (1.8 m) ✿ **Early to late summer**
◌◌ **Z5 pH5.5–7.5**

The dainty blooms of *Lonicera × americana* mingle freely with those of *Clematis montana* var. *wilsonii*. Maintaining a balance between two such vigorous climbers is difficult unless the two are planted some distance apart and trained toward each other. Hard pruning will be needed every few years, being more severe on the dominant climber. Instead, each could be trained to horizontal wires on a wall, but an unnatural effect, with honeysuckle and clematis alternating evenly, is best avoided.

*Lonicera × heckrottii* 'Gold Flame' here contrasts with golden hop (*Humulus lupulus* 'Aureus'). The hop dies back in winter, allowing the honeysuckle, which should be planted some distance away, to be pruned or retrained. The hop's vigorous new shoots need to be trained out sideways from the time they emerge and thinned occasionally later.

## *Lonicera × americana*

Like most deciduous climbing honeysuckles, *L. × americana* can be draped over a large shrub or small tree, or mingled with other climbers on a wall. Its long, elegant florets give a filigree effect, contrasting well with flowers of more solid outline, and they have a strong scent. Harmonies with similar tones, such as mid-pink roses, are best seen at close range, while a more contrasting companion works better from a distance: try carmine, strong red, white, palest buff, pink or yellow flowers, or purple foliage. After an abundant early summer flush, there is still enough bloom to combine with late summer flowering Viticella clematis. The similar *L. × italica* ♀ is often supplied under this name.

**Perfect partners:** *Clematis* 'Etoile Violette' p.158 **A**, *C.* 'Kermesina', *Cotinus coggygria* 'Royal Purple', *Prunus cerasifera* 'Nigra', *Rosa* 'Climbing Iceberg', *R.* 'Goldfinch'

**H: 30 ft. (9 m)** ❀ **Early summer to autumn**
◊◊ ▢-▪ **Z6 pH5–8**

## *Lonicera caprifolium* ♀
ITALIAN HONEYSUCKLE

Vigorous enough to scramble into a small tree, this deciduous honeysuckle has a creamy yellow tint that suits it to combinations with white, rich gold and even soft orange, or with purple foliage. Close-range harmonies with pale yellow or peach are attractive. Most clones have a pink tint in their florets; 'Anna Fletcher' lacks this, and therefore may be used in contrasts with light to mid-blue flowers. This species needs to be trained outward when young to prevent it growing straight up. Occasional pruning is needed to prevent it overwhelming a supporting shrub, or to maintain balance with another climber.

**Perfect partners:** *Clematis montana*, *Corylus maxima* 'Purpurea', *Eccremocarpus scaber*, *Magnolia grandiflora*, *Rosa* 'Madame Alfred Carrière', *R.* 'Maigold', *R.* 'Paul Noël'

**H: 20 ft. (6 m)** ❀ **Late spring to late summer**
◊◊ ▢-▪ **Z5 pH5–8**

*Lonicera caprifolium* has been trained out across *Cotinus coggygria* 'Royal Purple' to stop it smothering the bush. Common ivy (*Hedera helix*) provides winter furnishing.

## *Lonicera × heckrottii*

The coral-red trumpets of the deciduous or semi-evergreen *L. × heckrottii* have golden orange mouths, giving a rich coral-orange effect, a good contrast for chartreuse foliage. Freely produced in summer, they are brilliant carmine in bud, and fragrant. The oval or elliptical leaves, reddish purple when young, mature to a lustrous blue-green, especially on their underside, making a striking combination with the flower color. The flowerheads are a little congested and less elegant than in some honeysuckle species. *L. × heckrottii* combines well with salmon-pink, peach or apricot flowers, and is also pleasing with buff or gold, and with bronze or purple foliage. More vigorous 'Gold Flame' is brighter and more yellow in the mouth.

**Perfect partners:** *Berberis × ottawensis* f. *purpurea* 'Superba', *Cotinus coggygria* 'Royal Purple', *Philadelphus coronarius* 'Aureus', *Rosa* 'Buff Beauty', *R.* 'François Juranville'

**H: 13 ft. (4 m)** ❀ **Early to late summer**
◊◊ ▢-▪ **Z6 pH5–8**

Above: *Lonicera periclymenum* 'Belgica' in its second flush of flower, with Viticella clematis 'Polish Spirit'. The clematis does not show up well from a distance, so this combination is best seen at close range. *L.p.* 'Graham Thomas' would also succeed here, flowering more profusely with the clematis.

Right: Soft yellow *Lonicera periclymenum* 'Graham Thomas' harmonizes with cream *Lilium* 'Roma', both growing well in sun or partial shade. The less formal *L. martagon* var. *album* might better match the honeysuckle's semi-wild habit.

## *Lonicera periclymenum*
### COMMON HONEYSUCKLE, WOODBINE

The semi-wild appearance of this vigorous deciduous honeysuckle suits it to wilder parts of the garden. It has tubular, two-lipped flowers, which are white to crimson or soft yellow on the outside, and white aging to yellow within. 'Belgica' (early Dutch honeysuckle) flowers mainly in early summer, with some later blooms; creamy yellow 'Graham Thomas' ♀ blooms from midsummer to early autumn, as does crimson and cream 'Serotina' ♀. Yellow sorts combine well with white, gold or soft blue; pink and cream clones can be used with white or mid- to deep pinks; and crimson and cream ones are especially good with peach or rich pink.

**Perfect partners:** *Ceanothus* × *delileanus* 'Gloire de Versailles', *Clematis* 'Kermesina', *Rosa* 'Cerise Bouquet', *R.* 'Climbing Iceberg', *R.* 'François Juranville'

H: 23 ft. (7 m) ❀ Early summer to autumn
◊◊ ▢-▢ Z5 pH4–8

## *Lonicera* × *tellmanniana*

This superb but scentless deciduous honeysuckle has a single flush of flowers in golden orange, a color so rich that it is perhaps best in more cultivated garden areas. It contrasts well with chartreuse foliage or purple flowers, and harmonizes with cream, yellow, orange or red flowers, and with bronze or purple foliage. The plant is rather too big and vigorous to grow over shrubs, and its display can be too diffuse if grown through a small tree. It is, however, ideal for a shady wall; it will also thrive in sun, provided the root run is cool and moist. Its slightly more vigorous parent *L. tragophylla* ♀, which can be used in the same ways, produces flowers that are closer to pure yellow.

**Perfect partners:** *Clematis* 'Moonlight', *C.* 'Niobe', *Fremontodendron* 'California Glory', *Hedera helix* 'Buttercup', *Philadelphus coronarius* 'Aureus', *Rosa* 'Leverkusen'

H: 16 ft. (5 m) ❀ Late spring to early summer
◊◊ ▢-▢ Z6 pH5–8

*Lonicera* × *tellmanniana* and *Hedera colchica* 'Sulphur Heart' make a pleasing partnership, but are best planted some distance apart to avoid root competition. The ivy will cling to the wall, allowing the honeysuckle to be trained over it.

Varied leaf shapes and sizes create a pretty pattern when *Parthenocissus henryana* is grown with the ivy *Hedera colchica* 'Sulphur Heart'. A sunny site intensifies the colors of both.

## *Parthenocissus henryana* ♔

This self-clinging deciduous climber can attach itself to walls or tree trunks without support. The silvery markings at the center of the leaflets are more pronounced when grown in shade, although the fiery scarlet autumn color tends to be brighter in sun. When the stems have climbed to the top of their support, they will flow gracefully downward, making a veil of dainty foliage. It can also be grown over ground cover, but if this is too flat the elegantly draped effect may be lost. Growth is not as profuse as that of Boston ivy and Virginia creeper (right), making it much more amenable to combinations, and it is especially effective with gold autumn color or berrying plants such as the larger pyracanthas. Since the foliage of *P. henryana* is small and delicate, it is best seen at close range. In colder gardens it succeeds best on a wall.

**Perfect partners:** *Celastrus orbiculatus*, *Cotoneaster salicifolius* 'Rothschildianus', *Juniperus* × *pfitzeriana* 'Pfitzeriana Aurea', *Lindera obtusiloba*, *Vitis* 'Pulchra'

**H: 33 ft. (10 m) ( ❋ Summer)**
 ◊◊ ▢-■ Z7 pH5.5–8

## *Parthenocissus quinquefolia* ♔
### VIRGINIA CREEPER

This deciduous self-clinging climber is very useful for covering brickwork and tall fences, although it looks more natural tumbling downward (through large trees, for example), than growing tightly up against a wall. Its divided leaves make for a fairly delicate effect, and provide superb autumn color. It works best mixed with a plant that grows away from the wall a little, allowing the creeper to cascade from its partner's outermost twigs, forming intriguing, uneven patterns. Its vigor can be a problem, but regular pruning will prevent it from blocking guttering.

**Perfect partners:** *Ilex* × *altaclerensis* 'Camelliifolia', *Juniperus squamata* 'Blue Carpet' p.110 **A**, *Malus* × *zumi* 'Golden Hornet', *Pyracantha* 'Soleil d'Or', *Robinia pseudoacacia* 'Frisia'

**H: 50 ft. (15 m) ( ❋ Summer)**
 ◊◊ ▢-■ Z4 pH5.5–8

**Above:** The autumn color of *Parthenocissus quinquefolia* breaks up an expanse of a cream-variegated ivy (*Hedera colchica* 'Dentata Variegata'), creating attractive patterns.

**Opposite:** A mature common ivy (*Hedera helix*) produces elegant sprays of rich green foliage, seen distinctly against Virginia creeper's bright autumn leaves.

## *Parthenocissus tricuspidata* ♔
### BOSTON IVY

The lobed leaves of *Hedera helix* 'Oro di Bogliasco' sit easily with *Parthenocissus tricuspidata*, fiery red in autumn.

The lobed leaves of Boston ivy turn a brilliant red to purple color in autumn. The uses and cultivation requirements of this vigorous, self-clinging deciduous climber are similar to those of Virginia creeper (above). However, the greater vigor and more solid outline of the leaves of Boston ivy make it harder to integrate with other plants. It looks especially good planted on the back of the wall and allowed to fall over the top to form a curtain across the face. 'Lowii' is less vigorous with smaller, deeply lobed leaves; 'Veitchii' turns deep purple in autumn, forming a striking contrast with scarlet-tinted foliage.

**Perfect partners:** *Celastrus orbiculatus*, *Fraxinus excelsior* 'Jaspidea', *Liriodendron tulipifera*, *Pyracantha atalantioides* 'Aurea', *P. rogersiana* f. *flava*

**H: 65 ft. (20 m) ( ❋ Summer)**
 ◊◊ ▢-■ Z5 pH5.5–8

A

The large, pink-tinted flowerheads of *Schizophragma hydrangeoides* 'Roseum', grown at the foot of a sunny wall, contrast in form with the tiny stars of *Trachelospermum jasminoides*. The grassy leaves of *Iris unguicularis* add foliage contrast and promise a winter display.

## *Schizophragma hydrangeoides* 'Roseum' ♔

A deciduous climber that attaches itself by means of aerial roots, this is a hydrangea relative with "lacecap" flowers, creamy white in the species and soft rose-pink in 'Roseum'. It is a rather tender plant that needs a mild climate with plenty of moisture and some shade. In areas where frost is a possibility, it is best sited on a west-facing wall to avoid sun-scorch on frosted shoots and to minimize any rain-shadow effects caused by the wall. It can also be grown up a tree, initially attached firmly to a support until climbing freely. It combines well with pink or red flowers, such as berberidopsis and mandevillas, with purple foliage, and with white-variegated ivies, and is effective with other climbers that have contrasting leaves, such as some ampelopsis or parthenocissus. The creamy white flowers of *S. hydrangeoides* itself goes well with gold-variegated or yellow-green foliage.

**Perfect partners:** *Ampelopsis brevipedunculata* var. *maximowiczii* 'Elegans', *Hedera algeriensis* 'Gloire de Marengo', *H. helix* 'Buttercup', *Sambucus nigra* 'Guincho Purple'

**H: 40 ft. (12 m)** ❀ **Mid- to late summer**
◊◊ ▢-◼ ◼ **Z5 pH5.5–7.5**

## *Tropaeolum speciosum* ♔
FLAME FLOWER

This perennial relative of the annual nasturtium, with herbaceous stems growing from fleshy tuberous roots, flowers most prolifically if the roots are kept cool and moist, with the shoots in full sun. It can be used to stunning effect with the roots protected by the base of a broad hedge, while the stems grow over the face of the hedge, especially one with fine, dark foliage such as yew. This combination of hedge and elegant creeper is immensely effective and hard to better, although flame flower can also be used to form an integral part of a hot-colored scheme. A partially shaded woodland garden is a suitable setting, with the climber draped across shrubs, especially those with bronze foliage or dark evergreens, or as a striking contrast with yellow-green foliage.

**Perfect partners:** *Acer palmatum* (purple-leaved), *Amelanchier lamarckii*, *Hydrangea serrata* 'Rosalba' p.108 **C**, *Ilex aquifolium*, *Rhododendron luteum*, *Tropaeolum tuberosum* p.178 **C**

**H: 13 ft. (4 m)** ❀ **Midsummer to mid-autumn**
◊◊ ▢-◼ ◼ **Z7 pH5–6.5**

Spectacular trails of *Tropaeolum speciosum* drape themselves across a somber hedge of common yew (*Taxus baccata*). The surface of the hedge is angled toward the sun, encouraging the flame flower to bloom profusely.

*Tropaeolum tuberosum* 'Ken Aslet' flowers from midsummer, coinciding with the entire season of the flame flower (*T. speciosum*). Its trumpet-shaped blooms and peltate leaves harmonize with those of its companion but differ sufficiently to create a most effective combination.

## *Tropaeolum tuberosum*
AÑU

This is a tuberous herbaceous perennial with twining stems and relatively small yellow, orange or red flowers. T. t. var. *lineamaculatum*, does not flower until autumn, but its selection 'Ken Aslet' ♔ is in bloom from midsummer onward. It is good with warm hues like red, salmon, peach, apricot and burnt orange, with bronze foliage, and yellow-green foliage or flowers. It can be planted on supports such as stakes, or allowed to trail over shrubs such as warm-colored roses or philadelphus. It combines well with red-, yellow- or orange-flowered morning glories, nasturtiums, canary creeper and other tropaeolums, and golden hops.

**Perfect partners:** *Berberis* × *ottawensis* f. *purpurea* 'Superba', *Humulus lupulus* 'Aureus', *Rosa* 'Geranium', *Sambucus nigra* 'Aurea', *Vitis vinifera* 'Purpurea'

**H: 13 ft. (4 m)** ❀ **Early to mid-autumn**
◊◊ ▢-◼ ◼ **Z8 pH5.5–7**

When *Clematis* 'Perle d'Azur' starts to bloom in midsummer, the leaves of *Vitis vinifera* 'Purpurea' are downy gray, becoming gradually less so but more flushed with purple as the season advances. At all stages, the color of the vine and its handsome leaves flatter the clematis and punctuate its almost too solid sheet of bloom.

## *Vitis vinifera* 'Purpurea' ♛

The leaves of the claret vine emerge downy and gray, and only start to assume purplish tints from midsummer, becoming deep maroon-purple before they are shed. This handsome foliage is a good foil for cool-coloured flowers in early summer, including clematis and roses, and continues to blend with these colors in late summer as it turns purple; by late autumn the tone is distinctly reddish and blends equally well with autumn-coloring foliage and hot colors. During summer its grayish coloring complements climbers such as *Solanum crispum* and its cultivars and maurandyas. Its autumn tints go well with the lighter, brighter colors of other true vines and free-fruiting species or Rambler roses. Good drainage is a strong influence on fine autumn color, and heavy soils should be lightened by incorporating coarse material at planting time.

**Perfect partners:** *Acanthus spinosus, Buddleja fallowiana, Celastrus orbiculatus* Hermaphrodite Group, *Clerodendrum bungei* p.87 **B**, *Parthenocissus henryana, Rosa* 'Albertine' p.186 **A**, *R. rugosa* p.208 **B**, *Vitis coignetiae*

**H: 23 ft. (7 m) (** ✿ **Early summer)**
◊-◊◊◊ ☐-■ Z6 pH5–7.5

## *Wisteria sinensis* ♛
CHINESE WISTERIA

This is a vigorous, deciduous twining climber suitable for growing on trellises, pergolas and walls; it can also be trained as a standard, used perhaps as a focal point or at intervals to punctuate a border, while in areas with hot summers it may be allowed to scramble into trees. The long racemes of usually lilac-blue flowers are borne with extraordinary profusion and combine successfully with early-flowering clematis such as *C. montana* cultivars, early Rambler roses like the Banksian cultivars and ceanothus. Laburnums' strong yellow looks good with *W. sinensis* 'Alba' ♛. Chinese wisteria is a superb plant for pergolas or arcades because the pendent racemes of flowers hang down within the framework, although *W. japonica* 'Multijuga' ♛, with racemes 18 in. (45 cm) long, is sometimes even more spectacular. Where trained lower down a wall or other structure, or when used as a standard, wisteria's pendulous blooms can interact with shorter shrubs, such as genistas or berberis, or with herbaceous or bulbous plants, such as taller alliums or (especially with white wisteria) crown imperials. Wisteria enjoys plenty of moisture at its roots and is a classic climber for training along rustic bridges and fences near ponds, where its lavish display can be reinforced by reflections in the water.

**Perfect partners:** *Allium hollandicum, Ceanothus* 'Concha', *Euphorbia griffithii* 'Dixter', *Fritillaria imperialis, Fi.* 'Maxima Lutea', *Syringa vulgaris* 'Charles Joly' p.143 **A** ☐ p.111 **A**

**H: 30 ft. (9 m)** ✿ **Late spring**
◊◊ ☐-■ Z5 pH6–8

In areas with warm summers, *Wisteria sinensis* will produce plentiful bloom without severe annual pruning, allowing a much more informal effect than would be seen on spur-pruned plants kept trained close against a sunny wall. This delightful informality is here beautifully enhanced by swags of white *Clematis montana*, which is of comparable vigor and will remain, at least for a few years, in equilibrium with the wisteria.

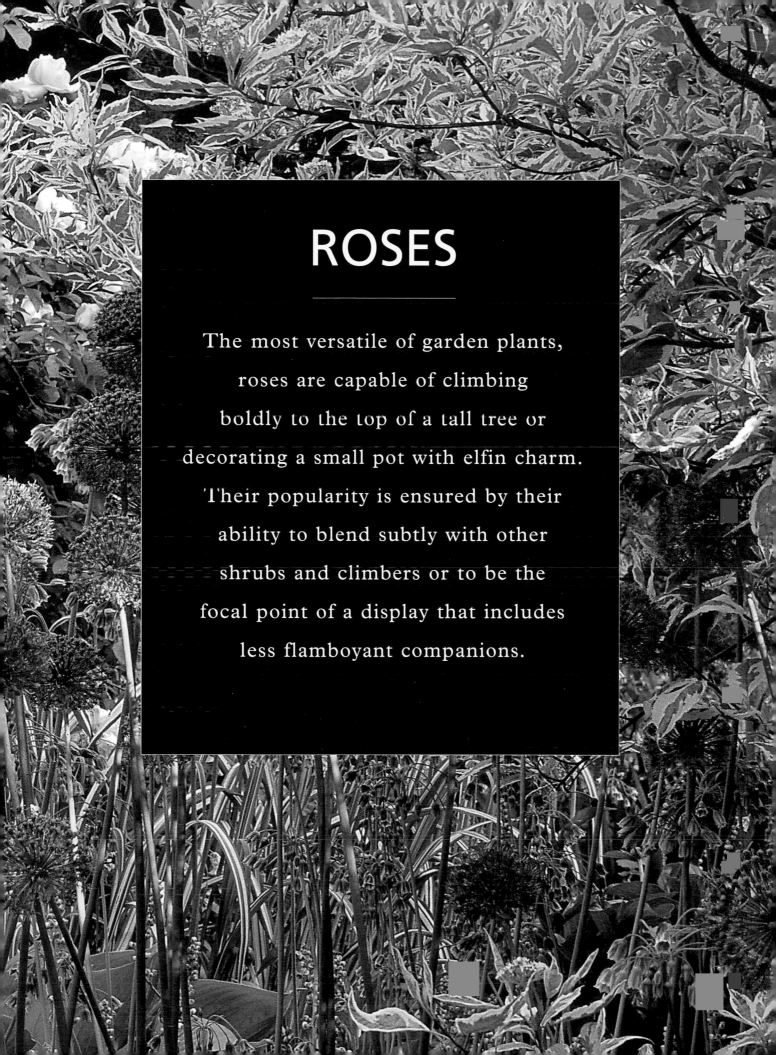

# ROSES

The most versatile of garden plants, roses are capable of climbing boldly to the top of a tall tree or decorating a small pot with elfin charm. Their popularity is ensured by their ability to blend subtly with other shrubs and climbers or to be the focal point of a display that includes less flamboyant companions.

**For centuries, the rose** has intrigued gardeners and plant breeders alike. As a result of this fascination and the untiring work of the plant breeders, there are now roses for almost every garden situation: swooning shrubs laden with scented flowers for borders and shrubberies, elegant climbers to festoon pergolas and arches, rampant ramblers to adorn trees and walls, neat and tidy bushes to use as bedding, and minute patio plants to fill pots, window boxes and raised beds.

Rose flowers come in an enormous variety of colors and forms, and many are beautifully fragrant. Some rose plants flower only once a year while others bloom sparsely but more or less continuously over a long period or produce several flushes of blooms. While the leaves are rarely the reason they are grown, plenty of roses do have attractive and healthy foliage. A few species and varieties also have brightly colored hips that extend the season of interest.

Because the rose genus is so large, it has been divided into different categories according to habit of growth and the form and presentation of the flowers. These categories include Climbing and Rambler roses, old and modern

Long after their flowers have faded, many Shrub and Climbing roses continue to delight the eye with their late summer and autumn display of colorful hips, while also offering sturdy support for later flowering climbers such as clematis and perennial sweet peas, as here in a border in Vita Sackville-West's Sissinghurst garden.

Shrub roses, Hybrid Teas and Floribundas, and Ground Cover roses. Many of the categories are further subdivided. All this can make choosing a rose seem a difficult task. However, it simplifies matters to consider the two main ways that roses are used in gardens: the shrubby roses and many of the climbers are perfect for integrating into the garden as a whole, while the larger-flowered roses, such as the Hybrid Teas and Floribundas, are suitable for more formal presentations.

## Roses in beds and borders

The type of rose that is ideal for growing in mixed borders or shrubberies tends to produce large trusses of fairly informal, softly colored flowers on plants with ample foliage. Apart from the modern "old" roses, most of these are shrubs that have one main flush of bloom with perhaps a second sprinkling later in the season. There is also a huge variety of species roses that are excellent used in this way.

All these roses will complement a wide variety of herbaceous plants, as well as each other, and they are very versatile because they may be left to grow into large masses or pruned regularly to produce small plants with more blooms. They are less useful as accent plants as their soft forms and usually indistinct foliage mean they are not very remarkable once flowering is over.

Although a little too brash for some tastes, the bright scarlet, white-eyed blooms of Floribunda rose Eye Paint can provide a racy element in imaginative combinations with softer colors such as the delicate pink of *Silene dioica*.

*Rosa* Pretty Polly, a small Floribunda or Patio rose of great quality, has the perfect combination of dense and shrubby but informal habit and outstanding flower color to be a success in a container, especially beside a border of complementary coloring.

Although often used for formal arrangements (see below), some of the larger-flowered roses with their clear colors and freedom of flowering can be invaluable in mixed borders. Memorable and long-lasting effects can be achieved by interspersing the strong-colored types with cannas, dahlias and scarlet salvias, or using the paler-colored ones with gray foliage plants – artemisias, cranesbills or pinks, for example.

## Formal rose beds

Roses suitable for planting alone or in geometric beds usually produce large flowers of exquisite shape in a steady trickle over long periods. Unlike many of their forebears, most of the recent introductions have compact growth, numerous flowers and good resistance to disease. However, their habit of growth is gaunt and their foliage is sparse and, therefore, formal rose gardens require careful complementary planting if they are to be attractive for more than a few weeks of the year. Edging the beds with

box or lavenders or, less formally, with stachys, London pride or other low-growing evergreens will provide a longer season of interest as well as emphasize the geometry of the beds in a way that the roses themselves cannot. In the summer, carpets of violas or cranesbills will furnish the garden more fully at ground level and will harmonize with most rose colors. As in mixed borders, standard roses can be used to introduce greater height, and climbers – roses or others – can be grown up pillars, over arches or on trellis to ensure year-round structure.

## Planting notes

Roses are grown for their flowers, so they are always best where these can be fully appreciated, especially if they are fragrant. Even the taller shrubs should be planted near the front of borders, where they will also produce a useful variation in height. Where roses are grown over arches, careful tying in is necessary to keep the thorns away from eyes, skin and clothes.

Opposite: Roses can play an important role as members of a mixed border or shrubbery. Here, Shrub roses, with their soft, fairly informal habit, can come to the fore while in bloom and, if they have little or no recurrence, will then blend in comfortably for the rest of the season.

Below: A trio of trained roses – the white Rambler 'Wedding Day' and the sumptuous purple Rambler 'Bleu Magenta', along with the shorter Hybrid Tea 'Botany Bay' – decorates the upper level of a pergola above a lower tier of Shrub roses and catmint in a high-summer celebration.

# Climbing & Rambler Roses

CLIMBING ROSES may be divided into two main classes: Ramblers and Large-flowered Climbers (including Climbing Hybrid Teas and Climbing Floribundas). Among the old roses, all Noisettes and Boursaults are Climbers, while Bourbons, Chinas, Hybrid Perpetuals and Teas include a few climbing varieties.

Ramblers include hybrids of the fragrant *R. multiflora* and glossy-leaved *R. wichurana*, as well as the stronger growing species roses, including rampant kinds like *R. filipes* (known botanically as *Synstylae* roses). They produce vigorous new shoots near the base of the plant each year, which flower the following year. Flowered stems are normally cut out immediately after flowering, but this can be difficult if the rose is closely combined with another climber; in this case, it is usually possible to prune both rose and companion in late winter. Shorter-growing Ramblers are ideal for pillars and as ground cover or, if grafted onto tall stems, as weeping standards. Varieties of middling vigor make stems long enough to reach over a pergola or arcade, or along a catenary; they can also sprawl into large shrubs or small trees; some may be trained against walls, although disease can be a problem here. The most vigorous sorts are best in a wild garden, where they can be left to scramble unrestrained into trees.

Large-flowered Climbers usually have fewer main stems, each of which provides flowering sideshoots for several years. Pruning, in late winter, consists of cutting back both main stems and sideshoots, and removing some older stems to encourage strong new growth. With their few stems and often coarse foliage these roses can look rather gaunt on a pergola or pillar, less noticeably so on a wall, but growing them in close association with another climber can improve their appearance.

A

## *Rosa* 'Albertine' ♧

This Wichurana Rambler flowers just once, at the height of summer, but so lavishly that the dark green foliage can disappear beneath the exuberant display. The fully double salmon-pink blooms, borne singly or in small sprays, emerge from copper-red buds and are deliciously scented. The rose is vigorous enough to be grown on a pergola or an arcade, and also succeeds trained against a wall. It is outstanding when associated with purple, bronze, red or copper-flushed foliage, and combines particularly well with blood-red, peach, apricot, cream or white flowers. Yellow-green flowers make good partners, but yellow-green foliage may tend to overwhelm it. This rose is rather prone to mildew, particularly when grown against a wall, where

Trained to mingle agreeably against a wall, the double flowers of *Rosa* 'Albertine' and the lobed leaves of the ornamental vine *Vitis vinifera* 'Purpurea' complement each other beautifully in both color and shape. It is unusual for this vine to be so strongly purple-flushed when *R.* 'Albertine' is in full bloom, except when grown in a nutrient-poor soil in a dry, sunny situation or hot climate.

air flow is restricted, but is relatively healthy if allowed to scramble freely into small trees or to develop as a sprawling, rather lax bush in the open garden.

**Perfect partners:** *Jasminum officinale* 'Aureum', *Lonicera × italica* Harlequin, *Photinia × fraseri* 'Red Robin', *Physocarpus opulifolius* 'Diabolo', *Rosa* 'American Pillar' p.187 **A**

**H: (16 ft.) (5 m)  S: 13 ft. (4 m)** ❁ **Midsummer**
◊◊ ▪-▪ **Z5  pH5.5–7.5**

## *Rosa* 'American Pillar'

This robust Wichurana Rambler has clusters of single, white-eyed, rich carmine flowers borne in one exuberant summer display, and glossy, deep green foliage. It is excellent for growing on pergolas or in trees, and may be trained on walls, although here it tends to suffer from mildew. It is valuable for creating brilliant, large-scale effects. Partnerships with lighter carmine or crimson flowers and purple or red-flushed foliage work well, and the blooms make pleasing contrasts with yellow-green flowers or dazzling clashes with orange. Its brashness can be tempered by combining it with silver foliage.

**Perfect partners:** *Acacia baileyana* 'Purpurea', *Cotinus coggygria* 'Royal Purple', *Eucalyptus kybeanensis*, *Euphorbia sikkimensis*, *Knautia macedonica*, *Senecio viravira*

**H: (16 ft.) (5 m)  S: 13 ft. (4 m)**
❀ **Mid- to late summer**
▬▬▬▭ ◊◊ ▮-▮ **Z5  pH5–7.5**

The strongly colored single blooms of *Rosa* 'American Pillar' are here combined with the more delicate pink rose *R.* 'Albertine' and *Helichrysum petiolare*. The helichrysum, with its elegant sprays of gray-green foliage tipped with clusters of creamy flowers, is an ideal companion for the roses in warmer climates, where it can be grown outdoors year-round, trained against a wall for shelter.

## *Rosa banksiae* 'Lutea' ♀

DOUBLE YELLOW BANKSIAN ROSE

The graceful, arching stems of this lovely Banksian rose look best if they are trained only loosely against a wall, allowing the swags and sprays of soft butter-yellow flowers to display themselves with a natural informality.

Each tiny bloom is fully double and lightly scented. This rose makes good contrasts with blue flowers, and harmonizes with white, cream, peach and apricot. Plants with yellow-variegated foliage, variegated ivies and many kinds of clematis are excellent partners. This is the hardiest of the Banksian roses, suitable for growing against a sheltered, sunny wall. In

areas with cool summers, plants may thrive but tend not to flower so profusely. Unlike most other Ramblers, pruning once every five to 10 years is usually enough. Single yellow *R.b.* 'Lutescens' is more fragrant than 'Lutea', as are double white *R.b.* var. *banksiae* (formerly known as *R.b. alba* or *R.b. alba-plena*) and single white *R.b.* var. *normalis*. None of these is as hardy as the double yellow form.

**Perfect partners:** *Acacia dealbata*, *Aquilegia chrysantha*, *Ceanothus arboreus* 'Trewithen Blue', *Euphorbia characias* subsp. *wulfenii* 'Purple and Gold', *E. griffithii* 'Dixter', *Hedera colchica* 'Dentata Variegata', *Kerria japonica* 'Pleniflora', *Ribes* × *gordonianum*, *Wisteria sinensis*

**H & S: 20 ft. (6 m)** ❀ **Late spring**
▬▬▭▮ ◊◊ ▮-▮ **Z7  pH5.5–7**

Many evergreen ceanothus coincide with *Rosa banksiae* 'Lutea'. Here, rich blue flowers of *Ceanothus* 'Concha' contrast perfectly with the rose's butter-yellow pompons. Looser training of the rose would also be effective, resulting in trails of blooms cascading over the clouds of blue.

## *Rosa* 'Brenda Colvin'

This *Synstylae* Rambler, with single pale pink flowers that fade as they age, inherits the vigor of its parent, *R. filipes* 'Kiftsgate' (facing page). Too vigorous to respond to annual pruning, it is not recommended for use on a wall; however, it can cover the largest pergola, will scramble through a medium-sized tree and may be used on a large, informal hedge. Where its strongly colored flowers and foliage can seem unnaturally bright, it is best combined with white flowers and with gray or delicately red-flushed foliage. Bolder pairings with, for example, rich pink flowers or strongly red-flushed foliage would be more successful on a large pergola; a robust vine would be a good companion, as would another Rambler of equal vigor, perhaps with double flowers.

**Perfect partners:** *Chamaecyparis lawsoniana* 'Pembury Blue', *Lonicera japonica* var. *repens*, *Prunus cerasifera* 'Pissardii', *Pyrus salicifolia* 'Pendula', *Rosa* 'Seagull'

H: 30 ft. (9 m)  S: 20 ft. (6 m)  ✿ Midsummer
○○ ■-■  Z5  pH5–7.5

The large-flowered *Clematis* 'Comtesse de Bouchaud' is an excellent partner for *Rosa* 'Brenda Colvin', echoing the rose's pink buds and the palest blush of its young blooms. However, the rose is so vigorous that the clematis will occupy only a part of its spread.

*Rosa* 'Climbing Paul Lédé' harmonizes beautifully with the cinnamon-pink of *Verbascum* 'Helen Johnson', bronze fennel (*Foeniculum vulgare* 'Purpureum') in the foreground, and distant red-leaved Japanese maples, leavened by the grayish shoots of *Cotoneaster simonsii* and white-variegated holly (*Ilex aquifolium* 'Silver Queen'). The blue-green of the obelisk and seat complement the scheme perfectly.

## *Rosa* 'Constance Spry' ♕

The large, fully double pink blooms of this versatile, once-flowering modern Shrub rose have the sweet fragrance of myrrh. The first of David Austin's English roses (see p.200), this is an unruly cultivar with long, pliable branches that demand a lot of space and management when grown as a shrub, and it is often treated as a climbing rose instead. When trained against a wall, it tends to bloom a little before the main flowering season of old roses, and so is best positioned behind the earliest of these, together with other precocious plants such as philadelphus or early-flowering clematis, and those with silver or purple-flushed foliage. With its vigorous habit and large flowers, it is suited to large-scale schemes, although its short flowering season may be a limitation. This can be redeemed by training a Viticella clematis over and through the rose stems.

**Perfect partners:** *Clematis* 'Princess Diana', *C.* 'Venosa Violacea', *Deutzia* × *elegantissima* 'Rosealind', *Philadephus* 'Manteau d'Hermine', *Vitis vinifera* 'Purpurea'

H & S: 10 ft. (3 m)  ✿ Early summer
○○ ■-■  Z5  pH5–7.5

## *Rosa* 'Climbing Paul Lédé'

The first flush of double, yellowish buff blooms on this Climbing Tea rose is highly prolific, and may be followed by occasional later flowers right through until autumn. It is particularly attractive combined with warm tints such as copper, peach and apricot, and is also good with glaucous foliage. Since its flowers are quite large, it may be used for contrast with a smaller-flowered climber, and looks outstanding behind tall herbaceous plants with differently shaped flowers, such as those with slender spikes or flat heads. It is deliciously scented and is useful for training on a pillar, obelisk or pergola; when grown against a wall it is prone to fungal diseases.

**Perfect partners:** *Achillea* 'Inca Gold', *Agastache* 'Firebird', *Elaeagnus* 'Quicksilver', *Hemerocallis* 'Penelope Vestey', *Hosta sieboldiana* var. *elegans*, *Stipa arundinacea*

H: 11 ft. (3.5 m)  S: 8 ft. (2.5 m)
✿ Midsummer to mid-autumn
○○ ■-■  Z7  pH5.5–7

Although *Rosa* 'Constance Spry' flowers earlier than many of the large-flowered Climbing roses, if moderately pruned (with all sideshoots cut back substantially), it will coincide in season with *R.* 'Rambling Rector', whose small, informal white florets contrast effectively in size and color with the lush and glorious blooms of its partner.

The delicate butter-yellow of *Rosa* 'Easlea's Golden Rambler' is a rare choice to combine with rich pink and red. This partnership with red valerian (*Centranthus ruber*) succeeds only through the sheer size, sumptuousness and profusion of the rose: smaller flowers of this hue would be visually overwhelmed by their more colorful partners.

## *Rosa* 'Easlea's Golden Rambler' ♔

The fragrant, soft butter-yellow flowers of this Wichurana Rambler are borne singly or in a cluster, in a single flush in early summer; they are large and fully double, with long, strong stems, and are excellent for cutting. This vigorous plant is suitable for training on a pergola or large pillar, and also against a wall, although here it may suffer from fungal diseases. It combines well with gold, white and warm colors such as peach or apricot, and with bronze-flushed, yellow-green, glaucous or gold-variegated foliage. Blue flowers make a fine contrast. This rose is good in an early summer garden; it can also be used to support a later-flowering clematis.

**Perfect partners:** *Clematis* 'Alba Luxurians', *Cornus alba* 'Spaethii', *Cotinus* 'Grace', *Digitalis purpurea* 'Sutton's Apricot', *Euphorbia griffithii* 'Dixter', *Lonicera periclymenum* 'Belgica', *Paeonia delavayi*, *Philadelphus* 'Innocence', *Potentilla fruticosa* 'Primrose Beauty'

**H: 20 ft. (6 m)  S: (16 ft.) (5 m)** ❀ **Early summer**
◌◌ ■-■ **Z5 pH5–7.5**

## *Rosa filipes* 'Kiftsgate' ♔

This is the most vigorous of all the *Synstylae* Ramblers, and in time it can smother even a moderately large tree. Because it is too territorial to be manageable when grown against a wall, and annual pruning and training make little impact on its vigor, it is perhaps best planted in a wild garden, where it can be scramble harmlessly into medium-sized or large trees (preferably robust, locally native species rather than cultivated ornamentals). Its spectacular flush of single, sweetly scented, creamy white blooms is followed in autumn by a glittering display of sprays of orange-red hips. These combine well with Virginia creeper, Boston ivy and other plants with fine autumn tints that can be trained through the same trees as the rose.

**Perfect partners:** *Acer platanoides* 'Crimson King', *Ampelopsis megalophylla*, *Fagus sylvatica*, *Fraxinus angustifolia* 'Raywood', *Parthenocissus quinquefolia*, *Vitis coignetiae*

**H: 33 ft. (10 m)  S: 65 ft. (20 m)** ❀ **Midsummer**
◌◌ ■-■ **Z5 pH5–7.5**

The dark, richly colored foliage of a purple plum (*Prunus cerasifera* 'Pissardii') makes a dramatic foil for the profuse, creamy white flowers of *Rosa filipes* 'Kiftsgate'. The rose will ultimately suppress even the largest plum unless pruned, although a comparable combination of the rose with a fairly mature, purple-leaved maple or beech, or even a large, dark green conifer, would work well.

Swags of *Rosa × fortuneana*, studded with charmingly informal, evenly spaced, creamy white blooms, drape themselves through the sumptuous purple flowers of the lilac *Syringa vulgaris* 'Charles Joly'. The rose could also be allowed to tumble through a large, blue-flowered, evergreen ceanothus or a purple-leaved shrub, or used on a wall or pergola together with a purple wisteria.

## *Rosa × fortuneana*

The great virtue of this lovely Chinese hybrid is that it flowers early, in late spring, when its informal, ruffled, double creamy white, scented blooms can be draped over larger shrubs in flower at the same time. It can also be trained against a wall, although here it is most successful if it is allowed to cascade freely over other climbers and wall shrubs. This pretty rose is generally believed to be a cross between the double white Banksian rose (*R. banksiae* var. *banksiae*) and Cherokee rose (*R. laevigata*). As such it requires a warm climate with mild winters.

**Perfect partners:** *Abutilon × suntense* 'Jermyns', *Allium hollandicum* 'Purple Sensation', *Ceanothus* 'Dark Star', *Clematis* 'Niobe', *Iris* 'Victoria Falls', *Paeonia rockii*, *Vitis vinifera* 'Purpurea', *Wisteria floribunda* 'Domino'

**H: 15 ft. (4.5 m)  S: 8 ft. (2.5 m)** ❀ **Late spring**
◌◌ ■-■ **Z7 pH5.5–7**

The rich, recessive purple of the late-flowering *Clematis* 'Venosa Violacea', its blooms enlivened by their star of pale petal centers, makes an attractive foil for *Rosa* 'Karlsruhe', providing a contrast of floral form. They make excellent companions, both remaining in flower for several months.

## *Rosa* 'Karlsruhe'

This moderately vigorous modern Climber is suitable for training on a pillar or against a wall. It has masses of glossy dark green foliage, and its scented, fully double pink flowers, borne in clusters of up to 10, appear in a prolific early flush, with some later blooms occurring. It goes well with coral-red, peach, apricot, cream or white flowers and with red-flushed or bronze foliage, and makes an excellent companion for deep red flowers, such as some clematis cultivars. One of the parents of this rose is *R.* × *kordesii*, a hybrid between *R. wichurana* and *R. rugosa*, both noted for their hardy nature.

**Perfect partners:** *Clematis* 'Rouge Cardinal', *Lilium* Pink Perfection Group, *Phlox paniculata* 'Windsor', *Phygelius* × *rectus* 'Salmon Leap', *Weigela florida* 'Foliis Purpureis'

**H: 8 ft. (2.5 m)  S: 6 ft. (1.8 m)**
✿ Midsummer to mid-autumn
⬛⬜ ◌◌ ⬛-⬛ Z5 pH5.5–7

Left to its own devices to form a mound of stems, *Rosa multiflora* is charming in more informal parts of the garden, with the added bonus of powerful fragrance. Here, white foxgloves (*Digitalis purpurea* f. *albiflora*) echo its color and add bold vertical accents, while *Clematis* × *durandii* provides a gentle contrast in flower shape and color.

## *Rosa multiflora*

This intensely fragrant Japanese species can be grown as a Rambler or as a freestanding shrub, when it will form a broadly spreading mound. It is most at home in a wild garden, where it can be left to scramble over hedges and into small trees. Its large clusters of single creamy white blooms are followed in autumn by tiny orange-red hips, which can be worked into a planting scheme with other berrying or autumn-coloring plants. In a wild garden it looks effective with plants of contrasting floral form or habit such as cow parsley, honeysuckles, foxgloves and bold grasses. 'Grevillei' (syn. 'Platyphylla'), or the seven sisters rose, is an old Chinese cultivar of similar habit, with sweetly scented blooms in shades of soft pink, deep lilac and white.

**Perfect partners:** *Cotoneaster lacteus*, *Eremurus robustus*, *Lunaria rediviva*, *Paeonia lactiflora* 'Bowl of Beauty', *Philadelphus coronarius* 'Variegatus', *Selinum wallichianum*, *Verbascum* 'Gainsborough', *Viburnum rhytidophyllum*

**H: (16 ft.) (5 m)  S: 10 ft. (3 m)** ✿ Midsummer
⬛⬜ ◌◌ ⬛-⬛ Z5 pH5–7.5

The bold boss of stamens at the center of each bloom of *Rosa* 'Mermaid' and the hint of yellow in its petals harmonize with the variegation of the ivy *Hedera colchica* 'Sulphur Heart'. Keeping the latter pruned close to the wall with the rose stems held just clear of the ivy allows occasional pruning or retraining of the rose and facilitates maintenance.

## *Rosa* 'Mermaid' ♔

The Macartney rose (*R. bracteata*) and an unknown double yellow Tea rose are the parents of this vigorous but slightly tender hybrid, which bears large, scented, single, pale canary-yellow flowers with a central boss of golden anthers. It is perpetual-flowering and in mild climates holds its glossy, dark green foliage all winter. Where summers are hot, it may thrive in the open garden or over a pergola, but in cooler climates flowering may be sparse unless it is given the protection of a warm wall. It should be allowed plenty of space while young because ultimately growth is very vigorous and can cover a large wall. Its flowers blend well with golden yellow, peach or apricot flowers and yellow-green foliage, and contrast with soft blues and rich purples.

**Perfect partners:** *Ceanothus* 'Pershore Zanzibar', *Clematis* 'Helios', *Corokia* × *virgata* 'Red Wonder', *Cytisus battandieri*, *Fremontodendron* 'Pacific Sunset', *Jasminum officinale* Fiona Sunrise, *Lilium lancifolium* 'Flore Pleno', *Phygelius* × *rectus* 'African Queen', *Piptanthus nepalensis*

**H & S: 20 ft. (6 m)** ✿ Early summer to mid-autumn
⬛⬜ ◌◌ ⬛-⬛ Z6 pH5.5–7

## *Rosa* 'New Dawn' ♈

This Climbing rose has relatively large, semi-double, pale pink flowers, often borne singly but also in clusters, particularly earlier in the summer. After a prolific early flush of freshly fragrant blooms, it continues to flower, rather less profusely, until autumn. With its vigor and delicate coloring, 'New Dawn' is a good choice for a wild garden, scrambling into trees or over hedges. It may be grown as a lax bush, and is also effective trained on a pergola.

Some shade is acceptable, so a wall facing away from the sun is another possible site. It looks great with white, lime green, deep pink or red flowers, and with purple-flushed foliage; honeysuckles make exceptionally attractive partners. 'New Dawn' is a sport of 'Doctor W. Van Fleet', an even more vigorous, rose that might be used as an alternative if flowers are needed only in early summer.

**Perfect partners:** *Centranthus ruber*, *Cestrum parqui*, *Deutzia* × *hybrida* 'Mont Rose', *Lonicera periclymenum* 'Belgica', *Persicaria bistorta* 'Superba', *Viburnum sargentii* 'Onondaga'

**H: 10 ft.** (3 m) **S: 8 ft.** (2.5 m)
✿ **Early summer to mid-autumn**
◌◌ ▮-▮ Z5 pH5.5–7

In this pleasingly delicate association, the marks at the base of the florets of *Philadelphus* 'Belle Etoile' echo the color of the buds and flowers of *Rosa* 'New Dawn'. This combination would be easier to manage if only a few odd stems of rose were trained in from a nearby wall, rather than allowing the two plants to tangle.

Roses grown on a wall need not be combined solely with other wall plants. Freestanding shrubs often make good companions as do biennials such as this Scotch thistle (*Onopordum nervosum*), which punctuates the rich blooms of *Rosa* 'Pink Perpétué' with a bold structure of pale leaves.

## *Rosa* 'Pink Perpétué'

A hybrid derived from crossing 'Danse du Feu' with 'New Dawn', this Climbing rose has fully double, deep pink flowers with a pleasant fragrance said to be of green apples, borne in clusters from summer into autumn. The stems, which are moderately vigorous and bear small, glossy leaves with purple tints, provide good coverage for pillars or for the lower part of a sunny wall. The latter site encourages free production of the charming flowers, which have a slight touch of iridescence, making 'Pink Perpétué' equally useful for lighting darker corners and walls. It is a good companion for late-flowering clematis and Ramblers with smaller flowers, and mixes well with dark red or light to mid-pink flowers, and with red or silver foliage.

**Perfect partners:** *Berberis thunbergii* 'Rose Glow', *Clematis* 'Duchess of Albany', *Cotinus coggygria* 'Royal Purple', *Phygelius aequalis* Sensation, *Rosa* 'Narrow Water'

**H: 10 ft.** (3 m) **S: 8 ft.** (2.5 m)
**Midsummer to mid-autumn**
**Z5 pH5.5–7**

## *Rosa* 'Rambling Rector' 🏆

This is a once-flowering Rambler, with the vigor and powerful, delicious fragrance of its parent, *R. multiflora* (see p.190). Its large clusters of small, semi-double flowers open cream and age to white. The central boss of golden anthers turn brown with age and are then not so appealing at close range. This is scarcely significant for large-scale effects in sites such as a wild garden, and in full bloom an established plant is a breathtaking sight. The display continues into autumn as shiny, rounded red hips follow the flowers. The rose's extraordinary vigor makes pruning and training difficult, and it is perhaps best planted where it can be allowed to grow without restraint – scrambling into a small or medium-sized tree, for example, or tumbling over an unsightly wall. It combines well with honeysuckles and small-flowered clematis.

**Perfect partners:** *Clematis* 'Perle d'Azur', *Lonicera periclymenum* 'Graham Thomas', *Parthenocissus henryana*, *Rosa* 'Constance Spry' p.188 **C**, *Vitis vinifera* 'Purpurea'

**H & S: 20 ft.** (6 m) **Midsummer**
**Z5 pH5–7.5**

An intimate combination of three different flowers usually succeeds if each is distinct in at least two of the three major characteristics – size, shape and color – while achieving pleasing harmonies or contrasts. This combination of *Rosa* 'Rambling Rector', the Chilean potato tree cultivar *Solanum crispum* 'Glasnevin' and *Clematis* 'Hagley Hybrid' meets this criterion, creating an attractive, harmonious effect.

*Rosa* 'Seagull', growing along a catenary swag from the left of the picture, makes a charming combination where it meets the luscious pink blooms of the Climbing Bourbon rose *R.* 'Blairii Number Two', growing from the right. The vigor of 'Seagull' is more than enough for it to grow up its catenary pole and over halfway along the rope slung between this and the next pole – an essential requirement for roses used in this way.

Grafted onto a standard-sized stock (4 ft./1.2 m), *Rosa* 'Sander's White Rambler' makes a dome of cascading white blooms, here surrounded by a contrasting carpet of lavender (*Lavandula angustifolia*). A taller stock would give longer, more dramatic trails of blooms, the curtain of stems broken in places toward the ground, allowing underplanting to continue beneath the rose.

## *Rosa* 'Sander's White Rambler' ♛

This superlative Wichurana Rambler is fairly late-flowering, producing sprays of rather formal, double, scented white blooms once in mid- to late summer. The flowers are especially attractive with mid-blues and pastels, and with glaucous or silver foliage. The moderate growth is suitable for pillars and for training on pergolas. It is also superb for growing as a weeping standard in beds and borders, where plants should have their cascades of bloom uncluttered by neighbors. It is an excellent for ground cover, both on the level, with its long, relaxed stems fanned out evenly and pegged down, and over banks, where it can be allowed to trail informally.

**Perfect partners:** *Acanthus mollis*, *Campanula lactiflora*, *Catananche caerulea*, *Clematis* 'Silver Moon', *Cynara cardunculus*, *Delphinium* 'Blue Nile', *Lupinus arboreus* (blue), *Miscanthus sinensis* var. *condensatus* 'Cosmopolitan', *Rhamnus alaternus* 'Argenteovariegata', *Salvia aethiopis*

**H & S: 13 ft. (4 m)** ❈ **Mid- to late summer**
◊◊ ■-■ **Z5 pH5–7.5**

## *Rosa* 'Seagull' ♛

The vigor of this Multiflora Rambler, which bears large sprays of fragrant, mainly single but also semi-double creamy white blooms with prominent golden stamens, makes it suitable for a wild garden, where it can grow through a medium-sized tree or over a large hedgerow. It is also useful for covering a large pergola or wall and is excellent with honeysuckles or the yellow-green foliage of golden hops. It goes well with white, peach or apricot flowers, and with silver foliage.

**Perfect partners:** *Campanula latifolia* 'Gloaming' p.248 **B**, *Elaeagnus* 'Quicksilver', *Eryngium* × *oliverianum*, *Humulus lupulus* 'Aureus', *Jasminum officinale* Fiona Sunrise, *Ligustrum lucidum* 'Excelsum Superbum', *Lonicera periclymenum* 'Belgica', *Philadelphus* 'Innocence'

**H: 20 ft. (6 m) S: 13 ft. (4 m)** ❈ **Midsummer**
◊◊ ■-■ **Z5 pH5–7.5**

## *Rosa* 'Sophie's Perpetual'

This perpetual-flowering Climbing China rose is a very old rose of unknown origin. It bears small, deliciously fragrant, loosely double flowers, cerise-carmine on their outer petals and shading to a rich pink center with silvery highlights. It is moderately vigorous and ideal for growing on pillars, pergolas and walls, where it goes well with other climbers such as clematis or honeysuckles of similar growth habit. Its color blends with deep crimson or pale pink flowers, and with silver or deep purple foliage, and makes effective contrasts with yellow-green foliage or flowers.

**Perfect partners:** *Buddleja fallowiana* var. *alba*, *Cotinus coggygria* 'Royal Purple', *Geranium* × *oxonianum* 'Winscombe', *Liatris spicata*, *Ruta graveolens*, *Weigela* 'Victoria'

**H: 8 ft. (2.5 m) S: 4 ft. (1.2 m)**
❈ **Early summer to mid-autumn**
◊◊ ■-■ **Z6 pH5.5–7**

The vibrant cerise blooms of *Rosa* 'Sophie's Perpetual' glow against the dusky purple of the Viticella clematis *C.* 'Venosa Violacea'. The pruning of the clematis, cutting it almost to the ground in late winter, is easier than that of a woody climber intertwined with the rose.

# Old shrub roses

NO GROUP OF GARDEN PLANTS has a greater power for evoking the romance of the past than the old shrub roses. Their intricately shaped blooms, heady fragrance and petals with sumptuous textures of satin or velvet are exquisite at close range, yet borne in enough profusion for grand effect. Although some do have a short flowering season – just a few glorious weeks at the height of summer – the beauty and quality of these plants offer more than adequate compensation.

The style of the flowers usually reflects the taste of the age when they were bred. Early 19th-century varieties, such as 'Charles de Mills', generally have formal, flat, intricately quartered blooms; high Victorian sorts, such as Bourbons, are usually globular and opulent; while those of the *fin de siècle* often have narrower, more elegant buds from which unfurl gracefully scrolled petals. A few (*R. gallica* 'Versicolor', for example) are even more ancient, associated with the Wars of the Roses, the Crusades or even the world of classical antiquity. Mixed with other old-fashioned plants, they are essential for bringing Old-World charm into any garden.

Hard annual pruning is seldom necessary; removal of weak, old or spindly stems and shortening the longest ones will usually suffice, although occasionally removing large old branches helps to ensure a succession of vigorous flowering stems. However, where smaller bushes are needed, many respond to harder pruning, giving a later, longer flush of larger blooms. Those with long, whippy stems benefit from training, either to a frame or by building up a structure from their own branches. If the flowers nod, higher training ensures that they face the viewer.

Their foliage is generally indifferent, and tedious when they are planted en masse; their appearance is much improved by combining them with plants of boldly contrasting leaf form or color.

## *Rosa* 'Charles de Mills' ♔

The flat, formally quartered, fully double blooms of this fragrant rose are perhaps the most perfect and fascinating of all the Gallica roses. Like its relatives, it flowers just once, in a color that varies according to climate and situation, from deep carmine to crimson, sometimes taking on purplish tints as the blooms age. It is suitable for the second or third rank of a border, and may be pruned each year to less than 40 in. (1 m) high, when it is ideal for bedding or rose parterres and for interplanting with alliums such as *A. cristophii*. It blends well with mauve, purple and pink flowers and with purple foliage. It can be contrasted with lime green, yellow-green and, in areas and climates where it takes on the darkest tints, with soft pale yellow. Sometimes said to be the same as 'Charles Lemayeux', 'Charles Lemoine' or 'Charles Wills', in fact the parentage and origin of this rose are not known for certain.

**Perfect partners:** *Allium* × *hollandicum* 'Purple Sensation', *Aquilegia* 'Apple Blossom', *Knautia macedonica*, *Salvia nemorosa* 'Rose Queen', *S. officinalis* 'Purpurascens', *Sambucus nigra* 'Gerda'

**H & S: 4 ft.** (1.2 m) ❀**Early to midsummer**
◊◊ ▢-▮ **Z4 pH5.5–7**

The superlative rich crimson blooms of *Rosa* 'Charles de Mills' contrast in size and color with the pale-leaved white rose campion (*Lychnis coronaria* 'Alba'), which is echoed in the distance by a white Rambler rose. Harmonious crimson Texensis Group clematis *C.* 'Gravetye Beauty' winds around the nearby post.

Purplish crimson *Rosa* 'De Rescht' clashes gently with Shirley poppies, most of which are a bright scarlet color. A hedge of dwarf box (*Buxus sempervirens* 'Suffruticosa') furnishes the front of the border, adding a touch of crisp formality lacking in the other plants.

## *Rosa* 'De Rescht' ♔

This is a recurrent-flowering Portland Damask rose of short to moderate height. Its fully double flowers are exquisitely scented and formally quartered, and vary in color from deep carmine to rich crimson, taking on purplish tints as they age. It suits the same combinations as 'Charles de Mills' (facing page). Other excellent repeat-flowering Portland Damasks include 'Arthur de Sansal', which is compact with upright growth and slightly deeper in color, and 'Indigo' (syn. 'Pergolèse'), 4 ft. (1.2 m) high, with smaller, more distinctly quartered flat flowers. Good pink cultivars are 'Madame Knorr' ♔ (syn. 'Comte de Chambord') and soft pink 'Marchesa Boccella' ♔ (syn. 'Jacques Cartier').

**Perfect partners:** *Cleome hassleriana* 'Cherry Queen', *Geranium phaeum*, *Monarda* 'Prärienacht', *Stachys macrantha*, *Teucrium hircanicum*, *Veronica spicata* 'Rotfuchs'

**H: 3 ft. (90 cm)  S: 2 ft. (60 cm)**
❀ Midsummer to mid-autumn
◐◐ ▣-■ Z5 pH5.5–7

## *Rosa* 'Fantin-Latour' ♔

Although sometimes classed as a Centifolia, the foliage of this once-flowering, pale rose-pink variety shows the influence of a China-derived rose such as a Bourbon. It is quite vigorous, so good in the middle or toward the back of a mixed border. Its very sweetly perfumed, fully double flowers, which are flat when fully open, harmonize well with white, deep pink, light crimson, mauve, lavender or lime green, and contrast well with yellow-green foliage and flowers. It is also very good with silver, red or purple-flushed foliage, and with a Viticella clematis such as 'Minuet'.

**Perfect partners:** *Alchemilla mollis*, *Digitalis purpurea*, *Eremurus robustus*, *Euphorbia palustris*, *Geranium* × *oxonianum* 'Julie Brennan', *Lychnis coronaria* Oculata Group, *Rosa* 'Impératrice Joséphine' p.195 C

**H: 5 ft. (1.5 m)  S: 4 ft. (1.2 m)**
❀ Early to midsummer
◐◐ ▣-■ Z5 pH5–7.5

The charming, soft pink blooms of *Rosa* 'Fantin-Latour' contrast in size and form with the slender spires of the perennial toadflax *Linaria purpurea* 'Canon Went' while matching its color exactly. Mixed foxgloves (*Digitalis purpurea*) echo the shape of the toadflax, which has a slender enough habit to weave itself through the rose, integrating the whole scheme perfectly.

Sumptuous blooms of *Rosa* 'Impératrice Joséphine' are here set above a sea of silvery rose campion (*Lychnis coronaria* 'Alba' and pink-eyed *L.c.* Oculata Group), with a bush of the paler pink *R.* 'Fantin-Latour' behind (top left). A yellow-green leaved shrub in the background provides piquancy, saving the scheme from potential blandness.

## *Rosa* × *francofurtana* 'Frankfurt rose' ♔

This is thought to be a cross between *R. gallica* and *R. pendulina* (syn. *R. alpina*). Formerly known as a Turbinata rose and now classed as a Gallica, this is surpassed by its hybrid 'Impératrice Joséphine' ♔, a sprawling shrub with plentiful, almost thornless stems and fairly dense, large foliage. Its semi-double (sometimes fully double) rose-pink flowers, shaded and veined with lilac, are large, fragrant and loosely formed, with slightly wavy petal margins. Although not recurrent, they are so beautiful that this plant deserves to be placed near the front of a border. It combines well with white, crimson, mauve, lilac and lavender flowers, and with purple, red-flushed or yellow-green foliage.

**Perfect partners:** *Centaurea* 'John Coutts', *Hosta* 'Buckshaw Blue', *Hyssopus officinalis* 'Roseus', *Lonicera nitida* 'Red Tips', *Salvia sclarea*, *Viburnum sargentii* 'Onondaga'

**H & S: 4 ft. (1.2 m)**  ❀ Early to midsummer
◐◐ ▣-■ Z4 pH5.5–7

# *Rosa gallica* 'Versicolor' ♛
## ROSA MUNDI

This ancient Gallica rose is easy to grow, very
floriferous and flowers only once. Its virtually
unscented, loosely semi-double blooms are
reddish pink, striped pale pink, with bold
golden anthers. In some seasons, many or
most of the blooms can be an unmarked red.
It is compact in habit, and grows densely
enough to make a hedge. Since it responds
well to fairly hard pruning it can also be used
for a parterre, where it looks effective with the
apothecary's rose (*R. gallica* var. *officinalis* ♛),
of which it is a sport. Also sometimes called
the red rose of Lancaster, this has light red,
fragrant blooms and more vigorous growth,
up to 5 ft. (1.5 m) tall; where they are grown
together, pruning needs to reflect the habit
differences. Both combine well with crimson,
pale pink, white and yellow-green flowers,
and with red-flushed or yellow-green foliage.

**Perfect partners:** *Campanula latiloba* 'Hidcote
Amethyst', *Dianthus* 'Pink Mrs. Sinkins',
*Galega* 'His Majesty', *Geranium sylvaticum*,
*Lilium candidum*, *Viola cornuta*

**H: 31 in. (80 cm)  S: 40 in. (1 m)**
❀ **Early to midsummer**
◌◌ ▣-■ Z4 pH5.5–7

**Right:** The large, informal blooms of Rosa Mundi (*Rosa
gallica* 'Versicolor'), extravagantly splashed and striped with
palest pink, contrast in size with the slightly taller cranesbill
*Geranium psilostemon*, its magenta flowers veined and eyed
with glistening black.

**Below:** The recessive tints of blue love-in-a-mist (*Nigella
damascena*) and dusky crimson-purple *Rosa* 'Tuscany Superb'
set off the bright flowers of Rosa Mundi (*R. gallica*
'Versicolor'), while the white rose campion (*Lychnis coronaria*
'Alba') leavens the ensemble. Fairly hard annual pruning
keeps 'Tuscany Superb' to the same height as Rosa Mundi.

## *Rosa* 'Madame Pierre Oger'

A rose of flawless beauty, 'Madame Pierre Oger' benefits from being seen at close range. Like most other Bourbons, it is repeat-flowering, with fragrant, nodding, globular, double blooms, in white shaded with the most delicate pink. It makes quite long, slender growth that is well suited to training, preferably on a fence or trellis. The subtle pink and white flowers can easily be upstaged by strong colors, so they are best combined with flowers in cool pastel colors and silver or smoky purple-gray foliage. 'Madame Pierre Oger' is a sport of 'Reine Victoria', which has flowers of similar shape but in rose-pink, borne on a more vigorous bush.

**Perfect partners:** *Achillea* 'Forncett Candy', *Aconitum napellus* subsp. *vulgare* 'Carneum', *Berberis temolaica*, *Campanula lactiflora* 'Loddon Anna', *Lavatera maritima*

**H: 6½ ft. (2 m)  S: 4 ft. (1.2 m)**
❀ **Early summer to mid-autumn**
 ◌◌ ▢ ▮ Z5 pH5 7

*Rosa* 'Madame Pierre Oger', its slender stems here bowed by the weight of its full, globular blooms, has flowers of great delicacy, their faint hint of pink toning with the red in the striking, contrasting dark leaves of purple berberis (*B. thunbergii* f. *atropurpurea*).

## *Rosa* × *odorata* 'Mutabilis' ♔

Also known as 'Tipo Ideale', this floriferous China rose blooms from early summer until the frosts, producing scarcely fragrant single flowers that open apricot and age through rich pink to red. With its shrubby habit, it can be grown in borders, including lightly shaded ones, as hedging and in containers. Its coloring combines well with warm colors such as cream, apricot, peach, coral-pink and soft red, and it is strong enough to survive partnerships with hot colors such as orange, vermilion and scarlet. It makes fine contrasts

with yellow-green, and associates well with purple or deep red foliage. It needs very little pruning in its formative years. Even mature bushes flower on very spindly shoots and require minimal seasonal attention.

**Perfect partners:** *Asclepias curassavica*, *Canna* 'Phasion', *Eccremocarpus scaber*, *Fuchsia magellanica* 'Versicolor', *Penstemon barbatus*, *Phygelius* × *rectus* 'African Queen'

**H: 3¼–4 ft. (1–1.2 m)  S: 2–3 ft. (60–90 cm)**
❀ **Early summer to mid-autumn**
 ◌◌ ▢-▮ Z7 pH5–7

The chameleon colors of *Rosa odorata* 'Mutabilis' embrace the soft yellow, pink and red found in the blooms of *Alstroemeria* 'Charm', creating a perfect harmony. Both contrast gently with the lilac blooms of the herbaceous *Clematis* 'Arabella' and spires of the perennial toadflax *Linaria purpurea*.

## *Rosa* 'Prince Charles'

This is a vigorous Bourbon rose, with veined and crinkled double flowers that open light crimson and assume maroon then lilac-magenta tints as they age. It is excellent in an early summer border, combining well with purple foliage and mauve, lilac or pink flowers, and making an attractive contrast with yellow-green or lime green. Its arching growth is strong enough to support a clematis that will supply color after the roses have finished flowering. Viticellas are outstanding for this purpose, especially a white cultivar such as *C.* 'Little Nell', or purple *C.* 'Purpurea Plena Elegans'.

**Perfect partners:** *Centaurea montana*, *Geranium sanguineum* 'Cedric Morris', *Linaria purpurea*, *Malva moschata*, *Phuopsis stylosa*, *Verbascum* 'Megan's Mauve'

**H: 5 ft. (1.5 m)  S: 4 ft. (1.2 m)**
❀ **Early to midsummer**
━━▬▬ ◌◌ ▢-▮ Z5 pH5–7

The purplish crimson blooms of *Rosa* 'Prince Charles' blend perfectly with the pink Damask rose *R.* 'La Ville de Bruxelles' and the large amethyst flowerheads of *Allium cristophii*, backed by a cloud of white *Crambe cordifolia*. Adding another relatively tall allium, for example *A.* 'Globemaster', between the roses would help break up their undistinguished foliage and unify the scheme.

## *Rosa* 'Reine des Centifeuilles'

Centifolia roses are once-flowering shrub varieties derived from the cabbage rose (*R.* × *centifolia*). One of the best is 'Reine des Centifeuilles', although unscented; it bears double blooms that are flatter, larger, and more formal than is usual for this class. The petals are also more open and less tightly packed. A good rose for a mixed border, its clear pink color blends well with white, crimson, deep pink, lilac, lavender and mauve flowers, and with purple-flushed foliage. 'Reine des Centifeuilles' is more tolerant of cool, wet weather than most Centifolias.

**Perfect partners:** *Cirsium rivulare* 'Atropurpureum', *Corylus maxima* 'Purpurea', *Erigeron* 'Quakeress', *Eryngium giganteum*, *Salvia verticillata* 'Purple Rain', *Silybum marianum*

**H & S: 5 ft. (1.5 m)** ☀ **Early to midsummer**
◌◌ ▨-▨ Z5 pH5–7.5

The intricately pleated blooms of *Rosa* 'Reine des Centifeuilles' harmonize perfectly with the pink toadflax *Linaria purpurea* 'Canon Went'. The toadflax contrasts in shape, as does the lavender goat's rue (*Galega orientalis*), which adds a second harmonious color.

A

B

## *Rosa* 'Tuscany Superb' ♔

The strongly fragrant, semi-double deep crimson blooms of this once-flowering Gallica rose assume purplish tints as they age. They are flat and slightly larger than those of 'Tuscany' (the old velvet rose), and display fewer prominent anthers at their center. The velvety blooms merit inspection at close range, and combine particularly well with pink, purple, lilac and mauve flowers, and with purple foliage; they also make effective contrasts with yellow-green foliage or flowers, and with white-flowered, silver-leaved plants. Although this rose is commonly grown as a freestanding shrub – most often in a border, hedge or tub – it produces numerous new upright canes from the base each year, and

The bright blooms of white rose campion (*Lychnis coronaria* 'Alba'), and its silvery stems and leaves, help lift the sumptuous but recessive colors of *Rosa* 'Tuscany Superb'. Sky-blue love-in-a-mist (*Nigella damascena*) is even more recessive in color than the rose, letting its partners dominate, although its blooms and feathery leaves add charm to the scheme.

so can be trained against a fence, for example. In this case, it may be pruned by removing all the older canes after flowering.

**Perfect partners:** *Aquilegia vulgaris* var. *stellata* 'Royal Purple', *Astrantia major* 'Ruby Wedding', *Galactites tomentosa* 'Alba', *Geranium* 'Sirak', *Rosa gallica* 'Versicolor' p.196 **B**

**H & S: 4 ft. (1.2 m)** ☀ **Early to midsummer**
◌◌ ▨-▨ Z4 pH5–7.5

## *Rosa* 'Zéphirine Drouhin'

This is a repeat-flowering Bourbon rose with attractive foliage, tinged bronze-purple when young, and completely unarmed stems, hence its popular name of the thornless rose. Its sweetly fragrant semi-double blooms, which appear continually until the frosts, suit cottage garden planting schemes, and they vary in color between carmine-pink and carmine-magenta. They combine effectively with crimson, purple, lavender and lilac flowers, and with purple foliage; they also make good contrasts with yellow-green foliage and flowers. Excellent companion plants include alliums, nicotianas and cranesbills. It may be pruned in the form of a shrub for growing in a larger border or as a tall hedge; alternatively, it can be grown as a climber. If trained against a wall,

it can suffer from mildew and blackspot, but on a pillar or pergola or trained on an open wire fence, where the flow of air is less restricted, it is relatively healthy. Its paler-flowered sport, 'Kathleen Harrop', is equally attractive but slightly less vigorous.

**Perfect partners:** *Cotinus coggygria* 'Royal Purple', *Lupinus* 'Blueberry Pie', *L.* 'Plummy Blue', *Nicotiana sylvestris*, *Persicaria bistorta*, *Phlox paniculata* 'Mother of Pearl'

**H 10 ft. (3 m) S: 6½ ft. (2 m)**
☀ **Midsummer to mid-autumn**
◌◌ ▨-▨ Z5 pH5–7

**Opposite:** *Rosa* 'Zéphirine Drouhin', variable in color and here almost at the palest end of its potential color range, blends perfectly with the rich crimson blooms of the Viticella clematis *C.* 'Madame Julia Correvon', which also provides a contrast of flower shape.

A

# Larger species & larger modern Shrub roses

APART FROM THEIR SIZE, the roses in this section have no shared characteristics but fall into a number of categories, each with its own distinct traits and uses.

The species and their primary hybrids tend to be more elegant than the highly bred cultivars. Many are single-flowered and often attractive also for their hips and autumn color. Some, such as *R. moyesii* and *R. glauca* ♀ and their hybrids, have a vase-shaped habit, with tall, arching stems that are bare at the base. The ruggedness of such stems can seem out of place in sophisticated borders, but in more naturalistic planting it is a positive virtue.

The Rugosa roses, many of them raised around 1900, and so on the cusp of old and modern, have glistening parsley-green foliage that, for some, is almost too vibrant for soft, old-fashioned schemes. They are, however, immensely useful for their hardiness, fragrance, continual blooming and autumn color. They can make an impenetrable thorny hedge.

Hybrid Musk roses, their rich fragrance derived not from the musk rose but mainly from *R. multiflora* (see p.190), usually have loosely double blooms in clusters borne continually from summer to autumn. Their colors include peach, apricot and soft yellow, rare in old roses but gentle enough to blend with them, as well as vibrant carmines and scarlets suited to more flamboyant schemes.

David Austin's English roses were bred to combine the floral form of the old roses with the colors and continual flowering of modern varieties. Selected for the English climate, many perform even better in hotter areas such as California, South Africa or the Mediterranean. Meilland's Romantica Series produces similar roses for the Mediterranean climate.

## *Rosa* Bonica ('Meidomonac') ♀

This is a superlative modern Shrub rose bearing clusters of slightly fragrant, fully double, rose-pink flowers from midsummer to mid-autumn. The color is close enough to primary pink to be used with both salmons and peaches, and also with cool colors such as mauve, lilac and lavender. It looks good, too, with crimson or white flowers, and silver, glaucous or red foliage, and makes effective contrasts with yellow-green foliage and flowers. It is excellent as a hedge, or in the second rank of a mixed border, either as a single plant or in loose groups, preferably with contrasting foliage such as that of daylilies or miscanthus. To hide the base

The large, loosely but charmingly informal pink flowers of *Rosa* Bonica contrast effectively with the dark, dusky pincushion blooms of *Knautia macedonica*, which furnish the rose's stems.

of the shrub, it can be allied with lavenders, catmints, hostas, shorter grasses or a similar mound-forming plant in front.

**Perfect partners:** *Cosmos bipinnatus* 'Daydream', *Nepeta* 'Six Hills Giant', *Penstemon* 'Alice Hindley', *Phlox paniculata* 'Eventide', *Verbena bonariensis*, *Vernonia noveboracensis*

**H: 3 ft.** (90 cm) **S: 4 ft.** (1.2 m)
✳ **Midsummer to mid-autumn**

 ◊◊ ■-■ Z5 pH5–7.5

The buff-apricot blooms of *Rosa* 'Buff Beauty' are here complemented by the boldly contrasting flower and leaf shape of the bright yellow columbine *Aquilegia chrysantha*. Several other columbines, particularly the North American species and their long-spurred hybrids, have warm-colored flowers, suiting them perfectly to combinations with soft yellow, peach or apricot roses.

## *Rosa* 'Buff Beauty' ♥

From early summer through to autumn, this Hybrid Musk rose bears large clusters of sweetly scented double blooms that vary in color from pale or medium buff-yellow to buff-apricot, making it especially suitable for blending with white or warm tints such as apricot, soft yellow or burnt orange, as well as with bronze foliage and yellow-green foliage or flowers. Associations with Spuria irises, daylilies and bronze sedges are excellent. It makes a large, branching shrub with strong, arching growth, heavy flower trusses and dark green, sometimes purple-tinted foliage. It can be prone to mildew in sites where airflow is restricted. In an open border it provides a handsome background to the superb autumn flower display.

**Perfect partners:** *Alchemilla mollis*, *Amaranthus hybridus* 'Hot Biscuits', *Bupleurum fruticosum*, *Carex testacea*, *Eupatorium rugosum* 'Chocolate', *Foeniculum vulgare* 'Purpureum', *Hemerocallis* 'Cynthia Mary', *Iris* 'Elixir'

**H & S: 5 ft.** (1.5 m) ❀ **Early summer to mid-autumn**
 ◊◊ ■-■ **Z5 pH5–7.5**

## *Rosa* 'Carmenetta'

This hybrid between *R. glauca* and *R. rugosa* inherits the typical Rugosa hardiness and vigor, combined with the foliage and loose, open clusters of single, unscented carmine-pink flowers characteristic of *R. glauca* (see p.203). In 'Carmenetta', the flowers are followed by an attractive autumn display of hips. Its thorny stems, which tend to become bare at the base, form a statuesque vase shape and look good with cranesbills, Spuria irises, campanulas or glaucous hostas. It is strong-growing, especially on light sandy soils where the good drainage can protect it against rust, and makes an excellent tall windbreak.

**Perfect partners:** *Clematis* × *durandii*, *Geranium phaeum* 'Rose Air', *G. pyrenaicum* 'Bill Wallis', *Hesperis matronalis*, *Hosta sieboldiana* 'Blue Angel', *Miscanthus sinensis* 'China'

**H: 8 ft.** (2.5 m)  **S: 6½ ft.** (2 m)
❀ **Early to midsummer**
■■■ ◊◊ ■-■ **Z4 pH5–7.5**

Although the bare stems of *Rosa* 'Carmenetta' may seem a little rugged for the most sophisticated sites, in more informal settings they can be dramatic and attractive, lifting a cloud of smoky foliage and pink flowers above the carpet of plants beneath. Here, the display includes large pinkish purple alliums (*Allium cristophii*), a variegated weigela and the upright *Campanula latiloba* and *C.l.* 'Hidcote Amethyst'.

## *Rosa* 'Cerise Bouquet' ♥

This is a large, sturdy modern Shrub rose, with grayish leaves and clusters of loosely double, but fairly refined, unscented carmine-red flowers. These appear in a main flush in summer, with a few more in autumn. One of its parents is *R. multibracteata*, from which it inherits its curiously bracted flower stalks. It is very vigorous, able to hold its own in a wild garden, although here the brightly colored flowers might be hard to place. It makes an arching, sprawling shrub for the back of a border or for large-scale planting with big, bold shrubs and larger herbaceous plants.

*Crambe cordifolia* is one of relatively few herbaceous plants that can match the gigantic scale of *Rosa* 'Cerise Bouquet', particularly if several plants are grouped together. Here, the vibrant blooms of the rose are contrasted with the crambe's clouds of tiny white flowers against an azure sky.

It may also be trained on a wall. 'Cerise Bouquet' combines well with crimson, cerise-pink or purple flowers and purple foliage, and makes a fine contrast with yellow-green foliage and flowers. Sweet peas climbing through its stems and a pink Rambler rose scrambling into it look marvellous.

**Perfect partners:** *Achillea* 'Summerwine', *Atriplex hortensis* var. *rubra*, *Lychnis coronaria*, *Malva sylvestris* 'Zebrina', *Persicaria amplexicaulis*, *Weigela florida* 'Foliis Purpureis'

**H & S: 13 ft.** (4 m) ❀ **Early summer to mid-autumn**
■■■ ◊◊ ■-■ **Z5 pH5–7.5**

With the simplicity of a briar rose but with larger, more strongly colored blooms, *Rosa* 'Complicata' is ideally suited to a more natural style of gardening using semi-wild flowers, for example this cultivated variant of common foxglove (*Digitalis purpurea*).

## *Rosa* 'Complicata' ♛

Although classed as a Gallica rose on the grounds of having *R. gallica* in its parentage, this vigorous shrub is quite unlike other Gallica hybrids in that it has large single flowers and a lax, arching habit capable of scrambling into large shrubs and even small trees. The solitary, pale-centered pink blooms, which are delicately scented, are followed by conspicuous round orange hips. It goes well in a wild garden, where it can be grown as a sprawling shrub, associated with flowers such as foxgloves and oxeye daisies. It can also be incorporated successfully into a flowering hedgerow, perhaps combined with other roses such as Ramblers and woven through with honeysuckles, and looks good in a mixed border, where it combines well with contrasting spikes of flowers.

**Perfect partners:** *Filipendula rubra* 'Venusta', *Leucanthemum × superbum* 'Horace Read', *Lonicera periclymenum*, *L. tatarica* 'Hack's Red', *Lythrum salicaria*, *Stemmacantha centaureoides*

**H: 6½ ft. (2 m) S: 8 ft. (2.5 m)**
⚘ **Early to midsummer**
▓▓▓▓░░ ◌◌ ▓-▓ Z4 pH5–7.5

## *Rosa* 'Excellenz von Schubert'

Variously identified as a Polyantha rose or as a Lambertiana, derived from a cross between 'Madame Norbert Levavasseur' and 'Frau Karl Druschki', this Shrub rose may be regarded as a forerunner of Hybrid Musks. Its sturdy arching stems bear large clusters of very lightly scented, fully double flowers, varying between dark carmine-rose and deep lavender-pink, shaded with lilac, and borne recurrently into autumn; they are followed by scarlet hips. This is a rose to be cherished for its continual display. It combines pleasingly with red or purple foliage, and with deep crimson, purple or pink flowers. It can also be grown on its own as a loose hedge.

**Perfect partners:** *Dianthus* 'Laced Monarch', *Galtonia candicans*, *Heuchera* 'Magic Wand', *Lamium maculatum* 'Beacon Silver', *Lavandula angustifolia* 'Hidcote Pink'

**H & S: 5 ft. (1.5 m)** ⚘ **Midsummer to late autumn**
▓▓▓▓░░ ◌◌ ▓-▓ Z5 pH5.5–7

The stems of *Rosa* 'Excellenz von Schubert' arch down to meet snow-in-summer (*Cerastium tomentosum*), its silver foliage and white flowers contrasting with the rich coloring of the rose. The ground-covering snow-in-summer could be underplanted with bulbs.

Extended groups of roses are often more pleasing and effective than single plants dotted around the garden. Here, a simple scheme depends on the repetition of delicate pink *Rosa* 'Felicia' and the contrasting green seedheads of *Allium hollandicum*. These draw the eye along the group toward the bright Hybrid Musk rose 'Vanity'.

## *Rosa* 'Felicia' ♛

This Hybrid Musk rose bears clusters of strongly scented, double, soft rose-pink blooms, with salmon and silver overtones, that blend with white, deep pink, crimson or soft red flowers, with warm colors such as peach or coral, and also with apple-green. One of the more vigorous Hybrid Musks, it is a bushy, wide-spreading shrub with strong branching stems and plenty of dark green leaves. It is useful in the second rank of a border, combined with silver or bronze foliage, or planted behind contrasting foliage such as that of Tall Bearded irises, catmints, or lavenders. Noted for its long flowering season that ends with a flourish – bushes often blooming lavishly in mid-autumn – it is handsome as a specimen shrub, and is good for cutting. It also makes a sturdy, weather-proof hedge, even on light, dry soils.

**Perfect partners:** *Eupatorium capillifolium* 'Elegant Feather', *Iris* 'Jane Phillips', *Nepeta grandiflora* 'Dawn to Dusk', *Potentilla nepalensis* 'Miss Willmott' ❑ p.125 **B**

**H: 5 ft. (1.5 m) S: 6½ ft. (2 m)**
⚘ **Midsummer to late autumn**
▓▓▓▓░░ ◌◌ ▓-▓ Z5 pH5–7.5

## *Rosa* 'Geranium' ♥

The single, soft cherry-red flowers of this *R. moyesii* seedling are borne from early to midsummer. The unscented blooms are relatively short-lived and are rarely produced in sufficient profusion to make a powerful impact. They are followed, however, by a display of pendent, flagon-shaped scarlet hips, which are among the showiest of the genus. Coloring in late summer and lasting well into the winter, they make a distinctive contribution to hot color schemes and to autumn plantings, harmonizing with orange or scarlet flowers and bronze foliage, and contrasting with yellow-green, blue or purple. The plant grows into a tall, arching bush, often bare at the base, with delicate, ferny foliage. It makes an impressive autumn feature when planted with larger miscanthus,

Rubellum or Korean chrysanthemums, and asters. Occasionally, one of the older, woodier branches should be pruned out.

**Perfect partners:** *Achillea* 'Fanal', *Canna* 'Wyoming', *Crocosmia* 'Lucifer', *Helenium* 'Bruno', *Helianthus* 'Monarch' p.283 **A**, *Kniphofia* 'Timothy', *Lobelia* × *speciosa* 'Cherry Ripe' p.307 **B**, *Phygelius capensis* ❑ p.422 **C**

**H: 8 ft.** (2.5 m)  **S: 5 ft.** (1.5 m)
✿ **Early to midsummer**
　　　　　　　◊◊　▪-▪ **Z4  pH5.5–7**

The scarlet hips of *Rosa* 'Geranium' are borne in sufficient profusion to make a bold effect, their uniformly nodding poise giving a distinct pattern to the bush. Here, they harmonize with other reds – *Penstemon* 'Andenken an Friedrich Hahn' and the unusual Anemone-flowered Group dahlia *D.* 'Comet' – together with maiden grass (*Miscanthus sinensis* 'Gracillimus') for foliage contrast.

In autumn, the vermilion hips of *Rosa glauca* are fully formed – plump and glistening – and the foliage is glaucous overlaid with a purple flush, turning to shades of orange, red and amber toward the end of the season. The orange flowers of common montbretias (*Crocosmia* × *crocosmiiflora*) harmonize perfectly with the rose's fruits, while the leaves provide good contrast in color and form.

## *Rosa glauca* ♥

This is one of a few roses that are grown mainly for their foliage, which in this species is glaucous blue-green, flushed with purplish red if sited in full sun. It tends to make a vase-shaped, arching shrub that is often bare at the base. Small, single, slightly fragrant flowers, carmine-pink with white centers, appear in early summer, followed by a lavish display of orange-red hips; the leaves, too, assume autumnal tints. In summer it goes well with cool colors, purples, blues, mauves, carmine-pinks and white, and with purple foliage; if grown in light shade to avoid the red foliar flush, it is also effective with yellow flowers. In autumn it makes a brilliant display with hot-colored crocosmias, Korean and Rubellum chrysanthemums and dahlias, as well as other autumn-coloring shrubs such as smoke bush, berberis or euonymus, and with larger grasses such as miscanthus.

**Perfect partners:** *Crocosmia* 'Dusky Maiden', *Euonymus alatus*, *Kniphofia* 'Sunningdale Yellow' p.303 **B**, *Lilium speciosum* p.377 **B**, *Miscanthus sinensis* 'Malepartus', *Onopordum nervosum* p.439 **A**, *Salvia guaranitica*

**H: 6½ ft.** (2 m)  **S: 5 ft.** (1.5 m)
✿ **Early to midsummer**
　◊◊　▪-▪ **Z4  pH5.5–7**

## *Rosa* Graham Thomas ('Ausmas') ♔

This is one of David Austin's English roses, producing flattish flowers like those of many old Shrub roses. The fully double blooms have a good Tea rose fragrance and are borne singly and in clusters, from early summer through to autumn, in a color that varies from light to mid butter-yellow, occasionally taking on amber tints. It creates excellent harmonies with warm colors – soft orange, peach, apricot and cream – and makes a fine contrast with blue. It combines well with yellow-green flowers and foliage, and with silver or glaucous foliage. Vigorous and freely branching as a specimen shrub, it may also be trained against a fence or trellis. In warm climates it can produce very long stems.

**Perfect partners:** *Aquilegia vulgaris* 'Mellow Yellow', *Eschscholzia californica* 'Apricot Flambeau', *Hemerocallis* 'Golden Chimes', *Nigella damascena* 'Oxford Blue', *Salvia patens*

**H: 4 ft.** (1.2 m) **S: 5 ft.** (1.5 m)
❀ **Early summer to mid-autumn**
◖◗ ◊◊ ▦-▦ **Z5 pH5–7.5**

**Right:** Rich blue, columnar flowerheads, such as the vertical spikes of *Delphinium* 'Cristella', make a highly effective contrast with the large, round blooms of the yellow rose *R.* Graham Thomas, while the horizontal plates of *Achillea* 'Coronation Gold' provide another contrast of form in a harmonious color. The cone-shaped panicles of lavender *Buddleja* 'Lochinch' behind the delphinium will continue the contrast after the delphinium has finished.

**Below:** In a combination similar in some ways to the one shown on the right, but this time in harmonious colors, *R.* Graham Thomas contrasts in form with the horizontal plates of creamy *Tanacetum macrophyllum* and the sulfur-yellow spikes of the lupin *Lupinus* 'Chandelier'.

In this hot-colored scheme, *Rosa* 'Helen Knight' is paired with the wallflower *Erysimum cheiri* 'Fire King' and the creamy yellow goblets of the peony *Paeonia mlokosewitschii*. The rose has been encouraged to produce blooms on the lower part of the bush by pruning some of the main stems back by about two-thirds of their length.

## *Rosa* 'Helen Knight'

This early-flowering species hybrid, usually classed as a Shrub rose, is the result of a cross between upright yellow-flowered *R. ecae* and sprawling Scotch rose (*R. pimpinellifolia*). 'Helen Knight' has single, unscented, saucer-shaped yellow flowers in one flush, on arching reddish brown or maroon stems that bear the typical ferny leaves of *R. ecae*. It is successful trained as a climber on walls and pillars, and may be used with warm- or hot-colored, late spring flowers such as wallflowers, tulips, late narcissi, early peonies and crown imperials.

Early cranesbills, brunneras, omphalodes, deeper colored forget-me-nots and similar blue flowers make attractive companions, as do yellow-green plants such as euphorbias.

**Perfect partners:** *Erysimum* × *marshallii*, *Euphorbia polychroma*, *Filipendula ulmaria* 'Aurea', *Fritillaria imperialis*, *Iris* 'Saltwood', *Polemonium caeruleum*, *Potentilla recta*, *Tanacetum vulgare* 'Isla Gold', *Tulipa* 'Golden Artist'

**H & S: 6½ ft. (2 m)** ❀ **Late spring**
◊◊◊ ▢-▮ Z4 pH5.5–7

The mauve-pink blooms of *Rosa* 'Lavender Lassie' combine well with the foliage of the weeping silver pear (*Pyrus salicifolia* 'Pendula'), contrasted here with dark green yew. With lighter pruning, the rose could scramble to the top of the pear, studding its entire surface with flowers.

## *Rosa* 'Highdownensis'

A seedling from *R. moyesii*, this large Shrub rose has copper-flushed foliage, especially on the new growth, and in summer deep cerise-pink, unscented single flowers borne on arching stems. These are followed by large, flagon-shaped plum-red hips. As with *R. glauca* (see p.203), this shrub's summer display makes it suitable for combinations with cool colors, whereas in autumn it blends particularly well with hot shades. Its stems are covered with colorful bristles and prickles. Occasional pruning out of one of the large, old branches can help to maintain a continuous supply of vigorous, flowering and fruiting stems with the brightest coloring.

**Perfect partners:** *Chrysanthemum* 'Mary Stoker', *Crocosmia* × *crocosmiiflora* 'Queen of Spain', *Kniphofia* 'Royal Standard', *Rudbeckia fulgida* var. *sullivantii* 'Goldsturm', × *Solidaster luteus*, *Stokesia laevis*, *Strobilanthes atropurpurea*

**H: 10 ft. (3 m) S: 6½ ft. (2 m)**
❀ **Early to midsummer**
◊◊ ▢-▮ Z5 pH5–7.5

Toward the back of a mixed border, *Rosa* 'Highdownensis' displays its elegant, rich pink blooms on a gracefully arching bush. The tender, shrubby *Artemisia arborescens* furnishes the foot of the rose with attractive silvery foliage. In front, the ancient double red campion *Silene dioica* 'Flore Pleno' has blooms that match exactly those of the rose, unifying the scheme.

## *Rosa* 'Lavender Lassie' ♕

A hybrid Shrub rose of similar parentage to the Hybrid Musks, 'Lavender Lassie' produces a tidy bush of moderate size, with large trusses of fragrant, mauve-pink pompon flowers opening from midsummer through to autumn. Their pretty, fully double shape and delicate coloring make this a suitable plant for mixing with old roses or for combining with cool colors, particularly pastel shades, and also with cerise. 'Lavender Lassie' is an outstanding partner for plants with silver, purple or glaucous foliage. Light pruning can emphasize its upright growth and encourages long stems, allowing it to be trained like a climbing or pillar rose or to scramble freely into a shrub, such as a silver elaeagnus.

**Perfect partners:** *Campanula punctata* 'Pantaloons', *Hebe* 'Mrs. Winder', *Hemerocallis* 'Grape Velvet', *Monarda* 'Aquarius', *Saponaria officinalis* 'Rosea Plena', *Sidalcea* 'Elsie Heugh', *Thalictrum delavayi* 'Hewitt's Double'

**H: 6½ ft. (2 m) S: 4 ft. (1.2 m)**
❀ **Midsummer to late autumn**

◊◊ ▢-▮ Z5 pH5–7.5

## *Rosa* 'Maigold' ♔

The strong, upright growth of this climbing Pimpinellifolia hybrid rose is useful for training against a fence or wall or around a pillar. Without support, it is also an attractive shrub, its prickly stems arching gracefully to form a large sprawling bush, well furnished with healthy foliage. Its large amber-yellow blooms are semi-double or loosely double and very fragrant, most of them borne in clusters in a single flush in late spring or early summer. Their gentle color and a relaxed growth habit make 'Maigold' suitable for less formal areas of the garden, even for a wild garden, where it can scramble through other shrubs or over a hedge. It blends well with warm colors, glaucous foliage and yellow-

The soft amber-yellow, loosely informal blooms of *Rosa* 'Maigold', borne on an arching bush, here contrast effectively with the blue flowers of *Iris sibirica*. The subdued blooms of the allium relative *Nectaroscordum siculum*, naturalized throughout the area, neither add to nor detract from the color scheme but provide a quiet charm.

green foliage or flowers, and makes a stunning contrast with blue flowers. Attractive partners include Bearded and Siberian irises, larger euphorbias and early peonies.

**Perfect partners:** *Euphorbia sikkimensis*, *Geranium himalayense*, *Iris* 'Blenheim Royal', *I.* 'Butter and Sugar', *Lupinus arboreus*, *Scrophularia buergeriana* 'Lemon and Lime'

**H & S: 8 ft.** (2.5 m) ❀ **Late spring to early summer**
◊◊ ■-■ Z5 pH5–7.5

## *Rosa* 'Nevada' ♔

This is a vigorous modern Shrub rose whose arching branches are studded with flowers, and can be trained against a wall to produce a short climber about 8 ft. (2.5 m) high. It is reputedly derived from a cross between a Hybrid Tea and *R. moyesii*, from which it gets its arching habit. Its lightly scented, semi-double blooms open palest yellow, fading in cool climates to white, while in hot situations they take on pinkish tints. In warm climates, they appear repeatedly from summer through to autumn, but in cooler areas there are few flowers after the first flush. Rain often marks the blooms with red spots, and this can limit the possible color combinations. It is perhaps best with warm-colored flowers, from yellow through apricot to peach. It also works well with silver or bronze foliage.

**Perfect partners:** *Eucalyptus gunnii*, *Hemerocallis* 'Prairie Sunset', *Lupinus* 'African Sunset', *Potentilla fruticosa* 'Abbotswood', *Rhamnus alaternus* 'Argenteovariegata'

**H & S: 6½ ft.** (2 m)
❀ **Early summer to early autumn**
◊◊ ■-■ Z4 pH5–7

Newly opened blooms of *Rosa* 'Nevada', each with a central boss of golden anthers, retain a hint of yellow in their petals, harmonizing here with yellow and orange Welsh poppies (*Meconopsis cambrica*). Other white flowers, namely white sweet rocket (*Hesperis matronalis* var. *albiflora*) and, across the path, *Spiraea* 'Arguta', unify the scheme.

In this pleasingly subtle combination, the delicate pink of *Rosa* Peach Blossom is echoed in the pink-flushed leaves of *Fuchsia magellanica* 'Versicolor'. A carpet of silver-green lamb's ears (*Stachys byzantina*) furnishes the front of the bed, while a cloud of *Crambe cordifolia* fills the background.

## *Rosa* Peach Blossom ('Ausblossom')

This David Austin English rose bears blush-pink flowers with a light almond fragrance. Deadheading the earliest blooms encourages the plant to produce more later on, or the spent flowers can be left to form an autumn crop of attractive hips. The loosely semi-double blooms have an informal charm that suits them to planting in cottage garden style. Their delicate coloring combines well with other cool pastels such as pink, mauve, lilac and pale lavender, and with white flowers and silver or purple-flushed foliage, such as silvery white stachys, or purple ajugas and smoke bush, and dark-leaved *Viola riviniana* Purpurea Group. With its fairly upright, bushy habit and size, this rose suits the second row in a border.

**Perfect partners:** *Achillea* 'Apfelblüte', *Astrantia maxima*, *Lavatera* 'Pavlova', *Malva moschata* f. *alba*, *Phlox maculata* 'Rosalinde', *Saponaria officinalis* 'Rosea Plena'

**H: 3 ft. (90 cm)  S: 4 ft. (1.2 m)**
✿ **Midsummer to mid-autumn**
▭▬ ◊◊ ▢-▉ Z5 pH5–7.5

Cranesbills are effective plants for carpeting in front of and beneath roses. Here, *Geranium clarkei* 'Kashmir Purple' – a useful cultivar flowering from early to late summer – weaves itself through the arching stems of the cherry-red Hybrid Musk rose *R.* 'Robin Hood'.

## *Rosa* 'Penelope' ♛

One of the most reliable Hybrid Musks, 'Penelope' flowers prolifically from midsummer until late autumn, especially if deadheaded after the first main flush. It makes a rather dense, spreading bush and bears large trusses of exceptionally fragrant, semi-double blooms that can vary in color according to climate and situation from pale peach to cream, with deeper shading toward the center. Its color is especially effective with warm colors such as peach, apricot and pale pink, and with bronze-flushed foliage. It goes well with daylilies that have bronzy copper flower tones, bronze sedges or red-flushed berberis. Blue flowers also make good companions, particularly delphiniums and salvias such as *S.* × *superba* cultivars.

**Perfect partners:** *Berberis thunbergii* 'Pink Queen', *Carex comans* (bronze), *Hemerocallis* 'Ruffled Apricot', *Iris* 'Champagne Elegance', *Persicaria virginiana* Compton's form, *Stokesia laevis* 'Peach Melba', *Uncinia egmontiana*

**H & S: 5 ft. (1.5 m)** ✿ **Midsummer to late autumn**
▭▬ ◊◊ ▢-▉ Z5 pH5–7.5

Trained to cover a post and wire fence, this fairly yellow *Rosa* 'Penelope' is seen here in a classic partnership with a columnar flower, the relatively short foxglove *Digitalis purpurea* Foxy Group. This shorter variant interacts with the rose more effectively than if a taller sort, such as *D.p.* 'Sutton's Apricot', had been used.

## *Rosa* 'Robin Hood'

'Robin Hood' has small flowers, freely borne in clusters over a long season. Unlike most of the other Hybrid Musks, the flowers are only faintly scented. They are a slightly dusky cherry-red, which forms an effective backdrop for other, brighter shades. The flowers deepen with age and are followed by clusters of tiny brown hips. Being close to primary red, this rose is equally suited to growing with vermilion or bright carmine-pink flowers, and also combines well with purple or red foliage. Yellow-green foliage or flowers make an excellent contrast. It is good as a flowering hedge and also looks attractive planted in tubs and other large containers.

**Perfect partners:** *Cotinus coggygria* Golden Spirit, *Geranium* 'Lydia', *Hypericum androsaemum* 'Albury Purple', *Leycesteria formosa* Golden Lanterns, *Sidalcea* 'Mrs. Borrodaile'

**H: 4 ft. (1.2 m)  S: 3 ft. (90 cm)**
✿ **Midsummer to late autumn**
 ◊◊ ▉-▉ Z5 pH5–7.5

## *Rosa* 'Roseraie de l'Haÿ' ♔

Constantly in flower from early summer until autumn, this Rugosa rose bears semi-double, rich magenta-crimson blooms, unfurling from narrow buds and strongly scented. Unlike most Rugosas, it produces very few hips, so it is grown mainly for its flowers even though the foliage does assume good autumn tints. It makes a very thorny bush that can be used as a hedge. If not grafted onto a rootstock, its own roots produce suckers that eventually form an impenetrable barrier that tolerates some shade. Its rich color can be used in harmonies with cool shades such as blue and purple, or in contrasts with bright yellow, vermilion or yellow-green. It works well with purple or glaucous foliage, and looks very attractive with a perennial pea or small-flowered clematis scrambling through it.

**Perfect partners:** *Atriplex hortensis* var. *rubra*, *Clematis* 'Princess Diana', *C. recta* 'Velvet Night', *Hypericum androsaemum* 'Albury Purple', *Lathyrus grandiflorus, Nepeta govaniana*

**H & S: 6½ ft. (2 m)** ❀ **Early summer to late autumn**
◊◊ ▢-◼ **Z4 pH5.5–7**

If *Rosa* 'Roseraie de l'Haÿ' is pruned only lightly or not at all, it will bloom in late spring, making possible dazzling combinations such as this with tree lupin (*Lupinus arboreus*), the young leaves of *Lysimachia ciliata* 'Firecracker', and a richly colored broom. Each brings its own contrasting texture and structure to the ensemble.

## *Rosa rugosa*

In cultivation *R. rugosa* has single, mid-carmine flowers with broad petals, crinkled and thin-textured and a prominent central boss of golden yellow anthers. The blooms, borne singly or in small clusters, are followed in autumn by large, round orange-red hips, and the leaves turn butter-yellow. Its flower color suits it to summer combinations with cool shades such as pale carmine-pink, magenta, crimson, mauve, lilac, lavender, blue or purple, together with purple or silver foliage, and to contrasts with yellow-green. In autumn it goes well with warm colors such as peach, apricot and soft orange, and bronze or red-flushed foliage. Like 'Roseraie de l'Haÿ' (left), it makes a suckering shrub if

In autumn, the flowers of *Rosa rugosa* become few and far between and its fat, glistening hips take over the display. Here, the hips harmonize with the mahogany leaves of the claret vine *Vitis vinifera* 'Purpurea' and the rusty seedheads of *Sedum* 'Herbstfreude', whose glaucous foliage and that of *Hebe albicans* provide gentle contrast.

grown on its own roots. 'Rubra' ♔ has slightly deeper, light magenta flowers and 'Alba' ♔ bears large, very delicate, single white flowers.

**Perfect partners:** *Crocosmia* × *crocosmiiflora* 'Mars', *Kniphofia rooperi, Miscanthus sinensis* 'Sioux', *Phormium* 'Pink Panther', *Phygelius* × *rectus* 'Salmon Leap', *Rudbeckia laciniata* 'Herbstsonne'

**H & S: 3¼–8 ft. (1–2.5 m)**
❀ **Early summer to mid-autumn**
 ◊◊ ▢-◼ **Z3 pH5.5–7**

## *Rosa* 'Sally Holmes'  ♛

This is an outstanding Shrub rose for the second or third rank of a border. Its flowers, creamy white and single with a central boss of golden anthers, are borne in large clusters in summer and autumn, and make a strong visual impact. Its parentage is similar to that of the Hybrid Musk roses, hence its rich fragrance. If pruned fairly hard, it may be treated as a Floribunda, whereas lighter pruning allows it to achieve more substantial size. This versatile rose looks especially effective with silver or glaucous foliage. Dramatic combinations can be made with yellow flowers that reflect the golden centers of the rose blooms, or with blue flowers to create a contrast to the anthers. Annual climbers such as morning glories can be planted as companions and allowed to weave informally across and through medium- to large-sized groups.

**Perfect partners:** *Campanula lactiflora* 'Prichard's Variety', *Clematis* × *durandii*, *Consolida ajacis*, *Convolvulus tricolor* 'Royal Ensign', *Coreopsis verticillata* 'Grandiflora', *Geranium* 'Brookside', *Geum* 'Lady Stratheden'

**H: 6½ ft. (2 m)  S: 3¼ ft. (1 m)**
✿ **Midsummer to late autumn**
▨▨ ◊◊ ▨-▨ **Z5  pH5–7.5**

*Rosa* 'Sally Holmes' is here pruned hard, as for a Floribunda, keeping it compact and spectacularly floriferous. *Potentilla fruticosa* 'Goldfinger' furnishes the rose's base and harmonizes with its golden yellow anthers. Deadheading the rose encourages plentiful later bloom.

A

# Hybrid Teas & Floribundas

HYBRID TEAS (Large-flowered roses), popular for the size and often superb shape of their blooms, and the very floriferous Floribundas (Cluster-flowered roses) are the largest and most commonly grown classes of bush rose, both of them available in a wide range of colors. Generally, bush roses are best combined with plants of other genera rather than planted in the traditional way – massed in beds or as a series of sentry singles in clashing colors, with their usually coarse foliage and stiff habit on view. Mound-forming plants, or even box edging, in front of the roses can mask their unsightly bases, while foliage of attractive texture or architectural form to either side and behind will ensure that the onlooker scarcely notices the leaves of the roses but instead concentrates on the undoubted beauty of the flowers.

The scale of the flowers and the bushes themselves also needs consideration. Large blooms, particularly if brightly colored, can look far too big in a tiny garden, unless there is a deliberate attempt to use oversized plants throughout. A single bush, or a whole bed of them, might not match the scale of planting of the rest of the garden: three, five or more bushes, perhaps loosely grouped, and with other plants woven through them, might provide a more fitting scale.

Hybrid Teas are traditionally pruned in late winter, removing weak or spindly shoots, shortening the main stems and sideshoots to outward-facing buds and removing occasional older main stems to ensure a constant supply of vigorous flowering wood. For Floribundas, the main stems are pruned more severely to encourage larger new shoots, each of which will provide a cluster of blooms in early summer, followed later in the season by smaller sprays on the sideshoots.

A

Pruning in this way allows light and air between the plants, making it possible to underplant with spring flowers, such as bulbs, wood anemones or primroses. The young rose leaves, if red, can harmonize attractively or clash dramatically with the plants beneath. If rose bushes are underplanted, pruning may need to take place earlier than usual, even in autumn in mild climates; it is usually impracticable to mulch in spring, but a friable organic mulch that will not impede the emerging shoots of spring flowers could be applied in autumn instead.

If the scale of the planting requires a bigger or taller rose than the traditional

The tall Floribunda *Rosa* Anne Harkness blooms a little later than others of its group, continuing into the autumn. Its habit makes it eminently suitable for use in a mixed border, where it can be combined with midsummer or later flowers in warm or hot colors, ideally using several bushes of the rose to relate the scale of the group to that of other planting and to avoid a spotty effect. Here, Anne Harkness is partnered by vermilion sprays of *Crocosmia paniculata* and the acid yellow-green buds of goldenrod; it would also combine well with dahlias.

Floribunda, then lighter pruning can be a solution. The cultivars 'Chinatown' ♀, 'Frensham', Iceberg ('Korbin') ♀, and 'Yesterday' ♀ work particularly well on a larger scale. More sizable bushes look very effective lightly draped with annual or herbaceous climbers, for instance morning glories or perennial peas.

*Rosa* Avalanche is here combined with the charming annual umbellifer *Orlaya grandiflora*, its lacy flowers and fernlike foliage contrasting with the altogether more solidly substantial rose. Other annual umbellifers such as *Ammi majus* could be used in the same way with roses.

## *Rosa* Avalanche ('Jacay')

This Floribunda rose has cream flowers fading to white. The flowers are not fully double and often reveal the yellow anthers at the center of the bloom. The shade of cream is inclined more toward apricot or peach than yellow, so this rose tends to go best with warm tints such as peach or apricot. It also works well with glaucous or silver foliage, as well as with bronze-flushed or white- or gold-variegated leaves. It looks particularly attractive planted with other white flowers, especially umbellifers, gypsophilas, sea kale and other plants with flowerheads of similarly contrasting form or size.

**Perfect partners:** *Achillea* 'Hella Glashoff', *A.* 'Hoffnung', *Artemisia* 'Powis Castle', *Eschscholzia californica* 'Alba', *Hakonechloa macra* 'Alboaurea', *Verbascum* (Cotswold Group) 'Gainsborough'

**H: 4 ft.** (1.2 m)  **S: 3 ft.** (90 cm)
❀ **Midsummer to late autumn**
 ◊◊ ☐-◼ Z5 pH5–7.5

The flat, formal, rich red flowers of *Rosa* 'Europeana' and its red-flushed young leaves combine perfectly with the salmon and scarlet, dark-centered blooms of sprawling *Potentilla nepalensis* 'Roxana'.

## *Rosa* 'Europeana'

Opulent and richly colored, this fine Floribunda rose has fully double, relatively flat blooms, and profuse foliage that emerges dark red and matures to green. The flower color suits sumptuous schemes, especially plantings with coral, rich salmon-pink or vermilion flowers, and contrasts with lime green or yellow-green foliage and flowers. The young red leaves make an eye-catching combination with late spring bulbs such as narcissi, tulips or crown imperials, perhaps underplanted with primroses. Its attractive flower formation is very striking at close range. Relatively upright and tall for a Floribunda, it is good for the second or third rank of a border, where it mixes well with bronze- or purple-leaved plants including medium-sized shrubs and phormiums, and dark-leaved dahlias and crocosmias.

**Perfect partners:** *Alchemilla mollis*, *Dahlia* 'Tally Ho', *Lychnis* × *arkwrightii* 'Vesuvius', *Narcissus* 'Ambergate', *Nicotiana* 'Lime Green', *Primula* Cowichan Venetian Group, *Tulipa* 'Couleur Cardinal'

**H & S: 24 in.** (60 cm)
❀ **Midsummer to late autumn**
 ◊◊ ☐-◼ Z5 pH5–7.5

Pruned hard, as usual for a Floribunda, *Rosa* 'Chinatown' is compact with a prolific first flush of flowers, produced at an ideal height to contrast with those of the catmint *Nepeta* 'Six Hills Giant'. Deadheading the rose will encourage blooming into the autumn. The catmint will also produce later flowers if cut back after its first flush.

## *Rosa* 'Chinatown' ♈

Although classed as a Floribunda, this is a vigorous, disease-resistant rose that may be lightly pruned for use as a shrub rose, or a medium-sized hedge, or even espaliered like a short climbing rose on a wall or fence. It may be grown in the second or third rank of a border. Its very large, fully double yellow flowers have notched and slightly crimped petals, giving each bloom a rather frilly outline, and they appear continuously throughout summer. The yellow of the flowers is pure enough to contrast well with blue, and it also looks good with pale yellow, cream and warm colors such as peach and apricot, as well as yellow-green foliage and flowers or gold-variegated leaves. Good companions include gold-variegated grasses, Spuria irises, *Iris sibirica* cultivars and hosta cultivars that tolerate strong sun.

**Perfect partners:** *Achillea* 'Lucky Break', *Delphinium* Summer Skies Group, *D.* 'Sungleam', *Hosta* 'Sum and Substance', *Iris* 'Cambridge', *I. orientalis*, *Miscanthus sinensis* 'Strictus', *Nigella damascena* 'Miss Jekyll', *Verbascum* (Cotswold Group) 'Cotswold King'

**H: 4 ft.** (1.2 m)  **S: 3 ft.** (90 cm)
❀ **Early summer to late autumn**
◊◊ ☐-◼ Z5 pH5–7.5

## *Rosa* 'Frensham'

This rose, with its pure scarlet, semi-double flowers, was the first truly popular red-flowered Floribunda. If only lightly pruned, this vigorous cultivar can achieve the size of a Shrub rose, so allowing its use toward the back of a border and in larger-scale plantings. With its exceptionally strong, robust habit and very prickly stems it makes a good hedge, although it can be prone to mildew if grown this way. Its bright coloring works well with hot tints such as orange, vermilion and golden yellow, or warm colors such as peach and coral. It also combines happily with bronze, purple or red-flushed foliage, and makes effective contrasts with yellow-green flowers and leaves and lime-green flowers.

**Perfect partners:** *Dahlia* 'Bednall Beauty' p.419 **B**, *Hemerocallis* 'Root Beer', *Kniphofia* 'Green Jade', *Nicotiana langsdorffii* 'Cream Splash', *Persicaria microcephala* 'Red Dragon'

**H: 4 ft.** (1.2 m) **S: 30 in.** (75 cm)
❀ **Midsummer to late autumn**
◖◗ ◊◊ ◼-◼ **Z5 pH5–7.5**

In this border of red, yellow and creamy white flowers combined with dusky foliage, the rich scarlet *Rosa* 'Frensham' and the dark-leaved loosestrife *Lysimachia ciliata* 'Firecracker' are leavened by the sulfur-yellow candelabra of *Verbascum* 'Vernale' and the fluffy yellow panicles of the meadow rue *Thalictrum flavum* subsp. *glaucum*. White roses in the background complete the scheme.

## *Rosa* Evelyn Fison ('Macev')

The rich scarlet, double blooms of this slightly fragrant Floribunda rose lend it to sumptuous combinations with salmon-pink, coral or vermilion, and striking contrasts with yellow-green or lime green. With its even, compact habit, it is suitable for places at the front of a border, perhaps behind a rank of mounded, sprawling plants. It may also be used as a bedding rose, especially if widely spaced at 24 in. (60 cm) or slightly more, when it can be interspersed with another plant of similar height and contrasting foliar or floral form. This might be an annual such as an alonsoa or zinnia, one of the taller French marigolds, or a tall nicotiana in lime green or rich salmon-pink. Other suitable companions might include a

The orange flowers of *Crocosmia* 'Vulcan' and its bold, pleated leaves contrast in form with scarlet *Rosa* Evelyn Fison, with golden *Ligularia dentata* and yellow *Verbascum chaixii* adding further warmth. The deep purplish blue flowers of *Aconitum* 'Spark's Variety' and dark-leaved *Berberis thunbergii* f. *atropurpurea* provide a useful foil.

hardy herbaceous plant such as a crocosmia, a tender perennial such as a dahlia, a grass such as a pennisetum or, for contrast, a yellow-green foliage plant.

**Perfect partners:** *Cosmos sulphureus* 'Polidor', *Eupatorium capillifolium* 'Emerald Feather', *Potentilla* 'Monsieur Rouillard', *Tagetes patula* 'La Bamba', *Tithonia rotundifolia*

**H: 27 in.** (70 cm) **S: 24 in.** (60 cm)
❀ **Midsummer to late autumn**
◖◗ ◊◊ ◼-◼ **Z5 pH5–7.5**

Rosa 'Gruss an Aachen' can vary a little in color according to climate and situation and is here pale pink, rather than its usual pale apricot-blush, allowing it to combine even more harmoniously with the foxglove *Digitalis purpurea* Foxy Group. Because the foxglove is relatively short, its spires of bloom can be seen in close conjunction with the rose, providing a contrast of form.

## *Rosa* 'Gruss an Aachen'

This fragrant perpetual variety, perhaps best classed as a Hybrid Tea, makes a fairly short, upright bush, with flattened, fully double blooms opening from apricot-pink buds to creamy white with a pale apricot-pink center. Its old-fashioned floral form associates well with old roses and with David Austin's English cultivars. The delicate flower color is especially attractive with other warm tints, such as apricot, pink, salmon-pink, coral, peach or yellow, and with bronze-tinted or silver foliage. Its neat habit suits it to bedding and, if fairly widely spaced, it can be used with other harmonious flowers or foliage, or it may be underplanted, for example with pinks.

**Perfect partners:** *Campanula punctata* 'Bowl of Cherries', *Dianthus* 'Doris', *Geranium* 'Mavis Simpson', *Lavandula angustifolia* 'Miss Katherine'

**H & S: 18 in.** (45 cm)
✳ **Midsummer to late autumn**
◊◊ ▢-▦ Z6 pH5.5–7

## *Rosa* Iceberg ('Korbin') ♛

One of the most beautiful and elegant of the Floribundas, the slightly fragrant, relatively thin-petaled, loosely double flowers of this rose are borne singly or in graceful sprays from midsummer, with a particularly strong flush in autumn. Their color is usually almost pure white, occasionally with a faint pinkish ivory flush towards the center, and is particularly suitable for leavening plantings of pink and darker-colored roses. It is also very attractive with silver or glaucous foliage and lime green or yellow-green flowers. This rose may be lightly pruned to produce a shrub up to about 6 ft. (1.8 m) high, perfectly at home when planted among old-fashioned roses; it also makes a good hedge, which benefits from having short, cushion-forming plants such as lavenders in front to disguise its unsightly vase-shaped bases.

**Perfect partners:** *Echinops sphaerocephalus* 'Arctic Glow', *Hemerocallis* 'Gentle Shepherd', *Lobelia × speciosa* 'La Fresco', *Lupinus* 'Storm', *Salvia nemorosa* 'Ostfriesland', *Sidalcea candida*

**H: 4–6 ft.** (1.2–1.8 m) **S: 3 ft.** (90 cm)
✳ **Midsummer to late autumn**
◻◻ ◊◊ ▢-▦ Z5 pH5–7.5

In a pretty planting scheme depending solely on flowers rather than foliage, the large white blooms of *Rosa* Iceberg and deep pink *R.* Mary Rose and the dense flowerheads of red valerian (*Centranthus ruber*) contrast in form with the more diffuse pink blooms of *Kolkwitzia amabilis* and *Gypsophila elegans* 'Giant White'. The cranesbill *Geranium* 'Johnson's Blue' carpets the foreground.

Rosa Lilli Marlene is here combined with other red flowers, including bold-leaved *Crocosmia* 'Lucifer' (behind), its red tending slightly toward orange, and in front a carpet of sprawling *Potentilla* 'Gibson's Scarlet', with the foliage of purple plum (*Prunus cerasifera* 'Pissardii') providing a strong, dusky background.

## *Rosa* Lilli Marlene ('Korlima')

This is a compact Floribunda with large, semi-double, velvety bright crimson blooms, borne in clusters. With its neat and strongly branching habit, it is useful as a bedding rose and as a sturdy hedge. The rich coloring of its flowers, set against the dark, slightly bronzy foliage, is enhanced in combinations with purple, mauve and strong pink. It can be a dusky foil for brighter red or vermilion, and for yellow-green and yellow flowers. Although it is a rich enough shade to be welcome as a stabilizing component of red borders, this tends to make the flowers less visible from a distance, and specimen plants are best positioned at close range. This rose is prone to mildew and blackspot.

**Perfect partners:** *Anthemis tinctoria* 'Sauce Hollandaise', *Coreopsis verticillata* 'Moonbeam', *Hemerocallis* 'Golden Chimes' p.286 **B**, *Hypericum frondosum, Lathyrus chloranthus*

**H: 30 in.** (75 cm) **S: 2 ft.** (60 cm)
✳ **Midsummer to late autumn**
◊◊ ▦-▦ Z5 pH5–7.5

A

## *Rosa* 'The Fairy' ♆

Best classed as a Polyantha rose, this hybrid derives from a cross between a Polyantha (a small-flowered ancestor of Floribundas) and a Wichurana Rambler. From the latter it inherits a rather lax but graceful habit that suits it for use as a bush rose toward the front of a border, for ground cover or as a cascading plant tumbling over the edge of a dwarf wall; it may also be grafted as a semi-weeping standard. The foliage is neat and attractive, with tiny, glossy leaflets. Its large clusters of lightly fragrant blooms, each lasting for several weeks, comprise numerous pompon-like, double, rose-pink florets. These are most attractive with warm colors such as coral, apricot, peach and cream; they also look good with white or rich deep scarlet flowers and silver or red-flushed foliage, and form striking contrasts with yellow-green and lime green. Pleasing companion plants include miscanthus, hostas, alstroemerias, and old roses.

**Perfect partners:** *Carex muskingumensis* 'Ice Fountains', *Diascia barberae* 'Blackthorn Apricot', *Hosta* 'Krossa Regal', *Scabiosa* 'Chile Pepper', *Senecio cineraria*, *Stachys coccinea*

H: 24 in. (60 cm)  S: 4 ft. (1.2 m)
❀ Midsummer to late autumn
◊◊ ☐-■ Z5 pH5–7.5

Opposite: A cascading mound of *Rosa* 'The Fairy' here harmonizes perfectly with the blooms of *Alstroemeria* 'Charm'. The combination would be further enhanced by the addition of some handsome foliage, perhaps in darkest red or silvery green.

## *Rosa* Westerland ('Korwest') ♆

This is a vigorous, branching rose that may be pruned firmly as a Floribunda for beds and the front ranks of a border, or more lightly as a Shrub rose for positions further back in borders and for flowering hedges. Its stiff, upright stems are also suitable for training on walls and fences, where it can exceed its usual height by 24 in. (60 cm) or more. Its loose sprays of pleasantly scented, ruffled, double apricot blooms blend happily with other warm colors, such as cream, peach, coral, buff-yellow, soft orange or soft red, and contrast prettily and gently with yellow-green or lime green. Since its color is in the same range as many of David Austin's English roses, it associates well with many of

The soft apricot blooms of *Rosa* Westerland are borne on a bush tall enough to overtop the other, scarlet-flowered border plants in this scheme, which includes opium poppy (*Papaver somniferum*), Jerusalem cross (*Lychnis chalcedonica*) and a climbing nasturtium (*Tropaeolum majus*).

these. It may also be combined in plantings with daylilies, lilies and taller grasses, or with bronze-flushed shrubs such as smoke bush and *Berberis thunbergii* cultivars.

**Perfect partners:** *Hemerocallis* 'Lemon Bells', *Hypericum androsaemum* 'Albury Purple', *Lilium henryi*, *Miscanthus sinensis* 'Zebrinus', *Rosa* Molineux, *R.* Pat Austin ⌑ p.440 C

H: 6 ft. (1.8 m)  S: 4 ft. (1.2 m)
❀ Midsummer to late autumn
◊◊ ☐-■ Z5 pH5–7.5

## *Rosa* 'Yesterday' ♆

This is an upright bushy Polyantha or modern Shrub rose which, depending on the severity of pruning, may be grown in the middle of a border or nearer the front, or as a mounded ground-cover rose. Its numerous small, lightly scented flowers, which open flat, at first magenta and fading to a soft lilac-pink, are borne in sprays, generally toward the top of the bush. Apart from a tendency to become chlorotic in alkaline or poor soils, it is a trouble-free variety that combines well with cool colors such as mauve, lilac, lavender or blue, and with white or crimson flowers and purple or silver foliage. Lime green or pale lemon-yellow flowers contrast effectively with the magenta blooms.

**Perfect partners:** *Indigofera amblyantha*, *Lavandula* 'Pukehou', *Lupinus* 'Storm', *Lysimachia ephemerum*, *Physostegia virginiana* 'Summer Snow'

H: 5 ft. (1.5 m)  S: 4 ft. (1.2 m)
❀ Midsummer to late autumn
◊◊ ☐-■ Z5 pH5–6.5

In this scheme, depending for its success solely on flowers in soft magenta, ruby and contrasting white, *Rosa* 'Yesterday' overtops the exotic-looking *Rehmannia elata* behind a carpet of *Diascia barberae* 'Ruby Field' and *Viola cornuta* Alba Group. The rehmannia and diascia are perennial plants, but would need to be treated as annuals in cooler climates.

# Smaller species & smaller modern Shrub roses

IN TINY GARDENS and small-scale areas within larger ones, conventional bush and shrub roses can sometimes seem coarsely oversized, and roses that are smaller in height and spread, and often in flower and leaf, may look more appropriate.

Among these are the Scotch or Burnet roses, slender shrubs derived from *R. spinosissima*, with tiny flowers borne in great profusion in early summer, sometimes followed by rounded hips. Thriving in light soil and tolerant of some shade, they are ideal plants for a natural garden, suckering steadily but controllably into wide colonies.

*R.* 'Cécile Brunner' is entirely different in form, a diminutive China rose with perfect, high-pointed buds unfurling to pale pink flowers on frail-looking stems. Many of the Miniature and Patio roses follow in its wake. These are hybrids between the very tiny sports of China roses and the more robust and free-flowering modern Floribunda roses.

The smallest of the Miniatures, only 9–18 in. (23–45 cm) tall, are pretty little roses best used in pots so that they may be most easily appreciated at close range – and in colder climates be moved to shelter in winter since the roots are intolerant of freezing. The simpler roses among these may also find a home on a rock garden.

The somewhat larger Patio roses look more like plants than scale models or toys and can be used effectively in raised beds or containers, or perhaps along the outer edge of a terrace so that they can be viewed in detail from below. Many small rock plants, ground-cover plants and annuals are delicate enough in appearance to associate with Patio roses in these situations without overwhelming their small flowers and fine-textured foliage.

A

## *Rosa elegantula* 'Persetosa'
FARRER'S THREEPENNY BIT ROSE

Sometimes listed as *R. farreri* var. *persetosa*, this is a dainty early-flowering species Shrub rose, with tiny fernlike leaflets that are purple-flushed in full sun and turn purple and crimson in autumn, and arching stems densely covered with bristles. In time it can form a fairly large shrub, studded in late spring with tiny, lightly scented pink flowers and later with small orange hips. A graceful rose for the front of a shrub or mixed border, and for wilder, more natural parts of the garden, it combines well with purple foliage and with other flowers that bridge the gap between spring and summer, for example columbines, violas, early cranesbills and bugles planted under its rather sparse growth. It looks attractive with plants of different floral form, such as umbellifers, including

Although it can become a moderately sized shrub in time, the tiny flowers and leaves of *Rosa elegantula* 'Persetosa' suit it to a smaller scale of planting and to close-range viewing, for instance at the front of a bed or border. Here, its relatively sparse branches let through enough light for a complete carpet of mixed violas.

cow parsley, and with contrasting foliage such as the grassy leaves of earlier-flowering herbaceous irises. Compatible partners include sweet rocket, purple-leaved berberis, dipeltas, exochordas, kolkwitzias and other early roses in white, pink or crimson shades.

**Perfect partners:** *Anthriscus sylvestris* 'Ravenswing', *Aquilegia vulgaris* var. *stellata* 'Royal Purple', *Hosta* 'Buckshaw Blue', *Iris* 'Banbury Beauty', *Salvia lyrata* 'Burgundy Bliss'

H & S: 5 ft. (1.5 m)  ❋ Late spring to early summer
◊◊ ■-■ Z4 pH5.5–7

The sprawling habit of *Rosa* 'Raubritter' allows other flowers to be woven through its outer fringes. Here, dainty blue love-in-a-mist (*Nigella damascena*) mingles with the globular blooms of the rose.

## *Rosa* 'Raubritter'

This *R*. 'Macrantha' hybrid is an arching Shrub rose, useful for early and midsummer planting schemes for banks, ground cover and the front of beds and borders. Its spherical flowers, reminiscent of 'Reine Victoria', are shapely and sophisticated, a rich enough pink to suit dazzling combinations with cool-colored flowers, glaucous, silver, red or purple-flushed foliage, and other roses with a contrasting color or flower size, such as small-flowered white or deep red Ground Cover cultivars. It also contrasts effectively with yellow-green flowers, such as alchemillas or nicotianas. Good partners include pinks, irises (including late-flowering Tall Bearded kinds), hebes, cranesbills such as *Geranium* × *riversleaianum*, eryngiums, campanulas and dictamnus. If planted close to a large shrub or small tree, its branches can be encouraged to scramble upward, and they can be trained as a semi-weeping standard or to sprawl over a dwarf wall.

**Perfect partners:** *Achillea* 'Apfelblüte', *Hebe* 'Pink Pixie', *Iris* 'Pacific Mist', *I*. 'Dreaming Spires', *Lavatera* × *clementii* 'Kew Rose', *Nicotiana langsdorffii*, *Physostegia virginiana* 'Bouquet Rose', *Ruta graveolens*

**H: 3¼ ft. (1 m)  S: 6 ft. (1.8 m)**
❀ **Early to midsummer**
  ◇◇ ■-■ Z5  pH5.5–7.5

## *Rosa* Sweet Dream ('Fryminicot') ♛

Winner of numerous awards, this Patio rose is among the most popular rose varieties of all time. Like all Patio roses, its flowers and foliage are proportionately smaller than those of Hybrid Teas or Floribundas, making it especially useful for smaller gardens, intimate plantings and for containers. Its neat and bushy, almost cushionlike habit and dense, glossy foliage make it a good choice for edging beds and paths, planted either in small groups or as a continuous low hedge. The soft apricot coloring of its fragrant, perfectly formed flowers is particularly suitable for combinations with other warm tints such as peach, salmon, soft yellow and cream, as well as with bronze foliage and with yellow-green foliage and flowers. It contrasts memorably with the pure blue of plants like Belladonna Group delphiniums or *Salvia patens* cultivars. Despite its small size, it benefits from having low or cushion-forming plants in front, including smaller glaucous-leaved hostas, bronze sedges, a heuchera with purple or bronze foliage and also diascias, especially a rich salmon or coral (so-called apricot-colored) cultivar. This rose has been propagated by tissue culture, resulting in the distribution of several slightly different clones, some of which are exceedingly prone to blackspot and others that differ in flower color, tending more toward yellow.

**Perfect partners:** *Diascia barberae* 'Blackthorn Apricot', *Heuchera* 'Chocolate Ruffles', × *Heucherella* 'Chocolate Veil', *Hosta* 'Buckshaw Blue', *Lavandula* × *chaytoriae* 'Sawyers', *Persicaria microcephala* 'Red Dragon', *Stokesia laevis* 'Peach Melba'

**H: 16 in. (40 cm)  S: 14 in. (35 cm)**
❀ **Midsummer to late autumn**
■—■ ◇◇ ■-■ Z5  pH5–7.5

*Rosa* Sweet Dream blends harmoniously with a carpet of *Diascia* 'Salmon Supreme' and the loose, greenish cream panicles of dark-leaved *Heuchera villosa* 'Palace Purple', with the bold *Phormium* 'Sundowner' just visible behind. Deadheading the rose and shearing over the diascia after it has completed its first flush of flowers will ensure the display continues into the autumn.

# Ground Cover roses

THERE ARE TWO main kinds of Ground Cover roses. Some are vigorous, decidedly prostrate plants, most flowering only once, in the summer. Others are neater and more compact, and rather like low, spreading modern Shrub roses; many of the more recent cultivars bloom repeatedly, producing showy flowers over a long season from summer into autumn.

The more prostrate types have trailing stems that often root where they touch the ground and usually form dense mats or hummocks of cover. Some may be too strongly horizontal to associate well with border plants, but are excellent for clothing banks or slopes, especially in more naturalistic parts of the garden.

The shrubby types have arching stems, giving a rather mounded or dome-shaped habit. These roses are particularly pleasing when allowed to tumble over a bank or low wall, or over the edge of a large container. Although their blooms are generally too sophisticated for the edge of a woodland garden, for example, they are useful in making the transition from formal to more relaxed and lower-maintenance areas. Great swaths of one variety are best avoided, unless planting on the largest scale, but groups of roses in harmonious colors weaving among arching shrubs can look very attractive.

Perhaps the main point to bear in mind when using Ground Cover roses is that most are too open to be really effective in smothering weeds. It is therefore vital to ensure there are no perennial weeds in the soil before planting and to control annual weeds meticulously in the first year.

These roses do not need regular pruning but they can be cut back severely every few years, using loppers or a brush cutter; this will rejuvenate the planting, and allow the removal of any intrusive upright branches to maintain a low profile.

## *Rosa* 'Nozomi' ♛

This is a versatile Ground Cover or Miniature Climbing rose that can be trained against a low wall or fence, or as a weeping standard for use as a focal point or repeated accent in a border. It is effective draped over a bank, and in containers. The single, unscented flowers, which open palest blush-pink, take on grayish tints as they age, and the anthers turn black, giving the blooms a slightly subdued tone that blends pleasingly with white and muted colors such as old rose or dusky mauve, and also complements silver, purple or red-flushed foliage. Its trailing stems can be pegged down to improve coverage, and these will often root, extending the spread. It is one of the best Ground Cover roses for use as a backdrop for clematis, both Viticellas such as purple 'Royal Velours' to provide exciting color combinations and

*Rosa* 'Nozomi' here spreads itself gracefully across a carpet of yellow-green leaved heather (*Calluna vulgaris*), creating a pleasingly uneven mix of the two plants and a contrast of foliage and form. The rose will have almost completed its flowering before the heather starts to bloom.

later-flowering kinds like *C. integrifolia* 'Rosea'. In a wild garden this rose can be combined with white umbellifers such as wild carrots or cow parsley, and simple wild flowers, for example campions, cranesbills and yarrows.

**Perfect partners:** *Achillea* 'Apfelblüte', *Astrantia maxima*, *Geranium* 'Emily', *Salvia nemorosa* 'Amethyst', *S. officinalis* 'Purpurascens', *Stachys byzantina*, *Veronica* 'Ellen Mae'

**H: 3 ft.** (90 cm) **S: 6 ft.** (1.8 m) ❀ **Midsummer**
▬▬▬▭▬ ◌◌ ▭-▬ **Z5 pH5–7.5**

The sprawling habit of Ground Cover roses allows them to mingle more effectively than bush roses, such as Floribundas, with neighbouring plants. Here, *Rosa* Pink Bells blends harmoniously with a white musk mallow (*Malva moschata* f. *alba*) and a lavender-blue peach-leaved bellflower (*Campanula persicifolia*).

## *Rosa* Pink Bells ('Poulbells')

The arching growth of this Ground Cover rose is suitable for covering banks and low fences, and for training as a weeping standard. It is equally effective for large plantings and small groups. The dainty, fully double, rich pink flowers, with a mild scent, go well with flowers in cool colors – rich pink, white, mauve – and with red, purple or silver foliage. Effective partners include sages, catmints, lavenders, smoke bush, pinks in white or crimson, and lime green nicotianas.

It will host a white or deep carmine perennial pea or a Texensis or Viticella clematis, while its repeat-flowering into autumn combines with later flowers such as penstemons.

**Perfect partners:** *Lavandula angustifolia* 'Imperial Gem', *Monarda* 'Aquarius', *Nepeta* 'Six Hills Giant', *Penstemon* 'Evelyn', *Salvia verticillata* 'Purple Rain', *Sidalcea candida*

H: 30 in. (75 cm) S: 5 ft. (1.5 m)
❀ Midsummer to early autumn
 ◊◊ ☐-■ Z5 pH5–7.5

The silvery foliage of *Artemisia* 'Powis Castle' provides an effective foil for the cascading blooms of *Rosa* Surrey, a partnership for a more steeply banked border than suits many of the other, lower-growing Ground Cover roses.

## *Rosa* Suffolk ('Kormixal')

This relatively prostrate Ground Cover rose bears small, lightly scented, rich scarlet single flowers in large clusters almost continuously until autumn. Their slightly cut petals enclose a boss of golden anthers, and their florets tend to close as the anthers blacken with age. This dramatic coloring suits hot color schemes with yellow, orange or yellow-green flowers, and looks effective with lime green flowers and with yellow-green or red-flushed foliage. It is an excellent rose for interplanting with larger phormiums, dark-leaved heucheras, berberis and smoke bush, and with climbers such as tropaeolums, Texensis clematis or Chilean glory flower.

**Perfect partners:** *Hakonechloa macra* 'Aureola', *Hemerocallis* 'Lemon Bells', *Heuchera* 'Chocolate Veil', *Hypericum frondosum*, *Lamium maculatum* Golden Anniversary

H: 18 in. (45 cm) S: 36 in. (90 cm)
❀ Midsummer to late autumn
 ◊◊ ☐-■ Z5 pH5–7.5

The petals of *Rosa* Suffolk contrast dazzlingly with *Euonymus fortunei* 'Emerald 'n' Gold', while the golden anthers form a satisfying harmony with the variegation in the euonymus leaves. Both of these plants are low-growing and suited to the front of beds and borders.

## *Rosa* Surrey ('Korlanum') ♕

The frilly, double, richly colored blooms of this very fragrant Ground Cover rose are close enough to primary pink to mix well with colors such as mauve, carmine or white, warm tints like peach, apricot and cream, and more opulent shades. Associations with red, purple, silver or glaucous foliage work well, as do contrasts with yellow-green flowers or foliage. It is suitable for larger plantings, punctuated with a climber such as a perennial pea or clematis. Flowering continues late into the season, and the rose can then partner Japanese anemones, and other roses grown for late blooms such as some China and Hybrid Musk cultivars.

**Perfect partners:** *Anemone hupehensis* 'Bowles Pink', *Eryngium giganteum*, *Leymus arenarius*, *Penstemon* 'Osprey', *Sedum telephium* subsp. *maximum* 'Atropurpureum'

H: 31 in. (80 cm) S: 4 ft. (1.2 m)
❀ Midsummer to late autumn
◊◊ ☐-■ Z5 pH5–7.5

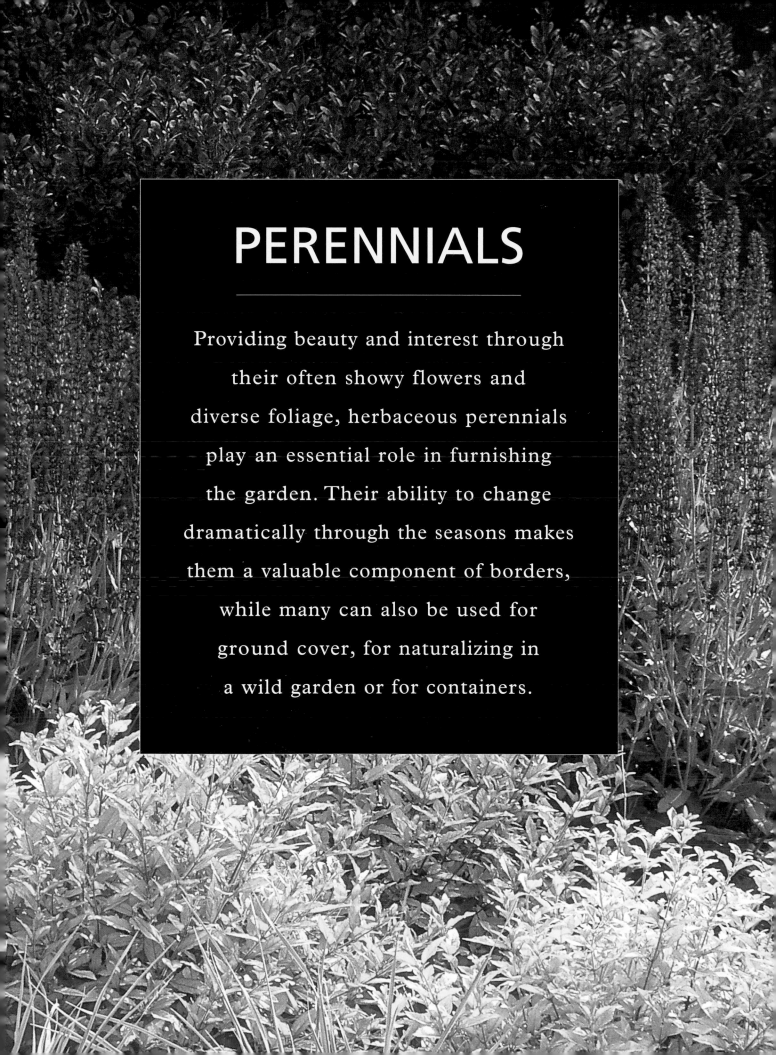

# PERENNIALS

Providing beauty and interest through
their often showy flowers and
diverse foliage, herbaceous perennials
play an essential role in furnishing
the garden. Their ability to change
dramatically through the seasons makes
them a valuable component of borders,
while many can also be used for
ground cover, for naturalizing in
a wild garden or for containers.

**Strictly, perennials are** any plants that live for two years or more and flower each year. Gardeners use the word mainly for herbaceous, nonwoody plants that die back to an overwintering rootstock.

The oldest herbaceous borders had single plants regularly spaced on a rectangular grid, with no attempt to order flower colors and little use of ornamental foliage. These were abandoned in Victorian times in favor of borders in which each sort of plant was massed in a group for maximum impact.

Gertrude Jekyll was perhaps the first to advocate borders based on a limited color range, with flowers of a single color, two pleasantly contrasting ones such as blue and yellow, or a spectrum of colors shifting gradually along the border's length. She recommended using hot colors near the house, passing from purple through orange to yellow, which would be contrasted with blue at the far end of the border to emphasize distance. Miss Jekyll was also an early advocate of the use of foliage color and form, both to enhance color schemes and to add structure to planting, a principle we regard as axiomatic today. She also favored the "drift," a long, narrow group of plants running at a shallow oblique angle to the border's front. This is especially useful in borders 10–13 ft. (3–4 m) deep, planted traditionally with groups that gradually and uniformly rise in height from front to back.

## Mixing form and color

Whatever the color scheme, a variety of flower forms generally gives the most pleasing effect. Flowers borne in spikes, such as those of lupins, delphiniums, verbascums and hardy salvias, provide useful vertical accents and can be contrasted with the flat plates of achilleas and clouds of crambe, gypsophila or thalictrum. Varied foliage helps too, for instance, fine-textured grasses, straps of daylilies, spiky sword-shaped leaves of crocosmias or handsomely architectural acanthus. Foliage color can also be used to complement a color scheme: silver,

glaucous or purple leaves blend well with cool shades, while red, bronze or yellow-green leaves are effective with hot ones. Pure blue flowers can be set off by yellow-green, glaucous or silver leaves. Variegation can provide accents, emphasize a bold leaf shape or give a lighter tone, but it can look frantic if used to excess.

Contrasts of form are easy to achieve and often successful. Harmonies are harder. A border planted solely with daylilies or hostas may become tedious, yet the gentle textures found in a grass garden can be immensely pleasing, the result of the most subtle variations of leaf color and form, particularly telling when they soften a formal pattern of beds. Yet monocot borders, with grassy, strap-shaped and spiky leaves, seem to fall between two stools, having neither enough harmony nor sufficient contrast. Even Gertrude Jekyll could not make a success of a border solely of Michaelmas daisies and had

This planting in the style of Gertrude Jekyll uses most of the plants she favored for the blue border. Blue echinops, perovskias, eryngiums and salvias are leavened by white cosmos, phlox and anemones, with drifts of tall cream antirrhinums. Foliage plays an important role, with silver stachys and artemisias, glaucous lyme grass and the bold thistle leaves of echinops providing structure and a variety of textures.

to resort to grasses such as miscanthus and an edging of neat foliage plants to provide the varied form and texture the asters lacked.

Even if we love a particular genus of perennials to the exclusion of all others, growing them in mixed company usually gives more satisfying results than a monoculture. The once-popular phlox border needs suitable companion plants both to hide the base of the phlox stems and to compensate for their rather dull leaves and amorphous flowerheads. A bed of hostas alone risks camouflaging the bold shape of individual plants, whereas combined with the contrasting leaves of ferns and grasses, each hosta can be appreciated distinctly. Even plants of more definite form, such as daylilies, lupins or delphiniums, benefit from two or three different companions to provide a foil. Many more than this, however, would risk diluting the essential character of the preferred genus, and result in something like any other border.

## All-year appeal

The main challenge in designing a traditional herbaceous border is to ensure it performs for as much of the year as possible. Two factors help: one, as discussed, is to make the most of foliage, not just for architecture and structure, but for color, too; the second is to incorporate tender perennials such as dahlias, cannas, penstemons or argyranthemums. These come from climates where frost does not curtail their yearly cycle: they do not have to rush to produce seed before the weather cuts them down, and so often flower incessantly. Some annuals can also be used in this way (see pp.406–455).

For winter, there are a few precious evergreen perennials, including hellebores, epimediums, periwinkles and bergenias and some of the newer heucheras. However, many gardeners relish the winter remains of herbaceous plants such as achilleas, sedums, cardoons and larger grasses such as miscanthus. Although the tidy-minded might prefer to cut back everything in autumn, those with a more relaxed attitude will leave these skeletons,

clearing them only to make room for bulbs and other early flowers. In this way even the herbaceous border can retain some form and structure through the winter months.

For creating a large and imposing display with a long season of interest, a mixed border is especially valuable. Combining herbaceous perennials mainly with shrubs, it is potentially the most attractive synthesis of garden plants.

## Numbers and spacing

There is a general convention among gardeners that perennials are best grouped in odd numbers and it is indeed difficult to avoid, say, a block of four or six plants looking self-consciously regular. Some, however, consider this a rule

Whereas a planting of variegated hostas alone would be tedious and would mask the individual beauty of the hosta, here the foliage of *H. crispula* is flattered by its companion plants, including ferns, *Hydrangea quercifolia*, Solomon's seal and the whorled leaves of martagon lilies.

made to be broken. An irregularly shaped group with odd plants of the same sort a little distance from it gives a more natural effect, and groups of the same sort of perennial can be repeated at intervals along the length of a border to provide a unifying theme.

Many books on perennials and nursery catalogues give a recommended spacing for plants within a group. Adjacent groups need spacing further apart than this if they are not to appear cramped. A rule of thumb is that the spacing between two groups should be three quarters the sum of their spacings: in other words, if one group has plants spaced at 16 in. (40 cm) and its neighbor has plants spaced at 24 in. (60 cm), the gap between the outermost plants of the two groups should be 30 in. (75 cm).

An old convention for herbaceous borders was that they should be twice as wide as the height of their tallest plants, with a path at the back to allow maintenance of hedges or wall plants. This gives a spacious feel to the planting but is a counsel of perfection that those of us with smaller gardens and narrower borders will neither want nor feel obliged to follow. It is perfectly possible to devise perennial border planting that is as tall as, or even taller than, the width of the border, giving a dramatically steep, even towering, effect. However, plants for such borders should have long, well-furnished, preferably flowering stems and should not bear their flowers only at the top. Using such paragons of the plant world, it is possible to achieve a border only three groups deep but 5 ft. (1.5 m) high with not a bare stem in sight.

## Frontline candidates

The choice of perennials for the front of beds and borders is perhaps the most crucial. Generally they should be of neat habit and/or should have attractive foliage. Spacious and gently rising borders can have low carpeters such as alpine pinks or lamb's ears in front, with mound-forming plants in the second rank to hide the ankles of taller plants behind. If the border is steeply banked, the carpeters must be dispensed with and the mounds must come to the fore. Some bold foliage, such as that of bergenias or hostas, toward the front can help define the border, anchoring it and giving it gravitas. Fluffs like catmint and gypsophila can set a tone of amorphous anonymity if used to excess, although they have ethereal charm when used in moderation with bolder plants.

Rebels may wish to flout the convention of designing the border as an evenly graded bank of flowers, gradually rising in height, and allow some tall plants to grow well forward of others of their own size. By contouring the heights of perennials more irregularly and dramatically, it is possible to create bays within the planting whose innermost recesses are hidden when the border is viewed obliquely from a distance – their contents will be revealed as a delightful surprise as the viewer moves along the border.

## *Acanthus spinosus* ♛

This stately plant has large, divided leaves, glossy, deep green with paler veins and spikes of pinkish white, foxglove-like florets, with magenta, purple-flushed calyces. It flowers profusely in sun, less so in shade, and while happy in poor, dry soil, it may lose its foliage there by midsummer or develop mildew. It makes a bold focal point near the front of a border, especially when set off by paler leaves or flowers, and works well with pink, mauve or mid- to light blue flowers or with soft yellow. Leaves of the Spinosissimus Group are deeply cut, with pale veins and almost white spines. *A. mollis* has less divided, glossier leaves.

**Perfect partners:** *Allium cristophii, Geranium* 'Johnson's Blue', *G.* 'Mavis Simpson', *Philadelphus coronarius* 'Aureus', *Rosa glauca*

**H: 5 ft. (1.5 m) S: 36 in. (90 cm)**
❀ **Early to late summer**
◊-◊◊ □-■ Z7 pH5–7.5

The handsome, architectural leaves and bold flower spikes of *Acanthus spinosus* act as a focal point in a sunny border, backed by the shrubby pale mauve-pink *Lavatera × clementii* 'Barnsley' and furnished in front by contrasting golden feverfew (*Tanacetum parthenium* 'Aureum') and the yellow-green flowerheads of lady's mantle (*Alchemilla mollis*).

In a garden of broad beds and hot-colored flowers in early summer, the horizontal plates of *Achillea* 'Coronation Gold' contrast with the vertical spires of a verbascum hybrid. The rich red flowers of Jerusalem cross (*Lychnis chalcedonica*), feathery heads of bronze fennel (*Foeniculum vulgare* 'Purpureum') and orange-yellow *Ligularia dentata* fill the gap between the two.

## *Achillea* 'Fanal'

'Fanal', one of the Galaxy hybrids, was the first yarrow to have bright scarlet flowers, making it useful for hot color schemes. However, the color fades with age through salmon-pink to buff – tints that make finding suitable neighbors a challenge. It is especially good with salmon-pink flowers and bronze foliage. If its older flowers do not harmonize with a particular scheme, they may be cut off; this will encourage new blooms, so extending the flowering period until autumn. Some other richly colored variants age more pleasantly – 'Feuerland' and 'Walther Funcke', for example.

**Perfect partners:** *Dahlia* 'Bishop of Llandaff', *Diascia* 'Salmon Supreme', *Elymus magellanicus, Foeniculum vulgare* 'Purpureum', *Monarda* 'Cambridge Scarlet'

**H: 30 in. (75 cm) S: 18 in. (45 cm)**
❀ **Early summer to mid-autumn**
◊-◊◊ □-■ Z3 pH5–7.5

## *Achillea* 'Coronation Gold' ♛

Some of the most valuable garden yarrows are derived from yellow-flowered species such as *A. clypeolata*. However, these gray-leaved sun-lovers do not thrive in heavy or damp soil, nor in cool summers, whereas hybrids from them can be more amenable.

*A.* 'Coronation Gold' is one of the best of medium height. It is easier to grow, longer-flowering and cleaner in color than its other parent *A. filipendulina*, and has better silver foliage. The flowers are held in horizontal plates, making it useful for balancing flowerheads of other form, especially spikes. It can produce good contrasts with mid-blue flowers, harmonizes well with hot colors, and is particularly good with silver-foliaged plants. Other compatible neighbors include salvias and many grasses of moderate size.

**Perfect partners:** *Artemisia ludoviciana, Campanula persicifolia, Coreopsis* 'Baby Gold', *Delphinium* 'Sabrina', *Hemerocallis* 'Sammy Russell' p.287 **C**, *Kniphofia* 'David' p.302 **C**, *Onopordum nervosum, Salvia nemorosa* 'Lubecca', *Stipa capillata, Viola cornuta*

**H: 36 in. (90 cm) S: 18 in. (45 cm)**
❀ **Early to late summer**
◊◊ ■ ■ Z3 pH5–7.5

The flowerheads of *Achillea* 'Fanal' open rich scarlet and turn to terracotta before aging through salmon to chamois. Here, the terracotta tones with the distant wall, while the scarlet chimes with the flowers of bold-leaved *Crocosmia* 'Lucifer'. The curious spherical seedheads of *Allium cristophii* are just tall enough to appear behind the achillea, playing their part in the ensemble.

Borne near eye level, the flat heads of *Achillea filipendulina* 'Gold Plate' appear as narrow yellow lines, a distinctive pattern that is even more pronounced in bright sun when underlined by the rich olive green of their undersides. The bold leaves of *Canna indica* 'Purpurea', *Dahlia* 'Blaisdon Red', orange heleniums and the tall sunflower *Helianthus* 'Velvet Queen' add exotic richness.

## *Achillea filipendulina* 'Gold Plate' ♔

This tall yarrows bears broad heads of yellow flowers. Its great height makes a striking impact but also reduces the area presented to the eye to a narrow, arched line. This effect is offset by the underside of the flowerheads, which in bright sunlight appear intense olive-green, emphasizing the graceful, arching habit. It is a good, drought-tolerant plant for the back of a border, especially pleasing when combined with blues and hot colors, spiked flowerheads and moderate to tall grasses such as *Miscanthus sinensis* 'Strictus' or 'Variegatus'. *A.f.* 'Neugold' and 'Altgold' bear their flowers below eye level.

**Perfect partners:** *Crocosmia* 'Lucifer', *Delphinium* 'Alice Artindale', *Eryngium* × *tripartitum*, *Hemerocallis* 'Stafford' p.287 **B**, *Salvia pratensis* 'Indigo' p.331 **A**

**H: 5 ft. (1.5 m) S: 24 in. (60 cm)**
☼ **Early to late summer**
⬛⬛⬛⬛ ◊-◊◊ ⬜-⬛ Z3 pH5–7.5

## *Achillea* 'Lachsschönheit' ♔

This delightful yarrow, also known as Salmon Beauty, is one of the Galaxy hybrids, bred from *A. millefolium* and *A.* 'Taygetea' in order to bring intermediate shades into achilleas' limited yellow or white-to-crimson color range. Its salmon-pink flowers age to beige. They are particularly effective with other salmon-pink or cream flowers and with bronze foliage. As with similar hybrids whose flowers change color as they age, they should be deadheaded if they pass to a shade that does not sit happily with those of their neighbors. It is useful for dry, sunny places and soils of poorer quality. 'Apfelblüte' (Appleblossom) has flowers ageing from pink to grayish white.

**Perfect partners:** *Berberis thunbergii* f. *atropurpurea*, *Delphinium* 'Sungleam', *Diascia barberae* 'Blackthorn Apricot', *Foeniculum vulgare* 'Purpureum', *Iris pallida* 'Variegata'

**H: 30 in. (75 cm) S: 18 in. (45 cm)**
☼ **Early to late summer**
⬛⬛⬛⬛ ◊-◊◊ ⬜-⬛ Z3 pH5–8

After opening rose pink, the flowers of *Achillea* 'Lachsschönheit' age to pale biscuit tints, harmonizing with the bronze leaves of *Heuchera villosa* 'Palace Purple', which furnishes in front. Removing the heuchera's flowers ensures fresh and healthy foliage.

In this cool-colored scheme, the profuse blooms of *Achillea millefolium* 'Cerise Queen' provide the mainstay of the display, aided by crimson *Knautia macedonica*, bold heads of agapanthus and a carpet of pansies. An additional bold-leaved plant at the front, perhaps one with glaucous or silver foliage, would give structure and anchor the design.

## *Achillea millefolium* 'Cerise Queen'

Pink variants of the yarrow *A. millefolium* are common in the wild, but examples that retain their color without developing grayish tints are rare, as are those that stand upright with little need for staking. 'Cerise Queen' succeeds on both counts and keeps its rich cerise coloring quite well, the small but plentiful flowerheads fading only slightly as they age. It is a good companion for crimson, blue or purple flowers, and for purple foliage; it also mixes well with white flowers and silver foliage. It tolerates hot, dry or sunny sites and poor soils, and benefits from frequent dividing. Another superlative hybrid, 'Summerwine', has very deep crimson flowers that do not become paler with age.

**Perfect partners:** *Artemisia schmidtiana* 'Nana', *Berberis thunbergii* 'Atropurpurea Nana', *Ruta graveolens* 'Jackman's Blue', *Salvia* × *superba* 'Superba'

**H: 24 in. (60 cm) S: 18 in. (45 cm)**
☼ **Midsummer to early autumn**
⬛⬛⬛⬛ ◊-◊◊ ⬜-⬛ Z3 pH5–8

The sumptuous, deep purplish blue flowers of monkshood (*Aconitum napellus*), borne on a tall and slender plant, provide a contrast with the dainty pink flowers of *Astrantia major* var. *rosea* in a steeply planted narrow border.

## *Aconitum napellus*
MONKSHOOD

This species bears light indigo-blue spires, which make a classic contrast with achilleas, particularly in soft yellow, and also work well with grasses, Japanese anemones and paler shades of blue, mauve, soft yellow and cream. Variants include subsp. *vulgare* 'Carneum', which is flesh pink, and grayish white subsp. *v.* 'Albidum', both producing the purest colors and largest flowers where summers are cool and moist. Annually dividing plants in early autumn encourages long spikes and prolonged flowering. Other choice species and cultivars include mid-blue and white *A.* × *cammarum* 'Bicolor' ♀ and white *A.* × *c.* 'Grandiflorum Album'. *A.* 'Spark's Variety' ♀ is deep purplish blue.

**Perfect partners:** *Anemone* × *hybrida* 'Honorine Jobert', *A.* × *h.* 'Elegans', *Aster* × *frikartii* 'Mönch', *Choisya ternata* Sundance, *Digitalis purpurea* f. *albiflora*, *Hosta* 'August Moon', *Miscanthus sinensis* 'Sarabande', *Stipa capillata*

**H: 5 ft. (1.5 m)  S: 12 in. (30 cm)**
❀ **Mid- to late summer**
 ◊◊ ▪ Z5 pH5–7.5

## *Acorus gramineus* 'Variegatus'

A variant of the Japanese rush (not a true rush, but a member of the arum family), *A. gramineus* 'Variegatus' (syn. *A.g.* 'Argenteostriatus') resembles a grass in impact, with its attractive cream-edged leaves and insignificant flowers. A dainty plant, ideal for small-scale planting schemes or viewing at close range, it enjoys moist, humus-rich soils, boggy sites and waterside beds. It looks effective with Candelabra primulas, calthas, smaller astilbes and small hostas. There are also several gold-variegated cultivars such as 'Oborozuki' and 'Ōgon'. *A. calamus* is similar but larger, and its cultivar 'Argenteostriatus' is a good choice for larger-scale plantings.

In rich, moist soil by a pond, *Acorus gramineus* 'Variegatus' can reach as high as 18 in. (45 cm), allowing it to overtop the vibrant vermilion Candelabra primula *P.* 'Inverewe'.

**Perfect partners:** *Astilbe* × *crispa* 'Perkeo', *Caltha palustris* 'Flore Pleno', *Hosta* 'Buckshaw Blue', *Primula japonica* 'Miller's Crimson', *P.j.* 'Postford White'

**H: 14 in. (35 cm)  S: 8 in. (20 cm)** ❀ **(Late spring)**
◊◊◊ ▪-▪ Z5 pH5–7

The elegant coppery fronds of *Adiantum aleuticum* 'Japonicum' emerge in mid-spring, contrasting attractively with the blue flowers of Siberian squill (*Scilla siberica*).

## *Adiantum aleuticum* 'Japonicum'

The leaves of this dainty maidenhair fern are bronze when they unfurl in spring. It is then most attractive among pure or greenish blue flowers. It associates happily with the blue of plants such as *Scilla siberica*, and some corydalis species, and with other ferns such as hart's tongue; smaller hostas and small epimediums, too, offer contrasting foliage. This fern also combines well with soft orange, cream and salmon-pink.

**Perfect partners:** *Corydalis flexuosa*, *Epimedium* × *versicolor* 'Cupreum', *E.* × *v.* 'Sulphureum', *Hosta* (Tardiana Group) 'Halcyon', *Pulmonaria saccharata*

**H: 24 in. (60 cm)  S: 18 in. (45 cm)**
◊◊-◊◊◊ ▪ Z8 pH5.5–7.5

## *Agapanthus* 'Loch Hope' ♀

Agapanthus have slim, handsomely arching foliage, which is usually deciduous. Umbels of generally blue flowers are held well above the leaves. They are stately, imposing plants, ideally suited to growing in the front or second rank of a border and in containers. Hybrids and cultivars are usually hardier than the parent species. 'Loch Hope' blooms later than most, in late summer and early autumn. It has tall, upright stems and deep blue flowers that do not develop the reddish tints that mar some hybrids as they age. It goes easily with grasses such as miscanthus, with silver foliage, and with blue, mauve, purple or pink flowers, and contrasts well with soft yellow flowers and gold foliage, such as that of golden hostas (in situations where some midday shade can protect the hosta leaves from scorching). Agapanthus need space on all sides for their magnificent foliage and flower stems to have maximum impact, so they should stand a little forward in the bed and not be near plants of their own height.

**Perfect partners:** *Elaeagnus* 'Quicksilver', *Euphorbia schillingii*, *Hosta* 'Sum and Substance', *Iris pallida* 'Variegata', *Miscanthus sinensis* 'Variegatus', *Sambucus nigra* 'Aurea', *Sisyrinchium striatum* 'Aunt May'

**H: 5 ft.** (1.5 m)  **S: 24 in.** (60 cm)
❀ **Late summer to early autumn**
�○�○   ■-■  **Z7  pH5–7.5**

Blue flowers and creamy yellow variegation can provide a pleasing contrast, as here with *Agapanthus* 'Loch Hope', the variegated pampas grass *Cortaderia selloana* 'Aureolineata' and *Helichrysum petiolare* 'Roundabout', each supplying a distinctive foliage effect.

The gentle coloring of *Agastache* 'Firebird' perfectly matches perfectly the variegation of *Berberis thunbergii* 'Rose Glow', whose darker tints and red stems add richness.

## *Agastache* 'Firebird'

This erect, bushy perennial has grayish foliage and slightly diffuse heads of flowers of almost indefinable color, somewhere between deep salmon-pink, coral and soft orange. It looks most effective with hot flower colors such as oranges and scarlets – calceolarias in burnt orange, for example, and scarlet penstemons – but is also attractive with peaches, apricots and creams. It mixes well with bronze foliage and silver-leaved plants such as *Plectranthus argentatus*. Sunny, dry positions are best, where it may be combined with other sun-lovers such as hemerocallis, achilleas and crocosmias. If grown in containers, it can then be moved under cover in winter.

**Perfect partners:** *Argyranthemum* 'Jamaica Primrose', *Artemisia* 'Powis Castle', *Crocosmia* × *crocosmiiflora* 'Lady Hamilton', *Dahlia* 'Bishop of Llandaff', *Diascia barberae* 'Ruby Field', *Foeniculum vulgare* 'Purpureum'

**H: 24 in.** (60 cm)  **S: 12 in.** (30 cm)
❀ **Midsummer to late autumn**
 ○-○○  ■-■  **Z7  pH5–7.5**

Above: The mildly invasive bugle (*Ajuga reptans*) is an excellent plant for providing a decorative infill between other late spring and early summer flowers, its recessive tints helping to highlight brighter blooms of bolder shape. Here, it harmonizes with pink, lilac and white *Symphytum ibericum* and flatters the handsome flowers of the Lenten rose (*Helleborus* × *hybridus*).

Below: Bugles can be used with other prostrate foliage plants to create a carpet of subtly varied textures and colors. Here, the dark foliage of *Ajuga reptans* 'Atropurpurea' is contrasted against the tiny, pale, glaucous leaves of *Hebe pinguifolia* 'Pagei'.

## Ajuga reptans
COMMON BUGLE

This European wild flower has dozens of cultivars that spread into carpets of evergreen foliage, often colored or variegated, with upright spikes of purple-blue, pink or white flowers. Choice varieties include 'Variegata', with leaves edged irregularly with cream, and 'Multicolor', mottled pink and cream. Vigorous 'Catlin's Giant' ♀ and 'Jungle Beauty' have larger leaves and blooms. Given good, rich soil, bugles make good ground cover under shrubs or at the front of borders, combined with pink, pale blue and mauve flowers. They associate well with late narcissi and cowslips, and with autumn crocuses and colchicums. Dark-leaved cultivars such as 'Purple Torch' and 'Atropurpurea' can be used as a dramatic background for pale flowers.

**Perfect partners:** *Chionodoxa* 'Pink Giant' p.356 **B**, *Colchicum agrippinum* p.357 **A**, *Dianthus* Allwoodii Alpinus Group, *Erysimum hieraciifolium*, *Iris pallida* 'Argentea Variegata', *Origanum vulgare* 'Aureum' p.316 **C**, *Primula veris*, *Tulipa clusiana* var. *chrysantha*

H: 6 in. (15 cm) S: 24–36 in. (60–90 cm)
✣ Late spring to early summer
 ◊◊-◊◊◊ □-■ Z3 pH5–7.5

In this scheme relying principally on foliage for its effect, billowing mounds of lady's mantle (*Alchemilla mollis*) flowers anchor the design at the front of the border. *Cornus alba* 'Aurea' provides matching yellow-green in the background, while the bold, bright green leaves of a crocosmia form a focal point. The pale foliage of *Rhamnus alaternus* 'Argenteovariegata' offers a gentler, lighter tone.

## Alchemilla mollis ♀
LADY'S MANTLE

This ground-cover plant is much tougher than its demure beauty suggests. The downy, scalloped leaves hold glittering droplets of rain or dew on their gray-green surface and, in summer, airy sprays of greenish yellow flowers appear like masses of tiny stars. It adds astringency to pink, mauve and blue flowers such as anchusas, and enhances yellows, oranges and scarlets. It can be planted in gravel, or used to soften the edges of paths, or along the front of a border, combined with lamb's ears, grasses and other spiky-leaved plants. Trimming plants after flowering stimulates fresh young foliage to appear two weeks or so later.

**Perfect partners:** *Calendula officinalis*, *Cotoneaster horizontalis* p.91 **C**, *Dianthus* Allwoodii Alpinus Group, *Elymus magellanicus*, *Euonymus fortunei* 'Emerald 'n' Gold', *Festuca glauca* 'Elijah Blue', *Geranium* 'Ann Folkard', *Lupinus arboreus* p.114 **B**, *Penstemon* 'Chester Scarlet' p.442 **C**, *Rosa* Graham Thomas, *Rubus cockburnianus* 'Goldenvale' p.137 **A**, *Viola cornuta* Lilacina Group

H: 16 in. (40 cm) S: 24 in. (60 cm)
✣ Early summer
 ◊◊-◊◊◊ □-■ Z3 pH4–8

## *Allium schoenoprasum*
CHIVES

A traditional edging for beds of other herbs, chives deserve wider use elsewhere in the garden. Plants form neat clumps of deep green, grasslike foliage, topped by tight, rounded heads of honey-scented mauve flowers. There are also good decorative cultivars such as clover-pink 'Forescate' and 'Pink Perfection', and several white forms. Clumps of chives are readily divided to provide plenty of plants for the front of sunny beds and borders, either in formal rows or as repeated groups. Their spiky, tufted shape and rich coloring make an exciting contrast to leafy herbs such as marjorams and purple- or gold-leaved sages, and in flower borders blend well with stachys, primroses and *Alchemilla mollis*. Chives can also be used to echo the shape of other alliums of different sizes but

In this extended grouping of plants of similar height, clumps of a vigorous, white-flowered form of chives (*Allium schoenoprasum*) and of a white columbine (*Aquilegia vulgaris* 'Nivea') are intermingled and repeated to give a ghostly harmony. Deadheading will keep the foliage of both plants healthy and encourage a little reblooming.

with similar flower color and form. Pulling out the flower stalks prevents self-seeding.

**Perfect partners:** *Allium moly, Allium Hollandicum* p.81 **B**, *Lavandula stoechas* subsp. *pedunculata* p.112 **C**, *Origanum vulgare* 'Aureum', *Salvia officinalis* 'Icterina', *S.o.* 'Purpurascens'

H: 12 in. (30 cm)  S: 9 in. (23 cm)
❀ Late spring to midsummer
◊-◊◊  ▣-▪  Z4  pH5.5–7.5

## *Alstroemeria* 'Apollo' ♀

Alstroemerias or Peruvian lilies have beautiful, often extravagantly marked flowers, small and lilylike in shape, with a distinctly aristocratic air. The blooms of most common species, borne on clumps of leafy, wiry stems, appear in early and midsummer, although some modern hybrids bloom later when other herbaceous flowers may be sparse. 'Apollo', soft white with a yellow throat, is an excellent choice for any border and may also be used for cutting. Like most alstroemerias, it makes an effective contrast with plants of radically different habit, especially delphiniums and others with tall, slim flower spikes, and may be planted in large groups in rose beds.

Other modern cultivars often have opulent coloring and contrasting markings – examples include the Princess and Little Princess Series, and broad-petaled Dutch hybrids such as 'Friendship' ♀ and 'Yellow Friendship' ♀. Most benefit from brushwood supports when stems are about two-thirds their eventual height.

**Perfect partners:** *Aconitum napellus, Campanula persicifolia, Delphinium* 'Sabrina', *Hydrangea paniculata* 'Grandiflora', *Rosa* 'Albertine', *R.* 'Felicia', *R.* 'Frensham'

H: 36 in. (90 cm)  S: 30 in. (75 cm) ❀ Midsummer
◊◊  ▣-▪  Z7  pH5.5–7.5

*Hydrangea arborescens* provides bulk and solidity next to a group of *Alstroemeria* 'Apollo'. The hydrangea flowerheads will mature to pure white while the alstroemeria remains in flower, harmonizing with its beautifully marked blooms.

This scheme of hot colors, with *Alstroemeria aurea* and harmonious *Crocosmia* 'Vulcan', is given greater depth by the recessive purplish blue tints of *Aconitum* 'Spark's Variety' in the background.

## Alstroemeria aurea

One of the easiest alstroemeria species (syn. *A. aurantiaca*), this typically has orange flowers. 'Dover Orange' and 'Orange King' are particularly rich selections. It looks best with hot colors and bronze foliage, but also contrasts effectively with bright pure blue or magenta; it is especially good with kniphofias, and soft orange or pale yellow achilleas. The plants are very vigorous and benefit from brushwood stakes inserted when about two-thirds their final height. Clumps can become congested, flowering less freely and for a shorter time. The best method of dividing them is to cut out portions after flowering and transplant them with their soil – the roots will not tolerate being teased out. In dry climates, plants are prone to red spider mite.

**Perfect partners:** *Achillea* 'Moonshine', *Cotinus coggygria* 'Royal Purple', *Geranium* 'Johnson's Blue', *Kniphofia* 'David', *Lychnis × arkwrightii* 'Vesuvius', *Rosa* 'Prince Charles'

H: 36 in. (90 cm)  S: 24 in. (60 cm)  ✿ Midsummer
━━◻◼◻  ◊◊  ◻-◼  Z7  pH5.5–7.5

## Alstroemeria ligtu hybrids

These are hybrids between *A. ligtu*, which has flowers varying in color from white to pale lilac or pinkish red, and *A. haemantha*, a variable, spreading species, with orange or dull red flowers streaked and splashed with yellow, maroon and purple. The hybrids vary considerably, but their most common color is salmon-pink with yellow inner petals marked with maroon. They are well suited to the front ranks of a border, where they go well with bronze-leaved heucheras. They are also very effective with white, soft orange and blue flowers, such as daylilies and *Polemonium caeruleum* or its white form *P.c.* subsp. *caeruleum* f. *album*, perhaps with acid green *Philadelphus coronarius* 'Aureus'.

**Perfect partners:** *Cistus × cyprius* p.86 **B**, *Geranium renardii*, *Heuchera villosa* 'Palace Purple', *Macleaya microcarpa* p.311 **A**

H: 30 in. (75 cm)  S: 24 in. (60 cm)  ✿ Early summer
━━◻◼◻  ◊◊  ◻-◼  Z7  pH5.5–7.5

The color of *Penstemon* 'Andenken an Friedrich Hahn' in the foreground is close enough to primary red to blend agreeably with the salmon flowers of the *Alstroemeria ligtu* hybrids beyond. They themselves harmonize with the color of the brick wall behind.

## Alstroemeria psittacina

This is not a showy plant, but it looks very appealing at close range. Its rich rust-red flowers with green-tipped segments are effective with lime green flowers, such as *Nicotiana langsdorffii* or the large-flowered *N.* 'Really Green'. Plants with many smaller scarlet blooms are good – alonsoas or *Salvia microphylla* cultivars, for example. It is also goes well with salmon-pink. It makes a sultry contribution to hot schemes, especially with tawny orange and yellow flowers such as

daylilies, achilleas or *Rudbeckia hirta*. Plants often make the best impression when positioned next to something of more solid habit and with bolder foliage.

**Perfect partners:** *Alonsoa warscewiczii*, *Cotinus coggygria* 'Royal Purple', *Euphorbia schillingii*, *Heuchera* 'Plum Pudding', *Phygelius × rectus* 'Salmon Leap'

H: 36 in. (90 cm)  S: 18 in. (45 cm)
✿ Midsummer to early autumn
━━◻◼◻  ◊◊  ◼-◼  Z7  pH5.5–7.5

The florets of *Alstroemeria psittacina* have their own internal contrast provided by the green tips to their red blooms. Mixing the alstroemeria with *Nicotiana* 'Lime Green', its flowers harmonizing with the tips but contrasting with the predominant scarlet, creates a striking combination. A background of *Berberis thunbergii* 'Rose Glow', its rich leaf color enlivened by splashes of pink, completes the picture.

Above: The elegant white flowers of *Anemone × hybrida* 'Honorine Jobert' rise above the spherical seedheads of *Allium cristophii*, nestling among the anemone's basal leaves. The allium just overtops the silvery edging provided by the foliage of *Senecio viravira* at the front of the border.

Below: The cross-banded *Miscanthus sinensis* 'Zebrinus' is of the right height to provide excellent contrast of form with the late Japanese anemone *A. × hybrida* 'Elegans'.

## Anemone × hybrida
JAPANESE ANEMONE

Japanese anemones derive mainly from two species: *A. hupehensis*, with its variant var. *japonica*, which has many narrow petals, and *A. vitifolia*. Their hybrid *A. × hybrida* and its cultivars are perhaps the most beautiful and useful to gardeners. The commonest include white 'Honorine Jobert' ♀ (sometimes called 'Alba', although in the United States this is a synonym of 'Lady Ardilaun'); pink 'Paxton's Original'; mid-pink 'Elegans' ♀, becoming paler with age; 'Lady Gilmour', with heavily frilled, light green leaves; and 'Margarete' (also incorrectly called 'Lady Gilmour'), with almost double, pale pink flowers. Japanese anemones are good with late roses such as Chinas and Hybrid Musks, with penstemons, pink chrysanthemums, asters such as *A. × frikartii* cultivars, and Michaelmas daisies, with smaller miscanthus cultivars such as *M. sinensis* 'Gracillimus', and with silver or purple foliage.

**Perfect partners:** *Arundo donax* var. *versicolor* p.412 **C**, *Aster novi-belgii* 'Marie Ballard', *Chrysanthemum* 'Clara Curtis', *Clematis* 'Alba Luxurians', *Rosa* 'Penelope' ❑ p.404 **B**

H: 4–5 ft. (1.2–1.5 m) S: 24 in. (60 cm)
❀ Late summer to mid-autumn
◆◆ ■ Z6 pH5–8

The cypress spurge (*Euphorbia cyparissias*) is slightly invasive, enabling it to grow through a carpet of *Anthemis punctata* subsp. *cupaniana*, punctuating it with its acid yellow-green flowerheads.

## Anthemis punctata subsp. *cupaniana* ♀

This carpeting plant is grown as much for its neat silver foliage as for the white flowers with their yellow centers. These appear mainly in early summer, although some blooms may be produced later, even into the autumn, encouraged by shearing plants after the main flowering period. Shearing also helps to keep them tidy and improves their color late in the season; untrimmed plants often turn grayish green. At the front of a border it can tumble over adjacent paving or edging stones, and it also succeeds well in a gravel garden. It looks good with other silver foliage, with lavenders, sages and other Mediterranean plants, including Dwarf Bearded irises, and with lime green flowers such as euphorbias or compact grasses like the smaller *Stipa* species. In hot, dry beds it is effective when planted beneath agaves, such as *A. americana*, and even columnar cacti.

**Perfect partners:** *Festuca glauca* 'Elijah Blue', *Helleborus foetidus*, *Iris* 'Curlew', *Kniphofia* 'Goldelse' p.303 **A**, *Lavandula angustifolia* 'Hidcote', *Myosotis alpestris*, *Salvia × sylvestris* 'Mainacht', *Stipa tenuissima*, *Tulipa* 'Ballerina' p.392 **B**, *T.* 'Fantasy' p.395 **B**

H: 12 in. (30 cm) S: 36 in. (90 cm) ❀ Early summer
◆ ■ Z3 pH5.5–7.5

In this richly colored combination at the front of a border, orange *Anthemis sancti-johannis* and its companions – light magenta *Stachys macrantha*, purplish blue *Campanula latiloba* 'Highcliffe Variety' and dusky pinkish crimson *Astrantia major* 'Rubra' – are allowed to flop forward over the adjoining path.

## Anthemis sancti-johannis

The true species of this herbaceous perennial is distinctive for the richness and intensity of its orange flowers, with short petals surrounding a central disk, although plants sold under this name are sometimes inferior hybrid seedlings. It is an outstanding source of hot color for the front of a border, harmonizing with other oranges, as well as scarlets, yellows, creams, peaches and apricots. It makes a striking contrast with violet-blue flowers and combines well with many geums and bronze-leaved heucheras.

It can be short-lived, especially where drainage is less than perfect, and can suddenly disappear unless cut back immediately after flowering.

**Perfect partners:** *Alonsoa warscewiczii*, *Calendula officinalis* 'Gitana Orange', *Campanula glomerata* 'Joan Elliott', *Geum* 'Lady Stratheden', *G.* 'Mrs. J. Bradshaw', *Hemerocallis* 'Golden Chimes', *Heuchera villosa* 'Palace Purple', *Lychnis* × *arkwrightii* 'Vesuvius'

**H & S: 24 in.** (60 cm) ❀ **Early to midsummer**
 ○ ☐ **Z5 pH5.5–7.5**

## Anthemis tinctoria
YELLOW CAMOMILE

The front or second rank of a well-drained border or gravel garden suits this showy plant, also known as dyer's camomile, ox-eye camomile or golden marguerite. The bright yellow flowers make excellent contrasts with blues and harmonize with hot orange and red. It flowers so prolifically that it may exhaust itself unless sheared back after its first flush. 'E.C. Buxton' and 'Wargrave Variety', both pale creamy yellow, and even paler 'Sauce Hollandaise' are very good with silver plants. The hybrid *A.* 'Grallagh Gold' is golden yellow, and *A.* Susanna Mitchell ('Blomit') has white flowers.

**Perfect partners:** *Achillea* 'Moonshine', *Aconitum* 'Spark's Variety', *Bidens ferulifolia* p.413 **B**, *Centaurea macrocephala*, *Clematis* × *diversifolia* 'Blue Boy' p.157 **A**, *Lavandula angustifolia* 'Hidcote', *Mimulus cardinalis*, *Rosa* 'Buff Beauty', *R.* **Graham Thomas**, *Tanacetum parthenium*

**H: 24–36 in.** (60–90 cm) **S: 24 in.** (60 cm)
❀ **Early to midsummer**
 ○-○○○ ☐-■ **Z4 pH5.5–7.5**

The soft yellow flowers of *Anthemis tinctoria* 'E.C. Buxton' here provide a contrast with the slender spires of purple toadflax (*Linaria purpurea*) and the magenta, black-eyed blooms of the cranesbill *Geranium* 'Ann Folkard'. The cranesbill's yellowish green foliage harmonizes with the lemon daisylike flowerheads while also contrasting with its own flowers and those of the toadflax.

Beneath a canopy of deciduous trees in late spring, *Aquilegia canadensis* and wild sweet William (*Phlox divaricata*) form a carpet of gently contrasting flowers.

## Aquilegia canadensis ♔
CANADIAN COLUMBINE

This dainty perennial has finely divided leaves, fernlike and dark green, and elegant, nodding flowers with scarlet sepals and lemon-yellow petals tapering to red spurs. *A. formosa* is similar but has bluish green foliage. Both species flower in late spring and early summer, and produce a much more refined effect than common columbine, which is bigger and beefier. Plants associate well with Dwarf and Intermediate Bearded irises, with Siberian wallflowers and with the bronze foliage of some heucheras, especially those with reddish flowers. They harmonize with hot or warm colors such as peach and scarlet, although too much strong color easily overpowers their natural daintiness. They are good with cream or lime green.

**Perfect partners:** *Erysimum* × *marshallii*, *Euphorbia amygdaloides* var. *robbiae*, *Heuchera villosa* 'Palace Purple', *Iris* 'Curlew', *I.* 'Rocket' p.300 **C**

**H: 15 in.** (38 cm) **S: 8 in.** (20 cm)
❀ **Late spring to early summer**
○○ ☐-■ **Z3 pH4.5–7.5**

# *Aquilegia vulgaris*
COMMON COLUMBINE

This is a very variable species, with single or double flowers, with or without spurs, and in colors ranging from white, pink and pale blue to deep blue, crimson and purple-black. 'Nivea' ♀ (also known as 'Munstead White') has nodding, single white flowers and gray-green leaves. *A.v.* var. *stellata* has spurless double flowers. Its famous variant is 'Nora Barlow' ♀, with petals that are reddish pink at the base, passing through white to green at the tips. Bold, single flowers and less double variants of var. *stellata* have most impact at a distance, whereas complex, fully double types work best at close range. They are all very effective with irises, early roses, early cranesbills, hostas and martagon lilies, as well as with purple foliage and umbel-shaped flowerheads such as pink cow parsley. All these aquilegias tolerate shade but are not very long-lived. Periodically raising replacements from seed is advisable, but only a few will produce true seedlings, and only then if plants have been growing in isolation.

**Perfect partners:** *Allium schoenoprasum* (white) p.231 **A**, *Anthriscus sylvestris* 'Broadleas Blush', *Centaurea montana* 'Alba' p.249 **C**, *Hosta* (Tardiana Group) 'Halcyon', *Iris sibirica* 'Cambridge', *Paeonia lactiflora* 'Albert Crousse'

**H: 24–36 in.** (60–90 cm)  **S: 18 in.** (45 cm)
✿ **Late spring to early summer**
◌◌ ☐-■  **Z3 pH4.5–7.5**

Right: A mauve-flowered strain of *Aquilegia vulgaris* var. *stellata* harmonizes perfectly with the spherical flowerheads of *Allium hollandicum* 'Purple Sensation' around silvery *Seriphidium nutans*.

Below: An informal mix of *Aquilegia vulgaris* in pinks and whites, plus lavender-blue *A.* 'Hensol Harebell', combines pleasingly with cranesbills, including the mourning widow (*Geranium phaeum*) in the foreground, the wood cranesbill (*G. sylvaticum*) just behind it and white *G. phaeum* 'Album'. All would flower equally well in semi-shade.

## *Arrhenatherum elatius* subsp. *bulbosum* 'Variegatum'
VARIEGATED BULBOUS OAT GRASS

The striped form of the bulbous oat grass is a brilliantly white-variegated plant for the front of a border. Ideally it is grown in moist soil, and in full sun in areas where summers are cool; in hotter climates a little shade is advisable. Plants look attractive with dark or silver foliage, such as purple-gray *Sedum telephium* 'Matrona' or *Stachys byzantina* 'Big Ears', and produce good contrasts with richly colored flowers including *Hemerocallis* 'Red Rum' and harmonies with pastel blues and mauves. This grass is best kept away from mat-forming plants because its rhizomatous roots spread fairly freely underground and may become entangled with those of its neighbors. The foliage is prone to rust, and it should be clipped back near or just after flowering time, otherwise by late summer the plant looks rather untidy.

**Perfect partners:** *Allium cristophii*, *Artemisia stelleriana* 'Boughton Silver', *Crocosmia* 'Lucifer', *Hemerocallis* 'Stafford', *Ophiopogon planiscapus* 'Nigrescens'

**H & S: 12 in.** (30 cm)
( ❀ **Midsummer to early autumn)**
�○-◊◊ ☐-■ **Z4 pH5–7.5**

Linear foliage, including the white-striped *Arrhenatherum elatius* subsp. *bulbosum* 'Variegatum', sword-shaped crocosmia, and arching, gold-banded pampas grass (*Cortaderia selloana* 'Aureolineata'), is contrasted with clouds of the goldenrod *Solidago* 'Goldenmosa' in a combination suitable for a broad, informally planted bed.

## *Artemisia alba* 'Canescens' ♀

Few other silver foliage plants can rival the daintiness of this wormwood cultivar, whose lacy leaves are divided into threadlike sections that coil into twists and curlicues. The flowering stems form delicate spires, but the flowers themselves are insignificant. This is a plant for well-drained soils, in a forward position in a border. It is charming with cranesbills, pinks, smaller campanulas and, above all, old roses, and it harmonizes with soft colors such as pinks, blues and mauves. It also works well with less dainty artemisias such as *A. stelleriana* in white schemes. The foliage contrasts effectively with bolder shapes, and with dark or glaucous foliage, like that of Dwarf or Intermediate Bearded irises; companions of differing leaf form but closely allied coloring, such as silver-green *Convolvulus cneorum*, can also prove satisfying.

**Perfect partners:** *Campanula* 'Burghaltii', *Dianthus* 'Doris', *Geranium sanguineum* var. *striatum* p.278 **A**, *Iris* 'Grapesicle', *Nemophila menziesii*, *Nigella damascena*, *Rosa* 'Charles de Mills', *R.* 'Fantin-Latour'

**H: 18 in.** (45 cm) **S: 12 in.** (30 cm)
❀ **Midsummer to early autumn**
�○ ☐ **Z5 pH5.5–7.5**

Deadheading *Artemisia alba* 'Canescens' after its first flush of flowers has here produced an uncharacteristically late second crop of filigree spires of buds in early autumn, contrasting with the solid, flat flowerheads of *Sedum* 'Herbstfreude', nestling in front of the variegated dogwood *Cornus alba* 'Elegantissima'.

## *Artemisia ludoviciana*

For much of the season, the slender stems
of this wormwood bear willowy leaves, some
with cut or forked ends, in clear silvery white,
although later they turn dull green as the
white flowers assume brownish tints with age.
The remedy is to cut growth back by half
when 30 in. (75 cm) high, which stimulates
plants to bush out and remain fresh and
silver. 'Silver Queen' ♀ has lax stems 36 in.
(90 cm) high; the more refined var. *latiloba*,
24 in. (60 cm) tall, is broader, with more
silvery, largely uncut leaves. All are good
in silver foliage schemes or with plants such
as lavenders and cistus, and associate well
with flowers in pastel pinks, mauves and pale
blues. They make good contrasts with richer
colors like crimson, and with dark foliage.

**Perfect partners:** *Cistus × purpureus*,
*Geranium tuberosum* p.279 **A**, *Hebe* 'Watson's
Pink' p.104 **C**, *Iris* 'Nightfall' p.298 **B**,
*Penstemon* 'Chester Scarlet' p.442 **C**, *Rosa*
'Carmenetta', *Tulipa* 'Palestrina' p.400 **B**

**H: 4 ft. (1.2 m) S: 24 in. (60 cm)**
❀ **Midsummer to early autumn**

 ◊-◊◊ ▢-▣ **Z4 pH5.5–7.5**

**Above:** A subtle interplay of leaf shapes in silvery gray-
green is achieved by combining *Artemisia ludoviciana* var.
*latiloba* and filigree *Senecio cineraria*, interlaced with bronze-
tinged umbels of dill (*Anethum graveolens*), giving a delicate
association best appreciated at close range.

**Below:** The typical species *Artemisia ludoviciana* has leaves
more lobed and divided than its variety above, making a
less bold but daintier effect. Here, wood forget-me-nots
(*Myosotis sylvatica*), self-seeded the previous summer,
spangle the young artemisia foliage with sky-blue flowers.

In a broad and shallowly banked grouping, a carpet of
compact silvery *Artemisia schmidtiana* 'Nana' spreads before
tussocks of bronze sedge (*Carex flagellifera*), in front of the
handsome spurge *Euphorbia characias*.

## *Artemisia schmidtiana* ♀

The silky, glistening silver foliage of this
species makes a strong impact at the front of
a border. A well-known variant, 'Nana' ♀, is
only 3½ in. (8 cm) or so high and produces a
very low, spreading mat of foliage. The small
yellow flowers of this and the species itself
are usually best cut off. These are some of the
easier, more tolerant silver plants to grow
and may be used with a wide range of other
silver-leaved plants and Mediterranean
natives such as lavenders, sages, pinks and
cistus. They go well with flowers in pastel
pinks, mauves and pale blues, or contrasted
with dark foliage and richly colored flowers.

**Perfect partners:** *Berberis thunbergii*
'Atropurpurea Nana', *Cistus × purpureus*,
*Dianthus* Allwoodii Alpinus Group, *Lavandula
lanata*, *Rosmarinus officinalis* Prostratus
Group, *Rosa* Pink Bells, *Salvia officinalis*
'Purpurascens'

**H: 12 in. (30 cm) S: 18 in. (45 cm)**
(❀ **Mid- to late summer)**

◊-◊◊ ▢-▣ **Z4 pH5.5–7.5**

## *Artemisia stelleriana* 'Boughton Silver'

Sometimes known as dusty miller, this semi-evergreen (syns *A.s.* 'Mori' and 'Silver Brocade') is a sprawling, prostrate plant with deeply indented silvery leaves, and flowers of similar color borne in sprays. It is ideal for the front of a border, for a gravel or rock garden, or for softening the edge of a path. A good partner for cool-colored flowers and silver or glaucous foliage, it is attractive when fronting mound-forming plants such as rue, lavenders, rosemaries, helichrysums, smaller cistus, perovskias, lavender cottons and other artemisias, together with dianthus, marjorams, and smaller irises. It also mixes well with other sprawling plants that grow at a similar rate, including smaller cranesbills, gray-leaved veronicas, stachys and sedums, and may be underplanted with bulbs such as alliums.

**Perfect partners:** *Dianthus* Allwoodii Alpinus Group, *Hebe pinguifolia* 'Pagei', *Lavandula angustifolia* 'Hidcote', *Origanum vulgare* 'Aureum', *Perovskia* 'Blue Spire', *Salvia officinalis* 'Kew Gold', *Sedum spectabile* 'Brilliant'

H: **6 in.** (15 cm)  S: **16 in.** (40 cm)
✿ **Midsummer to early autumn**
◐-◐◐  ▨-■  Z4  pH5.5–7.5

Although *Artemisia stelleriana* 'Boughton Silver' is far less vigorous than *Geranium* 'Ann Folkard', planting the artemisia near to the limit of the cranesbill's spread prevents it being overwhelmed by its neighbor and allows an attractive intermingling of the two.

## *Aruncus dioicus*
GOAT'S BEARD

This statuesque herbaceous perennial has elegantly divided leaves and imposing plumes of tiny creamy white flowers, male and female on separate plants (as the females produce copious quantities of invasive seed, only the male form has the ♀). It is a choice plant for mixed or herbaceous borders, for waterside planting or for use as a specimen, especially against a dark background. It harmonizes

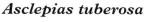

with astilbes and contrasts with delphiniums, achilleas, campanulas and Shrub roses, while its color, which mixes with most others, is very effective with yellow, pure white, warm peach or apricot, and yellow-green foliage or flowers. Good partners include euphorbias, ligularias, telekias, golden philadelphus or elder, and medium-sized bamboos. 'Kneiffii' is a smaller, dainty plant with leaflets reduced to threadlike strips; upright 'Glasnevin' has narrower plumes; and 'Southern White' has branching spikes and tolerates hot summers.

**Perfect partners:** *Achillea* 'Lachsschönheit', *Astilbe* 'Red Sentinel', *Heuchera* 'Pewter Moon', *Ligularia dentata* 'Desdemona', *Philadelphus intectus* p.120 **A**, *Rosa* 'Highdownensis'

**H: 6 ft.** (1.8 m) **S: 4 ft.** (1.2 m)
✣ **Early to midsummer**
◌◌-◌◌◌ ☐-■ Z3 pH4.5–7.5

The splendid architectural form of goat's beard (*Aruncus dioicus*) makes it a good choice where a specimen plant is needed, as here where it contrasts with a crisply formal opening through a hedge of beech (*Fagus sylvatica*). A pair of clipped box (*Buxus sempervirens*) in containers, one on either side, echoes the formality of the beech.

## *Asclepias tuberosa*
BUTTERFLY WEED

Hot summers and good drainage are essential for this tuberous herbaceous perennial if it is to continue flowering late in the season. Its flowers are usually vermilion with a golden yellow center, but there are numerous selections such as golden 'Hello Yellow', 24–30 in. (60–75 cm) high, and Gay Butterflies Group, also 24–30 in. (60–75 cm), in a range of colors including scarlet, gold, pink and orange. It looks very effective with other hot-colored perennials, such as hedychiums, and with dahlias, late-flowering euphorbias and alstroemerias, kniphofias, leonotis, cannas, rudbeckias, heleniums, arctotis hybrids, salvias and roses. It is also good with bronze foliage, yellow-green foliage and flowers, and annuals such as salvias, tagetes and ursinias.

**Perfect partners:** *Arctotis* × *hybrida* 'Flame', *Canna indica* 'Purpurea', *Hedychium coccineum* 'Tara', *Kniphofia* 'Sunningdale Yellow', *Tagetes patula* 'Striped Marvel'

**H: 18–36 in.** (45–90 cm) **S: 12 in.** (30 cm)
✣ **Midsummer to early autumn**
◌◌ ☐-■ Z4 pH5.5–7.5

This vibrant combination of orange butterfly weed (*Asclepias tuberosa*) and the mauve, dark-centered flowers of narrow-leaved *Echinacea tennesseensis* provides a contrast of floral form on plants of similar height. Both are wild flowers of the North American prairies.

Growing in a crevice in a limestone rockery, the bold unfurling fronds of hart's tongue fern (*Asplenium scolopendrium*) are furnished from spring into summer with the azure-blue blooms of *Lithodora diffusa* 'Heavenly Blue'.

## *Asplenium scolopendrium* ♀
HART'S TONGUE FERN

This hardy evergreen fern has strap-shaped leaves, 2–24 in. (5–60 cm) long, that are often crested, wavy or forked. The simplest kinds can look almost tropical when grown well. It is a shade-loving species for moist conditions, and mixes well with hardier begonias, ivies, asarums and other ferns such as athyriums and polystichums. Its evergreen foliage complements spring bulbs such as snowdrops and cyclamens, and provides interest under deciduous shrubs when these are out of leaf. Good selections include the ruffled Crispum Group, such as 'Crispum Bolton's Nobile' ♀; Fimbriatum Group, with narrow, deeply serrated fronds; and Ramocristatum Group, with divided, crested fronds. The leaves of 'Kaye's Lacerated' ♀ are more or less triangular and deeply cut at the edges.

**Perfect partners:** *Asarum shuttleworthii*, *Convallaria majalis* p.252 **A**, *Cyclamen coum*, *Galanthus nivalis*, *Hedera helix* 'Manda's Crested', *Lobelia richardsonii* p.433 **B**

**H & S: 2–24 in.** (5–60 cm)
◌◌-◌◌◌ ☐-■ Z4 pH4–8

## Aster divaricatus

The wiry, nearly black stems of this aster (syn. *A. corymbosus*) bear heart-shaped leaves. From midsummer onward, they also carry starry white flowers that associate well with almost any other color. This shade-tolerant species has a graceful habit, and looks best when allowed to drape forward naturally over other plants, particularly if these will accept some shade later in the year. The sprawling aster growth might interfere with the flowers of its neighbors, unless these are produced earlier in the season – as with heucheras, bergenias and bugles, for example. It is

perhaps at its best in a woodland garden, whose shade few late flowers tolerate so well. Although the rhizomatous roots eventually spread to form loose groups, for full impact it should be planted closely in generous drifts to produce a delicate haze of white stars. *A. macrophyllus* is a more robust plant of similar temperament, with pale violet flowers, fading to white.

**Perfect partners:** *Achillea millefolium* 'Cerise Queen', *Anemone* × *hybrida* 'Elegans', *Deschampsia cespitosa*, *Miscanthus sinensis* 'Gracillimus', *Rhus* × *pulvinata* Autumn Lace Group, *Salvia* × *superba* 'Rubin'

**H & S: 24 in. (60 cm)**
❀ **Midsummer to mid-autumn**
◌◌ ☐-■ Z4 pH5–7.5

In a classic combination, suitable for the front of a bed or border, the dainty flower stems of *Aster divaricatus* drape themselves over the bold leaves of mixed bergenias. The starlike aster flowers will continue into autumn.

## Aster × frikartii 'Mönch' ♛

Many consider this to be the finest aster for long display. Its soft lavender-blue flowers with a yellow disk go well with almost any color except lavender or lilac. The flowers harmonize with blues and purples, and contrast dramatically with orange – some late-flowering crocosmias, for example, or the early autumn tints of *Vitis coignetiae*. They also look very pleasing with silver foliage, chrysanthemums or dahlias, particularly the soft pale yellow, rose-pink and purple kinds. It benefits from staking with brushwood, which should be worked into the plant when about two-thirds of its flowering height, and is best replanted in fresh ground every three years or so. It is always advisable to purchase plants from stock that is known to be vigorous and free-flowering.

**Perfect partners:** *Chrysanthemum* 'Clara Curtis', *Dahlia* 'Pink Michigan', *Echinacea purpurea* 'Magnus', *Heliopsis helianthoides* 'Patula' p.284 **A**, *Rudbeckia fulgida* var. *sullivantii* 'Goldsturm', *Stipa tenuissima*, *Verbena bonariensis*

**H: 31 in. (80 cm)  S: 16 in. (40 cm)**
❀ **Midsummer to mid-autumn**
◌-◌◌ ☐-■ Z5 pH5.5–7.5

Although the camera sees its color as lying between lilac and mauve, *Aster* × *frikartii* 'Mönch' has petals of soft lavender, contrasting with the flowers' yellow centers. In this lively long-flowering summer scheme, *Aster novae-angliae* 'Harrington's Pink' supplies abundant smaller harmonious blooms. Both asters are resistant to tarsonemid mites.

**Above:** The lavender-blue *Aster novi-belgii* 'Marie Ballard' is sufficiently definite in color to be contrasted with the rich yellow, dark-centred daisy-like flowers of *Rudbeckia fulgida* var. *deamu*, also providing a contrast of floral form.

**Left:** *Aster novi-belgii* cultivars are often associated with impressionistic swirls of lavender and mauve, although bolder colors are available, such as carmine 'Carnival' here.

## Aster novi-belgii

MICHAELMAS DAISY, NEW YORK ASTER

Michaelmas daisies provide immensely useful color from late summer to mid-autumn, although most cultivars bloom only for about a month. Colors range from crimson, purple, and nearly blue, through all the paler shades to white, with individual flowers varying from single to fully double, and from about ½–2½ in. (1–7 cm) across. They are good with other late summer and autumn flowers such as Japanese anemones, chrysanthemums and dahlias, in pink, white, crimson or soft yellow. They also combine well with strongly textured or structured plants such as miscanthus, pampas grass and some of the later-flowering kniphofias. Plants need spraying against mildew and tarsonemid mites, and all but the shortest need staking. It is best to divide them annually in spring, replanting a vigorous section of rhizome, but they can be left undisturbed for up to three years before they start to decline.

**Perfect partners:** *Anemone* × *hybrida* 'Honorine Jobert', *Chrysanthemum* 'Wedding Day', *Cortaderia selloana* 'Aureolineata', *Cotinus* 'Flame', *Dahlia* 'Pink Michigan' p.422 **C**, *Kniphofia rooperi*, *Miscanthus sinensis* 'Morning Light', *Vitis coignetiae*

**H: 12–48 in.** (30–120 cm) **S: 12–16 in.** (30–40 cm)
❀ **Late summer to mid-autumn**
◌◌-◌◌◌ ▢-▦ **Z3 pH4.5–8**

## Astilbe × arendsii hybrids

These astilbes need waterside or bog planting, or a damp border. They produce dazzling displays in colors from crimson and scarlet to mauve-pink, rose-pink and salmon, and in white. In waterside and boggy sites, the least vibrant colors are most useful, particularly if they also have a graceful, arching habit. They can be planted with water-loving iris species, *Ranunculus aconitifolius*, white zantedeschias, and glaucous-leaved hostas, with aruncus or sorbarias to echo their form. For brighter, more highly colored schemes, crimson and rich pink cultivars can be grown with purple foliage and with flowers in similar tones. Scarlet cultivars may be mixed with variegated and gold-leaved plants, such as hostas or dogwoods, with bronze foliage

Soft pink *Astilbe* × *arendsii* 'Ceres' is a late-flowering, gently colored cultivar suited to subtle associations. Here, it harmonizes with the purplish, pink-splashed leaves of *Berberis thunbergii* 'Rose Glow'.

or with ligularias. All contrast well with strap- or grassy-leaved irises. Astilbes are best divided in early autumn and are very prone to vine weevil attacks.

**Perfect partners:** *Aruncus dioicus*, *Cornus alba* 'Elegantissima', *Hosta sieboldiana* var. *elegans*, *Iris pseudacorus* 'Variegata', *I.* 'Cambridge', *Ligularia dentata* 'Othello', *Lobelia cardinalis* 'Queen Victoria', *Sorbaria sorbifolia*

**H: 20–48 in.** (50–120 cm) **S: 18 in.** (45 cm)
❀ **Late spring to midsummer**
◌◌◌ ▢-▦ ▦ **Z5 pH5.5–7**

The erect, carmine-pink spires of *Astilbe chinensis* var. *taquetii* 'Superba', contrasted with orange *Crocosmia* 'Vulcan' and yellow kniphofias and daylilies, help to emphasize the straight geometric lines of this formal garden area.

The intricate flowers of *Astrantia major* 'Hadspen Blood', their dusky pink umbels enclosed in a ruff of crimson bracts, harmonize perfectly with the dark foliage of *Berberis thunbergii* 'Atropurpurea Nana'.

## *Astilbe chinensis* var. *taquetii* 'Superba' ♈

This astilbe, which flowers unusually late, has a stiffly upright habit useful for semi-formal accents in a formal border or at the water's edge. Its color is best in shade, combining well with mauve, lavender, lilac, purple and other cool hues, and contrasting with soft yellow, yellow-green and white flowers or variegated foliage; it also blends with silver or purple foliage. Good companions are lythrums, perennial lobelias, filipendulas, monardas, and late-flowering euphorbias, and plants such as hostas or larger sedges and grasses, including bamboos. 'Purpurlanze' is tall and branching, with magenta spikes; *A.c.* var. *pumila* ♈ is mauve-pink; and *A.c.* 'Visions' has spreading magenta-pink panicles.

**Perfect partners:** *Carex grayi, Euphorbia schillingii, Filipendula camtschatica, Hosta* 'Shade Fanfare', *Lysimachia clethroides, Mimulus aurantiacus, Phyllostachys nigra*

H: 4 ft. (1.2 m) S: 24 in. (60 cm)
✿ Late summer to mid-autumn

 ◊◊-◊◊◊◊ ▢-◾ ◾ Z4 pH5.5–7

## *Astilbe* 'Red Sentinel'

This early-flowering astilbe is suitable for bog gardens and waterside plantings, and also for borders where the soil does not become dry in summer. Its rich red flowers and dark foliage are very close to primary red, mixing happily with mauve-pink or rose-pink plants, including other astilbes and later-flowering primulas such as Candelabra hybrids, and with hot colors; it can also be contrasted with yellow-green foliage and flowers. It makes an effective partner for euphorbias, earlier-flowering ligularias and mimulus, and combines well with the contrasting foliage of grasses, sedges, smaller bamboos and hostas. Other good companions include plants with red-flushed foliage, including Japanese maples, and moisture-tolerant lilies like *L. superbum*.

**Perfect partners:** *Acer palmatum* f. *atropurpureum, Euphorbia amygdaloides* var. *robbiae, Iris ensata, Primula* Inshriach hybrids, *Sasa veitchii*

H: 36 in. (90 cm) S: 20 in. (50 cm) ✿ **Early summer**
▅▅▅ ◊◊-◊◊◊◊ ▢-◾ ◾ Z4 pH5.5–7

In this brightly colored waterside planting, *Astilbe* 'Red Sentinel' stands out against the yellow-green foliage of the dogwood *Cornus alba* 'Aurea'. In between, the lofty flowers of *Hosta* 'Tall Boy' are starting to unfurl. All three plants benefit from the pond's moisture.

## *Astrantia major* 'Hadspen Blood'

Although blooming mainly in summer, this astrantia bears some autumn flowers, all in a dusky ruby-red that is an excellent foil for richer crimson, brighter carmine, magenta and rich pink. It also combines effectively with white flowers and with dark-leaved heucheras and smaller purple-leaved berberis or ornamental cherries. It can be partnered by roses, especially old roses in crimson or dusky pink, shrubby lavateras, *Geranium psilostemon* cultivars and hybrids, *Achillea millefolium* cultivars and *Phlox maculata* cultivars, and looks very attractive with magenta species gladioli and light green *Gladiolus tristis* var. *concolor*. Other dark-flowered cultivars include 'Ruby Cloud', 'Ruby Wedding' and rather variable 'Claret'.

**Perfect partners:** *Cotinus* 'Flame', *Foeniculum vulgare* 'Purpureum', *Heuchera villosa* 'Palace Purple', *Phormium* 'Bronze Baby', *Rosa* 'Charles de Mills'

H: 24 in. (60 cm) S: 18 in. (45 cm)
✿ **Early to late summer**

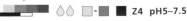 ◊◊ ▢-◾ ◾ Z4 pH5–7.5

In this complex tapestry of varied leaf forms, the boldly margined foliage of *Astrantia major* 'Sunningdale Variegated' is the focal point. It is joined by pale-spotted lungwort and glaucous-leaved roseroot (*Rhodiola rosea*), nestling against golden marjoram (*Origanum vulgare* 'Aureum').

## *Astrantia major* 'Sunningdale Variegated' ♕

This brightly variegated cultivar has spring foliage splashed with cream, darkening to green by midsummer. It is a choice plant for spring edging and for sparkling combinations with white or yellow tulips and late narcissi, or with blue flowers such as brunneras or omphalodes. The dusky pink flowers appear in early summer, but when the brightness of the leaves has diminished, so 'Sunningdale Variegated' is primarily a plant for early foliage effects, and is especially satisfying with yellow, white or blue flowers, and with yellow-green foliage and flowers. Among its many suitable partners are early-leafing hostas, bluebells, forget-me-nots, rock cress, aurinias, primroses, polyanthus and euphorbias.

**Perfect partners:** *Acer palmatum* var. *dissectum, Aconitum napellus, Diascia barberae* 'Blackthorn Apricot' p.258 **C**, *Hebe ochracea* p.104 **A**, *Spiraea japonica* p.141 **C**

H: 24 in. (60 cm) S: 18 in. (45 cm)
❉ Early to late summer

▮▮▮▮ ◌◌ ▢-▮ ▮ Z4 pH5–7.5

## *Athyrium filix-femina* ♕
LADY FERN

With its love of moisture, this deciduous fern thrives in bog or waterside plantings, woodland gardens and shady city gardens that are not too dry. It is perhaps most effective in subdued schemes based on shades of green, especially in late spring and early summer, when the lacy foliage is at its freshest. It contrasts well with hart's tongue ferns, smaller bamboos, grasses and sedges, and may be grown through a carpet of low ground cover, when the repeated pattern of its shuttlecock-shaped clumps of fronds can make an arresting statement. Strikingly different kinds include feathery 'Vernoniae' ♕; 'Frizelliae' ♕, the tatting fern, with fan-shaped lobes along the frond midribs; and 'Victoriae', which has narrow pinnae that branch to form crosses.

**Perfect partners:** *Asplenium scolopendrium, Carex grayi, Fargesia murielae* 'Simba', *Hedera algineriensis* 'Ravensholst', *Milium effusum* 'Aureum', *Pachysandra terminalis*

H: 6 in.–5 ft. (15 cm–1.5 m) S: 8–40 in. (20 cm–1 m)
▮▮▮▮ ◌◌-◌◌◌ ▢-▮ ▮ Z4 pH4–7.5

On a shady bank in late autumn, the arching fronds of a lady fern (*Athyrium filix-femina* Cruciatum Group) form a delicate tracery of criss-crossed pinnules above the autumn fern (*Dryopteris erythrosora*), an evergreen named for the bronze color of its young fronds.

## *Aubrieta* 'Argenteovariegata' ♕

This evergreen perennial with purple blooms and leaves edged in creamy white is good for rock gardens, sunny banks, walls, troughs and border edgings. If cut back after flowering, it produces a new crop of variegated leaves and shoots, which add interest when the plant is out of flower. Its color harmonizes with white, soft yellow, purple or lilac flowers, and contrasts with yellow-green flowers and foliage. Good companions include early-flowering euphorbias, soft yellow wallflowers, aurinias, white rock cress, smaller narcissi, ipheions, chionodoxas and small spring-

Purple *Aubrieta* 'Argenteovariegata' and white-flowered *Arenaria montana*, two plants of similar stature, flower shape and size but of contrasting flower color, make a pleasing pattern on a sunny bank in spring.

flowering shrubs such as daphnes or spiraeas. Plants are short-lived and are best increased by summer cuttings every three or four years.

**Perfect partners:** *Erysimum* 'Moonlight', *Euphorbia polychroma* 'Major', *Ipheion uniflorum, Narcissus bulbocodium, Spiraea japonica* 'Goldflame' (foliage)

H: 2 in. (5 cm) S: 24 in. (60 cm)
❉ Mid- to late spring

▮▮▮▮ ◌◌ ▢-▮ ▮ Z5 pH5.5–8

Rich lilac aubrieta makes an attractive foil for the bold white flowerheads of perennial candytuft (*Iberis sempervirens*) in late spring.

## *Aubrieta* cultivars

These easy, mat-forming, evergreen perennials are suitable for rock gardens, sunny banks, walls, hanging baskets and spring bedding. Over a hundred cultivars are available, in showy colors from ruby-red to lavender-blue, and shades between these and white. They are effective with spring bulbs, such as smaller narcissi and tulips, and with rock cress, perennial candytufts, primroses, polyanthus and smaller bedding violas. Plants in walls can become sparse in summer, but revive during winter to flower profusely in spring. Good seed-raised cultivars include the Royal Series. 'Novalis Blue' is very close to sky-blue, and the Bengal hybrids include semi-double flowers in red and purple.

**Perfect partners:** *Arabis alpina* subsp. *caucasica* 'Variegata', *Euphorbia amygdaloides* var. *robbiae* p.266 **B**, *Ipheion uniflorum*, *Muscari armeniacum*, *Narcissus* 'Hawera', *Primula* 'Guinevere', *Tulipa clusiana* p.394 **A**, *Viola tricolor*

**H: 2–6 in.** (5–15 cm) **S: 12 in.** (30 cm)
✺ Mid- to late spring
◌◌ ▢-▩ Z4–5 pH5.5–8

## *Aurinia saxatilis* ♛

A sub-shrubby and mound-forming plant, this easy evergreen perennial (syn. *Alyssum saxatile*) suits the same situations as *Aubrieta* cultivars (left), with which it can be planted. It is an excellent edging plant for the front of a border, and associates well with small white or cream narcissi, smaller tulips, ipheions, perennial candytufts, rock cress, primroses, polyanthus and wallflowers. A large expanse of aurinias can appear dull in texture, so they are best arranged in diffuse groups among plants of contrasting form, such as bulbs or, in a larger rock garden, dwarf conifers. 'Citrina' ♛ is lemon-yellow; 'Compacta' is shorter and neater, and more suitable for smaller planting schemes; 'Dudley Nevill' is apricot, also relatively compact; and 'Variegata' has leaves edged in creamy white.

**Perfect partners:** *Cerastium tomentosum*, *Erysimum linifolium* 'Variegatum', *Ipheion uniflorum*, *Juniperus horizontalis* 'Bar Harbor', *Muscari armeniacum*, *Narcissus* 'Actaea'

**H: 10 in.** (25 cm) **S: 18 in.** (45 cm)
✺ Late spring to early summer
 ◌◌ ▢-▩ Z4 pH5.5–8

Grown through gravel scree at the front of a sunny bed, the compact lemon-yellow *Aurinia saxatilis* 'Citrina' and gold *A.s.* 'Compacta' form spreading mats smothered with bloom in late spring, with white-flowered perennial candytuft (*Iberis sempervirens*) and the slightly taller spurge *Euphorbia polychroma* 'Major' beyond. Deadheading the aurinias will encourage some later blooming.

Two plants with attractive silvered foliage suited equally to containers or the front of beds and borders, *Ballota pseudodictamnus* and the feathery-leaved wormwood *Artemisia* 'Powis Castle' create a pleasing picture of contrasting foliage form.

## *Ballota pseudodictamnus* ♛

Woolly gray-green leaves and white stems characterize this mound-forming, sub-shrubby perennial, which is excellent in a white garden. It may also be grown in front of roses, in a gravel garden and at the front of a border, where it goes well with lavenders, shrubby phlomis, helianthemums and similar Mediterranean plants, as well as with silver foliage plants of contrasting form such as artemisias. Its white or pinkish white flowers are insignificant. Plants blend pleasingly with other blooms of almost any color, except hot or strong shades. The plant keeps its leaves all through the year; annual clipping in spring helps to maintain a neat and tidy habit.

**Perfect partners:** *Cistus* × *purpureus*, *Helianthemum* 'Rhodanthe Carneum', *Lavandula angustifolia* 'Hidcote', *Phlomis fruticosa*, *Rosa* 'Felicia', *Rosmarinus officinalis* 'Roseus', *Salvia officinalis* 'Purpurascens'

**H: 18 in.** (45 cm) **S: 24 in.** (60 cm)
(✺ Late spring to early summer)
◌◌ ▢-▩ Z7 pH5.5–7.5

The airy indigo spires of *Baptisia australis*, recessive in color and less visually insistent than the lupins they resemble, form a pleasing background for the sumptuous cupped pink blooms of *Rosa* 'Aloha'.

## *Baptisia australis* ♀

The indigo-blue flowers of this herbaceous perennial are borne in airy spikes, reminiscent of a lupin. A plant for the second or third rank of a border, it has a quiet charm that makes it suitable for supporting roles with foliage and flowers of more definite form and stronger color, such as delphiniums, roses, cranesbills and Tall Bearded irises. It blends well with silver and glaucous foliage, and with other cool colors, especially cream – the flowers of some *Anthemis tinctoria* cultivars, for example. Its blooms are a little too diffuse and too subtly colored, however, to succeed in strong contrasts with colors such as yellow. Its spikes of large, dark gray seedpods may be cut for indoor decoration.

**Perfect partners:** *Artemisia ludoviciana*, *Dahlia* 'Requiem' p.423 **A**, *Delphinium* 'Sabrina', *Geranium* × *oxonianum* 'Wargrave Pink', *Rosa glauca*, *Spiraea nipponica* 'Snowmound'

**H: 4 ft. (1.2 m) S: 24 in. (60 cm)** ❀ **Early summer**
◊-◊◊ ▢-▓ **Z3 pH5.5–7.5**

## *Bergenia cordifolia* 'Purpurea' ♀

This bergenia is one of the most outstanding foliage plants, preeminent in a genus noted for handsome leaves. Its pink flowers complement the leathery, shiny, rounded leaves, which are deep green and assume a purple flush in winter. Tolerating soils ranging from dry to very moist, it is an indispensable plant for a woodland or gravel garden, and for the front of a border, especially in full sun, which encourages the richest purple coloring. Winter-flowering plants such as *Cyclamen coum* variants, early crocuses, winter heaths, snowdrops and winter aconites make the most satisfying companions, but this bergenia also combines well with evergreen heucheras, smaller evergreen shrubs such as euonymus and dogwoods with colored winter stems, and with foliage of contrasting form – evergreen grasses, sedges and ferns, for example. It will also tolerate, even thrive in light shade, and so may be grown in front of a relatively lax plant, such as codonopsis or one of the floppier species of aster, that will sprawl over the bergenia for part of the year. It is propagated in early autumn by dividing clumps and replanting vigorous young sections of rhizome at the soil surface; this practice can prevent a build-up of vine weevil infestation if done once every five years or so.

**Perfect partners:** *Carex comans* (bronze), *Codonopsis ovata*, *Cornus alba* 'Sibirica', *Crocus tommasinianus*, *Eranthis hyemalis*, *Erica carnea* 'Springwood White', *Euonymus fortunei* 'Silver Queen', *Hedera colchica* 'Sulphur Heart'

**H: 24 in. (60 cm) S: 30 in. (75 cm)**
❀ **Late winter to late spring**
◊◊ ▢-▓ **Z3 pH4.5–7.5**

Glossy purple above and red below, the foliage of *Bergenia cordifolia* 'Purpurea' is most richly tinted in late winter and early spring, coinciding in season with delicate white snowdrops (*Galanthus nivalis*).

## *Bergenia* 'Morgenröte' ♔

The rich carmine flowers of this evergreen perennial, borne clear of the leaves on strong stems, appear in mid- to late spring and again in early summer or mid-autumn, especially if plants are deadheaded. It is a good partner for early irises and for crimson, purple or pink primulas, including polyanthus and Candelabra varieties. Its late flowers go well with plants that have distinctly different form and foliage, such as astilbes. It also creates striking contrasts with the bright yellow-green of euphorbias and *Alchemilla mollis*, orange Candelabra primulas and crown imperials. It combines well with purple-leaved *Berberis thunbergii* and *B.t.* 'Atropurpurea Nana', although the effect may be leaden without the addition of some paler-colored foliage.

**Perfect partners:** *Erythronium revolutum*, *Euphorbia polychroma* 'Major', *Fritillaria imperialis* 'The Premier', *Primula* Cowichan Garnet Group, *Tulipa* 'Prinses Irene'

H & S: 18 in. (45 cm) ❄ Mid- to late spring
◊◊ ☐-◼ ◼ Z4 pH4.5–7.5

Although in sunny situations and warm climates, the second flowering of *Bergenia* 'Morgenröte' can begin very shortly after the first flush ends (provided the plant has been deadheaded), it can sometimes reach a spectacular climax in mid-autumn, coinciding in season with *Sedum* 'Herbstfreude', as here. Both are handsome-leaved plants that work especially well at the front of a border.

The tiny sky-blue florets of *Brunnera macrophylla* harmonize with the larger, changeable pink to blue flowers of pulmonarias. This excellent combination is particularly suitable for positions near the front of a bed or border, in humus-rich soil and partial shade.

## *Buphthalmum salicifolium*

A remarkably long flowering season, from early summer to early autumn, and profuse flowering are notable qualities of this plant. It is a good choice for a sunny spot, ideally in poor soil. Its tendency to flop looks effective at the front of a border, spilling onto a path perhaps, or over edging. The rich gold flowers complement other hot colors, and also combine well with purple-leaved plants, such as heucheras or dwarf berberis. Fairly amorphous in appearance, it looks best with contrasting foliage, such as that of short, yellow-green or gold-variegated grasses or some irises – Tall Bearded irises flower at the same time whereas Intermediate and Dwarf Bearded irises flower earlier.

**Perfect partners:** *Achillea* 'Martina', *Crambe maritima*, *Delphinium* (Belladonna Group) 'Völkerfrieden', *Iris orientalis*, *Verbascum* (Cotswold Group) 'Gainsborough'

H & S: 24 in. (60 cm)
❄ Early summer to early autumn

◊-◊◊ ☐-◼ ◼ Z4 pH5–8

## *Brunnera macrophylla* ♔

This herbaceous perennial has dainty blue forget-me-not flowers and bold, heart-shaped leaves, silver spotted in some variants. Its slightly coarse appearance makes it suitable for wilder settings, or for underplanting in a rose garden, especially with early yellow roses. It blends well with other early yellow flowers, such as primroses and cowslips, with gold-edged hostas, and with Bowles golden grass. White or soft yellow tulips and late narcissi are also excellent partners. Two brightly variegated cultivars are 'Hadspen Cream' ♔ which has yellowish, cream-edged leaves that tolerate full sunlight, and the bold, creamy white variegation of 'Dawson's White', which can burn in hot sun. This cultivar needs moisture and grows relatively slowly.

**Perfect partners:** *Erythronium californicum* 'White Beauty' p.361 **A**, *Hosta* 'Zounds', *Juniperus squamata* 'Filborna' p.110 **B**, *Narcissus* 'Hawera', *Primula veris*, *Rosa spinossima* 'Grandiflora', *Tulipa* 'Golden Oxford' p.396 **A**

H: 18 in. (45 cm) S: 24 in. (60 cm)
❄ Mid- to late spring
◊◊ ☐-◼ ◼ Z4 pH4–7.5

In this long border entirely of yellow-flowered plants, *Buphthalmum salicifolium* is backed by evening primrose (*Oenothera biennis*), with the marigold *Tagetes tenuifolia* 'Lemon Gem' furnishing in front. Bold or grassy foliage could be included to add varied form and texture.

## *Caltha palustris* ♉
KINGCUP, MARSH MARIGOLD

This member of the buttercup family is a moisture-loving plant, equally successful in damp ground, bog gardens and waterside sites, and even as a pond plant in water up to 8 in. (20 cm) deep. Its bold, golden yellow flowers and glossy, fleshy, round leaves, which form dramatic clumps, are particularly suited to naturalizing in small colonies in swampy or marginal positions. This plant goes well with primroses and polyanthus, especially those in pale yellow or orange, with evergreen sedges and grasses with yellow-green or bronze foliage, and with early-leafing ferns. 'Flore Pleno' ♉ makes a smaller plant, with complex, fully double flowers that merit viewing from close range, while the variant often sold as *C. polypetala* is larger and more vigorous, with particularly large, single flowers. Creamy white *C.p.* var. *alba* produces its flowers in early spring, often before the leaves appear. It is a compact plant, suitable for sheltered, moist or boggy situations, and looks especially attractive combined with *Primula denticulata* and *P. rosea*.

**Perfect partners:** *Brunnera macrophylla*, *Carex oshimensis* 'Evergold', *Hosta fortunei* var. *albopicta*, *Lysichiton americanus* p.310 **A**, *Ranunculus ficaria* 'Brazen Hussy'

**H: 6–16 in. (15–40 cm)  S: 18 in. (45 cm)**
❀ **Early to late spring**
Z4  pH5–7.5

Alongside a stream, the heart-shaped leaves and glossy yellow flowers of kingcups (*Caltha palustris*) emerge at the same time as the strikingly striped foliage of *Iris pseudacorus* 'Variegata'. The combination will remain colorful for some two months, although the iris' variegation will begin to fade by summer.

The dusky lilac-gray bells emerging from maroon buds of *Campanula* 'Burghaltii' are the only colored flowers in this scheme of white blooms and silvery foliage, including feathery *Artemisia pontica*, spiky *Eryngium giganteum*, white *Papaver orientale* and *Lychnis coronaria* 'Alba', but their muted color does not disturb its tranquillity.

## *Campanula* 'Burghaltii' ♉

The upright stems of this unusual and striking hybrid bear long, tubular, pendent flowers in a subtle shade of lilac-gray. It is good at the front of a border, perhaps set off by a carpeting plant in the foreground. It can be grown in full sun in areas where summers are cool, but elsewhere it retains its color best when shaded from bright sun. Its delicate coloring is most attractive partnered with rich shades of mauve, purple and campanula-blue, or with pure white or cream. It makes a charming combination with silver-leaved plants such as artemisias, and with pale-colored pinks, and also works well with smoky purple foliage. 'Van-Houttei' is a similar hybrid but with darker flowers.

**Perfect partners:** *Artemisia ludoviciana*, *Dicentra* 'Stuart Boothman', *Geranium clarkei* 'Kashmir Purple', *G.* 'Sue Crûg', *Heuchera* 'Pewter Veil', *Nepeta* × *faassenii*

**H: 24 in. (60 cm)  S: 12 in. (30 cm)**
❀ **Early to midsummer**
Z4  pH5–7.5

This cool combination features *Campanula* 'Kent Belle' and the double-flowered feverfew *Tanacetum parthenium* 'Rowallane'. *Perovskia* 'Blue Spire' grows through the feverfew and will take over its display in late summer.

## *Campanula* 'Kent Belle' ♔

This superlative hybrid campanula tolerates shade sufficiently to merit a place in partially shaded borders or lighter parts of a woodland garden. Its rich purplish blue coloring mixes well with cool shades such as mauve, lilac, pink and blue, as well as white, cream or soft yellow, and looks very attractive with silver or glaucous foliage. It can partner cranesbills, thalictrums, echinops and aconites, including cream and pale yellow cultivars, and can be planted among old roses and hydrangeas. It contrasts effectively with yellow-green flowers and foliage, including alchemillas and variegated grasses. If cut back immediately after flowering, it will continue producing new flowering shoots into autumn.

**Perfect partners:** *Aconitum lycoctonum* subsp. *vulparia*, *Hosta fortunei* var. *albopicta* f. *aurea*, *Lamium maculatum* 'White Nancy', *Potentilla fruticosa* 'Primrose Beauty'

**H: 36 in. (90 cm)  S: 24 in. (60 cm)**
✿ **Early to late summer**
 ◊◊ ▣-▪ Z5 pH5–7.5

The sturdy and statuesque spikes of the pinkish buff perennial foxglove *Digitalis* × *mertonensis* give structure to this grouping, while the more diffuse stems of *Campanula persicifolia alba* planted through it leaven the effect.

## *Campanula latifolia*
### BROAD-LEAVED BELLFLOWER

This robust herbaceous campanula is suitable for perennial or mixed borders and wild or woodland gardens, and can be naturalized in coarse grass. Its flowers vary in color from white to deep purplish blue. White variants, sometimes known as 'Alba', are particularly good with other white or pale flowers, with contrasting dark foliage, and with orange lilies. Deep lavender-blue var. *macrantha* and rich lavender-blue 'Brantwood' are suitable for the same combinations as *C.* 'Kent Belle' (above). 'Gloaming', pale grayish lavender, is good with pure white and cream flowers; 'Pallida' is even paler and can be used in the same way where a ghostly effect is required.

**Perfect partners:** White: *Anthriscus sylvestris* 'Ravenswing', *Delphinium* 'Alice Artindale', *Lilium* 'Enchantment'
Blue: *Aruncus dioicus*, *Echinops bannaticus* 'Taplow Blue', *Geranium* × *oxonianum* 'Wargrave Pink'

**H: 36–48 in. (90–120 cm)  S: 24 in. (60 cm)**
✿ **Early to midsummer**
 ◊◊ ▣-▪ Z4 pH4.5–7.5

In a semi-wild setting, trailing stems of the white-flowered Rambler rose *R.* 'Seagull' drape down to the ground, from a bank of shrubs behind, to interact with the ghostly bells of *Campanula latifolia* 'Gloaming' planted at the front of the shrubbery in partial shade.

## *Campanula persicifolia*
### PEACH-LEAVED BELLFLOWER

Garden selections of this variable species have flowers that may be bell-shaped or almost flat, single or double, and pure white to campanula-blue. 'Hampstead White' is an extremely graceful double; 'Fleur de Neige' ♔ has well-formed white double flowers; and plants grown as *alba* are more or less pure white, blending with almost any color and excellent in white schemes or with silver foliage. Blue-flowered variants combine with cool colors and with glaucous or silver foliage, and are effective with white, cream or soft yellow Shrub and Ground Cover roses. All benefit from being placed behind plants such as pinks, catmints, lavenders or hostas. They complement plants of contrasting floral form, such as artemisias, achilleas and salvias.

**Perfect partners:** Blue: *Nepeta* 'Six Hills Giant', *Rosa* 'Nozomi', *Thalictrum delavayi*
▢p.219 **A**
White: *Hosta fortunei*, *Scabiosa* 'Butterfly Blue' p.332 **B**

**H: 24–48 in. (60–1.2 m)  S: 12 in. (30 cm)**
✿ **Early to midsummer**
 ◊◊ ▣-▪ Z4 pH5–7.5

## Campanula takesimana

This herbaceous bellflower with a strong creeping rootstock grows best in light to partial shade, although it tolerates more sun in areas with cool summers. A pale grayish pink with maroon spots inside, its flowers go well with plants with purple, red-flushed or white-variegated leaves, including heucheras, bugles and rodgersias, and it is outstanding with white or deeper pink and with soft yellow-green or lime green flowers, such as nicotianas. It is an attractive partner for astilbes, lilies and cranesbills, and good with contrasting foliage such as the strap-shaped leaves of larger grasses and more shade-tolerant irises, or the bold leaves of hostas. In moist, humus-rich soils, it can be invasive.

**Perfect partners:** *Ajuga reptans* 'Multicolor', *Astilbe* × *arendsii* 'Venus', *Helictotrichon sempervirens*, *Heuchera* 'Plum Pudding', *Lilium candidum*, *Rodgersia pinnata* 'Superba'

**H: 24 in.** (60 cm) **S: 18 in.** (45 cm)
✿ **Early to midsummer**
⬛⬜ ◊◊ ⬜-⬛ ⬛ Z5 pH5–7.5

At the front of a semi-shady border, the substantial, dusky gray-pink bells of *Campanula takesimana* harmonize perfectly with clouds of tiny heuchera flowers, providing a contrast of floral form.

## Cautleya spicata 'Robusta'

This is a handsome relative of ginger, growing from a tuberous rootstock and happy in partial shade, although in areas with cool summers it can be grown successfully in full sun. It is a plant for the second or third rank of a border, where its broad leaves and spikes of yellow florets emerging from rich maroon bracts have an almost tropical appearance that suits hot-colored schemes. Its two-toned flowers go well with yellows and maroons or scarlets, including plants such as late-blooming achilleas, dahlias, cannas, later-flowering crocosmias, chocolate cosmos, kirengeshomas, scarlet lobelias and hedychiums. It is an attractive companion for tender perennials such as coleus, and for plants with deep red or bronze foliage – dark-leaved heucheras, for example – and makes effective contrasts with yellow-green.

**Perfect partners:** *Canna* 'Erebus', *Crocosmia* × *crocosmiiflora* 'Carmin Brillant', *Euphorbia schillingii*, *Hedychium coccineum* 'Tara', *Lobelia cardinalis* 'Queen Victoria'

**H: 36 in.** (90 cm) **S: 18 in.** (45 cm)
✿ **Late summer to mid-autumn**
⬛⬜ ◊◊ ⬜-⬛ ⬛ Z7 pH5–7.5

The maroon calyces of *Cautleya spicata* 'Robusta' match the flowers of chocolate cosmos (*C. atrosanguineus*) in front, and harmonize with the foliage of *Dahlia* 'David Howard' behind. The color of its small, hooded, yellow flowers is reflected in those of *Heliopsis helianthoides* (left), *Hypericum kouytchense* (top right) and *Calceolaria angustifolia* (bottom right).

## Centaurea montana
MOUNTAIN KNAPWEED

The glory of this traditional cottage garden plant is the intricacy of its deep blue flowers. It is an attractive choice for the front of a border, together with pinks, lavenders and columbines, or cushion-forming plants such as catmints, and is good for providing color between the main flush of spring flowers and most of the summer flowering plants. It can be combined with Bearded irises, achilleas, dicentras, early cranesbills, daylilies and silver foliage plants such as artemisias, and used for contrasts with soft yellow including trollius. Useful variants include: pure white 'Alba'; pink 'Carnea'; blue 'Gold Bullion' with yellow-green leaves; creamy white 'Ochroleuca'; and amethyst 'Parham'.

**Perfect partners:** *Achillea* 'Moonshine', *Artemisia schmidtiana*, *Centranthus ruber* p.250 **A**, *Digitalis lutea* p.260 **B**, *Kniphofia* 'Atlanta', *Tulipa* 'Elegant Lady' p.395 **A**

**H: 18 in.** (45 cm) **S: 24 in.** (60 cm)
✿ **Early summer**
⬛⬜ ◊◊ ⬜-⬛ ⬛ Z3 pH4.5–7.5

In a sunny border in late spring, the boldly shaped flowers of white mountain knapweed (*Centaurea montana* 'Alba'), extravagantly flared outward from their black-netted knops, bring light into this cottage garden mixture of columbines (*Aquilegia vulgaris*) in various colors.

A charming late spring association, with a variety of flower forms, mixes the typical rich pink valerian (*Centranthus ruber*), deep blue mountain knapweed (*Centaurea montana*) and the long-flowering cranesbill *Geranium* 'Johnson's Blue'.

## Centranthus ruber

RED VALERIAN

Easy to grow, and highly attractive to bees and butterflies, red valerian bears rose-pink flowers from late spring to late summer. It enjoys a position in a sunny border but is seen at its best when naturalized in walls or stony banks. Two common color variants are white 'Albus', with the most glaucous leaves, and deep red 'Atrococcineus'. Each breeds true in isolation, but if grown near another variant seedlings can be mixed, with colors ranging from white to deepest black-red. Of these, delicate pale pink variants are among the most desirable for planting with silver foliage and in soft color schemes. The rose-red form complements yellow-green and rose-pink flowers and bronze foliage, but does not go well with strong, bright shades. Its slightly diffuse habit benefits from association with more structural plants such as Bearded irises.

**Perfect partners:** *Deutzia longifolia* 'Vilmoriniae' p.53 **C**, *Euphorbia polychroma* 'Major' p.268 **B**, *Rosa* 'Easlea's Golden Rambler' p.189 **A**, *R.* Iceberg p.213 **B**

H & S: 36 in. (90 cm)
❋ Late spring to late summer
━━ ◌ - ◌◌◌ ▢ - ▨ Z5 pH5–8

## Chaerophyllum hirsutum 'Roseum'

The ferny foliage and lacy pink flowers of this cultivar are especially attractive in late spring; if plants are deadheaded, they flower again on and off throughout summer. It is suitable for fairly informal plantings and for a wild garden, although it is also invaluable in more sophisticated schemes – combined with white-edged hostas and late tulips, for example, perhaps in a bed nearer the house. It can look effective with contrasting foliage, such as that of Siberian irises, and with white flowers or purple foliage, and harmonizes prettily with columbines of all colors. Other good companions include late primulas (such as *Primula japonica* cultivars), *Paeonia officinalis* cultivars, and grasses, which provide a fine contrast in texture. It prefers moist soil in a reasonably sunny position.

**Perfect partners:** *Cotinus coggygria* 'Royal Purple', *Hosta fortunei* 'Francee', *Iris* 'Cambridge', *Miscanthus sinensis* 'Morning Light', *Tulipa* 'White Triumphator'

H & S: 24 in. (60 cm)
❋ Late spring to early summer
 ◌◌ ▢ - ▨ Z5 pH4–7.5

This pleasing planting scheme for spring, good in either sun or partial shade, combines lacy pink *Chaerophyllum hirsutum* 'Roseum' with the maroon flowers of the mourning widow cranesbill (*Geranium phaeum*), to give a subtle and subdued combination suitable for wilder parts of a garden or even for naturalizing.

# Chrysanthemum

FLORISTS' CHRYSANTHEMUM

Chrysanthemums are immensely useful for providing late color, with plants flowering from midsummer until the onset of frost and even later in the case of the hardiest kinds. Thousands of cultivars are available, the majority of them raised specifically to produce cut flowers or pot plants and of only limited hardiness outdoors (usually Zone 9).

Varieties that belong to the Early-flowering Outdoor Groups may be used outdoors when grown from spring cuttings taken from stools overwintered under glass, but their hardiness is generally limited to Zone 9. A few varieties prove hardy enough for Zone 8, including the excellent scarlet 'Pennine Signal' ♀, 30 in. (75 cm) tall and flowering in late summer and early autumn. Early-flowering kinds such as this should be deadheaded to extend their flowering period into autumn (this does not benefit later-flowering ones, however, since their season is limited by frost). Most early kinds flower for a month or two – pot-grown plants of these can be valuable for replacing summer bedding that is exhausted early.

The hardiest chrysanthemums are divided into three main groups: Pompon, Korean and Rubellum chrysanthemums; all are generally hardy to Zone 5. Those in the Pompon Group have globular, tightly packed, fully double flowerheads. Among those recommended are 'Anastasia' (pink, 24 in./60 cm, mid- to late autumn); 'Bronze Elegance' (24 in./60 cm, late autumn); 'Bronze Fairy' (18 in./45 cm, autumn); 'Jante Wells' (vivid golden yellow, 12 in./30 cm, midsummer to autumn); 'Mei-kyo' (deep carmine, 24 in./60 cm, late autumn); 'Nantyderry Sunshine' ♀ (mid-yellow, 24 in./60 cm, mid- to late autumn); and 'Salmon Fairie' ♀ (18 in./45 cm, autumn). Korean chrysanthemums are early, outdoor spray chrysanthemums, mostly with single or semi-double flowers, and include 'Ruby Mound' (24 in./60 cm, autumn) and 'Wedding Day' (white with a green eye, 30 in./75 cm, autumn). Rubellum chrysanthemums, hybrids derived from *C. zawadskii* (syn. *C. rubellum*), have single, semi-double or double blooms. They include 'Apricot' (single, 30 in./75 cm, autumn); 'Clara Curtis' (single, clear pink, 30 in./75 cm, late summer to mid-autumn); 'Emperor of China' (double pink with quilled petals, foliage red-tinted in autumn, 4 ft./1.2 m, late summer and autumn); 'Mary Stoker' (single pink, tinted apricot-yellow, 30 in./75 cm, late summer and early autumn);

'Mrs Jessie Cooper' (semi-double, red, 30 in./75 cm, late summer and early autumn); and 'Nancy Perry' (semi-double, deep pink, 30 in./75 cm, late summer and early autumn).

A fourth kind that is increasingly used for outdoor display is the Charm Group ("cushion mums"), raised originally for pot-plant cultivation. They are generally compact and form neat mounds of single flowers. Although most are not hardy in areas colder than Zone 9, the Yoder Series contains many varieties claimed to survive in Zone 8 – Bravo ('Yobra') ♀, which is deep red, 12 in./30 cm tall, and flowers in late summer to mid-autumn, is a typical example. They generally make dwarf plants that are good for carpeting and for bedding in the front of borders. By planting irregular groups with a few single plants scattered away from the main colony, the shortest of the plants, especially pale pink, crimson or wine-purple kinds, would be very effective planted as a carpet beneath *Nerine bowdenii*.

Chrysanthemums may be combined with asters – blue asters, for example, are good partners for wine-purple, carmine, crimson,

The golden amber flowers of *Chrysanthemum* 'Honey', one of the Early-flowering Outdoor Intermediate Group, combine with the flat, deep rose flowerheads of *Sedum spectabile* 'Septemberglut' to provide warm tints toward the front of a border in early autumn.

white or soft yellow chrysanthemums. They also work well with dahlias and Japanese anemones, and with schizostylis or grasses for foliage contrast. Hot-colored chrysanthemums are particularly satisfying companions for grasses that are yellow-variegated or that turn red, bronze or orange in autumn, and for shrubs that color well in autumn, such as smoke bush.

**Perfect partners:** *Anemone* × *hybrida* 'Honorine Jobert', *Aster novi-belgii* 'Ada Ballard', *Cortaderia selloana* 'Aureolineata', *Cotinus* 'Flame', *Dahlia* 'Requiem', *Rhus* × *pulvinata* Autumn Lace Group, *Schizostylis coccinea* 'Major'

**H: 8–60 in. (20–150 cm)  S: 12–24 in. (30–60 cm)**
✾ **Midsummer to mid-winter**
◾️◾️◾️◾️ ◊◊ ◻️-◼️ **Z5–9  pH5.5–7**

## *Convallaria majalis* ♟

LILY-OF-THE-VALLEY

This species has attractive foliage and richly scented white flowers, which are best seen at close range (they are also superb for cutting). Excellent in woodland gardens, it can also be planted in mixed or shrub borders under deciduous shrubs, such as azaleas and roses, or with violets, wood anemones, spring bulbs and primroses. It combines well with plants with contrasting foliage – for example, early or evergreen ferns, blue mertensias and corydalis. It is quite invasive, and best grown away from choice, slow-growing plants. 'Fortin's Giant', 12 in. (30 cm), is the boldest variety, and the best at longer range; bright, striped 'Vic Pawlowski's Gold' is only 6 in. (15 cm), slow-growing and good at close range; 'Hardwick Hall', 10 in. (25 cm), has leaves with cream margins.

**Perfect partners:** *Anemone nemorosa, Arum italicum* 'Marmoratum', *Chelidonium majus, Corydalis flexuosa, Erythronium* 'Pagoda', *Mertensia virginica, Primula vulgaris*

H: **6–12 in.** (15–30 cm)  S: **12 in.** (30 cm)
❀ **Late spring**

 ◊◊-◊◊◊ ▨-■ ■ Z4 pH4.5–7.5

The bold leaves and bell-shaped florets of lily-of-the-valley (*Convallaria majalis*) combine with the unfurling fronds of hart's tongue fern (*Asplenium scolopendrium*) and the contrasting foliage of *Polystichum setiferum* Divisilobum Group, a soft shield fern in which the tiny pinnules are separate and do not overlap, giving a lacy effect.

A

Although *Achillea* 'Coronation Gold' is rather taller than *Coreopsis* 'Sterntaler', it nods down to mingle with its companion, their golden yellow flowerheads producing a close color harmony.

## *Coreopsis* 'Sterntaler'

'Sterntaler' is a hybrid of *C. lanceolata*, a long-flowering perennial that may be grown as an annual, whose various cultivars range in height from 10 to 24 in. (25–60 cm). 'Sterntaler' forms clumps of numerous wiry stems, each sporting a bright golden yellow flower with a brown disk – these make fine, long-lasting cut flowers. In areas with hot summers, especially in dry soils, the display may be short-lived; but a cool season will prolong flowering, and deadheading will extend the display into autumn. It is an excellent choice for the front or second rank of a border, and has maximum impact when combined with hot colors or in deliberate clashes with, for example, magenta or gentian-blue. Owing to its slightly amorphous shape, it benefits from a position next to plants with bold leaf forms or interesting textures, such as grasses.

**Perfect partners:** *Aconitum napellus*, *Delphinium* 'Blue Nile', *Geranium* 'Johnson's Blue', *G. psilostemon*, *Hakonechloa macra* 'Alboaurea', *Helictotrichon sempervirens*

**H & S:** 16 in. (40 cm)
❀ Late spring to late summer

⬛🟦🟦⬜ ◊-◊◊ ⬜-⬛ Z4 pH5.5–7.5

## *Cortaderia selloana*
### PAMPAS GRASS

Although its reputation has suffered slightly from crude and overenthusiastic Victorian use, this is an excellent plant for dramatic focal points, catching the eye with its fountain of foliage and creamy plumes of flowers that remain attractive all winter. Pampas grasses are extremely variable: they range in height from 4 to 10 ft. (1.2–3 m), and in hardiness from Zone 5 to Zone 9; flowering times vary from late summer to mid-autumn. To be sure of selecting the most suitable variety, it is best to buy a named, predictable clone.

'Sunningdale Silver' ♀ is perhaps the tallest clone at 10 ft. (3 m), with magnificent feathery, silvery white plumes in late autumn; however, it is hardy only to Zone 8, and is unreliable and shy-flowering in cool conditions. For paler tones, 'Albolineata' and 'Aureolineata' ♀ are effective variegated cultivars that flower in early autumn, are 6½ ft. (2 m) high, and hardy only to Zone 8. 'Pumila' ♀, 5 ft. (1.5 m) high and hardy to Zone 6, is very reliable, flowering profusely in early autumn. Its numerous stiff, silvery cream flowerheads are upright and lack elegance, but the foliage, markedly shorter than in the larger cultivars, arches beautifully to produce a handsome specimen plant for smaller gardens, especially as a feature near water. *C. richardii* ♀, 8 ft. (2.5 m) high and hardy to Zone 8, flowers in midsummer, producing slim, parchment-colored plumes that move freely in the breeze. It is earlier flowering, starting in midsummer, and the plumes arch expansively so that flowering plants can occupy a significantly larger area of ground than their basal leaf clumps, and this should be allowed for when placing companions.

The arching habit of most pampas grasses needs space to display itself to full effect, so plants are best positioned slightly forward of their rank in the border, surrounded by shorter neighbors, including other grasses and stately herbaceous perennials such as inulas, thalictrums, *Knautia macedonica*, *Scabiosa japonica* var. *alpina* and richly colored daylilies. All pampas grasses look best in more natural plantings, in scattered or informal groups. They grow naturally in vast colonies spreading across South American plains, hence their slightly artificial appearance when grown as lonely specimens in a lawn or as a front garden centerpiece. This can be remedied by combining them within a community of larger grasses, where they create effective textural harmonies with plants such as miscanthus and molinias, perhaps against a background of bamboos, or by integrating them as focal points in lavish autumn planting schemes with Michaelmas daisies, Japanese anemones and taller chrysanthemum cultivars.

**Perfect partners:** *Acer griseum*, *Agapanthus* 'Loch Hope' p.229 **A**, *Anemone* × *hybrida* 'Lady Gilmour', *Arrhenatherum elatius* subsp. *bulbosum* 'Variegatum' p.236 **A**, *Aster novi-belgii* 'Fellowship', *Chrysanthemum* Rubellum Group, *Cotinus* 'Flame', *Deschampsia cespitosa*, *Euonymus hamiltonianus* subsp. *sieboldianus* p.97 **C**, *Picea pungens* 'Koster', *Rhus* × *pulvinata* Autumn Lace Group, *Sedum* 'Herbstfreude' p.333 **B**, *Stipa calamagrostis*

**H:** 4–10 ft. (1.2–3 m) **S:** 6 ft. (1.8 m)
❀ Late summer to mid-autumn

⬛🟦🟦⬜ ◊◊-◊◊◊ ⬜-⬛ Z5–9 pH4.5–8

In this combination of plants liking a sunny site, pampas grass (*Cortaderia selloana*) and the shorter, variegated Spanish dagger (*Yucca gloriosa* 'Variegata'), joined also by a relatively hardy opuntia cactus, have great similarity of coloring, proportions and outline, making a harmonious grouping with a pronounced vertical emphasis.

*Corydalis flexuosa* and *Dicentra* 'Pearl Drops' harmonize well together, coming from related genera with the shared characteristics of compound pinnate leaves and relatively small florets. The dicentra's white flowers help leaven the intense blue of the corydalis.

## *Corydalis flexuosa* ♔

This exquisite plant, with its greenish blue flowers falling above daintily ferny foliage, brings a rare color to late spring and early summer plantings. Each floret is enlivened by a white throat. The most common cultivars include 'Blue Panda', 'China Blue', 'Père David' and 'Purple Leaf', all of them effective when combined with soft yellow primroses and soft pink polyanthus, or harmonized with meconopsis. They make telling partners for yellow-green flowers or foliage, for example *Hosta fortunei* var. *albopicta* f. *aurea*, and look outstanding contrasted with the foliage of grasses or more boldly shaped plants. Corydalis flower longest in moist, cool conditions.

**Perfect partners:** *Leucojum aestivum* 'Gravetye Giant' p.371 **B**, *Meconopsis betonicifolia*, *Primula* 'Guinevere' p.325 **B**, *Roscoea cautleyoides* p.329 **A**, *Smilacina racemosa* p.335 **B**

H: **12–15 in.** (30–38 cm) S: **8–12 in.** (20–30 cm)
❀ **Late spring to early summer**
 ◊◊ ◼ ◼ Z5 pH4.5–7

## *Crambe maritima* ♔

### SEA KALE

The chief glory of sea kale is its dramatically curled, frilled glaucous foliage. It also bears small white flowers followed by pea-sized glaucous pods, which when borne profusely are highly decorative. It is effective in sunny gravel gardens and maritime sites, and enjoys the same conditions as many late spring and early summer flowering bulbs, which make excellent partners. A group will produce superlative foliage effects at the front of a border, especially if full and luxuriant growth is sustained by supplying the roots with plenty of well-rotted manure. It can be grown with restrained carpeting plants such as small-leaved sedums or low-growing nigellas, and harmonizes well with other brassicas such as curly or black kale.

**Perfect partners:** *Brassica oleracea* (Acephala Group) 'Nero di Toscana', *Eryngium giganteum*, *Nigella damascena*, *Pyrus salicifolia* 'Pendula' p.127 **C**, *Sedum* 'Bertram Anderson'

**H & S: 24 in.** (60 cm) ❀ **Early summer**
◼◼◼◼ ◊-◊◊ ◻-◼ Z5 pH5.5–8

The burgeoning leaves and flower stems of sea kale (*Crambe maritima*) help to hide the dying foliage of *Allium hollandicum* while harmonizing with its mauve flowers and the foliage of an achillea behind.

## *Crocosmia* × *crocosmiiflora* cultivars
MONTBRETIA

*C.* × *crocosmiiflora* is one of the most useful plants for late summer and autumn display. The flowers are striking, especially as an ingredient of hot color schemes, and the grassy foliage is good for offering effective contrasts with other leaf textures. 'Carmin Brillant' ♀ is one of the most floriferous cultivars. Its color – almost pure red rather than carmine – harmonizes with yellows and oranges, and provides good contrasts with yellow-green flowers and golden or bronze foliage. It benefits from fairly frequent division and replanting, to keep it flowering well and to ensure longer, more branched, and longer-lasting flower spikes. 'Lady Hamilton' has similar qualities of foliage and texture. Its soft orange color is effective not only with hot, strong colors – bright yellows, golds and rich scarlets – but also the softer tones of peach and apricot; it is also very attractive with bronze foliage. All montbretias prefer a moderately rich soil that remains reasonably moist at all times. They are prone to red spider mite in dry conditions.

**Perfect partners:** *Aralia elata* 'Aureovariegata' p.79 **B**, *Hypericum forrestii* p.109 **A**, *Persicaria amplexicaulis* p.320 **A**, *Rosa glauca* p.203 **B**, *Stipa calamagrostis*

**H: 20–36 in.** (50–90 cm) **S: 9 in.** (23 cm)
❀ Midsummer to early autumn
◊◊ ☐-■ Z5–8 pH5–7.5

**Above:** Among the many cultivars of *Crocosmia* × *crocosmiiflora*, 'Lady Hamilton' is one of the finest and is an ideal candidate for including in planting schemes where hot, strong colors prevail. Here, its soft orange flowers combine effectively with bright yellow *Rudbeckia fulgida* var. *deamii* in a bold, long-lasting, midsummer to early autumn scheme. The two contrast not only in the color of their flowers, but also in flower and foliage shape.

**Left:** *Crocosmia* × *crocosmiiflora* 'Solfatare' ♀ has a softer flower color than many other cultivars. Here, the pale orange-yellow flowers and bronze-flushed leaves combine well with *Sedum telephium* 'Arthur Branch'. *S.t.* subsp. *maximum* 'Atropurpureum', whose glaucous leaves and stems are flushed deep purple, also makes an effective companion. Ornamental grasses, preferably with plain green leaves, can be planted among groups of montbretias.

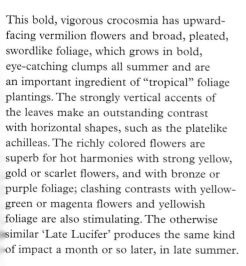

## *Crocosmia* 'Lucifer' ♀

This bold, vigorous crocosmia has upward-facing vermilion flowers and broad, pleated, swordlike foliage, which grows in bold, eye-catching clumps all summer and are an important ingredient of "tropical" foliage plantings. The strongly vertical accents of the leaves make an outstanding contrast with horizontal shapes, such as the platelike achilleas. The richly colored flowers are superb for hot harmonies with strong yellow, gold or scarlet flowers, and with bronze or purple foliage; clashing contrasts with yellow-green or magenta flowers and yellowish foliage are also stimulating. The otherwise similar 'Late Lucifer' produces the same kind of impact a month or so later, in late summer.

**Perfect partners:** *Dahlia* 'Arabian Night' p.419 **A**, *Helenium* 'Wyndley' p.282 **B**, *Hemerocallis fulva* 'Flore Pleno' p.286 **A**, *Monarda* 'Adam' p.314 **C** ☐pp.77 **A**, 213 **C**, 226 **C**, 372 **A**

**H: 4 ft.** (1.2 m) **S: 9 in.** (23 cm) ❀ **Midsummer**
◊◊ ☐-■ Z5 pH5–7.5

The widely planted *Crocosmia* 'Lucifer' is a deserved favorite for including in exotic foliage displays. To be really effective it needs to be planted in bold groups or drifts. Here, it combines well with the pinkish purple flowers of a perennial mallow (*Malva sylvestris* subsp. *mauritanica*) and the swordlike leaves of New Zealand flax (*Phormium tenax*), which echo those of the crocosmia. Various other phormiums would also make good companions, especially bronze- or purple-leaved cultivars.

## *Cynara cardunculus* 🏆

CARDOON

This is an extremely variable herbaceous plant bearing numerous thistlelike flowers, which emerge from a scaly head that is sometimes tinged purple. Its silvery gray leaves are deeply divided, usually spiny, and up to 4 ft. (1.2 m) long at the base of the plant. As a foliage plant, cardoon is handsomely architectural, at its best in late spring and early summer when the leaves are young. It is particularly impressive standing clear of other plants of similar height, perhaps as one-year-old dot plants in white or blue spring bedding or in beds and borders to punctuate less dramatic foliage, or as part of a scheme of silver foliage and white flowers. Its season of maximum glory coincides with plants such as delphiniums, Oriental poppies, lupins, earlier cranesbills, peonies, columbines, foxgloves, early roses and philadelphus. Cardoons can also be used with plants that look similar, such as centaureas and echinops, to give plantings a unifying theme. To prolong the season of good foliage effect, the flower stems can be removed in summer. Globe artichokes (Scolymus Group cultivars) have less silvery, sometimes green leaves that are not spiny, and may be used in similar situations.

**Perfect partners:** *Delphinium* 'Sungleam', *Digitalis lutea*, *Geranium pratense* 'Mrs. Kendall Clark', *Hemerocallis* red-flowered cultivars p.287 **C**, *Papaver orientale*

**H: 3¼–8 ft.** (1–2.5 m) **S: 4 ft.** (1.2 m)
**Early summer to early autumn**
**Z7 pH5–7.5**

In a complex grouping consisting principally of plants with silvery foliage, the large, boldly divided leaves of cardoon (*Cynara cardunculus*) form the focal point, furnished with the felted leaves of lamb's ears (*Stachys byzantina*), and highlighted by the bright cream variegation of gardener's garters (*Phalaris arundinacea* var. *picta*) backlit by the sun.

The intricate blue pompon florets of *Delphinium* 'Alice Artindale', borne on a narrow, erect spike, are given an effective backdrop by golden hops (*Humulus lupulus* 'Aureus'), trained against a wall.

## *Delphinium* 'Alice Artindale'

The double flowers of this delphinium combine shades of gray, green, blue and mauve, and have an old-fashioned formality that deserves viewing at close quarters, especially with other old-fashioned plants such as double sweet rocket or old roses. It benefits from combinations with cool mauve, rich blue (including other delphiniums, such as those of the Belladonna Group), purple and white flowers, and is sufficiently strongly colored to be contrasted with soft pale yellow. The bold shape of its tall slim flower spikes can be used to provide vertical accents, especially if contrasted with clouds of crambe and horizontal flowerheads such as achilleas, and can be echoed by the spikes of plants such as lupins or veronicas. It is an excellent partner for onopordums and galegas, and for plants with glaucous or silver foliage.

**Perfect partners:** *Achillea* 'Moonshine', *Galega orientalis*, *Hesperis matronalis* 'Lilacina Flore Pleno', *Lupinus* 'Polar Princess', *Onopordum nervosum*, *Rosa* 'Fantin-Latour'

**H: 5 ft.** (1.5 m) **S: 24 in.** (60 cm)
**Early to midsummer**
**Z3 pH5–7.5**

## *Delphinium* 'Sabrina'

This compact cultivar suits small-scale plantings and narrow borders and, if thinned at an early stage, will usually stay upright without staking. It has broad, dense spikes of mid-blue white-eyed flowers that go especially well with other pure blue flowers and silver or glaucous foliage, and make an effective contrast with yellow-green or yellow. It can be used with larkspurs, cornflowers, achilleas, campanulas, baptisias, smaller philadelphus, Tall Bearded irises and taller cranesbills and euphorbias. Other relatively short cultivars are Blue Jade Group, 4 ft. (1.2 m), pale blue with a brown eye; 'Blue Tit', 3¼ ft. (1 m), indigo-blue with a black eye; 'Cupid', 3 ft. (90 cm), pale sky-blue with a white eye; 'Lord Butler' ♀, also pale blue with a white eye, 4½ ft. (1.4 m); and 'Mighty Atom' ♀, also 4½ ft. (1.4 m), in deep lavender-blue.

**Perfect partners:** *Achillea* 'Coronation Gold', *Baptisia australis*, *Campanula persicifolia*, *Iris* 'Jane Phillips', *Philadelphus* 'Beauclerk', *Rosa* 'Maigold'

**H: 4 ft. (1.2 m) S: 24 in. (60 cm)**
❀ **Early to midsummer**
■□ ◊◊ □-■ Z3 pH5–7.5

Although many delphiniums would be too tall to interact with the Peruvian lily *Alstroemeria* 'Vesuvius', the relatively short *Delphinium* 'Sabrina' scarcely overtops it and contrasts strikingly with its rich vermilion flowers.

## *Delphinium* 'Sungleam' ♀

'Sungleam' bears numerous stems of blooms in a soft, pale butter-yellow that combines well with rich golden yellows, creams, whites and yellow-green foliage or flowers. It produces stunning contrasts with blue flowers, especially those in pale to mid-blue, and looks effective with glaucous foliage, yellow-green leaved shrubs such as golden elder or philadelphus, larger gold achilleas and Shrub roses in warm tints of yellow peach and apricot – some of David Austin's English roses, for example. Other good partners are crambes, spartiums, larger hypericums, earlier flowering kniphofias and, for contrast, baptisias and campanulas. 'Butterball' is similar but with flowers in a paler yellow.

**Perfect partners:** *Baptisia australis*, *Crambe maritima*, *Kniphofia* 'Goldelse', *Philadelphus coronarius* 'Aureus', *Potentilla fruticosa* 'Primrose Beauty', *Rosa* Graham Thomas, *Sambucus nigra* 'Aurea'

**H: 5 ft. (1.5 m) S: 24 in. (60 cm)**
❀ **Early to midsummer**
■□ ◊◊ □-■ Z3 pH5–7.5

The vertical spikes of *Delphinium* 'Sungleam' are echoed by the upright racemes of golden-flowered, dark-stemmed *Ligularia stenocephala*. The round flowerheads of the giant scabious (*Cephalaria gigantea*) exactly match the delphinium in color, while on the wall behind, pineapple broom (*Cytisus battandieri*) also has upright, albeit shorter, yellow racemes, unifying the design.

## *Deschampsia cespitosa*
### TUFTED HAIR-GRASS

This tussock-forming grass has airy panicles of flowers that are typically purplish in color, although some sorts are greenish yellow. A good plant for moist borders, bog gardens and waterside positions, it looks good among shorter plants such as heaths and heathers, other grasses, rushes, hostas, small gunneras and ferns. It can also be used in beds with mound- or hummock-forming plants such as hardy salvias. Selections include early-flowering 'Goldschleier' (Golden Veil) (4 ft./1.2 m) and 'Bronzeschleier' (Bronze Veil) (3 ft./90 cm); 'Tardiflora' (3 ft./90 cm), starts flowering only in midsummer. Blends of two or three cultivars are attractive, particularly if backlit by sun.

**Perfect partners:** *Arrhenatherum elatius* subsp. *bulbosum* 'Variegatum', *Calluna vulgaris* 'Blazeaway', *Juncus effusus* f. *spiralis*, *Rudbeckia hirta* Rustic Dwarfs Group, *Salvia nemorosa*

**H: 24–60 in. (60–150 cm) S: 24–40 in. (60–100 cm)**
❀ **Late spring to late summer**
■■□ ◊◊-◊◊◊ □-■ Z4 pH4.5–7

In autumn, the seedheads of tufted hair-grass (*Deschampsia cespitosa*) take on parchment tints and glow against the sun, aided by the aging leaves and red stems of the dogwood *Cornus sanguinea* 'Anny', with the magenta flowers of *Geranium* 'Ann Folkard' for contrast.

A bed of China roses including *Rosa* 'Hermosa' is underplanted with mixed pinks (*Dianthus* Allwoodii Alpinus Group). The pinks have attractive glaucous foliage and include exactly the same range of colors as the roses, providing neat furnishing between and in front of them.

*Diascia barberae* 'Blackthorn Apricot' flowers freely at the feet of a clump of *Astrantia major* 'Sunningdale Variegated', whose bright leaf edges darken to green once spring passes into summer. The apricot-pink diascia harmonizes with the astrantia's pink-flushed flowers.

## *Dianthus* Allwoodii Alpinus Group

The Allwoodii Pinks, once known as *D. × allwoodii*, crossed with alpine pink (*D. alpinus*) has resulted in this group of superb hybrids. Distinguished by compact growth, freedom from disease and a long flowering season, these neat garden pinks have flowers in often brilliant colors, from white through pink to red, some with a contrasting eye. They are versatile plants, at home in a gravel garden or at the front of a border, and may be used as edging or for carpeting beneath loosely branched China or Polyantha roses. They are good partners for other pink, red and white flowers, and contrast well with acid yellow-green flowers such as *Alchemilla mollis*.

**Perfect partners:** *Ajuga reptans* 'Atropurpurea', *Artemisia schmidtiana*, *Euphorbia seguieriana* subsp. *niciciana*, *Lavandula angustifolia* 'Hidcote', *Rosa* 'Cécile Brünner'

H: 6 in. (15 cm)  S: 12–18 in. (30–45 cm)
❀ Early to midsummer
◊-◊◊  ▣-■  Z4  pH5.5–8

## *Dianthus* 'Haytor White' ♔

This easy and floriferous pink, with pure white, sweetly scented flowers on tall stems, is one of the Devon Series, bred for the cut-flower market. It can be grown in gravel or in a border, both at the front and in the second rank behind a low carpeting plant. It can be used to leaven rich colors or to form harmonies with paler tones, and is a good candidate for white and silver schemes. As with other Devon Series cultivars – 'Devon Cream', yellow with a light magenta flush, 'Devon Wizard' ♔, purple with a ruby eye, and rich crimson 'Devon General', for example – occasional high-potash feeding results in stouter, more numerous flower stems.

**Perfect partners:** *Diascia barberae* 'Ruby Field', *Festuca glauca*, *Geum* 'Mrs. J. Bradshaw', *Iris sibirica* 'White Swirl', *I.* 'Symphony', *Lavandula lanata*, *Papaver orientale* 'Cedric Morris', *Rosa* 'Frensham', *R.* Iceberg

H: 18 in. (45 cm)  S: 16 in. (40 cm)
❀ Early summer to early autumn
◊-◊◊  ▣-■  Z4  pH5.5–8

In this carpet of white flowers with silvery and white-variegated foliage, *Dianthus* 'Haytor White' supplies abundant bloom in front of the filigree leaves of *Senecio cineraria* and the neatly white-edged evergreen spindle, *Euonymus fortunei* 'Emerald Gaiety'.

## *Diascia barberae* 'Blackthorn Apricot' ♔

This sprawling, mat-forming plant suits sites near the front of a border where it can weave through its neighbors, especially restrained shrubs of similar height such as some of the smaller hebes. It flowers over a long season, covering itself with loose masses of apricot-pink blooms with downward pointing spurs well into autumn. Plants benefit from being cut back after the first main flush of bloom, but this should not be done during prolonged dry weather. It is good with grasses, small sedums and dianthus, and makes attractive combinations with peach, cream, white or brick-red flowers, and with bronze or glaucous foliage. Its strong, clear coloring is enhanced by partners with soft blue flowers or gold-variegated or yellow-green foliage, especially the contrasting forms of smaller ferns.

**Perfect partners:** *Alchemilla mollis*, *Cerinthe major* 'Purpurascens', *Eryngium giganteum*, *Helichrysum petiolare*, *Lavandula angustifolia* 'Hidcote', *Plectranthus argentatus*

H: 10 in. (25 cm)  S: 20 in. (50 cm)
❀ Early summer to early autumn
◊◊  ▣-■  Z8  pH5.5–7.5

## *Diascia barberae* 'Ruby Field' ♀

This popular cultivar bears masses of rich coral-colored flowers from early summer onward. Its slightly sprawling growth benefits from shearing after the first flush of bloom; provided there is adequate moisture at their roots, plants will bear a strong second flush of flowers lasting into autumn. It is good at the front of a border or for underplanting loosely branched roses, making harmonies with peach, cherry-red, salmon or white flowers, and contrasts with pale sulfur-yellow or acid yellow-green. Since its growth is rather amorphous, it benefits from close association with plants of more definite form.

**Perfect partners:** *Euphorbia schillingii*, *Penstemon* 'Pennington Gem', *Phygelius aequalis* 'Yellow Trumpet', *P.* × *rectus* 'Salmon Leap', *Rosa* 'Yesterday' p.215 **B**

**H: 10 in.** (25 cm)  **S: 20 in.** (50 cm)
⚘ **Early summer to early autumn**
◐◐ ▦ Z8 pH5.5–7.5

A

In a steeply banked planting, coral-pink *Diascia barberae* 'Ruby Field' furnishes the base of *Penstemon* 'Schoenholzeri', whose colorful racemes of flowers fill the gap at the foot of a wall-trained *Carpenteria californica*.

B

## *Dicentra eximia*

This rhizomatous dicentra has glaucous ferny foliage and nodding racemes of pink flowers that are longer and more elegant than those of the otherwise similar *D. formosa*. It is an invaluable plant for woodland gardens or semi-shady borders, and grows best in climates with cool summers and adequate moisture. In hotter, dryer weather it tends to become untidy by midsummer, dying back and only reviving when cooler, moister conditions return. It is attractive with crimson, white or palest pink flowers, and also with purple-flushed foliage such as that of some newer heuchera cultivars. It harmonizes well with ferns and looks effective with contrasting foliage – that of smaller grasses and hostas, for example. The richer pink forms may be used with yellow-green flowers or foliage.

**Perfect partners:** *Arum italicum* 'Marmoratum', *Asplenium scolopendrium*, *Epimedium* × *versicolor* 'Neosulphureum' p.263 **A**, *Heuchera* 'Plum Pudding'

**H: 24 in.** (60 cm)  **S: 18 in.** (45 cm)  ⚘ **Late spring**
◐◐ ▦ Z4 pH5.5–7.5

The fernlike leaves of *Dicentra eximia*, the broad, lobed foliage of the cranesbill *Geranium* × *oxonianum* and the simple, lance-shaped leaves of *Spiraea japonica* 'Goldflame' combine in a pleasing interplay of different foliage forms at the front of a border. The dicentra's flowers clash gently with the spiraea's yellow-green young leaves.

## *Dicentra* 'Pearl Drops'

Like *D. eximia* (below left), this is a good choice for a woodland garden or semi-shady border, but it spreads rather more freely, its rhizomes tending to weave among adjacent plants. Its flowers are white with a hint of pink and brown, a subdued coloration that qualifies this cultivar for planting schemes where form and texture are paramount: it is effective with smaller grasses, for example, with ferns and glaucous-leaved plants, and creates an exciting contrast of leaf form with hostas and other plants of dramatically different shape. Its glaucous leaf color blends well with pure blue flowers like brunneras, forget-me-nots and omphalodes. Pink flowers are also attractive partners.

**Perfect partners:** *Brunnera macrophylla*, *Corydalis flexuosa* p.254 **A**, *Hosta* (Tardiana Group) 'Halcyon', *Hyacinthoides hispanica*, *Myosotis sylvatica*, *Omphalodes cappadocica*

**H: 12 in.** (30 cm)  **S: 18 in.** (45 cm)
⚘ **Mid-spring to early summer**
◐◐ ▦ Z4 pH5.5–7.5

Glaucous *Dicentra* 'Pearl Drops' weaves between mid-green male ferns (*Dryopteris filix-mas*) and epimediums to create a tapestry of shapes. This combination succeeds solely on the variety of foliage forms and colors, although it is not impaired by the dicentra's pinkish white flowers.

C

## *Dicentra spectabilis* ♔

BLEEDING HEART, DUTCHMAN'S BREECHES

This herbaceous perennial has divided leaves and heart-shaped, pendent flowers, strung out on slender, drooping stems like a row of rose-pink lockets; the shape of the individual florets is emphasized by the white inner petals. The plants form fairly upright clumps, the neat foliage and long flower stalks arching out from the center. Bleeding hearts are desirable plants for a woodland garden, accompanied by heucheras, tellimas, tiarellas and herbaceous saxifrages. They can be grown at or near the front of a lightly shaded border with plants of similar stature, or in isolation, surrounded by a carpet of white bugles, creeping small-leaved gunneras, or *Mitella breweri*. They associate well with pale pink or crimson flowers or, in brighter situations, with pale pink, white or soft, pale yellow tulips. In moist, cool growing conditions, bleeding hearts remain attractive for longer than in areas with hot summers, where they will die back by midsummer. Pure white-flowered 'Alba' ♔ is more vigorous, with paler green leaves, while 'Goldheart' is a gold-leaved variety, although the combination of foliage color with rich pink flowers is not to everyone's taste.

**Perfect partners:** *Ajuga reptans* 'Variegata', *Gunnera magellanica*, *Heuchera* 'Pewter Moon', *Saxifraga granulata*, *Tellima grandiflora*, *Tiarella trifoliata*, *Tulipa* 'Spring Green'

**H: 4 ft. (1.2 m)  S: 24 in. (60 cm)**
❀ **Late spring to early summer**
⬜⬛ ◌◌◌ ⬛ ⬛ Z3 pH5.5–7.5

The nodding pink and white racemes of *Dicentra spectabilis* create a contrast of form and color with the yellow-green flowerheads of the spurge *Euphorbia polychroma*.

In an appealing association for a lightly shaded position, the pale yellow flowers of straw foxglove (*Digitalis lutea*) are offset by the spidery, deep blue heads of mountain knapweed (*Centaurea montana*).

## *Digitalis lutea*

STRAW FOXGLOVE

The straw foxglove is smaller and less showy than its more common cousin, the yellow foxglove (*D. grandiflora*), but it is more dependably perennial and has a compelling elegance. Plants form clumps of smooth, toothed leaves and discreetly pretty spikes of small, creamy yellow, tubular flowers. It makes very attractive vertical accents in a woodland garden, with blue cranesbills or meconopsis, or in a sunny or lightly shaded border, especially if given a position of prominence slightly forward from its peers. It may be contrasted with flowers or foliage of different form, such as grasses and ferns, and its soft yellow coloring associates well with blue shades or with gold and white. It is also sufficiently muted to succeed close to pink.

**Perfect partners:** *Astrantia major* 'Sunningdale Variegated', *Corydalis flexuosa*, *Dryopteris affinis*, *Geranium* 'Johnson's Blue', *Meconopsis betonicifolia*, *Milium effusum* 'Aureum'

**H: 24 in. (60 cm)  S: 12 in. (30 cm)**
❀ **Early to midsummer**

⬜⬛ ◌◌ ⬛ ⬛ Z4 pH5.5–7.5

## *Dryopteris affinis* ♛
GOLDEN MALE FERN

This long-lived, robust species is more refined than the common male fern (*D. filix-mas*). It is loveliest in spring, when its pale green fronds emerge, unfurling with contrasting golden brown scales on the leaf stalks and mid-ribs, and radiating outward around a central hollow, producing a charming shuttlecock effect. This fern makes fine contrasts with broad-leaved plants such as hostas and bergenias, and with grasses. Attractive companions include gold, sulfur-yellow, apricot and soft orange flowers, such as geums or trollius, and primulas – for instance *Primula bulleyana* or *P. cockburniana*. It is particularly effective with earlier flowering lilies that tolerate shade, such as martagon lilies. The ferns are best grouped in irregularly scattered colonies, allowing each plant space to develop its distinctive shape. In late winter, surviving fronds should be cut off to make way for new spring growth.

**Perfect partners:** *Geum rivale* 'Leonard's Variety', *Hosta* 'Gold Standard', *Lilium martagon* var. *album*, *Rodgersia pinnata* p.328 **B**, *Trollius × cultorum* 'Alabaster'

**H: 6–48 in.** (15–120 cm) **S: 6–36 in.** (15–90 cm)
◊◊-◊◊◊ ■ Z4 pH5–7.5

The emerging yellow-green, orange-flushed fronds of *Dryopteris affinis* create a striking contrast of form with the handsome bronze-tinged foliage of *Rodgersia podophylla*.

## *Echinacea purpurea*
PURPLE CONEFLOWER

A slightly coarse perennial for sunny borders or prairie meadows, purple coneflower has slightly muted, deep magenta flowers, each with a central golden brown cone. Its petals may descend strongly to give the impression of a shuttlecock or, in some varieties, stand out almost horizontally, and the bold floral shape can be used to make a pronounced accent. Plants combine well with purple or crimson flowers, or with purple foliage and grasses such as silky brown-flowered *Calamagrostis × acutiflora*, and contrast with soft pale yellow or rich deep orange flowers. Creamy white 'White Lustre' and 'White Swan' contrast effectively in hot color schemes, and blend well with soft yellow, peach and apricot, or with bronze foliage.

**Perfect partners:** *Achillea* 'Summerwine', *A.* 'Taygetea', *Aster novi-belgii* 'Chequers', *Cotinus coggygria* 'Royal Purple', *Helenium* 'Kupferzwerg', *H.* 'Septemberfuchs', *Miscanthus sinensis* 'Sarabande', *Monarda* 'Prarienacht', *Rhus × pulvinata* Autumn Lace Group

**H: 24–48 in.** (60–120 cm) **S: 18 in.** (45 cm)
❀ Midsummer to mid-autumn
◊◊ ■ Z3 pH5.5–7.5

**Above:** In a border of mainly mauve-pink flowers, *Echinacea purpurea* provides bold floral shape behind a froth of tiny blooms of *Heuchera villosa* 'Palace Purple', with *Lychnis coronaria* Oculata Group, large heads of *Phlox maculata* and the narrow, dark spikes of *Persicaria amplexicaulis* 'Atrosanguinea'.

**Below:** Floriferous *Echinacea purpurea* 'Magnus' is here joined by the smaller, harmoniously colored flowers of *Verbena bonariensis* and *Aster × frikartii*.

## *Echinops bannaticus* 'Taplow Blue' ♀

With its rich, steely blue flowerheads and lobed leaves, this is a splendid plant for borders and wild gardens and for naturalizing. It blends with cool mauve, lilac, lavender or purple, soft yellow or acid yellow-green, white and pure blue, and with glaucous or silver foliage. The shapely leaves can be used to echo other thistlelike plants such as onopordums, cardoons and centaureas, and contrast with miscanthus cultivars and other taller grasses, and shrubs such as silver-leaved elaeagnus or pollarded silver willow. Suitable partners are repeat-flowering Shrub roses, pillar-trained clematis, taller campanulas such as *C. lactiflora* cultivars and *Hydrangea paniculata* cultivars. *Echinops ritro* ♀ is similar but a little shorter, as are its rich blue variants subsp. *ruthenicus* ♀ and 'Veitch's Blue'.

**Perfect partners:** *Centaurea macrocephala*, *Cynara cardunculus*, *Eryngium bourgatii* 'Picos Blue', *Miscanthus sinensis* 'Morning Light', *Onopordum nervosum*, *Rosa* 'Felicia'

**H: 4 ft. (1.2 m) S: 24 in. (60 cm)**
✿ **Mid- to late summer**
◊◊ ▢-■ **Z3 pH5.5–7.5**

A purple plum (*Prunus cerasifera* 'Pissardii') provides a sumptuous setting for the silvered leaves and steely blue globes of *Echinops bannaticus* 'Taplow Blue'. A shrub such as purple-leaved smoke bush (a *Cotinus coggygria* cultivar) could be used as an alternative to the plum.

A

B

## *Elymus magellanicus*

This short-lived perennial grass differs from other elymus and leymus species in that it is relatively small, lax in habit and prefers cool summers. Its foliage is a bright silvery blue, which is valuable at the front of a border or in a gravel garden for growing through low ground-cover plants such as acaenas, black mondo grass, bugles or sedums. It combines effectively with glaucous- or silver-leaved plants such as lamb's ears, smaller artemisias, smaller glaucous hostas and glaucous oxalis species, with white or blue annuals like heliophilas and nigellas, and yellow-flowered annuals such as smaller California poppies and hunnemannias. Good contrasts can be made with yellow-green plants such as euphorbias, and with the soft yellow of some smaller achilleas. Its flower spikes, which are

In a simple but effective combination using cool colors and contrasting form, the narrow blue-green leaves of *Elymus magellanicus* arch gracefully in front of mauve-flowered musk mallow (*Malva moschata*).

narrow and the same color as the foliage, add little to the effect, although allowing the plant to seed is often the best means of ensuring its survival. Similar species include *E. hispidus*, or blue wheatgrass, which is a more erect plant, and the blue fescues, which have narrower, stiffly upright leaves.

**Perfect partners:** *Achillea* 'Moonshine', *Eschscholzia caespitosa* 'Sundew', *Geranium* 'Mavis Simpson' p.277 **C**, *Ophiopogon planiscapus* 'Nigrescens'

**H: 6 in. (15 cm) S: 18 in. (45 cm)**
✿ **Early to late summer**
◊◊ ▢-■ **Z4 pH5.5–7.5**

## *Epimedium* × *versicolor*

This shade-tolerant hybrid is rather variable. Its typical cultivar, 'Discolor' (syn. 'Versicolor'), is deciduous, with young red leaves maturing to green and flowers of dusky deep pink and yellow, while 'Sulphureum' ♀, is evergreen with sulfur-yellow flowers. 'Neosulphureum' is similar but with fewer leaflets, and 'Cupreum' resembles 'Discolor' but with coppery flowers. All are ground-cover plants, the copper or pink cultivars going well with warm-tinted spring flowers, while the yellow ones blend with rich yellow narcissi, primroses and rhizomatous anemones, and blue flowers such as forget-me-nots, brunneras and omphalodes. They are also attractive with euphorbias and white, cream, green or soft yellow hellebores, or, for contrast, with early-leafing ferns and grasses.

**Perfect partners:** *Anemone ranunculoides*, *Brunnera macrophylla*, *Helleborus* × *hybridus* (primrose), *Luzula sylvatica* 'Aurea', *Milium effusum* 'Aureum', *Myosotis sylvatica*

**H & S: 12 in. (30 cm)** ❀ **Mid- to late spring**
◊◊ ▢-◼ ◼ **Z5 pH5–7.5**

This pleasing mixture combines two mildly invasive plants that have contrasting leaf form: *Epimedium* × *versicolor* 'Neosulphureum' with its red-flushed, heart-shaped leaflets and the feathery, glaucous-leaved *Dicentra eximia*.

In mid-spring, a carpet of *Epimedium* × *youngianum* 'Niveum' topped with tiny white florets forms a foil for a handsome rosette of *Meconopsis napaulensis*, which has yet to extend its summer flower spike. The dark green leaves and yellowish green flowerheads of the hybrid spurge *Euphorbia* × *martini* make an effective backdrop.

## *Epimedium* × *youngianum* 'Niveum' ♀

Gently spreading, rather variable *E.* × *youngianum* is sometimes almost evergreen and bears flowers that may or may not have spurs. 'Niveum' has small white flowers, few of which have spurs, and bronze-flushed young foliage. The leaves are most effective with warm-tinted flowers, including tulips, primroses and smaller narcissi, and with other plants with bronzed or reddish foliage, such as bugles and some euphorbias and sedges. White flowers – pachyphragmas and narcissi –

are also good partners. 'Merlin' has purple-flushed young leaves and large, short-spurred mauve flowers, while 'Roseum', also purple-flushed, has smaller mauve-pink flowers.

**Perfect partners:** *Ajuga reptans* 'Atropurpurea', *Anemone nemorosa* 'Vestal', *Cardamine trifolia*, *Euphorbia amygdaloides* 'Purpurea', *Hosta fortunei* 'Albomarginata' p.292 **A**

**H: 8 in. (20 cm) S: 12 in. (30 cm)** ❀ **Mid- to late spring**
◊◊ ▢-◼ ◼ **Z5 pH5–7.5**

## *Erigeron* cultivars
FLEABANE

Most garden fleabanes are herbaceous plants for the front of borders, rock gardens or gravel gardens. Their single or double daisy-like flowers have a central disc of yellow florets within petals that are usually in shades from white through rich carmine to lavender-blue. Purple, lavender or lilac fleabanes are especially pleasing with other blooms in the same range and in yellow-green or soft yellow. Their slightly soft texture works well with plants of more definite form, such as fescues, eryngiums, artemisias, and sedums. Cultivars include deep lavender-blue 'Dunkelste Aller' ♀ (Darkest of All), 'White Quakeress' and mauve-pink 'Foersters Liebling' ♀.

**Perfect partners:** *Artemisia alba* 'Canescens', *Ballota pseudodictamnus*, *Eryngium* × *tripartitum*, *Euphorbia seguieriana* subsp. *niciciana*, *Festuca glauca* 'Elijah Blue'

**H: 10–30 in. (25–75 cm) S: 12 in. (30 cm)** ❀ **Early to midsummer**
◊◊ ▢-◼ ◼ **Z5 pH5.5–7.5**

The bright pink flowers of *Erigeron* 'Gaiety' and the magenta blooms of rose campion (*Lychnis coronaria*) are borne at the same height and mingle together attractively if plants of each are grown close to each other.

## Erodium trifolium

Plants in the genus *Erodium* are known as storksbills or heron's bills, and are close relatives of the very similar cranesbills. *E. trifolium* (syn. *E. hymenodes*) is a fairly sprawling species, its relaxed, spreading shape suiting it to the front of a border and to rock, scree and gravel gardens. The soft coloring of its dull green toothed leaves and simple flowers in two shades of pink, delicately spotted with brown, blends especially well with mauves, blues, carmines and crimsons, and even soft yellows; purple-leaved plants are good companions, too. Plants can be short-lived, lasting four to five years in light soils, and only two on clay. Fortunately, they self-seed readily.

**Perfect partners:** *Dianthus* Allwoodii Alpinus Group, *Festuca glauca* 'Elijah Blue', *Geranium* × *antipodeum* 'Chocolate Candy', *Lysimachia nummularia* 'Aurea', *Molinia caerulea* 'Variegata'

**H: 12 in.** (30 cm)  **S: 18 in.** (45 cm)
✿ **Early to late summer**
�○ ▨ **Z8 pH6–8**

The exquisitely shaped flowerheads of *Eryngium alpinum* are perhaps most effectively displayed against a simple, contrasting background, as provided here by *Berberis thunbergii* 'Rose Glow'.

## Eryngium alpinum ♔

These European or Old World eryngiums have rounded, lobed or pinnate leaves and flowers often flushed with blue as they age. American or New World species bear strap-like leaves and usually smaller green or cream flowers.

*E. alpinum* has striking conical heads of florets in summer, each cone surrounded by a ruff of feathery bracts, and blue-tinted foliage. The maturing flowers assume clear blue shades, especially in 'Amethyst', 'Slieve Donard' and 'Superbum'. The cultivars are suitable for the second rank of a herbaceous border, combined with magenta, pink, mauve, purple and soft yellow flowers, and purple-leaved plants. They are effective with other flowers of contrasting shapes, such as the flattened, soft yellow heads of some achilleas, and glaucous or yellow-banded grasses.

**Perfect partners:** *Achillea* 'Taygetea', *Cotinus coggygria* 'Royal Purple', *Geranium pratense* 'Plenum Violaceum', *Lythrum virgatum* 'The Rocket', *Miscanthus sinensis* 'Strictus', *Phormium* 'Bronze Baby', *Phygelius* × *rectus* p.121 **C**

**H: 20–30 in.** (50–75 cm)  **S: 18 in.** (45 cm)
✿ **Midsummer to early autumn**
�○ ▨ **Z5 pH5.5–7.5**

## Eryngium bourgatii 'Picos Blue'

*E. bourgatii* develops deeply divided, dark green leaves with a lighter central zone or veining that emphasizes the crisp outline. 'Picos Blue' has more strongly colored flowers, which age to lavender-blue. With smaller blooms than *E. alpinum* (above), it needs to be seen at close quarters – the front of a border is ideal, with grassy or sword-leaved plants such as Dwarf Bearded irises. 'Oxford Blue' ♔ is a purer silvery blue.

**Perfect partners:** *Berberis thunbergii* 'Aurea', *Iris sibirica* 'Harpswell Happiness', *Phalaris arundinacea* var. *picta* 'Feesey', *Philadelphus coronarius* 'Aureus', *Phormium* 'Yellow Wave', *Potentilla fruticosa* 'Primrose Beauty', *Sisyrinchium striatum* 'Aunt May'

**H: 18 in.** (45 cm)  **S: 12 in.** (30 cm)
✿ **Mid- to late summer**
�○ ▨ **Z5 pH5.5–7.5**

*Erodium trifolium* will scramble into shrubby, yellow-flowered *Halimium lasianthum* to add its flowers to those of its support. Both like a sunny, well-drained site.

The color of *Eryngium bourgatii* 'Picos Blue' is strong enough to contrast with yellow-green dogwood (*Cornus alba* 'Aurea') and box (*Buxus sempervirens* 'Latifolia Maculata').

## *Eryngium maritimum*
SEA HOLLY

This species has grayish blue-green foliage and bracted gray-green flowers with a slightly blue cast. Such striking plants belong at the front of a border, where they blend well with pink, magenta, mauve, purple and soft yellow flowers, and purple foliage. They look most effective with achilleas and glaucous and yellow-banded grasses. Their rather open, irregular habit can be disguised by growing them through gravel or a carpet of prostrate plants, such as alpine pinks. They tolerate the salt-laden winds of coastal gardens but are not always easy to establish; like most eryngiums, they need very porous soil and may rot in moist conditions.

**Perfect partners:** *Achillea filipendulina* 'Gold Plate', *Dianthus* 'Doris', *Helictotrichon sempervirens*, *Miscanthus sinensis* 'Zebrinus', *Tamarix ramosissima* 'Pink Cascade'

**H & S: 12 in. (30 cm)** ❀ **Mid- to late summer**
◖ ▢ **Z5  pH5.5–7.5**

The silvery blooms of *Eryngium maritimum*, here supported by encircling *Lavandula angustifolia*, are strikingly decorative; they become tinged with blue as they age.

**Left:** Even before its stems and flowerheads flush blue, the pale, glaucous *Eryngium* × *tripartitum* makes an effective display against a dark background of *Salvia* × *superba*.

**Right:** The wiry habit of *Eryngium* × *tripartitum* allows it to support scrambling plants such as *Rehmannia elata* and the cranesbill *Geranium* × *riversleaianum* 'Russell Prichard'.

## *Eryngium* × *tripartitum* ♔

The prettily divided leaves are arranged in a basal rosette, which develops widely spaced, pale gray-green flowering shoots that assume blue tints as buds develop. Its dainty flowers are violet-blue, with darker bracts, and are borne in great profusion. As they fade, they develop parchment-colored tints lasting into autumn, and they deserve to be left through winter until the spring tidy. The tallish clumps look well combined with magenta, pink, mauve, purple and soft yellow flowers, and

with some of the larger grasses. They will also support restrained climbers and scramblers, for example the smaller convolvulus species.

**Perfect partners:** *Achillea* 'Moonshine', *Allium sphaerocephalon* p.351 **B**, *Eupatorium maculatum* 'Atropurpureum', *Geranium* 'Ann Folkard', *Hemerocallis* 'Golden Chimes', *Miscanthus sinensis* 'Morning Light'

**H: 30 in. (75 cm)  S: 18 in. (45 cm)**
❀ **Midsummer to early autumn**
◖ ▢ **Z5  pH5.5–7.5**

## *Eupatorium maculatum* 'Atropurpureum' ♱

*E. maculatum*, or Joe Pye weed, is a large, imposing perennial with tall, stout stems that sport pointed leaves arranged in neat whorls. In the choice selection 'Atropurpureum', the leaves are purple-tinted, while the rounded heads of the tiny florets are a dusky purplish pink and borne in two main flushes, first in midsummer and again in early autumn. This cultivar thrives in rich soil with plenty of moisture, and so makes a good choice in a moist wild garden or beside water, planted in bold groups; it also stands out at the back of a moist border. It is best combined with muted colors, such as dusky pink or cream. Good companions include Japanese anemones, pampas grass and similar tall grasses, and plumed or spiky flowers such as artemisias and later aconites.

**Perfect partners:** *Aconitum napellus* subsp. *vulgare* 'Carneum', *Anemone* × *hybrida* 'Lady Gilmour', *Cortaderia selloana* 'Pumila', *Sedum* 'Herbstfreude' p.333 **B**

**H & S: 12 in. (30 cm)**
❀ Midsummer to early autumn
Z5 pH5.5–7.5

The creamy plumes of *Artemisia lactiflora* provide a contrast of form next to the rounded, dusky pink heads of *Eupatorium maculatum* 'Atropurpureum'.

## *Euphorbia amygdaloides* var. *robbiae* ♱
MRS. ROBB'S BONNET

This robust wood spurge has upright stems that bear rosettes of glossy, dark green foliage, capped in mid-spring by rounded heads of acid green flowers. It is best in an informal tapestry of low-growing plants in a woodland setting – perhaps among carpets of other flowers, such as aubrietas. It combines well with wood anemones, Bowles' golden grass and other early-leafing grasses, and with some evergreen sedges. Its deep green foliage and yellow-green flowers harmonize well with hot colors, and makes a good contrast with blues, purples, cream and pale yellow.

Grown beneath aubrietas on a dwarf wall, the yellow-green flowers of *Euphorbia amygdaloides* var. *robbiae* provide a sharp color contrast through mid- and late spring.

**Perfect partners:** *Allium hollandicum* 'Purple Sensation', *Anemone sylvestris*, *Arum creticum* p.354 **C**, *Berberis thunbergii* f. *atropurpurea*, *Carex elata* 'Aurea', *Geranium phaeum* p.276 **A**, *Rosmarinus officinalis* 'Sissinghurst Blue', *Viola* 'Huntercombe Purple'

**H & S: 20 in. (50 cm)**
❀ Mid-spring to early summer
Z7 pH5–8

## *Euphorbia cyparissias*
CYPRESS SPURGE

This varible, wandering species is known by its slender, dense, feathery foliage, with less glaucous coloring than many euphorbias. In late spring it bears yellow-green flowers, at times tinged with orange. This plant goes well near the front of a border or in gravel, with bugles and other mat-forming plants of comparable size and vigor. It contrasts with purples and blues, and combines well with pale yellow, cream and hot colors. In full sun, plants may develop fine autumn tints. Less invasive kinds include 'Fens Ruby' (syns 'Clarice Howard', 'Purpurea'), with purple-flushed leaves; and 'Orange Man'.

**Perfect partners:** *Anthemis punctata* subsp. *cupaniana* p.233 **C**, *Geranium pratense* 'Mrs. Kendall Clark' p.276 **B**, *Helianthemum* 'Fire Drago p.105 **B**

The slightly sprawling habit of cypress spurge (*Euphorbia cyparissias*) allows it to meander through the variegated *Hosta* (Tardiana Group) 'June' and the contrasting cranesbill *Geranium himalayense* 'Plenum'.

**H: 6–20 in. (15–20 cm) S: 12–24 in. (30–60 cm)**
❀ Late spring to midsummer
Z4 pH5.5–8

## *Euphorbia dulcis* 'Chameleon'

Within this species, autumn coloring is richest in 'Chameleon'. Its loose, airy clouds of small leaves are bronze-green flushed purple, turning orange, scarlet and crimson in autumn, especially if grown in full sun. By comparison, the yellowish green flowers, aging to bronze-purple in early summer, are insignificant. It can be planted in a woodland garden or near the front of a border, to mingle with more structured neighboring plants, and also in gravel, where it can seed itself. It is attractive in hot-colored schemes, and mixes well with orange, scarlet and yellow flowers, or with silver foliage.

**Perfect partners:** *Allium nigrum* p.351 **A**, *Brachyglottis* (Dunedin Group) 'Sunshine', *Erysimum cheiri* (mixed) p.426 **C**, *Euphorbia griffithii* 'Dixter', *Geranium sylvaticum* f. *albiflorum*, *Tulipa* 'Orange Favourite'

**H: 16 in.** (40 cm) **S: 12 in.** (30 cm)
✿ **Mid-spring to early summer**
◐–◐◐ ▣ Z4 pH5–8

In a sunny position, *Euphorbia dulcis* 'Chameleon' assumes dark bronze tints, contrasting dramatically with the silvery wormwood *Artemisia* 'Powis Castle'.

**Left:** In spring, the orange and bronze tints of *Euphorbia griffithii* 'Dixter' harmonize with golden feverfew (*Tanacetum parthenium* 'Aureum'), tulips and the wallflower *Erysimum cheiri* 'Fire King'.

**Above:** In mid- to late autumn, *Euphorbia griffithii* 'Dixter' turns fiery scarlet, harmonizing with the golden blooms of *xerochrysum bracteatum* 'Dargan Hill Monarch'.

## *Euphorbia griffithii* 'Dixter' ♀

*E. griffithii* is a very variable species that has given rise to numerous superior clones, of which 'Dixter' is probably the best. It has dark foliage with a distinct red flush, turning dazzling orange and scarlet in autumn. From late spring or early summer, it is crowned by heads of orange-red bracts that look good in a hot color scheme. It makes an outstanding partner for contrasting leaf shapes such as those of grasses. Other commendable cultivars include 'Fern Cottage', with burnt orange bracts and yellow and gold autumn shades; 'King's Caple', with brick-red flowers and good autumn color; and 'Robert Poland', a strong plant with bright red bracts.

**Perfect partners:** *Berberis thunbergii* f. *atropurpurea*, *Cytisus* × *praecox* 'Warminster', *Helictotrichon sempervirens*, *Photinia* × *fraseri* 'Birmingham' p.121 **A**, *Primula* Inshriach hybrids p.325 **A**, *Pyrus salicifolia* 'Pendula'

**H: 24 in.** (60 cm) **S: 18 in.** (45 cm)
✿ **Late spring to midsummer**
◐◐ ▢–▣ Z5 pH5–7.5

## *Euphorbia myrsinites* ♀
MYRTLE SPURGE

This Mediterranean species is a sun-lover for hot, dryish sites. Its serpentine stems are covered with glaucous leaves, evergreen or semi-evergreen, and from late spring they bear rounded, greenish yellow flowerheads, which in some forms turn pink or purple as they age. If grown on its own in bare soil, the gaps between the stems would be too noticeable, so it is best planted in gravel, or where it can sprawl over the edge of borders; or it can be combined with aubrietas and other smaller carpeters. It mixes well with hot colors, purple or bronze foliage, and blue or purple flowers. Good partners include smaller fescues and other glaucous grasses, and small, sun-loving bronze sedges.

**Perfect partners:** *Aubrieta* 'Argenteovariegata', *Carex comans* (bronze), *Festuca glauca* 'Elijah Blue', *Muscari latifolium* p.378 **B**, *Sedum* 'Bertram Anderson' p.333 **A**

H: 6 in. (15 cm)  S: 12 in. (30 cm)
❀ Late spring to midsummer
◐ ▢ Z5 pH5.5–8

Spreading clumps of myrtle spurge (*Euphorbia myrsinites*), grown through gravel at the front of a border, contrast with *Berberis thunbergii* 'Atropurpurea Nana' in late spring.

## *Euphorbia polychroma* 'Major' ♀

This euphorbia (syn. *E. epithymoides*) is grown for its bright greenish yellow bracts. 'Major' is shorter and more compact than the species, and has striking autumn color. Its solid clumps are best grown as individually and are good in muted color schemes. Plants mix well with many mid- or late spring bulbs. Pale yellow, cream, apricot, peach, orange and scarlet are go well, while blue makes a fine contrast. 'Midas' is a little taller; 'Orange Flush' has darker foliage, orange flower tints and bright autumn color; and 'Sonnengold' is tinted purple, then rich orange or brown.

*Euphorbia polychroma* 'Major' sets off *Centranthus ruber* in late spring, while spires of foxgloves add vertical accents.

**Perfect partners:** *Aurinia saxatilis* 'Citrina' p.244 **B**, *Deutzia longifolia* 'Vilmoriniae' p.93 **C**, *Dicentra spectabilis* p.260 **A**, *Euphorbia characias* subsp. *wulfenii* 'Lambrook Gold' p.98 **A** and **B**, *Fritillaria pyrenaica* p.363 **C**, *Tulipa* 'Spring Green' p.401 **C**

H: 16 in. (40 cm)  S: 20 in. (50 cm)
❀ Mid-spring to early summer
◐-◐◐ ▢ Z5 pH5.5–8

## *Euphorbia rigida*

Also sold under the name *E. biglandulosa*, this euphorbia is impressive when out of flower. It has very glaucous, upright stems that bear pointed, very fleshy glaucous leaves, and yellowish green flowerheads from early spring. It is similar to *E. myrsinites* (left), but its large, bold leaves make a stronger statement, and it has fewer, more succulent stems, so clumps are less likely to develop into a solid circle of radiating branches. It is best grown through carpets of very small prostrate plants at the front of a border or in gravel. This species combines well with blue, purple and yellow flowers, and with bronze foliage such as that of smaller sedges; its flowers make a dramatic partnership with orange.

**Perfect partners:** *Acaena microphylla* 'Kupferteppich', *Aubrieta* cultivars (blue or purple), *Carex comans* (bronze), *Erodium trifolium*, *Sedum* 'Bertram Anderson'

The fleshy glaucous rosettes of *Euphorbia rigida* make a bold, small-scale accent between the diminutive cranesbill *Geranium subcaulescens* 'Splendens' and violas.

H & S: 18 in. (45 cm)
❀ Early spring to early summer
◐ ▢ Z7 pH5.5–8

*Euphorbia schillingii* contrasts strikingly with scarlet Jerusalem cross (*Lychnis chalcedonica*) in midsummer.

## *Euphorbia schillingii* ♆

*E. schillingii* makes an impressive statement in mixed and herbaceous borders. It increases freely into clumps of tall, upright stems, with deep green, elliptical leaves highlighted by conspicuous white veins. The bright greenish yellow, branching heads of flowers are large and eye-catching, and last over a long season from midsummer into autumn. The foliage produces good autumn tints, scarlet in hot climates or buttery yellow where summers are cooler. This euphorbia can be planted in the middle ranks of a border, ideally in loose, scattered groupings, as a repeated accent. It is an extremely useful ingredient of hot color schemes, and makes a startling contrast with blues and purples. Hostas, other glaucous foliage plants and grasses are good companions. In exposed borders it benefits from a little brushwood support when stems are two-thirds their eventual height.

**Perfect partners:** *Asclepias tuberosa, Cerinthe major* 'Purpurascens', *Helictotrichon sempervirens, Hosta sieboldiana* var. *elegans, Lobelia siphilitica, Ruta graveolens* 'Jackman's Blue', *Salvia nemorosa* 'Ostfriesland'

**H: 36 in.** (90 cm) **S: 24 in.** (60 cm)
❀ **Midsummer to mid-autumn**

◐◐ ■ Z8 pH5–7.5

## *Euphorbia seguieriana* subsp. *niciciana*

This is an easy-to-grow plant from south-east Europe, with lively coloring and supremely elegant form. It produces clumps of slender, woody-based stems, well clad with narrow blue-green foliage and topped by large heads of vibrant yellow-green bracts. Its impressive clumps look best when surrounded by shorter neighbors, well away from the competition of other tall plants. It combines well with purples and blues, as well as mid- to pale yellows, cream and orange. Fescues and other grasses are perfect companions, sharing its love of sunshine and sharp drainage.

**Perfect partners:** *Allium cristophii, Crocosmia* 'Lucifer', *Festuca glauca* 'Elijah Blue', *Heuchera* 'Plum Pudding', *Nepeta* 'Six Hills Giant', *Leymus arenarius, Miscanthus sinensis* 'Zebrinus', *Monarda* 'Prärienacht'

**H: 20 in.** (50 cm) **S: 18 in.** (45 cm)
❀ **Early summer to early autumn**

◐ ■ Z8 pH5.5–8

In a gravel garden, *Euphorbia seguieriana* subsp. *niciciana* provides contrasting color and variety of form with the purple racemes of *Salvia nemorosa* 'Ostfriesland' and the white-flowered sun rose *Helianthemum* 'The Bride'.

## *Ferula communis*
GIANT FENNEL

This majestic perennial is highly prized as a foliage plant, its broad clump of feathery green leaves building up over several seasons to make an impressive mound of lacy, finely cut plumes. From its center, a robust stem eventually soars to 6½–10 ft. (2–3 m), even to 16 ft. (5 m) in some cases, bearing masses of umbels of yellow-green flowers. After this, plants usually die, although they can be allowed to self-seed. Giant fennel can be planted in the middle or near the front of the border, contrasted with neighbors with broad or spiky leaves such as hostas or irises; the flowers are so airy and softly colored that they combine well with most colors except pink. It tolerates a fair amount of shade, but to flower freely it should be grown in full sun.

In mid-spring, the giant fennel (*Ferula communis*) makes a dramatic fountain of feathery fronds among the strap-shaped leaves of bulbs such as snowdrops and eye-catching foliage plants including the boldly variegated *Arum italicum* 'Marmoratum'.

**Perfect partners:** *Dicentra* 'Pearl Drops', *Hosta* (Tardiana Group) 'Halcyon', *Iris* 'Jane Phillips', *I. pallida* 'Variegata', *Miscanthus sinensis* 'Variegatus', *Onopordum nervosum, Phormium tenax* 'Veitchianum', *Yucca gloriosa*

**H: 11 ft.** (3.5 m) **S: 4 ft.** (1.2 m)
❀ **Early to midsummer**

◐–◐◐ ■ Z7 pH5.5–8

## *Festuca glauca*
BLUE FESCUE

This small grass has softly arching blue-green foliage (becoming greener in winter) that is evergreen in climates with relatively mild winters. Especially suited to small-scale plantings, it is attractive in gravel gardens, at the front of borders and as an edging to beds. It combines well with blue, soft yellow, cream or white flowers, other glaucous or silver-leaved plants, and foliage of contrasting form, such as that of smaller glaucous hostas, smaller yellow-flowered achilleas, anthemis and eryngiums. Intensely blue-green cultivars are 'Azurit', slightly more upright than most; 'Blaufuchs' ♀ (Blue Fox), and 'Blauglut' (Blue Glow); and 'Elijah Blue', bright silvery blue-green and long-lived. 'Harz' is a deeper, duller color with purple-tipped leaves, good in beds of mixed blue-green fescues.

**Perfect partners:** *Achillea × lewisii* 'King Edward', *Anthemis punctata* subsp. *cupaniana*, *Artemisia schmidtiana*, *Eryngium maritimum*, *Hosta* (Tardiana Group) 'Halcyon'

**H: 4–12 in.** (10–30 cm)  **S: 8–20 in.** (20–50 cm)
❀ **Late spring to midsummer**
◐-◐◐ □-■ **Z4 pH5.5–7.5**

The leaves of *Festuca glauca* 'Blauglut' are sufficiently blue to be set off by companions with yellow-green foliage and flowers, as here with *Juniperus × pfitzeriana* Gold Sovereign among a carpet of heathers.

In a waterside planting in midsummer, the feathery, rich rose-pink flowerheads of *Filipendula* 'Kahome' provide a contrast of form with the delicately colored daylily *Hemerocallis* 'Dresden Dream'.

## *Filipendula* 'Kahome'

This hybrid meadowsweet, with rose-pink flowers and slightly bronze-flushed foliage, suits bog gardens, waterside sites and beds or borders that do not dry out. Its rich flower color is useful in blends with cool colors such as mauve, purple, lilac, lavender and white, and contrasts with yellow-green foliage and flowers. The deeply cut leaves and fluffy flowerheads allow harmonies with the similar form of astilbes and can be contrasted with the more solid outline of hostas or the foliage of moisture-loving irises, sedges and grasses such as phalaris, and ferns like *Athyrium filix-femina* cultivars. Good companions include lythrums, monardas, white filipendulas, and purple, glaucous or gray foliage.

**Perfect partners:** *Carex grayi*, *Hosta fortunei* 'Francee', *Iris pseudacorus* 'Variegata', *Lythrum salicaria* 'Morden Pink', *Phalaris arundinacea* var. *picta* 'Feesey'

**H: 16 in.** (40 cm)  **S: 18 in.** (45 cm)
❀ **Mid- to late summer**
◐◐ □-■ ■ **Z4 pH5–7.5**

## *Filipendula ulmaria* 'Aurea'
GOLDEN MEADOWSWEET

Yellow-green leaves approach pure gold in fairly well-lit sites and are at their brightest in late spring and early summer, when the creamy white flowers appear. 'Aurea' is then very effective for harmonies with hot colors or contrasts with blue in waterside plantings, bog gardens and moist borders, especially with early-leafing ferns, ranunculus, moisture-loving irises, Candelabra and Sikkimensis primulas, and late spring bulbs like crown imperials, bluebells and muscari. It is an attractive partner for euphorbias, brunneras, forget-me-nots, wallflowers, honesty, sweet rocket, blue, yellow or red columbines, and shrubs such as spiraeas, especially cultivars of *Spiraea japonica* with yellow-green leaves.

**Perfect partners:** *Aquilegia vulgaris* (blue), *Brunnera macrophylla*, *Hyacinthoides hispanica*, *Iris* 'Cambridge', *Matteuccia struthiopteris*, *Myosotis sylvatica*, *Omphalodes cappadocica*, *Primula* Inshriach hybrids

**H: 30 in.** (75 cm) **S: 18 in.** (45 cm)
❀ **Late spring to early summer**
 ◊◊-◊◊◊ ▢-■ Z3 pH4–7.5

In early summer, the bright foliage of golden meadowsweet (*Filipendula ulmaria* 'Aurea') contrasts with the flowers of the cranesbill *Geranium* 'Johnson's Blue'. The combination will remain colorful for several months.

In this mixture of herbs, a pleasing effect is achieved solely through the use of different kinds of foliage. The feathery leaves of fennel and bronze fennel (*Foeniculum vulgare* and 'Purpureum') are joined by the larger, bolder leaflets of angelica (*Angelica archangelica*) and by the narrow-leaved Spanish sage (*Salvia lavandulifolia*).

## *Gentiana asclepiadea* ♔
WILLOW GENTIAN

This easy-to-grow gentian bears intense, deep pure blue flowers. It can be grown in borders in partial or full shade, but seems to perform best in a woodland setting, particularly in the shade of beech or oak. Its elegant arching habit looks best surrounded by shorter plants such as ferns, late-flowering saxifrages, shade-loving grasses and sedges, and Japanese anemones, particularly white cultivars. It combines effectively with white or pale blue flowers and contrasts with yellow flowers like patrinias, or yellow-green foliage and flowers. Good companions include white or yellow tricyrtis, yellow-green hostas and ground-covering ivies, kirengeshomas, hydrangeas, late-flowering lilies, white-variegated grasses and plants with white or yellow berries.

**Perfect partners:** *Anemone* × *hybrida* 'Honorine Jobert', *Geranium* 'Johnson's Blue', *Hedera helix* 'Buttercup', *Hosta* 'Sum and Substance', *Lilium lancifolium* var. *splendens*

**H: 36 in.** (90 cm) **S: 24 in.** (60 cm)
❀ **Midsummer to early autumn**
◊◊ ▢-■ Z5 pH5–7.5

## *Foeniculum vulgare*
COMMON FENNEL

This aromatic herbaceous perennial can be grown in wild or gravel gardens, and in borders. Its feathery foliage is best in late spring and early summer, when spangled with the flowers of companions such as *Gladiolus tristis*, moricandias, *Omphalodes linifolia*, calochortus, alliums, nigellas, forget-me-nots and heliophilas. Its own flowers, borne later in the season, are yellowish green. It can also be used purely as a foliage plant, providing a complete contrast with grasses and sedges, ferns, angelicas or hostas. Bronze fennel, *F.v.* 'Purpureum', combines well with mauve, purple and hot-colored flowers.

**Perfect partners:** *Achillea* 'Coronation Gold' p.226 **B**, *Dahlia* 'Glorie van Heemstede' p.421 **A**, *Geranium* × *oxonianum* f. *thurstonianum* p.275 **B**, *Hedychium coccineum* 'Tara' p.282 **A**, *Rosa* 'Climbing Paul Lédé' p.188 **B**

**H: 6 ft.** (1.8 m) **S: 20 in.** (50 cm)
❀ **Mid- to late summer**
▬ ◊-◊◊ ▢-■ Z4 pH5.5–8

The rich blue flowers of *Gentiana asclepiadea* stand out dramatically against the yellow-green foliage of *Rubus cockburnianus* 'Goldenvale'. Grown in light shade, the rubus leaves remain bright and avoid being scorched by the sun.

# Geraniums

GERANIUMS, or cranesbills, are among the most popular herbaceous plants, reflecting their versatility and prettiness, and the fact that they are generally easy to cultivate. Many grow naturally in dappled shade in woods or hedgerows. Others are meadow plants, upright in habit and suitable for a herbaceous border. Some are scramblers, able to weave through shrubs and across banks or providing good ground cover. There are hummock-forming alpine species, superb for a gravel garden, rock garden or (the easier ones) the front of a border. A few, such as the monocarpic, tender *G. maderense* ♀ and the rather hardier, longer-lived *G. palmatum* ♀, are not herbaceous but form bold rosettes of leaves borne on a woody stem. There are also some annuals, although these tend to be rather straggly with tiny flowers.

The flowers of cranesbills are cool-colored, from soft lavender-blue to magenta and paler tints to white; they are often attractively veined – dramatic black on magenta, for example. The blooms are borne scattered across the clump, seldom in such profusion that they overwhelm their neighbors, making them ideal in a supporting role to stars of the border such as delphiniums, peonies, or old roses. One exception is *G. × magnificum* ♀, which for a brief couple of weeks can produce a solid sheet of blue capable of disrupting the balance with and between its companions, unless used in a scattered drift or grown in partial shade to control its flower production. There is a handful of *G. pratense* cultivars that have double flowers; although these perhaps lack the pleasing simplicity of the single blooms, they have their own charm and are longer-lasting.

The foliage of cranesbills is usually tidy and respectable, without showing any strong form or texture, which must be supplied by companion plants such as irises, daylilies or grasses. There are some silvery leaved sorts, and chocolate-

**Above:** An informal mix using cranesbills in a sunny glade, including pale grayish blue *Geranium pratense* 'Mrs. Kendall Clark' (foreground and center), magenta *G. psilostemon* and rich blue *G. × magnificum*, with cardoons (*Cynara cardunculus*), delphiniums, lupins, poppies and roses.

**Left:** Deep pink *Geranium × oxonianum* f. *thurstonianum* and lavender-blue *G. ibericum* mingle harmoniously in this border planting, with contrasting iris leaves and the erect, deep blue spikes of *Veronica austriaca* subsp. *teucrium*.

or purple-leaved cultivars are on the increase. Most are sufficiently late-leafing to be underplanted with spring bulbs or with wood anemones and celandines.

Many cranesbills are excellent when used as ground cover, although the vigor and ultimate size of the chosen sort need to be carefully tailored to the neighboring plants. While smaller kinds such as *G. × cantabrigiense* are not problematic,

the larger *G. macrorrhizum* and *G. × oxonianum* cultivars are so large and vigorous that they can suppress nearby roses, for example. *G. procurrens* is beautiful but irrepressible, rooting wherever it touches the ground, and only practicable where there is plenty of space.

Deadheading is usually desirable to keep the clumps looking tidy, prevent excess seedlings and maintain good basal foliage. Snapping off the spent flower stems within the dome of basal foliage leaves no trace of interference. However, cutting the whole group to the ground with shears may be simpler. New foliage is usually produced within a couple of weeks.

*Geranium albanum* weaves through the outer branches of *Weigela* 'Florida Variegata', beneath which grows a carpet of self-seeded wood forget-me-nots (*Myosotis sylvatica*). The sprawling habit of this cranesbill allows it to meander through its neighbors, its scattering of dainty flowers uniting them all into an intimately mixed ensemble.

## *Geranium albanum*

A rather sprawling cranesbill, with bright pink flowers, this species is suitable for the front of a border or for ground cover, especially when intermingled with small shrubs with a fairly open habit, or small species or Ground Cover roses. It also looks effective associated with periwinkles, *Omphalodes linifolia* and low-growing annuals such as forget-me-nots. Its blooms are rather small, and the foliage can predominate in nitrogen-rich soil, so for a good flowering display plants are best grown in rather poor soil or even in gravel. Because growth tends to die back during summer, it is a good idea to combine this species with a late-blooming plant such as *Aster divaricatus*, which can fill the cranesbill's space in late summer and autumn.

**Perfect partners:** *Cistus* × *cyprius*, *Convolvulus cneorum*, *Erysimum* 'Bowles Mauve', *Lavandula lanata*, *Rosa* 'Nozomi', *R.* 'The Fairy', *Vinca minor* 'La Grave'

H & S: 18 in. (45 cm)   Late spring to midsummer   ◇◇   ▣-▦   Z7   pH5.5–7.5

## *Geranium* × *cantabrigiense*

This cranesbill is capable of making dense carpets of ground cover and is useful for underplanting shrubs that tend to have clear stems such as some roses. It has neat, glossy foliage that assumes tints of scarlet, flame and yellow before it dies in autumn, and flowers that vary from palest pink to a rich carmine-pink. It thrives in sun or partial shade, and is suited to the front of a border. 'Biokovo' is palest blush-pink; 'Cambridge', a richer shade of pink; and 'Karmina', a deeper carmine-pink. All go well with bergenias and plants with contrasting foliage such as ferns, sedges and glaucous grasses. They make a superb foil for summer-flowering bulbs.

**Perfect partners:** *Bergenia* 'Abendglut', *Carex comans* 'Frosted Curls', *Dryopteris affinis*, *Festuca glauca* 'Elijah Blue', *Heuchera cylindrica* 'Greenfinch', × *Heucherella alba* 'Rosalie', *Lilium* 'Joy', *Molinia caerulea* 'Variegata', *Rosa glauca*

H: 12 in. (30 cm)   S: 24 in. (60 cm)
Early to midsummer   ◇◇   ▣-▦   Z5   pH5–7.5

*Geranium* × *cantabrigiense* 'Cambridge', grown through gravel to edge a bed, is infiltrated by the mildly invasive variegated apple mint, *Mentha suaveolens* 'Variegata'. The cream edges to the mint's leaves highlight their shape, producing a pleasing pattern.

## *Geranium* 'Ann Folkard' ♀

This sprawling cranesbill has black-veined magenta flowers and contrasting yellow-green leaves. It gives its most dazzling display when newly in bloom, especially when set against yellow-green foliage and flowers such as euphorbias or *Alchemilla mollis*, pale yellow plants such as some achilleas, or carmine or crimson flowers. Leaves are at their brightest in sun. This versatile cultivar is most suitable for ground cover or as a carpet through which other plants can be grown: small shrubs such as *Potentilla fruticosa* cultivars, herbaceous perennials or summer bulbs such as lilies.

*Geranium* 'Ann Folkard' is, like *G. albanum* above, a plant that will sprawl through its neighbors, drawing them into a unified whole. Its flowers contrast with its foliage: combining it with the mauve blooms of *Allium cristophii* and yellow-green leaves of golden marjoram (*Origanum vulgare* 'Aureum') gives a scheme in which all the flowers contrast with all the leaves.

**Perfect partners:** *Anthemis tinctoria* p.234 **B**, *Artemisia stelleriana* 'Boughton Silver' p.238 **A**, *Cytisus nigricans* p.92 **B**, *Deschampsia cespitosa* p.257 **C**, *Geranium sylvaticum* 'Mayflower' p.278 **C**, *Heuchera villosa* 'Palace Purple' p.288 **A**, *Lilium* 'Joy' p.375 **A**, *Populus alba* 'Richardii' p.125 **A**, *Rhus* × *pulvinata* Autumn Lace Group p.134 **A**, *Rosa* 'De Rescht'

H: 24 in. (60 cm)   S: 36 in. (90 cm)
Midsummer to mid-autumn   ◇◇   ▣-▦   Z5   pH5–7.5

A

## *Geranium* × *antipodeum* 'Chocolate Candy'

This cultivar is suitable for rock gardens and sunny borders with good drainage, where it associates most easily with plants from a similar climate and needing similar conditions – plants from New Zealand or the Chilean Andes, for example. Its deeply colored foliage looks best in a forward position, mixed with black mondo grass, heucheras and other dark-leaved cranesbills such as *G. pratense* Midnight Reiter strain. Its flowers are a strong enough pink to contrast with yellow-green flowers or, even more dramatically, with silver foliage, and they also associate well with crimson and other cool colors such as mauve, lilac or purple. Good partners include small euphorbias, oxalis, campanulas, marjorums, smaller penstemons, alchemillas, erodiums, smaller hebes and other small or prostrate cranesbills.

**Perfect partners:** *Artemisia alba* 'Canescens', *Celmisia spectabilis*, *Hebe ochracea*, *Heuchera* 'Plum Pudding', *Ophiopogon planiscapus* 'Nigrescens', *Spiraea japonica* 'Goldflame'

H: 10 in. (25 cm)   S: 20 in. (50 cm)
❁ Early summer to early autumn
 ◊◊ ☐-▓ Z8 pH5.5–7.5

Opposite: The variety of flower and foliage sizes and colors adds interest to this pretty mixture of three cranesbills, in which soft pink *Geranium* 'Dusky Crûg', bright pink *G.* × *antipodeum* 'Chocolate Candy' and soft magenta *G. psilostemon* 'Bressingham Flair' all harmonize agreeably.

*Geranium* 'Johnson's Blue' is a superlative and floriferous mound-forming plant for the front of beds and borders, flowering profusely over several months, especially if grown in a fairly sunny situation. Here, it is used to furnish beneath Jerusalem sage (*Phlomis fruticosa*), providing a contrast of color and floral form.

## *Geranium* 'Johnson's Blue' ♛

With flowers as near to true blue as any cranesbill, this superlative hybrid performs well in partial shade and also tolerates full sun. Combinations with yellow flowers are perhaps the most striking, especially early-flowering roses, daylilies, columbines and Bearded irises; it is also attractive with yellow-green foliage or flowers and with white and other cool-colored flowers. It mixes well with baptisias, centaureas, anthericums, philadelphus, alchemillas, catmints, pinks and campanulas, as well as with contrasting foliage plants, including yellow-green, glaucous or variegated hostas and glaucous grasses such as elymus and helictotrichons.

It makes dramatic partnerships with flowers of contrasting shape and size – camassias or veronicas, for example – and with those of similar shape but distinctively different color, such as violas in soft yellow, purple and deep or very pale blue.

**Perfect partners:** *Allium hollandicum* p.349 **A**, *Centranthus ruber* p.250 **A**, *Filipendula ulmaria* 'Aurea' p.271 **A**, *Iris chrysographes* p.297 **A**, *Lamium maculatum* p.304 **A**, *Lilium pyrenaicum* var. *pyrenaicum* p.376 **C**, *Rosa* Iceberg p.213 **B**, *Spiraea japonica* p.141 **C**

H: 16 in. (40 cm)   S: 24 in. (60 cm)
❁ Early summer to mid-autumn
 ◊◊ ☐-▓ Z4 pH5–7.5

## *Geranium* × *oxonianum*

This clump-forming plant is useful for a woodland garden and for naturalizing, and can be used in a mixed border, beneath roses or to create a tapestry of ground cover. Its flowers are various shades of pink: cultivars tending toward rose-pink mix well with warm colors such as peach and apricot, but are often close enough to primary pink not to clash with mauves and blues; mauve-pink cultivars are best with cool- or white-flowered

In this subtly subdued but satisfying combination, the dusky magenta-pink flowers of the cranesbill *Geranium* × *oxonianum* f. *thurstonianum* harmonize with the purple-flushed leaves of bronze fennel (*Foeniculum vulgare* 'Purpureum'). The squirting cucumber (*Ecballium elaterium*) provides foliage interest in front, while the white flowers of the love-in-a-mist *Nigella damascena* 'Miss Jekyll Alba' leaven the whole.

plants; pale rose-pink cultivars combine with soft yellow. All blend with silver, glaucous or purple-flushed foliage – artemisias or glaucous hostas, heucheras and bergenias, for example – and with contrasting foliage such as that of irises. 'A.T. Johnson' ♛ is silvery pink; 'Claridge Druce', mauve-pink and vigorous; 'Phoebe Noble', deep magenta; 'Prestbury Blush', almost white; 'Rose Clair' and 'Wargrave Pink' ♛ are both rose-pink.

**Perfect partners:** *Cotinus coggygria* 'Royal Purple' p.90 **B**, *Dicentra eximia* p.259 **B**, *Hebe stenophylla* p.104 **B**, *Hosta* 'Sum and Substance' p.295 **A**, *Kniphofia* 'Atlanta' p.302 **B**, *Philadelphus* 'Beauclerk' p.119 **A** ❏ p.118 **A**

H: 12–24 in. (30–60 cm)   S: 16–30 in. (40–75 cm)
❁ Late spring to mid-autumn
 ◊◊ ☐-▓ ▓ Z5 pH4.5–8

The somber maroon flowers of the mourning widow cranesbill (*Geranium phaeum*) are not easily visible from a distance, and tend to be upstaged by dazzling colors such as magenta, but combining them, as here, with Mrs. Robb's bonnet (*Euphorbia amygdaloides* var. *robbiae*) draws attention to them without their being overwhelmed.

In a steeply banked, sunny planting of mainly cool but rich colors, Armenian cranesbill (*Geranium psilostemon*) grows beneath blush-pink *Rosa* Heritage, with *Sedum* 'Herbstfreude' in front. *Viola* 'Mercury' and *Dianthus* 'Laced Monarch' furnish the front of the border. In a less steep position, a plant of intermediate height could be used between the cranesbill and the viola.

## Geranium phaeum
MOURNING WIDOW CRANESBILL

This rather variable species tolerates dry shade well, but also performs well in full sun and is vigorous enough to be naturalized in grass and in a woodland garden. Its flowers, usually purplish black with a white center, are best appreciated at close range and are useful for providing a base note for plantings with brighter flowers, such as pink, mauve or purple, and with purple-flushed foliage. White 'Album' is good for lighting up a shady corner; 'Blue Shadow' may be dusky amethyst or lavender, depending on light levels; 'Joan Baker' is pale lavender-blue; and 'Lily Lovell' is dusky purple with yellowish green leaves.

**Perfect partners:** *Aquilegia vulgaris* p.235 **B**, *Chaerophyllum hirsutum* 'Roseum' p.250 **B**, *Digitalis purpurea* f. *albiflora*, *Heuchera* 'Plum Pudding', *Tellima grandiflora*

**H: 27–36 in.** (70–90 cm) **S: 18 in.** (45 cm)
✿ **Late spring to early summer**
○○ □-■ Z4 pH4.5–7.5

## Geranium psilostemon
ARMENIAN CRANESBILL

This is a candidate for the middle ranks of a border. Its flowers are intense magenta, accentuated by shining black veins and a black center, making it suitable with cool colors and for almost shocking contrasts with soft yellow, yellow-green or orange. It combines well with glaucous, silver or purple foliage, and makes good contrasts with yellow-green foliage. Striking effects can be achieved with contrasting form and foliage – larger miscanthus cultivars or larger hostas, for example. 'Bressingham Flair' is a lighter magenta, slightly shorter, and useful where harmonies of cool shades are needed.

**Perfect partners:** *Cotinus coggygria* 'Royal Purple', *Foeniculum vulgare*, *Geranium* × *antipodeum* 'Chocolate Candy' p.274 **A**, *Gladiolus communis* subsp. *byzantinus* p.366 **A**, *Hosta sieboldiana* var. *elegans*, *Iris* 'Braithwaite', *Lathyrus odoratus* 'Matucana' p.173 **B**, *Miscanthus sinensis* 'Zebrinus', *Papaver orientale*, *Phygelius aequalis* 'Yellow Trumpet' p.121 **B**, *Rosa gallica* 'Versicolor' p.196 **A**

**H: 40 in.** (1 m) **S: 24 in.** (60 cm)
✿ **Early to late summer**
○○ □-■ Z4 pH5–7.5

## Geranium pratense
MEADOW CRANESBILL

This cranesbill is good in a border, but also sufficiently robust to be naturalized in long grass and woodland gardens. It mixes with white flowers, silver foliage and Shrub roses in cool colors and warm peach or apricot, and contrasts with soft yellow flowers and yellow-green foliage or flowers. It works well with glaucous hostas and larger grasses, especially white- or gold-variegated miscanthus. In grass, it looks effective with variants of *Achillea millefolium*. *G.p.* f. *albiflorum* embraces white-flowered 'Galactic'; 'Mrs. Kendall Clark' ♀, pale grayish blue; Victor Reiter strain, lavender-blue with bronze or purple-flushed foliage; subsp. *stewartianum* 'Elizabeth Yeo', almost pure pink; and robust, double-flowered lavender 'Plenum Violaceum' ♀.

**Perfect partners:** *Achillea millefolium* 'Lilac Beauty', *Artemisia alba* 'Canescens', *Hosta* (Tardiana Group) 'Halcyon', *Miscanthus sinensis* 'Variegatus', *Rosa* 'Buff Beauty'

**H: 24–36 in.** (60–90 cm) **S: 24 in.** (60 cm)
✿ **Early to midsummer**
○○ □-■ Z4 pH4.5–8

The streaked, soft blue flowers of *Geranium pratense* 'Mrs. Kendall Clark' are contrasted with the yellow-green inflorescences of cypress spurge (*Euphorbia cyparissias*). A deeper blue cranesbill would also be effective.

# Geranium renardii ♡

A charming plant for the front of a border or for rock gardens, this short, clump-forming herbaceous perennial flowers best in a sunny site. Its downy leaves are sage-green, almost silvery in relatively nutrient-poor soil, and incised with a network of deep veins, while the white flowers are veined with lavender. It is an excellent partner for silver foliage and blue to violet flowers. Its lavender-blue variant, 'Whiteknights', is more richly colored and will stand combinations with cream and contrasts with delicate yellow. Lilac-colored 'Tcschelda', and 'Zetterlund', also lilac but with violet veins, are attractive with smaller catmints, pinks, artemisias and glaucous hebes, blue fescues, sages and the silver (or lime-encrusted) *Ligulatae* saxifrages.

**Perfect partners:** *Anthemis tinctoria* 'E.C. Buxton', *Festuca glauca* 'Blaufuchs', *Hebe pinguifolia* 'Pagei', *Nepeta × faassenii*, *Salvia officinalis* 'Purpurascens'

**H & S: 12 in.** (30 cm) ✿ **Early summer**
◊◊ ▢-▦ **Z6 pH5.5–7.5**

*Geranium renardii*, with its fascinatingly felted and netted leaves and pale blooms, is an excellent plant for the front of a border, here harmonizing with the coppery flowers of *Geum rivale* 'Leonard's Variety'.

# Geranium × riversleaianum

This hybrid between *G. endressii* and *G. traversii* has produced several cultivars, two of which are particularly useful for ground cover and for the front of a border, or rock or gravel garden. 'Mavis Simpson' is a sprawling plant that will also scramble effectively over its neighbors and into small open shrubs like cistus, olearias, escallonias and tree poppies. Its satiny rose-pink flowers and grayish green foliage arc cxccllcnt with cool purplc foliage plants such as purple sage and flowers such as pinks, catmints, campanulas, bugles, smaller penstemons and violas. More robust 'Russell Prichard' ♡ has bright magenta flowers that look great with purple, silver or glaucous foliage, and yellow-green, soft yellow or orange flowers. Good companions include soft yellow achilleas, agapanthus, alchemillas, daylilies and euphorbias.

**Perfect partners:** *Achillea* 'Moonshine', *Dianthus* 'Doris', *Eryngium × tripartitum* p.265 **C**, *Festuca glauca* 'Elijah Blue', *Heuchera villosa* 'Palace Purple' p.288 **A**, *Lilium speciosum* p.377 **B**

**H: 9 in.** (23 cm) **S: 40 in.** (1 m)
✿ **Early summer to early autumn**
◊◊ ▢-▦ **Z6 pH5.5–7.5**

**Above:** In an attractive partnership for the front of a border, *Geranium × riversleaianum* 'Russell Prichard' weaves among the stems of tricolor sage (*Salvia officinalis* 'Tricolor'), its magenta flowers matching the flushed tips of the sage's young shoots.

**Below:** The soft pink flowers and slightly gray foliage of *Geranium* 'Mavis Simpson' are suited to more delicately colored schemes and combinations with silvery or glaucous foliage, as here with the contrasting form of the grass *Elymus magellanicus*.

The delicate blooms of *Geranium sanguineum* var. *striatum* show among a tracery of silvery *Artemisia alba* 'Canescens', the artemisia's filigree foliage letting through the light the cranesbill needs to flower.

## Geranium sanguineum var. striatum ♀

With its sprawling mound of deeply cut, dark green leaves, this plant is invaluable for the front of a border or a rock garden. In full sun it gives the best display of its delicate pink, crimson-veined flowers. These combine pleasingly with cool colors or purple leaves, and their color is usually strong enough to contrast with yellow-green flowers – euphorbias, for example – or with very pale yellow flowers such as those of some violas. It goes well with polemoniums, heucheras, violas in dusky deep pink, mauve, purple and blue, and shorter alliums that flower in early summer. Other good companions include early roses and campanulas, and columbines.

**Perfect partners:** *Allium cristophii, Berberis thunbergii* 'Atropurpurea Nana', *Dictamnus albus* var. *purpureus, Euphorbia schillingii, Salvia nemorosa* 'Lubecca' p.330 **B**

**H: 6 in.** (15 cm) **S: 8 in.** (20 cm)
❀ **Early summer to late autumn**
◊◊ ☐-■ Z4 pH5.5–7.5

## Geranium sylvaticum
WOOD CRANESBILL

This versatile plant tolerates some shade and may be naturalized in sunnier parts of wild or woodland gardens. It blooms before the bulk of summer flowers, so its natural allies include violas, polemoniums, columbines and brunneras, as well as shrubs like brooms, rhododendrons, daphnes and lilacs. Blue-flowered sorts, including 'Mayflower' ♀, are very effective with cool colors, glaucous, silver or variegated foliage, and yellow-green foliage and flowers. White umbellifers, soft yellow deciduous azaleas, ceanothus and early yellow roses are excellent partners. White-flowered variants ("Album' and f. *albiflorum*) mix especially well with silver, glaucous or white-variegated foliage and blue flowers, and with contrasting floral forms, such as the lacy heads of umbellifers or the spikes of lupins.

**Perfect partners:** *Anthriscus sylvestris* 'Ravenswing', *Aquilegia vulgaris* (mixed) p.235 **B**, *Milium effusum* 'Aureum', *Polemonium caeruleum, Rhododendron* 'Narcissiflorum'

**H: 30 in.** (75 cm) **S: 24 in.** (60 cm)
❀ **Late spring to early summer**
◊◊ ☐-■ Z4 pH5–7.5

**Above:** The relatively upright *Geranium sylvaticum* f. *albiflorum* is tall enough to mingle with the lower branches of this purple smoke bush (*Cotinus coggygria* 'Royal Purple'), its flowers contrasting with the dark foliage.

**Below:** In a semi-shady border in late spring, the harmonious, similarly sized blooms of *Geranium sylvaticum* 'Mayflower' ♀ and *Viola cornuta* 'Rosea', enlivened by their white eyes, are separated by the contrasting yellow-green leaves of *Geranium* 'Ann Folkard'.

## *Geranium tuberosum*

This tuberous-rooted perennial has deeply divided leaves and rosy-purple flowers that appear in late spring and early summer, and can partner the same plants as *G. sylvaticum* and its derivatives (facing page), together with biennials such as sweet Williams. It dies back quickly after blooming, and needs to be followed by a late-sown annual like nicotiana, a perennial bedding plant or a pot-grown tender perennial to continue the display. It also thrives when naturalized in sunnier parts of a wild or woodland garden, where it mixes well with later flowering rhododendrons and azaleas. It succeeds with cool colors and white flowers, including early white roses and philadelphus, and purple foliage such as that of purple cow parsley and some heucheras.

**Perfect partners:** *Dianthus barbatus*, *Heuchera villosa* 'Palace Purple', *Nicotiana* Domino Series, *Philadelphus* 'Belle Etoile', *Rosa × fortuneana*

**H & S: 12 in.** (30 cm)
**Late spring to early summer**
**Z7 pH5.5–7.5**

The mauve flowers of *Geranium tuberosum* match those of trailing *G. pyrenaicum* 'Bill Wallis', although the two differ substantially in scale. In late spring, the silvery foliage of *Artemisia ludoviciana* is just emerging; as *G. tuberosum* dies back, the artemisia will become much taller, largely filling the gap left by the cranesbill.

A

At the peak of their flowering in early summer, yellow *Geum* 'Lady Stratheden' and scarlet *G.* 'Mrs J. Bradshaw' combine to give a dazzling display. Deep red or yellow-green foliage or blood-red flowers could enhance the effect.

## *Geum* 'Lady Stratheden' ♛

This hybrid thrives at the front of a sunny or partially shaded border, where it will flower all summer long. Its ruffled, semi-double blooms are a rich, soft yellow that works well with hot colors and bronze foliage, and with warm shades such as apricot, peach and buff. Roses in these colors make good companions, as do early lilies and daylilies. It blends with cream flowers such as *Paeonia* × *lemoinei* cultivars, and looks effective with mid-blue or lavender-blue flowers such as columbines, *Trachymene coerulea*, *Nigella damascena* and *Salvia pratensis* Haematodes Group. Its slightly coarse foliage benefits from finer or contrasting neighbors, including yellow-green grasses. 'Mrs. J. Bradshaw' ♛ has scarlet flowers. Both hybrids come true from seed.

**Perfect partners:** *Achillea* 'Fanal', *Aconitum* 'Ivorine', *Aquilegia* 'Hensol Harebell', *Geranium* 'Johnson's Blue', *Hakonechloa macra* 'Alboaurea', *Lilium* 'Enchantment', *Phormium* 'Bronze Baby', *Rosa* 'Buff Beauty'

**H: 20 in. (50 cm) S: 24 in. (60 cm)**
❀ **Early summer to early autumn**
◊◊ ■ **Z5 pH5.5–7.5**

## *Gunnera manicata* ♛

Often called giant rhubarb, this magnificent monster of a plant can make gardens of more modest size look junglelike. Its conical flower spikes, 40 in. (1 m) high and covered with frilled reddish bracts, sometimes nestle beneath the leaves. It revels in moist places, especially waterside sites where reflections double its impact. It is best combined with similarly dramatic plants – bamboos and other large grasses such as arundos or the biggest miscanthus – and with plants of semi-tropical appearance, such as bananas, cannas, colocasias, palms, tetrapanax, the biggest ligularias and eupatoriums and stooled paulownias or catalpas. Companions should be grouped on a similar scale to avoid being overwhelmed. *G. tinctoria* (syn. *G. chilensis*) is similar, but shorter at 5 ft. (1.5 m) high.

**Perfect partners:** *Canna* 'Erebus', *Catalpa bignonioides* (stooled), *Eupatorium purpureum*, *Hosta sieboldiana* var. *elegans* p.294 **C**, *Ligularia stenocephala*, *Miscanthus sacchariflorus*, *Tetrapanax papyrifer* (stooled)

**H: 8 ft. (2.5 m) S: 13 ft. (4 m)** ❀ **(Early summer)**
◊◊◊ ■ ■ **Z7 pH5.5–7.5**

Backed by the elegant, arching canes of the bamboo *Fargesia murielae*, *Gunnera manicata* creates an exotic, almost tropical effect. Its leaves are echoed by the much smaller umbrellalike foliage of *Darmera peltata* that furnishes the front of the planting.

In this pleasing late spring association for partial shade, the oak fern (*Gymnocarpium dryopteris*) unfurls lacy new fronds between the lavender-speckled blooms of *Viola sororia* 'Freckles' and the sky-blue flowers of the wood forget-me-not (*Myosotis sylvatica*).

## *Gymnocarpium dryopteris* ♀

OAK FERN

This hardy deciduous fern has divided, wavy-edged fronds, resembling tiny, unfurling oak leaves, that become a bright, rich green with age. It is useful for moist, shady situations, especially as ground cover, either alone or partnered with contrasting foliage such as grasses and sedges, or the loose shuttlecocks of hart's tongue fern. Shade-lovers with white or very pale flowers that appear in late spring look most effective. A classic partner is *Ornithogalum nutans*, whose nodding, silvery white flowers stand above the fern's emerald-green new foliage, which in turn masks the bulb's rather untidy leaves. In cool soils the fern's slender, creeping rhizomes eventually produce a carpet of dainty foliage that looks deceptively fragile throughout the season, but in drier soils and warmer summers or in limey soil growth is usually sparser.

**Perfect partners:** *Asplenium scolopendrium*, *Carex siderosticha* 'Variegata', *Hesperis matronalis* var. *albiflora*, *Lunaria annua* var. *albiflora*, *Milium effusum* 'Aureum'

**H: 8 in.** (20 cm) **S: 18 in.** (45 cm)
Z3 pH5–7.5

The gracefully arching leaves of *Hakonechloa macra* 'Alboaurea', with their striking variegation of yellow and white, furnish the front of a border beneath the bold, dark green foliage of *Hosta tardiflora*.

## *Hakonechloa macra* 'Alboaurea' ♀

This arching, deciduous grass has green and gold leaves occasionally streaked with white. It is attractive at the front of a border or on a moist bank, and looks effective in containers, where it is best grown on its own, with companions in adjacent pots. It mixes easily with glaucous foliage and the contrasting leaf shapes of ferns, hostas or bergenias, and contrasts well with bronze or purple foliage. Blue flowers such as lower-growing veronicas and corydalis are good partners, but pairings with early spring flowers should be avoided. The plant may become flat in the center unless brushwood is worked through the foliage. 'Aureola' ♀ has slightly shorter, wider leaves without the white streaks.

**Perfect partners:** *Bergenia cordifolia* 'Purpurea', *Corydalis flexuosa*, *Cotinus coggygria* Rubrifolius Group, *Erodium glandulosum*, *Festuca glauca*, *Lychnis* × *arkwrightii* 'Vesuvius', *Veronica austriaca* subsp. *teucrium*

**H: 9 in.** (23 cm) **S: 18 in.** (45 cm)
❀ **Early to mid-autumn**
Z5 pH5–7.5

## *Gypsophila paniculata* 'Compacta Plena'

The airy clouds of blushed white, formal, double blooms produced by this slow-growing, spreading form of baby's breath are indispensable for softening hard edges, such as those at the side of paths or against edging stones. It is very much a front-of-border plant, ideal for growing next to spring bulbs or biennials such as sweet Williams or early perennials such as Oriental poppies, since it will happily fill the gap that is left once these have been removed or died back.

'Compacta Plena' makes a good foil for plants with deeper pink, carmine or crimson flowers, and with glaucous or silver foliage, particularly if they have a bold, substantial form. 'Bristol Fairy' ♀ is taller at 24 in. (60 cm), with larger, double white flowers up to ¾ in. (1.5 cm) across, but it is inclined to be short-lived, except on sharply drained, alkaline soils. *G.* 'Rosenschleier' (syn. 'Rosy Veil') ♀ is a hybrid with double pink flowers and will grow 16–20 in. (40–50 cm) high by about 3¼ ft. (1 m) wide.

The airy flowers of *Gypsophila paniculata* 'Compacta Plena' help to soften the almost too solid color of Chinese pink *Dianthus chinensis* (Princess Series) 'Princess Salmon'.

**Perfect partners:** *Convolvulus cneorum*, *Dahlia* 'Bednall Beauty', *Diascia rigescens*, *Geranium* 'Mavis Simpson', *Helianthemum* 'Ben Hope'

**H: 10 in.** (25 cm) **S: 24 in.** (60 cm)
❀ **Mid- to late summer**
Z4 pH6–8

## *Hedychium coccineum* 'Tara' ♔

This is a relatively hardy orange-flowered cultivar of the scarlet ginger lily, *H. coccineum*. It is a rhizomatous herbaceous perennial that can be grown in beds and borders, in a greenhouse or in large containers, and its foliage and flowers add an exotic ingredient to plantings. It may be used with other hot-colored plants, including tender species such as shrubby and sub-shrubby salvias, dahlias, phygelius, leonotis and cannas, as well as with hardier plants such as ligularias, crocosmias or kniphofias, and with bright annuals and bedding plants such as alonsoas, impatiens and larger tagetes. The flowers contrast effectively with the glaucous foliage of plants like *Nicotiana glauca* and hostas. They are also good with yellow-green foliage and flowers, including late-flowering euphorbias, cautleyas and later-flowering lilies. Deep orange *H. densiflorum* 'Assam Orange' is a good, clump-forming ginger lily.

**Perfect partners:** *Alonsoa warscewiczii*, *Canna* 'Striata', *Kniphofia caulescens*, *Leonotis leonurus*, *Phygelius* × *rectus* 'Moonraker', *Salvia coccinea* 'Lady in Red'

**H: 6½ ft. (2 m) S: 3 ft. (90 cm)**
❀ **Late summer to mid-autumn**
◊◊ ▢-■ **Z8 pH5.5–7.5**

The tropical-looking spikes of *Hedychium coccineum* 'Tara' are here set in a haze of seedheads of common fennel (*Foeniculum vulgare*), beneath the golden honey locust (*Gleditsia triacanthos* 'Sunburst').

The rich golden yellow, outward-facing flowers of *Helianthus decapetalus* 'Soleil d'Or', seen here with *Helenium* 'Mahogany', are borne on the upper half of an erect plant, allowing it to punctuate borders with bright highlight.

## *Helenium* 'Wyndley'

Sneezeweeds are invaluable late-flowering hardy herbaceous perennials, providing solid color in a range from yellow through orange to rusty red and mahogany. 'Wyndley' has yellow petals flushed and streaked orange, and makes a strong impact in hot schemes in mixed or herbaceous borders, especially with plants of more definite form, such as dahlias, crocosmias, cannas, tender shrubby salvias, hedychiums and late-flowering lilies. Other good partners include yellow-green foliage and flowers such as hostas and late-flowering euphorbias, bronze foliage, yellow-variegated grasses and annuals such as larger tagetes, alonsoas, rudbeckias, coreopsis and sunflowers. 'Blütentisch' ♔ is golden yellow flecked with brown; and mahogany-red 'Moerheim Beauty' ♔ flowers in early to midsummer.

**Perfect partners:** *Euphorbia sikkimensis*, *Hosta* 'August Moon', *Kniphofia* 'Wrexham Buttercup', *Miscanthus sinensis* 'Zebrinus', *Tagetes patula* 'Striped Marvel'

**H: 24 in. (60 cm) S: 18 in. (45 cm)**
❀ **Early to late summer**
◊◊ ▢-■ **Z4 pH5.5–7.5**

In this glowing combination for midsummer, the flowers of the sneezeweed *Helenium* 'Wyndley', with golden petals shaded warm orange around a mahogany disk, are just overtopped by the vermilion *Crocosmia* 'Lucifer'.

## *Helianthus decapetalus* 'Soleil d'Or'

An upright plant with fully double golden yellow flowers, this perennial sunflower is useful in a herbaceous or mixed border, especially where the intricacy of its flowers can be appreciated at fairly close range. It associates well with hot-colored flowers, including dahlias, kniphofias, crocosmias and later-flowering daylilies, and with yellow-green foliage, including that of shrubs such as golden elders. Effective contrasts can be made with glaucous foliage and with blue flowers such as *Ceanothus* × *delileanus* cultivars and with taller late-flowering salvias. Good companions include repeat-flowering Shrub roses in white, cream or soft yellow, larger grasses such as miscanthus cultivars, and other late-flowering daisies such as rudbeckias and heleniums. 'Loddon Gold' ♔ has more reflexed petals of a slightly paler yellow.

**Perfect partners:** *Canna* 'Striata', *Coronilla valentina* subsp. *glauca*, *Hemerocallis fulva* 'Flore Pleno', *Kniphofia rooperi*, *Rosa* Graham Thomas, *Sambucus nigra* 'Aurea'

**H: 5 ft. (1.5 m) S: 3 ft. (90 cm)**
❀ **Late summer to mid-autumn**
◊◊ ▢-■ **Z5 pH5–7.5**

## *Helianthus* 'Monarch' ♀

The semi-double golden yellow flowers of this tall herbaceous perennial sunflower make a strong statement in hot-colored schemes, such as those suggested for *Helianthus decapetalus* 'Soleil d'Or' (facing page). In addition, the yellowish brown disk at the center of each flower helps it to harmonize with tawny colored flowers, such as heleniums and some annual sunflowers, and with bronze-colored foliage, including purple smoke bush and bronze or purple cultivars of hazel and larger berberis. The quality of its blooms is so high that 'Monarch' was traditionally grown for exhibition, disbudding each stem to leave a solitary bloom, which then grew to 6 in. (15 cm) or more across. Its height can be reduced and its flowering delayed slightly by pinching out in late spring and early summer.

**Perfect partners:** *Berberis* × *ottawensis* f. *purpurea* 'Superba', *Corylus maxima* 'Purpurea', *Cotinus coggygria* 'Notcutt's Variety', *Helianthus* 'Pastiche'

**H: 6½ ft. (2 m) S: 3 ft. (90 cm)**
❀ **Early to mid-autumn**
■□ ▬▬▬▬ ◊◊ □-■ **Z5 pH5–7.5**

The golden yellow flowers of *Helianthus* 'Monarch' lose some impact from being upward facing, although their size and profusion compensate. Here, they make a fine show with the yellow-edged leaves of the dogwood *Cornus alba* 'Spaethii' and the vermilion hips of *Rosa* 'Geranium'.

The blue-green leaves of blue oat grass (*Helictotrichon sempervirens*) harmonize with the fleshy foliage of *Sedum spectabile* 'Rosenteller', while contrasting gently with its rich rose flowerheads in late summer and early autumn.

## *Helictotrichon sempervirens* ♀
### BLUE OAT GRASS

This tufted evergreen grass bears silvery blue-green leaves and spikes of flowers that mature to straw-yellow tinged with purple. Like other blue-green grasses such as *Elymus* species and *Festuca glauca* cultivars, it is a good plant for use toward the front of a border or in a gravel garden, especially if surrounded by shorter plants. It harmonizes particularly well with blue, white or pink flowers and silver or glaucous foliage, and contrasts well with yellow-green foliage or flowers. When the seedheads assume their straw tints, blue oat grass also looks good with apricot-colored flowers such as repeat-flowering roses, *Mimulus aurantiacus* (syn. *M. glutinosus*), verbenas and achilleas, or with *Stipa gigantea* and other grasses that have seedheads of a similar color. Plants benefit from being shorn almost to ground level in late winter.

**Perfect partners:** *Achillea* 'Walther Funcke', *Centranthus ruber* 'Albus', *Euphorbia polychroma* 'Major', *E. rigida*, *Geranium* 'Johnson's Blue', *G.* × *oxonianum* 'Wargrave Pink'

**H & S: 40 in. (1 m)** ❀ **Late spring to midsummer**
■□ ▬▬▬▬ ◊-◊◊ □-■ **Z4 pH6–8**

## *Heliopsis helianthoides* 'Patula'

This long-flowering daisy, with rich golden yellow blooms, semi-double and gently frilled, is an invaluable plant for hot borders, perhaps combined with other yellow or orange flowers such as ligularias or inulas, especially if their flamboyance is slightly soothed by plum or brown foliage – as in *Dahlia* 'Bishop of Llandaff' – and grasses like miscanthus or carex. It is also good in late herbaceous or mixed borders, especially on clay. 'Patula' can be mixed with perennials such as cannas, larger hypericums, later-flowering daylilies and kniphofias, late lilies in yellow or orange, heleniums and other daisies in warm colors. It works well with gold-variegated foliage and yellow-green foliage or flowers, and with blue or purplish blue, including echinops and *Buddleja davidii* cultivars. *H.h.* var. *scabra* 'Benzinggold' produces large golden single blooms into mid-autumn.

**Perfect partners:** *Ceanothus* × *delileanus* 'Gloire de Versailles', *Echinops bannaticus* 'Taplow Blue', *Hypericum forrestii*, *Rosa* 'Grace', *Rudbeckia laciniata* 'Herbstsonne'

**H: 3–4 ft. (90–120 cm)  S: 24 in. (60 cm)**
❀ **Early summer to early autumn**
⬤⬤ ☐-◼ **Z4 pH5–7.5**

In a partnership that will last from summer into autumn, the softly frilled, golden yellow, daisylike flowers of *Heliopsis helianthoides* 'Patula' mingle easily with the lavender-blue blooms of *Aster* × *frikartii* 'Mönch'.

In a semi-shady border, the profuse, apple-green, dark-rimmed flowers of stinking hellebore (*Helleborus foetidus*) contrast gently with the pale pink flowering currant *Ribes sanguineum* 'Carneum'.

## *Helleborus foetidus* ♔
STINKING HELLEBORE

With its handsome foliage and early apple-green flowers, stinking hellebore is an essential element of the winter garden. It is an evergreen perennial that is strictly herbaceous because it produces leafy stems in one season that bear flowers the next, before dying. It combines well with bergenias, evergreen heucheras, ground-covering ivies, *Euonymus fortunei* cultivars, fatshederas, sarcococcas and galax, and with early-flowering bulbs such as snowdrops, *Crocus tommasinianus* variants and winter aconites. Other early hellebores, such as *H. niger* variants, *H.* × *nigercors* and *H.* × *ericsmithii*, also make good companions. The most common of its variants is the Wester Fisk Group, in which the leaf stalks and especially the flower stems are flushed with rich deep red. However, this is a very variable group.

**Perfect partners:** *Cornus alba* 'Sibirica' p.88 **B**, × *Fatshedera lizei*, *Galanthus nivalis*, *Galax urceolata*, *Heuchera* 'Plum Pudding', *Iris unguicularis* p.301 **B**, *Mahonia aquifolium* 'Apollo', *Sarcococca hookeriana* var. *humilis*, *Tulipa* 'White Triumphator' p.403 **B**

**H & S: 18 in. (45 cm)** ❀ **Midwinter to mid-spring**
⬤⬤ ☐-◼ **Z6 pH5.5–8**

# *Helleborus* × *hybridus*
LENTEN ROSE

This name covers all the hybrid stemless hellebores, available in a huge variety of floral forms, markings and colors ranging from nearly black through deep wine-purple to crimson, pink and white, together with cream, soft yellow and yellow-green, often with dark blotches or spots. They are excellent plants for the front of a border or a woodland garden, and excel in small city gardens. They can be combined with much the same late winter and spring flowers as for *H. foetidus* (facing page), but their flowers often continue appearing later and so are also effective with small to medium-sized bulbs such as narcissi, scillas, smaller tulips, muscari and

erythroniums, as well as with primroses and polyanthus, brunneras, omphalodes and winter heaths. They also associate pleasingly with hepaticas, pachyphragmas, cardamines, corydalis and epimediums, and with the contrasting foliage of sedges and evergreen grasses and ferns. Other good partners include witch hazels, magnolias, mahonias, early cyclamens, anemones including wood anemones, pulmonarias, evergreen heucheras and smaller early-flowering rhododendrons. Named cultivars are becoming available, including rich deep purple 'Thanksgiving', which is in bloom on Thanksgiving Day.

**Perfect partners:** *Ajuga reptans* p.230 **A**, *Buxus sempervirens* 'Marginata' p.82 **A**, *Eranthis hyemalis*, *Erythronium* 'Pagoda',

**Left:** The pale green flowers of *Helleborus* × *hybridus* are enlivened by the bright yellow-green of Bowles golden grass (*Milium effusum* 'Aureum').

**Right:** This near-black selection from *Helleborus* × *hybridus* Ballard's Group would scarcely be visible from a distance but is fascinating at close range, especially when partnered by the distinctively marked snowdrop *Galanthus* 'Armine'.

**Below:** Recent hellebore breeding has resulted in strains with stronger yellow flowers that are more outward-facing, allowing the speckling at the center of the bloom to be seen. Here, a primrose *Helleborus* × *hybridus* is joined by *Narcissus* 'Tête-à-tête' and *Cyclamen hederifolium*.

*Magnolia* × *soulangeana* 'Alba', *Narcissus* 'February Silver', *Primula vulgaris* subsp. *sibthorpii*, *Rhododendron hippophaeoides* p.131 **A** ❏ p.304 **B**

**H: 18 in. (45 cm)  S: 24 in. (60 cm)**
❀ Midwinter to mid-spring

Z4  pH5–7.5

## *Hemerocallis fulva* 'Flore Pleno'

Daylilies are almost indestructible plants and are invaluable assets in any garden scheme, producing superlative single or double flowers – some deliciously scented – in a wide range of colors, from late spring to late summer depending on the cultivar. Although individual blooms are short-lived, a constant succession of buds ensures a long display of color. (The flowers are worth cutting while still in bud.) The leaves provide a useful shape and texture, punctuating expanses of dull, broad-leaved foliage and harmonizing with grasses and spiky irises. Plants are hardy and quickly multiply into fat clumps, and, although not always floriferous in colder regions, they flower profusely in warm sites.

'Flore Pleno' is a double cultivar with a long flowering season. The advantage of double flowers is that the individual florets last for two days, twice as long as those of most single cultivars. Whereas many modern varieties have ceded the classic daylily flower shape to a more rounded outline, congested in the center in the case of double flowers, 'Flore Pleno' retains the clear lilylike symmetry of six outer petals. Its color – soft orange with deeper red markings at the base, sometimes hidden by other petals – blends well with bronze foliage and flowers in hot colors, such as red, yellow or orange. Dahlias are particularly good companions – dark-leaved 'Bishop of Llandaff', for instance. Plants are best in the second rank of a border, where their bases will be hidden.

**Perfect partners:** *Cotinus coggygria* 'Notcutt's Variety', *Iris pallida*, *Kniphofia* 'Bees Sunset', *Lilium* African Queen Group p.372 **A**, *L.* 'Connecticut King' p.374 **B**, *Lobelia* × *speciosa* 'Cherry Ripe' p.307 **B**

**H: 30 in.** (75 cm) **S: 4 ft.** (1.2 m)
❀ **Mid- to late summer**

◊◊ ☐-■ **Z3 pH5–7.5**

In this hot-colored scheme, *Hemerocallis fulva* 'Flore Pleno' harmonizes with vermilion *Crocosmia* 'Lucifer', while the superlative lemon-yellow *Lilium* Citronella Group echoes the flower shape of the daylily. Adding a bronze foliage plant with more rounded leaves could be effective.

The rufous-red reverses to the outer petals of *Hemerocallis* 'Golden Chimes' unite this combination with the richly colored *Rosa* Lilli Marlene and the deep bronze foliage of *Heuchera villosa* 'Palace Purple'.

## *Hemerocallis* 'Golden Chimes' ♔

The daylily species *H. dumortieri* produces rich, deep yellow blooms, dark brownish or mahogany on the reverse, with buds of the same dark color. It has passed these qualities on to 'Golden Chimes', a dainty, long-flowering cultivar, with slender, grassy foliage, especially suitable for small gardens. The trumpet-shaped blooms, each lasting into a second day, are comparatively small, but they are borne in copious numbers in generously branching sprays. 'Corky' ♔ has paler, lemon-yellow flowers. Plants belong in the second rank of a border, together with hot colors and bronze foliage, and also cream flowers. Purple or blue flowers are best avoided. Bronze-leaved heucheras with coral-red or scarlet flowers are superb companions.

**Perfect partners:** *Canna* 'Wyoming', *Dahlia* 'Moonfire', *Fuchsia* 'Thalia', *Phygelius aequalis* 'Yellow Trumpet', *Rosa* Westerland, *Sisyrinchium striatum* 'Aunt May'

**H: 36 in.** (90 cm) **S: 24 in.** (60 cm)
❀ **Early to late summer**

◊◊ ☐-■ **Z4 pH5–7.5**

The elegant, starry flowers of *Hemerocallis* 'Hyperion' seem to leap forward when set against a contrasting background of recessive, soft lavender *Clematis* 'Perle d'Azur'.

## *Hemerocallis* 'Hyperion'

This well-loved hybrid is one of the oldest still in existence. It retains its popularity because of its fresh coloring – a clear, sharp yellow without a trace of orange – but it is its bold and elegant flower shape that makes it so useful. The flowers are held well above the slim, grassy foliage, making this a good plant for the middle ranks of a border where it can mix with tall neighbors more successfully than other daylily cultivars. 'Hyperion' goes well with all kinds of blue, even shades with a hint of lavender. The flowers are especially effective grown among those of a contrasting shape – roses, for example, particularly a very pale yellow such as Windrush ('Ausrush'), or with orange, peach, apricot and red. Similarly colored 'Marion Vaughn' ♀ is very fragrant and flowers well into late summer.

**Perfect partners:** *Agapanthus* 'Lilliput', *Aralia elata* 'Aureovariegata', *Clematis* 'Prince Charles', *Helictotrichon sempervirens*, *Kniphofia* 'David', *Miscanthus sinensis* 'Zebrinus', *Phormium* 'Duet', *Rosa* Benjamin Britten, *R.* Grace, *Yucca flaccida* 'Golden Sword'

**H: 36 in.** (90 cm)  **S: 30 in.** (75 cm)  ❊ **Midsummer**
 ◌◌ ▢-◼ **Z5  pH5–7.5**

## *Hemerocallis* red-flowered cultivars

Red cultivars are a favorite choice for the second or third rank of red borders, and they mix well with dark blue, yellow and cream (but not white, which can be too harsh), together with bronze foliage. They are generally very hardy, but the blooms of many are easily blemished in cold or wet weather. Evergreen red cultivars are particularly sensitive to the cold, although a few such as rich scarlet 'Amadeus' are markedly more weatherproof. Some of the oldest are among the best, including 'Cherry Cheeks', cherry-red with a prominent white midrib on each petal; 'Stafford' in a rich opulent shade with contrasting midribs; and 'Sammy Russell', with smaller starlike tile-red blooms.

**Perfect partners:** *Artemisia ludoviciana*, *Corylus maxima* 'Purpurea', *Deschampsia cespitosa*, *Heuchera villosa* 'Palace Purple', *Kniphofia* 'Wrexham Buttercup', *Ligularia dentata* 'Desdemona' p 306 **A**

**H: 6–48 in.** (15–120 cm)  **S: 12–36 in.** (30–90 cm)
❊ **Midsummer**
◌◌ ▢-◼ **Z5  pH5–7.5**

**Above:** In a relatively steeply banked border, tall stems of *Achillea filipendulina* 'Gold Plate' provide a contrast of floral and foliage form with the rich red *Hemerocallis* 'Stafford'. They are backed by purple smoke bush (*Cotinus coggygria* 'Royal Purple'), whose foliage harmonizes perfectly with the daylily.

**Below:** *Hemerocallis* 'Sammy Russell' is here combined with *Achillea* 'Coronation Gold', showing the effective use of the achillea's grayish, feathery leaves and flat flowerheads as a contrast for the gently flared blooms of the daylily. Cardoons (*Cynara cardunculus*) provide bold, architectural foliage behind.

A

## *Heuchera villosa* 'Palace Purple'

In its best selections, chosen for outstanding leaf color, this popular heuchera is a handsome plant with metallic, deep coppery bronze foliage. There are numerous inferior seedlings, less richly colored than 'Palace Purple', but *H. v.* Bressingham Bronze ('Absi') is particularly fine, with shiny, almost black leaves that provide reliable foliage cover. It is an excellent choice where dramatic dark foliage is needed, perhaps for contrast with lighter leaves or flowers. Both plants enjoy a position in sun or partial shade (although full sun produces the most opulent coloring), and both can be grown in the front of a border, in a lightly shaded woodland garden or as ground cover.

These plants associate well with late spring bedding, providing a foil for lighter or brighter bulbs and biennials, including late-flowering narcissi, tulips, hyacinths, wallflowers, epimediums and erythroniums, combining with both cool-colored flowers and those in warmer shades such as burnt orange, apricot and peach. White or cream flowers and white-variegated leaves create dramatic contrasts. Other attractive companions include low-growing plants such as cranesbills, bergenias, shorter ferns and sedges, and hostas. Exciting contrasts can be made with silver-leaved plants or yellow-green foliage and flowers.

The tiny heuchera flowers are borne in airy sprays, but their brownish buff color is neither showy nor effective. If they are thought to detract from the impact of the foliage, the stems can be removed as they start to develop. Plants can be left for three to four years before division is necessary. This should be done in early autumn.

**Perfect partners:** *Achillea* 'Lachsschönheit' p.227 **B**, *Aralia elata* 'Aureovariegata', *Echinacea purpurea* p.261 **B**, *Hemerocallis* 'Golden Chimes' p.286 **B**, *Pelargonium* 'Paul Crampel' p.442 **A**, *Rosa* Sweet Dream p.217 **B**

**H: 20 in.** (50 cm) **S: 18 in.** (45 cm)
✿ Late spring to early summer
◌◌ ☐-■ ■ Z4 pH5.5–7.5

At its best, the foliage of *Heuchera villosa* 'Palace Purple' is glistening and sumptuously dark and, as here, makes a fine contrast with the yellow-green leaves of *Geranium* 'Ann Folkard'. Sprawling *G.* × *riversleaianum* 'Russell Prichard' furnishes in front, its flowers a touch paler than those of 'Ann Folkard' but in perfect harmony.

The extraordinarily rich foliage color of *Heuchera* 'Plum Pudding' makes it suitable for opulent schemes with other dark foliage and flowers intended to be seen at close range. Here, its companions are *Tulipa* 'Queen of Night' and the wallflower *Erysimum cheiri* 'Purple Queen'.

## *Heuchera* 'Plum Pudding'

The leaves of this neat heuchera are distinctly lobed, and have a strong purple overlay to their metallic silver flush, making them a superb choice for rich color schemes with purple, magenta, carmine, crimson, pink or mauve flowers. The foliage is at its most colorful from late spring to early summer as the new leaves expand, and it is then very attractive with tulips, wallflowers, polyanthus and primroses, both in spring bedding schemes and as an edging plant. The flower spikes are best removed as they develop, to encourage the production of good foliage. Plants benefit from division every three years.

**Perfect partners:** *Crocus goulimyi* p.358 **B**, *Erysimum* 'Bowles Mauve', *Gaura lindheimeri* 'Siskiyou Pink', *Primula* 'Tawny Port', *P.* 'Wanda', *Tulipa* 'Red Shine'

**H: 16 in. (40 cm) S: 12 in. (30 cm)**
❀ **Late spring to late summer**
▭▬▬ ◊◊ ▭-▪ ▪ **Z4 pH5.5–7.5**

## *Heuchera* 'Rachel'

This compact heuchera is widely regarded as a recent improvement on *H. micrantha* var. *diversifolia* 'Palace Purple' (facing page). Its rounded, maplelike leaves are rich copper-bronze, with a gleaming metallic finish between the veins and fine rosy-purple undersides. Small coral-pink flowers are borne in tall airy sprays, with some repeat flowering after the first flush. It is useful for the front of a border and for edging, and is particularly good with flowers in coral, peach or apricot, and with red-flushed or dark purple foliage. It is excellent beneath roses, especially those with small, soft-colored flowers and dark foliage.

**Perfect partners:** *Allium cristophii*, *Festuca glauca* 'Elijah Blue', *Geranium* × *riversleaianum* 'Russell Prichard', *Rosa* Pink Bells, *Stachys byzantina*, *Tulipa* 'Burgundy'

**H: 12 in. (30 cm) S: 18–24 in. (45–60 cm)**
❀ **Early to late summer**
▭▬▬ ◊◊ ▭-▪ ▪ **Z4 pH5.5–7.5**

The warm yet not too strongly colored leaves of *Heuchera* 'Rachel' work well with cool flowers such as this white musk mallow (*Malva moschata* f. *alba*). Warm "fruity" colors of high summer also make effective partners for this heuchera.

In a lightly shaded bed in late spring, the dainty, starlike pink flowers of × *Heucherella alba* 'Rosalie' harmonize with the much larger blooms of the strikingly variegated red campion *Silene dioica* 'Clifford Moor'. Bigger groups of each, planted farther apart so that they remain more distinct, would allow the attractive foliage and blooms of both to be more clearly seen and make the harmony between them even more apparent.

## × *Heucherella alba* 'Rosalie'

This hybrid between a heuchera and a tiarella is grown mainly for its flowers, which appear as a froth of pale pink spikes – well suited to subdued schemes or as a foil for showier flowers. It needs reasonably good light to flower profusely, but will thrive satisfactorily in lightly shaded woodland, perhaps growing beneath pink or white azaleas. It is good for the front of a border or for ground cover, and combines prettily with columbines, smaller violas and *Primula sieboldii* cultivars. Its

cultivation needs are the same as those of *Heuchera villosa* 'Palace Purple' (facing page), except that it requires dividing every two to three years in autumn.

**Perfect partners:** *Aquilegia vulgaris* (mixed), *Dicentra spectabilis*, *Geum rivale* 'Leonard's Variety', *Rhododendron* 'Palestrina', *Rosa glauca*, *Stachys byzantina* 'Silver Carpet'

**H: 16 in. (40 cm) S: 12–18 in. (30–45 cm)**
❀ **Late spring to midsummer**
▭▬▬ ◊◊ ▭-▪ ▪ **Z4 pH5.5–7.5**

# Hostas

HOSTAS, OR PLANTAIN LILIES, are immensely popular plants for shade, and several thousand new varieties have been developed in the last few decades. They are useful especially for their tiny or exotically large foliage, which can be green, glaucous or yellow-green, often variegated with white or yellow. Most also flower prolifically, the beauty of the blooms sometimes rivaling that of the leaves. Some hostas, such as *H. plantaginea* and its hybrids, have the added bonus of fragrant flowers.

All hostas grow well in partial shade and some even in full shade; some can take full sun, although variegated or yellow-green kinds can become scorched, except in areas with the coolest summers. Hostas are superlative plants for a woodland garden, and are also excellent for beds and borders, but they can look unnaturally exotic in a wild garden. Particularly associated with Japanese gardens, they look at home with other Japanese plants with contrasting foliage, including bamboos, smaller maples, moisture-loving irises, primulas, sedges, ferns and hydrangeas. Hostas work well when underplanted with late winter or spring bulbs, wood anemones or celandines – as the bulbs enter their summer dormancy, the hosta's leaves unfurl to hide their dying foliage. They are also excellent in containers, where they are perhaps most effective planted alone, with harmonies or contrasts provided by different subjects in adjacent pots.

In small gardens, the biggest sorts such as *H. sieboldiana* and its hybrids tend to be too large for general use or ground cover, although they are useful as strong accents, repeated if necessary at intervals along a border. Similarly, variegated or yellow-green cultivars can be rather strident if used to excess, although they too make effective accents; green- or glaucous-leaved hostas are perhaps the best for extensive plantings such as ground cover. The tiniest

A

This planting mainly of hostas, including (clockwise from right) the cream-edged *H. fortunei* 'Spinners', bright blue-gray *H.* (Tardiana Group) 'Halcyon', yellow-green variegated *H. sieboldiana* 'Frances Williams', and the large, deeply puckered *H.s.* var. *elegans*, is saved from monotony by the addition of the contrastingly smaller leaves and flowers of cranesbills, including *Geranium* × *oxonianum*.

species and cultivars are well suited to small-scale schemes and to groupings that are to be viewed at close range.

Some, especially the largest-leaved sorts, can take up to five years to adopt their full size and characteristic habit. Conversely, if left many years without division, the leaves can become congested and reduced in size, obscuring the shape of individual leaves. Tiny species such as *H. venusta* ♀, often dismissed for use as ground cover because so many plants are needed for a reasonably sized group, can be propagated by division up to three times a year, even in full growth, provided the offsets are kept moist. In fact, the neat, dark green leaves and entrancing flowers of this species make it exceptionally beautiful for large drifts of ground cover. This

method also works for suckering cultivars such as 'Ginko Craig'. With slow-growing cultivars the quickest means of propagation is to cut the central bud from a healthy crown and divide the remaining base plate with its octopus of roots vertically into three.

Slugs and snails can ruin the effect of hostas, particularly those with delicate, thin leaves. They should be controlled, especially when their populations start to increase in late winter and spring.

## *Hosta* 'August Moon'

Grown for its large yellow-green leaves and pale lavender, nearly white flowers, this is one of the most sun-tolerant yellow-green hostas, its fine color appearing less striking when plants are grown in shade. 'August Moon' is bold enough for a large garden or for use as a strong accent in a medium-sized or small site. It makes good harmonies with gold or white flowers, and contrasts strikingly with blue or purple, or with foliage that differs markedly in color (purple, glaucous and bronze) or form (grasses, sedges and ferns). Japanese maples, berberis and other smaller shrubs are an excellent background for this hosta. Other yellow-green cultivars of similar size include 'Birchwood Parky's Gold', with lavender flowers and slightly smaller, heart-shaped, wavy-edged leaves, and 'Gold Edger', with thicker, more slug-resistant leaves. 'Aspen Gold', 36 in. (90 cm) wide, has rounded, cupped, puckered leaves; *H. tokudama* 'Golden Medallion', similarly cupped and crimped, makes a slightly taller, less broad mound of foliage; while 'Golden Prayers' is smaller, with thick leaves.

**Perfect partners:** *Acer palmatum* f. *atropurpureum*, *Berberis thunbergii* f. *atropurpurea*, *Carex oshimensis* 'Evergold', *Gentiana asclepiadea*, *Hakonechloa macra* 'Alboaurea', *Hosta sieboldiana* var. *elegans*, *Matteuccia struthiopteris*, *Primula japonica* 'Postford White'

**H: 28 in. (70 cm)  S: 30 in. (75 cm)** ❀ **Midsummer**
○○-○○○ ■-■ **Z3 pH5–7.5**

Although even a wispy clematis planted among hostas could obscure the pattern of their handsome rosettes of leaves, the occasional trailing stem wandering from an adjacent wall or supporting shrub can create a charming incident. Here, *Clematis* 'Etoile Violette' contrasts with the bright foliage of *Hosta* 'August Moon'.

In this dramatic grouping, handsome foliage, some of it glaucous or yellow-green, is contrasted with the salmon-pink flowers of the Hybrid Musk rose *R.* 'Cornelia' and *Rodgersia pinnata* 'Maurice Mason'. The striking blue-green *Hosta* 'Buckshaw Blue' contrasts with Bowles golden sedge (*Carex elata* 'Aurea'), while the spurge *Euphorbia palustris* fills the space beneath the rose.

## *Hosta* 'Buckshaw Blue'

Pale lilac-colored flowers and strongly blue-green leaves that are ribbed and puckered produce a bold shape toward the front of a border. It combines well with other glaucous or silver foliage and with pink, lilac or white flowers, and stands out against yellow-green foliage or flowers and leaves of contrasting shape, such as those of grasses, astilbes or ferns. It is an excellent choice for a woodland garden, especially with blue flowers, although it leafs too late to be combined effectively with late spring flowers such as omphalodes or forget-me-nots. It goes well with old roses, and the bronze or purple leaves of Japanese maples, berberis, and similar smaller shrubs.

**Perfect partners:** *Acer palmatum* 'Bloodgood', *Astilbe chinensis* var. *taquetii* 'Superba', *Euphorbia schillingii*, *Festuca glauca* 'Elijah Blue', *Meconopsis betonicifolia*, *Milium effusum* 'Aureum', *Rodgersia pinnata* 'Superba', *Rosa* 'Reine des Centifeuilles'

**H: 14 in. (35 cm)  S: 24 in. (60 cm)** ❀ **Midsummer**
○○-○○○ ■-■ **Z3 pH5–7.5**

## *Hosta fortunei*

One of the great benefits of this pale lilac-flowered hosta is that its leaves appear early enough to be combined with late spring flowers, unfolding while wood anemones and celandines are still in bloom, and going well with azaleas, bluebells, forget-me-nots, brunneras, epimediums and meconopsis.

The species itself is rarely seen compared to its many variants. One of the most common of these is var. *albopicta* ♀, with young leaves that emerge with green edges and a pale yellow center, darkening to green in summer. Its foliage is useful where an emphatic plant of moderate size is needed. Another good choice is var. *albopicta* f. *aurea* ♀, which emerges brilliant light yellow-green, making dramatic combinations with blue spring flowers and striking contrasts with dark ground cover such as purple bugles. One of the most floriferous variants is var. *hyacinthina* ♀, with lilac blooms and glaucous leaves with a narrow silvery edge. Its sports include 'Gold Standard', with yellow, green-edged leaves, the centers aging to cream and so remaining brightly variegated in summer. 'Crowned Imperial' has white-edged leaves, while 'Aoki' has very puckered, less glaucous leaves and mauve flowers. The leaves of 'Albomarginata', white-edged and often quite narrow, are suitable where a less emphatic note is needed, while 'Antioch' has even longer, more pointed leaves, with a broader cream margin fading to white. 'Francee' is another white-variegated sport with bold, white-edged leaves emerging later than most *H. fortunei* variants; it is among the best of the white hostas and makes a good specimen plant for pots or containers. With leaves narrowly edged in yellow, var. *aureomarginata* ♀ (syn. 'Obscura Marginata') is useful where more subtle variegation is needed, such as in a woodland garden.

**Perfect partners:** *Acer palmatum* Dissectum Atropurpureum Group, *Anemone nemorosa* 'Leeds' Variety', *Brunnera macrophylla*, *Chelidonium majus*, *Dryopteris erythrosora*, *Epimedium* × *versicolor*, *Geranium* × *oxonianum*, *Hyacinthoides non-scripta*, *Myosotis sylvatica*, *Omphalodes cappadocica*, *Primula* 'Rowallane Rose' p.326 **B**, *Ranunculus ficaria* 'Brazen Hussy', *Rehmannia elata*, *Rhododendron* 'Blue Peter' p.129 **C**, *R. luteum*, *Viburnum plicatum* 'Mariesii'

H & S: 24–36 in. (60–90 cm)  ❀ Midsummer
◊◊-◊◊◊  ■-■ Z3 pH5–7.5

**Top:** The white margins of *Hosta fortunei* 'Albomarginata' strikingly accentuate each rosette of leaves among a carpet of woodland plants – *Viola sororia* 'Freckles' and the dainty white *Epimedium* × *youngianum* 'Niveum'.

**Above:** Brightly white-variegated *Hosta fortunei* 'Francee' nestles against leaves that contrast in color and form. The pale deadnettle *Lamium maculatum* 'Beacon Silver' furnishes in front, while the attractively lobed leaves of *Kirengeshoma palmata* provide pleasingly different foliage to the left.

**Left:** Newly emerging *Hosta fortunei* var. *albopicta* f. *aurea*, placed where it is lit by the sun, is given yet more prominence by being set among a contrasting carpet of bluebells (*Hyacinthoides non-scripta*), whose recessive tints make the hosta seem even brighter.

**Opposite:** Hostas are useful for furnishing beneath the spreading branches of their compatriots, the Japanese maples. Here, *Hosta fortunei* var. *hyacinthina* and *H.f.* var. *aureomarginata*, edged in creamy yellow, cover the ground beneath *Acer palmatum* Dissectum Atropurpureum Group, which is echoed in hue by *Plantago major* 'Rubrifolia'.

The yellow-green, brightly gold-tipped leaves of *Hosta* 'Hydon Sunset' contrast with the soft lavender, red-eyed flowers of another inhabitant of deciduous woodland, *Phlox divaricata* subsp. *laphamii* 'Chattahoochee'. Both need relative freedom from slugs and snails if they are to succeed.

## Hosta 'Hydon Sunset'

The foliage of this small hosta – probably a derivation from *H. nakaiana* – emerges brilliant yellow-green, but darkens to green. Its diminutive leaves, perfectly to scale with smaller gardens and intimate planting schemes, combine well with plants intended for late spring and early summer impact. The foliage needs shade for best results, as in a woodland garden, for example, where the plant looks good with corydalis, small ferns such as maidenhairs, smaller tiarellas and bugles. A similar but rather smaller hosta,

confusingly called just 'Sunset', has leaves of paler gold, a color that is maintained throughout summer and into autumn.

**Perfect partners:** *Adiantum aleuticum* 'Japonicum', *Ajuga reptans* 'Atropurpurea', *Asplenium scolopendrium* 'Kaye's Lacerated', *Corydalis flexuosa* 'China Blue', *Heuchera villosa* 'Palace Purple', *Pulmonaria saccharata*, *Tiarella wherryi* 'Bronze Beauty'

**H: 14 in. (35 cm) S: 8 in. (20 cm)** ❁ **Midsummer**
◊◊-◊◊◊ ■-■ **Z3 pH5–7.5**

## Hosta 'Shade Fanfare' ♛

This large-leaved hosta has bright yellow-green foliage, edged with creamy white, and turning white with age; lavender-colored flowers are borne in summer. It needs to be grown in shade, but it is such a brilliantly colored cultivar that, unlike 'Hydon Sunset' (above), it may look out of place in a woodland garden. Instead, it can be used as a bold focal point in a shady border, or as the focus of a group of containerized plants. It associates best with blue, white or yellow flowers, including companions such as cranesbills and forget-me-nots, as well as with ferns. Against a background of dark foliage, plants make a particularly striking impact.

**Perfect partners:** *Dryopteris affinis*, *Fatsia japonica*, *Geranium* 'Johnson's Blue', *Hedera algeriensis* 'Ravensholst', *Hydrangea macrophylla* 'Mariesii Perfecta', *Lobelia siphilitica*, *Myosotis sylvatica*, *Primula florindae*, *Schizophragma hydrangeoides*

**H: 20 in. (50 cm) S: 18 in. (45 cm)** ❁ **Midsummer**
◊◊-◊◊◊ ■-■ **Z3 pH5–7.5**

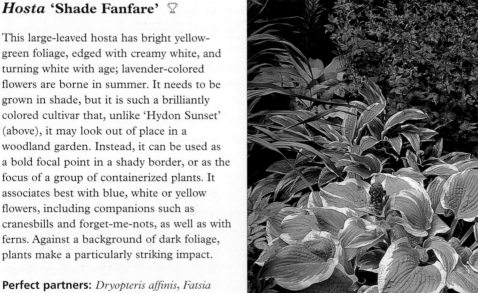

Three harmonious hostas – (from front to back) the white and creamy yellow variegated 'Shade Fanfare', gold-edged 'Yellow Splash' and yellow-green 'Sun Power' – provide a contrast with the rich mauve flowers of the cranesbill *Geranium nodosum*. Placing 'Shade Fanfare', the largest and boldest of the three, at the back might help to draw the eye into the grouping.

*Hosta sieboldiana* var. *elegans* is a large and splendid hosta, capable almost of matching in magnificence the *Gunnera manicata* towering above it in this waterside planting. In front, the variegated yellow flag (*Iris pseudacorus* 'Variegata') provides a vertical accent, while *Primula vialii* adds a bold focus of color, with rich mauve flowers emerging from startlingly contrasting scarlet calyces.

## Hosta sieboldiana var. elegans ♛

This large hosta, with conspicuously veined and puckered glaucous foliage and lilac-colored blooms, tolerates full sun in areas with cool summers. Its size suits the second rank of a border, in large-scale plantings and combinations with bold, even tropically lush plants. It is very successful with blue, purple, white, yellow or yellow-green, and combines with *Iris sibirica* cultivars, Japanese maples, larger ferns and larger grasses. 'Big Daddy' has cupped, rounded, very veined, crinkled leaves; 'Big Mama', smoother, less glaucous leaves; 'Blue Angel' ♛, nearly white flowers; and 'Blue Seer' is narrower leaved.

**Perfect partners:** *Acer shirasawanum* 'Aureum', *Euphorbia schillingii*, *Iris sibirica* 'Harpswell Happiness', *Lilium leichtlinii* var. *maximowiczii* p.376 **B**, *Miscanthus sinensis* 'Zebrinus', *Philadelphus coronarius* 'Aureus', *Pleioblastus viridistriatus*, *Rosa glauca*

**H: 40 in. (1 m) S: 4 ft. (1.2 m)**
❁ **Mid- to late summer**
◊◊-◊◊◊ ■-■ **Z3 pH5–7.5**

Big and bold *Hosta* 'Sum and Substance' is furnished to the ground with leaves and so can be used at the very front of steeply banked borders. Here, the vigorous, tall cranesbill *Geranium* × *oxonianum* 'Claridge Druce' leavens the hosta's solidity with contrastingly small foliage and flowers.

## *Hosta* 'Sum and Substance' ♛

This very large hosta is perhaps the most sun-tolerant of the yellow-green kinds, with thick leaves that are relatively unpalatable to slugs and snails. Except in areas with particularly hot summers, a position in full sun is beneficial, producing a brighter, richer yellow coloring that combines well with purple, blue, yellow or white flowers, and with glaucous foliage. It is impressive both in large pots and in partnership with the largest, most exotic kinds of foliage plant, such as large grasses and ferns, bamboos, herbaceous aralias, cannas, sumachs and stooled catalpas. As with other very large-leaved cultivars, such as glaucous gray-green 'Snowden', profuse watering is essential in dry weather.

**Perfect partners:** *Ailanthus altissima* (stooled), *Aruncus dioicus, Gunnera manicata, Hosta sieboldiana* var. *elegans, Lysimachia punctata, Miscanthus sacchariflorus, Paulownia tomentosa* (stooled), *Phyllostachys nigra*

H: 30 in. (75 cm)  S: 4 ft. (1.2 m)
❀ Early to midsummer

 ◊◊ ▨-■ Z3 pH5–7.5

## *Hosta* (Tardiana Group) 'Halcyon' ♛

Most Tardiana Group hostas combine the glaucous foliage of one parent, *H. sieboldiana* var. *elegans*, with the prolific flowers and neat, relatively small leaves of the other, the late-flowering *H. tardiflora*. The majority are glaucous-leaved, although a few have yellow-green or variegated foliage. The leaves of 'Halcyon' – intensely blue-green when grown in shade, more gray-green in full sun – are lance-shaped when young, becoming broader with age. It is ideal for a woodland garden or the front of a border, and is very effective with blue, purple, yellow or white flowers; it makes good contrasts with yellow-green foliage and flowers, and with feathery, grassy, or pinnate foliage. As an edging with roses, it is the right height to mask the base of bushes.

**Perfect partners:** *Aralia racemosa, Astilbe* 'Red Sentinel', *Campanula* 'Kent Belle', *Choisya ternata* Sundance, *Gentiana asclepiadea, Lysimachia clethroides, Rosa* 'Frensham'

H: 24 in. (60 cm)  S: 40 in. (1 m)
❀ Early to late autumn

◊◊ ▨-■ Z5 pH5–7.5

The broad, glaucous foliage of *Hosta* (Tardiana Group) 'Halcyon' makes a fine contrast with the feathery mid-green fronds of common fennel (*Foeniculum vulgare*). It would be possible to use this combination on a larger scale, planting mature clumps of the hosta, irregularly spaced, with larger plants of the fennel in the gaps, although the site must not be too shady for the sun-loving fennel. In this way, the characteristic rosettes of the hostas would give a pattern to the planting, while the fennel would form billowing mounds of soft green plumes between. The fennel would flower before its companion but would retain lacy seedheads overtopping the hosta as it came into bloom.

Rhizomatous anemones such as the wood anemone (*A. nemorosa* and its cultivars) flower at the same time as early-leafing hostas such as *Hosta undulata* var. *albomarginata* emerge, making them excellent and attractive companions, especially in a woodland garden.

## *Hosta undulata* var. *albomarginata*

Bright, white-edged leaves emerge light yellowish green in mid-spring, early enough to combine with celandines and wood anemones. Its coloring is highly effective with blue or yellow flowers such as brunneras, omphalodes, meconopsis, yellow epimediums and doronicums; it is also outstanding for underplanting yellow-flowered deciduous azaleas. Its spikes of flowers have purple, trumpet-shaped florets, while its leaves darken to rich green in summer. *H.u.* var. *univittata* ♛ has a central white stripe; var. *erromena* ♛ is all-green; and var. *undulata* ♛ has yellow-green streaks and a central area of white.

**Perfect partners:** *Epimedium* × *versicolor* 'Sulphureum', *Hydrangea macrophylla* 'Générale Vicomtesse de Vibraye' p.107 **A**, *Rhododendron* 'Kirin' p.131 **B**

H: 36 in. (90 cm)  S: 18 in. (45 cm)
❀ Early to midsummer

 ◊◊ ▨-■ Z3 pH5–7.5

# Irises

THE VERY DIVERSE genus *Iris* embraces several thousand immensely useful garden plants. Herbaceous and rhizomatous sorts are considered here; those that grow from corms are discussed under Bulbs (see pp.369–371). *I. ensata* ♀, *I. japonica* ♀, and their hybrids and cultivars enjoy moist conditions and are superlative plants for waterside planting. Cultivars of *I. ensata* have large, exotically marked flowers, showy from a distance but needing close-range inspection for their intricacy to be appreciated. *I. chrysographes* cultivars and the related *I. delavayi* ♀ tend to be taller with grassier leaves and flowers in sumptuously dark colors; they too benefit from moist or waterside conditions and close-range viewing, their dusky blooms being scarcely visible from a distance. The hundreds of cultivars and hybrids of *I. sibirica* ♀ are also excellent marginal plants, but can be grown in a border provided the soil does not dry out. They make a classic combination with late-flowering deciduous azaleas in situations that are neither too arid nor too shady.

Species such as the evergreen *I. unguicularis* ♀, a precious winter-flowering iris, are suited to dry, sun-baked spots. *I. foetidissima* ♀ is invaluable in dry shade, and has attractively glossy, dark evergreen foliage and brilliant vermilion seeds, displayed for several months after its pods split open in autumn. It will grow happily at the foot of a hedge where few other plants would survive.

The Californian Hybrids, derived from species such as *I. douglasiana* ♀, *I. innominata* and *I. chrysophylla*, make evergreen, fairly low-growing clumps of foliage with flowers in a range of colors, often attractively veined, usually in mid- to late spring but occasionally into summer.

Spuria irises, which are derived from species such as *I. crocea* ♀, *I. monnieri*, *I. orientalis* ♀ and *I. sanguinea* ♀, are the tallest and latest-flowering irises, making

**Above:** The Tall Bearded iris *I.* 'Kent Pride' is classed as a Plicata cultivar (having a pale ground edged with a darker color). Brown varieties such as this can be combined with bronze or purple foliage (here, *Heuchera* 'Rachel') and purple or warm-colored flowers.

**Left:** Tall Bearded irises such as *I.* 'Nightfall' can supply an accent among lower planting, as here with poached egg plant (*Limnanthes douglasii*) and dark-leaved heucheras.

narrow clumps with deciduous grassy foliage. Tolerating light shade, their habit suits them to planting in borders.

Perhaps the most valuable irises are the sun-loving Bearded cultivars, which vary in size from the Miniature Dwarf Bearded sorts at about 8 in. (20 cm) high to Tall Bearded kinds at 28 in. (70 cm) or more. As a rough rule, the shortest sorts flower earliest, in mid-spring, while the tallest

continue into early summer, their foliage providing a useful contrast for old roses.

Irises are propagated by division after flowering, with young, short sections of vigorous rhizome replanted at the surface (not buried). Care should be taken not to arrange them all facing the same way, so that they move inexorably in one direction, leaving bare rhizome behind. The base of the plants, particularly if they are used toward the front of a border, can look unattractive but can be masked by interplanting with a low carpeting plant such as an acaena, or with a later-flowering bulb such as *Allium flavum*. Some varieties are remontant, flowering reliably a second time in late summer.

At the front of a border in early summer, the deep purple-black flowers of *Iris chrysographes*, although recessive in color and hard to see from a distance, show distinctly against the much paler flowers of *Geranium* 'Johnson's Blue', and their upright stems provide a strong vertical accent.

## *Iris chrysographes* ♀

A waterside position is ideal for this moisture-loving species, which usually has deep ruby-red or dark purple flowers, although it also occurs in paler tones such as yellow and violet. Plants with purplish blooms look most effective with other mauve or lighter purple flowers, such as cranesbills and tradescantias (provided the ground is not too waterlogged), while the red variants work well with lythrum cultivars, monardas and late-flowering primulas. Related species that enjoy similar conditions include purple *I. delavayi* ♀, 5 ft. (1.5m) tall, and yellow *I. forrestii* ♀, 16 in. (40 cm), both flowering in midsummer.

**Perfect partners:** *Astilbe* 'Red Sentinel', *Lythrum virgatum* 'Dropmore Purple', *Monarda* 'Cambridge Scarlet', *Primula capitata*, *Tradescantia* (Andersoniana Group) 'Purple Dome'

H: 16–20 in. (40 50 cm)  S: 12 in. (30 cm)
❀ Early to midsummer
◊◊-◊◊◊ ☐-☐ Z4 pH5.5–7

The rich purple blooms of *Iris* 'Grapesicle' dominate the smaller but harmoniously colored flowers of honesty (*Lunaria annua*) and wood forget-me-nots (*Myosotis sylvatica*) in this late spring border, with the glaucous foliage of opium poppy (*Papaver somniferum*) behind.

## *Iris* 'Curlew'

This Intermediate Bearded iris blooms before the main flush of summer bloom, making it a particularly valuable source of color for combining with late wallflowers, columbines, species roses, euphorbias and early peonies. It is a superlative plant for the front of a border, where its soft yellow blooms blend well with cream, orange and yellow-green flowers, together with warm colors such as peach and apricot, and with yellow-green or bronze foliage, including bronze-flushed cultivars of *Euphorbia griffithii* and sedges. Blue is an effective contrast, with the exception of the strongest blues, which can dominate the soft coloring of the iris.

**Perfect partners:** *Aquilegia vulgaris* (blue or yellow), *Carex oshimensis* 'Evergold', *Euphorbia griffithii* 'Dixter', *E. polychroma* 'Major', *Heuchera villosa* 'Palace Purple', *Paeonia mlokosewitschii*, *Rosa* 'Helen Knight', *Valeriana phu* 'Aurea'

H: 18 in. (45 cm)  S: 16 in. (40 cm)
❀ Late spring to early summer
◊-◊◊ ☐-☐ Z4 pH5.5–8

In a bed of relatively low plants in late spring, *Iris* 'Curlew' stands above the golden orange Siberian wallflower (*Erysimum × marshallii*), with golden feverfew (*Tanacetum parthenium* 'Aureum') adding piquancy.

## *Iris* 'Grapesicle'

This Standard Dwarf Bearded iris blooms in mid- and late spring, coinciding with late spring bulbs and forget-me-nots. Its relatively small, rich plum-purple flowers are more graceful than those of some large-flowered modern cultivars. It is an elegant plant for gravel gardens or the front of borders, where it may be planted with smaller columbines, shorter perennial wallflowers and mauve flowers such as early cranesbills. It combines well with purple foliage, and may be contrasted with soft yellow – poached egg plant, for example – or with acid yellow-green foliage and flowers, such as euphorbias. *I. pumila atroviolacea* is darker purple.

**Perfect partners:** *Aquilegia canadensis*, *Erysimum* 'Wenlock Beauty', *Geranium tuberosum*, *Heuchera villosa* 'Palace Purple', *Ipheion uniflorum* 'Wisley Blue', *Limnanthes douglasii*, *Moricandia moricandioides*

H & S: 12 in. (30 cm)  ❀ Mid- to late spring
◊-◊◊ ☐-☐ Z4 pH5.5–8

## *Iris* 'Lavinia'

The gentle coloring and pretty markings of this Californian Hybrid go well with mauve or lilac, and with purple-flushed foliage; effective contrasts can also be made with rich deep purple. It works well at the front of a border, with ipheions, dicentras, columbines, moricandias, early cranesbills, prostrate rosemary and chives. All Californian Hybrids need sharply drained soil, dry at the surface but with adequate moisture beneath, and with that proviso they can be grown in a gravel garden. Derived originally from West Coast and Californian species, they are not very hardy and some need warm summers to flower well; in cooler regions, cultivars derived mainly from selections from Oregon or Washington State tend to flower better.

**Perfect partners:** *Allium schoenoprasum*, *Dicentra peregrina*, *Erodium trifolium*, *Geranium tuberosum*, *Heuchera* 'Plum Pudding', *Rosmarinus officinalis* Prostratus Group

**H & S: 16 in.** (40 cm)
✽ **Late spring to early summer**
◊◊ ■-■ Z7 pH5–7

In early summer, the maroon markings of *Iris* 'Lavinia' match those of *Erodium pelargoniiflorum*, while their flowers and foliage provide a contrast of size and form.

A

## *Iris* 'Nightfall'

B

A Tall Bearded iris, 'Nightfall' has light purple standard petals and deep purple, almost black falls. Its flowers retain some of the classic fleur-de-lis outline of older Tall Bearded cultivars, and associate happily with old roses and alliums such as *A. aflatunense* or *A. hollandicum* and its cultivars. It harmonizes with mauve, pink and crimson, and looks opulent planted beside pale yellow flowers such as achilleas, and with yellow-green foliage and flowers. Purple or silver foliage plants are effective partners, as are lupins, cranesbills, shorter delphiniums, peonies,

Two-toned *Iris* 'Nightfall' contrasts dramatically with the pale silvery leaves of *Artemisia ludoviciana*.

Mediterranean plants such as phlomis and santolinas and plants of more diffuse habit, such as variants of *Thalictrum aquilegiifolium*.

**Perfect partners:** *Cistus* × *argenteus* 'Silver Pink', *Delphinium* 'Mighty Atom', *Lupinus* 'Chandelier', *Paeonia lactiflora* 'Albert Crousse', *Rosa* 'Tuscany Superb'

**H: 30 in.** (75 cm) **S: 24 in.** (60 cm)
✽ **Late spring to early summer**
◊◊ ■-■ ■ Z4 pH5.5–8

## *Iris orientalis* ♀

This splendid Spuria iris has grassy foliage, which makes a good foil for old roses, and white and yellow flowers that work well with rich crimson, purple or blue. They harmonize with white and cream, soft colors such as peach and apricot, rich golden yellow and yellow-green, and with glaucous foliage such as that of larger hostas. Suitable companions include peonies, lupins and delphiniums, and medium-sized shrubs such as philadelphus, and rhododendrons. Like most Spuria irises, it tolerates all but very dry soil. 'Shelford Giant' ♀ is about twice as high as *I. orientalis*, with creamier flowers. Other choice Spuria irises are *I. spuria* itself, in various colors such as blue, white, violet or yellow; *I.* Monspur Group, which comprises blue and violet hybrids including 'Monspur Cambridge Blue'; *I.* 'Sunny Day' ♀, with rich yellow flowers; and 'Clarke Cosgrove' ♀, which is lilac with yellow on its falls. 'Lydia Jane' ♀ is yellow shading to cream, a coloring shared by the more substantial 'Sierra Nevada'.

**Perfect partners:** *Berberis thunbergii* 'Aurea', *Delphinium* 'Sabrina', *D.* 'Sungleam', *Hosta sieboldiana* var. *elegans*, *Lupinus* 'Polar Princess', *L.* 'Thundercloud', *Paeonia lactiflora* 'Instituteur Doriat', *Rhododendron* Blinklicht Group, *Rosa* 'Charles de Mills'

**H: 40 in.** (1 m) **S: 24 in.** (60 cm)
✽ **Late spring to early summer**
◊◊-◊◊◊ ■-■ Z4 pH5–7.5

**Opposite:** This combination is unified by the golden markings on the falls of *Iris orientalis* and traces of yellow, in the anthers of *Clematis* 'Sylvia Denny' and in the cream variegation of *Philadelphus coronarius* 'Variegatus'.

A

## Iris pallida

This is a Bearded iris which in the typical sub-species *I.p.* subsp. *pallida* ♀ has gray-green leaves and soft lavender-blue blooms. It is one of the best for general use, effective with cool colors or white flowers and with silver, gray or purple foliage, and a pleasing partner for early roses, lupins, delphiniums and Mediterranean plants such as phlomis, cistus or rosemary. The foliage of *I.p.* subsp. *cengialtii* ♀ is less gray, and its flowers violet-blue with slightly paler standard petals. *I.p.* 'Variegata' ♀ produces yellow-striped leaves that make a strong accent and contrast gently with its flowers; and 'Argentea Variegata' has white-striped leaves. Both supply bold accents towards the front of a border, and can be repeated at intervals to give a unifying theme.

**Perfect partners:** *Anemone apennina* p.352 **A**, *Cistus* × *skanbergii*, *Lupinus* 'Gallery White', *Phlomis fruticosa*, *Rosa* 'Maigold', *Rosmarinus officinalis* 'Aureus'

**H: 36 in. (90 cm) S: 24 in. (60 cm)**
❀ **Late spring to early summer**
◊-◊◊ ▪-▪ Z4 pH5.5–8

The boldly striped sword-like leaves of the Bearded iris *I. pallida* 'Variegata' supply strong form to this grouping with *Penstemon* 'Pink Endurance', whose diffuse flower spikes open after those of the iris have faded.

## Iris pseudacorus 'Variegata' ♀
### VARIEGATED YELLOW FLAG

Like *I. pseudacorus* itself, this is a moisture-loving plant which also thrives in ordinary border soil that is not too dry. Its leaves emerge boldly variegated with yellow, but become greener in summer; the flowers are yellow with brown markings. It makes a strong accent in waterside plantings, especially when grown through darker-leaved plants such as purple bugles or heucheras, and mixes well with warm or hot colors, yellow-green foliage and flowers, and white flowers. Good partners include Candelabra primulas, euphorbias, ligularias, calthas and *Trollius* cultivars. It makes an inspired contrast with meconopsis, and also with the markedly different foliage of ferns.

In late spring, *Iris pseudacorus* 'Variegata' contrasts effectively with purple bugle (*Ajuga reptans* 'Atropurpurea').

**Perfect partners:** *Caltha palustris* p.247 **A**, *Hosta sieboldiana* var. *elegans* p.294 **C**, *Hydrangea arborescens* p.106 **B**, *Lysichiton americanus* p.310 **A**, *Primula florindae*

**H: 4 ft. (1.2 m) S: 30 in. (75 cm)**
❀ **Early to midsummer**
◊◊-◊◊◊ ▪-▪ Z5 pH4–7.5

## Iris 'Rocket'

The profuse apricot-colored flowers of this Tall Bearded iris blend particularly well with warm colors such as peach, apricot, soft yellow or soft scarlet, and with bronze foliage and yellow-green foliage or flowers. Plants can be combined with early yellow roses, euphorbias, columbines in warm colors, geums and dark-leaved heucheras, as well as with shrubs such as brooms, helianthemums, halimiums, halimiocistus, phlomis and santolinas. 'Supreme Sultan' is butterscotch-yellow with crimson-brown falls; and 'Beyond' is creamy apricot-yellow.

**Perfect partners:** *Aquilegia chrysantha* 'Yellow Queen', *Berberis thunbergii* f. *atropurpurea*, *Cytisus* × *praecox* 'Warminster', *Helianthemum* 'Ben Hope'

**H: 30 in. (75 cm) S: 24 in. (60 cm)**
❀ **Late spring to early summer**
◊-◊◊ ▪-▪ Z4 pH5.5–8

In late spring, the warm amber tints of *Iris* 'Rocket' blend perfectly with a bicolored columbine (a hybrid of *Aquilegia canadensis*), while providing a contrast of floral form.

# *Iris sibirica* ♈
## SIBERIAN IRIS

This has rich purplish blue flowers, smaller and less showy than most cultivars, but still invaluable for waterside planting in wild gardens. Flowering profusely in sunny, moist sites, it tolerates light shade and soil that is not too dry. Its hybrids have flowers that are marked and veined at the top of their broad, nearly horizontal falls. Among the best are 'Cambridge' ♈, which is almost pure light blue; 'Oban' ♈, in rich blue edged with white; 'Dreaming Spires' ♈, with deep purple falls and mid lavender-blue standards; the reddish purple 'Ruffled Velvet' ♈; 'Shirley Pope' ♈, which is very dark purple with a white flash; 'Crème Chantilly' ♈, in pale cream fading to white; cream and yellow 'Harpswell Happiness' ♈; 'White Swirl' ♈, with dramatic flaring falls; and 'Wisley White' ♈, white with yellow markings. All look effective with deciduous azaleas, meconopsis, euphorbias, Candelabra primulas and larger ferns, as well as small to medium-sized shrubs such as philadelphus, variegated dogwoods, deutzias and silver-leaved willows. Other partners could include peonies and cranesbills.

**Perfect partners:** *Astilbe* 'Fanal', *Cornus alba* 'Sibirica Variegata', *Rhododendron* 'Narcissiflorum', *Rosa* 'Maigold' p.206 **A**, *Salix exigua, Trollius × cultorum* 'Canary Bird'

**H: 20–48 in. (50–120 cm)  S: 18 in. (45 cm)**
❀ **Early to midsummer**

 ◊◊-◊◊◊ ■-■ Z4 pH5–7.5

In early summer, the flowers of *Iris sibirica*, borne above its leaves, combine attractively with those of white sweet rocket (*Hesperis matronalis* var. *albiflora*).

# *Iris unguicularis* ♈
## ALGERIAN IRIS

An evergreen, winter-flowering iris from the Mediterranean, *I. unguicularis* has sweetly scented flowers in colors ranging from white through pale lilac to violet-blue. It is slightly tender and in cooler climates needs to be grown at the foot of a warm, sunny wall; it also prefers a soil fairly low in nutrients. It is suitable for combining with other winter-flowering plants such as snowdrops, *Cyclamen coum* variants, early crocuses and hellebores; the more richly colored forms also pair well with corylopsis. 'Alba' has white thin-petaled flowers that are rather poorly shaped, 'Mary Barnard' is rich violet and 'Walter Butt' has large pale lilac flowers. All are best propagated by dividing clumps in late summer.

**Perfect partners:** *Corylopsis pauciflora, Crocus chrysanthus* hybrids, *Galanthus nivalis, Helleborus × hybridus* (yellow), *Jasminum nudiflorum* p.172 **A**, *Lonicera × purpusii* ☐p.178 **A**

**H: 16 in. (40 cm)  S: 24 in. (60 cm)**
❀ **Late autumn to early spring**

■ ◊ □-■ Z8 pH6–7.5

A lilac-flowered variant of *Iris unguicularis* contrasts gently with the pale apple-green, maroon-lipped flowers of stinking hellebore (*Helleborus foetidus*) in late winter.

In early spring, the white of the snowdrop *Galanthus elwesii* var. *monostictus* leavens the rich lavender flowers of *Iris unguicularis* 'Mary Barnard', behind silvery cyclamen leaves.

A purple smoke bush (*Cotinus coggygria* 'Royal Purple') forms a harmonious background for the crimson pincushionlike flowerheads of *Knautia macedonica.*

## Knautia macedonica

This clump-forming herbaceous perennial has pincushion flowerheads usually of the deepest crimson, but in the wild it varies from crimson to pale pink or mauve, and these variants are sometimes available as "Melton pastels." It is good for the front of a border, where it will blend with other cool colors and can be used as a foil for flowers of a brighter red. It contrasts well with peach-colored flowers, including roses, and yellow-green or lime green flowers (but it can be overwhelmed by solid areas of yellow-green foliage), and also with glaucous or silver foliage, such as that of grasses and artemisias. Exceptionally pretty partnerships can be made with nicotianas, penstemons, eryngiums, daylilies, phlox, thalictrums and pinks, and with flowers of contrasting form, including pink gypsophilas, linarias and veronicas.

**Perfect partners:** *Achillea millefolium* 'Cerise Queen' p.227 **C**, *Allium sphaerocephalon* p.351 **C**, *Clematis* × *durandii* p.156 **C**, *Malva sylvestris* p.434 **B**, *Rosa* Bonica p.200 **A**

**H: 24 in. (60 cm)   S: 18 in. (45 cm)**
❀ Mid- to late summer
◊◊ ▨-■ Z5  pH5–7.5

## Kniphofia 'Atlanta'

A vigorous and hardy evergreen perennial, this red hot poker bears yellow flowers that open from orange-red buds, favouring combinations with bronze foliage or yellow, orange or scarlet flowers, and making a telling contrast with blue flowers or yellow-green foliage and flowers. Its spiky gray-green leaves look imposing at the front of a border, especially with glaucous foliage plants. It is effective with late spring and early summer bulbs such as earlier daylilies, Bearded irises, and early Shrub roses in yellow or other warm tints, and creates thrilling clashes with magenta species gladioli. Other good partners are anthericums, baptisias, alchemillas, and sea kale, as well as delicate woodland plants.

**Perfect partners:** *Camassia cusickii* 'Zwanenburg', *Gladiolus communis* subsp. *byzantinus*, *Hemerocallis* 'Golden Chimes', *Iris pallida* 'Variegata', *Rosa* 'Maigold'

**H: 4 ft. (1.2 m)   S: 24 in. (60 cm)**
❀ Late spring to early summer
◊◊ ▨-■ Z7  pH5.5–7.5

## Kniphofia 'David' ♔

This mid-season herbaceous perennial bears flowers that open soft yellow from coral-red buds, and slender green foliage that can be a little untidy and is therefore best hidden by other plants in front. The color of its flowers suggests much the same combinations as for 'Atlanta' (below left), but its later timing also allows associations with achilleas, phygelius, lilies, later roses including larger bush roses, and crocosmias. With its festive coloring, it is a good partner for annuals and bedding plants such as *Mimulus aurantiacus* and its variants, arctotis hybrids, verbascums, poppies, penstemons, calceolarias and larger French marigolds. Its spiky outline is a useful accent in a border and can add rhythm to a landscape of mainly round or branching flowers, such as rudbeckias or heliopsis.

**Perfect partners:** *Alonsoa warscewiczii*, *Arctotis* × *hybrida* 'Flame', *Papaver rhoeas* Angels' Choir Group, *Rosa* 'Chinatown', *Tagetes patula* 'Striped Marvel'

**H: 30 in. (75 cm)   S: 18 in. (45 cm)**
❀ Early to midsummer
◊◊ ▨-■ Z6  pH5.5–7.5

Groups of yellow and red *Kniphofia* 'Atlanta', repeated at intervals and contrasted with silvery evergreen *Brachyglottis* (Dunedin Group) 'Sunshine', provide rhythm and accent along this border in late spring, together with lavender catmints and the pink cranesbill *Geranium* × *oxonianum*.

In this early summer planting of warm-colored flowers at the foot of a sentinel Irish yew (*Taxus baccata* 'Fastigiata'), the flat flowerheads of *Achillea* 'Coronation Gold' contrast with the vertical pokers of *Kniphofia* 'David' and the yew, joined by the coral blooms of *Phygelius aequalis*.

# *Kniphofia* yellow cultivars

Red hot pokers with pure yellow flowers are remarkably versatile plants that can be used for fiery hot-colored schemes and equally effectively as brilliant highlights among softer blue or cream flowers. Many excellent cultivars are available, flowering at different times, so their contribution to color schemes can be extended over a long season.

*K.* 'Goldelse' flowers fairly early, and has grassy foliage and narrow spikes of golden yellow blooms that combine well with catmints, baptisias, cranesbills, campanulas, Tall Bearded irises and smaller delphiniums such as Belladonna Group cultivars, and they coincide with many shrub and bush roses in warm colors. It is also a good partner for shrubs such as halimiocistus, hypericums, lavenders and *Potentilla fruticosa* cultivars.

*K.* 'Wrexham Buttercup' is beefier and more substantial than 'Goldelse', with broader foliage and flowers that open yellow from yellow-green buds, and age to gold. It starts flowering with roses and delphiniums, but continues into the season of later summer bedding plants and tender perennials.

*K.* 'Sunningdale Yellow' ♀ is a pure yellow poker that remains in bloom longer than most other cultivars, coinciding with blue flowers such as cultivars of *Salvia farinacea* and *S. patens*, argyranthemums in white, cream or yellow, later-flowering cannas and bedding plants such as smaller-flowered zinnias.

All these kniphofias provide strong vertical accents in borders and they can make memorable statements among agapanthus, daylilies, smaller grasses such as hakonechloas and smaller *Miscanthus sinensis* cultivars, and blue-green grasses, including *Elymus* species, helictotrichons and larger fescues. Other good companions include glaucous-leaved hostas (together with yellow-green and gold-variegated hostas in areas with cool summers), later-flowering catmints including yellow-flowered species, achilleas, and nicotianas in white or green.

**Perfect partners:** Early cultivars: *Baptisia australis*, *Campanula latifolia* 'Gloaming', × *Halimiocistus wintonensis* 'Merrist Wood Cream', *Nepeta* 'Six Hills Giant'
**Later cultivars:** *Agapanthus* 'Loch Hope', *Canna* 'Striata', *Salvia* × *superba*

**H: 30–48 in.** (75–120 cm) **S: 18–30 in.** (45–75 cm)
✿ **Early summer to early autumn**
◊◊ ▨-▪ Z6 pH5.5–7.5

**Above:** In early summer, an imposing clump of *Kniphofia* 'Goldelse' rises from a carpet of white-flowered *Anthemis punctata* subsp. *cupaniana*, the kniphofias harmonizing with the golden centers of the daisies.

**Above:** Vertical accents of *Kniphofia* 'Sunningdale Yellow', backed by dusky *Rosa glauca*, echo the primrose blooms of *Anthemis tinctoria* 'Wargrave Variety', joined by golden feverfew (*Tanacetum parthenium* 'Aureum').

**Below:** The vertical pokers of *Kniphofia* 'Wrexham Buttercup' contrast with the horizontal layers of the variegated dogwood (*Cornus controversa* 'Variegata') and the flat plates of a creamy achillea.

A

**Above:** The dusky magenta blooms of the spotted deadnettle (*Lamium maculatum*) mingle and harmonize with the long-flowering cranesbill *Geranium* 'Johnson's Blue'.

**Below:** Mixing different sorts of spotted deadnettle (*Lamium maculatum*) introduces variety to a carpet of ground cover: here, the plain species is joined by *L.m.* 'Album' beneath a Lenten rose (*Helleborus* × *hybridus*). A silver-leaved deadnettle could also be used.

## Lamium maculatum
SPOTTED DEADNETTLE

This is a low-growing rhizomatous perennial, with flowers in dusky magenta, pink or white, and silver-marked leaves. Cultivars with almost entirely silver leaves, such as 'White Nancy' ♀ and pink-flowered 'Beacon Silver', tolerate shade and are useful for ground cover, effective with cool-colored flowers and white-variegated or darkest green foliage. They look good with heucheras, ivies, asarums, tiarellas, sedges, hostas and bugles. Gold-variegated 'Anne Greenaway' and Golden Anniversary ('Dellam') and yellow-green 'Aureum' mix well with hot-colored flowers, yellow-green or gold-variegated foliage and contrasting foliage, such as dicentras or early-leafing ferns.

**Perfect partners:** *Asarum europaeum*, *Colchicum autumnale* p.357 **B**, *Dicentra eximia*, *Hosta fortunei* 'Francee' p.292 **C**, *Saxifraga fortunei*, *Tiarella cordifolia*

**H: 6–12 in.** (15–30 cm)  **S: 36 in.** (90 cm)
✽ **Late spring to late summer**

 ◌◌ ▢-▮ ▮ **Z4  pH4.5–8**

B

C

By adding a shorter aster such as lilac *Aster turbinellus* in front of tall and narrow *Leucanthemella serotina*, a steep bank of autumn flowers can be created with blooms of matching form but contrasting size.

## Leucanthemella serotina ♀

This very erect rhizomatous herbaceous perennial is immensely useful for its late white daisylike flowerheads, each with a central yellowish green disk. Formerly *Chrysanthemum uliginosum*, it is as choice as any white chrysanthemum, its 3½ in. (8 cm) blooms lasting until the first frosts. It can be used in a wild garden, bog garden or at the back of a moist border, where it combines well with taller, late-flowering perennials such as boltonias and the tallest asters. Late flowering and berrying roses such as some of the Hybrid Musks and cultivars or hybrids of *R. moyesii* make good companions, as do autumn-coloring shrubs, including amelanchiers, sumachs, aronias, berberis, callicarpas, clethras and cotinus, together with enkianthus, linderas, deciduous azaleas and guelder roses. It is also attractive with taller eupatoriums, actaeas and late aconites.

**Perfect partners:** *Actaea simplex* (Atropurpurea Group) 'Brunette', *Amelanchier lamarckii*, *Aster novi-belgii* 'Sarah Ballard', *Euonymus alatus*, *Helianthus* 'Monarch'

**H: 6 ft.** (1.8 m)  **S: 3 ft.** (90 cm)
✽ **Early to late autumn**

 ◌◌-◌◌◌ ▢-▮ ▮ **Z5  pH4.5–7.5**

## Leucanthemum vulgare
OXEYE DAISY

This herbaceous perennial is admirably suited to a wild garden and for naturalizing in grass, competing successfully even with vigorously growing grass. In these wild situations it can be used with other fairly strong-growing perennials, such as some umbellifers (it can follow on from cow parsley, for example), meadow buttercups and other robust species of ranunculus, and other naturalized or wild flowers such as red or white campions and yarrows; it also combines well with heracleums, columbines, chaerophyllums, trollius and vigorous cranesbills. More refined forms suitable for including as part of a border scheme are 'Maistern' (May Star), which is 20 in. (50 cm) high and produces large early flowers, and 'Maikönigin' (May Queen), also very early and taller, at 28 in. (70 cm).

**Perfect partners:** *Anthriscus sylvestris, Aquilegia vulgaris, Chaerophyllum hirsutum* 'Roseum', *Geranium phaeum, Heracleum mantegazzianum, Ranunculus repens* var. *pleniflorus, Silene dioica, Trollius europaeus*

**H: 12–36 in. (30–90 cm)  S: 18–24 in. (45–60 cm)**
✿ **Late spring to early summer**
⬛⬜ ◊◊ ⬜-⬛ **Z3  pH4.5–7.5**

In grassland that is neither nutrient rich nor very impoverished, oxeye daisy (*Leucanthemum vulgare*) can be naturalized attractively with wild flowers liking similar regimes, such as meadow buttercup (*Ranunculus acris*).

## Leymus arenarius
LYME GRASS

This is a vigorous herbaceous rhizomatous grass (syn. *Elymus arenarius*) with vividly blue-gray leaves and stiff wheatlike flower spikes. It can be grown in a border or a gravel garden, but it is invasive and needs confining or siting away from less robust plants, ideally in fairly nutrient-poor, sharply drained soil. It contrasts well with yellow and mixes happily with other blue plants as well as sea kale, thrifts, horned poppies, eryngiums, pinks and other grasses. If restricted in a border, it can partner similar plants, together with other blue-flowered or glaucous-leaved plants and, for contrast, silver foliage or

Spreading clumps of *Leymus arenarius* are usually loose enough for slender plants of contrasting form and color, such as purple toadflax (*Linaria purpurea*), to be grown though their fringes, creating a pleasing mixture.

yellow flowers. Examples include artemisias, glaucous hebes, irises, ballotas, erigerons, anthemis, gypsophilas and yellow achilleas.

**Perfect partners:** *Achillea filipendulina* 'Gold Plate', *Anthemis tinctoria, Armeria pseudarmeria, Ballota pseudodictamnus, Glaucium corniculatum, Nepeta* 'Six Hills Giant' p.315 **C**

**H: 4 ft. (1.2 m)  S: 3 ft. (90 cm)**
✿ **(Midsummer to early autumn)**
 ◊-◊◊ ⬜-⬛ **Z4  pH5.5–7.5**

**Top:** In this combination of dark leaves and hot colors, bronze-green leaved *Ligularia dentata* 'Desdemona' is joined by the yellow spires of *L. stenocephala*, the flat heads of *Achillea filipendulina* 'Gold Plate' and a rich red daylily (*Hemerocallis* 'Stafford'), against a background of purple smoke bush (*Cotinus coggygria* 'Royal Purple').

**Above:** Mauve-pink and orange can be difficult colors to combine pleasingly but can be less contentious if slightly muted tones are used, as in this selection of *Ligularia dentata* and *Clematis* 'Hagley Hybrid'. They sit easily alongside *Hydrangea aspera* subsp. *sargentiana*, with its felted leaves and lilac flowerheads edged with white.

## Ligularia dentata
GOLDEN GROUNDSEL

The leaves of this handsome if slightly coarse plant (syns *L. clivorum, Senecio clivorum*) are kidney-shaped or rounded, and heart-shaped at the base. Their color is green in the typical species, purplish green in 'Othello' and bronze-green with purple undersides in 'Desdemona' ♀. Golden groundsel is very successful in waterside plantings and as ground cover. Ideally it should receive morning sun but needs some shade in the afternoon. It blends well with other hot colors, or soft yellow, apricot or peach, and also looks effective with purple foliage and other plants with a similarly bold, almost tropical effect. Satisfying contrasts can be achieved with the foliage of daylilies, irises, ferns and grasses, and with flowers in blue, purple, yellow-green or even shocking pink.

**Perfect partners:** *Achillea* 'Coronation Gold' p.226 **B**, *Camassia leichtlinii* 'Semiplena' p.355 **C**, *Iris pseudacorus* 'Variegata', *Rosa* Evelyn Fison p.212 **A**

**H: 3–5 ft. (90–150 cm) S: 3 ft. (90 cm)**
❀ **Midsummer to early autumn**
◊◊◊ ▪-▪ Z4 pH4.5–7.5

## Ligularia stenocephala

This is an excellent plant for large-scale effects by water, where reflections can double the impact of its bold spikes of yellow flowers, which are borne on dark stems above triangular leaves with jagged edges. It goes well with hot colors as well as pale yellow, cream and yellow-green, and may be contrasted with blue or purple flowers, with bronze foliage plants, and with the different leaf forms of plants such as grasses, ferns, irises and daylilies. Like *L. dentata* (left), it needs moisture and sun, with afternoon shade.

*L. przewalskii* has much more jagged leaves and a less solid flower spike, while their hybrid *L.* 'The Rocket' ♀ is intermediate.

**Perfect partners:** *Astilbe* 'Red Sentinel', *Carex pendula, Delphinium* 'Sungleam' p.257 **B**, *Deschampsia cespitosa, Lobelia speciosa* 'Cherry Ripe', *Rodgersia pinnata* 'Superba'

**H: 5 ft. (1.5 m) S: 3 ft. (90 cm)**
❀ **Early to late summer**
◊◊◊ ▪-▪ Z5 pH4.5–7.5

In this classic combination of moisture lovers, *Ligularia stenocephala* towers over *Lysimachia ciliata*, a contrast in form but a blend of colors. The loosestrife, whose star-shaped flowers have red-brown centers, grows up to 4 ft. (1.2 m) tall. Other large-scale plants to combine with these two include *Gunnera manicata* and *Rodgersia podophylla*.

In this combination for a well-drained sunny site, blue *Linum narbonense* contrasts with the yellow-flowered, prostrate broom *Genista sagittalis*. An attractive, sub-shrubby spurge, *Euphorbia characias*, gives bold architectural form to the planting.

## Linum narbonense

This sun-loving flax has delicate, saucer-shaped flowers in silky blue, with a white eye. It is at its best in the morning, as the color tends to fade by the afternoon. It needs sharp drainage and prefers an open site, although it can be grown at the front of a border among low, carpeting plants. It is good with other sun-lovers such as lavenders, phlomis, cistus, helianthemums and similar plants from the Mediterranean, South Africa and California. It harmonizes with glaucous or silver foliage, and pink, white, or mauve flowers, and makes a fine contrast with sulfur-yellow flowers. The dome-shaped plants look effective with the contrasting form of achilleas or grasses. 'Heavenly Blue' ♈ is a superlative selection.

**Perfect partners:** *Achillea* 'Moonshine', *Cistus* × *cyprius*, *Hakonechloa macra* 'Alboaurea', *Phlomis fruticosa*, *Rosmarinus officinalis* 'Roseus', *Ruta graveolens* 'Jackman's Blue'

**H: 12–24 in.** (30–60 cm) **S: 18 in.** (45 cm)
❋ Early to midsummer

 ◊-◊◊ ◻-■ Z5 pH5.5–8

## Lobelia × speciosa 'Cherry Ripe'

The exotic flower spikes of this bronze-leaved herbaceous perennial are cherry-red, and suited to hot color schemes and more subtle plantings with peach, apricot or soft orange flowers and purple or bronze foliage. It is a shade of red that mixes equally well with scarlet or crimson. Like most of the herbaceous lobelias, 'Cherry Ripe' is suitable both for waterside schemes and for herbaceous borders provided the soil is adequately moist and fairly well drained. As with all the older lobelia clones, viral disease can be a problem, and any plants with symptoms such as distorted leaf blades or streaks in the flowers should be destroyed.

**Perfect partners:** *Carex pendula*, *Corylus maxima* 'Purpurea', *Hosta sieboldiana* var. *elegans*, *Iris pseudacorus* 'Variegata', *Ligularia dentata* 'Desdemona', *Lysimachia ciliata* 'Firecracker', *Mimulus aurantiacus*, *Osmunda regalis*

**H: 36 in.** (90 cm) **S: 12 in.** (30 cm)
❋ Midsummer to early autumn

◊◊-◊◊◊ ■ Z6 pH5–7.5

The narrow, upright habit of *Lobelia* 'Cherry Ripe' and its long racemes of blooms make it especially useful for steeply banked borders such as this. In a predominantly red scheme, the lobelia is joined by *Dahlia* 'Grenadier', the scarlet lips of *Rosa* 'Geranium', and the double-flowered daylily *Hemerocallis fulva* 'Flore Pleno'.

In this extensive planting of hot-colored flowers, *Lobelia cardinalis* 'Queen Victoria' has to be grouped several plants deep for its slender spikes to give the impression of solid color. Its partners here include *Dahlia* 'Bishop of Llandaff', heleniums, and crocosmias.

## Lobelia cardinalis 'Queen Victoria' ♈

Brilliant scarlet flowers and purple foliage make this a fine candidate for hot color schemes and red borders, and for dramatic contrasts with yellow-green foliage or flowers. It is also effective with plants of contrasting form, such as grasses and golden hostas or ligularias. Plants tend to look unsatisfactory on their own and are better arranged in fairly generous groups. Most are now grown from seed, sown in early spring to flower by mid- to late summer. Other useful seed-raised lobelias include the Fan and Kompliment Series, both best treated as annuals or biennials. They are available in blue, purple and pink, as well as scarlet and deep red.

**Perfect partners:** *Canna* 'Erebus' p.415 **B**, *Dahlia* 'Alva's Doris' p.418 **A**, *Hosta* 'Sum and Substance', *Ligularia dentata* 'Desdemona', *Molinia caerulea* 'Variegata'

**H: 36 in.** (90 cm) **S: 12 in.** (30 cm)
❋ Midsummer to mid-autumn

 ◊◊-◊◊◊ ■ Z6 pH5–7.5

## *Lupinus* hybrids

Among the most popular of border perennials, lupins are often showy plants, on average 3–4 ft. (90–120 cm) high, with densely packed spikes of bloom arising from clumps of soft green palmate leaves. The large pea flowers come in a vast range of colors – varying tones of pink and red, lilac and blue, orange and yellow – as well as white, and including bicolors (often white with another color). The main flowering period is early summer, but if the first flush is removed as the flowers fade, further spikes will usually be produced in late summer and autumn.

White cultivars generally are good partners for silver foliage and other white flowers, and perhaps make most impact with pastel shades. The contrast they make with richer colors,

particularly with hot colors, can be a little severe, and a cream or a broken white lupin might be a more satisfactory choice. Good white cultivars include 'Pope John Paul', 'Noble Maiden' in the Band of Nobles Series ♀, and 'Gallery White' in the (20 in./50 cm) Gallery Series. 'Polar Princess' (4 ft./1.2 m) is one of the finest, with magnificent spikes of pure white flowers, but these are followed by relatively little secondary branching, so the flowering season is comparatively short. 'Thundercloud' is one of the best purple lupins, its color being effective not only when

**Far left:** Vigorously grown young lupins, such as the superb *Lupinus* 'Polar Princess', here making strong vertical accents against the silvery foliage of *Elaeagnus commutata*, will produce solid, columnar racemes of almost unnatural regularity in their first year of flowering, although they will bear numerous spires of varied size in subsequent years.

**Left:** In this purple, lavender and yellow-green scheme, *Euphorbia characias* subsp. *wulfenii* echoes the bold verticals of *Lupinus* 'Thundercloud', along with catmint (*Nepeta* 'Six Hills Giant') and *Erysimum* 'Bowles Mauve'.

combined with harmonious tones such as those of blue cranesbills, or mauve or crimson flowers, but also when contrasted with yellow-green flowers or foliage, and with soft yellow flowers such as some achilleas.

All of the taller lupins are very useful for adding vertical accents and subdued focal points to a border, although they may need staking. They are best positioned in the second or third rank, slightly forward from other plants of similar height to give their spikes more prominence. They associate well with euphorbias and catmints, and make an arresting contrast with the globe-shaped flowerheads of early alliums.

Lupin aphid can disfigure plants and introduce viral disease, causing mottling of the leaves; slugs may also be a problem, and may require controlling.

**Perfect partners:** *Allium cristophii*, *A. sphaerocephalon*, *Artemisia ludoviciana*, *Iris orientalis*, *Paeonia lactiflora* 'Duchesse de Nemours', *Papaver orientale* 'Black and White', *Rosa* Graham Thomas p.204 **A**

H: 36–48 in. (90–120 cm)  S: 24 in. (60 cm)
❀ Early summer
◊◊ ▢-▪ ▪ Z3  pH5.5–7.5

## *Lychnis* × *arkwrightii* 'Vesuvius'

With its rich bronze-purple foliage and red-vermilion flowers, this eye-catching perennial (syn. *Silene* × *arkwrightii* 'Vesuvius') is ideal for a hot color scheme, and also makes a startling contrast with acid yellow-green flowers or foliage. Some cultivars of *L.* × *haageana* are very similar in coloring and habit, and these include seed-raised 'Molten Lava' which can be used in the same way as *L.* × *arkwrightii* 'Vesuvius'. For optimum impact, place them next to a plant of more definite structure or with interestingly textured foliage, such as a grass. These cultivars require fairly rich soil and sun, and suffer from slug damage.

**Perfect partners:** *Berberis thunbergii* f. *atropurpurea*, *Choisya ternata* Sundance, *Euphorbia schillingii*, *Hemerocallis* 'Golden Chimes', *Phormium* 'Bronze Baby', *Stipa gigantea*

H: 18 in. (45 cm)  S: 12 in. (30 cm)
❀ Early to midsummer
◊◊ ▢-▪ ▪ Z6  pH5.5–7.5

In this dramatic grouping reminiscent of a Japanese ikebana arrangement, the vivid flowers of *Lychnis* × *arkwrightii* 'Vesuvius' contrast with the brightly variegated grass *Hakonechloa macra* 'Aureola', around the spiky foliage of a dark form of *Eucomis comosa*. The scheme could be repeated in a larger planting, replacing the grass with a less fiercely contrasting one if desired.

## *Lychnis coronaria* ♧
ROSE CAMPION

This silver-leaved plant is long-flowering and profuse, with flowers in a range of colors. The species itself is usually magenta-pink, and combines well with pink, crimson, mauve or purple flowers, and with silver or glaucous foliage of contrasting form, such as that of artemisias and grasses; soft yellow makes a pleasing contrast. It is best placed in the front or second rank of a border, and also succeeds in gravel gardens. It is fairly short-lived, but self-seeds freely. To keep colored forms separate, plants of different shades should be grown apart. The many variants include the Atrosanguinea Group, which is purplish red, and contrasts well with salmon or soft yellow; it is excellent with old roses, catmints, and lavenders. Pure white 'Alba' ♧ can partner yellows, apricots and peaches, as well as pink and red through to blue.

**Perfect partners:** *Campanula* 'Burghaltii' p.247 **B**, *Echinacea purpurea* p.261 **B**, *Erigeron* 'Gaiety' p.263 **C**, *Gladiolus communis* subsp. *byzantinus* p.366 **A**, *Malva sylvestris* p.434 **B**, *Rosa* 'Charles de Mills' p.194 **A**, *R. gallica* 'Versicolor' p.196 **B**, *R.* 'Impératrice Joséphine' p.195 **C**, *R.* 'Tuscany Superb' p.198 **B**

**H: 31 in. (80 cm)  S: 18 in. (45 cm)**
�֎ **Mid- to late summer**
◊-◊◊  ▫-▪  ■ Z4  pH5–8

**Right:** A gently contrasting salmon pelargonium scrambles into rose campions (magenta *Lychnis coronaria* and white *L.c.* 'Alba') to give a vibrant color combination.

**Below:** In a sunny display in midsummer, *Lychnis coronaria* 'Alba' combines with a lemon daylily (*Hemerocallis* 'Baroni'), the bold and elegant shape of the daylily blooms contrasting with those of the campion.

In boggy ground alongside a stream in early spring, the handsome golden spathes of the yellow skunk cabbage (*Lysichiton americanus*) harmonize with the cream and yellow stripes of the variegated yellow flag (*Iris pseudacorus* 'Variegata'), underplanted with kingcups (*Caltha palustris*).

## *Lysichiton americanus* ♥

YELLOW SKUNK CABBAGE, BOG ARUM

This waterside plant has an alien appearance in spring when its hooded yellow spathes emerge, surrounding upright greenish flowers with a slightly unpleasant scent. The large, glossy, rather coarse leaves appear much later. It is an excellent companion for water irises, whose foliage provides contrast at flowering time and later when the yellow skunk cabbage is in leaf. The foliage is particularly useful for creating a luxuriant primeval effect with other large-leaved partners such as gunneras. Plants harmonize with early yellow flowers such as calthas and the moisture-loving *Narcissus bulbocodium* and *N. jonquilla*. They provide good contrast with blue flowers such as brunneras and forget-me-nots, and with larger evergreen ferns. *L. camtschatcensis* ♥ is similar but smaller, with white spathes.

**Perfect partners:** *Brunnera macrophylla*, *Caltha leptosepala*, *C. palustris* var. *alba*, *Cornus alba* 'Sibirica', *Dryopteris affinis*, *Gunnera manicata*, *Iris chrysographes*, *I. ensata* cultivars, *Myosotis sylvatica*, *Osmunda regalis*, *Primula rosea*, *Rodgersia pinnata* 'Superba'

**H:** 3¼ ft. (1 m)  **S:** 5 ft. (1.5 m)
❀ **Early to mid-spring**
◊◊◊ ▪-▪ Z7 pH5–7

## *Lysimachia ciliata* 'Firecracker' ♥

Although producing nodding yellow flowers in summer, 'Firecracker' is primarily grown for its foliage, reddish purple in closely space whorls. It is useful from spring, when it can make a harmonious or contrasting backdrop to tulips and late narcissi, until autumn, when the leaves take on attractive tints. It looks good with pink, salmon-pink or mauve flowers before its own flowers appear, and makes a fine subject for hot color schemes. Boggy or waterside situations are ideal. Because it is invasive and needs to be kept under control, it should not be grown where the questing roots are likely to tangle with those of neighbors that resent disturbance.

**Perfect partners:** *Hemerocallis* 'Stafford', *Ligularia stenocephala*, *Narcissus* 'Actaea', *Rosa* 'Frensham' p.212 **B**, *R.* 'Roseraie de l'Haÿ' p.208 **A**, *Tulipa* 'Palestrina'

**H:** 4 ft. (1.2 m)  **S:** 24 in. (60 cm)
❀ **Mid- to late summer**
◊◊-◊◊◊ ▪ Z3 pH5–7.5

The emerging chocolate shoots of *Lysimachia ciliata* 'Firecracker' in late spring provide a strong color contrast in this mixed planting of yellow tulips, which includes the Lily-flowered cultivar *T.* 'West Point' (top), emphasizing the bold shape of the flowers.

## *Lysimachia nummularia* 'Aurea' ♥

GOLDEN CREEPING JENNY

The bright yellow-green foliage of this superb carpeting plant spreads rapidly, making an good foil for plants such as white colchicums – even magenta ones – or clumps of ferns. It will intermingle with other carpeters of comparable vigor, for example contrasting purple bugles, bronze acaenas or the white-splashed wild strawberry, *Fragaria* × *ananassa* 'Variegata', and may be used in hanging baskets, although it must have moist soil and can scorch in full sun. The flowers are yellow

The bright yellow-green foliage and pale stems of golden creeping Jenny (*Lysimachia nummularia* 'Aurea') mingle with the glaucous, pinnate foliage of *Acaena saccaticupula* 'Blue Haze' to create a carpet that could be underplanted with blue, white or yellow bulbs. Although both plants have similar vigor, maintaining a balance between the two might require occasional division and replanting.

and rather camouflaged by the leaf color, and are more charming seen against the fresh green foliage of *L. nummularia*, which is a more rampant carpeter for cool, damp places.

**Perfect partners:** *Acaena microphylla* 'Kupferteppich', *Ajuga reptans* 'Atropurpurea', *Colchicum speciosum*, *C.s.* 'Album', *Hebe pinguifolia* 'Pagei', *Lobelia richardsonii*, *Matteuccia struthiopteris*, *Muscari armeniacum*, *Myosotis sylvatica*, *Scilla siberica* 'Spring Beauty', *Viola* 'Huntercombe Purple' p.340 **B**

**H:** 2 in. (5 cm)  **S:** indefinite  ❀ **Midsummer**
◊◊-◊◊◊ ▪-▪ Z4 pH4.5–7.5

The tall plumes of *Macleaya microcarpa* in early summer harmonize both with the brick wall behind and with the group of mixed *Alstroemeria* ligtu hybrids in front. A soft shield fern (*Polystichum setiferum*) furnishes the base of the alstroemerias, while *Convolvulus sabatius* provides a splash of contrasting blue in the foreground.

## Macleaya microcarpa

The color of the tall, airy flower spikes of this plume poppy lies somewhere between brick-red, coral and salmon. It harmonizes with other flowers in all these colors, and contrasts with soft blue ones. With its scalloped foliage, the plant is very effective among or in front of shrubs, and with perpetual-flowering roses such as some old Chinas, Teas and Hybrid Musks, and many of the David Austin English rose cultivars. It combines well with alstroemerias, and with grasses, hostas and other contrasting glaucous or silver-leaved plants, and its form is enhanced by a background of bronze or purple foliage. *M.m.* 'Kelway's Coral Plume' ♀ is particularly fine. The rootstock is restlessly invasive so that plants tend to wander from their original positions.

**Perfect partners:** *Alstroemeria aurea*, *Campanula latifolia* 'Gloaming', *Cotinus coggygria* 'Notcutt's Variety', *Dahlia* 'Glorie van Heemstede' p.421 **A**, *Rosa* Peach Blossom

**H: 7 ft.** (2.2 m) **S: 3 ft.** (90 cm)
✽ Early to midsummer

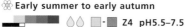 ◊◊-◊◊◊ ■ Z4 pH5.5–7.5

## Malva moschata f. alba ♀

The white form of the musk mallow varies in habit and in the size and number of its blooms. The best forms produce neat plants that are almost covered with broad, glistening white flowers in summer. The purity of the color, set against the deep green of the crisp, prettily cut leaves, is immensely effective with other white flowers, pastel shades and silver foliage, and with yellow-green or glaucous leaves. The plants are excellent at the front of a border, growing with companions such as pinks, alchemillas and catmints. Cultivated forms of musk mallow, selected for their tidy, compact growth habit, are only about half the height of the wild species, which can reach 36 in. (90 cm).

**Perfect partners:** *Artemisia schmidtiana*, *Astrantia maxima*, *Heuchera* 'Rachel' p.289 **B**, *Hydrangea arborescens*, *Rosa* Pink Bells p.219 **A**, *Veronicastrum virginicum* 'Album'

**H: 36 in.** (90 cm) **S: 24 in.** (60 cm)
✽ Early summer to early autumn

◊◊ □-■ Z4 pH5.5–7.5

An upright *Miscanthus sinensis* cultivar produces a fountain of foliage behind *Malva moschata* f. *alba* in a simple scheme of subdued colors. The deeply cut leaves of the musk mallow give a strong contrast of form with the ribbonlike foliage of the grass.

## Matteuccia struthiopteris ♀
OSTRICH-PLUME FERN, SHUTTLECOCK FERN

Spring is the best season for this deciduous fern, when the young extending foliage forms a plume of light yellowish green shuttlecocks. It is also attractive in autumn as the fronds assume russet tints, and the dark brown fertile fronds will often persist through much of winter. It perhaps looks its best combined with yellow or blue spring flowers, such as forget-me-nots, omphalodes, brunneras, epimediums and erythroniums, and is very effective with a carpet of lower-growing

In early spring at the front of a border alongside a path, the young shuttlecocks of the ostrich-plume fern (*Matteuccia struthiopteris*) make a bold statement and help draw attention to an imposing terracotta pot. Pure blue-flowered *Omphalodes cappadocica* 'Cherry Ingram' sits at the base of the ferns and hides the edge of the path.

plants beneath and between the plumes. This moisture-loving fern is excellent in bog gardens or waterside plantings, and for moist, dappled shade, especially with deciduous azaleas. The underground shoots spread freely in all but the heaviest soils.

**Perfect partners:** *Arum italicum* 'Marmoratum' p.355 **A**, *Erythronium revolutum* p.361 **C**, *Pyrus salicifolia* 'Pendula' p.127 **C**, *Tulipa* 'Sweet Harmony' p.402 **A**

**H: 4 ft.** (1.2 m) **S: 3 ft.** (90 cm)
◊◊-◊◊◊ ■ ■ Z2 pH5.5–7

## *Meconopsis betonicifolia* ♈
### TIBETAN BLUE POPPY

The exquisite flowers of this species (syn. *M. baileyi*) are a rare pure blue, slightly greenish in areas with moist soils and cool summers, a little more purple after a hot or dry spring. It tends to be short-lived so is best divided or resown every two years or so in early to mid-spring. It is superlative with light yellow, white or cream flowers, and with yellow-green foliage or flowers and bronze foliage. It is especially attractive with ferns with light green spring foliage, and with other greenish blue flowers on plants of contrasting form, such as corydalis.

*M. grandis* ♈ has larger, more symmetrical flowers, but it is not so perennial. The hybrid between the two species, *M.* × *sheldonii* ♈, combines superior flower shape and size with longer life. *M.b.* var. *alba* has delicate, purest white flowers, borne over good foliage that is more glaucous than the typical species.

**Perfect partners:** *Astilbe* × *arendsii* 'Irrlicht', *Corydalis flexuosa*, *Hosta fortunei* var. *albopicta* f. *aurea*, *Matteuccia struthiopteris*, *Primula florindae*, *Rhododendron* 'Polar Bear', *Rodgersia pinnata* 'Superba'

**H: 4 ft. (1.2 m) S: 18 in. (45 cm)** ✿ **Early summer**
○○○ ■ **Z7 pH5–6.5**

In a partially shaded glade blessed with moist, humus-rich soil, Tibetan poppies (*Meconopsis betonicifolia*) and white foxgloves (*Digitalis purpurea* f. *albiflora*) create a classic combination of blue and white, the spikes of the foxgloves providing bold accents and contrast of form.

## *Milium effusum* 'Aureum' ♈
### BOWLES GOLDEN GRASS

Woodland gardens and shady borders are the best sites for this yellow-green grass, which can become untidy and scorched when it is planted in full sun. It is easy to grow and showiest in mid- to late spring, although its fine color will persist into summer if grown in moist cool conditions. With its readiness to self-seed, it may become a weed. It is best treated as a short-lived perennial, as older plants tend to look rather disheveled. Blue, pale yellow, cream or white flowers, glaucous foliage, and yellow-green foliage of contrasting form – hostas, for example – are all outstanding partners. Mass planting in blocks hides its natural grace, and it looks better scattered as individual tussocks, perhaps

Bowles golden grass (*Milium effusum* 'Aureum') has sown itself through silverweed (*Potentilla anserina*), an invasive plant with silvery glaucous foliage, to create a charming spring mixture.

through a carpet of low-growing plants such as bugles. It is very effective, too, growing through forget-me-nots, blue corydalis, geums, bluebells, brunneras and omphalodes, and with white, cream or yellow erythroniums.

**Perfect partners:** *Ajuga reptans* 'Atropurpurea', *Geranium* 'Johnson's Blue', *Geum* 'Lady Stratheden', *Helleborus* × *hybridus* p.285 **A**, *Hosta* (Tardiana Group) 'Halcyon'

**H: 24 in. (60 cm) S: 12 in. (30 cm)**
✿ **Late spring to midsummer**
 ○○-○○○ ■-■ ■ **Z5 pH5–7.5**

By late autumn, the sere seedheads of *Miscanthus sinensis* take on parchment tints but remain attractive, especially if rimed with frost or lit by the sun. The faded heads of other border plants can, if left, combine with them to create interesting patterns of contrasting forms in subdued fawns and russets, as here with the flat plates of *Achillea filipendulina*.

## *Miscanthus sinensis*

This grass varies wildly in height, habit, hardiness and flowering, and it is advisable to choose a named cultivar with particular qualities, rather than buy a plant simply as *Miscanthus sinensis*. There are narrow forms that can be incorporated into borders, whereas more arching cultivars need space to show their natural grace. Most hold their seedheads well and so are very useful for a winter garden, particularly if sited where they are backlit by the sun or sunlit against a dark evergreen backdrop. The most floriferous are often so prolific that the individual grace of the flowerheads or seedheads is not obvious: maroon-flushed 'Gewitterwolke', for example, although impressive at 6 ft. (1.8 m) and with excellent foliage, bears flowers in such profusion that it can look very congested.

All cultivars may be grown with autumn-flowering plants such as helianthus, asters and chrysanthemums, but with their loosely informal growth and subtle colorings they are more effective where not overwhelmed by strong color. The following cultivars are all hardy to Zone 5. Some of the most useful non-variegated kinds include 'Gracillimus' (maiden grass), which is narrow-leaved with a pale central vein, 6 ft. (1.8 m) tall, and good as a specimen or for planting in borders, but shy to flower where summers are cool. 'Sarabande', 4 ft. (1.2 m), has similar narrow gray-green foliage but is floriferous, with flowers that emerge pink-flushed, ageing to silver. 'Graziella', 5 ft. (1.5 m), is also narrow-leaved with prolific pink-flushed flowers that turn silver, as do the spreading pink panicles of 'Flamingo', 4 ft. (1.2 m). 'Silberturm', 8 ft. (2.5 m), has silvery plumes. Those of 'Grosse Fontäne', 6½ ft. (2 m), cascade in a fountain of long fingers; 'Kleine Fontäne' is 3¼ ft. (1 m). Free-flowering and also 3¼ ft. (1 m) high is 'Kleine Silberspinne', with narrow

leaves held horizontally and maroon-flushed plumes aging to silver. *M.s.* var. *condensatus*, with broad leaves and thick, silvery culms, reaches 10 ft. (3 m) and flowers in mid-autumn. More diminutive kinds, such as 'Little Kitten', 12 in. (30 cm) tall, narrow-leaved and flowering in early autumn, are invaluable for smaller gardens and for containers.

**Perfect partners:** *Aster* × *frikartii* 'Mönch', *Eupatorium purpureum* subsp. *maculatum*, *Helianthus decapetalus* 'Soleil d'Or', *Malva moschata* f. *alba* p.311 **B**, *Rosa* 'Geranium' p.203 **A**, *Verbascum* 'Helen Johnson' p.339 **B**

**H: 1–10 ft.** (30 cm–3 m)  **S: 2–6 ft.** (60 cm–1.8 m)
✿ **Midsummer to late autumn**

◊◊ ■-■ ■  **Z5–7  pH5–7.5**

In mid-autumn, *Miscanthus sinensis* 'Undine' stands gracefully behind lilac-tinted *Aster lateriflorus* 'Horizontalis' in front of creamy plumes of *Artemisia lactiflora*, with silvery *M.s.* 'Silberfeder' silhouetted against a dark yew hedge.

The cream-striped *Miscanthus sinensis* 'Variegatus' here seems almost identical in tone to silvery *Elaeagnus* 'Quicksilver', differing in form and texture, but blending to give a gentle and elegant combination.

## *Miscanthus sinensis* 'Variegatus'

This arching foliage plant looks good surrounded by lower plants. Narrower variegated kinds for growing in borders include 'Silberpfeil', 7 ft. (2.2 m), fairly free-flowering but rather bare at the base. 'Morning Light', 5 ft. (1.5 m), has narrow, white-edged leaves. More spreading cultivars with marginal variegation include 'Dixieland', 5 ft. (1.5 m), a brighter and stronger plant than 'Variegatus'. *M.s.* var. *condensatus* 'Cabaret', 8 ft. (2.5 m), has broad, white-centered leaves, while equally tall var. *c.* 'Cosmopolitan' is green with white edges. 'Zebrinus', 7 ft. (2.2 m), has arching leaves with transverse gold or beige variegation, and a spreading habit. 'Strictus' (porcupine grass), of similar height, has stiffly angled, variegated leaves.

**Perfect partners:** *Anemone* × *hybrida* 'Elegans' p.233 **B**, *Chrysanthemum* Rubellum Group, *Crocosmia* 'Lucifer', *Echinacea purpurea*, *Rhus* × *pulvinata* Autumn Lace Group, *Rodgersia podophylla* p.328 **C**

**H: 5 ft.** (1.5 m)  **S: 3¼ ft.** (1 m)
✿ **Early to mid-autumn**

 ◊◊ ■-■ ■  **Z5  pH5–7.5**

A

This mid-autumn scheme has a strong vertical theme. *Molinia caerulea* 'Variegata' in the foreground furnishes the base of *Actaea simplex* Atropurpurea Group, its white bottle-brushes borne above dark leaves. In the distance are the upright buff seedheads of the feather reed grass, *Calamagrostis* × *acutiflora* 'Strictus'.

## *Molinia caerulea* 'Variegata' ♔
### VARIEGATED PURPLE MOOR GRASS

This is a neat herbaceous grass, with clumps of brightly cream-striped leaves and spikes of purplish flowers that turn parchment color in winter. Tolerant of a wide range of soils, it can be used at the front of a border and as an edging to beds. Its top growth is usually shed by late winter, allowing it to be under- or interplanted with early-flowering bulbs such as snowdrops, and since it is rather late leafing in spring it suits summer and autumn schemes. It harmonizes with yellow or cream and contrasts with blue flowers or glaucous foliage. Other effective partners include lavenders, nigellas, smaller yellow tagetes, California poppies, fescues and lyme grasses.

**Perfect partners:** *Delphinium grandiflorum* 'Blue Butterfly', *Heliophila coronopifolia*, *Hosta* (Tardiana Group) 'Halcyon', *Nemophila menziesii*, *Nigella damascena* 'Miss Jekyll'

**H: 36 in.** (90 cm) **S: 24 in.** (60 cm)
❀ **Midsummer to mid-autumn**

 ◊◊-◊◊◊ ▫-▪ ■ Z5 pH5.5–7.5

C

Pale pink *Monarda* 'Beauty of Cobham', used toward the front of a border of predominantly purple flowers and dark foliage, helps to leaven an otherwise dull combination featuring the smoke bush (*Cotinus coggygria* 'Foliis Purpureis') and purple loosestrife (*Lythrum salicaria* 'Feuerkerze').

## *Monarda* 'Adam'

This is a fairly compact, clump-forming rhizomatous perennial, with sturdy upright square stems bearing fragrant, dark green mintlike leaves. The comparatively large, hooded flowers are borne in dense terminal whorls. Although not sufficiently intense for hot-colored schemes, their sumptuous shade of cherry-red is a color that deserves prominence, and plants make exciting accents and highlights within borders, especially if partnered by acid yellow-green foliage and flowers, or soft yellow flowers, such as some achilleas and daylilies, or euphorbias. Other good companions include liatris, catmints, hardy salvias and eryngiums. Like many red monardas, it tends to be susceptible to powdery mildew, especially on dry soils or if massed within a tightly packed border.

**Perfect partners:** *Achillea filipendulina* 'Gold Plate', *Aster divaricatus*, *Deschampsia cespitosa*, *Rudbeckia fulgida* var. *deamii*, *Salvia coccinea* 'Coral Nymph'

**H: 31 in.** (80 cm) **S: 18 in.** (45 cm)
❀ **Mid- to late summer**

 ◊◊ ▫-▪ ■ Z4 pH5–7.5

B

In this border of brightly colored flowers for midsummer to autumn, the relatively compact, cherry-red *Monarda* 'Adam' takes center stage. In front are golden heleniums and crimson *Phlox paniculata*, while behind, *Crocosmia* 'Lucifer', achilleas and dark-leaved *Ricinus communis* provide both structure and bold color.

## *Monarda* 'Beauty of Cobham' ♔

Although tolerating any soil that does not dry out in summer, this rhizomatous herbaceous perennial prefers damp conditions, in which it will gradually spread to form a moderately sized clump. It is an attractive subject for moist herbaceous or mixed borders, and also for waterside plantings. The pale pink flowers suit combinations with other cool colors, such as purple, mauve, crimson, white and lavender, while the purple calyces harmonize particularly well with purple foliage. 'Beauty of Cobham' can be partnered very pleasingly with the glaucous foliage of *Hosta sieboldiana* or *H.* Tardiana Group. It is an outstanding partner for astilbes, filipendulas, perennial lobelias, lythrums, later-flowering thalictrums, persicarias, plume poppies and grasses such as *Miscanthus sinensis* cultivars. Like most monardas, it benefits from frequent division.

**Perfect partners:** *Aster* × *frikartii* 'Mönch', *Astilbe* × *arendsii* 'Ceres', *Lobelia* × *speciosa* 'Fan Scharlach', *Lythrum virgatum* 'Dropmore Purple', *Thalictrum delavayi* 'Hewitt's Double'

**H: 36 in.** (90 cm) **S: 18 in.** (45 cm)
❀ **Mid- to late summer**

 ◊◊ ▫-▪ ■ Z4 pH5–7.5

# Nepeta govaniana

This Himalayan herbaceous perennial expands in moist cool conditions to form a clump of erect pointed foliage and airy racemes of subdued creamy yellow flowers, borne in summer. It is an especially charming companion for flowers in yellow or yellow-green, white or warm colors such as apricot, and glaucous, gold-variegated or yellow-green foliage, including hostas with yellow-green leaves and grasses such as *Miscanthus* or *Molinia* cultivars. It combines well with later-flowering daylilies, repeat-flowering Shrub roses, agapanthus, willow gentians, hedychiums and ligularias. Other good partners include *A. amellus* and *A.* × *frikartii* cultivars, blue or white hydrangeas, kniphofias and later-flowering lilies, as well as hypericums, *Ceanothus* × *delileanus* cultivars, caryopteris, perovskias and similar shrubs.

**Perfect partners:** *Agapanthus* 'Loch Hope', *Caryopteris* × *clandonensis* 'Heavenly Blue',

The airy primrose flowers of *Nepeta govaniana*, rising above a cushion of feathery *Artemisia* 'Powis Castle' and a cream achillea, contrast with the nearby lavender-blue catmint *Nepeta* 'Six Hills Giant' in midsummer.

*Hydrangea macrophylla* 'Mariesii Perfecta', *Lilium* African Queen Group, *Perovskia* 'Blue Spire', *Rosa* **Crown Princess Margareta**

H: 36 in. (90 cm) S: 24 in. (60 cm)
Midsummer to early autumn
Z5 pH5.5–7.5

# Nepeta 'Six Hills Giant'

This vigorous herbaceous perennial succeeds in large-scale plantings, with shrubs such as roses or philadelphus, or in front of fairly tall herbaceous plants like *Phlox paniculata* cultivars and some campanulas. It is good with cool colors and soft yellow, especially flowers such as daylilies or achilleas that contrast with its own slightly amorphous form. Where summers are cool, it associates well with glaucous-leaved hostas. Many Mediterranean plants, including cistus and lavenders, make pleasing partners; grasses such as blue fescues, helictotrichons or lyme grasses are also effective, as are Bearded irises, cranesbills and peonies. The lavish top growth of 'Six Hills Giant' benefits from being cut hard back after the first flush of bloom. It will at once start to revive, quickly producing a new foliage and blooming again in late summer, when it can combine well with Japanese anemones and penstemons.

**Perfect partners:** *Geranium* × *oxonianum* 'A.T. Johnson', *Lupinus* 'Thundercloud' p.308 **B**, *Paeonia lactiflora* 'Albert Crousse', *Rosa* 'Chinatown' p.211 **B**

H: 30 in. (75 cm) S: 36 in. (90 cm)
Early to late summer
Z5 pH5.5–7.5

The lavender-blue flowers of the catmint *Nepeta* 'Six Hills Giant' sprawl across a gravel path next to the contrasting yellow blooms of Jerusalem sage (*Phlomis fruticosa*), harmonizing with the glaucous lyme grass (*Leymus arenarius*), confined in a verdigrised laundry copper.

# Oenothera speciosa 'Siskiyou'

Good drainage and a sunny site are essential for this rhizomatous, clump-forming herbaceous perennial, so it is well suited to a rock or gravel garden, where it can grow with Mediterranean plants such as lavenders, marjorams and teucriums. Its delicate pink flowers, attractively veined and embellished with a yellow base, are perhaps most successful with cool-colored flowers, since the yellow eye scarcely provides enough color to participate in associations with warmer tints such as peach or salmon. Plants can be grown at the front of a border, with room to allow the cushions of growth to develop symmetrically. They look best in evenly spaced groups, perhaps interplanted with carpeting or cushion-forming plants.

**Perfect partners:** *Cistus* × *argenteus* 'Silver Pink', *Helianthemum* 'Wisley White', *Lavandula* 'Regal Splendour', *Origanum* 'Kent Beauty', *Stipa gigantea*, *Teucrium fruticans*

H & S: 12 in. (30 cm) Early to late summer
Z5 pH5.5–7.5

*Allium senescens* has here grown through the fringes of *Oenothera speciosa* 'Siskiyou', its mauve flowerheads harmonizing with the satin-pink blooms of the oenothera but providing a contrast of floral form.

Pink purslane (*Claytonia sibirica*) has here sown itself around *Omphalodes cappadocica* and mingles its mauve flowers with those of the omphalodes to give a charming and harmonious combination.

## *Omphalodes cappadocica* ♔

With its preference for moisture and partial shade, this clump-forming rhizomatous evergreen succeeds in woodland gardens, beneath deciduous trees where it gets winter sun and some summer shade; it also makes a neat edging plant in shady borders. Its early flowering season allows combinations with spring bulbs. The rich blue of its flowers contrasts well with yellow or white flowers, such as celandines and primroses. Other good partners are scillas and evergreen sedges and ferns. Notable selections are intense blue 'Cherry Ingram' ♔, white-centered 'Starry Eyes', 'Lilac Mist' and rich blue 'Parisian Skies'.

**Perfect partners:** *Carex oshimensis* 'Evergold', *Epimedium* × *versicolor* 'Sulphureum', *Hosta fortunei* var. *albopicta*, *Matteuccia struthiopteris* p.311 **C**, *Muscari latifolium*

H: 9 in. (23 cm)  S: 16 in. (40 cm)
❀ Late spring to early summer
◊◊-◊◊◊ ☐-■ ■ Z6 pH5.5–7.5

The glistening dark foliage of black mondo grass (*Ophiopogon planiscapus* 'Nigrescens') contrasts with the glaucous leaves of acaenas, forming a carpet beneath. The cranesbill *Geranium sessiliflorum* subsp. *novae-zelandiae* 'Nigricans' has smoky foliage intermediate in color between that of its two companions.

## *Ophiopogon planiscapus* 'Nigrescens' ♔

BLACK MONDO GRASS

This is an evergreen perennial lilyturf (also available as 'Arabicus', 'Black Dragon' and 'Kokuryû') that spreads slowly but steadily by means of rhizomes. Its glistening straplike foliage is closer to black than almost any other plant, while its insignificant flowers – small, white and sometimes tinged with lilac – are followed by dark green berries that are shaded black with turquoise undertones. This ground-cover plant makes a good foil for contrasting foliage and flowers, especially bulbs such as colchicums, and for specimen shrubs like Japanese maples. It can also be used to make a patchwork of ground-cover foliage with leaves of contrasting form, either in harmonizing dusky colors such as those of dark-leaved heucheras, or together with contrasting pale-leaved plants like smaller yellow-green hostas or silver lamiums. It is an excellent choice for creating abstract carpet bedding designs on a large scale.

**Perfect partners:** *Acer palmatum* Dissectum Atropurpureum Group p.77 **B**, *Cyclamen hederifolium* f. *albiflorum* p.360 **A**, *Heuchera villosa* 'Palace Purple', *Iris* 'George' p.369 **B**

H: 8 in. (20 cm)  S: 12 in. (30 cm)  ❀ Midsummer
◊◊ ☐-■ ■ Z6 pH5–7

## *Origanum vulgare* 'Aureum' ♔

GOLDEN MARJORAM

The bright yellow-green young foliage of this rhizomatous, clump-forming, aromatic perennial approaches pure gold in sunny sites, deepening to green by midsummer. Cutting plants to the ground when the foliage becomes lackluster produces a second crop of young leaves but removes the mauve-pink flowers. It associates well with sisyrinchiums, annual or clump-forming convolvulus, blue-green fescues and smaller achilleas, and is attractive with nasturtiums, rosemary, borage, hyssop and white-flowered herbs such as camomile and feverfew. It tolerates clipping as a component of a knot garden, and can be used to fill a parterre or in the front of borders, mixed with glaucous foliage or blue flowers, hot colors such as orange and gold or gold-variegated foliage.

**Perfect partners:** *Anthemis punctata* subsp. *cupaniana*, *Astrantia major* 'Sunningdale Variegated' p.243 **A**, *Geranium* 'Ann Folkard' p.273 **B**, *Salvia officinalis* 'Purpurascens'

H & S: 18 in. (45 cm)  ❀ Early to late summer
◊◊ ☐-■ ■ Z4 pH5.5–8

The new foliage of golden marjoram (*Origanum vulgare* 'Aureum') is at its brightest in late spring to early summer when, as here, it contrasts dramatically with the flowers and foliage of purple bugle (*Ajuga reptans* 'Atropurpurea').

In a glade in a woodland garden, the double-flowered evergreen azalea *Rhododendron* 'Amoenum' provides dramatic color behind a carpet of *Paeonia emodi*. A paler azalea, perhaps in soft yellow, would also be pleasing.

## Paeonia emodi

Despite its relatively short flowering season, this herbaceous peony has prettily divided foliage that remains attractive all summer. Its deliciously scented, pure white flowers have golden anthers, a combination that perhaps works best with blue, yellow or yellow-green flowers, or with warm colors; it also looks good with glaucous or yellow-green foliage. Compatible partners are trollius, smilacinas, dicentras, columbines, corydalis, epimediums and early cranesbills, together with shrubs like deciduous azaleas, early yellow roses, *Potentilla fruticosa* cultivars and kerrias. It can be combined with plants of contrasting foliage, including early-leafing hostas, Bowles golden grass and yellow-green sedges.

**Perfect partners:** *Carex elata* 'Aurea', *Corydalis flexuosa* 'China Blue', *Epimedium* × *versicolor* 'Sulphureum', *Hosta fortunei* var. *albopicta* f. *aurea*, *Rosa* 'Helen Knight'

**H & S: 30 in.** (75 cm) ✿ **Late spring**
◊◊ ▢-▨ ■ **Z6  pH5.5–7.5**

## Paeonia lactiflora

This north-east Asian herbaceous peony has single white blooms, 3½–4 in. (8–10 cm) across, with a central mass of pale yellow stamens. It is the parent of several thousand cultivars in a wide range of floral forms – single, semi-double, double (sometimes ruffled) and 'Imperial' cultivars, in which the stamens are transformed into a nest of smaller petals – and in colors from white to deep red and soft yellow. Most retain the species' mahogany-tinted foliage, which often colors brightly in autumn, together with a wonderful lingering fragrance. Among the best cultivars are 'Bowl of Beauty' ♡, soft pink with a creamy white center; 'Festiva Maxima' ♡, double white with red flecks; and 'Sarah Bernhardt' ♡, double pink fading at the edges. The rich spring leaf tints combine well with forget-me-nots and make a fine setting for gold foliage and bright spring bulbs.

**Perfect partners:** *Alstroemeria* 'Apollo', *Aquilegia vulgaris* (mixed), *Chionodoxa forbesii* p.356 **A**, *Iris* 'Jane Phillips', *Papaver orientale* 'Black and White', *Rosa* 'Charles de Mills'

**H: 30–36 in.** (75–90 cm)  **S: 24 in.** (60 cm)
✿ **Early to midsummer**
◊◊ ▢-▨ ■ **Z4  pH5.5–7.5**

In early summer, the rose-pink blooms of *Paeonia lactiflora* 'Albert Crousse' harmonize closely, both in color and floral form, with those of *Rosa* Gertrude Jekyll. Upright alliums in purplish mauve (*Allium aflatunense* and the taller *A. giganteum*) add contrast of form, their ramrod stems providing repeated vertical accents, while distant dark foliage gives depth to the perspective.

Carmine *Paeonia lactiflora* 'Auguste Dessert' is here daringly juxtaposed against yellow loosestrife (*Lysimachia punctata*). Although the contrast of form certainly succeeds, some gardeners might prefer to achieve it with spires of a more harmonious color, perhaps using a lupin or delphinium that would also blend agreeably with pale pink *P.l.* 'Noemi Demay' behind.

## Paeonia lactiflora 'Auguste Dessert'

One of the most pleasing cultivars of this highly variable species, 'Auguste Dessert' has deep green foliage that assumes crimson tints in autumn, and vivid carmine flowers, shaded rose-pink and edged with silvery white. Its floral form resembles that of many old roses, with which it can produce good harmonies, but it is even better when contrasted with rose cultivars of distinctly different flower size, color or form. The hint of blue in its coloring makes white too stark a contrast, but the shade suits combinations with cool colors – especially purple, crimson and magenta – or contrasts with yellow-green or soft yellow, such as euphorbias or achilleas. Other fine partners include *Dianthus* Devon Series, dictamnus, mauve-pink campanulas, cranesbills, thalictrums, Tall Bearded irises and alchemillas. Like all double peonies, the full blooms are heavy, especially after rain, and plants benefit from a wire hoop support.

**Perfect partners:** *Centaurea montana*, *Delphinium* 'Bruce', *Dictamnus albus* var. *purpureus*, *Lupinus* 'Thundercloud', *Potentilla fruticosa* 'Primrose Beauty', *Rosa* 'Complicata'

**H & S: 30 in.** (75 cm) ❀ **Early to midsummer**
◊◊ ☐-■ ■ Z4 pH5.5–7.5

Double-flowered *Papaver* 'Fireball' is here combined with the yellow-green leaves of golden feverfew (*Tanacetum parthenium* 'Aureum'), lemon Welsh poppies (*Meconopsis cambrica*) and yellow and red columbines. In a slightly less sunny site, the fading of 'Fireball' from vermilion toward salmon might be lessened and the effect improved.

## Paeonia mlokosewitschii 🏆

MOLLY THE WITCH

The downy grayish green foliage of this herbaceous peony remains handsome throughout summer. It has a relatively short flowering season, but its soft yellow blooms with their golden anthers combine especially well with warm-colored flowers, such as early yellow and cream roses, geums, Siberian wallflowers, columbines, chaenomeles and *Potentilla fruticosa* cultivars. It makes satisfying harmonies with yellow-green foliage and flowers, including euphorbias, perfoliate alexanders, Bowles golden grass, yellow-green sedges and early-leafing hostas, as well as glaucous plants like dicentras. For contrast it can be partnered with blue flowers.

**Perfect partners:** *Brunnera macrophylla*, *Carex elata* 'Aurea', *Cytisus* × *praecox* 'Warminster', *Dicentra eximia*, *Kerria japonica* 'Picta', *Rosa* 'Helen Knight' p.205 **A**

**H & S: 30 in.** (75 cm) ❀ **Late spring**
◊◊ ☐-■ ■ Z5 pH5.5–7.5

In this delightful, late spring planting scheme, soft yellow *Paeonia mlokosewitschii* sits companionably with the moisture-loving *Euphorbia palustris* behind, while the dark blue Tall Bearded iris in front makes a subtle contrast.

## Papaver 'Fireball'

A hybrid of the Oriental poppy, 'Fireball' has informal double flowers that open vermilion and age (in sunny sites and warm climates) to salmon-pink. These colors allow it to mix well with flowers in warm tints such as peach, salmon or apricot; however, in areas where it does fade, association with hot colors can make it seem jaded by comparison. Effective partners include geums, columbines, *Potentilla fruticosa* cultivars, Dwarf and Intermediate Bearded irises and bronze foliage plants such as heucheras, bronze sedges and *Berberis thunbergii* cultivars. This herbaceous plant can be invasive and needs a situation where its roots can spread without overwhelming its neighbors, and this, together with its slightly ragged and informal charm, suits it to a cottage garden style of planting.

**Perfect partners:** *Aquilegia canadensis*, *Berberis thunbergii* 'Rose Glow', *Carex comans* (bronze), *Geum* 'Coppertone', *Iris* 'Golden Muffin', *Potentilla fruticosa* 'Sunset'

**H & S: 12 in.** (30 cm) ❀ **Late spring to early summer**
◊-◊◊ ☐-■ ■ Z4 pH5.5–7.5

## *Papaver orientale* cultivars

Garden hybrids of the Oriental poppy vary in height from 2 to 5 ft. (60 to 150 cm), and may be any shade between white, vermilion, blood-red and crimson. A few have double flowers, and these bloom for slightly longer, but they lack the charming simplicity of the single flowers. All can be grown in herbaceous or mixed borders and gravel gardens, ideally set forward of companions of their own height so that the leaves at the base of the plants get plenty of sunlight. Their spectacular glistening blooms, often marked with an attractive dark basal blotch, appear before most other summer flowers, but plants have a tendency to die back after flowering, leaving an awkward gap in borders. One solution is to plant poppies in drifts, flanked by annuals or summer bedding plants that later grow into the vacant space: dahlias, nicotianas, argyranthemums, osteospermums, and cosmos are all suitable for this purpose.

The more intense poppy colors are suited to hot schemes with, for example, columbines, lupins, Siberian wallflowers, Bearded irises, and early alstroemerias and for contrasts with yellow-green foliage and flowers. Those tending toward orange contrast effectively with blue flowers such as delphiniums and baptisias, while white-flowered cultivars combine well with silver, bronze or purple foliage plants. Cultivars with salmon flowers can be combined with warm tints such as peach and apricot, while those in the color range mauve-pink to carmine blend pleasantly with cool colors. All are good with roses, brooms and tree peonies.

**Above:** Extravagantly ruffled salmon flowers of *Papaver orientale* 'Prinz Eugen' are joined by the lilac blooms of sweet rocket (*Hesperis matronalis*) in this narrow border.

**Above left:** In an early summer combination, scarlet black-blotched *Papaver orientale* 'Avebury Crimson' is contrasted with a gentian-blue *Anchusa azurea* cultivar.

**Perfect partners:** *Alstroemeria ligtu* hybrids, *Campanula* 'Burghaltii' p.247 **B**, *Delphinium* 'Alice Artindale', *Iris* 'Symphony' p.370 **A**, *Lupinus* 'The Governor'

H: 2–5 ft. (60–150 cm)  S: 18–36 in. (45–90 cm)
❀ Late spring to midsummer
  Z4  pH5.5–7.5

In this sharp but striking partnership that will last into the autumn, the acidic, slightly greenish yellow blooms of *Patrinia scabiosifolia* are set off by the purple-flowered *Verbena bonariensis*, both plants of similar branching habit.

## *Patrinia scabiosifolia*

This herbaceous perennial, invaluable for providing late flower color, has deeply divided leaves and loose, airy heads of small yellow flowers, tinted slightly with green. It is useful for weaving in drifts through mixed or herbaceous borders, where it can harmonize with hot colors such as orange, yellow and scarlet, and with yellow or yellow-green plants, especially late-flowering euphorbias, larger hostas with yellow-green or gold-variegated leaves and yellow-variegated grasses such as miscanthus or cortaderia cultivars. Effective contrasts can be made with blue or rich purple, using late aconites for example, and with the quite different form of late-flowering daisies in hot colors, including heleniums, rudbeckias, and helianthus. It is particularly successful with salvias, dahlias and other late-flowering tender perennials.

**Perfect partners:** *Aconitum napellus*, *Cortaderia selloana* 'Aureolineata', *Crocosmia* × *crocosmiiflora* 'Lady Hamilton', *Euphorbia schillingii*, *Helenium* 'Septemberfuchs'

H: 36 in. (90 cm)  S: 18 in. (45 cm)
❀ Late summer to mid-autumn
  Z5  pH5.5–7.5

The brick-red flower spikes of *Persicaria amplexicaulis* harmonize with sprays of burnt orange montbretia (*Crocosmia* × *crocosmiiflora*) in late summer.

## Persicaria amplexicaulis

The flowers of this moisture-loving knotweed (syn. *Polygonum amplexicaule*) are a slightly impure brick-red, and appear prolifically in sunny sites. They work well with salmon, peach or burnt orange and with bronze foliage, and may be contrasted with yellow-green foliage or flowers. With its rather divergent flower stems and slightly coarse leaves, the plant is more at home in informal, waterside or bog gardens. It is best combined with plants of bold form – rodgersias or white-flowered hostas, for example – or with contrasting foliage such as that of grasses, ferns and crocosmias. 'Firetail' ♀ has brighter red flowers, and 'Inverleith' is a rich deep red. The flowers attract wasps, so planting near sitting areas should be avoided.

**Perfect partners:** *Euphorbia schillingii*, *Hosta* 'Honeybells', *Ligularia dentata* 'Desdemona', *Phalaris arundinacea* var. *picta* 'Feesey', *Rodgersia pinnata* 'Elegans'

**H: 12–48 in.** (30–120 cm) **S: 18–48 in.** (45–120 cm)
❀ **Midsummer to early autumn**
○○-○○○ ☐-■ ■ Z5 pH5–7.5

## Phalaris arundinacea var. *picta* 'Picta' ♀
GARDENER'S GARTERS

Bright stripes in the leaves carry a hint of cream, which enhances their appearance when grown among yellow, apricot or peach-colored flowers. There are a number of other similar variegated clones. 'Aureovariegata' and 'Luteovariegata' are both more yellow; the leaves of 'Tricolor' have a distinct pink flush for combining with purple foliage and pink, red or mauve flowers; 'Feesey' is shorter, brighter with a faint pink flush, and less invasive. Plants are best in moist, rich situations: in poor or dry soil in the sun, the foliage can become untidy in summer.

**Perfect partners:** *Achillea* 'Lachsschönheit', *Crocosmia* × *crocosmiiflora* 'Solfatare', *Cynara cardunculus* p.256 **A**, *Hemerocallis fulva*, *Tulipa* 'Ballerina' p.392 **B**

**H: 30–40 in.** (75–100 cm) **S: 40 in.** (1 m)
❀ **Late spring to early summer**
○○ ☐-■ ■ Z4 pH5–7.5

The bright variegation of *Phalaris arundinacea* var. *picta* 'Picta' contrasts boldly with the dark foliage of *Berberis thunbergii* 'Rose Glow'. Behind, carmine *Clematis* 'Madame Julia Correvon' harmonizes with the berberis.

## Phlomis russeliana ♀

This variable species has handsome leaves – mid-green and long, with a heart-shaped base – and hooded flowers that can range from almost pure light yellow to fawn. They are borne in dense whorls on upright stems, producing a distinct rhythm and pattern when plants are grown in large groups. This is the best way to make an impact because single specimens tend to have too few flowers to be effective. The color is very good with warm hues such as soft yellow, apricot, peach and cream, as well as with yellow-green flowers or foliage.

This selection of *Phlomis russeliana* has flowers of clear yellow, rather than brownish buff, which make a fine contrast with lavender-blue flowers such as those of the catmint *Nepeta sibirica*. The phlomis is sufficiently strongly colored to be seen against a background of the harmonious cream variegation of the privet *Ligustrum ovalifolium* 'Argenteum'.

Since the species varies in the number of flowers it develops, it is best to obtain plants from a clone of known quality. Plants can tolerate some shade, although they produce more flowers when in full sun.

**Perfect partners:** *Cornus alba* 'Spaethii', *Cytisus* × *kewensis*, *Digitalis purpurea* f. *albiflora*, *Euphorbia characias* subsp. *wulfenii*, *Geranium sanguineum* var. *striatum*, × *Halimiocistus wintonensis* 'Merrist Wood Cream'

**H: 36 in.** (90 cm) **S: 30 in.** (75 cm)
❀ **Late spring to early autumn**
○ ☐-■ ■ Z4 pH5.5–7.5

## *Phlox divaricata* subsp. *laphamii* 'Chattahoochee' ♔

With its purple-tinted stems and long, prolific display of lavender flowers with purplish red eyes, this prostrate plant is a good subject for growing with purple foliage – purple-leaved heucheras, for example – or with crimson, purple, mauve or mauve-pink flowers. It is also useful for underplanting sparsely branched roses in these colors. It looks effective in a woodland garden, at the front of a border and in containers, and makes a pretty carpeting plant, but would benefit from more structured partners such as green hostas with a narrow white leaf edge. The color goes well with yellow-green foliage or flowers. Partial shade is the best aspect, but it will tolerate full sun where summers are cool. Plants are relatively short-lived, and very susceptible to slug damage.

**Perfect partners:** *Alchemilla mollis, Aquilegia canadensis, Cornus florida, Heuchera* 'Plum Pudding', *Hosta* 'Hydon Sunset' p.294 **A**, *Primula japonica, Rosa* 'Charles de Mills', *Symphytum* 'Goldsmith' p.337 **C**

**H: 6 in.** (15 cm)  **S: 12 in.** (30 cm)
❀ **Late spring to early autumn**

◊◊-◊◊◊  ☐-■  ■ Z4 pH5.5–7.5

As the first blooms of *Phlox divaricata* subsp. *laphamii* 'Chattahoochee' open, they are set off by the salmon flowers and cream variegation of *Pulmonaria rubra* 'David Ward'.

## *Phlox maculata*
MEADOW PHLOX

This upright perennial has narrow, conical flowerheads, loosely branched in some cultivars, in colors from mauve to lilac. These shades are good with purple, white, crimson or blue flowers and with purple foliage, and contrast well with sulfur- or lemon-yellow. There are several excellent cultivars: 'Alba' is white, 'Alpha' ♔ mauve, and 'Omega' ♔ white with a magenta eye. 'Natascha', slightly shorter than the species, has cylindrical spikes of white and pink striped flowers. 'Princess Sturdza' is one of the finest selections with a color between mauve and lilac. All are suitable for borders in sun or partial shade,

Although strong yellow and mauve can make an uneasy alliance, the slightly paler yellow daylily *Hemerocallis* 'Marion Vaughn' and *Phlox maculata*, here with teasel (*Dipsacus fullonum*), make a more pleasant contrast.

and for waterside planting, where the flowers should be scattered or sparsely grouped.

**Perfect partners:** *Achillea* 'Moonshine', *Atriplex hortensis* var. *rubra, Campanula latifolia* 'Brantwood', *Cotinus coggygria* 'Royal Purple', *Echinacea purpurea* p.261 **B**, *Lupinus* 'Polar Princess', *Macleaya cordata*

**H: 36 in.** (90 cm)  **S: 18 in.** (45 cm)
❀ **Early to midsummer**

 ◊◊-◊◊◊  ☐-■  ■ Z4 pH5.5–7.5

In midsummer, the cream-variegated foliage of *Phlox paniculata* 'Norah Leigh' harmonizes with a white agapanthus, while its mauve-pink flowers blend happily with the Oriental hybrid lily *Lilium* 'Black Beauty' and the Regal pelargonium *P.* 'Pompeii', a cultivar that will bloom outdoors even in climates with barely warm summers.

## Phlox paniculata 'Norah Leigh'

This perennial phlox is grown for its creamy white foliage rather than for its flowers, which are mauve-pink with magenta eyes. It is good in borders, placed a little forward so the leaves are clearly visible. This also benefits growth because, with so little green in the leaves, the plant's constitution is slightly weakened and it is less able to compete with its neighbors. The flower color restricts partners to crimson, purple, pink, mauve or blue flowers and contrasting purple foliage. Other variegated cultivars include 'Pink Posie', in deeper pink, and 'Harlequin', in magenta-purple, both less brightly variegated and therefore a little more vigorous. It is essential to get stock free from stem eelworm, which kills the lower leaves.

**Perfect partners:** *Campanula* 'Kent Belle', *Corylus maxima* 'Purpurea', *Geranium* × *oxonianum* 'Claridge Druce', *Heuchera* 'Plum Pudding', *Rosa* 'De Rescht'

**H: 40 in.** (1 m) **S: 24 in.** (60 cm)
❀ Midsummer to mid-autumn
◖◖ ▣-▨ **Z4 pH5.5–7.5**

A pale blend of green and cream, *Phormium* 'Duet' and the scented pelargonium *P.* 'Lady Plymouth' make a good focal point for a container where subtle color is needed.

## Phormium 'Bronze Baby'

New Zealand flax (*Phormium tenax* ♥) has upright, swordlike leaves. 'Bronze Baby' is useful as a focal point in smaller gardens or for pots. It is not as emphatic as larger phormiums, because of its size and also because it grows unevenly, with some leaves arching and others borne at an angle. It is best used as a secondary accent, such as in a bedding scheme to echo a focal point provided by a larger purple phormium or a cordyline, and also as a contrast with paler foliage and flowers, especially in sky-blue or yellow-green. It is good with soft orange or peach, with hot colors such as scarlet and with coral or apricot diascias. A loose group may be underplanted with carpeting plants such as Million Bells Series petunias.

**Perfect partners:** *Diascia* 'Dark Eyes', *Phygelius* × *rectus* 'Pink Elf', *Potentilla fruticosa* 'Tangerine', *Skimmia japonica* 'Rubella', *Verbena* 'Lawrence Johnston'

**H & S: 24 in.** (60 cm) ❀ Midsummer
◖◖-◖◖◖ ▣-▨ **Z8 pH5–7.5**

To produce a sumptuous effect at the height of the summer, in either a bed or a good-sized container, the richly colored *Phormium* 'Bronze Baby' can be planted through a carpet of flaming scarlet verbenas.

## Phormium 'Duet' ♥

The leaves of this phormium bear creamy white variegation, mainly near the edges. It is a spreading cultivar, with leaves fairly close to the ground while young, although older plants are stiffer and more upright, especially in areas with hot summers. The plant makes a quieter accent than more upright cultivars such as *P. tenax* 'Variegatum' ♥, so the effect is more relaxed, while the variegation tends to emphasize the leaf shape and the plant's habit. It is useful for the front of a border or for growing in gravel, especially through a contrasting carpet of Tapien Series verbenas or purple bugles. It combines well with paler blue flowers such as pimpernels, and with rich yellow or warm colors such as apricot and peach. It needs adequate moisture to develop into impressive clumps.

**Perfect partners:** *Ajuga reptans* 'Atropurpurea', *Anagallis monellii*, *Hemerocallis* 'Golden Chimes', *Lysimachia nummularia* 'Aurea', *Verbena* Tapien Pink

**H: 40 in.** (1 m) **S: 4 ft.** (1.2 m) ❀ Midsummer
◖◖-◖◖◖ ▣-▨ **Z8 pH5–7.5**

## *Phormium tenax* 'Veitchianum'

This variegated New Zealand flax is extremely spiky, and therefore suitable for the most emphatic accents. With the broad, creamy yellow stripes on its dark green leaves, it is especially effective when used as a contrast to plants with purple foliage, and when grown with strong blue flowers or in harmonies with gold or yellow-green. As with most other plants, the price of brighter variegation is reduced hardiness. *P.t.* 'Variegatum' ♀ has narrower creamy yellow stripes and is less striking than more brightly variegated clones, but it is hardier. Purple-flushed forms are also less hardy. Purpureum Group ♀ is recommended, and has some variation in intensity of color; it harmonizes with flowers in hot colors and makes a fine contrast with yellow-green foliage.

**Perfect partners:** *Bergenia cordifolia* 'Purpurea', *Penstemon* 'Andenken an Friedrich Hahn' p.442 **B**, *Pittosporum tenuifolium* 'Purpureum', *Verbena* Tapien Violet

**H: 8 ft.** (2.5 m) **S: 6 ft.** (1.8 m) ❀ **Midsummer**
◌◌-◌◌◌ ◻-◼ **Z7 pH5–7.5**

In this striking combination relying on foliage effect alone, the creamy yellow striped leaves of *Phormium tenax* 'Veitchianum' make a bold statement between dark-leaved cannas and *Berberis* × *ottawensis* f. *purpurea* 'Superba'.

Jacob's ladder (*Polemonium caeruleum*) contrasts with *Spiraea japonica* 'Gold Mound', accompanied by black pansies, achilleas and wood forget-me-nots (*Myosotis sylvatica*) in a charming incident that could be equally effective used on a larger scale.

## *Polemonium caeruleum*
JACOB'S LADDER

The flowers of this easy herbaceous perennial have cool campanula-blue petals and orange anthers. They form effective contrasts with soft yellow flowers and yellow-green flowers or foliage, and harmonize with mauve or purple flowers or silver foliage. Garden forms are usually about 16 in. (40 cm) tall, suiting them to the front ranks of a border. They can seem rather leafy and a little coarse, and are best used in more informal areas. Other polemoniums of merit include *P.c.* subsp. *caeruleum* f. *album*, with pure white flowers, and *P. foliosissimum* subsp. *foliosissimum* ♀ (syn. *P. archibaldiae*), which is soft lavender, flowers longer and is self-sterile.

**Perfect partners:** *Achillea* 'Moonshine', *Allium cristophii*, *Artemisia schmidtiana*, *Euphorbia characias* subsp. *wulfenii*, *Stachys byzantina* 'Silver Carpet'

**H: 24 in.** (60 cm) **S: 16 in.** (40 cm) ❀ **Early summer**
◌◌-◌◌◌ ◼-◼ **Z4 pH5–7.5**

In a lightly shaded site, the soft shield fern (*Polystichum setiferum*) contrasts strongly in form with the sub-shrubby spurge *Euphorbia characias*. This is a simple but striking combination that needs no color other than green.

## *Polystichum setiferum* ♔

SOFT SHIELD FERN

This evergreen fern tolerates a wide range of conditions, including dry shade, and is useful in woodland and rock gardens, at the front of borders and in small city gardens. The soft fronds are bright green and arranged like a shuttlecock, with dense brown scales on the stems and leaf buds. There are several cultivars, all of which grow successfully through low ground cover such as acaenas, bugles or small spreading ivies, or with ferns of contrasting form – hart's tongues, for example. Among the most attractive variants are Acutilobum Group, with erect fronds and wedge-shaped pinnules; Congestum Group, with overlapping pinnae; lacy Divisilobum Group and crested 'Divisilobum Iveryanum' ♔; and the very feathery Plumosodivisilobum Group. 'Pulcherrimum Bevis' ♔ is tall and bold, with evenly spaced pinnae.

**Perfect partners:** *Acaena saccaticupula* 'Blue Haze', *Ajuga reptans* 'Catlin's Giant', *Arisaema erubescens* p.354 A, *Convallaria majalis* p.252 A, *Macleaya microcarpa* p.311 A

**H: 24–48 in.** (60–120 cm) **S: 18–36 in.** (45–90 cm)
◌·◌◌◌ □-■ ■ Z5 pH4.5–7.5

## *Potentilla* 'Etna'

This clump-forming cinquefoil has mid- to dark green leaves overlaid with silver hairs, and sprawling stems bearing semi-double, blood-red flowers. It is most effective against a lighter background, such as silver or yellow-green foliage or paler flowers, in hot yellow or orange, or warm peach, apricot and rich salmon. At the front of a border, it can trail over carpeting plants such as variegated ivies, acaenas or golden creeping Jenny, or grow into a small glaucous hebe, hypericum or phygelius. It mixes well with violas, pinks and zinnias, alchemillas, smaller pelargoniums, coleus and California poppies, and with plants of similar habit, such as nasturtiums, bidens and *Helichrysum petiolare* cultivars.

**Perfect partners:** *Artemisia ludoviciana* 'Silver Queen', *Berberis thunbergii* 'Aurea', *Hebe* 'Red Edge', *Hedera helix* 'Glacier', *Phygelius* × *rectus* 'Pink Elf'

**H: 18 in.** (45 cm) **S: 24 in.** (60 cm)
❀ **Early to late summer**
◌◌ □-■ ■ Z5 pH5–7.5

Against a background of dark foliage, blood-red *Potentilla* 'Etna' scrambles forward across the floriferous seed-raised *Viola* 'Prince John', whose bright yellow blooms highlight those of the potentilla.

In two colors that lie to either side of primary deep pink, coral *Potentilla nepalensis* 'Miss Willmott' and soft magenta *Stachys macrantha* 'Superba' contrast gently, the potentilla scrambling around, into and over its companion.

## *Potentilla nepalensis* 'Miss Willmott' ♔

This clump-forming cinquefoil makes a looser plant than *P.* 'Etna' (above), and its flowers vary from salmon-pink to deeper cherry-pink. It is just as effective trailing over other plants at the front of a border, although its color is more telling from a distance. Its flowers combine well with warm tints such as peach and apricot, and with purple foliage plants like dark-leaved heucheras. It can be contrasted with small amounts of yellow-green flowers. Good partners are diascias, soft orange or ruby-red violas, smaller purple- or bronze-leaved shrubs and silver foliage plants, including *Senecio viravira* and *Helichrysum petiolare* cultivars. For dramatic effect, it can be trained into low-growing roses of significantly different color, such as very pale pink or rich red.

**Perfect partners:** *Berberis thunbergii* 'Atropurpurea Nana', *Diascia barberae* 'Blackthorn Apricot', *Heuchera villosa* 'Palace Purple', *Rosa* 'Europeana'

**H: 18 in.** (45 cm) **S: 24 in.** (60 cm)
❀ **Early to late summer**
◌◌ □-■ ■ Z5 pH5–7.5

## *Primula elatior* ♀
OXLIP

Like its cousin *P. vulgaris*, the common primrose, this herbaceous perennial tolerates heavy soils and wet conditions. It is suitable for naturalizing in grass or in sunny glades in a woodland garden, as well as more subdued plantings at the front of a border. It combines well with white, blue or yellow flowers, and also blends attractively with warm-colored tints such as peach and apricot. It can be naturalized with lady's smock, pasque flowers and smaller narcissi. In less natural settings it looks good with such spring plants as wood anemones, brunneras, omphalodes, muscari

In this design, soft yellow oxlips (*Primula elatior*) are joined by the purple chequered blooms of snake's head fritillary (*Fritillaria meleagris*) and white *Fm.* var. *unicolor* subvar. *alba*, along with a semi-wild, self-seeded pink polyanthus.

and forget-me-nots, and with foliage of contrasting form, particularly yellow-green grasses and sedges.

**Perfect partners:** *Anemone nemorosa* 'Allenii', *Cardamine pratensis*, *Milium effusum* 'Aureum', *Narcissus* 'Sun Disc', *Omphalodes cappadocica*, *Pulsatilla vulgaris*

**H: 12 in.** (30 cm) **S: 10 in.** (25 cm)
✿ Mid-spring to early summer
  Z5 pH5.5–8

## *Primula* 'Guinevere' ♀

This is a herbaceous perennial with dark foliage and freely borne pink flowers, which looks most attractive at the front of a border. It may also be used for ground cover between deciduous shrubs such as shrub or bedding roses. It blends well with cool colors such as blue, mauve, deeper pink, crimson and white, and purple or red-flushed foliage. Its flower color is strong enough to contrast well with yellow-green flowers and can hold its own with other primroses and polyanthus in distinctly different colors. Good companions include epimediums, corydalis, cardamines and hellebores, and bulbs such as muscari, scillas, ipheions, snake's head fritillaries and smaller white narcissi.

**Perfect partners:** *Euphorbia polychroma* 'Major', *Heuchera villosa* 'Palace Purple', *Primula* 'Wanda', *Pulmonaria saccharata*, *Scilla siberica*

The smoky bronze foliage and soft pink flowers of *Primula* 'Guinevere' harmonize with the dainty blue blooms and feathery leaves of *Corydalis flexuosa*.

**H: 6 in.** (15 cm) **S: 8 in.** (20 cm)
✿ Early to late spring
 Z5 pH5.5–7.5

Growing in moist ground, the warm colors of *Primula* Inshriach hybrids blend agreeably with the bronze leaves and vermilion bracts of *Euphorbia griffithii* behind.

## *Primula* Inshriach hybrids

These are herbaceous perennial Candelabra primulas, in colors that range from yellow through orange to scarlet, together with paler tones such as apricot and coral-pink. All blend well with warm colors, bronze foliage and white or yellow-green flowers. They thrive in waterside sites, in bog or woodland gardens and in very moist borders, where they can associate with bronze rodgersias, yellow-green hostas, *Euphorbia griffithii* cultivars and the contrasting foliage of stenanthiums, veratrums and yellow-green or bronze moisture-loving ferns and sedges. Other good partners are early-flowering astilbes, ligularias, gold-variegated or yellow-green leaved dogwoods, and some Sikkimensis primulas.

**Perfect partners:** *Carex elata* 'Aurea', *Cornus alba* 'Spaethii', *Iris orientalis*, *Matteuccia struthiopteris*, *Primula sikkimensis*, *Rodgersia pinnata* 'Superba', *Veratrum nigrum*

**H: 30 in.** (75 cm) **S: 18 in.** (45 cm)
✿ Late spring to early summer
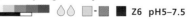 Z6 pH5–7.5

## *Primula japonica*

With its tiers of flowers in purplish red to
white, this Candelabra primula is superb for
naturalizing in a bog garden, beside water or
in dappled shade. It combines best with pink,
crimson and purple flowers, purple-leaved
plants, and the contrasting foliage of Siberian
or *Laevigatae* irises, sedges, grasses and ferns.
Yellowish green spring foliage, such as on
ostrich-plume ferns, makes a good contrast.
While the plant mixes well with other
primulas such as polyanthus and primroses,
hybrids may result, possibly marring color
schemes. 'Miller's Crimson' ♀ is richly hued
with deep crimson eyes; 'Postford White' ♀
has florets with carmine eyes.

**Perfect partners:** *Astilbe* × *arendsii* 'Venus',
*Dryopteris affinis*, *Iris ensata* cultivars, *I. sibirica*
'Cambridge', *Ligularia dentata* 'Othello',
*Molinia caerulea* 'Variegata'

**H & S: 18 in.** (45 cm)
❀ **Late spring to early summer**
▨▨▨▨ ◊◊◊ ▢-▣ ▉ Z4 pH5–7.5

In this streamside planting through a woodland glade, soft
crimson *Primula japonica* stands above a carpet of wild
sweet William (*Phlox divaricata*) in cool lavender, growing
in moist ground by the water's edge.

## *Primula* 'Rowallane Rose'

This Candelabra primula, producing rich
salmon flowers with a yellow eye, thrives
in waterside or bog gardens. It looks most
attractive with soft orange, salmon or peach
companions, with soft yellow flowers such as
those of geums and deciduous azaleas, and
with bronze foliage. For contrast it may be
planted with grasses, including those with
yellow-green leaves, and yellow-green or
yellow-variegated hostas. 'Rowallane Rose'
is a sterile hybrid that needs propagating
by division. 'Inverewe' ♀ (syns 'Keillour
Copper' and 'Ravenglass Vermilion') is also
sterile, with dark flower stems 24 in. (60 cm)

In a warm-colored waterside scheme, the rich salmon
candelabra of *Primula* 'Rowallane Rose' overtop the soft
yellow-edged leaves of *Hosta fortunei* var. *aureomarginata*,
both plants supplying strong architectural form.

tall, and intense vermilion flowers that make
it suitable for hot color schemes or
combinations with bronze foliage.

**Perfect partners:** *Carex comans* (bronze),
*Geum* 'Lady Stratheden', *Hakonechloa macra*
'Alboaurea', *Ligularia dentata* 'Desdemona',
*Rhododendron* 'Narcissiflorum'

**H & S: 18 in.** (45 cm)
❀ **Late spring to early summer**
 ◊◊◊ ▢-▣ ▉ Z6 pH5–7.5

## *Primula veris* ♢
COWSLIP

Rich yellow petals of cowslip flowers emerge from pale apple-green calyces, suggesting harmonies with other apple-green flowers such as *Helleborus* × *sternii* and some selections from *H.* × *hybridus*. Plants may be naturalized in grass, in borders in a wild garden or in light, dappled shade in woodland. Here it is effective with blue flowers such as forget-me-nots, omphalodes or brunneras, and with other primulas such as primroses. It harmonizes with glaucous-leaved plants, and with yellow-green foliage, although this might camouflage the cowslip so the two are best separated with a contrasting plant. It combines well with hot colors, but avoid bold planting schemes.

**Perfect partners:** *Brunnera macrophylla, Dicentra eximia, Hyacinthoides hispanica, Omphalodes cappadocica, Primula vulgaris* subsp. *sibthorpii, Pulmonaria angustifolia*

**H & S: 10 in.** (25 cm)
✽ **Mid-spring to early summer**
◌◌ ▢-▧ ■ Z5 pH6–8

At the edge of a border, cowslips (*Primula veris*) are contrasted with wood forget-me-nots (*Myosotis sylvatica*), while the yellow-green leaved *Philadelphus coronarius* 'Aureus' behind harmonizes with the cowslips.

## *Pulmonaria* 'Lewis Palmer' ♢

This lungwort (syn. 'Highdown') has flowers that open dusky carmine touched with purple, ageing to rich blue, and leaves lightly spotted with silver-green. Growing best in full spring sunshine, with light shade in summer, it is effective in woodland gardens and semi-shady borders, and as ground cover under late-leafing deciduous shrubs, such as *Hibiscus syriacus*, that do not hide the flowers. It contrasts well with soft yellow or yellow-green flowers, and with golden grassy foliage such as Bowles golden sedge, and it harmonizes with ferns, early-leafing hostas and white or sulphur narcissi.

**Perfect partners:** *Carex elata* 'Aurea', *Hosta fortunei* var. *albopicta* f. *aurea, Milium effusum* 'Aureum', *Narcissus* 'Tête-à-tête' p.385 **A**, *Rhododendron* Cilpinense Group p.130 **B**

**H: 14 in.** (35 cm) **S: 10 in.** (25 cm)
✽ **Early to mid-spring**
◌◌-◌◌◌ ▢-▧ ■ Z5 pH5–7.5

In a sumptuous but cool-colored combination for moist, humus-rich soil, *Pulmonaria* 'Lewis Palmer' is set against the glowing crimson winter heath, *Erica carnea* 'Myretoun Ruby'.

## *Pulmonaria saccharata*
JERUSALEM SAGE

The flowers open pink and mature to blue, over leaves that are spotted with silvery green. The mix of pink and blue works well with blue, pink, crimson, purple or white flowers, and with purple or glaucous foliage. It is a good partner for polyanthus and primroses in these colors, and for foliage of contrasting form, such as grasses and ferns. Like all lungworts, it prefers spring sun, with dappled shade in summer, and is suitable for a woodland garden or for underplanting late-leafing deciduous shrubs. The silvery leaf spots coalesce in Argentea Group ♢, the best clones of which have leaves that are entirely silvery green. 'Alba' has pure white flowers.

**Perfect partners:** *Anemone nemorosa* 'Leeds Variety', *Bergenia cordifolia* 'Purpurea', *Corydalis flexuosa* 'Purple Leaf', *Dicentra eximia, Erythronium californicum* 'White Beauty', *Primula* 'Guinevere', *P.* 'Tawny Port'

**H: 12 in.** (30 cm) **S: 24 in.** (60 cm)
✽ **Early to late spring**
◌◌-◌◌◌ ▢-▧ ■ Z4 pH5–7.5

If cut back after flowering in spring, Jerusalem sage (*Pulmonaria saccharata*) will bear handsome, healthy foliage into the autumn. Here, it forms a carpet for the scrambling, herbaceous *Clematis* 'Praecox', whose milk-white blooms in late summer create a pleasing pattern with the spots on the pulmonaria's leaves.

A

Standing prominently at the edge of a bed, in front of a carpet of pure blue *Ceratostigma willmottianum* and a sentinel clump of New Zealand flax (*Phormium tenax*), the exotic trumpets of *Rehmannia elata* mingle with racemes of the smaller, paler pink blooms of *Diascia rigescens*.

## Rehmannia elata ♈

The large, showy flowers of this rehmannia, appearing in early summer, resemble those of incarvilleas, and are rich carmine-pink tending towards magenta, with yellow markings in the throat. Most attractive with cool colors and purple foliage, they also contrast well with soft yellow or yellow-green. They are superb in semi-tropical schemes, and good partners for flowers of contrasting form, such as pink gypsophilas, thalictrums and purple salvias that produce flowers in a spike. Although the woody stems are relatively tender, plants grow again readily from shoots produced from the rootstock, provided frost does not penetrate too deeply into the soil. Where the rootstock is likely to become frozen in winter, plants are best treated as tender bedding for summer display.

**Perfect partners:** *Eryngium* × *tripartitum* p.265 **C**, *Gypsophila* 'Rosenschleier', *Nigella damascena* p.438 **B**, *Rosa* 'Yesterday' p.215 **B**, *Salvia nemorosa* 'Ostfriesland'

H: **24 in.** (60 cm)   S: **18 in.** (45 cm)
❈ **Early to late summer**

 ◊◊ ▢-▨ ▮ Z9 pH5.5–7.5

## Rodgersia pinnata

This rhizomatous herbaceous perennial is a superb plant for watersides and bog gardens. It has pinnate foliage and pyramidal panicles of flowers in yellowish white, pink or red, later developing mahogany-red seedheads that remain decorative into autumn. It is an attractive plant that can complement pink and crimson flowers, and pink- or red-flowered sorts may be contrasted with yellow-green flowers such as late euphorbias. Good partners include filipendulas, persicarias, lilies and perennial lobelias, cannas, later-blooming monardas and contrasting foliage such as grasses and ferns. 'Alba' is yellowish white; 'Buckland Beauty' is rosy-red; 'Elegans' has sweet-scented, creamy white flowers; and 'Superba' ♈ is relatively tall, with red-flushed leaves and bright pink flowers.

**Perfect partners:** *Hosta* 'Buckshaw Blue' p.291 **B**, *Lilium speciosum*, *Lobelia cardinalis* 'Queen Victoria', *Mimulus cardinalis*, *Monarda* 'Beauty of Cobham', *Persicaria amplexicaulis*

H: **36–48 in.** (90–120 cm)   S: **24–30 in** (60–75 cm)
❈ **Mid- to late summer**

◊◊-◊◊◊ ▢-▨ ▮ Z5 pH5–7.5

C

Grasses, like ferns, provide a telling contrast of form with rodgersias. Here, the bronze-flushed palmate foliage of *Rodgersia podophylla* is joined by the elegant cream-striped *Miscanthus sinensis* 'Variegatus'.

B

Ferns are classic partners for rodgersias, liking similar conditions and providing an effective contrast of form. In this moist, semi-shady bed, the bold leaves of *Rodgersia pinnata* furnish the base of golden male fern (*Dryopteris affinis*), its orange-tinged fronds just unfurling.

## Rodgersia podophylla ♈

This rhizomatous herbaceous perennial thrives in the same conditions as *R. pinnata* (above), preferring damp or moist sites but tolerating any position as long as the soil does not dry out completely. It produces panicles of greenish cream flowers that suit mixtures with warm tints and yellow-green foliage and flowers. Its palmate leaves, usually with five leaflets, are bronze when young, maturing to green, and later providing bright reddish bronze autumn tints that harmonize well with a whole range of late-coloring trees and shrubs, including maples, linderas, aronias, clethras and stephanandras, as well as smoke bush, deciduous berberis, euonymus, azaleas, sumachs and autumn-coloring grasses.

**Perfect partners:** *Acer palmatum* 'Ōsakazuki', *Deschampsia cespitosa*, *Dryopteris affinis* p.261 **A**, *Euphorbia schillingii*, *Kirengeshoma palmata*, *Rhododendron luteum*

H: **3–5 ft.** (90–150 cm)   S: **24–30 in.** (60–75 cm)
❈ **Early to late summer**

 ◊◊-◊◊◊ ▢-▨ ▮ Z5 pH5–7.5

## *Roscoea cautleyoides* ♀

This exotic-looking relative of ginger is a tuberous herbaceous perennial, with white, yellow or magenta-purple flowers. It generally prefers humus-rich soil, good drainage and some shade, and so makes an excellent plant for woodland gardens, partially shaded rockeries and shady borders. The commonest variant is 'Kew Beauty' ♀, with large, pale creamy yellow flowers that suit combinations with flowers in warm tints, stronger yellows, yellow-green or white, and yellow-green or gold-variegated foliage. It is particularly attractive with ferns, smaller sedges, grasses and hostas (especially purple-flowered ones), later-flowering woodland plants including patrinias, and later-flowering lilies, as long

as these are not too strongly colored. Good magenta-purple selections are available, including 'Early Purple' and 'Purple Giant'.

**Perfect partners:** *Acer palmatum* var. *dissectum, Carex siderosticha* 'Variegata', *Dryopteris affinis, Hosta* 'Ginko Craig', *Lilium regale, Meconopsis betonicifolia, Molinia caerulea* 'Variegata', *Patrinia triloba* var. *palmata*

**H: 18 in.** (45 cm) **S: 12 in.** (30 cm)
✿ **Early to midsummer**

⬛⬛⬛⬜⬜ ◊◊ ⬜-⬛ **Z6 pH5–7.5**

In a semi-shaded bed of moist, humus-rich soil in early summer, the soft, creamy yellow, orchidlike blooms of *Roscoea cautleyoides* contrast in size, shape and color with the striking blue flowers of *Corydalis flexuosa*. A shady rock garden also makes a good home for roscoea.

The combination of *Rudbeckia fulgida* var. *deamii* with a richly colored *Aster amellus* or *A.* × *frikartii* cultivar provides months of dramatically contrasting display, as here with *A.a.* 'King George'.

## *Rudbeckia fulgida* var. *deamii* ♀

This clump-forming herbaceous perennial has neat growth and prolific, bright golden yellow single daisy flowers, each with a mahogany-colored center. It is very useful for hot-colored schemes and contrasts with blue or purple, and also succeeds with perennials and grasses planted in a naturalistic way in relatively nutrient-poor soil. It combines well with heleniums, daylilies, dahlias and other yellow daisies such as coreopsis, and looks outstanding with the contrasting foliage of larger grasses like *Miscanthus sinensis* cultivars. Effective with bronze shrubs and sedges, and yellow-green foliage and flowers such as nicotianas or feverfews, it can also be used with annuals – including larger tagetes, zinnias and annual coreopsis – and with tender perennials like coleus, *Helichrysum petiolare* cultivars, argyranthemums, and osteospermums.

**Perfect partners:** *Aster novi-belgii* 'Marie Ballard' p.241 **B**, *Bidens ferulifolia, Crocosmia* × *crocosmiiflora* 'Lady Hamilton' p.255 **A**, *Hemerocallis fulva* 'Flore Pleno', *Nicotiana langsdorffii, Plectranthus argentatus* p.445 **A**, *Rudbeckia laciniata* 'Herbstsonne', *Zinnia* 'Chippendale'

**H & S: 36 in.** (90 cm)
✿ **Late summer to mid-autumn**

⬛⬛⬜⬜ ◊◊ ⬜-⬛ **Z4 pH5.5–7.5**

## *Rudbeckia laciniata* 'Herbstsonne'

Long-flowering and unusually tall, this herbaceous perennial is a good candidate for the widest herbaceous borders, mixed borders and even shrubberies. Its rich yellow flowers with yellowish green centers blend well with hot-colored flowers and yellow-green, red or bronze foliage, and create memorable contrasts with blue flowers such as echinops or aconites. Suitable partners include taller heleniums, *Ceanothus* × *delileanus* cultivars and larger *Miscanthus* cultivars, and shrubs with colored foliage such as smoke bush, deciduous dogwoods, philadelphus, hazels, physocarpus or elders. It may be used imaginatively with pollarded trees with colored leaves – for example, poplars or catalpas kept to a comparable height by yearly pruning. Like many of the taller rudbeckias, the spreading rhizomes tolerate most moist soils as well as competition from other plants, making them an excellent choice for wildflower schemes in tall, rough grass. Here, they associate well with

Michaelmas daisies, goldenrods, elecampanes and eupatoriums to produce an exuberant late-season display. In a border, the plants need staking, but can be made bushier by pinching out the flowering stems at the end of spring. *R. maxima*, with drooping golden yellow petals around a prominent black central cone, is even taller at 9 ft. (2.7 m), and may be shortened in the same way.

**Perfect partners:** *Echinops bannaticus* 'Taplow Blue', *Nicotiana* 'Domino Red' p.437 **A**, *Populus alba* 'Richardii' (pollarded), *Sambucus nigra* 'Guincho Purple'

**H: 7 ft. (2.2 m)  S: 3 ft. (90 cm)**
✿ **Midsummer to early autumn**
▬▬▭ ◌◌ ▣-▪ **Z4  pH5.5–7.5**

In this grouping from a border filled with hot-colored flowers, *Rudbeckia* 'Herbstsonne', with broad, reflexed, golden yellow petals surrounding a prominent green cone, is the tallest element of the display. The variegated dogwood (*Cornus alba* 'Spaethii'), here partly mutated to an all-gold sport, provides bulk to its left, while *Heliopsis helianthoides* var. *scabra* 'Spitzentänzerin' echoes the color of the rudbeckia at a shorter height, with a coppery helenium to its left.

At the height of summer, the violet flowers of *Salvia nemorosa* 'Lubecca', borne on a 24 in. (60 cm) plant, are furnished at the base by a cushion of the delicate pink cranesbill, *Geranium sanguineum* var. *striatum*.

## *Salvia nemorosa*

This variable herbaceous perennial has a narrow, upright habit that suits herbaceous and mixed borders, where its shape can be echoed by veronicas, delphiniums and lupins, for example, and steeply banked borders, perhaps set against the horizontal plates of achilleas and the diffuse flowers of crambes or thalictrums. It is also a good candidate for naturalistic planting schemes, with grasses and daisylike flowers such as rudbeckias on free-draining, fairly nutrient-poor soil. Its long, narrow racemes of flowers, usually mauve-pink to lavender-blue and emerging from dark calyces, harmonize with cool colors and purple foliage and contrast with soft yellow, particularly old Shrub roses. Other suitable companions are silver-leaved artemisias, campanulas and Tall Bearded irises, biennials such as sweet Williams, and early-flowering annuals like nigellas. Useful cultivars include 'Amethyst' ♀, violet 'Lubecca' ♀, and purple 'Ostfriesland' ♀.

**Perfect partners:** *Achillea* 'Coronation Gold', *Delphinium* 'Sungleam', *Deschampsia cespitosa*, *Euphorbia seguieriana* subsp. *niciciana* p.269 **B**, *Rudbeckia fulgida* var. *deamii*

**H: 18–36 in. (45–90 cm)  S: 18–24 in. (45–60 cm)**
✿ **Early summer to early autumn**
▬▬▭ ◌-◌◌ ▣-▪ **Z4  pH5.5–7.5**

## *Salvia pratensis*
MEADOW CLARY

The rather diffuse spikes of this lavender-blue herbaceous salvia make a good foil for larger flowers like roses or those with more solid blooms such as delphiniums. It naturalizes well with achilleas, grasses and daisylike flowers. Haematodes Group ♀ produces pale lavender-blue flowers, mixing well with cool colors and silver or purple foliage, contrasting with soft yellow, and good with cranesbills, lavateras and Tall Bearded irises. 'Indigo' ♀ has rich lavender blooms.

**Perfect partners:** *Alchemilla mollis, Anthriscus sylvestris* 'Ravenswing', *Artemisia* 'Powis Castle', *Delphinium* 'Butterball', *Eryngium alpinum, Iris* 'Nightfall', *Rosa* 'Buff Beauty', *Stipa tenuissima, Thalictrum flavum*

**H: 30–40 in.** (75–100 cm) **S: 18 in.** (45 cm)
❀ **Early to midsummer**
◊◊ ▢-■ Z3–4 pH5.5–7.5

The long-flowering, airy, lavender blooms of *Salvia pratensis* 'Indigo' provide a pleasing contrast, of both color and form, beneath the horizontal flowerheads of *Achillea filipendulina* 'Gold Plate'.

## *Salvia* × *sylvestris* 'Mainacht' ♀

This salvia blooms about two weeks before *S.* × *superba* and *S. pratensis* and their variants (left), and therefore suits slightly different combinations with earlier-flowering shrubs and perennials in herbaceous and mixed borders. Its blooms are rich deep lavender-blue emerging from purplish black calyces, and it can be used with cool colors or contrasts with yellow or yellow-green. It goes well with honesty, sweet rocket, columbines, earlier cranesbills and peonies, early yellow Shrub roses, and daylilies, camassias, and Intermediate Bearded irises. Other selections include the slightly lighter 'Blauhügel' ♀, and 'Tänzerin' ♀, with lavender flowers emerging from purple calyces.

**Perfect partners:** *Aquilegia vulgaris* (mixed), *Camassia leichtlinii* 'Semiplena', *Geranium* × *oxonianum* 'A.T. Johnson', *Hemerocallis* 'Golden Chimes', *Hesperis matronalis* var. *albiflora, Lunaria annua* 'Variegata', *Paeonia lactiflora* 'Emperor of India', *Rosa* 'Maigold'

**H: 24 in.** (60 cm) **S: 12 in.** (30 cm) ❀ **Early summer**
◊◊ ▢-■ Z5 pH5.5–7.5

The sumptuous dark blooms of *Salvia* × *sylvestris* 'Mainacht' harmonize perfectly with *Geranium* 'Kashmir Blue'. The near-black calyces remain attractive after flowering and should be left, rather than deadheaded.

In midsummer, the richly colored flowers of *Salvia* × *superba* look striking beside the copper-red blooms of *Helenium* 'Moerheim Beauty'. Deadheading the salvia will encourage it to produce further flowers, prolonging the display.

## *Salvia* × *superba* ♀

This hybrid species of herbaceous salvia has narrow spikes of lavender-blue flowers emerging from deep reddish purple calyces. Its upright habit is similar to that of *S. nemorosa* (facing page) and it may be used in the same situations, especially in borders where it can provide a useful leitmotif with other vertical plants along the border, or a contrast to horizontal flowerheads or diffuse clouds of tiny blooms. The typical lavender-blue clone of the species, sometimes distinguished as *S.* × *s.* 'Superba', is sterile.

Another superlative cultivar is *S.* × *s.* 'Rubin' ♀ which, at 30 in. (75 cm) tall, is compact and bushy, and produces spikes of mauve-pink flowers emerging from purple calyces.

**Perfect partners:** *Achillea millefolium* 'Cerise Queen', *Echinacea purpurea, Eryngium* × *tripartitum* p.265 **B**, *Rudbeckia fulgida* var. *deamii, Thalictrum delavayi* 'Album', *Verbascum* (Cotswold Group) 'Gainsborough'

**H: 24–36 in.** (60–90 cm) **S: 18–24 in.** (45–60 cm)
❀ **Midsummer to early autumn**
◊-◊◊ ▢-■ Z4 pH5.5–7.5

A

In this scheme using bold form and primary colors, the nodding white flowerheads of *Sanguisorba tenuifolia* 'Alba' are backed by the stiffly upright grass *Calamagrostis × acutiflora* 'Strictus', with red *Papaver commutatum* 'Ladybird' and *Crocosmia masoniorum* 'Dixter Flame', blue *Campanula lactiflora* and yellow *Oenothera biennis*.

## *Sanguisorba tenuifolia* 'Alba'

This herbaceous perennial bears white, drooping, almost catkinlike inflorescences, enhanced by their prominent anthers. It is a invaluable component of white-flowered schemes, especially when combined with silver or glaucous foliage. It looks good when grown in a naturalistic way, with artlessly arranged plants emerging from a carpet of smaller flowers – these could be annuals like nigellas and poppies, or perennials such as shorter catmints, salvias and cranesbills, or the Little Princess Series of alstroemerias. Other good companions include artemisias, *Coreopsis verticillata* cultivars, later-flowering heucheras and annuals such as taller ageratums and coreopsis.

**Perfect partners:** *Artemisia ludoviciana, Clarkia amoena* Satin Series, *Geranium × oxonianum* 'Prestbury Blush', *Nepeta × faassenii* 'Alba', *Nigella damascena, Salvia × superba*

**H: 4 ft.** (1.2 m) **S: 24 in.** (60 cm)
✽ Mid- to late summer
 ◊◊ ▢-■ **Z4 pH5.5–7.5**

## *Scabiosa* 'Butterfly Blue'

The blooms of this long-flowering herbaceous perennial scabious are generally soft lavender, but may tend toward lilac in some climates and situations. They combine well with contrasting floral forms – the spikes of smaller penstemons, veronicas or salvias, for example – and with cool-colored flowers and silver or cream foliage. Attractive companions include shorter-growing roses, such as Ground Cover and Patio cultivars, artemisias, pinks, shorter eryngiums and gypsophilas, and annuals such as brachyscomes, clarkias, annual gypsophilas and *Salvia farinacea* cultivars. It also looks effective with tender perennials such as white or pink argyranthemums and purple or pink osteospermums.

**Perfect partners:** *Artemisia schmidtiana, Brachyscome iberidifolia, Eryngium bourgatii* 'Picos Blue', *Gypsophila paniculata* 'Compacta Plena', *Rosa* Pink Bells

**H & S: 18 in.** (45 cm)
✽ Midsummer to early autumn
 ◊◊ ▢-■ **Z4 pH5.5–8**

B

In this complex combination of cool-colored flowers graded in height at the front of a border, *Scabiosa* 'Butterfly Blue' is furnished in front by the glaucous foliage of *Mertensia simplicissima* and the brilliant crimson heads of *Dianthus deltoides* 'Leuchtfunk', and behind by the white *Campanula persicifolia alba*. Two alliums, blue *Allium caeruleum* and large-headed mauve *A. cristophii*, push their way through the other plants.

C

In a simple but effective partnership, the soft scarlet blooms of *Schizostylis coccinea* 'Major' harmonize with the tiny red berries of the herringbone cotoneaster (*C. horizontalis*), trained against a wall behind.

## *Schizostylis coccinea* 'Major' ♱

This red-flowered rhizomatous herbaceous perennial is immensely useful for its late flowers. It prefers moist soil, a sheltered site in cold gardens, and full sun. It can be grown in mixed borders and at the foot of a sunny wall, although here it must be kept moist, to sustain growth and keep flowering unchecked and to prevent attacks by red spider mite, its most serious pest. It is effective with other late flowers such as nerines, liriopes, asters (especially white-flowered cultivars), chrysanthemums and fuchsias, and combines well with autumn-coloring plants including grasses. Other good partners include late-flowering sedums and smaller late roses, white autumn crocuses and colchicums, and plants with bronze or purple foliage. It appears to grow best with a companion, rather than on its own.

**Perfect partners:** *Colchicum speciosum* 'Album', *Crocus speciosus* 'Conqueror', *Fuchsia magellanica* var. *gracilis, Nerine bowdenii, Sedum* 'Herbstfreude', *Stipa tenuissima*

**H: 24 in.** (60 cm) **S: 12 in.** (30 cm)
✽ Late summer to late autumn
 ◊◊ ▢-■ **Z6 pH5.5–7.5**

The warm, rosy-red flowers and purple foliage of *Sedum* 'Bertram Anderson', meandering through a clump of harmonious mauve *Allium senescens*, contrast with the glaucous foliage of the spurge *Euphorbia myrsinites*.

## *Sedum* 'Bertram Anderson' ♔

The fleshy leaves of this herbaceous perennial are perhaps its most outstanding feature. They are glaucous and flushed strongly with deep purple, a coloring that suits schemes with both glaucous-leaved plants and other purple foliage plants, and with cool-colored flowers. As well as being attractive throughout the time it is in leaf, it also has conspicuous pink flowers. It is a good plant for rock and gravel gardens, and for the front of a border, where its slightly sprawling habit does not look untidy. Even out of flower, it is a good plant for combining with pinks, catmints, glaucous fescues and sea kale, sprawling cranesbills, smaller hebes, dwarf hardy fuchsias and smaller hostas, provided these do not shade the sedum. It contrasts well with yellow-green foliage and flowers, including many smaller euphorbias.

**Perfect partners:** *Anthemis punctata* subsp. *cupaniana*, *Festuca glauca* 'Elijah Blue', *Fuchsia* 'Tom Thumb', *Geranium sanguineum* var. *striatum*, *Nepeta* × *faassenii*

**H: 10 in.** (25 cm) **S: 16 in.** (40 cm)
❅ Late summer to mid-autumn

◊-◊◊ □-■ Z4 pH5.5–8

## *Sedum* 'Herbstfreude' ♔

Alternatively called Autumn Joy, this fleshy herbaceous perennial has glaucous foliage that is handsome throughout the season, and glaucous green buds opening into flat flowerheads that start pink, slightly to the mauve side of primary pink, and age to brick-red. Plants look very effective with white flowers – including chrysanthemums, asters, Japanese anemones, colchicums and autumn crocus – and with lavender-blue flowers such as caryopteris and ceratostigmas. The flowerheads remain attractive throughout winter, when they become rusty-red and make colorful partners for the dried leaves and stems of small to medium-size grasses. 'Herbstfreude' excels in gravel gardens and in positions near the front of a border, especially if surrounded by low carpeting companions.

**Perfect partners:** *Allium karataviense* p.350 **A**, *Artemisia alba* 'Canescens' p.236 **B**, *Bergenia* 'Morgenröte' p.246 **A**, *Rosa rugosa* p.208 **B** ❑ p.276 **C**

**H: 18 in.** (45 cm) **S: 24 in.** (60 cm)
❅ Early to mid-autumn

◊◊ □-■ Z3 pH5.5–8

By mid-autumn, the brickish red flowers of *Sedum* 'Herbstfreude', here furnishing the front of a border, match those of *Eupatorium maculatum* 'Atropurpureum' behind, leavened by a white shrubby cinquefoil (*Potentilla fruticosa*), with dwarf pampas grass (*Cortaderia selloana* 'Pumila') supplying a bold focal point.

The glaucous, fleshy foliage and developing flowerheads of *Sedum spectabile* 'Iceberg' look attractive for many months, but the plant has a brief moment of true glory when the flowers open to a rich cream. Soon, however, they turn a rather less appealing brown. Here, they provide a contrast for the bold, light magenta racemes of *Physostegia virginiana* 'Vivid'.

## *Sedum spectabile* ♔

This is one of the parents of *S.* 'Herbstfreude' (above), sharing the qualities of its glaucous foliage, but flowering a little earlier, with bright mauve-pink blooms that combine well with cool colors and silver-gray, purple or glaucous leaves. It mixes well with Japanese anemones, earlier-flowering chrysanthemums, and blue fescues. Later-flowering cranesbills, eryngiums, penstemons and tender perennials like argyranthemums are other good partners. The flowers attract butterflies, and the seedheads remain decorative well into winter. Useful cultivars are 'Album', which opens pure white; bright pink 'Brilliant' ♔; rich carmine 'Carmen' and 'Meteor'.

**Perfect partners:** *Anemone* × *hybrida* 'Honorine Jobert', *Aster* × *fikartii* 'Mönch', *Chrysanthemum* 'Clara Curtis', *Festuca glauca* 'Blaufuchs', *Perovskia* 'Blue Spire' ❑ p.251 **A**

**H: 12–20 in.** (30–50 cm) **S: 18 in.** (45 cm)
❅ Late summer to early autumn

◊◊ □-■ Z3 pH5.5–8

## *Sedum telephium*

ORPINE

This extremely variable species has fleshy, glaucous leaves and light to rich carmine-pink flowers, which mix well with cool colors, purple foliage, and mauve, blue or carmine flowers. Forms with salmon or brick-red flowers are perhaps best with warm tints such as blood-red, salmon, peach or apricot, and with bronze foliage. Dark-leaved variants

include subsp. *maximum* 'Atropurpureum' ♀, which is slightly lax with very dark purplish red leaves, and *S.t.* 'Arthur Branch', with similar leaves, glowing red stems and a more upright habit. These are good clump-formers for the front of a dry, sunny border or for growing in gravel. In winter the seedheads turn a beautiful rusty red.

**Perfect partners:** *Crocosmia* × *crocosmiiflora* 'Solfatare' p.255 **B**, *Dahlia* 'Bishop of Llandaff' p.419 **C**, *Nemesia* 'Innocence' p.436 **B**, *Verbena* 'Lawrence Johnston' p.453 **A**

**H: 18–24 in.** (45–60 cm)  **S: 12–18 in.** (30–45 cm)
❀ **Late summer to early autumn**

◊-◊◊  ▢-▉  **Z4 pH5.5–8**

In this pair of matching mixed borders, the flowers of orpine (*Sedum telephium*) harmonize with the distant brick wall and with purple-leaved *Berberis* × *ottawensis* f. *purpurea* 'Superba', while contrasting with the yellow-green leaves of false acacia (*Robinia pseudoacacia* 'Frisia').

**A**

At the front of a border adjoining a stone path, the erect stems of creamy yellow *Sisyrinchium striatum* provide a strong accent. The plant's base is furnished by a carpet of rich blue-flowered *Veronica austriaca* subsp. *teucrium*, which spills over onto the path.

## *Sisyrinchium striatum*

The pale creamy yellow flowers of this clump-forming perennial blend especially well with blue. It is a good plant for the front of a border, where its grassy, upright habit can offer useful contrasts of texture and form with, for example, santolinas, violas or agastaches, and satisfying harmonies with glaucous or silver foliage, rich yellow flowers and yellow-green flowers or foliage. It thrives in gravel, perhaps with a carpeting plant at its base, and will tolerate even fairly heavy soils, although in these conditions it may be shorter-lived. It seeds itself readily. Timely deadheading can prevent this – and can also help to produce flowers into late summer or even autumn. The variegated 'Aunt May' is less hardy and requires good drainage.

**Perfect partners:** *Achillea* 'Moonshine', *Artemisia* 'Powis Castle', *Campanula persicifolia*, *Kniphofia* 'David', *Lavandula angustifolia* 'Hidcote', *Papaver orientale* cultivars

**H: 24 in.** (60 cm) **S: 12 in.** (30 cm)
❈ **Early to midsummer**

 ◊-◊◊ ☐-☐ **Z7 pH5.5–8**

The plumose flowerheads of the goldenrod *Solidago* 'Crown of Rays' contrast in color and form with the tender, sub-shrubby, fragrant, deep purple *Heliotropium* 'Marine', both of them exactly matched in height.

## *Solidago* 'Crown of Rays'

The dense flowering display of this goldenrod (also known as Strahlenkrone) is seen at its best in loosely spaced or scattered groups, with other plants threaded through. Alternatively, it may be grown in partial shade, which limits the profusion of its flower spikes. It is invaluable for the second rank of a herbaceous border, the golden yellow of its flowers looking especially fine with hot colors such as orange and scarlet, or with bronze foliage. Effective contrasts with blue or purple flowers can be achieved with shorter dahlias and *Aster* × *frikartii* cultivars, or some taller *Aster amellus* cultivars. It is also good with shorter heleniums and early-flowering Michaelmas daisies, and with contrasting textures such as provided by grasses of similar height.

**Perfect partners:** *Aster amellus* 'King George', *Crocosmia* 'Lucifer', *Dahlia* 'Grenadier', *Helenium* 'Wyndley', *Sambucus nigra* 'Guincho Purple' (stooled), *Stipa capillata*

**H: 24 in.** (60 cm) **S: 18 in.** (45 cm)
❈ **Mid- to late summer**

 ◊-◊◊ ☐-☐ **Z4 pH5.5–7.5**

## *Smilacina racemosa* ♧

FALSE SPIKENARD

This clump-forming perennial (syn. *Maianthemum racemosum*) is invaluable for a partially shaded woodland garden or border, especially if surrounded by shorter plants to display its slightly arching habit. Its creamy white flowers blend perhaps most effectively with blue, yellow or yellow-green, and with contrasting strong-colored flowers such as purple bugles or blue corydalis. It is good with contrasting foliage such as ferns, grasses and sedges. Sometimes it bears red berries, which can be useful for schemes in late summer and early autumn; the fruits do not, however, always last long enough for designs with autumn-coloring deciduous shrubs.

**Perfect partners:** *Ajuga reptans* 'Atropurpurea', *Brunnera macrophylla*, *Erythronium* 'Pagoda', *Euphorbia characias* subsp. *wulfenii* 'Lambrook Gold' p.98 **B**, *Polystichum setiferum*

**H: 30 in.** (75 cm) **S: 24 in.** (60 cm)
❈ **Mid- to late spring**

 ◊◊ ☐-☐ **Z4 pH5–7**

Toward the front of a bed in partial shade, a boldly arching clump of false spikenard (*Smilacina racemosa*), topped with creamy plumes of flower, is carpeted beneath with blue *Corydalis flexuosa*. A shield fern adds foliage of contrasting form in front and, like the smilacina, will remain handsome when the corydalis has finished flowering.

In late spring, the emerging flower stems of lamb's ears (*Stachys byzantina*) harmonize with the gray-leaved willow *Salix hastata* 'Wehrhahnii' behind. They are joined by self-seeded wood forget-me-nots (*Myosotis sylvatica*) and Miss Willmott's ghost (*Eryngium giganteum*).

## Stachys byzantina

LAMB'S EARS

An excellent carpeting plant, *S. byzantina* (syns *S. lanata*, *S. olympica*) is suitable for the front of a border and for gravel gardens, its rosettes of silvery gray leaves merging to form soft woolly mats, above which grayish white hairy stems bear whorls of small magenta flowers. It mixes well with other silver-leaved plants such as artemisias, and with lavenders, pinks and catmints. 'Big Ears' (syn. 'Countess Helen von Stein') has larger leaves that are slightly less white but very effective for longer-range viewing. 'Cotton Boll' (syn. 'Sheila McQueen') has longer leaves and abortive flower stalks studded with cottony balls. 'Silver Carpet' is also nonflowering and produces a very flat mat of growth. 'Primrose Heron' has yellow-green leaves, so goes well with gold or yellow-green flowers and adds zest to pink, mauve and soft blue schemes.

**Perfect partners:** *Allium moly* p.350 **B**, *Crocus vernus* 'Jeanne d'Arc' p.359 **B**, *Cynara cardunculus* p.256 **A**, *Rosa* Peach Blossom p.207 **A**, *Tulipa* 'Palestrina' p.400 **B**

**H & S: 18 in.** (45 cm)
❀ **Early summer to early autumn**
◊-◊◊ ☐-■ Z4 pH5.5–7.5

## Stipa calamagrostis

The habit of this grass varies from almost upright, with its bottle-brush spikes scarcely branching, to gracefully arching, with stems of fully branched blooms. The spikes start light green and age to biscuit, and at mid-season both colors appear on a mix of young and old spikes. The glaucous foliage turns warm brown by autumn. This is a drought-tolerant species that thrives in gravel gardens; it also looks attractive near the front of a border, especially surrounded by the shortest sedums or Charm chrysanthemums. The warm biscuit color blends with other warm tints, especially peach, copper and apricot flowers, and bronze foliage, and contrasts well with blue flowers. A stout wire hoop can provide support for the stems.

**Perfect partners:** *Acaena microphylla* 'Kupferteppich', *Ajuga reptans* 'Atropurpurea', *Ceratostigma willmottianum*, *Chrysanthemum* 'Bronze Fairy', *Colchicum autumnale*

**H: 3 ft.** (90 cm) **S: 4 ft.** (1.2 m)
❀ **Early summer to early autumn**
◊◊ ☐-■ Z5 pH5.5–7.5

In this subtle scheme relying on contrasting form and subdued coloring, the parchment plumes of *Stipa calamagrostis* arch over the pink-flushed flowers of *Sedum* 'Strawberries and Cream'.

Left: The glistening seedheads of *Stipa capillata* shimmer against the sun, providing a contrast of form with *Eryngium planum* 'Blaukappe', its flowerheads flushed steely blue.

## Stipa capillata

Like most stipas, *S. capillata* prefers full sun and good drainage and tolerates drought, so it is a superb plant for a gravel garden. It is a tough grass, developing into tall tussocks with hair-like, almost white seedheads that are so fine and insubstantial that, from a distance, they resemble a shimmering cloud. Plants look best in scattered groups, loosely woven through slightly taller companions, forming a radiant foil for plants with a more definite structure. Single plants are ineffective, and solid groups are too nebulous to make a strong impact. Eryngiums are perhaps the supreme partners for them. Others include phormiums (but only cultivars of moderate height, and those in muted colors), kniphofias and the more handsome salvias, such as *Salvia candelabrum*, *S. leucantha*, *S. splendens* 'Van-Houttei' and the densest white selections of shrubby *S. canariensis*.

Above: *Stipa tenuissima* differs from *S. capillata* in its smaller size, narrower habit of growth and denser panicles, suiting it to a smaller scale, including containers, as here.

**Perfect partners:** *Achillea* 'Fanal', *Aster × frikartii* 'Mönch', *Echinops ritro*, *Kniphofia* 'Sunningdale Yellow', *Phormium* 'Duet', *Rudbeckia fulgida* var. *sullivantii* 'Goldsturm'

H: **36 in.** (90 cm) S: **24 in.** (60 cm)
❀ **Early to late summer**
◊-◊◊ ▢-▮ Z6 pH5.5–7.5

## Symphytum 'Goldsmith'

This spreading rhizomatous comfrey has brightly variegated foliage, edged at first with gold but aging to cream, and bears pale blue, white-tipped flowers. Its bright young foliage works well with blue spring flowers, such as brunneras, forget-me-nots, omphalodes, meconopsis and corydalis, and it harmonizes with cream, white or yellow flowers – geums and doronicums, for example. It is also good with plants of contrasting form such as ferns and grasses. 'Goldsmith' is a good ground-cover plant, but it is very vigorous and large plantings can threaten the scale of other plant groups or of the garden itself. It is best grown in partial shade with adequate moisture. The foliage stays brightest, with less mildew, if the flowers are removed as they appear.

**Perfect partners:** *Corydalis flexuosa* 'China Blue', *Forsythia × intermedia* p.100 **A**, *Myosotis sylvatica*, *Omphalodes cappadocica*, *Viola* 'Molly Sanderson'

H: **14 in.** (35 cm) S: **18 in.** (45 cm)
❀ **Mid- to late spring**
◊◊-◊◊◊ ▢-▮ Z5 pH5–7.5

The gold-edged leaves of *Symphytum* 'Goldsmith' contrast with the red-eyed, soft lavender flowers of *Phlox divaricata* subsp. *laphamii* 'Chattahoochee'. Both are plants that relish partial shade and a moist, humus-rich soil.

A

In a semi-shaded site, the airy, pale green racemes of fringe cups (*Tellima grandiflora*) and the purple globes of *Allium hollandicum* contrast in color and form.

## Tellima grandiflora
FRINGE CUPS

This modest perennial, bearing kidney-shaped leaves, with scalloped edges and dainty spikes of pale green flowers, tolerates dry shade and so makes invaluable ground cover for a woodland garden. It is a good foil for plants of bolder shape or brighter color, especially red, orange and purple, as in alliums that flower in late spring. It goes well with most late spring bulbs, although it is best to avoid the largest, showiest kinds, such as Darwinhybrid Group tulips, which are likely to overwhelm the tellima. Forms with red-flushed stems and leaves, such as 'Pinky' and 'Purpurteppich', have pinkish flowers, but the variable Rubra Group may contain individuals that, neither a distinct green nor pink, are a slightly grubby brown. Plants are prone to infestation by vine weevils, especially if grown as a solid mat of ground cover.

**Perfect partners:** *Bergenia* 'Morgenröte', *Euphorbia griffithii* 'Dixter', *Hedera algeriensis* 'Gloire de Marengo', *Hyacinthoides hispanica*, *Narcissus* 'Actaea'

H: 24 in. (60 cm)  S: 18 in. (45 cm)
❀ Late spring to early summer
 ◌◌-◌◌◌ ◼-◼ ◼ Z4 pH5–7.5

## Trillium chloropetalum
GIANT WAKE ROBIN

The stems of this shade-loving perennial each bear three leaves, marbled with silver-green and/or maroon, and arranged around an erect flower, which can be greenish white, yellow or maroon-red. This trillium prefers humus-rich soil in a woodland garden, surrounded by lower-growing plants such as *Anemone nemorosa* cultivars, and looks effective with smaller, pale yellow, cream or white narcissi. Like all trilliums, the plants have the greatest impact when grown in groups of 15 or more crowns. They are slow to increase, but may be divided after flowering. To multiply plants quickly, the crowns can be lifted in early spring, the growing point excised, and the remaining stock cut vertically into three sections, which can then be replanted.

**Perfect partners:** *Alchemilla mollis*, *Anemone nemorosa* 'Leeds' Variety', *Arum italicum* 'Marmoratum', *Myosotis sylvatica*, *Narcissus* 'Hawera', *Omphalodes cappadocica*

H: 20 in. (50 cm)  S: 12 in. (30 cm)
❀ Late spring to early summer
 ◌◌-◌◌◌ ◼-◼ ◼ Z4 pH5.5–7.5

B

Grown in shade, the bold foliage and upright blooms of red-flowered *Trillium chloropetalum* var. *giganteum* ♥ make a strong statement. Its companions here are the yellow archangel *Lamium galeobdolon* 'Silberteppich' – one of very few shade-tolerant plants with silvery leaves – and foamflower (*Tiarella cordifolia*).

C

In the temporary light beneath deciduous trees in late spring, an imposing group of white wake robin (*Trillium grandiflorum*) furnishes the ground in front of an elegant trumpet daffodil.

## Trillium grandiflorum ♥
WHITE WAKE ROBIN

This has the largest trillium flowers, usually pure white but sometimes ageing with a pink flush. Unlike in *T. chloropetalum* (above), the leaves are only loosely arranged around each stem. Excellent in a woodland garden, with other spring flowers or growing through a carpet of bugles or wood anemones, it is also robust enough to associate with plants of similar height such as smaller pulmonarias or epimediums. It is perhaps best with pink, mauve or blue if its flowers have a pink flush.

Good variants include the formal double 'Snow Bunting' (sometimes sold as 'Flore Pleno') and the rose-pink 'Roseum'. Plants can be propagated as for *T. chloropetalum*, and should be protected from slugs.

**Perfect partners:** *Ajuga reptans* 'Catlin's Giant', *Anemone nemorosa* 'Robinsoniana', *Dicentra eximia*, *Epimedium* × *versicolor* 'Discolor', *Pulmonaria saccharata*

H: 16 in. (40 cm)  S: 12 in. (30 cm)
❀ Late spring to early summer
 ◌◌ ◼ ◼ Z4 pH5.5–7.5

In this use of contrasting bold foliage but harmonious flowers, *Veratrum nigrum* furnishes in front of the elegant hybrid plume poppy, *Macleaya* × *kewensis*. The poppy's biscuit-colored flowers are borne in panicles similar in shape to those of the veratrum.

## *Veratrum nigrum* ⟁

This architectural plant has broad, deeply pleated basal leaves, topped by tall, branched panicles of deep maroon flowers in summer. With its handsome appearance, it merits space away from other plants that might vie for attention. Combinations with bright colors and bronze- or purple-leaved shrubs tend to camouflage its grandeur, and it is best associated with more subdued tones, such as soft brick-red or orange, peach, apricot or light to mid-blue; it also benefits from a background of pale foliage to show off its flowers. Asiatic or martagon lilies in warm shades make excellent companions. Partial shade is ideal for this plant. It is very prone to slug and snail damage.

**Perfect partners:** *Cercidiphyllum magnificum*, *Cornus alba* 'Sibirica Variegata', *Lilium* 'Enchantment', *L. martagon*, *Meconopsis betonicifolia*, *Saxifraga fortunei*

**H: 6 ft.** (1.8 m)  **S: 24 in.** (60 cm)
✿ **Mid- to late summer**
 ◊◊-◊◊◊ ▮ ▮ Z4  pH5.5–7.5

## *Verbascum* 'Helen Johnson'

The unusually subtle coloring of this lovely perennial – peachy buff flowers borne over silver gray-green, woolly leaves – is difficult to combine effectively, since it is easily overwhelmed by brighter, brasher tones. Plants look most effective when sited with warm colors such as peach, apricot or soft orange, and with bronze or silver foliage, and they make a telling contrast with pale to mid-sky-blue flowers. Warm-colored achilleas, artemisias, or glaucous grasses make pleasing companions; in fact, glaucous foliage generally offers the most attractive and gentle contrast to the color of the flowers. Some stocks have mutated during micropropagation to lose much of their silvery hairy covering, turning the foliage a darker, duller gray-green – these are best avoided. The plants need sun and sharp drainage if they are to thrive, and are prone to attack by mullein moth.

**Perfect partners:** *Anthriscus sylvestris* 'Ravenswing', *Artemisia ludoviciana*, *Clematis* 'Pastel Blue', *Rosa* 'Climbing Paul Lédé' p.188 **B**, *Stipa calamagrostis*

**H: 36 in.** (90 cm)  **S: 12 in.** (30 cm)
✿ **Early to late summer**
▬▬▮▮ ◊-◊◊ ▯-▮ Z4  pH6–7.5

In this charming mix of flowers, *Verbascum* 'Helen Johnson' stands behind young leaves of the grass *Miscanthus sinensis* and the yellow plate-like heads of *Achillea clypeolata*, with white sweet rocket (*Hesperis matronalis* var. *albiflora*) in the background. The grouping would be most effective on a larger scale, with more space given to each plant.

Rich blue, low-growing *Veronica austriaca* subsp. *teucrium* 'Crater Lake Blue' provides a foil for the flowers of *Osteospermum* 'Pink Whirls', with their spoon-tipped petals.

## *Veronica austriaca* subsp. *teucrium*

This mat-forming speedwell has long-lasting racemes of rich blue flowers. Hybrids include gentian-blue 'Kapitän' and rich, deep 'Crater Lake Blue' ♀, both 12 in. (30 cm) tall, and vivid sky-blue 'Shirley Blue' ♀, just 2–4 in. (6–10 cm). All harmonize with white, pink, and pale blue flowers, such as osteospermums and violas, and contrast with the glaucous foliage of Tardiana Group hostas, eryngiums, sea kale, and many grasses. They need full sun to produce a solid sheet of blue. *V. prostrata* ♀, 6 in. (15 cm) tall, and *V.p.* 'Loddon Blue', 8 in. (20 cm), have similar uses, while *V.p.* 'Trehane' has yellow-green leaves that are useful for combining with other yellow-green foliage plants of bolder form.

**Perfect partners:** *Crambe maritima, Eryngium* × *tripartitum, Euonymus fortunei* 'Emerald 'n' Gold', *Salvia* × *sylvestris* 'Mainacht', *Sisyrinchium striatum* p.335 **A** p.272 **B**

**H: 4–20 in.** (10–50 cm) **S: 6–18 in.** (15–45 cm)
✿ Late spring to midsummer
 Z4 pH5.5–7.5

## *Viola* 'Huntercombe Purple' ♀

The flowers of this mat-forming perennial viola are intense purple-blue and produced profusely throughout much of spring. In areas where late spring and summer are cool, intermittent blooms continue appearing until late summer, when there is a distinct second flush of blue flowers. The plant is particularly effective as a contrast with yellow flowers, and yellow-green flowers or foliage, and blends harmoniously with cool colors such as pink, mauve and blue, or with glaucous and silver foliage plants. It can be used beneath widely spaced roses with an open branch structure – some of the China roses, for example – and may be combined with short-growing purple foliage plants. 'Martin' ♀ is similar, with flowers perhaps a little darker. Plants are vulnerable to aphid attack, which can curtail flowering.

**Perfect partners:** *Ajuga reptans* 'Atropurpurea', *Humulus lupulus* 'Aureus' p.170 **C**, *Rosa* × *odorata* 'Mutabilis', *Stachys byzantina* 'Primrose Heron'

**H: 6 in.** (15 cm) **S: 12 in.** (30 cm)
✿ Mid-spring to late summer
Z5 pH5.5–7.5

The rich flowers of *Viola* 'Huntercombe Purple' contrast effectively with the yellow flowers of golden garlic (*Allium moly*) and the yellow-green foliage of golden creeping Jenny (*Lysimachia nummularia* 'Aurea').

In this softly pretty planting scheme, the dusky pink flowers of *Viola* 'Nellie Britton' match exactly those of the speedwell *Veronica spicata* 'Erika', whose foliage is lightly silvered, harmonizing with the white-edged leaves of *Ajania pacifica*.

## *Viola* 'Nellie Britton' ♀

This viola (syn. 'Haslemere') is one of the most successful hybrids, with its small, dainty flowers in an uncommon shade of dusky mauve-pink (pink is a relatively rare color among viola cultivars). It works well with cool shades such as cream, lilac, blue and palest sulfur-yellow. It makes a pleasing association at the front of a border with silver, purple or glaucous foliage, especially blue fescues or some of the smaller Tardiana Group hostas – 'Blue Blush', 'Blue Moon' or 'Hadspen Blue', for example. 'Vita' is similar, although the flowers are a little larger and a slightly purer shade of pink.

**Perfect partners:** *Epimedium* × *versicolor* 'Sulphureum', *Hebe pinguifolia* 'Pagei', *Helichrysum petiolatum, Heuchera* 'Plum Pudding', *Myosotis sylvatica, Nemophila menziesii*

**H: 6 in.** (15 cm) **S: 12 in.** (30 cm)
✿ Late spring to midsummer
 Z5 pH5.5–7.5

## *Yucca flaccida* 'Golden Sword' ♛

Yuccas are invaluable as focal points, especially the stiff-leaved, stem-forming species such as *Y. aloifolia*, *Y. elephantipes* ♛, and *Y. gloriosa* ♛. Clump-forming species are less strident in their effect, particularly if the leaves tend to flop, as they do in *Y. filifera* and *Y. flaccida* and its cultivars 'Ivory' ♛ and 'Golden Sword' ♛, so these can be used for gentler impact. The almost stemless 'Golden Sword' is grown for its foliage, which has bright gold central variegation. Best planted near the front of a sunny border or gravel garden, it makes greater impact when surrounded by lower plants. It harmonizes with glaucous grasses, bronze or strap-shaped foliage, and hot colors, and contrasts well with blue flowers such as agapanthus.

**Perfect partners:** *Agapanthus* 'Loch Hope', *Crocosmia* × *crocosmiiflora* 'Lady Hamilton', *C.* 'Lucifer', *Helictotrichon sempervirens*, *Hemerocallis* red-flowered cultivars, *Kniphofia* 'Bees Sunset', *Phormium* 'Bronze Baby', *Phygelius* × *rectus* 'African Queen', *Watsonia fourcadei*

**H: 6 ft. (1.8 m)  S: 4 ft. (1.2 m)**
✿ Mid- to late summer
◊-◊◊  ☐-■  Z4  pH5.5–7.5

In this combination for foliage effect that would work equally well with the plants more widely spaced through low ground cover, *Yucca flaccida* 'Golden Sword' is joined by the grass *Stipa arundinacea* and the shrubby honeysuckle *Lonicera nitida* 'Baggesen's Gold'.

A

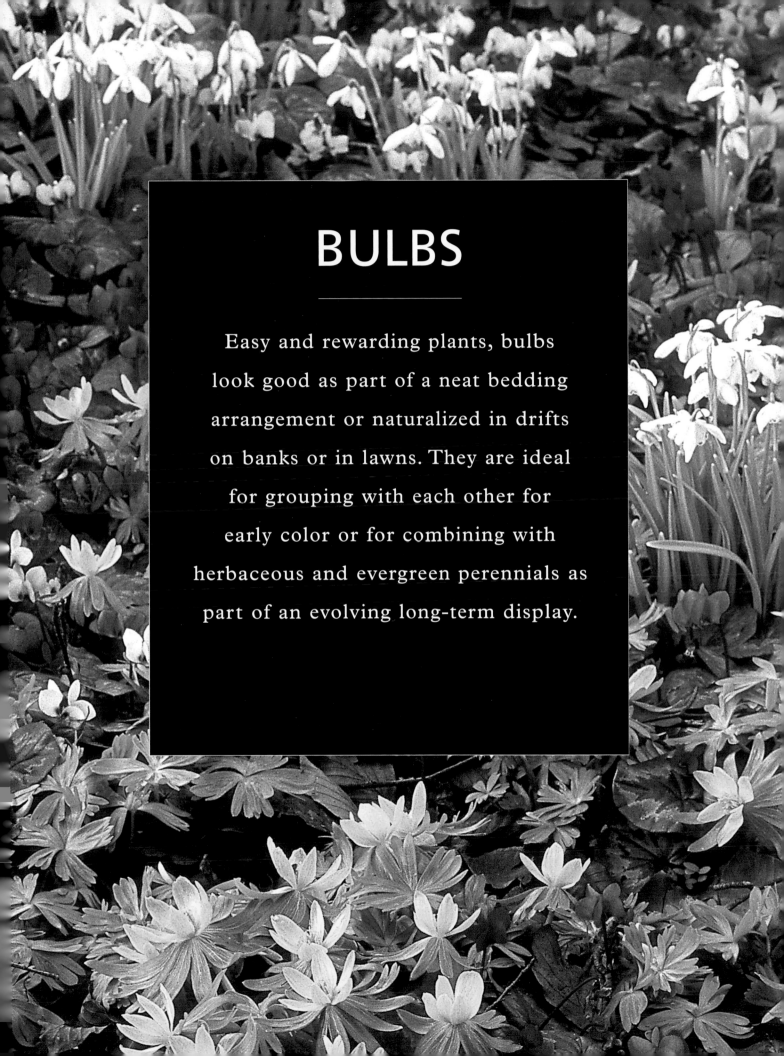

# BULBS

Easy and rewarding plants, bulbs
look good as part of a neat bedding
arrangement or naturalized in drifts
on banks or in lawns. They are ideal
for grouping with each other for
early color or for combining with
herbaceous and evergreen perennials as
part of an evolving long-term display.

**In gardening, the word bulb** is used very loosely to refer to any plant with a more or less swollen, underground storage organ that can be dried and sold as a conveniently packaged object: bulb catalogs offer true bulbs (daffodils, lilies, muscari, tulips), corms (crocosmias, crocuses, gladioli) and assorted tubers, tuberous roots and rhizomes (aconites, anemones, dahlias). Strictly speaking, however, a bulb is a compressed shoot with fleshy leaves packed with food, arranged around a flattened "stem," the basal plate.

The vast majority of these "bulbous" plants share a common lifestyle as perennials, returning annually to their underground resting state. They come from a range of natural habitats, including desert margins, alpine pastures and deciduous woodlands, most requiring them to grow, flower and die down in the short space of time that the conditions are favorable. Bulbs also usually have short-lived brightly colored blooms, a quality needed to attract pollinating insects, and many have fairly uninteresting, often strap-shaped foliage. In other respects, such as height and flower presentation and form, they are very varied.

## Gardening with bulbs

In reasonably sheltered gardens, there can be bulbs in flower all the year round – from the earliest snowdrops, crocuses and scillas, through phalanxes of narcissi, tulips and fritillaries, to imposing lilies and gladioli, irises and zantedeschias, then bright amaryllis, nerines and sternbergias, before finally the autumn and winter flowering crocuses and colchicums. The spring-flowerers are perhaps the most magical of bulbs, pushing up through near-frozen ground to produce seemingly fragile blooms of beautiful proportions, but all bulbous plants have a contribution to make, and most are perfect for a wide range of companion planting.

Bulbs are inexpensive when bought in bulk, and some suppliers are willing to sell even quite small quantities fairly cheaply. While crocuses, daffodils and tulips are among the most popular, other good value bulbs include chionodoxas, scillas and snake's head fritillaries. Alliums, lilies and tigridias, although slightly more costly, are well worth the outlay for their statuesque habit or exotic flowers.

Many bulbs are easy to grow. If they are chosen to suit the situation, they will spread and flower with increasing abundance each year with no effort required on the part of the gardener. In fact, the majority of bulbous plants benefit from being left undisturbed year after year. Because they are essentially pre-packed plants with their own supply of food, they are almost guaranteed

Tulip cultivars are among the brightest and most reliable bulbs for providing color in spring. Here, their large solid blooms on stout stems make brilliant highlights above a carpet of traditional bedding plants that includes wallflowers and forget-me-nots.

to produce a flower in the first year they are planted. This is especially the case with tulips, where the flower is already formed inside the bulb before it begins to grow.

## Bedding and borders

Bulbs are very useful for creating early bedding displays. Tulips, especially, are effective planted alone or through a carpet of forget-me-nots, pansies, polyanthus or wallflowers to produce a colorful carpet of flowers in mid- to late spring. Hyacinths are also ideal for short-term color, although they must be combined with similarly low-growing companions. After flowering, the bulbs and their partners are removed to make way for summer bedding.

An underplanting of bulbs can be as gorgeous, or as naturalistic and subdued as befits the setting, using them to cover all available bare ground, woven in loose drifts among the emerging plants. The biggest, boldest and brightest sorts should be used with conviction but be restricted to more sophisticated and showy planting, perhaps near the house. The leaves of perennials and deciduous shrubs will cover the dying bulb foliage after they have flowered. (Bulbs are best mixed with other plants when used for edging, otherwise there will be a gap when they retreat below ground.)

Summer flowering bulbs can be integrated into borders and used in much the same way as herbaceous plants. Lilies are perfect for pairing with tall delphiniums or placing in front of Shrub or Climbing roses, both combinations being popular in cottage gardens, while gladioli and irises will provide strong focal points among cranesbills and other plants with lax or rounded forms, or punctuation for those with soft foliage, such as fennel and artemisias.

## Bulbs in pots

Most bulbs are ideal for pot culture and many will enjoy the special conditions that can be created; for example, lime-hating lilies can

As well as being indispensable for bedding displays and drifts of early color in mixed borders, bulbs are also very effective when massed in a dedicated bulb border such as this, in which tulips, narcissi and crown imperials provide height behind leucojums, erythroniums, muscari and snake's head fritillaries.

be grown in containers of ericaceous compost in chalk or limestone areas. Pots of early bulbs can be forced to make them flower even earlier, providing long-lasting delight in late winter and early spring. Window boxes bring the flowers closer to eye level, where their delicate markings and, with some, wonderful scent can be more fully appreciated. As the weather gets warmer, containers of pale tulips with forget-me-nots or bright hyacinths with polyanthus can decorate terraces and patios. Lilies, perhaps underplanted with annuals, make ideal subjects for large pots later in the summer, while many even later-flowering bulbs – nerines and sternbergias – also benefit from being in containers. Growing them in this way allows for the provision of free drainage and winter protection. If the bulbs are left undisturbed, they will respond with ever greater freedom of flowering year on year.

## Naturalizing bulbs

Many spring flowering bulbs are perfect for naturalizing in grass or under trees. Where they are in grass, it can be left uncut until mid-summer, meaning less work for the gardener; an attendant benefit is that the grass will gradually be colonized by wild flowers, which prefer the meadowlike maintenance routine. Delicate drifts of cowslips and snake's head fritillaries or, in more shaded sites, carpets of cyclamens, anemones and primroses are the rewards for such relaxed gardening.

**Opposite:** In this border at Great Dixter, ribbons of hot-colored tulips create vivacious contrasts with the more demure coloring of forget-me-nots, ornamental cherries and euphorbias.

**Below:** Colonies of dwarf bulbs such as muscari, smaller narcissi and fritillaries will become denser and more lavish if they are left undisturbed to multiply and spread. Larger tulips and narcissi in pots can be lifted after flowering to make way for summer bedding.

## *Allium carinatum* subsp. *pulchellum* ♀

The slightly diffuse flowerheads of this slender plant are made up of dainty amethyst florets that droop until pollinated, after which they turn upward. The plants are ideal for interweaving with shorter ground-cover plants, and when combined with cranesbills, catmints or eryngiums. Their coloring works well with silver, glaucous or purple foliage, and cool flower colors such as crimson, lavender, pale pink, pale mauve and white, and is strong enough to contrast successfully with yellow-green foliage and flowers or pale sulfur-yellow flowers. A white-flowered variant is *A.c.* subsp. *pulchellum* f. *album* ♀. These ornamental onions readily self-seed.

**Perfect partners:** *Artemisia stelleriana* 'Boughton Silver', *Heuchera* 'Amethyst Myst', *Populus alba* 'Richardii' p.125 **A**

H: 18 in. (45 cm)  S: 2 in. (5 cm)
✤ Mid- to late summer

 ◊-◊◊ ▢-▨ ■ Z6 pH5–7.5

The delicate, amethyst flowers of *Allium carinatum* subsp. *pulchellum* are intimately mixed with the taller, starry flowerheads of *Eryngium × oliverianum*, to striking effect. This combination would perhaps work even better with an eryngium that grows to the same height as the allium – for example *E. bourgatii* 'Picos Blue'.

## *Allium cristophii* ♀

This ornamental onion produces stout stems topped with bold globes of mauve, starry flowers that mature to parchment-colored seedheads, almost as eye-catching as the flowers themselves. Its broad leaves start to die back at flowering time and are best hidden by foliage from neighboring plants. It can be interplanted with bush roses and old shrub roses, although these need to be pruned fairly hard to allow sunlight to reach the allium leaves early in the year and to match the height of its flowerheads. The color of these, varying between pale silvery grayish mauve and rich amethyst, combines attractively with cool shades, while the most richly colored forms can be contrasted with pale yellow flowers or yellow-green foliage and flowers. Good companions include Bearded irises, catmints and shorter, silver-leaved artemisias. Although this allium prefers a sharply drained site, even gravel, it will grow in any good soil, where it self-seeds readily.

**Perfect partners:** *Allium sphaerocephalon* p.351 **C**, *Anemone × hybrida* 'Honorine Jobert' p.233 **A**, *Geranium* 'Ann Folkard' p.273 **B**,

**Above left:** *Allium cristophii* flowers at exactly the same height as *Nigella damascena* 'Miss Jekyll', the leaves of the nigella hiding the allium's untidy dying foliage.

**Above:** The same combination is attractive in seed, the silvery seedheads of the ornamental onion contrasting effectively with the nigella's brown pods.

*Lavandula stoechas* subsp. *pedunculata* p.112 **C**, *Rosa* 'Prince Charles' p.197 **C**, *Spiraea japonica* (yellow-green leaved) p.141 **C** ❑ pp.201 **B**, 226 **C**, 332 **B**

H: 18 in. (45 cm)  S: 12 in. (30 cm)
✤ Early to midsummer

◊-◊◊ ▢-▨ ■ Z4 pH5–8

## *Allium hollandicum* ♀

This is perhaps the easiest and most useful ornamental onion for general garden use, with bold heads of mauve flowers borne on slender stems. The spherical flowerheads, often confused with those of the taller lilac *A. aflatunense*, form an effective pattern when repeated through a border, especially with late-flowering tulips and other late spring bulbs, early roses and bedding plants such as wallflowers. Other suitable companions include Bearded irises, columbines and later-flowering deciduous azaleas. It looks effective with cool colors, white flowers and silver or purple foliage, in a gravel garden or fairly well-drained border. 'Purple Sensation' ♀ is a mixture of three, more richly colored clones, perhaps the best of which is 'Purple Surprise' ♀. Their color contrasts with yellow-green foliage and flowers, and with fairly strong yellow flowers. All variants of this species and the closely related *A. aflatunense* self-seed readily and must be kept separate if they are to remain distinct. Their seedheads change from green to parchment by late summer.

**Perfect partners:** *Aquilegia vulgaris* var. *stellata* p.235 **A**, *Clematis montana* var. *rubens* p.162 **B**, *Crambe maritima* p.254 **B**, *Galactites tomentosa* p.428 **C**, *Laburnum × watereri* 'Vossii' p.111 **A**, *Tellima grandiflora* p.338 **A**, *Tulipa* 'Red Shine' p.401 **B** ❑pp.173 **B**, 202 **C**

H: 36 in. (90 cm) S: 12 in. (30 cm) ❀ Late spring
▰▱▱▰▰▰ ◇-◇◇ ▢-▰ ▰ Z4 pH5–7.5

**Right:** The amethyst *Allium hollandicum* and *A.h.* 'Purple Sensation', together with the royal blue *Anchusa azurea* 'Loddon Loyalist' and purplish blue *Geranium* 'Johnson's Blue', make a striking contrast against the background of yellow-green foliage of *Robinia pseudoacacia* 'Frisia' and *Philadelphus coronarius* 'Aureus'.

**Below:** Used as late spring bedding in harmonious colors, the spherical *Allium hollandicum* contrasts with the initially cup-shaped then flat *Tulipa* 'Blue Parrot'. Here, both are set in a carpet of blue wood forget-me-nots (*Myosotis sylvatica*).

## *Allium karataviense* ♀

This short, relatively early-flowering
ornamental onion bears globes of mauve-
flushed flowers at the same time as its broad,
purple-flushed, grayish green leaves. The
seedheads remain attractive after flowering
and dry to a pleasing parchment color
by mid- to late summer, by which time
the leaves have disappeared. Although
appealing in flower, it is valued more for
its architectural form, the plants making
a bold statement that can be enhanced by
companions with small leaves and flowers.
It is good for a rock garden or gravel garden,
or for growing in a sink or shallow trough,
and also for the front of a border, where it
can be grown through low ground-cover
plants such as bugles or smaller cranesbills.
Good companions include silver, purple or
glaucous foliage plants, and flowers in cool
colors, particularly mauve, purple, pink, or
crimson and white. Plants self-seed freely.

**Perfect partners:** *Acaena saccaticupula* 'Blue
Haze', *Ajuga reptans* 'Arctic Fox', *Festuca
glauca* 'Blaufuchs', *Geranium* 'Mavis Simpson',
*Sedum* 'Red Rum'

**H: 8 in.** (20 cm) **S: 12 in.** (30 cm) ❀ **Late spring**
▨ ◊ ▢-▨ ■ **Z4 pH5–7.5**

The delicately colored, spherical flowerheads and bold,
strap-shaped leaves of *Allium karataviense* contrast
effectively in form with the succulent *Sedum* 'Herbstfreude'.

## *Allium moly*

A bright display can be guaranteed from this
clump-forming ornamental onion, which is
suitable for the front of a border, or in a rock
or gravel garden. It has glaucous foliage and
sharp yellow flowers that harmonize with hot
colors and contrast effectively with blue or
purple. Plants also go well with glaucous or
silver foliage and late spring bedding such as
shorter, richer blue alpine forget-me-nots and
shorter late-flowering tulips. 'Jeannine' ♀ has
broad glaucous foliage and bolder flowers, at
times with two flower stems per bulb. They
flower most profusely in full sun, although
this may scorch the leaf tips.

**Perfect partners:** *Artemisia schmidtiana*
'Nana', *Carex comans* (bronze), *Euphorbia
cyparissias* 'Fens Ruby', *Heuchera* 'Can-can',
*Rumex flexuosus*, *Viola* 'Huntercombe
Purple' p.340 **B**

**H: 8 in.** (20 cm) **S: 2 in.** (5 cm)
❀ **Late spring to early summer**
▨ ◊-◊◊ ▢-▨ ■ **Z4 pH5–7.5**

**Above:** Planted beneath a clump of lamb's ears (*Stachys
byzantina*), *Allium moly* spangles the silvery gray stems with
its bright umbels of yellow flowers.

**Below:** The bold yellow flowers of *Allium moly* 'Jeannine'
are scattered randomly among the smaller-flowered purple
*Viola* 'Gustav Wermig' to form a striking color contrast.

Tall white flowerheads of *Allium nigrum*, borne aloft on parallel ramrod stems, are here contrasted with the shorter, rich purple-leaved *Euphorbia dulcis* 'Chameleon'.

## Allium nigrum

The starry flowers of this undemanding, tall ornamental onion are borne in domed umbels on extremely straight stalks. Their color is usually creamy white with a green vein at the center of each petal, but at times they are flushed with mauve, while the nectaries in the middle of each floret are either green or black. The most common cultivated variants lack the mauve flush and are perhaps most arresting when combined with white flowers or contrasting dark foliage. The stiff upright stems look good planted as a group in a gravel garden, and can make a striking accent for repeating at intervals along a sunny border. It is advisable to grow the plants among later-leafing herbaceous perennials so that the allium foliage receives adequate light during its active growth, but is hidden from view as it dies back.

**Perfect partners:** *Actaea simplex* (Atropurpurea Group) 'Brunette', *Aster lateriflorus* 'Lady in Black', *Berberis thunbergii* 'Helmond Pillar', *Geranium phaeum*, *Lysimachia ciliata* 'Firecracker'

**H: 24 in.** (60 cm)  **S: 8 in.** (20 cm)
❀ **Late spring to early summer**

▬▬▭▭◼ ◊ ◻-◼ ◼ Z4 pH5–7.5

## Allium sphaerocephalon
ROUND-HEADED LEEK

This is an easy bulb for a gravel garden or sunny border, where it is useful as a unifying theme if repeated at intervals in informal drifts. Its magenta-purple flowerheads are invaluable in a late summer border, although it needs to be grown in generous quantities to be really effective. The flower color goes well with cool shades, particularly pink, lilac and lavender, and can be contrasted with pale yellow flowers or with yellow-green foliage and flowers such as late-flowering euphorbias. Its slender growth allows it to weave prettily through groups of other plants, although the flower stems often lean at divergent angles, producing a confusing impression that may be avoided by growing the plants through an airy, branching perennial neighbor such as an eryngium or gypsophila.

**Perfect partners:** *Bupleurum rotundifolium*, *Eryngium planum* 'Blaukappe', *Euphorbia palustris*, *Gaura lindheimeri* 'Whirling Butterflies', *Gypsophila paniculata* 'Flamingo'

**H: 24 in.** (60 cm)  **S: 3 in.** (8 cm)
❀ **Early to late summer**

 ◊-◊◊ ◻-◼ ◼ Z4 pH5–7.5

**Above:** Save for a ruff of narrow bracts, the egg-shaped flowerheads of *Eryngium* × *tripartitum* match the larger ones of *Allium sphaerocephalon* and harmonize in color.

**Below:** In this equally harmonious scheme, *Knautia macedonica* matches *Allium sphaerocephalon* perfectly in color, along with lilac *Viola cornuta*, blue cornflowers (*Centaurea cyanus*) and bold seedheads of *Allium cristophii*.

## *Anemone apennina* ♛

This is not a true bulb but a rhizome, sold dry by bulb merchants and often requiring a full season after planting to produce reliable results. Its many "petals" are in fact strap-shaped sepals, which are typically bright lavender-blue and very good in combinations with cool colors such as pink, crimson, mauve and lilac, or with glaucous or yellow-green foliage. Invaluable for naturalizing, it can be used to create a carpet through which to grow larger spring flowers and bulbs, such as narcissi, primroses, polyanthus, cowslips, erythroniums and (in sunnier sites) smaller fritillaries. It is also attractive with early leafing perennials, lesser celandine and its variants, particularly those in soft yellow or white, and with spring bedding. Other uses include underplanting in herbaceous and mixed borders, even beneath bush roses, and combining with late-leafing hostas and other herbaceous plants that unfurl their leaves when the anemone's foliage starts to die back. It enjoys humus-rich soils and a sunny site in cool climates, although in warmer areas it can tolerate a considerable amount of shade, such as that of deciduous woodland.

**Perfect partners:** *Epimedium × youngianum* 'Niveum', *Euphorbia polychroma* 'Major', *Hosta* 'Blue Arrow', *Primula* 'Guinevere', *Ranunculus ficaria* 'Salmon's White', *Tulipa praestans* 'Unicum', *Valeriana phu* 'Aurea' ❑ p.397 **B**

H: 6 in. (15 cm)  S: 8 in. (20 cm)
❋ Early to mid-spring
◌◌ ☐-◼ ◼ Z5 pH5–7.5

In spring, when the daggerlike leaves of Bearded irises (here, *Iris pallida* 'Variegata') are too small to hide the bare earth between each shoot, the addition of a small plant such as the pretty, bright lavender-blue *Anemone apennina* can complete the picture perfectly.

*Anemone blanda* has a loose habit that makes it suitable for more naturalistic plantings, as well as for beds and borders. In informal situations it contrasts well with soft yellow flowers such as those of primroses (*Primula vulgaris*).

## *Anemone blanda* ♛

Although similar in appearance, cultivation, and uses to *Anemone apennina* (left), and differing only in minor botanical details such as the nodding habit of its mature seedheads, this is an outstandingly versatile species for garden use because of its large number of color variants. These include 'Ingramii' (rich lavender-blue with a purple reverse to the sepals), 'Violet Star' (amethyst-violet flowers), 'Charmer' (rich mauve-pink) and 'Radar' ♛ (magenta flowers with a white center). One of the most useful is 'White Splendour' ♛, which is white with a mauve-flushed reverse, and blends with almost any other color; it is perhaps most effective with blue flowers such as muscari, forget-me-nots, blue hyacinths and omphalodes. Although in its Mediterranean homeland this anemone grows in full or partial shade, in cooler gardens the flowers require full sun to open completely.

**Perfect partners:** *Hyacinthus orientalis*, *Muscari armeniacum* 'Valerie Finnis', *Omphalodes cappadocica*, *Primula veris*, *Scilla siberica* p.389 **B**, *Tulipa clusiana* p.394 **B**

H: 8 in. (20 cm)  S: 12 in. (30 cm)
❋ Early to mid-spring

◌◌ ☐-◼ ◼ Z4 pH5–7.5

## *Anemone coronaria*
## Saint Bridgid Group

This group of tuberous herbaceous perennials includes scarlet, crimson, purple or lavender-blue selections, with all shades between these and white. They are easily raised from seed, or may be bought as a mixture or as single-colored cultivars. Mixtures can be used for naturalizing, to create a millefleurs tapestry effect, and blend well with bluebells, cowslips and primroses, producing an attractive carpet in a fairly sunny glade. The single colors are useful for planned color schemes – semi-double, deep lavender-blue 'Lord Lieutenant', for example, goes with pale lilac, white or sulfur-yellow, while semi-double, white 'Mount Everest' combines with almost any other color, especially blue.

**Perfect partners:** *Allium neopolitanum, Amelanchier × grandiflora* 'Ballerina', *Cornus florida, Iris pallida, Magnolia* 'Susan', *Narcissus poeticus* var. *recurvus, Tulipa* 'Maywonder'

H: 16 in. (40 cm)   S: 6 in. (15 cm)
✿ Mid- to late spring

 ◌-◌◌ ☐ Z5 pH5–7

A limited color range of *Anemone coronaria* Saint Bridgid Group and single anemones combine with bluebells (*Hyacinthoides non-scripta*) in this semi-natural, delightfully simple planting. The bluebells provide contrast in floral form in a harmonious but distinct color.

## *Anemone nemorosa* ♔
WOOD ANEMONE

This rhizomatous species is excellent for naturalizing in woodland, and for planting among late-leafing perennials and taller bulbs in borders. There are many double or single cultivars with green, lavender, pink or white flowers, a few with a green ruff. Good whites include tall, large-flowered 'Lychette', 'Leeds' Variety' and 'Wilks Giant', and the double 'Vestal' ♔. Pale pink 'Lismore Pink' is good with deep pink flowers. Pale lavender-blue cultivars such as large-flowered 'Blue Beauty' and 'Robinsoniana' ♔ blend effectively with deeper lavender-blue and white. Richer lavender blue cultivars, including 'Allenii' ♔, harmonize with other lavender-blue flowers and contrast with pale sulphur-yellow or yellow-green foliage and flowers.

**Perfect partners:** *Anemone × lipsiensis, Arum italicum* 'Marmoratum', *Corydalis solida, Dryopteris erythrosora, Hosta undulata* var. *albomarginata* p.295 **C**, *Lathyrus vernus, Muscari armeniacum* p.378 **A**, *Primula denticulata* 'Snowball', *Scilla bifolia* p.388 **A**, *Trillium grandiflorum*

H: 3–8 in. (8–20 cm)   S: 12 in. (30 cm)
✿ Early to late spring

◌◌ ☐-☐ ■ Z4 pH4.5–7.5

This charmingly natural and informal mix of mainly woodland flowers would brighten any lightly shaded area. With no pretensions to color scheming yet no clashes, *Anemone nemorosa* is joined by *Muscari armeniacum*, primroses (*Primula vulgaris*), *Cyclamen repandum* and Siberian squill (*Scilla siberica*).

## *Anemone pavonina*
POPPY ANEMONE

This tuberous-rooted herbaceous perennial is similar in appearance, color range, and cultivation needs to *A. coronaria*, differing mainly in the shape of its leaves, which are deeply cut and lobed. Its garden uses match those of *A. coronaria* Saint Bridgid Group (left), but it is easier to grow and longer lived, with a more elegant appearance that is especially appealing when the plants are naturalized. Good companions include early-flowering ceanothus, daphnes, exochordas, shrubby, spring-flowering ornamental cherries, white flowering currants, spiraeas, viburnums, magnolias, and dwarf lilacs.

**Perfect partners:** *Cytisus × kewensis, Exochorda × macrantha* 'The Bride', *Prunus tenella* 'Fire Hill', *Ribes sanguineum* White Icicle, *Spiraea × vanhouttei, Syringa meyeri* var. *spontanea* 'Palibin', *Viburnum × burkwoodii*

H: 10 in. (25 cm)   S: 6 in. (15 cm)
✿ Mid- to late spring

 ◌ ☐ Z8 pH5–7

A pleasing carpet of *Anemone pavonina* in a range of colors, some with white eyes, is shown here growing through grass on a sunny bank together with the smaller-flowered common daisies (*Bellis perennis*).

The upright flowers of *Arisaema erubescens* look to left and right, like a family of meerkats peering anxiously over the undergrowth. Seen here above the fronds of the shield fern *Polystichum setiferum* (Divisilobum Group) 'Herrenhausen', their extravagantly striped and blotched stems and their backing of radiating leaflets are as attractive as their hooded spathes.

## Arisaema erubescens

Arisaemas are tuberous or rhizomatous perennials with palmate leaves on blotched and spotted stalks, and slightly sinister-looking hooded flowers, usually in subdued colors and often striped and veined. Those of tuberous *A. erubescens* are brownish pink, red or purple, and covered with a whitish bloom. Their curious beauty is best seen at close range, perhaps growing through a carpet of ground cover, preferably of a significantly different color and low enough to reveal the distinctive leaf shape and attractive flower stalks. This is a plant for quiet color schemes, and blends well with warm shades such as brick-red, soft orange, peach or apricot. It is useful for a woodland garden and looks good with hostas, ferns, ivies and epimediums, but it is possibly most effective surrounded by small, finely textured foliage.

**Perfect partners:** *Adiantum pedatum*, *Epimedium* × *warleyense* 'Orangekönigin', *Geum* 'Georgenburg', *Heuchera* 'Green Ivory', *Polygonatum falcatum*

H & S: 12 in. (30 cm)
 Late spring to early summer
 ◊◊ ◻-◼ ◼ Z6 pH4.5–6.5

The sculptural yellow spathes and bright yellow spadices of *Arum creticum* combine perfectly with the yellow-green inflorescences and purple-flushed leaves of Mrs Robb's bonnet (*Euphorbia amygdaloides* var. *robbiae*).

## Arisaema triphyllum
JACK-IN-THE-PULPIT

A familiar native wild flower of the north-eastern United States, this is a tuberous perennial with a hooded white, purple and green spathe surrounding the central purple or green spadix. In early summer the leaves die back and the spathe shrivels, to be followed in autumn by orange-red berries. The muted flowers are effective above a fine-textured ground-cover plant of rather different leaf color, such as a pale or deep shade of green or yellow-green. The purple flush on the inside of the spathe, and also on the leaf and flower stalks, suits combinations with crimson and dusky maroon flowers.

**Perfect partners:** *Aquilegia canadensis*, *Dicentra* 'Pearl Drops', *Euphorbia polychroma*, *Geranium* × *oxonianum* 'Lace Time', *Hosta* 'August Moon', *Iris* × *fulvala*

H: 18 in. (45 cm) S: 12 in. (30 cm)
 Late spring to early summer
◊◊ ◻-◼ ◼ Z4 pH4.5–6.5

The handsome leaves and elegant striped spathe of *Arisaema triphyllum* stand clear and uncluttered above the gray-green filigree foliage and racemes of wine-colored flowers of *Dicentra* 'Bacchanal'.

## Arum creticum

This striking tuberous perennial bears glossy, rich green, arrow-shaped leaves and curved, soft pale yellow spathes surrounding a bright yellow spadix – a coloring that goes well with other late spring flowers in blue, yellow, white or yellow-green, and with yellow-green or glaucous foliage. Attractive companions include muscari, omphalodes, yellow-green grasses and sedges, smaller anthemis, smaller narcissi and late-flowering species tulips. It can be propagated by separating the offsets from the main tuber, but established tubers may pull themselves well into the ground, and care should be taken not to sever the main one. Although tender, given a sheltered sunny site this species can survive over winter in cold areas. In hot areas it needs some shade.

**Perfect partners:** *Anthemis punctata* subsp. *cupaniana*, *Corydalis flexuosa*, *Euphorbia amygdaloides* 'Purpurea', *Milium effusum* 'Aureum', *Narcissus* 'Hawera', *Tulipa sprengeri*

H: 18 in. (45 cm) S: 12 in. (30 cm)  Late spring
◊◊ ◻-◼ ◼ Z7 pH5–7.5

## *Arum italicum* 'Marmoratum' ♡

In areas where its white-veined leaves are not injured by cold weather, this cultivar is very useful for combining with winter-flowering bulbs such as winter aconites, early crocuses, snowdrops and *Cyclamen coum* variants, as well as winter heaths, bergenias and small evergreen shrubs such as *Euonymus fortunei* cultivars. In spring it blends well with sedges and evergreen ferns, narcissi, smaller species tulips, bugles, primroses, polyanthus, cowslips, evergreen epimediums and smaller mahonias. It is happy in sun or partial shade, although its leaf markings are stronger in sun, and it can be grown in a woodland garden or toward the front of a border, where its pale green flower spikes are good with late-leafing perennials. There is a second season of interest in autumn, when showy orange-red berries develop on the spikes these are enhanced by low ground cover such as an unvariegated, plain green or yellow-green ivy.

**Perfect partners:** *Ajuga reptans* 'Catlin's Giant', *Erica carnea*, *Narcissus* 'Tête-à-tête', *Skimmia japonica* 'Rubella' p.145 **B**, *Vinca minor* 'Illumination' ❏ pp.101 **C**, 269 **C**

H: 12 in. (30 cm)  S: 8 in. (20 cm)
❀ Late spring to early summer
▬▬▬▭▮ ◌◌ ▢-▨▮ Z7 pH5–7.5

**Above:** In late spring, the eye-catching white-veined leaves of *Arum italicum* 'Marmoratum' combine effectively with foliage of contrasting form, including that of snowdrops, lady's mantle (*Alchemilla mollis*), ostrich-plume fern (*Matteuccia struthiopteris*) and a mahonia, to create an intricate pattern for close-range viewing.

**Below:** In autumn, the glossy evergreen foliage of *Sarcococca confusa* provides a pleasing foil for the glistening vermilion berries of *Arum italicum* 'Marmoratum'.

The creamy white, star-shaped flowers of *Camassia leichtlinii* 'Semiplena' are borne on stiffly upright stems above an underplanting of vibrantly colored, magenta and yellow columbines. The very dark background, which is provided by *Berberis thunbergii* f. *atropurpurea* above and *Ligularia dentata* 'Desdemona' below, sets off the creamy camassia flowers to dramatic effect.

## *Camassia leichtlinii* 'Semiplena'

This elegant bulbous perennial blooms after most spring bulbs, but before the main flush of summer flowers. Its double florets give the flower spike extra substance, prolonging flowering and enhancing the display. Their soft, creamy color blends with many others, especially warm shades such as peach, apricot, soft orange and scarlet; it is also good with soft powder blues and deep blues. The leaves can be rather untidy at flowering time, but biennials or hardy annuals, such as nigellas, can be planted in front to screen the foliage as it dies back. The plants look most effective in loose groups or drifts, blended with yellow or red columbines, geums, late-flowering deciduous azaleas, early yellow roses and glaucous, yellow-green, or yellow-variegated foliage. Good contrasts can be made with purple or red-flushed foliage.

**Perfect partners:** *Ceanothus* 'Concha', *Eupatorium rugosum* 'Chocolate', *Geranium × oxonianum*, *Lunaria annua* 'Variegata', *Rosa* 'Helen Knight'

H: 31 in. (80 cm)  S: 9 in. (23 cm)
❀ Late spring to early summer
▬▬▭▭▮ ◌◌ ▢-▨▮ Z4 pH5–8

## *Chionodoxa forbesii*

This spring-flowering bulb has star-shaped, soft lavender flowers, with pale centers. It is useful for underplanting in herbaceous or mixed borders, where it may be combined with bugles or acaenas. The color blends well with cream, pale yellow, bluish pink, mauve, purple, blue and white, and with purple, glaucous or silver foliage. It contrasts reasonably well with yellow-green. The species has 4–12 florets per stem, while the similar *C. luciliae* bears only one or two.

**Perfect partners:** *Acorus gramineus* 'Ōgon', *Ajuga reptans* 'Arctic Fox', *Dianthus gratianopolitanus*, *Erica carnea* 'Springwood White', *Festuca glauca*, *Narcissus* 'Geranium' p.382 **A**, *Ranunculus ficaria* 'Coffee Cream' ❑ p.336 **A**

**H: 6 in.** (15 cm) **S: 4 in.** (10 cm)
❀ **Early to mid-spring**
〇-〇〇 ▢-▨ **Z4  pH5–8**

Tulips and a carpet of *Chionodoxa forbesii* surround the dark shoots of a *Paeonia lactiflora* cultivar. The bulbs will have finished flowering before the peony casts them into shade, making them useful for underplanting herbaceous plants.

## *Chionodoxa* 'Pink Giant'

The soft mauve-pink of this chionodoxa mixes with much the same colors as *C. forbesii* (above) – white, cream, mauves, blues and purples – although it is too delicate to go satisfactorily with yellow-green. It is a sport of *C.f.* 'Rosea', which differs from the species only in color. 'Pink Giant' is larger in all respects, enabling it to overtop more neighbors, including wood anemones, and to grow through taller carpeting plants. *C. forbesii* 'Blue Giant' is equally large and has the lavender flowers of the species, while pure white *C.f.* 'Alba' resembles the species in size and is particularly pretty in plantings with silver foliage, intended to be seen at close range.

**Perfect partners:** *Acaena caesiiglauca*, *Aubrieta* 'Gloriosa', *Dianthus* 'Dewdrop', *Lathyrus vernus*, *Narcissus bulbocodium* p.379 **B**, *Ophiopogon planiscapus* 'Nigrescens'

**H: 6 in.** (15 cm) **S: 4 in.** (10 cm)
❀ **Early to mid-spring**
〇-〇〇 ▢-▨ **Z4  pH5–8**

A carpet of neat, dark-leaved bugle (*Ajuga reptans* 'Atropurpurea') provides an effective foil for the mauve-pink flowers of *Chionodoxa* 'Pink Giant'.

The starry, checkered pink flowers of *Colchicum agrippinum* stand out dramatically against the foil of a dark-leaved cultivar of *Ajuga reptans*. This bugle is a useful companion for both early and late bulbs.

## *Colchicum agrippinum* ♔

Colchicums (sometimes erroneously called autumn crocuses) are versatile bulbs that flower from late summer until mid-autumn, before their leaves appear. They are supremely effective naturalized in grass or flowering through a carpet of low ground cover. *C. agrippinum* has obscure origins but is probably a hybrid of *C. variegatum*, the species with the most strongly checkered flowers but a difficult plant to grow, whereas *C. agrippinum* is robust and increases well, and withstands being naturalized. It blooms in the middle of the colchicum season, and combines well with flowers in mauve, blue, purple, white and pink shades on the blue side of primary pink, and also with purple foliage – for example, a carpet of purple-leaved violets. Perhaps the most markedly checkered of the easier garden colchicums, it mixes well with true autumn crocuses such as *Crocus speciosus* ♔ and its cultivars.

**Perfect partners:** *Achillea clavennae, Ajania pacifica, Cyclamen hederifolium* 'Silver Cloud', *Haloragis erecta* 'Wellington Bronze', *Scabiosa* 'Butterfly Blue', *Zephyranthes candida*

**H & S: 3 in.** (8 cm)
❀ **Late summer to early autumn**
▬▬▭▬ ◊◊ ▭-▪ **Z5 pH5–7.5**

## *Colchicum autumnale*
MEADOW SAFFRON

This easy, mid-season colchicum is one of the best for naturalizing in grass, which may be mowed until the flowers emerge in early autumn. It can also be grown in beds or borders through a carpet of ground cover. The most useful cultivar for general planting is 'Nancy Lindsay' ♔, which is exceptionally prolific with flowers of rich glowing pink. Double forms include 'Pleniflorum', whose star-shaped flowers in the typical mauve-pink color of the species are not so profuse or richly colored as *C.* 'Waterlily' ♔, a prodigious hybrid cultivar which tends to flop under the weight of its blooms. *C.a.* 'Alboplenum' has starry, double white flowers that are not absolutely pure white.

**Perfect partners:** *Aster thomsonii* 'Nanus', *Convolvulus sabatius, Diascia* 'Lilac Belle', *Geranium* 'Pink Spice', *Hebe pimeleoides* 'Quicksilver', *Hosta* 'Blue Blush',

Cutting back a carpet of *Lamium maculatum* after its first flush of flower provides fresh new foliage and some late bloom to flatter meadow saffron (*Colchicum autumnale*).

*Origanum laevigatum* 'Herrenhausen', *Verbena* 'Silver Anne'

**H: 4 in.** (10 cm)   **S: 3 in.** (8 cm)
❀ **Late summer to early autumn**
▬▬▭▬ ◊◊ ▭-▪ **Z5 pH5–7.5**

## *Colchicum speciosum* 'Album' ♔

*Colcheum speciosum* ♔ is notable for its late flowering time and its rich magenta-pink flowers, which have broad petals and an immaculate goblet shape. *C.s.* 'Atrorubens' has large purple-pink flowers with glowing red stalks. The species is perhaps surpassed in loveliness by the pure white *C.s.* 'Album', whose superlative blooms have a touch of yellow towards the base of their petals and are borne on yellow-green stems. This looks particularly effective when grown through a carpet of silver foliage or if starkly contrasted against the leaves of a dusky plant such as a purple-leaved bugle or violet.

**Perfect partners:** *Anthemis punctata* subsp. *cupaniana, Ceratostigma willmottianum* Forest Blue, *Fuchsia* 'Mr. West', *Liriope muscari, Nerine bowdenii, Penstemon digitalis* 'Husker Red', *Petunia* 'Purple Wave'

**H: 7 in.** (18 cm)   **S: 4 in.** (10 cm)
❀ **Early to mid-autumn**
▬▬▭▬ ◊◊ ▭-▪ **Z6 pH5–7.5**

Tender carpeting plants such as shrubby *Helichrysum petiolare* 'Variegatum' can be used to furnish the naked flowers of *Colchicum speciosum* 'Album', the yellow tints in the colchicum's blooms harmonizing perfectly with the foliage.

The dark, ferny, basal leaves of *Anthriscus sylvestris* 'Ravenswing' make an effective background for the blooms of *Crocus* 'Ladykiller', a cultivar derived principally from *C. biflorus*, although the closely related *C. chrysanthus* is also thought to be involved in its parentage.

## Crocus chrysanthus hybrids

These cormous plants are cultivars of *Crocus chrysanthus* (which is yellow), *C. biflorus* (white, purple, or blue) and of hybrids between the two. They vary in color, often with bold markings, and many increase freely even when naturalized in grass. Their habit suits gravel, rock and scree gardens, and the front of borders. Generalizations about color combinations are difficult, except to point out that golden or orange cultivars do not mix well with lavender-blue or purple. Attractive cultivars include 'Blue Pearl' ♀ (white with pale lavender-blue outer petals); 'Cream Beauty' ♀; 'Ladykiller' ♀ (white with deep purple markings); and 'Zwanenburg Bronze' ♀ (yellow with broad maroon bands).

**Perfect partners:** *Carex morrowii* 'Variegata', *Erica carnea* 'Vivellii', *Lamium maculatum*, *Narcissus* 'Eystettensis', *Viola* 'Magnifico', *V. riviniana* Purpurea Group

**H: 3 in.** (8 cm)  **S: 2 in.** (5 cm)
※ **Late winter to early spring**
◌-◌◌  ▢-▣  Z4  pH5.5–8

## Crocus goulimyi ♀

This fairly easy autumn-flowering crocus, with sweetly scented lilac flowers, is suitable for growing in gravel or rock gardens and at the front of sunny beds or borders. It looks especially fine with white or deep violet variants of *Crocus speciosus*, dark bugles, contrasting forms of *Cyclamen hederifolium*, or a dusky background of purple heucheras. Other easy autumn crocuses include lilac *C. cartwrightianus* ♀ and pure white *C.c.* 'Albus' ♀. *C. pulchellus* ♀ has pretty, dark-veined lavender flowers and is a good choice for naturalizing; its hybrid, 'Zephyr' ♀, is pale lilac. *C. speciosus* ♀ naturalizes and self-seeds readily, and its excellent selections include pure white 'Albus' ♀ and violet 'Oxonian'.

**Perfect partners:** *Acaena microphylla* 'Kupferteppich', *Ajuga reptans* 'Braunherz', *Festuca glauca*, *Geranium* × *antipodeum* 'Chocolate Candy', *Hebe* 'Mrs. Winder', *Verbena* 'Silver Anne'

**H: 4 in.** (10 cm)  **S: 2 in.** (5 cm)  ※ **Mid-autumn**
◌-◌◌  ▢-▣  Z6  pH5.5–8

The naked lilac flowers of *Crocus goulimyi* have a telling backcloth provided by the handsome evergreen *Heuchera* 'Plum Pudding', its purple leaves overlaid (except on its veins) with a metallic sheen. The heuchera should be divided and replanted every two years or so in mid-spring rather than the usual early autumn to avoid impairing its foliage when the crocus comes into bloom.

## Crocus × luteus 'Golden Yellow' ♀
DUTCH YELLOW CROCUS

Dutch yellow crocus is derived from *C. angustifolius* ♀, from which it inherits the dark stripes at the base of its petals, and *C. flavus*. It is easily grown, and vigorous enough to naturalize successfully in grass, and it multiplies freely into expanding clumps, although as a hybrid its flowers are sterile and cannot produce seeds. It looks effective at the front of beds or borders, especially growing through low ground cover, alone or in association with other early spring bulbs such as smaller narcissi and snowdrops,

The goblets of *Crocus* × *luteus* 'Golden Yellow' are set off beautifully by a surrounding carpet of naturalized *Cyclamen coum* in shades of magenta. The cyclamen provides both attractive foliage and contrasting blooms – paler pink variants would form a less effective combination with the orange-yellow crocus. Snowdrops could be added for extra sparkle.

and *Crocus chrysanthus* hybrids in white, cream or pale yellow. It makes pleasing combinations with muscari or scillas in white or pale to mid-blue shades.

**Perfect partners:** *Ajuga reptans* 'Catlin's Giant', *Carex comans* (bronze), *Euphorbia myrsinites*, *Galanthus nivalis*, *Heuchera* 'Blackbird', *Lysimachia nummularia* 'Aurea', *Narcissus* 'Tête-à-tête', *Scilla siberica* 'Spring Beauty'

**H: 3 in.** (8 cm)  **S: 2 in.** (5 cm)
※ **Late winter to early spring**
◌-◌◌  ▢-▣  Z4  pH5–8

## *Crocus tommasinianus* ♔

A superlative crocus for growing through low ground cover or grass, this species has pale lilac to reddish violet flowers, often with silver markings. It is excellent with snowdrops, *Cyclamen coum*, or *Crocus chrysanthus* hybrids in white, pale blue or lilac, and with pale yellow flowers such as earlier, smaller narcissi. It is also good with winter heaths or beneath yellow witch hazel. This crocus self-seeds freely. There are various forms that bloom from midwinter to mid-spring: 'Eric Smith' has purple-speckled buds opening to pure white flowers in mid- and late winter; f. *albus* is pure white and flowers in late winter to early spring; and 'Ruby Giant' and 'Whitewell Purple' are larger and slightly later, flowering from late winter to mid-spring.

**Perfect partners:** *Daphne bholua* 'Darjeeling', *Eranthis hyemalis* p.360 **B**, *Galanthus elwesii* var. *monostictus* p.364 **A**, *Helleborus × hybridus*, *Prunus × subhirtella* 'Autumnalis', *Viburnum × bodnantense* 'Dawn' ❑ pp.365 **A**, 369 **B**

**H: 3 in. (8 cm) S: 2 in. (5 cm)**
❀ **Midwinter to mid-spring**
�△-◇◇ ▢-▣ **Z5 pH5–8**

The heart-shaped leaves and pale flowers of *Cyclamen coum* f. *pallidum*, enlivened by a burgundy blotch at the base of each petal, blend attractively with the violet blooms of *Crocus tommasinianus*. Both plants will self-seed readily, making them ideal for naturalizing.

## *Crocus vernus* cultivars

The flowers of *Crocus vernus* cultivars vary from white and lilac to lavender or deep purple, and first appear in late winter or early spring, a week or two after *C. tommasinianus* (left) and *C. chrysanthus* hybrids (facing page) start to flower. Robust plants that multiply freely, they look effective with winter heaths, *Cyclamen coum* variants and snowdrops, or with purple or silver foliage. The deepest purples are not so useful for naturalizing, whereas striped varieties provide a lighter, paler tone for growing in grass. Attractive cultivars include light violet 'Flower Record'; 'Graecus' (soft lavender); 'Jeanne d'Arc' (pure white with a hint of purple); mid-lavender 'Queen of the Blues'; and 'Vanguard' (pale lilac with deeper lilac-gray outer petals). Good purples are 'Remembrance' and

The small, white-lined foliage of *Crocus vernus* 'Jeanne d'Arc' is echoed exactly by the much larger, handsome evergreen leaves of *Iris foetidissima* 'Variegata'. Lamb's ears (*Stachys byzantina*), planted throughout to give later ground cover, could be replaced with a more evergreen carpeting plant such as a small-leaved ivy.

'Paulus Potter', while 'Pickwick' and 'Striped Beauty' are striped. When naturalizing, choose closely related colors and plant in uneven, overlapping drifts.

**Perfect partners:** *Chionodoxa forbesii*, *Heuchera* 'Purple Petticoats', *Lamium maculatum* 'Beedham's White', *Primula vulgaris* subsp. *sibthorpii*, *Vinca minor* 'Argenteovariegata'

**H: 4–5 in. (10–13 cm) S: 2 in. (5 cm)**
❀ **Late winter to late spring**
◇-◇◇◇ ▢-▣ **Z4 pH5–8**

## *Cyclamen hederifolium* ♔

Although fairly tolerant of sun in areas with cool summers, this easy autumn cyclamen revels in dappled shade, in beds or at the front of borders, in a woodland garden or beneath deciduous trees and shrubs in bare ground. The flower color ranges from white to magenta-red, and the variable leaf shape resembles a narrow ivy leaf, often with silver markings. A tuberous plant appearing first in late summer, usually without leaves, it mixes well with colchicums and autumn crocuses. Purple foliage offers a fine contrast with the white forms or harmonies with pink to magenta-red ones; white f. *albiflorum* is particularly striking with near-black foliage. 'Rosenteppich' has deep magenta-pink to magenta-red and 'Ruby Glow' is even deeper magenta or magenta-purple, sometimes paling at the margins, while 'Silver Cloud' has fully silver leaves and pink flowers.

**Perfect partners:** *Arum italicum* 'Marmoratum', *Buddleja davidii* 'Dartmoor', *Caryopteris* × *clandonensis*, *Ceratostigma willmottianum*, *Colchicum agrippinum*, *Crocus speciosus*, *Hedera helix* 'Glacier', *Nerine bowdenii*, *Salvia officinalis* 'Purpurascens' ❏ pp.285 **C**, 369 **A**

**H: 4–5 in.** (10–13 cm)   **S: 6 in.** (15 cm)
✽ **Late summer to mid-autumn**
◌◌ ▨ ▪ **Z5  pH5–8**

The white flowers of *Cyclamen hederifolium* f. *albiflorum* stand out dramatically against black mondo grass (*Ophiopogon planiscapus* 'Nigrescens'). The leaves of the cyclamen will overtop those of the ophiopogon in spring.

*Eranthis hyemalis*, each bloom surrounded by a decorative ruff of leaves, creates a striking color contrast with the early-flowering *Crocus tommasinianus* 'Whitewell Purple'.

## *Eranthis hyemalis* ♔
### WINTER ACONITE

This tuberous plant may be naturalized beneath deciduous trees or shrubs, where it looks charming when flowering with the first spring bulbs, such as early snowdrops, pure white *Cyclamen coum* f. *albissimum* and light to mid-blue early scillas. It will seed itself readily on bare ground. All winter aconites are also useful for borders, underplanted in positions where they are later covered by deciduous foliage. Cilicica Group (syn. *E. cilicica*) has larger flowers of a more golden yellow, and bronze-flushed foliage. Tubergenii Group (the hybrid between the typical species and Cilicica Group) has extra vigor, and bears golden flowers and bronze-flushed foliage, particularly noteworthy in the cultivar 'Guinea Gold' ♔.

**Perfect partners:** *Carex buchananii*, *Euphorbia amygdaloides* 'Purpurea', *Galanthus nivalis*, *Hamamelis* × *intermedia*, *Leucothoe* Scarletta, *Vinca minor* ❏ pp.365 **A**, 379 **B**

**H & S: 2 in.** (5 cm)   ✽ **Late winter to early spring**
◌◌ ▨ ▪ **Z5  pH5.5–7.5**

## *Erythronium californicum* 'White Beauty' ♚

Erythroniums are among the most graceful of all spring bulbs. The European dog's-tooth violet (*E. dens-canis* ♀), with white, pink or purple flowers and dappled leaves, is well-known, but some North American species and hybrids are more vigorous. *E. californicum* 'White Beauty' has creamy white flowers and bold foliage, veined and shaded silvery green and bronze. It looks good in a woodland or as underplanting in a border where it is exposed to sun while in leaf. Its delicate color looks best with blue or rich yellow. The foliage contrasts well with ferns, corydalis, grasses and sedges, particularly in bronze or yellow-green. Pure white *E.* 'Minnehaha' is taller.

**Perfect partners:** *Athyrium filix-femina, Carex flagellifera, Corydalis flexuosa, Dicentra spectabilis* 'Alba', *Epimedium × perralchicum, Hepatica nobilis, Muscari latifolium, Myosotis sylvatica, Primula bulleyana*

**H: 10 in.** (25 cm)  **S: 6 in.** (15 cm)
❀ Mid- to late spring
 Z5 pH5–7.5

The boldly shaped cream and yellow flowers of *Erythronium californicum* 'White Beauty' contrast in size and color with the tiny blue florets of *Brunnera macrophylla*.

## *Erythronium* 'Pagoda' ♚

This vigorous hybrid produces slender stems of sulfur-yellow flowers, above a clump of bold, fresh green leaves, which – unlike those of its parent *E. californicum* 'White Beauty' (left) – lack any significant markings. Its other parent is *E. tuolumnense* ♀, from which it inherits its very free production of offsets. 'Kondo' is another yellow-flowered hybrid with the same parentage and closely related to 'Citronella', slightly later with clear yellow flowers and dark anthers, and 'Sundisc', with yellow horizontal petals and a red throat. All go well with blue, cream, white or orange flowers, and with bronze or yellow-green foliage, including grasses, sedges and ferns.

**Perfect partners:** *Dryopteris affinis, Geranium × oxonianum* 'Walter's Gift', *Geum* 'Lemon Drops', *Hosta* 'Golden Tiara', *Lathyrus aureus, Milium effusum* 'Aureum', *Omphalodes cappadocica, Ranunculus bulbosus* 'F.M. Burton'

**H: 12 in.** (30 cm)  **S: 6 in.** (15 cm)
❀ Mid- to late spring
Z5 pH5–7.5

The elegant blooms of *Erythronium* 'Pagoda', borne above handsome, unmarked green leaves, harmonize with a carpet of the much smaller *Anemone ranunculoides*, a rhizomatous species useful for spring ground cover.

*Erythronium revolutum* provides attractive blooms and ground cover between emerging fronds of the ostrich-plume fern (*Matteuccia struthiopteris*), its rich rose-pink flowers contrasting with the fern's bright green leaves. The fern foliage will splay out to cover most of the ground as the erythronium dies back.

## *Erythronium revolutum* ♚

The leaves of this species are heavily marbled with silvery green and bronze. Each stem bears up to four rose-pink flowers. 'Pink Beauty', in mauve-pink, and 'Rose Beauty', in deep pink with leaves strongly marked with bronze, are two fine cultivars; 'Joanna' is a hybrid with an unusual floral mix of pink and yellow. Johnsonii Group covers some good pink-flowered variants; the pretty, soft pink hybrid 'Rosalind' is a seedling of this group. All these erythroniums thrive in the same situations as *E. californicum* 'White Beauty'

(left) and combine with mauve, lilac, white, purple, cream or crimson flowers, and with purple, silver or glaucous foliage. They work well with small rhododendrons and, for foliage contrast, with ferns, grasses or sedges.

**Perfect partners:** *Camellia × williamsii* 'Donation', *Cardamine pentaphylla, Primula denticulata, Pulmonaria* 'Lewis Palmer', *Vinca minor* 'Gertrude Jekyll'

**H: 10–12 in.** (20–30 cm)  **S: 6 in.** (15 cm)
❀ Mid- to late spring
 Z5 pH5–7.5

A

The erect, pale apple-green racemes of *Eucomis pallidiflora* contrast with the elegant, pink, scented flowers of *Lilium speciosum* in a sheltered site at the foot of a wall.

## *Eucomis pallidiflora* ♀

In favored climates and sunny sites, the pale apple-green flowers and bold strap-shaped leaves of this bulb make a strong architectural accent. It suits the second rank of a border, together with white Japanese anemones or late lilies, and combines well with blue, white and yellow-green, and warm colors such as peach and apricot, as well as contrasting with rich pink. Other species commonly grown include *E. bicolor*, with pale green flowers edged maroon, maroon anthers and a topknot of bracts that gives the genus its common name of pineapple flower. *E. comosa* has a shorter topknot and taller spikes of whitish flowers, with narrow maroon edges and maroon ovaries; some of its selections have purple-flushed foliage and flowers.

**Perfect partners:** *Agapanthus* 'Loch Hope', *Clematis durandii*, *Dahlia* 'David Howard', *Fuchsia* 'Genii', *Melianthus major*, *Plectranthus argentatus*, *Ricinus communis* 'Carmencita', *Salpiglossis* 'Royale Chocolate'

**H: 24 in.** (60 cm) **S: 12 in.** (30 cm)
❀ Late summer to early autumn
◌◌ ▣-▪ Z8 pH5–7.5

## *Fritillaria imperialis*
CROWN IMPERIAL

This is an imposing, architectural spring bulb, creating bold focal points when planted in groups, and tall enough to interact with white lilacs, kerrias, physocarpus and other shrubs of medium height, or with deciduous azaleas if the soil is not too acid or too wet. Yellow cultivars work well with cream or blue flowers, yellow-green foliage and flowers, and glaucous foliage. Orange cultivars are good with cream, warm colors such as peach or apricot, and bronze foliage. The red cultivars combine with orange or scarlet, yellow-green foliage and flowers, and bronze foliage; they are outstanding planted with late tulips, late narcissi and early-leafing hostas. Among the best are 'Maxima Lutea' ♀, which is slightly shorter than the species; 'Sulpherino', in tangerine-orange with purplish veins; 'The Premier' is orange and flowers early; and 'Rubra Maxima' has large florets.

**Perfect partners:** *Chaenomeles speciosa* 'Geisha Girl', *Euphorbia characias* subsp. *wulfenii*, *Kerria japonica* 'Picta', *Philadelphus coronarius* 'Aureus' ❑p.391 **C**

**H: 30–48 in.** (75–120 cm) **S: 10 in.** (25 cm)
❀ **Mid- to late spring**
 ◌◌ ▣-▪ **Z5 pH5–7.5**

A statuesque group of burnt orange crown imperials (*Fritillaria imperialis*), among the tallest of spring bulbs, harmonizes with warm-colored tulips including the Single Early Group *Tulipa* 'Apricot Beauty'.

B

The nodding bells of snake's head fritillary (*Fritillaria meleagris*), with checkered markings in burgundy and dusky pink, are especially fine seen at close range. Here, they are daintily poised above Siberian squill (*Scilla siberica*).

## *Fritillaria meleagris* ♔

SNAKE'S HEAD FRITILLARY

Moist springs and cool, dryish summers best suit this subtly colored water meadow plant, with distinctive nodding flowers in checkered shades of dusky pinkish purple. It can be grown with plants that like similar conditions, such as *Saxifraga granulata* and *Cardamine pratensis* cultivars, and cream or white narcissi, especially the smaller kinds. Its subdued colors are effective with pink, mauve and white flowers, and with purple foliage. *F.m.* var. *unicolor* subvar. *alba* ♔ has faint white and pale greenish cream checkering; 'Aphrodite' is a large, fine selection of this, especially effective with blue flowers. The subtle markings of 'Jupiter' and 'Mars' benefit from being seen at close range.

**Perfect partners:** *Bergenia cordifolia* 'Purpurea', *Brunnera macrophylla* 'Dawson's White', *Heuchera* 'Plum Pudding', *Lathyrus vernus* 'Alboroseus', *Muscari armeniacum*, *Narcissus* 'Thalia', *Ornithogalum nutans* p.386 **C**, *Primula elatior* p.325 **A**, *Tulipa linifolia* Batalinii Group p.397 **B**

**H: 6–12 in.** (15–30 cm) **S: 6 in.** (15 cm)
❀ Mid- to late spring
○○-○○○ ■-■ Z4 pH5–7.5

## *Fritillaria persica*

This fritillary is a highly variable species with bell-shaped, pendent flowers, borne on sturdy stems, and lance-shaped leaves. Its most reliable cultivar is 'Adiyaman' ♔, 40 in. (1 m) high and best grown so that its glaucous foliage and plum-purple flowers are clearly seen from all sides. It harmonizes well with blue, purple, crimson and pink flowers on the blue side of primary pink, and with glaucous, silver or purple foliage. It makes effective contrasts with soft yellow and cream, and its dusky appearance can be enlivened by reds, deep pinks and red foliage on the orange side of primary red. Goes well with late tulips, cream or pale yellow late narcissi, and some *Ranunculus asiaticus* cultivars.

**Perfect partners:** *Erysimum* 'Bowles Mauve', *Lunaria annua* 'Variegata', *Pittosporum tenuifolium* 'Nigricans', *Ruta graveolens* 'Jackman's Blue'

**H: 24–48 in.** (60–120 cm) **S: 12 in.** (30 cm)
❀ Mid- to late spring
○-○○○ ■-■ Z6 pH5–8

In this scheme of rich reds and purples, the bold spikes of dusky bells of *Fritillaria persica* 'Adiyaman' harmonize with blood-red tulips and a Japanese maple (*Acer palmatum* f. *atropurpureum*), while the fritillary's glaucous foliage provides a pleasing contrast.

## *Fritillaria pyrenaica* ♔

This easy, vigorous fritillary will grace any sunny border, rock garden or gravel garden – especially if it is planted where its nodding flowers can be seen at close range. It is perhaps most effective combined with soft oranges, apricots, creams or soft yellows, or with yellow-green foliage and flowers such as early-flowering euphorbias. Similar associations suit other easy, subtly colored fritillaries, such as *F. acmopetala* ♔, with pale green flowers stained purple-brown on the inner petals; and *F. messanensis*, which has green flowers edged with brown-purple.

The bright yellow-green flowerheads of *Euphorbia polychroma* 'Major' provide an effective foil for the dusky maroon bells of *Fritillaria pyrenaica*.

**Perfect partners:** *Dicentra* 'Pearl Drops', *Plantago lanceolata* 'Golden Spears', *Salvia officinalis* 'Icterina', *Stachys byzantina* 'Primrose Heron', *Thymus vulgaris* 'Silver Posie'

**H: 18 in.** (45 cm) **S: 8 in.** (20 cm)
❀ Mid- to late spring
○-○○ ■-■ Z6 pH5–8

## *Galanthus elwesii* var. *monostictus* 🏆

This broad-leaved bulb, formerly called *G. caucasicus* hort., is useful for naturalizing or planting on a large scale, perhaps with early crocuses, winter aconites, winter heaths, early-flowering hellebores, *Cyclamen coum* and evergreens such as *Euonymus fortunei* cultivars, asarums and heucheras.

*G.e.* var. *m.* Hiemalis Group flowers in midwinter, while 'Washfield Colesbourne', a hybrid of *G. elwesii*, bears flowers with deep emerald-green inner petals. All can be grown through short ground-covering plants, and are equally happy in deciduous woodland or at the front of a sunny border.

**Perfect partners:** *Bergenia* 'Eric Smith', *Crocus sieberi*, *Hedera helix* 'Glymii', *Helleborus foetidus*, *Iris unguicularis* p.301 **C**

**H: 5–9 in.** (12–23 cm) **S: 6 in.** (15 cm)
**Late winter to mid-spring**
**Z5 pH5–7.5**

The bold foliage and relatively large flowers of the snowdrop *Galanthus elwesii* var. *monostictus* make a showy early display with mauve *Crocus tommasinianus*. Both are vigorous, cheap to buy in bulk and suited to naturalizing on a large scale in the open or under deciduous trees and shrubs.

## *Galtonia candicans* ♔

This useful bulb, flowering in late summer, has pendent, bell-shaped flowers, white with a light green basal tint, and long, strap-shaped leaves that tend to kink untidily. Its subtle hues look particularly effective in a white garden, planted together with blue or green flowers such as nicotianas, or weaving through a carpet of shorter bedding plants. Other good companions include agapanthus, dahlias, *Aster amellus* cultivars, sun-tolerant hostas and tender, late summer perennials – cannas, argyranthemums and late-flowering lilies, for example – while shorter fuchsias can be used to hide its foliage. It is excellent for taking the place of earlier flowers, such as Oriental poppies, after they have died back. Lesss hardy *G. viridiflora* has green, bell-like flowers that do not show up well against the green foliage unless seen at close range.

**Perfect partners:** *Agapanthus* 'Loch Hope', *Agastache* 'Firebird', *Artemisia lactiflora* Guizhou Group, *Dahlia* 'Bednall Beauty', *Filipendula rubra* 'Venusta', *Lilium* 'Black Beauty', *Nicotiana langsdorffii*, *Papaver orientale* 'Sultana'

**H: 4 ft. (1.2 m)  S: 12 in. (30 cm)** ❉ **Late summer**
◊◊ ▢-▣ ■ Z7 pH5.5–7.5

The white bells of *Galtonia candicans* overtop the old Dwarf Bedding Group dahlia *D.* 'Hatton Castle' in a striking late summer display. The dahlia disguises the galtonia's foliage, which tends to become untidy as flowering time nears. Other dahlias that would also make good companions for the galtonia are 'Gallery Art Deco' and 'Orange Nugget'.

**Above:** The showy flowers of the double snowdrop *Galanthus nivalis* 'Flore Pleno' sit prettily among other early flowers such as *Crocus tommasinianus*, winter aconites (*Eranthis hyemalis*) and *Cyclamen coum*. All are suited to naturalizing and all but the snowdrop will self-seed freely.

**Left:** The elegant single flowers of the common snowdrop (*Galanthus nivalis*) combine well with evergreen perennials and small shrubs such as the brightly variegated *Euonymus fortunei* 'Emerald 'n' Gold'.

## *Galanthus nivalis* ♔
COMMON SNOWDROP

This undemanding species resembles *G. elwesii* var. *monostictus* (facing page) in its uses, cultivation and combinations, although its smaller size is more suited to intimate planting schemes and tiny gardens. Many dozens of variants are cultivated. Perhaps the most useful is 'Flore Pleno' ♔, the double common snowdrop. Although this lacks the simplicity of the species, its longer-lasting flowers appear larger and showier, making more impact when naturalized. Other good cultivars include 'Lady Elphinstone', a double that has yellow markings on the inner petals, and 'Pusey Greentip', also double, with outer petals flushed green. The leaflike spathes of Sharlockii Group are split into two and overtop the flowers, while 'Viridapicis' has a long spathe, sometimes split into two, and green markings on the outer petals. Like all snowdrops, these are best transplanted when in green leaf or during the two or three months afterwards, when plants are dormant.

**Perfect partners:** *Arum italicum* 'Marmoratum', *Bergenia cordifolia* 'Purpurea' p.245 **B**, *Eranthis hyemalis*, *Hedera helix* 'Manda's Crested', *Heuchera villosa* 'Palace Purple', *Vinca minor* ▢ p.369 **C**

**H: 3–5 in. (8–13 cm)  S: 4 in. (10 cm)**
❉ **Late winter to mid-spring**
◊◊ ▢-▣ ■ Z4 pH4.5–8

## *Gladiolus communis* subsp. *byzantinus* ♔

The deep magenta, funnel-shaped flowers of this gladiolus species have an elegance that is lacking in some of the large-flowered gladiolus hybrids. The vibrant color blends well with soft shades such as mauves, pinks and blues, and with silver or purple foliage, and makes a striking contrast with flowers or foliage in soft yellow or yellow-green. Very easy to grow, vigorous and spreading readily from cormlets, it is an excellent choice for sunny sites with sharply drained soil. It combines authentically with other Mediterranean plants, especially if these are positioned where they can mask the sparse, rather untidy base of the gladiolus clumps.

**Perfect partners:** *Cistus* × *purpureus*, *Cytisus* × *praecox* 'Warminster', *Iris pallida*, *Lavandula stoechas* subsp. *pedunculata*, *Phormium* 'Bronze Baby', *Rosmarinus officinalis*

H: 36 in. (90 cm)  S: 12 in. (30 cm) ❀ **Early summer**
◐-◊◊ ▢-▢ Z7 pH5.5–7

Magenta-flowered *Gladiolus communis* subsp. *byzantinus* and *Geranium psilostemon* have contrasting flower shapes that combine well. Their rich color is leavened by the silver leaves of rose campion (*Lychnis coronaria*), which will add its own magenta blooms before the gladiolus fades.

A drift of showy *Gladiolus* 'Dancing Doll' (there is also a Butterfly Group cultivar of this name) is combined with other plants with vertical inflorescences, including pure blue *Salvia patens* and *Penstemon* 'Mother of Pearl'. These form an effective contrast with the rounded flowerheads of *Phlox paniculata* cultivars. *Gladiolus* 'Windsong' would look equally good in such a planting.

## *Gladiolus* Grandiflorus Group

Hybrid gladioli of the Grandiflorus Group are available in every color except pure blue, black and blue-green. The Giant-, Large- and Medium-flowered hybrids have great impact and an almost tropical exuberance that suits large-scale planting schemes. Their spikily habit makes bold accents, and any stiffness can be masked by planting shorter, mound-forming plants in front. They are excellent with dark-leaved dahlias or when echoing the habit of *Crocosmia paniculata* and *C. masoniorum* cultivars and hybrids. The Small- and Miniature-flowered Grandiflorus gladioli are more graceful and suitable for smaller gardens, but their dramatic potential is less.

**Perfect partners:** *Cleome hassleriana*, *Dahlia* 'Arabian Night', *Lavatera* × *clementii* 'Barnsley', *Miscanthus sinensis* 'Kleine Silberspinne', *Penstemon* 'King George V', *Phygelius* × *rectus*

H: 5–6 ft. (1.5–1.8 m)  S: 8 in. (20 cm)
❀ **Early to late summer**
◐-◊◊ ▢-▢ Z9 pH5.5–7

## *Gladiolus* small-flowered hybrids

There are several groups of small-flowered gladioli, with more graceful stems than those in the Grandiflorus Group (above), usually with fewer, smaller, more widely spaced flowers, and less disfigured by fading blooms. Most have slender, often kinked foliage, and benefit from carpeting plants in front. Nanus Group produces two or three slender spikes of loosely arranged blooms in early summer. Primulinus Group has one thin stem, with up to 23 buds in a zigzag arrangement, in early to midsummer. Tubergenii Group cultivars have slender flower spikes in early summer. All are effective near the front of a border.

**Perfect partners:** *Erysimum* 'Bowles Mauve', *Euphorbia palustris*, *Philadelphus* 'Manteau d'Hermine', *Phlomis purpurea*, *Rosa* Sweet Dream, *Spiraea japonica* 'Bullata'

H: 3¼–4 ft. (1–1.2 m)  S: 6 in. (15 cm)
❀ **Early to late summer**
◐-◊◊ ▢-▢ Z9 pH5.5–7

The sumptuous red blooms of *Gladiolus* 'Georgette', one of several of this name, harmonize in color but contrast in form with the dainty hanging bells of *Fuchsia magellanica* 'Versicolor', working well against the fuchsia's pale leaves.

## Gladiolus tristis var. concolor

*Gladiolus tristis* is a variable species with creamy white flowers, tinged yellowish green and flushed or dotted with mauve, red, brown or purple. In var. *concolor*, the creamy white grades to yellowish green at the center of each petal and toward the base of the flower. Worthy of a warm position in cooler gardens, its blooms have an exquisite scent, especially in the evening. Its color blends with almost any other, especially with blue, pure yellow and crimson flowers, yellow-green foliage and flowers, and glaucous foliage. The grassy foliage tends to kink, so it is best masked by growing it through other short, loosely cushioning plants. Superlative companions include forget-me-nots, dark sweet Williams

The cream flowers of *Gladiolus tristis* var. *concolor* create a gentle contrast with the lilac-mauve flowers of Single Late Group *Tulipa* 'Bleu Aimable' and the perfectly matching variegated honesty (*Lunaria annua* 'Variegata').

and hyacinths, and also tulips (except the most brilliantly colored kinds, which tend to upstage the gladiolus).

**Perfect partners:** *Brunnera macrophylla*, *Dianthus barbatus* Nigrescens Group, *Euphorbia* × *martini*, *Melissa officinalis* 'Aurea', *Prunus glandulosa* 'Alba Plena', *Spiraea japonica* 'Goldflame', *Tanacetum parthenium* 'Aureum'

**H: 18 in.** (45 cm)  **S: 6 in.** (15 cm)
❀ **Late spring to early summer**
◊-◊◊  Z9  pH5.5–7

## Hyacinthoides hispanica
SPANISH BLUEBELL

This vigorous bulb is a native of shady places but tolerates full sun and naturalizes well – although its flowerheads, with florets arranged round the stem, lack the informality of the common bluebell, which has one-sided spikes. It is also effective when used for underplanting borders or a woodland garden, where nearby plants can hide its dying leaves. The campanula-blue florets, with a deeper, purer blue midrib, go well with white or soft yellow flowers, yellow-green foliage and flowers, and glaucous foliage. They work with late narcissi, tulips, primroses, London pride and other pink or mauve flowers. Cultivars include blue 'Excelsior', white 'La Grandesse' and mauve-pink 'Rosabella'.

**Perfect partners:** *Euonymus fortunei* 'Silver Queen' p.97 **B**, *Euphorbia characias* subsp. *wulfenii*, *Lamium galeobdolon* 'Hermann's Pride', *Narcissus* 'Spellbinder', *Primula vulgaris*, *Saxifraga umbrosa*, *Symphytum* 'Goldsmith', *Tanacetum vulgare* 'Isla Gold', *Valeriana phu* 'Aurea'

**H: 16 in.** (40 cm)  **S: 6 in.** (15 cm)  ❀ **Late spring**
◊-◊◊  Z4  pH4–8

The soft flowers of the bluebell *Hyacinthoides hispanica* harmonize with the emerging glaucous leaves of the plume poppy (*Macleaya cordata*). The latter's leaves will expand to cover the fading flowers and foliage of the bluebell.

## *Hyacinthus orientalis*

The common hyacinth is popular as a fragrant indoor pot plant, but its potential outdoors is often neglected. Full-size bulbs produce coarse, rather heavy flower spikes when grown as individual plants or in small gardens, but permanent outdoor plantings form small clumps with slender flower spikes that seem more graceful and natural. The single or double flowers are available in most colors, except strong yellow and rich orange, and look very attractive mixed in drifts of different shades of the same color – three or four irregularly blended shades of blue, for example, can look good interplanted with taller, softer yellow narcissi. Ideal planting companions are white, yellow or orange narcissi, as are tulips, wallflowers, silver-leaved pulmonarias, polyanthus, *Prunus tenella* cultivars, exochordas, daphnes, rock cress and aubrietas. For a daintier effect, *H.o.* var. *albulus*, the white-flowered Roman hyacinth, has numerous, more slender spikes of flowers; and the blue-flowered var. *provincialis* has a similar habit. Good cultivars include 'Anna Marie' ♀ (pale pink); 'Blue Jacket' ♀ (deep blue); 'City of Haarlem' ♀ (soft primrose-yellow); 'Delft Blue' ♀ (soft blue); 'Gipsy Queen' ♀ (peach); 'Ostara' ♀ (purplish blue); 'Pink Pearl' ♀ (deep pink); 'L'Innocence' ♀ in white; and 'Borah' ♀, which has numerous, very slender lavender-blue spikes.

**Perfect partners:** *Arabis blepharophylla* 'Frühlingszauber', *Daphne mezereum* f. *alba*, *Erysimum cheiri* Prince Series, *Euphorbia polychroma* 'Major', *Lamium maculatum*, *Myosotis sylvatica*, *Narcissus* 'February Gold' p.380 **B**, *N.* 'Jetfire', *Nonea lutea*, *Primula* Cowichan Venetian Group, *Pulmonaria* Opal, *Viola* Ultima Series

**H: 8–12 in. (20–30 cm) S: 6 in. (15 cm)**
❋ Early to mid-spring
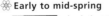 ◊-◊◊ ▢-▇ Z5 pH4.5–7.5

**Above right:** The dainty flower spikes of the hyacinth *Hyacinthus orientalis* var. *albulus* are ideal for a smaller scale of planting such as a window box. Here, they drape themselves gracefully over the box's edge, elegantly furnishing the brightly bicolored blooms of the relatively short Single Early Group *Tulipa* 'Keizerskroon'.

**Right:** This mixture of hyacinths is saved from dullness by the uneven grouping of three cultivars, white *Hyacinthus orientalis* 'L'Innocence', purplish blue 'Ostara' and the slightly deeper 'Blue Jacket'. Adding a fourth plant, perhaps a soft yellow narcissus or a yellow-green euphorbia such as *E. polychroma* 'Major', would also be effective.

The bright, early blooms of *Iris danfordiae* shine against the dark, attractively zoned foliage of *Cyclamen hederifolium*. A white-flowered variant of an early-blooming cyclamen, for example *C. coum*, could also be used.

## Iris danfordiae

This winter-flowering Reticulata iris, with bright chrome-yellow flowers enlivened by greenish markings at the base of the falls, is good for a rock or gravel garden, and for the front of a border, perhaps through a carpet of very low-growing ground cover. It can be combined with snowdrops, white *Cyclamen coum*, stinking hellebores and blue Reticulata irises, and makes a dramatic contrast with black mondo grass. Deep planting to a depth of about 8 in. (20 cm) can prevent bulbs disintegrating after flowering into tiny bulblets, the size of rice grains, which take many years to reach flowering size again. Like other Reticulata irises, the leaves become long and grassy after flowering; they must have full sun to guarantee blooms the following year.

**Perfect partners:** *Euphorbia myrsinites*, *Galanthus* 'S. Arnott', *Heuchera* 'Chocolate Veil', *Sedum spathulifolium* 'Purpureum', *Trifolium repens* 'Purpurascens'

**H: 4 in.** (10 cm)   **S: 2 in.** (5 cm)
✿ **Late winter to early spring**
◊-◊◊   Z5   pH6–7.5

## Iris 'George' ♛

Slightly easier to grow than *Iris danfordiae* (left), this winter-flowering Reticulata iris is less liable to divide into small, nonflowering bulblets and requires less sharp (although still good) drainage. Its plum-colored flowers, enlivened by a gold splash on the falls, mix well with the same plants as *I. danfordiae*, especially with pink and carmine variants of *Cyclamen coum* and early crocuses such as *C. tommasinianus* variants. It can be combined with winter heaths, although these can overwhelm 'George', and is also excellent in pots or bowls, especially with variegated ivies.

**Perfect partners:** *Ajuga reptans* 'Burgundy Glow', *Chionodoxa* 'Pink Giant', *Cyclamen hederifolium*, *Erica carnea*, *Primula vulgaris* subsp. *sibthorpii*

**H: 5 in.** (13 cm)   **S: 2 in.** (5 cm)
✿ **Late winter to early spring**
◊-◊◊   Z4   pH5–7.5

Black mondo grass (*Ophiopogon planiscapus* 'Nigrescens') provides a dusky background for the sumptuous purple blooms of *Iris* 'George'. Mauve *Crocus tommasinianus* will leaven the combination before the iris fades.

## Iris 'Joyce'

This Reticulata iris resembles 'George' (above) in being fairly easy to grow. It thrives in rock and gravel gardens and at the front of a border, in a carpet of low-growing ground cover or in combination with plants such as snowdrops, early scillas, stinking hellebore variants and other early-flowering hellebores, winter heaths (especially white-flowered cultivars) and early-flowering crocuses. Its blue flowers are suitable for contrasts with low-growing, yellow-green leaved evergreens such as *Euonymus fortunei* cultivars. Other good blue Reticulata cultivars include the rich blue 'Gordon' and 'Cantab', very pale blue with darker falls.

**Perfect partners:** *Calluna vulgaris* 'Beoley Gold', *Crocus* 'Blue Pearl', *Helleborus* × *sternii*, *Heuchera* 'Raspberry Regal', *Vinca minor* 'Illumination'

**H: 5 in.** (13 cm)   **S: 2 in.** (5 cm)
✿ **Late winter to early spring**
◊-◊◊   Z4   pH5–7.5

Pure blue *Iris* 'Joyce' harmonizes perfectly with the glaucous foliage of the rue *Ruta graveolens* 'Jackman's Blue', the variegated leaves of the periwinkle *Vinca major* 'Variegata' and common snowdrops (*Galanthus nivalis*). This scheme would work equally well on a larger scale, with the iris clumped less solidly and more intermingled with its partners.

A

## *Iris* 'Symphony'

Dutch irises are hybrids between variants of the Spanish iris, *I. xiphium*, and the frost-tender *I. tingitana*. Their flowering season extends beyond spring bulbs such as tulips and narcissi, bridging the gap between these and many summer flowers. 'Symphony' is an excellent cultivar, as is 'Apollo', both of them white and yellow bicolors. Other yellowish Dutch irises include 'Royal Yellow' and 'Golden Harvest', with golden yellow falls and paler standards; and 'Yellow Queen', in golden yellow, with an orange blotch on the falls. With their upright, narrow habit, they are all useful for planting among slightly

**Opposite:** The bright colors of Dutch Group *Iris* 'Symphony' shine among the orange flowers of *Geum* 'Prinses Juliana' and an Oriental poppy (*Papaver orientale*). Adding more of the iris and poppy, perhaps with some bronze foliage, would also be effective.

shorter herbaceous or biennial plants with simpler shapes or significantly different colors or with small to medium-sized shrubs such as smaller ceanothus, and shrub roses. They are excellent in loose drifts, associated with late spring and early summer bedding, forget-me-nots, Siberian wallflowers and early poppies. Their yellow tones go well with soft-colored flowers in apricot, peach or orange, and yellow-green or glaucous foliage, and contrast with blue flowers.

**Perfect partners:** *Aquilegia chrysantha* 'Yellow Queen', *Ceanothus* 'Puget Blue', *Erysimum* × *marshallii*, *Papaver nudicaule*, *Potentilla fruticosa* 'Hopleys Orange', *Rosa xanthina* 'Canary Bird', *Spiraea japonica* Golden Princess

**H: 26 in.** (65 cm)  **S: 4 in.** (10 cm)
❀ **Late spring to early summer**
Z7  pH5.5–7.5

The white, bell-shaped flowers of *Leucojum aestivum* 'Gravetye Giant' combine attractively with dainty blue *Corydalis flexuosa*. Adding a plant of intermediate height, perhaps with glaucous or yellow-green foliage, would help bridge the difference in height between the two.

## *Leucojum aestivum* 'Gravetye Giant' ♔

This is a vigorous cultivar of the summer snowflake, *L. aestivum*, a misleading name because its flowers are usually over by early summer. Unlike other *Leucojum* species, it grows well in moist borders and beside water. This rather leafy bulbous perennial is best fronted by shorter neighbors to disguise the imbalance between foliage and flowers. Its white blooms, with green tips, mix well with blue, soft yellow or yellow-green flowers, and with yellow-green or glaucous leaves. It associates prettily with Jonquilla narcissi, trollius and snake's head fritillaries, and with the contrasting foliage of early-leafing ferns, corydalis, brunneras and symphytums.

**Perfect partners:** *Doronicum* 'Miss Mason', *Dryopteris erythrosora*, *Epimedium* × *perralchicum* 'Frohnleiten', *Meconopsis cambrica*, *Nonea lutea*, *Primula denticulata*, *Trollius* × *cultorum* 'Alabaster', *Vinca major* 'Variegata' ❑ p.127 **C**

**H: 24 in.** (60 cm)  **S: 10 in.** (25 cm)
❀ **Mid- to late spring**
  Z4  pH5.5–7

Floating above a sea of azure wood forget-me-nots (*Myosotis sylvatica*), the bold shape of *Iris* 'Wedgwood' and the contrasting yellow flare on its falls prevent its soft blue flowers from being camouflaged among its neighbors. This subtle, hazy effect could be made brighter by leavening with white flowers, or more piquant by adding yellow-green.

## *Iris* 'Wedgwood'

This is one of several fine purplish blue Dutch irises, with yellow markings on the falls. Others include 'H.C. van Vliet', in dark violet-blue, with an orange blotch on its gray-blue falls; 'Imperator', in indigo-blue with an orange blotch on the falls; and 'Professor Blaauw' ♔, in violet-blue with a golden yellow blotch on the falls. All succeed in the same combinations as 'Symphony' (above), but especially with white or pale blue flowers, and in contrasts with soft yellow or yellow-green

flowers, and yellow-green or glaucous foliage. White Dutch irises such as 'White Bridge' are effective with yellow, blue, mauve and pink.

**Perfect partners:** *Cerinthe major* 'Purpurascens', *Dicentra spectabilis* 'Alba', *Euphorbia characias*, *Lunaria annua* var. *albiflora* 'Alba Variegata', *Smyrnium perfoliatum*, *Tulipa* 'Spring Green'

**H: 26 in.** (65 cm)  **S: 4 in.** (10 cm)
❀ **Late spring to early summer**
  Z7  pH5.5–7.5

## *Lilium* African Queen Group ♛

These lilies form a group of Aurelian hybrids derived from *L. henryi* ♛, *L. leucanthum* and *L. sargentiae*, and typically have large, trumpet-shaped flowers in shades of rich yellow and apricot-orange. 'African Queen' was selected as the best seedling of the group and has flowers in more intense colors: the petals are warm, deep tangerine-apricot inside and warm mahogany brown suffused with yellow outside. Its bold shape and beautiful lines, also characteristic of other lilies in this group, make a strong architectural impact and add a striking note of superlative quality wherever it is used. The dark stems contribute to the effect, making this an excellent plant to associate with bronze foliage and warm colors such as peach, apricot and soft orange. It is also strongly fragrant.

The African Queen Group are outstanding combined with yellow-green foliage such as that of some larger hostas, and are tall enough to interact with medium-sized shrubs such as Shrub roses, for instance some of David Austin's English roses. Like many other lilies, they can be very impressive mixed with other plants in large, deep containers, although pots should be turned frequently to prevent the lilies from leaning toward the light.

With their tall, narrow habit, most lilies look good weaving through shorter plants to create extended groups or drifts. If they are to thrive and increase, or at least maintain their size from year to year, they should not be crowded by companion plants of comparable size. Individual stems may need to be supported with stakes about one-third or half the ultimate height of the flowering stem, especially if the bulbs are grown where uneven lighting causes them to lean in the direction of the sun.

Like all lilies, these are very attractive to slugs and snails, and are also susceptible to viral diseases.

**Perfect partners:** *Canna* 'Phasion', *Foeniculum vulgare* 'Purpureum', *Hosta* 'Sum and Substance', *Physocarpus opulifolius* 'Diabolo', *Rosa* Graham Thomas, *Weigela* Briant Rubidor

**H: 6 ft. (1.8 m)  S: 8 in. (20 cm)**
❀ **Mid- to late summer**

▬▬▭▬ ◌◌ ▭-▬ ▬ Z5 pH5.5–7.5

This is a dramatic combination of warm colors consisting of *Lilium* African Queen Group, *Crocosmia* 'Lucifer' and the double daylily *Hemerocallis fulva* 'Flore Pleno'.

The warm orange *Lilium* Bellingham Group forms a striking contrast with sumptuous indigo *Delphinium* King Arthur Group, its blooms enlivened by their white eyes.

## *Lilium* Bellingham Group ♔

This is a strong-growing hybrid group derived from crosses between the brilliantly colored turkscap lily *L. humboldtii*, the leopard lily (*L. pardalinum* ♔) and the beautiful yellow *L. parryi*. Clones are vigorous and persistent, and can tolerate some shade. The unscented flowers range from clear yellow to bright orange-red, most of them spotted with rusty brown. The most common clones are a rich, hot orange, with exquisite markings that are best appreciated at close range. With their imposing stature and elegant habit, these lilies are ideal for large-scale plantings in sunny or partially shaded borders, and in open glades in a woodland garden. They all harmonize with hot colors and bronze foliage, and contrast well with blue, blue-purple or yellow-green flowers, and with yellow-green foliage. Suitable companions include yellow-green hostas, delphiniums, and late azaleas.

**Perfect partners:** *Anchusa azurea, Euphorbia palustris, Meconopsis* × *sheldonii, Osmanthus heterophyllus* 'Purpureus', *Rhododendron* 'Delicatissimum'

**H: 6½ ft. (2 m) S: 8 in. (20 cm)**
✹ **Early to midsummer**

Z5 pH5–7.5

## *Lilium* 'Black Beauty'

Robust and aristocratic in form, this scented Oriental Hybrid lily combines the deep crimson coloring and large flower size of one of its parents, *L. speciosum* var. *rubrum*, with the recurved flower shape, easy culture and vigor of its other parent, *L. henryi* ♔. With good cultivation in a humus-rich soil, it should produce a prodigious candelabra of blooms, each stem bearing dozens of flowers – as many as 150 have been reported on one stem. The complex architecture and geometry

This summer combination of flowers in similar shades of rose-pink and crimson includes the blooms of the Oriental Hybrid lily *Lilium* 'Black Beauty', upward-facing Texensis Group *Clematis* 'Duchess of Albany' and *Anisodontea capensis*. They form a close harmony that is charming and intricate at close range – although from a distance it would be hard to distinguish the individual blooms.

of a well-grown flower spike, with its secondary and tertiary branching, has a pleasing symmetry that can be destroyed if any limbs of the candelabra are lost through damage from slugs. 'Black Beauty' blends well with pink, crimson or white flowers, and can make a major impact in combination with glaucous foliage or grown beside deep purple leaves. It also looks attractive contrasted with pale apple-green.

**Perfect partners:** *Anemone* × *hybrida* 'September Charm', *Atriplex hortensis* var. *rubra, Buddleja davidii* 'Nanho Petite Indigo', *Fuchsia magellanica, Phlox paniculata* 'Harlequin', *Phygelius aequalis* Sensation, *Weigela florida* 'Foliis Purpureis'

**H: 6 ft. (1.8 m) S: 8 in. (20 cm)** ✹ **Midsummer**
Z6 pH5–6.5

Careful planting of the hybrid lavender *Lavandula* × *intermedia*, both in front of and behind *Lilium candidum*, has hidden the Madonna lily's untidy basal foliage.

## *Lilium candidum* ♛

MADONNA LILY

Cultivated forms of this traditional cottage garden plant have broad petals that give the trumpet-shaped flowers superlative substance and elegance. Because their leaves die as the flowers open, these powerfully scented lilies are best planted in a broad, shallowly banked border, behind a taller plant that will hide the foliage without overcrowding it. Alternatively, annuals such as nigellas or *Silene coeli-rosa*, and annual or perennial gypsophilas, can screen the dying foliage. This lily's simple beauty mixes especially well with blue, pink, mauve, apricot or peach flowers, and silver or glaucous foliage. It looks charming in large groups at the foot of a sunny wall, or planted with old roses, lavenders, catmints or pinks. These lilies thrive in lime-rich soil, and need plenty of sun and air around them.

**Perfect partners:** *Artemisia* 'Powis Castle', *Dianthus* 'Mrs. Sinkins', *Lavandula* × *chaytoriae* 'Sawyers', *Nepeta* 'Six Hills Giant', *Nigella damascena* 'Oxford Blue', *Rosa* 'De Rescht', *R. glauca*

**H: 5 ft.** (1.5 m) **S: 12 in.** (30 cm)
❀ **Early to midsummer**

 Z6 pH5.5–8

In this combination, *Lilium* 'Enchantment' contrasts boldly with *Lavandula* × *intermedia* Old English Group. Yearly mid-spring pruning of the lavender will be needed, in order to let in enough light for the lily to survive.

## *Lilium* 'Enchantment'

This early-flowering Asiatic Hybrid has rich orange, unscented blooms, in compact, egg-shaped flowerheads topped by a radiating crown of buds. The flowers have a strong shape that can provide a gentle focal point or, if plants are repeated along a border, will create an attractive pattern. Their color is very striking, especially in full sun, and can be difficult to combine with other plants, although they do associate well with hot colors, cream flowers and bronze foliage, and make effective contrasts with blue or yellow-green. Older cultivars such as this can suffer from an accumulation of viral disease, although choosing the largest bulbs helps to guarantee relative freedom from the disease.

**Perfect partners:** *Acanthus mollis* 'Hollard's Gold', *Achillea* 'Moonshine', *Alchemilla mollis*, *Campanula glomerata* 'Superba', *Canna indica* 'Purpurea', *Centaurea cyanus*, *Corokia* × *virgata* 'Bronze King', *Hemerocallis* 'Corky', *Lysimachia ciliata* 'Firecracker', *Phygelius* × *rectus* 'Sunshine', *Rosa* Amber Queen

**H: 36 in.** (90 cm) **S: 8 in.** (20 cm) ❀ **Early summer**
Z5 pH5.5–7.5

## *Lilium* 'Connecticut King'

This early-flowering Asiatic Hybrid lily is very vigorous and easy to grow, with upright stems bearing dark green, glossy foliage and unscented, sharp yellow, star-shaped flowers that face upward. The flower color makes a powerful impact and combines dramatically with hot oranges and reds. It also looks impressive with cream or strong blue flowers, and with glaucous foliage. Effective companions include yellow-variegated grasses and yellow-green hostas. Other similar yellow-flowered cultivars include 'Destiny', 'Sun Ray', and the considerably shorter Golden Pixie ('Ceb Golden').

**Perfect partners:** *Achillea* 'Inca Gold', *Coreopsis* 'Sunray', *Delphinium grandiflorum*, *Lychnis chalcedonica*, *Miscanthus sinensis* 'Zebrinus', *Tagetes patula* Favourite Series (mixed)

**H: 40 in.** (1 m) **S: 8 in.** (20 cm)
❀ **Early to midsummer**
Z5 pH5.5–7.5

Strong yellow *Lilium* 'Connecticut King' provides the focal point in this hot mixture of orange daylilies (*Hemerocallis fulva* 'Flore Pleno') and red *Crocosmia* 'Lucifer'.

## *Lilium* 'Joy' ♛

Often sold under the synonym 'Le Rêve', this Oriental Hybrid lily has bowl-shaped, soft pink flowers, with maroon spots on the lower half of the petals and contrasting yellow-green nectaries and rust-colored anthers. The ruffled margins and slightly reflexed petal tips give an elegant shape to the unscented flowers, which are borne on stalks long enough to allow each floret a separate identity. Although a slightly bluish pink, the flower color is close enough to primary pink to mix successfully with rose-pink, salmon, peach, magenta, crimson and white, and to combine well with glaucous or purple foliage. Plants are good in small groups in the middle rank of borders, among soft pink cranesbills and *Deutzia* × *elegantissima*, or they can be massed with lavenders, brachyglottis and roses.

**Perfect partners:** *Achillea millefolium* 'Lilac Beauty', *Astrantia major* 'Roma', *Berberis thunbergii* 'Pink Queen', *Campanula* 'Burghaltii', *Geranium pratense* Midnight Reiter strain, *Gypsophila paniculata* 'Flamingo', *Heuchera* 'Raspberry Regal', *Hosta* 'Krossa Regal', *Rosa glauca*, *Salvia officinalis* 'Purpurascens', *Stachys byzantina*

**H: 30 in.** (75 cm) **S: 8 in.** (20 cm) ❀ **Midsummer**
◊◊ ▢-▨ ■ **Z6 pH5–6.5**

*Lilium* 'Joy' harmonizes with the blooms of *Geranium* 'Ann Folkard', joined by gently contrasting bluish bracts of *Cerinthe major* 'Purpurascens', *Salvia patens* 'Cambridge Blue' and the sharp yellow-green leaves of the cranesbill.

## *Lilium lancifolium* var. *splendens* ♈

This handsome plant is a vigorous selection from the tiger lily (*L. lancifolium*, syn. *L. tigrinum*), grown for its large, soft orange-red, spotted turkscap flowers. It blends well with cream flowers and warm colors such as apricot, peach and coral, and with bronze or purple foliage. Lilac or purple flowers make striking contrasts, and yellow-greens are also effective. Since they are late-flowering, tiger lilies are useful partners for chrysanthemums, except those in the hottest colors or the kinds that form solid mounds of flowers.

**Perfect partners:** *Chrysanthemum* 'Mary Stoker', *Dahlia* 'Bishop of Llandaff', *Hydrangea arborescens* 'Annabelle', *Phygelius* × *rectus* 'Winchester Fanfare', *Verbena bonariensis*

**H: 5 ft. (1.5 m) S: 8 in. (20 cm)**
❀ **Late summer to early autumn**

Z4 pH5–6.5

In this pleasing contrast of color and form, *Lilium lancifolium* var. *splendens* mingles with *Lobelia* × *speciosa* 'Kompliment Blau'. Although the lobelia will often overwinter without protection in Zone 6 and warmer areas, it grows most vigorously if raised from seed each year.

## *Lilium leichtlinii* var. *maximowiczii*

The typical variety of *L leichtlinii*, *L.l.* var. *leichtlinii*, has yellow flowers and stoloniferous roots but is difficult to grow. *L.l.* var. *maximowiczii* is more vigorous with orange-red flowers resembling the tiger lily (*L. lancifolium*, above). Both are smaller, slimmer and more graceful than the tiger lily, bearing pendent, wide turkscap flowers, on green rather than dark colored stems. The tops of the plants benefit from being in sun, while their bases should be kept cool and shaded. They are used in the same way as *L. lancifolium* var. *splendens* (above),

The orange flowers and airy habit of *Lilium leichtlinii* var. *maximowiczii* here form an effective contrast with the bold glaucous foliage of *Hosta sieboldiana* var. *elegans*.

although they are more useful wherever a smaller or daintier plant is required, as in smaller beds or for viewing at close range.

**Perfect partners:** *Alchemilla mollis*, *Dryopteris affinis*, *Euphorbia schillingii*, *Geranium sylvaticum* 'Album', *Hypericum androsaemum* 'Albury Purple', *Lysimachia ciliata* 'Firecracker', *Tanacetum parthenium* 'Aureum'

**H: 4 ft. (1.2 m) S: 8 in. (20 cm)**
❀ **Late summer to early autumn**

Z4 pH5–6.5

## *Lilium pyrenaicum* var. *pyrenaicum*

Very easy and early flowering, this lily is good for naturalizing in grass and for growing in a bed, border or wild garden. With its yellow or greenish yellow turkscap flowers, it is best combined with cream or palest yellow flowers or contrasted with blue, although it is also effective with yellow-green flowers and foliage, with soft orange or apricot flowers, and with glaucous foliage. It blends well with blue cranesbills, early-flowering Shrub roses and silver foliage, provided this has a slight yellow flush or is accompanied by yellow flowers such as some phlomis or brachyglottis species. *L.p.* var. *rubrum* tends to be a stronger plant, with orange-red to blood-red flowers. Because of this greater vigor, it is usually var. *rubrum* that nurseries offer as *L. pyrenaicum*. As a result, purchases may produce yellow flowers unless *L. pyrenaicum* var. *pyrenaicum* is specified.

**Perfect partners:** *Aquilegia* 'Roman Bronze', *Brachyglottis monroi*, *Euphorbia griffithii*, *Geranium pyrenaicum* 'Bill Wallis', *Phlomis fruticosa*, *Rosa* English Garden

**H: 30 in. (75 cm) S: 8 in. (20 cm)** ❀ **Early summer**

Z3 pH5.5–7.5

At the foot of a sunny wall, the bright yellow flowers of *Lilium pyrenaicum* var. *pyrenaicum* harmonize with yellow *Fremontodendron* 'California Glory' and contrast with the early-flowering cranesbill, *Geranium* 'Johnson's Blue'.

## *Lilium speciosum* ♕

Light shade and an acidic soil are essential for this late-flowering lily, which revels in glades in woodland gardens, in partially shaded beds and borders, and in mixed containers. Its sweetly scented turkscap flowers are white or pink, shading through deeper carmine to a center spotted with deepest crimson. It goes well with purple or glaucous foliage, and purple, pink, crimson, white or pale green flowers. Plants may be combined with colchicums, actaeas, Japanese anemones and numerous airy asters such as variants of *A. cordifolius*. Late-flowering shrubs such as *Itea ilicifolia* and hydrangeas are also good companions. Among the best cultivated selections are var. *album*, in pure white with contrasting purplish brown stems, and the vigorous var. *rubrum*, with deep purplish stems and carmine flowers. All may need some staking.

**Perfect partners:** *Anemone* × *hybrida* 'Lady Gilmour', *Aster ericoides* 'Pink Cloud', *Eucomis pallidiflora* p.362 **A**, *Hydrangea aspera*, *H. paniculata*, *Tricyrtis formosana*

**H:** 3¼–5 ft. (1–1.5 m) **S: 8 in.** (20 cm)
❀ **Late summer to early autumn**
▮▮▮▮ ◌◌ ▢-▮ ▮ **Z5 pH5–6.5**

In this scheme of pinks and reds, *Lilium speciosum* is given space to arch gracefully over its neighbors, including the pink cranesbill *Geranium* 'Mavis Simpson'. It is backed by the hips and glaucous leaves of *Rosa glauca*.

## *Lilium regale* ♕

This vigorous and easy-to-grow species bears very sweetly scented, white trumpets shaded pink and brownish red on the reverse. Since it is inexpensive to buy, it is a good choice for ambitious schemes involving extended drifts or bold, repeated groups. It mixes well with most colors, in particular warm pinks, pale yellow-green or pale green flowers, and reddish foliage. 'Album', without the pinkish reverse to the petals, combines with almost any color, and is invaluable in white or silver schemes. Plants have a slight tendency to lean toward the light, and may require individual staking. They start growing very early and

In this white-flowered scheme, which would be equally effective with larger groups of each plant, *Lilium regale* is joined by *Hydrangea arborescens* 'Grandiflora', feverfew (*Tanacetum parthenium*), Miss Willmott's ghost (*Eryngium giganteum*) and the seedheads of *Allium aflatunense*.

their young shoots benefit from the shelter of evergreen shrubs such as skimmias, cistus, olearias, osmanthus and larger berberis.

**Perfect partners:** *Astilbe* × *arendsii* 'Cattleya', *Cryptotaenia japonica* f. *atropurpurea*, *Nicotiana langsdorffii*, *Oenothera fruticosa* 'Fyrverkeri', *Ruta graveolens*, *Weigela* 'Victoria'

**H: 6 ft.** (1.8 m) **S: 8 in.** (20 cm) ❀ **Midsummer**
▮▮▮▮ ◌◌ ▢-▮ ▮ **Z5 pH5–7.5**

The large blue spikes of *Muscari armeniacum* provide a strong foreground for the pale lavender-blue wood anemone *A. nemorosa* 'Robinsoniana' and the soft white *Narcissus* 'Thalia'. Because the grape hyacinth can spread rather rapidly, this grouping may be best in a semi-wild area.

## Muscari armeniacum ♀

Perhaps the easiest of several bulbous species commonly called grape hyacinths, this is a very free-flowering muscari with relatively large flower spikes. It is good for the front of a border and for gravel or rock gardens, and for underplanting late-leafing herbaceous plants and deciduous shrubs. Its foliage appears in autumn, but by flowering time the leaves have flopped, an affliction not shared to the same extent by *M. azureum* ♀ and *M. botryoides*. Planting among erythroniums, pulmonarias, wood anemones or euphorbias helps disguise this fault. Plants mix well with white, cream and soft yellow flowers, such as smaller narcissi, and with yellow-green foliage and flowers. 'Argaei Album' is white; 'Blue Spike' has larger, double flowers; and 'Saffier' is a paler campanula-blue.

**Perfect partners:** *Euphorbia dulcis* 'Chameleon', *Mahonia aquifolium* 'Apollo' p.115 **C**, *Puschkinia scilloides* p.387 **B**, *Tulipa linifolia* Batalinii Group p.397 **B** ❑ p.353 **B**

**H: 8 in. (20 cm) S: 6 in. (15 cm)**
❀ Mid- to late spring
◊◊ ▢-▣ ▮ Z4 pH5–7.5

## Muscari latifolium

This robust species is one of the largest grape hyacinths, with dusky deep purple-blue fertile florets, topped by paler sterile florets and borne in racemes above broad leaves. At close range the dark coloring provides an effective contrast for soft yellow and yellow-green foliage and flowers, and also blends well with mauve, lighter purple, blue and cream. It is useful for combining with euphorbias, wood anemones, erythroniums and smaller narcissi at the front of a border or in a rock garden, and for underplanting late-leafing herbaceous perennials. *M. neglectum* has narrower leaves and a similar color that is useful for the same combinations and close-range viewing.

**Perfect partners:** *Cardamine pentaphylla*, *Primula* 'Lady Greer', *Spiraea* × *vanhouttei* Pink Ice, *Valeriana phu* 'Aurea', *Vinca minor* 'Argenteovariegata', *Viola* 'Dawn'

**H: 8 in. (20 cm) S: 6 in. (15 cm)**
❀ Mid- to late spring
◊◊ ▢-▣ ▮ Z4 pH5–7.5

The dusky and recessive purple and royal-blue flowers of *Muscari latifolium*, most clearly visible at close range, are here contrasted with the yellow-green flowerheads of the glaucous-leaved myrtle spurge (*Euphorbia myrsinites*).

## Narcissus 'Actaea' ♀

This vigorous and easy late-flowering Poeticus narcissus has pure white petals surrounding a golden yellow cup edged with deep red. It can be contrasted with red foliage or mixed with hot colors, but is more effective with warm colors such as peach, apricot, soft yellow and soft orange, and with gently bronze-flushed foliage. Because white predominates in the flower coloring, it is unnecessary to harmonize with the yellow and orange of the cup. This bulb is suitable for beds and borders, for naturalizing in grass, and for underplanting deciduous shrubs, and looks very effective with azaleas, hardy hybrid rhododendrons, trollius, geums, primulas and kerrias. The flowers are larger and more solid in outline than those of *N. poeticus* and its variants, suiting it to extravagant effects, but *N. poeticus* has a more graceful, natural appearance. 'Actaea' needs regular dividing to prevent it becoming too congested.

**Perfect partners:** *Epimedium* × *warleyense* 'Orangekönigin', *Erythronium* 'Pagoda', *Geum rivale* 'Leonard's Variety', *Kerria japonica* 'Picta', *Rhododendron* 'Surrey Heath'

**H: 18 in. (45 cm) S: 8 in. (20 cm)** ❀ Late spring
◊◊ ▢-▣ ▮ Z4 pH5–7.5

Beneath a young birch, the russet young leaves of evergreen, mauve-flowered *Epimedium acuminatum* bridge the gap between the flowers of *Narcissus* 'Actaea' and those of the wood forget-me-not (*Myosotis sylvatica*).

# *Narcissus bulbocodium* ♀

HOOP-PETTICOAT DAFFODIL

With a preference for moist but well-drained conditions when in active growth and drier conditions in summer, this is a good choice for naturalizing in impoverished grass, such as an old meadow or grassland that has been regularly mown, with the cuttings habitually removed for some years. It may also be grown in a rock garden, provided moisture is adequate, while in beds and borders its small stature makes it liable to be overwhelmed by other plants. It looks most seductive mingling with pale blues, light pinks and similar softer colors, as well as white. Suitable neighbors include meadow flowers such as cardamines, snake's head fritillaries, snowdrops, *Leucojum aestivum*, spring-flowering cyclamens and violets. When naturalized in ideal conditions

it will self-seed prolifically, provided the sward is not cut before the seeds have had time to fall – here, mass planting will produce spectacular effects. However, the flaring, almost trumpet-shaped, deep yellow flowers, with their usually ruffled margins and ring of rudimentary outer petals, also merit closer examination. Of the numerous variants, the most useful for gardens is probably pale yellow var. *citrinus*.

**Perfect partners:** *Acaena microphylla* 'Kupferteppich', *Ajuga reptans* 'Jungle Beauty', *Cyclamen coum*, *Geranium sessiliflorum* subsp. *novae-zelandiae* 'Nigricans', *Ipheion uniflorum*, *Pulmonaria* Opal, *Ranunculus ficaria* var. *aurantiacus*, *Stachys byzantina* 'Primrose Heron', *Viola* 'Huntercombe Purple'

**H: 4–6 in. (10–15 cm)  S: 2 in. (5 cm)  ❀ Mid-spring**
◊◊◊ ▣-▪ ▪ Z6 pH5–6.5

Above: *Narcissus bulbocodium* and paler *N.b.* var. *citrinus* are naturalized with mixed shades of the dog's-tooth violet (*Erythronium dens-canis*). Both flower at the same height.

Below: Deep yellow *Narcissus bulbocodium* is here grown at the front of a bed with *Chionodoxa* 'Pink Giant' and, now out of flower, winter aconites (*Eranthis hyemalis*).

## *Narcissus* 'Eystettensis'
QUEEN ANNE'S DOUBLE DAFFODIL

Narcissus cultivars with slightly muddled or untidy flowers, such as doubles or those with split coronas, are sometimes considered inferior to the classic trumpet-flowered varieties, but they have their own unique beauty. 'Eystettensis' has charming blooms, each with six ranks of petals, decreasing in size toward the center of the flower. It is useful for beds and borders, especially at close range, but its vigor is not quite strong enough for naturalizing. Its soft pale yellow combines very successfully with blue flowers such as hyacinths, with rich gold, cream and

Sulfur-flowered *Narcissus* 'Eystettensis' grows through a carpet of glistening yellow blooms and near-black leaves of the celandine *Ranunculus ficaria* 'Brazen Hussy'.

white flowers, and with yellow foliage and flowers. It also contrasts effectively with dark foliage, such as purple-leaved bugles or the young crimson foliage of herbaceous peonies.

**Perfect partners:** *Doronicum* 'Little Leo', *Heuchera* 'Purple Petticoats', *Hyacinthus orientalis* 'Blue Magic', *Plantago lanceolata* 'Golden Spears', *Symphytum ibericum* 'All Gold'

H: 8 in. (20 cm)  S: 3 in. (8 cm)  ❀ **Mid-spring**
◊◊  ▢-■  ■  **Z4  pH5–7**

## *Narcissus* 'February Gold'  ♈

While lacking the elegantly swept-back petals of its parent *N. cyclamineus*, this Cyclamineus cultivar is early, vigorous and free-flowering, and one of the best for general garden use and for naturalizing. It usually flowers in early spring. With smaller blooms than Trumpet daffodils, it is ideal for small gardens, and its early season makes it suitable for mixing with plants such as crocuses, snowdrops, Reticulata irises and white-flowered winter heaths. Palest yellow, cream, white, blue and yellow-green are good color combinations. Other notable Cyclamineus cultivars include 'Bartley', which has a long, narrow trumpet and slender, reflexed petals, and 'Charity May' ♈, with greenish yellow petals and a yellow cup fading to white. All Cyclamineus cultivars bear one flower per stem.

**Perfect partners:** *Crocus chrysanthus* 'Cream Beauty', *Erica carnea* 'Springwood White', *Euphorbia characias*, *Helleborus* × *hybridus*, *Spiraea japonica* 'Gold Mound', *Trachystemon orientalis*

H: 12 in. (30 cm)  S: 4 in. (10 cm)  ❀ **Early spring**
◊◊  ▢-■  ■  **Z5  pH5–7.5**

The cheerful yellow blooms of *Narcissus* 'February Gold' are here contrasted with fragrant, dark-stemmed *Hyacinthus orientalis* 'Delft Blue', a combination that could equally be used in large containers or bedding.

## *Narcissus* 'February Silver'

This is a Cyclamineus narcissus, with slightly reflexed white petals and large yellow trumpets. It is similar to 'Jack Snipe' (see p.383) but a little larger and the trumpet is more flared and fluted. It flowers in early spring rather than in winter, a week or two after 'February Gold' (facing page) has started to bloom. It is a good choice for general use, for underplanting herbaceous plants or deciduous shrubs and for naturalizing in grass. Its pale coloring goes well with most other hues, especially blue or gold flowers and yellow-green foliage or flowers, and it also makes an

excellent foil for dusky purple blooms. Many other desirable hybrids have been created by crossing Trumpet daffodils with *N. cyclamineus*. Among the best bicolored hybrids are 'Dove Wings' ♀ (creamy white petals surrounding a long, primrose-yellow trumpet that fades gently with age); 'Foundling' ♀ (white with a rosy pink cup); and 'Jenny' ♀ (similar to 'Dove Wings', but with narrower, more pointed petals). 'Tracey' ♀ has white petals surrounding a soft lemon-yellow trumpet.

All these bicolors are effective massed in flower beds, with bare soil or dark plants to provide a contrasting background. 'February Silver' is particularly satisfying in generous

drifts through a leafy carpet of heathers or the basketry of bare stems of climbers such as *Hydrangea anomala* subsp. *petiolaris* and *Clematis* 'Praecose' planted as ground cover.

**Perfect partners:** *Centaurea montana* 'Gold Bullion', *Helleborus foetidus*, *Paeonia lactiflora* 'Crimson Glory', *Prunus* 'Shirotae' p.126 **B**, *Pulmonaria angustifolia* subsp. *azurea*

**H: 12 in.** (30 cm)  **S: 4 in.** (10 cm)  ❀ **Early spring**
⬜⬜⬜⬛  ◌◌  ⬜-⬛  ⬛  Z5  pH5–7.5

The pale *Narcissus* 'February Silver' and *Pulmonaria officinalis* 'Blue Mist' work well against the dusky maroon blooms of *Trillium sessile* and *Fritillaria persica*.

Grown through a carpet of *Chionodoxa forbesii*, a generous clump of *Narcissus* 'Geranium' contrasts in flower color and makes an imposing focal point.

## *Narcissus* 'Geranium' ♥

This narcissus is one of the Tazetta cultivars, which produce as many as 20 small flowers per stem. They have broad petals and small cups and are usually sweetly scented. Some inherit the tenderness of their parents, which might be any of the Section Tazetti, including *N. tazetta* itself, *N. papyraceus* (paper white narcissus) or *N. aureus*. The stout stems and broad leaves of most cultivars give them a slightly coarse appearance, but makes them excellent for cutting. 'Geranium' has white petals and small orange cups. These add piquancy to combinations with blue, purple or yellow-green, and harmonize with warm colors such as peach, yellow, apricot and soft orange. It is excellent for borders, for underplanting herbaceous plants and deciduous shrubs (including roses), and for naturalizing. It is also popular for forcing under glass, and for growing in containers.

**Perfect partners:** *Carex comans* (bronze), *Geranium* × *oxonianum* 'Spring Fling', *Hyacinthus orientalis* 'Gipsy Queen', *Nonea lutea*, *Sambucus nigra* 'Gerda', *Spiraea japonica* 'Goldflame'

**H: 14 in.** (35 cm)  **S: 6 in.** (15 cm)
❀ **Mid- to late spring**
⬛⬛⬜⬜ ◊◊ ⬜-⬛ ⬛ **Z4 pH5–7.5**

## *Narcissus* 'Hawera' ♥

'Hawera' is a Triandrus daffodil, with the graceful habit and bunched flowers of its parent *N. triandrus*, together with its slightly reflexed petals and rather rounded cup. The soft yellow coloring is excellent with golden yellow or cream, and contrasts well with mid- or pale blue flowers such as forget-me-nots, although it is not a strong enough shade to work successfully against the rich or deep blue of plants such as brunneras or bluebells. Its charming shape makes it a good choice for small gardens. Many Triandrus hybrids have been produced by crossing *N. triandrus* with the jonquil, *N. jonquilla*, combining the grace and delicate shape of the former with the jonquil's vigor and good constitution. They include 'April Tears' ♥, with which 'Hawera' is often confused. The two are similar in height and shape, but the flowers of 'April Tears' are a slightly deeper buttercup-yellow that is strong enough to contrast with rich blue flowers. 'Frosty Morn' is pure white and about 6 in. (15 cm) high, while the white 'Ice Wings' ♥ is taller at 14 in. (35 cm).

**Perfect partners:** *Hakonechloa macra* 'Aureola', *Ilex crenata* 'Golden Gem', *Luzula sylvatica* 'Taggart's Cream', *Omphalodes cappadocica*, *Ribes sanguineum* 'Brocklebankii', *Veronica peduncularis* 'Georgia Blue' ❏ p.119 **C**

**H: 9 in.** (23 cm)  **S: 3 in.** (8 cm)  ❀ **Late spring**
⬛⬛⬜⬜ ◊◊ ⬜-⬛ ⬛ **Z4 pH5–7**

The dainty, nodding, sulfur-yellow flowers of *Narcissus* 'Hawera' stand out well above a dense blue covering of wood forget-me-nots (*Myosotis sylvatica*).

A

*Narcissus* 'Jack Snipe' harmonizes perfectly at the foot of a bush of evergreen *Elaeagnus pungens* 'Frederici', although viewed from a distance the narcissus may be camouflaged.

## *Narcissus* 'Jack Snipe' ♈

This vigorous and easy Cyclamineus narcissus, with long-lasting, bicolored flowers in white and lemon-yellow, looks like a smaller version of 'February Silver' (see p.381), and is invaluable for smaller gardens, window boxes and other containers. It is excellent for the front of borders or as underplanting for later-leafing perennials, especially if planted in generous colonies. It flowers early enough to be useful with white winter-flowering heaths, and goes well with gold flowers and yellow-green flowers or foliage. It also makes outstanding contrasts with blue flowers such as scillas and muscari.

**Perfect partners:** *Erica* × *darleyensis* 'Jenny Porter', *Helleborus argutifolius* 'Pacific Frost', *Ipheion uniflorum*, *Muscari armeniacum* 'Valerie Finnis', *M. botryoides* 'Superstar'

**H: 8 in.** (20 cm)  **S: 3 in.** (8 cm)
❋ **Early to mid-spring**
  Z5  pH5–7

C

Grown beneath *Narcissus poeticus* var. *recurvus*, alpine forget-me-nots (*Myosotis alpestris*) provide an attractive foil for the elegant flowers of the narcissus.

## *Narcissus poeticus* var. *recurvus* ♈
PHEASANT'S-EYE NARCISSUS

This fragrant, late-blooming narcissus is invaluable for extending the flowering season towards early summer. It is vigorous and easily grown in beds and borders, planted in loose drifts where late-leafing shrubs can cover up its dying foliage. It is also successful naturalized in grass, where it can be used with late spring flowering bulbs, such as camassias, and wild flowers that match its simplicity. The small, red-rimmed yellow cup, giving a focus to each dainty white recurved bloom, barely provides enough color to influence combinations. As a result, it may be grown successfully with almost any color, although soft orange, sulfur-yellow, peach and apricot are possibly the most charming partners. The double *N.p.* 'Plenus' is even more fragrant and flowers very late.

**Perfect partners:** *Camassia quamash*, *Carex testacea*, *Cornus alba* 'Spaethii', *Diervilla* × *splendens*, *Hosta* 'Fire and Ice', *Mahonia aquifolium* 'Apollo', *Ranunculus aconitifolius* 'Flore Pleno', *Ribes* × *gordonianum*, *Viburnum carlesii*

**H: 14 in.** (35 cm)  **S: 6 in.** (15 cm)  ❋ **Late spring**
 ◊◊ ▢-▪ ▪ Z4  pH5–7.5

B

## *Narcissus* 'Jetfire' ♈

For a Cyclamineus narcissus, this has fairly large flowers that are richly colored in gold and strong orange, although the orange becomes paler with age in full sun. 'Jetfire' is a superb subject for bold bedding schemes, for grouping at the front of beds and borders, and for underplanting late-leafing perennials. Effective with flowers in reds, oranges and bright yellows, it also looks good with yellow-green foliage or flowers and in contrasts with cream or strong blue. Primroses, polyanthus, muscari and Greigii or Kaufmanniana tulips make fine companions. Narcissus hybrids like 'Jetfire', with small but conspicuous orange

This large-scale bedding-style combination of a white *Arabis alpina* cultivar with *Narcissus* 'Jetfire' could equally be repeated in smaller groups for underplanting in borders.

or red cups, are also useful for adding sparks of early warm color to shady corners. They include 'Beryl', yellow with an orange cup, and 'Foundling' ♈, white and rose-pink.

**Perfect partners:** *Erysimum* 'John Codrington', *Luzula sylvatica* 'Aurea', *Primula* Cowichan Blue Group, *Pulmonaria angustifolia*, *Tulipa* 'Orange Emperor'

**H: 8 in.** (20 cm)  **S: 3 in.** (8 cm)
❋ **Early to mid-spring**
◊◊ ▢-▪ ▪ Z5  pH5–7

In this informal planting *Narcissus pseudonarcissus* is scattered unevenly and naturalistically through a carpet of contrasting lavender-blue *Chionodoxa forbesii*.

## *Narcissus pseudonarcissus* ♀
LENT LILY

The flowers of this vigorous, easily grown species have slightly twisted, sulfur-yellow petals surrounding a golden yellow trumpet. With their natural grace, they look very much at home in wilder parts of the garden or naturalized in grass, although the plant is sufficiently showy to succeed almost anywhere, especially in beds and borders as underplanting for later-leafing herbaceous perennials and deciduous shrubs. It may be naturalized in drifts in more open woodland areas, and makes a charming display with primroses, cowslips and blue flowers such as bluebells. Its comparatively small scale also qualifies it for use in smaller gardens and close-range plantings.

The Tenby daffodil, *N. obvallaris* ♀, once classed as a subspecies of the Lent lily, is slightly shorter, equally vigorous and similar in appearance, but the flowers are more upright and a deeper shade of golden yellow.

**Perfect partners:** *Acorus gramineus* 'Ōgon', *Glechoma hederacea* 'Variegata', *Hyacinthoides hispanica*, *Hyacinthus orientalis* 'Delft Blue', *Primula veris*, *P. vulgaris*, *Pulmonaria* 'Apple Frost', *Vinca minor* 'La Grave'

**H: 10 in. (25 cm)  S: 4 in. (10 cm)** ❀ **Early spring**
◊◊ ▢-■ ■ Z4 pH5–7.5

## *Narcissus* 'Spellbinder' ♀

This daffodil has broad, overlapping mid-yellow petals, tinged yellowish green and paler at the base, and a flared, ruffled trumpet, aging almost to white. While vigorous enough for naturalizing in grass, its bold flowers are best used for large-scale schemes. Its slight greenish tinge suits greenish yellow, cream or white, and contrasts with blue. Other large Trumpet daffodils are 'Dutch Master' ♀ and 'Golden Harvest', both rich golden yellow. Large-cupped narcissi such as golden yellow 'Carlton' ♀ and double 'Golden Ducat' are equally useful for bold schemes. All associate well with hyacinths and Darwinhybrid tulips.

**Perfect partners:** *Anemone blanda*, *Carex flagellifera*, *Chamaecyparis obtusa* 'Fernspray Gold', *Euonymus fortunei* 'Silver Queen', *Fritillaria imperialis* 'Aureomarginata'

**H: 20 in. (50 cm)  S: 8 in. (20 cm)** ❀ **Mid-spring**
◊◊ ▢-■ ■ Z4 pH5–7.5

The newly opened blooms of *Narcissus* 'Spellbinder', which will become paler as the flowers age, are here prettily partnered by alpine forget-me-nots (*Myosotis alpestris*).

The charming round flowers of *Narcissus* 'Sun Disc', borne with elegance above grassy foliage, combine happily with the nodding azure flowers of Virginia bluebells (*Mertensia virginica*) at the front of a border.

## *Narcissus* 'Sun Disc' ♀

This miniature narcissus, one of the Jonquilla and Apodanthus cultivars, is a hybrid between *N. rupicola* and *N. poeticus*. It is useful in most parts of the garden, although its Alpine pedigree as a relative of *N. rupicola* especially qualifies it for growing in rock gardens and gravel gardens. (Other cultivars in this group derived from water-loving *N. jonquilla* tolerate high winter water tables and are better suited to waterside planting.) Its circular, pale yellow flowers, with a deep yellow cup, are particularly effective when contrasted with blue flowers or harmonized with white or golden yellow. 'Sundial' has the same parentage and is similar, flowering a little earlier and bearing smaller flowers with slightly darker mid-yellow petals and cup.

**Perfect partners:** *Arabis alpina* 'Flore Pleno', *Chrysosplenium davidianum*, *Hepatica nobilis*, *Ophiopogon jaburan* 'Vittatus', *Santolina pinnata* 'Edward Bowles', *Viola sororia* 'Freckles'

**H: 7 in. (18 cm)  S: 3 in. (8 cm)** ❀ **Mid-spring**
◊◊ ▢-■ ■ Z4 pH5.5–7.5

## *Narcissus* 'Tête-à-tête' ♧

Officially as a Miscellaneous daffodil, this dainty dwarf narcissus displays characteristics from both its parents, *N. cyclamineus* and *N. tazetta*. It flowers very early in the year, typically bearing two or three blooms per stem, in a strong yellow that looks spectacular when contrasted with other flowers in blue or purple, or harmonized with those in cream,

pale yellow, yellowish green, orange or white, including white kinds of winter heaths and Darley Dale heaths. 'Tête-à-têtc' is excellent for rock gardens and for the front of borders, and in smaller gardens; it looks pretty with other early spring flowers such as snowdrops, muscari, scillas and pulmonarias.

**Perfect partners:** *Crocus vernus* 'Purpureus Grandiflorus', *Scilla mischtschenkoana* p.389 **A**,

*Thuja occidentalis* 'Rheingold', *Uncinia egmontiana* ❑ pp.95 **A**, 285 **C**

**H: 6 in.** (15 cm)  **S: 3 in.** (8 cm)  ❀ **Early spring**
◊◊  ☐-▧  ■  Z4 pH5–7

Grown among a group of bright blue lungwort (*Pulmonaria* 'Lewis Palmer'), the strong yellow blooms of *Narcissus* 'Tête-à-tête' are borne at the same height, creating an effective contrast of color and form.

In this striking mixture of *Nerine bowdenii* with *Aster amellus* 'Veilchenkönigin', the aster grows between the slightly taller nerine bulbs, producing an almost solid carpet of bloom. In late autumn, the aster covers the nerine's leaves, but not until they start to die back.

In a subdued but charming scheme, the silvery green flowers of *Ornithogalum nutans* are joined by white snake's head fritillary (*Fritillaria meleagris* var. *unicolor* subvar. *alba*) and the smaller cream bells of *Symphytum ibericum*.

## *Nerine bowdenii* ♛

This autumn-flowering bulb has vibrant pink blooms, borne without the leaves and so benefiting from close association with other plants that can provide a foil to the flowers. Dark purple or silver foliage plants are good, together with markedly paler or darker flowers, perhaps white or palest pink, ruby, crimson, lavender or deep purple. It is especially effective with shorter *Aster amellus*, *A.* × *frikartii* and *A. novi-belgii* cultivars, and dark-leaved coleus. However, these must not obscure the nerine leaves from winter and spring sunlight, essential to help it store reserves for good flower production. 'Mark Fenwick' and 'Pink Triumph' are superior pink cultivars, 'Mollie Cowie' has variegated leaves and 'Alba' is off-white.

**Perfect partners:** *Artemisia stelleriana, Chrysanthemum yezoense, Convolvulus cneorum, Helichrysum petiolare, Pelargonium* 'Lady Plymouth', *Solenostemon* 'Palisandra'

**H: 18 in. (45 cm) S: 3½ in. (8 cm)**
✿ **Early to late autumn**
◊-◊◊ ▢-▇ Z8 pH5.5–7.5

## *Nerine* 'Zeal Giant' ♛

This relatively hardy large-flowered hybrid of *N. bowdenii* (above) is suitable for a sheltered, sunny spot, especially at the foot of a warm wall. With its large size and bright coloring, it is a better choice for grander schemes than *N. bowdenii*. It can be used in similar plant associations, and looks excellent with tender salvias, dark-leaved iresines and schizostylis, while its stronger coloring – close to primary pink – is a good match for brighter, more dazzling plantings, perhaps with a slightly tropical theme. It is good with red and purple foliage; combinations with magenta or vermilion can seem exciting or disconcerting, depending on personal taste. The bulbs are best left undisturbed, and clumps divided only when flowering declines.

**Perfect partners:** *Heliotropium arborescens,*

This combination of *Nerine* 'Zeal Giant' with coleus (*Solenostemon scutellarioides*) is highly effective: the coleus covers the nerine foliage only as the leaves start to die.

*Ipomoea batatas* 'Blackie', *Iresine herbstii* 'Brilliantissima', *Plectranthus argentatus*

**H: 21 in. (53 cm) S: 4 in. (10 cm)**
✿ **Early to late autumn**
 ◊-◊◊ ▢-▇ Z8 pH5.5–7.5

## *Ornithogalum nutans* ♛

The exquisite flowers of this bulbous species have white petals, each with a central silvery gray-green stripe, producing a subtle color scheme that merits close inspection and is especially good in combinations with silver or green foliage and white flowers. It is a shade-tolerant plant, with slightly untidy foliage, and benefits from being hidden at flowering time by other plants so only the flowers are seen. Good companions include blue flowers such as corydalis, meconopsis, brunneras and *Hyacinthus orientalis* cultivars. It also goes well with the green-striped petals of Viridiflora tulips and *Hosta undulata* varieties. En masse the ornithogalum flowers resemble filigree, so are best offset by bold foliage and flowers, such as those of pulmonarias, aspidistras, tulips and larger late narcissi.

**Perfect partners:** *Asplenium scolopendrium, Brunnera macrophylla* 'Dawson's White', *Geranium renardii, Helleborus foetidus, Hosta* 'Night before Christmas', *Omphalodes verna, Pulmonaria* 'Excalibur', *Tulipa* 'Spring Green'

**H: 12 in. (30 cm) S: 10 in. (25 cm)** ✿ **Late spring**
◊-◊◊ ▢-▇ Z6 pH5.5–7.5

## Ornithogalum pyramidale

Distinguished by its neatly conical heads of starry white flowers, this bulbous perennial has slightly untidy grassy foliage that is perhaps best masked by a companion plant, preferably one of contrasting floral form that does not obstruct the sun from reaching the ornithogalum's leaves until it is just about to flower. Many annuals are ideal for this, provided they are early flowering and feathery leaved – nigellas, for example – with plenty of small blooms that are not too strongly colored. Some biennials, such as a single-colored cultivar of *Silene coeli-rosa*, are suitable, as are white flowers for viewing at close range. Annuals or biennials in mixed colors are not suitable because they would add an intrusive note of visual confusion.

**Perfect partners:** *Cerinthe major* 'Purpurascens', *Echinops ritro* 'Veitch's Blue', *Eucalyptus gunnii, Eupatorium rugosum* 'Chocolate', *Nigella damascena* 'Miss Jekyll', *Osmanthus heterophyllus* 'Purpureus', *Phormium* 'Bronze Baby'

**H: 40 in. (1 m) S: 8 in. (20 cm)** ✿ **Early summer** ◊-◊◊ ▢-■ **Z7 pH5.5–7.5**

This combination uses the feathery silver leaves of tender shrubby *Artemisia arborescens* to hide the untidy dying foliage of *Ornithogalum pyramidale* and to fill in between the bulb's spindly flower stems. The artemisia can be grown from cuttings taken in late summer or early autumn, overwintered under glass and planted outside as soon as the danger of frost has passed.

In this pleasing partnership for a rock garden or the front of a bed or border, the harmonious colors and matching height and habit of *Muscari armeniacum* and *Puschkinia scilloides* are balanced by a contrast of form.

## Puschkinia scilloides

This spring-flowering bulb looks similar to a scilla. It bears delicate blue flowers, which are good with richer blues and white flowers, and with silver foliage. It is useful for combining with muscari, smaller white narcissi, ipheions and wood anemones, and contrasts effectively with very dark-leaved ground-cover plants such as black mondo grass or purple bugle. The flowers of *P.s.* var. *libanotica* are usually white and capable of blending with almost any other color; occasionally they are striped with blue, an attractive variation for isolated groups and drifts. *P.s.* var. *l.* 'Alba' is similar, but generally cleaner in color. Neither white form is as eye-catching as the species unless massed in bold patches among a contrasting dark ground-cover plant.

**Perfect partners:** *Ajuga reptans* 'Atropurpurea', *Festuca glauca, Fragaria* Pink Panda, *Ipheion* 'Rolf Fiedler', *Muscari armeniacum, Ophiopogon planiscapus* 'Nigrescens'

**H: 8 in. (20 cm) S: 3 in. (8 cm)** ✿ **Early spring** ◊-◊◊ ▢-■ **Z5 pH5.5–7.5**

## *Scilla bifolia* ♔

A mountain species most at home in relatively cool climates, this is an easy bulb, that is suitable for growing in a border or rock garden, or for naturalizing. The tiny, star-like lavender-blue florets make an effective contrast of scale with larger-flowered bulbs and spring plants, and benefit from close-range viewing. It is most attractive combined with white and deep blue flowers, and contrast well with soft yellow flowers, such as those of smaller narcissi. It goes with celandines, wood anemones and low ground cover such as bugles, and may be contrasted with yellow-green foliage and flowers, such as early-flowering euphorbias. 'Alba' is a white-flowered variant, although there are several forms of it, not all of them pure in color; the same caveat applies to 'Rosea', which is found in shades of mauve to pink. All variants associate well with smaller species tulips, smaller crocuses, ipheions, small-flowered winter violas, fritillaries and erythroniums.

**Perfect partners:** *Anemone nemorosa, Crocus chrysanthus* 'Cream Beauty', *Epimedium × youngianum* 'Niveum', *Euphorbia dulcis* 'Chameleon', *Helleborus × hybridus* (primrose), *Ipheion uniflorum, Milium effusum* 'Aureum', *Narcissus* 'Jack Snipe', *Ranunculus ficaria, Valeriana phu* 'Aurea'

H: 5 in. (13 cm)  S: 2 in. (5 cm)  ✺ Early spring
▬▬▬▬▬  ◊-◊◊  ▢-◼  Z6  pH5.5–7.5

The dainty lavender-blue flowers of *Scilla bifolia*, with their matching floret stems, and wood anemones (*Anemone nemorosa*) make a charming and informal combination, suitable for a sunny glade in a woodland garden or as underplanting beneath herbaceous plants or deciduous trees and shrubs. Scillas will happily grow through the crowns of other plants such as the Bearded irises seen here.

*Scilla mischtschenkoana* 'Tubergeniana' is the most richly colored variant of the species and is especially well-suited to contrasts with yellow. Here, it is perfectly matched in height with the dwarf *Narcissus* 'Tête-à-tête', attractively and neatly filling a narrow border between a path and a wall.

This carmine selection of *Tigridia pavonia*, flopping obligingly to place itself among the matching, sprawling *Verbena* 'Sissinghurst', creates a fascinating picture to be viewed at close range at the front of a border.

## *Scilla mischtschenkoana*

Suitable for edging, for the front of a border, or for a rock garden, this species has silvery blue flowers, marked with a darker stripe down the center of each petal and opening flatter than the more familiar *S. siberica* (below). The flowers of 'Tubergeniana' ♀ are a strong enough blue to contrast successfully with the soft yellow of, for example, smaller narcissi and crocuses, *Anemone* × *lipsiensis* and *A. ranunculoides* cultivars. Other good companions are early-flowering Reticulata irises and winter-flowering hellebores. Like most scillas, it looks charming beneath late-leafing perennials such as hostas and is worth planting liberally for early color.

**Perfect partners:** *Crocus chrysanthus* 'Blue Pearl', *C. sieberi* 'Albus', *Cyclamen coum* f. *pallidum* 'Album', *Galanthus plicatus*, *Helleborus* × *nigercors*, *Hosta* 'Blue Angel', *Iris* 'Cantab', *Primula vulgaris*, *Saxifraga* × *urbium* 'Aureopunctata'

**H: 5 in.** (13 cm) **S: 2 in.** (5 cm)
✿ **Late winter to early spring**
◊-◊◊ ■-■ Z4 pH5.5–7.5

## *Scilla siberica* ♀
SIBERIAN SQUILL

This rich colored scilla is useful as an edging plant and naturalized in lawns. Its flowers combine greenish blue and purplish blue, two gently clashing tones that add extra richness and vibrancy to the blooms, and produce dramatic contrasts with white, yellow or yellow-green flowers, such as early-flowering euphorbias, narcissi, smaller tulips, crocuses and snowdrops. *S.s.* 'Spring Beauty' is almost identical to the species, while subsp. *armena* has larger flowers borne singly on their stems. A white cultivar, 'Alba', blends with almost any other color.

**Perfect partners:** *Adiantum aleuticum* 'Japonicum' p.228 **C**, *Ajuga reptans* 'Arctic Fox', *Corydalis solida* 'Snowstorm', *Euphorbia myrsinites*, *E. polychroma* 'Candy', *Fritillaria meleagris* p.363 **A**, *Hyacinthus orientalis* 'Gipsy Queen', *Lamium maculatum* 'Roseum', *Plantago lanceolata* 'Golden Spears', *Tulipa kaufmanniana* ❑ p.353 **B**

**H: 6 in.** (15 cm) **S: 2 in.** (5 cm)
✿ **Early to late spring**
◊-◊◊ ■-■ Z5 pH5–7.5

White and blue flowers with rich green foliage invariably create a pleasing combination, as seen here in this small but charming group consisting of *Scilla siberica*, *Anemone blanda* 'White Splendour', with yellow eyes, and *Pulmonaria* 'Sissinghurst White'. This mix would be equally successful on a greater scale, with large, intermingling groups of each.

## *Tigridia pavonia*
PEACOCK FLOWER

This exotic-looking tender bulb has grassy foliage, and flowers in white, yellow, orange, pink, red and purplish red, marked and mottled dramatically with yellow and red. Each flower lasts only for a day, and although they appear in succession it is seldom in sufficient profusion to make an impact through color alone. They associate most effectively with yellow-green foliage and flowers, and dark foliage, especially neater plants with more attractive or shapely leaves. Good companions include cannas, coleus, *Hibiscus acetosella* and flowers in warm colors such as peach or apricot. Peacock flowers require warmth and sun. In cold areas, they need to be taken inside for winter.

**Perfect partners:** *Argyranthemum* 'Jamaica Primrose', *Canna* 'Champigny', *Dahlia* 'Roxy', *Phormium* 'Yellow Wave', *Salvia greggii* 'Peach', *Solenostemon* 'Walter Turner'

**H: 18 in.** (45 cm) **S: 9 in.** (23 cm)
✿ **Midsummer to early autumn**
◊◊ ■ Z9 pH5–7

# Tulips

TULIPS ARE AVAILABLE in a wide range of colors, including bicolors, making them particularly welcome after the more limited shades of the other key spring bulb, the daffodil. There are 15 groups or divisions of tulips, categorized mainly according to flower type or season, and they offer endless possibilities for effective associations, including combinations that are subtle in both color and form, and more adventurous contrasts between hot and cool colors, or strong elegant shapes overtopping massed smaller flowers. There are tulips suitable for formal bedding displays as well as those that are ideal for wilder areas of the garden.

Of the 15 categories, the most widely grown is the stately Single Late Group, formerly subdivided into the Darwin Group, the aristocrats of spring bedding, and the Cottage Group. As the name suggests, tulips in this group have single flowers that appear late in the season. They are also relatively tall. Single Early tulips are much shorter and a month or so earlier to flower but equally colorful. The Triumph Group is intermediate in height and season and was derived by crossing Single Early tulips with other cultivars. Large, single flowers produced on sturdy stems over a long season are typical of the Darwinhybrids, created by crossing *T. fosteriana* with the Darwin Group. Tulips from all these divisions are excellent for formal schemes or less formal displays in a mixed border. Some of the Darwinhybrids are suitable for naturalizing in grass.

The Double Early and Double Late Groups have peonylike blooms, often in subtle color blends. The flowers are susceptible to weather damage, but are good in pots and for sheltered bedding.

Tulips in the Parrot, Fringed and Lily-flowered Groups have flowers quite unlike the egg-shaped blooms of most of the other groups. Those of Parrot tulips are dissected and twisted, while the petals

of Fringed tulips have ragged edges. Lily-flowered tulips have an elegant tapering form. All these can be used for exotic effects in combination with other tulips or with a wide variety of foliage and early-flowering plants. For interesting color schemes, Viridiflora tulips have an attractive green stripe down the center of each petal, and the petals of Rembrandt tulips are "feathered" with darker colors.

Tulip bulbs should be planted about 4–6 in. (10–15 cm) deep in fertile soil in a

The earliest tulips bloom before their traditional spring-bedding partners, so pansies and violas are ideal alternative companions. Here, Forerunner Series makes a cool contrast to the bright pink Single Early tulip 'Christmas Cheer'.

sunny site in autumn. In areas with cool, wet climates, lifting the bulbs after flowering and replanting in autumn prevents the number of blooms diminishing; however, species tulips and those from the Greigii, Kaufmanniana and Fosteriana Groups can remain in the soil. These small-flowered tulips are ideal for rock gardens, pots or near border edges.

## *Tulipa* 'Abu Hassan'

This Triumph Group tulip has gold-edged, rich mahogany-red flowers, a very striking combination that emphasizes the flower shape and harmonizes especially well in hot color schemes. It is effective planted in drifts in a border, where it can partner sulfur-yellow or orange wallflowers, and plants with yellow-green leaves such as perfoliate alexanders, early-flowering euphorbias and shrubs with yellow-green foliage. It is also good with bronze foliage, soft yellow or cream hyacinths and narcissi, doronicums, kerrias, fritillaries, epimediums and early-leafing ferns. Triumph Group tulips are particularly useful for their mid-season flowering and their height.

**Perfect partners:** *Epimedium* × *perralchicum*, *Erythronium oregonum*, *Foeniculum vulgare* 'Purpureum', *Hyacinthus orientalis* 'City of Haarlem', *Narcissus* 'Binkie'

**H: 20 in.** (50 cm)   **S: 6 in.** (15 cm)   **Late spring**
◊   ▢-▮   ▮   **Z4 pH5–7.5**

Pale petal edges of *Tulipa* 'Abu Hassan' emphasize its flower shape, helping it to be seen distinctly against the orange-red and yellow wallflowers (*Erysimum cheiri*) beneath.

## *Tulipa* 'Angélique' ♚

The small flowers of this Double Late Group tulip open pale pink and deepen a little with age; its petals are edged and streaked with a lighter color, and the outer ones are flushed with green. This soft coloring allows it to mingle with cool-colored flowers in blue, mauve, purple or crimson, and with purple or silver foliage. As a bedding plant, it can be grown through forget-me-nots in white, pink or blue, or with a tulip of contrasting form. It goes well with rock cress, herbaceous plants such as the earliest cranesbills, hyacinths and the latest narcissi such as Poeticus cultivars.

**Perfect partners:** *Arabis blepharophylla* 'Frühlingszauber', *Aubrieta* 'Bressingham Pink', *Brunnera macrophylla*, *Convolvulus cneorum*, *Dicentra spectabilis*, *Heuchera* 'Can-can', *Narcissus* 'Actaea', *Pulmonaria* 'Lewis Palmer'

**H: 18 in.** (45 cm)   **S: 6 in.** (15 cm)   **Late spring**
◊   ▢-▮   ▮   **Z4 pH5–7.5**

The attractively edged blooms of *Tulipa* 'Angélique' stand clear of short alpine forget-me-nots (*Myosotis alpestris*) in front of the mauve wallflowers *Erysimum* 'Bowles Mauve'.

Tall scarlet *Tulipa* 'Apeldoorn', standing evenly spaced above a carpet of wallflowers (*Erysimum cheiri*), is overtopped by statuesque crown imperials (*Fritillaria imperialis*) in a mixture of harmonious colors.

## *Tulipa* 'Apeldoorn'

'Apeldoorn' is one of the most popular red-flowered Darwinhybrid Group tulips. Blooming in mid-season, it is useful for bedding and permanent planting in mixed and herbaceous, and is effective with hot-colored flowers or in contrasts with white and yellow-green foliage and flowers. Its large scarlet blooms look marvellous when grown through orange wallflowers or with early-flowering euphorbias, white or orange narcissi, yellow-green hellebores, leucojums, Candelabra primulas and polyanthus in hot colors, and plants with bronze or red-flushed foliage. Like all the Darwinhybrids, 'Apeldoorn' is remarkable for its vigor and persistence, even in cool, wet climates. While the color range of this group is more restricted than other tulip categories, there is enough choice to make wonderful sequences and blends – for example, from ivory through cream and soft yellow to apricot and orange.

**Perfect partners:** *Cornus alba* 'Elegantissima', *Erysimum* 'Apricot Twist', *Euphorbia* Redwing, *Kerria japonica* 'Golden Guinea', *Spiraea japonica* 'Goldflame'

**H: 22 in.** (55 cm)   **S: 6 in.** (15 cm)   **Mid-spring**
◊-◊◊   ▢-▮   ▮   **Z4 pH4.5–7.5**

## *Tulipa* 'Apricot Beauty' ♛

This is a Single Early Group tulip with pale
apricot flowers tinged with salmon. While
most of the group is fairly short, 'Apricot
Beauty' is relatively tall, allowing it to be
planted through a ground of lower plants.
It is superlative with warm-colored flowers,
but is also sufficiently strong in color to be
contrasted effectively with blue – early forget-
me-nots, for example – as well as with yellow-
green foliage or flowers and bronze foliage.
It mixes well with dark-leaved heucheras, soft
orange celandines, soft yellow rhizomatous
anemones and epimediums (particularly
those with copper-flushed foliage), and
makes charming associations with white
rock cress, early euphorbias, white narcissi,
primroses and polyanthus. Blooming at
the same time as the majority of narcissi,
all Single Early tulips are immensely useful
for early display.

**Perfect partners:** *Anemone* × *lipsiensis*, *Arabis
alpina* subsp. *caucasica*, *Epimedium* × *versicolor*
'Sulphureum', *Fritillaria imperialis* p.362 **B**,
*Ranunculus ficaria* var. *aurantiacus*

**H: 18 in.** (45 cm)  **S: 6 in.** (15 cm)  ❅ **Mid-spring**
◼◻◻◻  ◊  ◻-◼  ◼  **Z4 pH5–7.5**

*Tulipa* 'Apricot Beauty', toward the front of a permanently
planted bed, blends perfectly with the bronze-flushed
foliage of *Photinia* × *fraseri* 'Red Robin'. Yellow-green
foliage or scarlet flowers would also be effective here.

## *Tulipa* 'Ballerina' ♛

'Ballerina' is a fairly tall, fragrant tulip
belonging to the Lily-flowered Group.
All Lily-flowered tulips have blooms with
elongated petal tips and usually elegant
waists, although some cultivars have blooms
that open to a flat star, which, while exposing
a greater area of colored petal, can diminish
the graceful shape of the bloom. 'Ballerina'
has the characteristic tapering petals, blood-
red in the center, grading to vermilion, with
a narrow lemon-yellow edge (lighter cultivars
are sometimes sold under this name). It
may be used for the same combinations as
'Abu Hassan' (see p.391), although its subtly
graded hues produce a distinctly more restful
effect. Lily-flowered tulips bloom from mid-

Growing through the daisylike *Anthemis punctata* subsp.
*cupaniana* at the edge of a border, shapely *Tulipa* 'Ballerina'
adds pizzazz in front of brightly variegated gardener's
garters (*Phalaris arundinacea* var. *picta*).

to late season, and they overlap with all but
the Double Early, Single Early, Greigii and
Kaufmanniana groups, and can be used with
cultivars bearing different flower shapes.

**Perfect partners:** *Erysimum* Walberton's
Fragrant Sunshine, *Euphorbia* × *martini*,
*Heuchera* 'Amber Waves', *Kerria japonica*
'Picta', *Narcissus* 'Cassata', *Ribes alpinum*
'Aureum', *Spiraea japonica* 'FireLight'

**H: 22 in.** (55 cm)  **S: 6 in.** (15 cm)  ❅ **Late spring**
◼◻◻◻◻  ◊  ◻-◼  ◼  **Z4 pH5–7.5**

## *Tulipa* 'Blenda'

Belonging to the Triumph Group, 'Blenda' has deep rose flowers with a white or creamy white base. It blends well with cool colors such as blue, paler pink, crimson and purple, yet is rich enough to contrast strikingly with white or yellow-green flowers. It can look sumptuous partnered by crimson or purple flowers and dark foliage such as that of dusky heucheras or ornamental cherries. It goes well with hyacinths, bergenias, white narcissi and euphorbias (including bronze- or purple-leaved cultivars), and among flowering shrubs such as viburnums and rhododendrons.

**Perfect partners:** *Berberis* × *ottawensis* 'Silver Miles', *Bergenia* 'Brahms', *Camellia* × *williamsii* 'Garden Glory', *Exochorda* × *macrantha* 'The Bride', *Heuchera* 'Regina'

**H: 18 in.** (45 cm)  **S: 6 in.** (15 cm)
❀ **Mid- to late spring**
  ◊  ▢-▨  ■  **Z4  pH5–7.5**

Drifts of rose-pink *Tulipa* 'Blenda' and black-purple *T.* 'Queen of Night' alternate along a spacious and naturalistically planted border in light shade under a tree.

## *Tulipa* 'China Pink' ♛

One of the longest-lasting Lily-flowered tulips, 'China Pink' often remains in bloom throughout late spring, its rich pink flowers opening out into a star and gradually becoming paler as they age. It combines well with cool colors such as blue, mauve, purple and crimson, and with purple foliage such as that of berberis, as well as contrasting effectively with yellow-green foliage and flowers. It is particularly good with bergenias, heucheras, rock cress, forget-me-nots, primroses and polyanthus, with other bulbs such as hyacinths or later-flowering white narcissi, and with flowering shrubs such as exochordas, daphnes and smaller magnolias. It is a popular alternative to Darwinhybrid tulips, whose flowering period is very similar, and it is a good choice both for massed spring bedding and for planting in containers.

**Perfect partners:** *Berberis* × *ottawensis* f. *purpurea* 'Superba', *Heracleum minimum* 'Roseum', × *Heucherella alba* 'Rosalie', *Magnolia* × *loebneri* 'Leonard Messel', *Narcissus* 'Thalia', *Viola cornuta*

**H: 18 in.** (45 cm)  **S: 6 in.** (15 cm)  ❀ **Late spring**
◊  ▢-▨  ■  **Z4  pH5–7.5**

In moist ground and light shade, the ornamental rhubarb *Rheum palmatum* 'Atrosanguineum' makes an imposing focal point behind *Tulipa* 'China Pink', growing through a carpet of wood forget-me-nots (*Myosotis sylvatica*).

In an unusual but effective color scheme at the front of a border, dusky purple *Tulipa* 'Burgundy' is combined with soft blue wood forget-me-nots (*Myosotis sylvatica*), yellow wallflowers (*Erysimum cheiri* 'Primrose Bedder') and the yellow-green flowerheads of *Euphorbia polychroma*. Each plant plays a part, and omitting any one would impair the ensemble.

## *Tulipa* 'Burgundy'

This Lily-flowered tulip has slender petals grading from dusky purple in the center to a lighter magenta-purple toward the edge. It is useful for opulent combinations with other purple and crimson flowers and with dark or glaucous foliage and purple-leaved shrubs, or it can provide a base note in plantings with paler cool colors such as mauve, pink and blue, as well as contrasting soft yellow, cream or yellow-green. As it is a late flowerer, it can be used with early-leafing hostas, columbines, honesty and forget-me-nots. It looks outstanding growing through harmonizing plants such as moricandias or contrasting ones such as pale yellow wallflowers.

**Perfect partners:** *Aquilegia* 'Hensol Harebell', *Bergenia* 'Ballawley', *Dicentra* 'Bountiful', *Erysimum* 'Bowles Mauve', *Euphorbia amygdaloides* 'Purpurea', *Heuchera* 'Raspberry Regal', *Hosta* 'True Blue', *Milium effusum* 'Aureum', *Moricandia moricandioides*, *Viola* 'Martin'

**H: 20 in.** (50 cm)  **S: 6 in.** (15 cm)  ❀ **Late spring**
◊  ▢-▨  ■  **Z4  pH5–7.5**

## *Tulipa clusiana*

LADY TULIP

Relatively early to appear, lady tulip's flowers have white petals with a deep purple-black blotch at the base and the outer three petals stained crimson. It is useful for rock gardens, for the front of a border – where it can be grown through a mat of shorter plants – and for more intimate plantings. It mixes well with silver or purple foliage including heucheras, smaller winter violas, bergenias, corydalis, smaller daphnes and other bulbs such as muscari, rhizomatous anemones, later-flowering snowdrops, spring-flowering cyclamens and pink or white erythroniums. Useful variants include var. *chrysantha* ♀, with mainly yellow petals, good for blending with flowers in hot colors and with bronze or yellow-green foliage; 'Tubergen's Gem' is a selection of var. *chrysantha*. In *T.c.* 'Cynthia' ♀ the flowers are creamy yellow, flushed red on the outer petals and with a green edge.

**Perfect partners:** *Acaena microphylla* 'Kupferteppich', *Anaphalis triplinervis* 'Sommerschnee', *Anthemis punctata* subsp. *cupaniana*, *Chionodoxa* 'Pink Giant', *Convolvulus cneorum*, *Daphne cneorum* 'Eximia', *Heuchera* 'Quilter's Joy', *Lavandula* × *chaytoriae* 'Sawyers', *Stachys byzantina* 'Big Ears'

**H: 10 in. (25 cm)  S: 4 in. (10 cm)**
❁ **Early to mid-spring**
▢ ◊ ▢-◼ ◼  Z5  pH5.5–7.5

**Left:** The vibrant *Tulipa clusiana* var. *chrysantha* combines with bugle (*Ajuga reptans* 'Atropurpurea'), Siberian wallflowers (*Erysimum* × *marshallii*) and magenta aubrietas.

**Below:** More gently colored *Tulipa clusiana* in a semi-wild scheme mingles with bluebells (*Hyacinthoides non-scripta*) and anemones (*Anemone blanda* 'White Splendour').

Exuberantly splashed and streaked, carmine-red *Tulipa* 'Cordell Hull' makes a dramatic display above a carpet of pale blue wood forget-me-nots (*Myosotis sylvatica*).

## *Tulipa* 'Cordell Hull'

A Single Late Group tulip of Cottage Group origin, 'Cordell Hull' is rich carmine-red, splashed and blotched with white. It is close enough to primary red to favor schemes with both hot or cool colors, while its two-tone effect, although slightly obscuring the elegant shape of the blooms, adds sparkle to the overall impression. It combines well with red or purple foliage, and contrasts effectively with yellow-green foliage and flowers, including euphorbias. As with most members of the Single Late Group, it is relatively tall, and its height makes it suitable for growing through plants such as wallflowers, and partnering taller shrubs like deciduous azaleas, dark-leaved berberis, exochordas, kolkwitzias, camellias and smaller magnolias.

**Perfect partners:** *Berberis thunbergii* 'Red Chief', *Camellia* × *williamsii* 'Mirage', *Dianthus barbatus* 'Sooty', *Erysimum* 'Sweet Sorbet', *Hebe* 'Mrs Winder', *Magnolia stellata* 'Waterlily', *Penstemon digitalis* 'Husker Red'

**H: 22 in. (55 cm)  S: 6 in. (15 cm)** ❁ **Late spring**
◼▢ ◊ ▢-◼ ◼  Z4  pH5–7.5

## *Tulipa* 'Fantasy' ♛

All Parrot Group tulips, of which 'Fantasy' is one, have very ruffled and fringed petals that are often broader than those of the cultivars from which they have sported. 'Fantasy', a relatively late-blooming member of the group, has flowers in deep rose, paler toward the edges and on the outside, with a satin sheen and some green cresting near the tips of the petals. It is close enough to primary red to be combined with cool colors and purple foliage, silver or glaucous leaves, and white flowers, or with warm tints such as peach, coral and bronze; contrasts with yellow-green foliage or flowers are also excellent. It can be grown through spring bedding plants such as moricandias, and also combines effectively with dark-leaved heucheras and berberis.

**Perfect partners:** *Astrantia major* 'Sunningdale Variegated', *Cerinthe major* 'Purpurascens', *Cryptotaenia japonica* f. *atropurpurea*, *Prunus* × *cistena*, *Weigela* 'Victoria'

**H: 22 in. (55 cm) S: 6 in. (15 cm)** ❀ **Late spring** 
▬▬▭▬ ◊ ▭-▮ ▮ **Z4 pH5–7.5**

Here *Tulipa* 'Fantasy' is grown as bedding through *Anthemis punctata* subsp. *cupaniana*, a combination that could equally be used on a smaller scale in a border.

## *Tulipa* 'Elegant Lady'

This Lily-flowered Group tulip bears creamy yellow blooms that fade a little as they age, with streaks and flecks of deep magenta-pink. Its predominately yellow coloring suits contrasts with blue flowers and harmonies with white, rich golden yellow or warm tints such as peach and apricot, and with yellow-green foliage or flowers. It is tall enough to be grown through wallflowers and similar plants, and to be combined with flowering shrubs such as brooms, deciduous azaleas, mahonias, ceanothus and kerrias. Other good partners are later-flowering narcissi, fritillaries (including crown imperials) and hyacinths.

*Tulipa* 'Elegant Lady' contrasts gently with wood forget-me-nots (*Myosotis sylvatica*), the blue flowers of *Centaurea montana* and variegated honesty (*Lunaria annua* 'Alba Variegata') in a permanently planted border.

**Perfect partners:** *Berberis thunbergii* Bonanza Gold, *Heuchera* 'Purple Petticoats', *Coronilla valentina* subsp. *glauca* 'Citrina', *Corydalis lutea*, *Cytisus* × *praecox* 'Warminster', *Erysimum* 'Bredon', *Euphorbia characias* Silver Swan, *Kerria japonica* 'Picta', *Lathyrus aureus*

**H: 24 in. (60 cm) S: 6 in. (15 cm)** ❀ **Late spring** 
▬▭▬▬ ◊ ▭-▮ ▮ **Z4 pH5–7.5**

A

## *Tulipa* 'Golden Oxford'

This is a fragrant tulip of the Darwinhybrid Group, and is golden yellow with a narrow red edge to the petals. Although comparable in many respects to 'Jewel of Spring' (opposite page), it is slightly shorter, with deeper yellow flowers that have a less distinct edge to the petals. It combines well with hot colors and with bronze, red or yellow-green foliage, and contrasts effectively with white or blue flowers. Good companions include forget-me-nots, wallflowers, brunneras, later-flowering cream or white narcissi, hyacinths, bronze-leaved heucheras and yellow- or cream-variegated shrubs such as elaeagnus or holly cultivars. Like most Darwinhybrid Group tulips, it is relatively vigorous, and well suited to being planted permanently.

*Tulipa* 'Golden Oxford', planted permanently in a border and contrasted with blue *Brunnera macrophylla*, only just overtops the white Triandrus Group *Narcissus* 'Thalia' at the start of its flowering, although it will grow another 4 in. (10 cm) taller before its petals are shed.

**Perfect partners:** *Brunnera macrophylla*, *Ceanothus* Zanzibar, *Elaeagnus* × *ebbingei* 'Limelight', *Erysimum cheiri* 'Cloth of Gold', *Euonymus fortunei* 'Emerald 'n' Gold', *Euphorbia griffithii* 'Fireglow', *Heuchera villosa* 'Palace Purple', *Ilex aquifolium* 'Golden Milkboy', *Thuja occidentalis* 'Rheingold'

**H: 22 in.** (55 cm) **S: 6 in.** (15 cm)
❀ **Mid- to late spring**
　　　　　　　　◊-◊◊　▢-▥　▮ Z4 pH4.5–7.5

## *Tulipa* 'Greuze'

The blooms of this Single Late Group tulip are a rich deep magenta-purple. It can be used in combinations with cool colors – either rich and sumptuous, like crimson, strong blue, or purple and purple foliage, or delicate, paler tints such as mauve, pink and pale blue. It also contrasts effectively with soft yellow, yellow-green foliage and flowers, and (for those who dare) orange flowers. It is useful for growing through shorter plants such as hyacinths and forget-me-nots, and it also goes well with dark-leaved heucheras, dicentras, columbines, euphorbias and bergenias, and with shrubs such as deciduous azaleas, brooms and early yellow roses.

**Perfect partners:** *Aquilegia vulgaris* var. *stellata* 'Royal Purple', *Bellis perennis* 'Tasso Strawberries and Cream', *Cytisus* 'Hollandia', *Dicentra* 'Bountiful', *Erysimum* 'Sweet Sorbet', *Heuchera* 'Magic Wand', *Iris pallida* 'Variegata', *Rosa* 'Frühlingsgold', *Rubus microphyllus* 'Variegatus'

**H: 22 in.** (55 cm) **S: 6 in.** (15 cm) ❀ **Late spring**
　　　　　◊　▢-▥　▮ Z4 pH5–7.5

Although the camera sees them differently, to the naked eye *Tulipa* 'Greuze' and the wallflower *Erysimum cheiri* 'Purple Queen' are closely matched in color.

B

A

## *Tulipa* 'Jewel of Spring' ♈

This Darwinhybrid Group tulip is very similar in appearance to 'Golden Oxford' (opposite page), although its flowers are a slightly paler yellow, with the petals edged in a stronger red. Its paler coloring is still strong enough to contrast with blue flowers and to combine with hot or rich colors, while the extra touch of red around the petal margins provides a link with orange or red flowers, warm colors such as peach and apricot, and red-flushed foliage. It associates well with medium-sized shrubs such as elaeagnus and holly, while its typical Darwinhybrid Group tolerance of a little shade allows permanent planting under deciduous trees or in a semi-shaded border.

In this permanent planting of *Tulipa* 'Jewel of Spring', the yellow petals and their narrow red edging harmonize with the red-flushed, yellow-green young foliage of *Spiraea japonica* 'Goldflame'.

**Perfect partners:** *Carex comans* (bronze), *Euphorbia dulcis* 'Chameleon', *Lychnis × arkwrightii* 'Vesuvius', *Meconopsis cambrica* 'Muriel Brown', *Narcissus* 'Cheerfulness', *Nonea lutea*, *Paeonia lactiflora* 'Crimson Glory', *Symphytum* 'Goldsmith'

**H: 24 in.** (60 cm) **S: 6 in.** (15 cm)
**Mid- to late spring**
**Z4 pH4.5–7.5**

## *Tulipa linifolia* Batalinii Group ♈

Tulips of the Batalinii Group are rather variable, with pronounced blue-gray foliage and dainty flowers ranging from pale or bright yellow, flushed with bronze, through apricot to vermilion – colors that are particularly suited to combinations with other warm hues and bronze foliage, or to contrasts with blue. They are very easy to grow in rock or gravel gardens, and near the front of a border, where they can be planted through low carpeting plants such as acaenas or bugles. They succeed in small-scale schemes alongside the tiniest shrubs, including small glaucous-leaved hebes, and combine well with spring bulbs such as erythroniums, muscari, smaller narcissi, white snake's head fritillaries, ipheions and rhizomatous anemones. Useful selections include 'Apricot Jewel' (apricot with an orange flush) and 'Bright Gem' ♈ (sulphur-yellow with an orange flush).

**Perfect partners:** *Acaena microphylla* 'Pewter Carpet', *Chamaecyparis thyoides* 'Ericoides', *Festuca glauca* 'Elijah Blue', *Hebe pimeleoides* 'Quicksilver', *Ipheion uniflorum* 'Wisley Blue', *Pittosporum tenuifolium* 'Tom Thumb', *Salix* 'Boydii', *Saxifraga exarata* subsp. *moschata* 'Cloth of Gold', *Thymus × citriodorus* 'Silver Queen', *Uncinia egmontiana*, *Veronica peduncularis* 'Georgia Blue'

**H: 6 in.** (15 cm) **S: 4 in.** (10 cm)
**Early to mid-spring**
**Z5 pH4.5–7.5**

B

Apricot *Tulipa linifolia* Batalinii Group mingle with blue *Muscari armeniacum*, *Anemone apennina* and white snake's head fritillary (*Fritillaria meleagris* var. *unicolor* subvar. *alba*).

In this combination *Tulipa* 'Mariette' is planted through a carpet of alpine forget-me-nots (*Myosotis alpestris*) around the apothecary's rose (*Rosa gallica* var. *officinalis*). Harder pruning of the rose would allow the display to continue uninterrupted through the area it occupies.

## *Tulipa* 'Mariette'

This Lily-flowered Group cultivar has rich rose-pink flowers with a white base, and markedly reflexed petals. It is a little deeper in color than 'China Pink' (see p.393), and an inch or two taller, but is otherwise so similar in appearance that the two tulips can be combined to provide subtle variations in color and height, and also a slightly extended flowering season, because 'Mariette' flowers a few days later. Its deeper coloring is useful in more luxuriant, darker-hued schemes with, for instance, purple foliage. It mixes well with bergenias, heucheras and forget-me-nots, violas, primroses and polyanthus, and with other bulbs such as hyacinths and white narcissi. Exochordas, daphnes and smaller magnolias are suitable shrubby partners.

**Perfect partners:** *Cordyline australis* 'Purple Tower', *Magnolia* × *loebneri* 'Leonard Messel', *Tulipa* 'Marjolein' p.398 **B**, *Viola* (Sorbet Series) 'Yesterday, Today and Tomorrow'

H: 22 in. (55 cm) S: 6 in. (15 cm) ❀ Late spring
◊ ▢-◼ ◼ Z4 pH5–7.5

*Tulipa* 'Mariette' and its sport *T.* 'Marjolein' clash gently above a carpet of alpine forget-me-nots (*Myosotis alpestris*), while matching perfectly in form and habit.

## *Tulipa* 'Marjolein' ♛

A sport of 'Mariette' (left), this Lily-flowered Group cultivar has flame-colored flowers with a soft yellow base, but is otherwise identical. Its warm color goes well not only with scarlet or strong orange but also with soft or burnt orange, peach and apricot, as well as clashing agreeably with pink tulips such as 'Mariette' itself.

**Perfect partners:** *Chaenomeles* × *superba* 'Knap Hill Scarlet', *Erysimum* × *marshallii*, *Euphorbia characias*, *Filipendula ulmaria* 'Aurea', *Phormium* 'Bronze Baby'

H: 22 in. (55 cm) S: 6 in. (15 cm) ❀ Late spring
◼▢▢ ◊ ▢-◼ ◼ Z4 pH5–7.5

## *Tulipa* 'Negrita'

This is a sumptuous Triumph Group tulip, with rich royal purple flowers veined with darker purple. Although its coloring is best appreciated at close range, it is superlative for combinations with cool colors and contrasts with orange or yellow-green. It is invaluable for providing a base note in plantings of brighter flowers in, for example, magenta or carmine. Eye-catching designs can be made with lightly purple-flushed foliage, with mauve flowers and with euphorbias.

Sumptuous purple *Tulipa* 'Negrita' is bedded here through a gently contrasting orange wallflower (*Erysimum cheiri*) in a rich blend that shows up best at close range.

**Perfect partners:** *Ruta graveolens*, *Salvia officinalis* 'Tricolor', *Silene dioica* 'Graham's Delight'

H: 18 in. (45 cm) S: 6 in. (15 cm)
❀ Mid- to late spring
◼▢▢ ◊ ▢-◼ ◼ Z4 pH5–7.5

## *Tulipa* 'Orange Favourite'

The complex and very fragrant vermilion flowers of this Parrot Group tulip are shaded with coral and lighter orange, and have yellow at the base and flecks of green at the tips. The cut edges to the petals and subtle shadings within each bloom are especially pleasing when viewed at close range. Like many Parrot Group and double tulips, the extra weight of the flower may cause it to flop; in a container the stems tend to sprawl over the edge and arch back in an elegant curve. It suits hot-colored schemes and contrasts with glaucous foliage, yellow-green leaves or flowers, blue flowers, white rock cress and vinous purple wallflowers. A relatively late tulip, it goes well with brunneras, deciduous azaleas, shorter ceanothus, omphalodes and bronze- or purple-leaved shrubs such as berberis.

**Perfect partners:** *Anthriscus sylvestris* 'Ravenswing', *Berberis thunbergii* 'Golden Ring', *Euphorbia amygdaloides* 'Purpurea', *Omphalodes cappadocica*, *Rhododendron* 'Glowing Embers', *Rubus cockburnianus* 'Goldenvale', *Salvia officinalis* 'Icterina', *Thalictrum flavum* 'Illuminator'

**H: 20 in. (50 cm)  S: 6 in. (15 cm)** ✿ **Late spring**
◊ ▢-▨ ■ **Z4  pH5–7.5**

*Tulipa* 'Orange Favourite' and deep black-purple *T*. 'Queen of Night' are here closely planted and thoroughly mixed together at the front of a bed. This rich and exuberant combination depends on the identical flowering season of the two cultivars for its extraordinary effect.

## *Tulipa* 'Orange Wonder'

Although similar in coloring to 'Orange Favourite' (see p.399), this is a Triumph Group tulip, so it has a more regular and classically shaped flower, and a tendency to be more upright, which makes it more suitable for formal schemes and for bedding through a ground of lower plants. It produces attractive vermilion blooms, shaded with bronze and a paler orange toward the edge of the petals. It harmonizes with bronze foliage and hot colors, and contrasts particularly effectively with yellow-green foliage and flowers. White rock cress and purple wallflowers make exciting companions, as do purple-foliaged plants.

**Perfect partners:** *Chaenomeles speciosa* 'Geisha Girl', *Foeniculum vulgare* 'Purpureum', *Salvia officinalis* 'Icterina', *Trollius* × *cultorum* 'Orange Princess'

**H: 18 in.** (45 cm) **S: 6 in.** (15 cm)
✿ Mid- to late spring
◑ ◊ ◻-◼ ◼ Z4 pH5–7.5

A

In this informal planting, which is furnished in front by variegated stinking gladwyn (*Iris foetidissima* 'Variegata'), the vibrant blooms of *Tulipa* 'Orange Wonder' are effectively contrasted against a background of yellow-green perfoliate alexanders (*Smyrnium perfoliatum*).

## *Tulipa* 'Prinses Irene' ♆

This relatively short Triumph Group tulip has soft orange blooms, flamed with reddish purple and green down the center of the petals. Such a comparataively subdued color combination is good with soft colors such as peach, apricot and coral, or with bronze, glaucous or purple foliage, and contrasts well with blue flowers and yellow-green foliage or flowers. Its own foliage is attractively glaucous and contrasts pleasingly with its flowers. It is most appealing with geums, heucheras, wallflowers, forget-me-nots and euphorbias, and makes a good plant for containers.

**Perfect partners:** *Euphorbia cyparissias*, *Geranium* 'Ann Folkard', *Geum* 'Georgenburg', *Hebe ochracea*, *Lonicera nitida* 'Baggesen's Gold', *Myosotis alpestris* 'Royal Blue'

**H: 14 in.** (35 cm) **S: 6 in.** (15 cm)
✿ Mid- to late spring
◑ ◊ ◻-◼ ◼ Z4 pH5–7.5

The curiously striped, soft orange tones of *Tulipa* 'Prinses Irene' combine perfectly with *Geum* 'Beech House Apricot' in a scheme in which rich bronze foliage and/or yellow-green, blood-red or cream flowers could be added.

B

## *Tulipa* 'Palestrina'

A tulip belonging to the Triumph Group, 'Palestrina' has large, rich deep salmon flowers flushed with green on the outside. It goes well with warm colors, white flowers and bronze, red and silver foliage plants, and makes fine contrasts with yellow-green foliage and flowers. It blooms relatively late, and so is good with euphorbias, heucheras, geums and strong green foliage such as that of parsley.

**Perfect partners:** *Anaphalis triplinervis*, *Astelia chathamica*, *Choisya ternata* Sundance,

The warm salmon blooms of *Tulipa* 'Palestrina' glow against the silver foliage of lamb's ears (*Stachys byzantina*) and *Artemisia ludoviciana*, with a sprinkling of blue wood forget-me-nots (*Myosotis sylvatica*).

*Coronilla valentina* subsp. *glauca*, *Erysimum cheiri* 'Cloth of Gold', *Geum* 'Fire Opal', *Leymus arenarius*, *Lotus hirsutus*, *Lunaria annua* var. *albiflora* 'Alba Variegata', *Physocarpus opulifolius* 'Diabolo', *Ruta graveolens*, *Yucca filamentosa*

**H: 16 in.** (40 cm) **S: 6 in.** (15 cm) ✿ **Late spring**
◑ ◊ ◻-◼ ◼ Z4 pH5–7.5

C

The pale flowers of a ground of chamois-pink wallflower (*Erysimum cheiri* 'Eastern Queen') help to show up the rich, dark blooms of *Tulipa* 'Queen of Night'. The wallflower looks identical to one often sold (incorrectly) as *Erysimum* 'Ellen Willmott'.

When *Tulipa* 'Red Shine' is in full bloom, the ornamental onion *Allium hollandicum* 'Purple Sensation' passes it on its way upward as its own rich amethyst blooms begin to open. Both are vigorous and persistent enough to be used as permanent planting among herbaceous perennials that can hide their dying leaves.

## *Tulipa* 'Red Shine' ♛

The exceptionally long-lasting flowers of this Lily-flowered Group tulip are a deep primary red, with petals that are blunter than in most others of the group and only slightly reflexed at the tip. The blooms open slowly over weeks from their initial cup shape to form a star. 'Red Shine' works well with hot and cool colors, and makes an effective contrast with yellow-green foliage and flowers. It is goes excellently with purple foliage such as that of heucheras, purple sage and purple smoke bush, and also with honesty, columbines and bulbs such as crown imperials.

**Perfect partners:** *Cotinus coggygria* 'Royal Purple', *Euphorbia characias* subsp. *wulfenii*, *Fritillaria imperialis* 'Aurora', *Geum coccineum*, *Miscanthus sinensis* 'Zebrinus', *Salvia officinalis* 'Purpurascens'

H: 24 in. (60 cm)   S: 6 in. (15 cm)   ✽ Late spring
◊   ▢-▣   ▇ Z4 pH5–7.5

## *Tulipa* 'Queen of Night'

This magnificent Single Late Group tulip is even darker than 'Negrita' (see p.398), with black-purple flowers, shaded rich plum-purple. Although suitable for the same kinds of combinations – with cool colors and softly purple-flushed foliage, for example – the deep coloring makes it even less visible from a distance, and it needs to be planted where it can be seen clearly, perhaps against orange or yellow-green. Taller and later than 'Negrita', it is especially useful with another, brighter tulip, and possibly one of contrasting shape. It is outstanding planted through moricandias or similar shorter plants, and goes well with columbines, bergenias, dicentras, honesty and the earliest cranesbills.

**Perfect partners:** *Berberis thunbergii* 'Atropurpurea Nana' p.80 **B**, *Cynara cardunculus*, *Erysimum* 'Butterscotch', *Euphorbia polychroma* 'Major', *Heuchera* 'Plum Pudding' p.289 **A**, *Tulipa* 'Orange Favourite' p.399 **A** ❑ p.393 **A**

H: 24 in. (60 cm)   S: 6 in. (15 cm)   ✽ Late spring
◊   ▢-▣   ▇ Z4 pH5–7.5

## *Tulipa* 'Spring Green' ♛

This is a Viridiflora Group tulip of medium height. The typical green stripe down the center of the petals shades through yellowish cream to white toward the edges and tips; each petal is slightly twisted and reflexed, with a pointed tip, rather like a Lily-flowered tulip. This subtle color scheme goes well with white, yellow, yellow-green or green flowers, and yellow-green foliage. 'Spring Green' can be naturalized in wilder areas, where it complements flowers of contrasting floral form, such as early-flowering umbellifers. It works with blue flowers – forget-me-nots and omphalodes – and early white-flowered shrubs. Other good partners include hostas and early yellow roses.

**Perfect partners:** *Brunnera macrophylla* 'Dawson's White', *Exochorda serratifolia* 'Snow White', *Hosta* 'Fire and Ice', *Paeonia mlokosewitschii*, *Pulmonaria* 'White Wings', *Spiraea thunbergii* 'Mount Fuji', *Viburnum carlesii*

H: 20 in. (50 cm)   S: 6 in. (15 cm)   ✽ Late spring
◊   ▢-▣   ▇ Z4 pH5–7.5

This is a subtle combination consisting of *Tulipa* 'Spring Green', its blooms shaded from green through yellow-green and cream to white, and yellow-green *Euphorbia polychroma*.

A

## *Tulipa* 'Sweet Harmony' ♛

This Single Late Group tulip, with its lemon-yellow blooms grading softly to ivory-white at the petal edges, goes well with warm colors such as apricot, and with yellow-green flowers or foliage. It is an outstanding partner for white flowers, especially late narcissi, umbellifers, white honesty and white forget-me-nots, and it is also good associated with early-leafing, glaucous or yellow-green hostas and yellow-green euphorbias. Other suitable companions include brooms, genistas, kerrias and deep gold or ivory wallflowers.

**Perfect partners:** *Aquilegia vulgaris* var. *stellata* 'Greenapples', *Cytisus* × *kewensis*, *Euonymus fortunei* 'Silver Queen', *Genista lydia*, *Griselinia littoralis* 'Dixon's Cream', *Milium effusum* 'Aureum', *Ranunculus bulbosus* 'F.M. Burton', *Sambucus nigra* 'Madonna', *Sisyrinchium striatum* 'Aunt May', *Smyrnium perfoliatum*

**H: 22 in.** (55 cm)  **S: 6 in.** (15 cm)  ✿ **Late spring**
◊ ▢-▣ ■ **Z4  pH5–7.5**

Opposite: *Tulipa* 'Sweet Harmony' and the similarly colored *T.* 'Maja' of the Fringed Group are here planted through the emerging yellowish green fronds of the ostrich-plume fern (*Matteuccia struthiopteris*) beside a pond. Although the relatively damp, semi-shaded conditions are not ideal for tulips, which generally prefer a reasonably dry and sunny site, it is a stunningly successful combination, and helps to light up an otherwise fairly dark corner. Sadly, the tulips may be short-lived in such conditions.

## *Tulipa* 'West Point' ♛

As the sweetly scented flowers of this Lily-flowered Group tulip age, they open from a slender, narrowly tapered and reflexed form into a less elegant star shape. The bright yellow coloring works well with other hot colors, such as orange and red, with bronze or purple foliage, with yellow-green foliage and flowers or with white flowers. 'West Point' can be combined with other tulips flowering at the same time, preferably with a different floral form, but also looks good on its own in large containers. White honesty, early-flowering shrubs such as brooms and dark-leaved shrubs are suitable companions,

A classic combination is yellow tulips (here *T.* 'West Point') with rich blue alpine forget-me-nots (*Myosotis alpestris*).

as are hot-colored wallflowers, white or cream late-flowering narcissi, euphorbias, dark-leaved heucheras and geums.

**Perfect partners:** *Berberis thunbergii* 'Red Chief', *Fritillaria imperialis*, *Lysimachia ciliata* 'Firecracker' p.310 **B**, *Narcissus* 'Thalia', *Pentaglottis sempervirens*, *Tulipa* 'White Triumphator' p.403 **B**, *Viburnum sargentii* 'Onondaga'

**H: 20 in.** (50 cm)  **S: 6 in.** (15 cm)  ✿ **Late spring**
◊ ▢-▣ ■ **Z4  pH5–7.5**

## *Tulipa* 'White Triumphator' ♛

The greenish ivory buds of this Lily-flowered Group tulip mature to pure white blooms. The petals are less tapered and reflexed than those of 'West Point' (above right), giving a flower form that is less extreme but equally graceful. Its color looks outstanding in white flower schemes, with silver foliage or with yellow-green, yellow or blue flowers and glaucous or yellow-green foliage. It combines well with flowers of contrasting floral form (umbellifers, for example), smaller late-flowering narcissi and shrubs such as spiraeas, brooms, genistas and exochordas. Striking contrasts can be made by planting it through a carpet of purple-leaved plants such as heucheras, for example, or against dark evergreens such as yew, or intermingled with a dark-leaved cow parsley. It is suitable for naturalizing and for growing in large pots.

**Perfect partners:** *Anthriscus sylvestris* 'Ravenswing', *Atriplex halimus*, *Brunnera macrophylla* 'Betty Bowring', *Crambe maritima*, *Eupatorium rugosum* 'Chocolate', *Euphorbia characias* 'Portuguese Velvet', *Farfugium japonicum* 'Argenteum', *Foeniculum vulgare* 'Purpureum', *Geranium pratense* Midnight Reiter strain, *Melianthus major*, *Ornithogalum nutans*, *Potentilla fruticosa* 'Abbotswood', *Rosa glauca*, *Sambucus nigra* 'Gerda'

**H: 24 in.** (60 cm)  **S: 6 in.** (15 cm)  ✿ **Late spring**
◊ ▢-▣ ■ **Z4  pH5–7.5**

A sunny mix of three bulbs in graduated heights, white *Narcissus* 'Thalia', 14 in. (35 cm), yellow *Tulipa* 'West Point', 20 in. (50 cm), and the slightly taller *T.* 'White Triumphator', is here planted around the stinking hellebore (*Helleborus foetidus*). Through replanting, the flowering of the narcissus has been slightly delayed to coincide with the tulips.

**Above:** The rich coral-red flowers and swordlike foliage of *Watsonia* 'Stanford Scarlet' and spiky *Cordyline australis* 'Torbay Dazzler' create a bold, almost tropical effect.

**Below:** A clump of coral-red *Watsonia fourcadei* is here given ample room to display its imposing habit to the fullest. Its blooms contrast with large *Agapanthus praecox* subsp. *orientalis* and a smaller agapanthus. White Japanese anemones (*Anemone* × *hybrida*) leaven the rich colors.

## *Watsonia* species and cultivars

Watsonias are rather tender South African relatives of the gladiolus, growing from corms and requiring good drainage, but with ample moisture when in full growth. They are therefore good plants for stream banks, combined with other waterside plants like zantedeschias and tender perennials such as cannas. The flowers of *W. fourcadei* are pink, red, vermilion or, more rarely, purple, borne above the foliage in two-ranked spikes of long-tubed florets. Its colors associate well with warm and hot tints, and with bronze or red-flushed foliage. In frost-prone areas, spring-flowering watsonias can be lifted in autumn and stored as dried corms for planting as tender perennials, but summer-flowering species such as *W. fourcadei* are best not disturbed, although transplanting immediately after flowering is feasible.

**Perfect partners:** *Agapanthus* 'Loch Hope', *Agastache* 'Firebird', *Beschornia yuccoides*, *Canna* 'Cleopatra', *Dahlia* 'Bednall Beauty', *Hedychium gardnerianum*, *Hemerocallis* 'Frans Hals', *Kniphofia* 'Timothy', *Leonotis leonurus*, *Lobelia tupa*, *Nandina domestica*, *Phormium* 'Yellow Wave', *Phygelius* × *rectus* 'Sunshine', *Yucca gloriosa*

**H: 18–60 in.** (45–150 cm)  **S: 16 in.** (40 cm)
✿ **Early spring to early autumn**
◊◊ ▢ **Z9 pH5–7**

In hot climates, the arum lily (*Zantedeschia aethiopica*) will flower happily in partial shade, where it can be combined with other shade-loving plants such as the dainty *Begonia* 'Ricinifolia', with its elegant sprays of pink flowers.

## *Zantedeschia aethiopica* ♛
ARUM LILY

This rhizomatous perennial is happiest in moist soils and pond margins, where reflections can double its impact, but it does tolerate ordinary border soils if not too dry. The arrow-shaped, glossy deep green leaves are overtopped by the flowers, which consist of a white spathe surrounding a yellow spadix. Arum lilies provide a bold, tropical effect that combines well with Siberian irises, moisture-loving euphorbias, veratrums and larger ferns. Even after flowering, its foliage is a handsome companion for water cannas, hedychiums and hostas. It is slightly tender and in cold climates benefits from a thick mulch for protection. Useful cultivars include the relatively hardy 'Crowborough' ♛, 'Green Goddess' ♛ (green spathes), and 'Little Gem' and 'Childsiana'.

**Perfect partners:** *Astilbe* 'Deutschland', *Canna* 'Erebus', *Dryopteris filix-mas*, *Filipendula rubra* 'Venusta', *Iris* 'Butter and Sugar', *Rodgersia aesculifolia*

**H: 36 in.** (90 cm)  **S: 24 in.** (60 cm)
✿ **Late spring to midsummer**
◊◊-◊◊◊ ▢-▪ **Z8 pH5–7.5**

The atamasco lily (*Zephyranthes atamasca*) does not need full sun to flower in hot climates but benefits from a sunny position in colder climates. Here, it fills a border by a path beneath evergreen oaks (*Quercus ilex*).

## *Zephyranthes* species

ZEPHYR LILY

The zephyr lilies are rather tender bulbs, relatives of narcissi, with showy flowers in white, pink or yellow. The most widely grown species is *Z. candida*, 4–8 in. (10–20 cm) high and flowering in early to mid-autumn. It is useful for the front of a border, perhaps with Charm chrysanthemums, colchicums and autumn crocuses. Atamasco lily (*Z. atamasca*) is 8–12 in. (20–30 cm) high and has very large flowers, usually white but occasionally pale pink. It combines well with other spring bulbs, grown through compact ivy, bugles or arisaemas. Autumn-flowering *Z. rosea*, 6–8 in. (15–20 cm), bears rose-pink flowers with a greenish base, while *Z. grandiflora*, 4–8 in. (10–20 cm) has rose-pink flowers from midsummer to early autumn – both may be used in similar ways to *Z. candida*.

**Perfect partners:** *Aster thomsonii* 'Nanus', *Colchicum speciosum*, *Crocus speciosus*, *Cyclamen hederifolium*, *Hedera helix* 'Kolibri', *Nerine undulata*, *Sternbergia lutea*

H: 4–12 in. (10–30 cm)   S: 2–4 in. (5–10 cm)
❈ Late spring to mid-autumn
◊◊   Z8–10   pH5.5–7.5

## *Zigadenus elegans*

This very hardy bulb, with airy spikes of creamy green flowers, is a sun-lover for the front of a warm border, although it will tolerate some shade in areas with hotter summers. It needs very good drainage, so is good in a gravel garden. It looks attractive growing through low ground-cover plants, particularly against a background of dark foliage. The quiet color of its flowers combines well with glaucous foliage, and with other flowers in white, soft yellow, pure blue, very deep blue or purple and yellow-green such as summer-flowering euphorbias.

**Perfect partners:** *Agapanthus* 'Bressingham Blue', *Agastache rugosa*, *Eryngium alpinum* 'Blue Star', *Phygelius aequalis* 'Yellow Trumpet', *Verbena rigida*, *Veronica spicata*

H: 27 in. (70 cm)   S: 3 in. (8 cm)
❈ Mid- to late summer
◊-◊◊   -   Z5   pH5.5–7.5

An airy veil of green and cream flowers of *Zigadenus elegans* is enlivened by the brilliant magenta, dark-veined blooms of the sprawling, long-flowering cranesbill *Geranium wallichianum* 'Syabru' in front of a carpet of *G. macrorrhizum*.

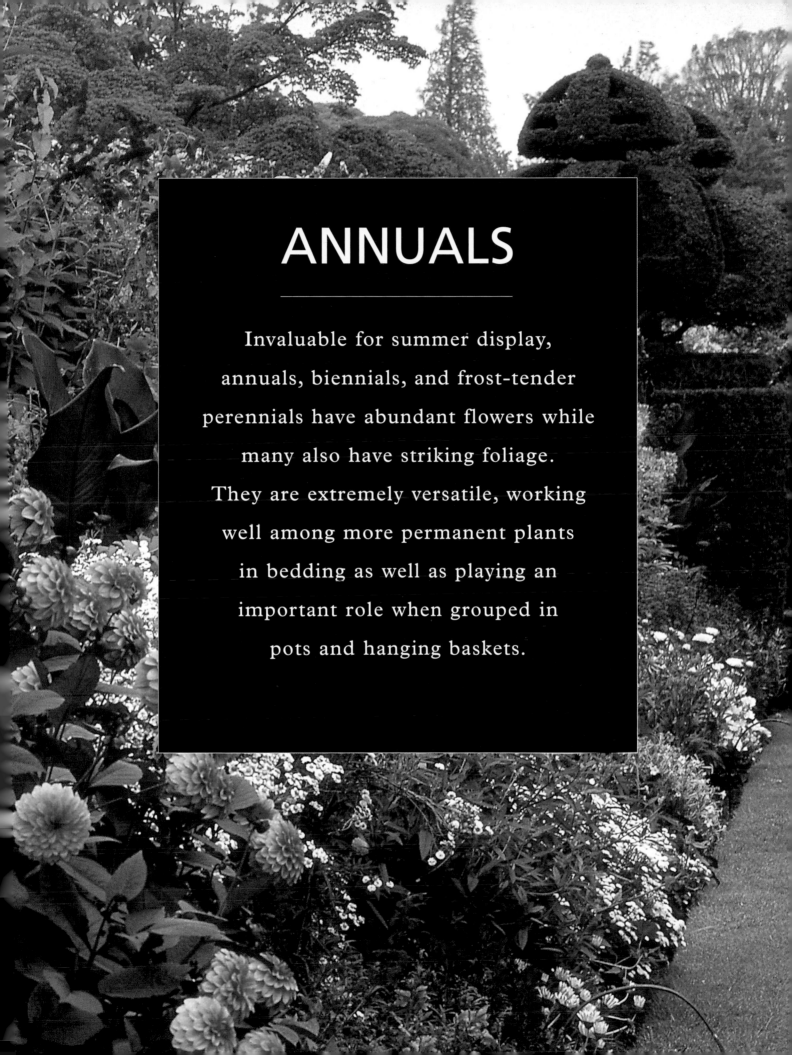

# ANNUALS

Invaluable for summer display,
annuals, biennials, and frost-tender
perennials have abundant flowers while
many also have striking foliage.
They are extremely versatile, working
well among more permanent plants
in bedding as well as playing an
important role when grouped in
pots and hanging baskets.

**Often the brightest flowers** and most spectacular foliage in gardens are provided by the shortest-lived plants – the annuals and biennials, and tender perennials that are used for summer display (those not reliably hardy in Zone 8 are included here). True annuals and biennials are plants that invest all their energy into one season of flower and seed production before dying. Tender perennials are from climates without cold winters; this means they evolved to flower freely over a very long period. The result in all cases is maximum flower power, a feature that plant breeders have often intensified by producing astonishing color ranges on compact and uniform plants.

The downside is that all such plants are temporary visitors, contributing nothing to the permanent structure of the garden. Most are costly in time and money to raise or buy, to plant and remove each year, and, in the case of tender perennials, perhaps to overwinter. However, most gardeners would consider the outlay well worth it as the impact of these plants begins instantly and increases rapidly as summer progresses. By selecting some of the taller-growing and larger annuals – cosmos, tithonias, cleomes, ricinus, Nicotiana sylvestris – an astonishing, albeit temporary, sense of maturity can be achieved in a new garden, especially if these are supplemented by climbing annuals such as sweet peas and morning glories on pillars, wigwams or trellises.

## Seed-raised plants

Hardy annuals are easy to sow where they are to flower, and thinned out to final spacings when they are established. One particularly delightful way of using them is in a mixture: many seed companies offer packets of mixed tall or short annuals, while more adventurous gardeners may like to concoct their own mixes for a particular range of colors or heights. The seeds can be sown sparsely in straight rows and thinned to small clumps of seedlings, 6–8 in. (15–20 cm ) apart.

Among the most popular and dependable of tender perennials, dahlias provide bold colors and strong shapes in borders from midsummer until the autumn frosts. Here, single-, double- and cactus-flowered cultivars in a range of sumptuous reds make a vibrant partnership, the effect enhanced by a background of deep purple foliage.

The fast-growing plants soon disguise the straight rows and go on to produce a colorful, ever-changing display as early flowerers are succeeded by progressively later ones.

Biennials need to be sown the year before they are required in flower and then put in their flowering positions in autumn or spring. Some hardy annuals can be treated in the same way. Being sown the previous late summer or autumn means they flower earlier on larger plants, thus widening the possible flowering combinations. Sweet peas are ideal for this treatment.

Half-hardy annuals and many tender perennials are also easy to raise from seed. In cold areas, this should be sown in pots or trays somewhere bright and warm, such as on a window sill or in a greenhouse, and the seedlings must not be planted in the garden until no further frosts are expected.

## Formal and informal bedding

Annuals and tender perennials are very popular for bedding. Plants used in spring displays are usually low-growing biennials, such as daisies and wallflowers, and bulbs are often included. The choice of plants for summer bedding is much wider and a huge range of effects can be achieved. Plants may be arranged in patterns or mixed loosely together to create a tapestry of mingled colors and varied forms. Careful selection of colors, forms and textures can produce gentle, romantic moods or bright, vibrant ones. For example, the vivid red salvia, once so popular for formal beds in public parks, is now available in a variety of softer colors which produce a much more delicate display. Where there is more space, taller-growing tender perennials with bold foliage can be used to produce exciting subtropical or junglelike areas in the garden: bananas, cannas, ricinus and eucalyptus are all excellent.

Although some gardeners devote entire beds to these comparatively short-lived displays, most prefer the informality that can be achieved with less concentrated planting – mixing groups of summer annuals among plants in a herbaceous or mixed border, for example. This can be done to fill gaps where permanent plants have not yet covered their allotted space, or planned as a regular part of the border's changing display. It is easy to find annuals in colors and forms that match the character of the border as a whole. Drifts of quiet color – pale antirrhinums, cosmos, lavateras and nigellas – will enrich a subtle bed, while cannas, dahlias, ricinus and many salvias, and will bring a border of hot-colored roses, kniphofias and purple-leaved shrubs to a fiery climax.

Imaginative compositions of annuals and tender perennials can supply an exciting patchwork of summer color. Here scarlet *Salvia coccinea* and pelargoniums are mized with clashing carmine impatiens and nicotiana. Some purple and bronze foliage, plenty of green, and some gentler pinks help mitigate the effect.

A well-branched plant of *Aeonium* 'Zwartkop' contrasts dramatically against the near-white stems of *Leucophyta brownii*. Both benefit from a sunny site with good drainage and relatively low nitrogen availability.

## *Aeonium* 'Zwartkop' ♈

Aeoniums are tender perennial succulents with rosettes of leaves that are fascinating for their geometrical perfection. The leaves of 'Zwartkop' age from bronze through deep chocolate to lustrous black. Single young rosettes are used in formal carpet bedding schemes, while more mature branching plants combine well in pots with a contrasting foliage plant – a glaucous-leaved lotus, for example. They are most effective with silver foliage but also excel in sumptuous dark schemes, such as red borders, or with hot colors and bronze foliage. In rich soil, use *A. arboreum* 'Atropurpureum' ♈, which is more erect and slightly lighter in color.

**Perfect partners:** *Cordyline australis* Purpurea Group, *Dahlia* 'Bishop of Llandaff', *Fuchsia* 'Thalia', *Lotus berthelotii*, *Plectranthus argentatus*, *Ricinus communis* 'Carmencita', *Senecio cineraria* 'Silver Dust'

H: **18 in.** (45 cm)  S: **14 in.** (35 cm)  ❀ **Late spring**
◊ ▢-▣ ▮ **Z10 pH5.5–7**

## *Ageratum houstonianum* **'Old Gray'**

'Old Gray' is one of the taller *A. houstonianum* cultivars, annuals that are distinguished by a loose growth habit that allows them to intermingle successfully with other annual and herbaceous plants toward the front of a border. The name is misleading because its flower color is soft lavender-blue; it mixes well with other lavender flowers and with blue, purple, mauve or white, as well as purple, glaucous or silver foliage. Its numerous tiny, fuzzy flowerheads provide an ideal foil for larger, bolder flowers such as marguerites, petunias, and osteospermums, while its slightly diffuse flowering habit combines well with heliotropes, an equally valuable foil for larger-flowered plants.

**Perfect partners:** *Argyranthemum gracile* 'Chelsea Girl', *Brachyscome iberidifolia* 'Summer Skies', *Helichrysum petiolare*, *Heliotropium arborescens* 'Princess Marina', *Osteospermum* 'White Pim', *Senecio cineraria* 'Cirrus'

H: **18 in.** (45 cm)  S: **12 in.** (30 cm)
❀ **Early summer to early autumn**
◊◊ ▢-▣ ▮ **Z10 pH5.5–7.5**

At the front of a border, the small flowerheads of *Ageratum houstonianum* 'Old Gray' and bicolored florets of *Nemesia* 'KLM' contrast in size with the larger, more solid flowers of *Petunia* (Pearl Series) 'Pearl Azure Blue' and *Salpiglossis* 'Kew Blue', all of them in harmonious shades.

A veil of shining scarlet florets of *Alonsoa warscewiczii* shows up brightly against the dusky, reddish purple foliage of a smoke bush (*Cotinus coggygria*) cultivar in a steeply banked detail at the front of a border.

## *Alonsoa warscewiczii*

This is a sub-shrubby perennial with broadly oval, serrated leaves that are evergreen where it survives the winter. Elsewhere, it is usually raised from seed as an annual, bearing clouds of tiny scarlet flowers on red stems. It is most useful for providing a contrast with larger, bolder blooms. It goes well with hot colors, peach and apricot shades, and bronze foliage, and looks effective with yellow-green foliage and flowers. The tiny, evenly spaced blooms create a shimmering effect if mixed with flowers of similar size in a clashing color, such as magenta or rich carmine-pink. 'Peachy-keen' has salmon-pink flowers.

**Perfect partners:** *Calceolaria* 'Camden Hero', *Canna indica* 'Purpurea', *Cordyline australis* Purpurea Group, *Dahlia* 'Bednall Beauty', *D.* 'Yelno Harmony', *Fuchsia* 'Thalia', *Lobelia* × *speciosa* 'Fan Orchidrosa', *Lysimachia nummularia* 'Aurea', *Nicotiana* 'Domino Red', *N.* 'Lime Green', *Pelargonium* 'Paul Crampel', *Salvia splendens* p.448 **C**

H: **18 in.** (45 cm)  S: **12 in.** (30 cm)
❀ **Early summer to mid-autumn**
◊◊ ▢-▣ ▮ **Z10 pH5–7.5**

The flattish, lacy heads of *Ammi majus* contrast in form and color with the blue columns of the larkspur *Consolida ajacis* 'Blue Spire', both of exactly the same height.

## Ammi majus

The white flowerheads of this hardy annual umbellifer have a distinctly lacy, ethereal beauty that create an excellent foil for flowers of bolder floral form and color. Other annuals, such as larkspurs, biennials, herbaceous perennials or shrubs (including Shrub roses) make good partners. It may be used to contrast with strong colors or to form gentle harmonies with pastel shades, and it is indispensable in a white garden. Large, well-branched plants are essential for maximum impact and prolonged flowering, so it is important to thin young plants in order to give them the generous space they need to develop fully.

**Perfect partners:** *Briza maxima*, *Lunaria annua* 'Variegata', *Paeonia lactiflora* 'Albert Crousse', *Rosa* 'Impératrice Joséphine', *Weigela* Lucifer

**H:** 24–36 in. (60–90 cm)   **S:** 12 in. (30 cm)
❀ **Early to midsummer**
◊◊ ▢-■ ■   76   pH5.5–7.5

## Antirrhinum majus
SNAPDRAGON

Snapdragons are short-lived perennials usually grown as hardy annuals. They are available in a wide range of sizes, and in colors from yellow through orange to scarlet, crimson, pink and white. Tall kinds are elegant, their tapering spires echoing the form of delphiniums, verbascums and lupins. White is the most versatile, yellow is excellent as a contrast for blue, while the hotter shades work well with red, bronze, and purple foliage. The Rocket Series, at 36 in. (90 cm), is a popular tall form. Intermediates such as the fairly rust-resistant Monarch Series, 18 in. (45 cm), and the Coronet and Sonnet Series, 16 in. (40 cm), are very useful in the second rank of a border. The shorter spikes of dwarf varieties are valuable for providing contrasts with flat-headed flowers such as achilleas.

**Perfect partners:** *Atriplex hortensis* var. *rubra*, *Cosmos bipinnatus* 'Sonata White', *Cotinus coggygria* 'Royal Purple', *Ricinus communis* 'Carmencita', *Verbena rigida*

**H:** 6–48 in. (15–120 cm)   **S:** 6–12 in. in. (15–30 cm)
❀ **Early summer to early autumn**
◊◊ ▢-■ ■   Z9   pH5.5–7.5

Spikes of *Antirrhinum majus* 'Black Prince' and the rounded flowerheads of sweet William (*Dianthus barbatus* Nigrescens Group) match perfectly in flower and foliage color.

The white petals and contrasting golden disks of *Argyranthemum foeniculaceum* hort., along with its feathery glaucous foliage, lift the recessive tints of lavender, lilac and indigo supplied by sea lavender (*Limonium latifolium*), the cranesbill *Geranium himalayense*, horned violets (*Viola cornuta*) and the annual clary, *Salvia viridis* 'Claryssa Blue'.

## Argyranthemum foeniculaceum hort.

The true *A. foeniculaceum* is a dainty foliage plant that has filamentous blue-green leaves and flowers shyly from mid-autumn to early midsummer. The plant known as *A. foeniculaceum* hort. (a tender evergreen shrubby marguerite, like the true species) is more free-flowering, with incessant white daisies and feathery, glaucous foliage that goes well with blue flowers, silver foliage and soft shades generally, while contrasting with soft yellow or rich flower colors. With its bright flowers and even growth habit, it is an excellent candidate for bedding or for the front of a mixed or herbaceous border, the plants developing into symmetrical domes that are useful for gentle punctuation along its length. They are also effective in pots combined with a trailing petunia or verbena.

**Perfect partners:** *Allium hollandicum* 'Purple Sensation', *Brachyscome iberidifolia* 'Summer Skies', *Heliotropium arborescens* 'Princess Marina', *Pelargonium* 'Paul Crampel', *Petunia* 'Frenzy Buttercup', *Phygelius aequalis* 'Yellow Trumpet', *Salvia farinacea* 'Victoria', *Senecio cineraria* 'Silver Dust', *Verbena* 'Silver Anne'

**H:** 30 in. (75 cm)   **S:** 24 in. (60 cm)   ❀ **All year**
◊◊ ▢-■ ■   Z9   pH5–7.5

## *Argyranthemum* 'Jamaica Primrose' ♕

This tender shrubby marguerite, with dark green leaves and abundant soft yellow, single daisy flowers borne incessantly throughout the year, is one of the more sizable cultivars of argyranthemum. With its large, bulky form, it is suitable for containers and for the second rank of herbaceous or mixed borders, where it is best placed forward of other plants of the same height to allow it space to achieve its full potential. Excellent in schemes with hot colors such as red and orange, the yellow is also a soft enough shade for use with warm apricot or peach. Good contrasts can be made with blue flowers such as agapanthus or perovskias, variegated foliage and glaucous or yellow-green foliage, for example that of some grasses. Annuals make good partners, including osteospermums, ageratums, tropaeolums, petunias, rudbeckias, zinnias, ursinias, salvias such as *S. farinacea* cultivars and yellow-green or green flowers, together with tender perennials such as cannas, calceolarias, cupheas, heliotropes, coleus and bidens. Where a smaller cultivar is needed, there are numerous alternatives, such as 'Cornish Gold' ♕, with green leaves, or *A. maderense* ♕, only 16 in. (40 cm) high, with dramatic blue-green foliage and soft yellow flowers that are particularly good with blue.

**Perfect partners:** *Agapanthus* 'Loch Hope', *Arundo donax* var. *versicolor*, *Dahlia* 'David Howard', *Helichrysum petiolare* 'Variegatum', *Nicotiana* 'Lime Green', *Nigella damascena* 'Miss Jekyll', *Perovskia* 'Blue Spire', *Salvia farinacea* 'Strata'

**H & S: 40 in.** (1 m) **Late spring to mid-autumn**
Z9 pH5–7.5

**Left:** Yellow-flowered *Potentilla aurea* and *P.* 'Gibson's Scarlet' scramble through *Argyranthemum* 'Jamaica Primrose', providing a contrast of flower size and foliage form at the front of a border in early summer.

**Below:** In late summer and early autumn, *Argyranthemum* 'Jamaica Primrose' remains in full bloom, combining beautifully with warm, bronze-orange *Rudbeckia hirta* Rustic Dwarfs Group and the sprawling yellow *Bidens ferulifolia*, which fills in the space in front of both, spilling onto the adjoining path. Foliage of contrasting form, either grassy or bold, in bronze, yellow-green or variegated with gold, could be added to the three daisies.

The distinctive, upright stems of the grass *Arundo donax* var. *versicolor* provide a striking accent among the harmonious flowers of yellow corn marigolds (*Glebionis segeta*), white Japanese anemones (*Anemone* × *hybrida* 'Honorine Jobert') and, behind, the shrubby *Bupleurum fruticosum*.

## *Arundo donax* var. *versicolor*

With its tall, upright habit and eye-catching variegation, the giant reed, a tender perennial grass, is an ideal choice for bold accents in mixed borders or semi-tropical bedding schemes; it also thrives in bog gardens and containers. The variegation usually emerges whitish, becoming cream with age, but there are clones that start cream and turn yellow by late summer. It makes a useful dot plant for summer plantings, and may also be planted in drifts for foliar contrast. It mixes successfully with many tender perennials such as dahlias, and *Nicotiana sylvestris*, and other larger plants grown as annuals. In herbaceous or mixed borders, it suits restrained schemes with silver foliage and white or blue flowers.

**Perfect partners:** *Canna indica*, *Cleome hassleriana* Color Fountain Series, *Dahlia coccinea*, *Melianthus major*, *Musa basjoo*, *Ricinus communis* 'Carmencita', *Verbena bonariensis*

**H: 6 ft.** (1.8 m) **S: 24 in.** (60 cm)
**(Mid- to late autumn)**
Z9 pH4.5–7.5

## *Atriplex hortensis* var. *rubra*
RED ORACH

This easy, slim annual has leaves flushed red or purple, and insignificant flowers followed by plumelike seedheads that turn parchment colored in autumn. Cultivars such as 'Rosea', 'Purpurea', 'Atrosanguinea', 'Cupreata' and the Plumes Series vary in leaf color from pink-flushed to crimson, copper or rich purple-black. Magenta, crimson and purple forms blend well with cool colors and purple foliage, while purple and bronze kinds combine with hot colors. In borders, they are effective sown in drifts, repeated at intervals, or allowed to weave through other plants. Red orach is invaluable in red borders, excellent with dahlias and contrasting lime green or yellow-green flowers, and also mixed with the yellow-green variant (golden orach).

**Perfect partners:** *Cotinus coggygria* 'Royal Purple', *Dahlia* 'Bishop of Llandaff', *Echinops bannaticus* 'Taplow Blue', *Eryngium giganteum*, *Hemerocallis* 'Stafford', *Nicotiana* 'Lime Green', *Plectranthus argentatus*

**H: 4 ft.** (1.2 m)  **S: 12 in.** (30 cm)
❁ (Early to midsummer)

The large, dusky purple-red leaves of *Atriplex hortensis* var. *rubra* fill in the gaps between and unify the cool colors of various perennials – *Allium giganteum*, with spherical flowerheads, pale blue *Campanula lactiflora* and *Salvia verticillata* 'Purple Rain'. In the foreground is a mound of contrasting yellow-green lady's mantle (*Alchemilla mollis*).

In this combination entirely of daisies, *Bidens ferulifolia* (centre) scrambles between the annual *Rudbeckia fulgida* var. *sullivantii* 'Goldsturm' (left), tender *Osteospermum* 'Buttermilk' (bottom) and hardy perennial *Anthemis tinctoria* 'E.C. Buxton' (right), unifying the ensemble. The varied flower sizes and contrasting dark centers of the rudbeckias and osteospermums add interest.

## *Brachyscome iberidifolia*
SWAN RIVER DAISY

This annual has single daisy flowers in white, mauve, purple or lavender-blue with a yellow or black central disk. It flowers profusely and can sprawl gracefully in baskets and pots, or at the front of a border. It is effective with cool colors, white flowers and plants of more definite structure, mainly silver or glaucous foliage plants such as sea kales. Good companions include alyssums, sage, lavender, catmint and pinks. For contrast, it can be grown with smaller yellow California poppies, yellow-green grasses and shorter euphorbias. Useful cultivars include Splendour Series, with black or yellow disks; Bravo Series, available in various colors; compact 'Brachy Blue', good for edging; and 'Summer Skies', in pastels and deeper tones.

**Perfect partners:** *Crambe maritima*, *Eschscholzia caespitosa* 'Sundew', *Heliotropium arborescens* 'Princess Marina', *Petunia* 'Frenzy Buttercup', *Verbena peruviana* 'Alba'

**H: 12–18 in.** (30–45 cm)  **S: 12 in.** (30 cm)
❁ Early to late summer

Z10  pH5.5–7.5

## *Bidens ferulifolia* ♈

This drought-resistant perennial, usually grown as an annual bedding plant, has divided, feathery leaves and golden yellow daisy flowers. If grown from seed, it is upright until pinched out, which causes it to sprawl, a valuable quality that allows it to weave through other plants and tumble over the edge of a pot or hanging basket, especially with other trailers such as *Helichrysum petiolare* or *Anagallis monellii* cultivars. At the front of a border, it can be grown with hot-colored flowers and foliage, including coleus, with contrasting hardy herbaceous plants such as achilleas or salvias, or between or through small to medium-sized shrubs such as Patio and Ground Cover roses.

**Perfect partners:** *Argyranthemum* 'Jamaica Primrose' p.412 **B**, *Caryopteris* × *clandonensis*, *Dahlia* 'Moonfire' p.422 **B**, *Solenostemon* 'Glory of Luxembourg'

**H: 8–24 in.** (20–60 cm)  **S: 12–40 in.** (30–100 cm)
❁ Late spring to late autumn

Z9  pH5–7.5

This charming incident with dark-eyed, vivid lavender *Brachyscome iberidifolia* set in a carpet of sweet alyssum (*Lobularia maritima*) could be repeated on a larger scale, perhaps with contrasting soft yellow or yellow-green foliage and flowers for greater impact.

The radiating purple-flushed leaves and magenta midribs of *Brassica oleracea* (Acephala Group) 'Red Peacock' make a focal point in this container planting, harmonizing with *Osteospermum* 'Pink Whirls', *Verbena* 'Hidcote Purple' (top) and sprawling *V. tenuisecta* (bottom). The bizarre form and eccentric charm of both the kale and the osteospermum add considerably to the effect.

## Brassica oleracea
## Acephala Group

ORNAMENTAL KALE

The most familiar ornamental kales (all of which are biennials) have feathery glaucous leaves that develop white, pink or magenta variegation at the onset of autumn, and make excellent winter bedding plants with, for example, winter pansies. Varieties include Peacock Series, 8–12 in. (20–30 cm), in red or white; Feather Series, 14 in. (35 cm), also red or white; slightly shorter Kamone Series, with fringed red or white heads; and Northern Lights Series, with large rosettes in white, pink or magenta. Several culinary kales are very ornamental: black kales such as 'Nero di Toscana' and 'Laciniato', with slim, arching and puckered blue-green leaves, resemble miniature palms and make striking foliage plants among shorter summer bedding.

**Perfect partners:** Colored kales: *Chrysanthemum* 'Anastasia', *Skimmia japonica* 'Rubella', *Viola* Universal Series
Black kales: *Crambe maritima*, *Petunia* Surfinia Blue, *Solenostemon* 'Lord Falmouth'

H & S: 12–18 in. (30–45 cm)
❀ (Late spring to midsummer)
◊◊ ☐-■ Z5–6 pH6–8

## Briza maxima
GREATER QUAKING GRASS

This curious grass can be spring-sown as a summer-flowering annual or autumn-sown as a biennial to flower in late spring and early summer. It remains attractive after flowering as its seedheads dry, but if autumn-sown these disintegrate by midsummer and it is then best replaced with summer bedding. It is most pleasing at close range, especially if sowings are thinned to produce erect, bushy plants 6–8 in. (15–20 cm) apart. This grass is good near the front of a border, loosely mixed with other overwintering biennials such as nigellas and Shirley poppies. It may also be grown in gravel, and looks particularly effective when allowed to seed itself.

**Perfect partners:** *Calendula officinalis* Pacific Beauty Series, *Centaurea cyanus*, *Nigella damascena* 'Miss Jekyll', *Papaver rhoeas* Angels' Choir Group

H: 18–24 in. (45–60 cm) S: 10 in. (25 cm)
❀ Late spring to late summer
◊-◊◊ ☐-■ Z4 pH5.5–7.5

Sown beneath a mature, sprawling plant of *Helianthemum* 'Ben Hope', the flowerheads of greater quaking grass (*Briza maxima*) mix thoroughly with the sun rose's flowers to offer an intriguing pattern of contrasting shapes and colors.

Floriferous orange *Calceolaria* 'Camden Hero' (bottom) is combined with other flowers that are rich but slightly muted in color, giving a warm but not searingly brilliant effect. Included are salmon *Stachys coccinea*, red *Mimulus aurantiacus* var. *puniceus* and a dark-leaved dahlia, all of them colorful from late spring, when they are planted out, until the first frosts.

## Calceolaria 'Camden Hero'

A tender perennial overwintered under glass from late summer cuttings, this is a short sub-shrub with a profuse display of striking flowers in a rare, rich shade of burnt orange. It is ideal for combining with hot colors and bronze foliage in a conspicuous position toward the front of a border. The bushy plants are very brittle, so work brushwood between them for support. If grown in the same site for a number of seasons, plants may become prone to fungal disease that can kill the entire group, so they should ideally be grown in a different place each year. 'Kentish Hero' is similar, slightly lighter in color and more free-flowering, but with even more brittle stems. Like 'Camden Hero', it flowers from late spring until the first frosts.

**Perfect partners:** *Calendula officinalis* Fiesta Gitana Series, *Canna* 'Durban', *Cordyline australis* Purpurea Group, *Dahlia* 'Moonfire', *Fuchsia* 'Genii', *Perilla frutescens* var. *crispa*, *Tagetes patula* 'Striped Marvel'

H & S: 12 in. (30 cm) ❀ Late spring to mid-autumn
◊◊ ☐-■ Z10 pH5–7

## *Calendula officinalis*

POT MARIGOLD

This cottage garden flower is a hardy annual that may be sown in autumn for blooms in early summer, or in spring for flowers from mid- or late summer. Grow shorter kinds such as the double Fiesta Gitana Series 🏆, at 8 in. (20 cm), at the front of a border or in gravel. Intermediate varieties include 'Lemon Queen' and 'Orange King', both 18 in. (45 cm) with double flowers; orange 'Radio', 18 in. (45 cm), with quilled petals; and 'Touch of Red', 16 in. (40 cm), in deep orange with bronze-red reverse. Taller kinds include Kablouna Series, 24 in. (60 cm), with anemone-centered blooms; the double Pacific Beauty Series, 24 in. (60 cm), in colors such as pale yellow and apricot; and The Prince Series, double, to 30 in. (75 cm). All blend well with other hot colors, and with yellow-green foliage and flowers and bronze leaves. They look good with lettuces, nasturtiums and parsley in potagers.

**Perfect partners:** *Briza maxima*, *Centaurea cyanus*, *Euphorbia schillingii*, *Nigella damascena* 'Miss Jekyll', *Papaver rhoeas* Angels' Choir Group p.440 **B**, *Stipa tenuissima*

**H: 12–28 in.** (30–70 cm) **S: 12–18 in.** (30–45 cm)
**Early summer to mid-autumn**
Z9 pH5.5–7.5

The bright flowers of the pot marigold *Calendula officinalis* (Fiesta Gitana Series) 'Gitana Orange' create a vibrant combination at the front of a border with a magenta-centered, purple-leaved ornamental cultivar of kale (*Brassica oleracea* Acephala Group) and a compact, variegated nasturtium (*Tropaeolum majus* Alaska Series).

This exotic combination, mainly of tender plants, includes salmon-pink *Canna* 'Erebus', scarlet *Lobelia cardinalis* 'Queen Victoria', the raylike umbels of papyrus (*Cyperus papyrus*), a dark-leaved canna and the cider gum (*Eucalyptus gunnii*). The canna's flowers act as the focal point of the group, harmonizing with the red blooms and contrasting gently with the glaucous foliage of the gum.

## *Canna* 'Erebus'

Cannas are tender, rhizomatous perennials used mainly for bedding and for summer display. They have bold foliage, sometimes dramatically colored or striped, and exotic-looking flowers in bright, brassy, hot colors that can introduce a hint of the tropics even to cooler gardens. 'Erebus' is less extroverted than most, with glaucous foliage and salmon-pink flowers. It is an excellent choice for less jazzy schemes together with cream, white, peach or apricot flowers and glaucous foliage, although it also looks good in brighter partnerships with scarlet or coral flowers, and with bronze or deep red foliage. Plant it behind or through a sprawling or spreading plant 8–12 in. (20–30 cm) high to conceal its base. It can vary from 3 ft. (90 cm) high in climates with cool summers to 10 ft. (3 m) in warmer areas.

**Perfect partners:** *Cordyline australis* Purpurea Group, *Dahlia* 'Alva's Doris', *Diascia rigescens*, *Fuchsia* 'Thalia', *Ricinus communis* 'Carmencita', *Verbena bonariensis*

**H: 4 ft.** (1.2 m) **S: 20 in.** (50 cm)
**Midsummer to early autumn**
Z9 pH5.5–7.5

## Cerinthe major 'Purpurascens'

This annual, sometimes grown as a biennial in warmer climates, has glaucous foliage and purple or brown flowers covered by bracts that vary from intense blue to deep purple. At close range, the luminosity of that area of the flower stem where the color changes from glaucous green to blue and purple is most remarkable, particularly at dusk. This effect is enhanced by neighbors with glaucous or silver foliage, soft yellow, white or blue flowers, yellow-green foliage and flowers, and contrasting foliage, such as grasses, irises or cardoons. Plants grown as biennials flower from late spring onward, combining well with Bearded irises, and may self-seed a late summer generation. Spring-sown plants look good with grasses such as small miscanthus.

**Perfect partners:** *Eschscholzia caespitosa* 'Sundew', *Euphorbia characias* 'Blue Hills', *Iris* 'Jane Phillips', *Lilium* 'Joy' p.375 **A**, *Miscanthus sinensis* 'Kleine Fontäne'

**H: 18 in.** (45 cm) **S: 12 in.** (30 cm)
✽ **Early to late summer**
⬛⬜🟦⬛ ◊◊ ⬜-⬛ **Z9 pH5.5–7.5**

This cool-colored combination consists of *Cerinthe major* 'Purpurascens' and lavender (*Lavandula angustifolia*) – both of them favorite food plants of bees – behind a clipped edging of dwarf box (*Buxus sempervirens* 'Suffruticosa').

## Cleome hassleriana
SPIDER FLOWER

The relatively tall height of this half-hardy annual makes it useful for growing at the back of an annual border or in drifts through a herbaceous or mixed border. Good cultivars include 'Violet Queen', 'Cherry Queen', 'Pink Queen', pure white 'Helen Campbell' ♀, and Color Fountain Series, a mixture sometimes available as separate colors, including a fine amaranth-purple. These cultivars mix well with cool pink, crimson, lilac, purple or white flowers, and with glaucous, purple and white-variegated foliage, such as some larger miscanthus cultivars. They are excellent with dahlias, asters such as larger China asters, while for a tropical effect they can be mixed with cannas, melianthus and larger-flowering tender solanums. Spider flowers require warm summers to thrive.

White and purplish crimson spider flowers (*Cleome hassleriana*) are ideally matched in height to *Verbena bonariensis*, whose small purple flowerheads produce a soft haze of contrasting blooms. In front, *Cosmos bipinnatus* closely corresponds with the colors of the spider flowers but provides a contrast of floral form.

**Perfect partners:** *Aster* × *frikartii* 'Wunder von Stäfa', *Crambe maritima*, *Dahlia* 'Gerrie Hoek', *Lathyrus rotundifolius* p.173 **C**, *Populus alba* 'Richardii' (stooled) p.125 **A**

**H: 4 ft.** (1.2 m) **S: 18 in.** (45 cm)
✽ **Mid- to late summer**
⬛⬜🟦⬛ ◊◊ ⬜-⬛ **Z10 pH5.5–7**

## *Consolida* species and cultivars
LARKSPUR

Garden larkspurs are annuals mainly derived from *C. ajacis* and *C. orientalis*, both with flowers in tightly packed spikes, and the airy *C. regalis*. Spike-forming cultivars usually make a single stiff flower stem, useful for repeated bold vertical accents; among the best are blue and white 'Frosted Skies' and dusky pink 'Early Gray', both 30 in. (75 cm) high. Good *C. regalis* cultivars include 'Snow Cloud', 30 in. (75 cm), with single creamy white florets; and members of Exquisite Strain, such as rich royal-blue 'Blue Cloud', 36 in. (90 cm), and 'Salmon Beauty', also 36 in. (90 cm), with a central flower spike followed by lateral spikes of semi-double blooms.

**Perfect partners:** *Ammi majus* p.411 **A**, *Antirrhinum majus* 'White Wonder', *Clarkia unguiculata* Royal Bouquet Series, *Lychnis coronaria* 'Alba', *Plecostachys serpyllifolia*

**H: 12–48 in.** (30–120 cm) **S: 9–12 in.** (23–30 cm)
❀ **Early to late summer**
 ◊◊ □-■ Z7 pH5.5–7.5

The columnar racemes of this attractive rich blue cultivar of *Consolida ajacis* are tall enough to appear among and just above the contrasting white flowers of an annual mallow (*Lavatera trimestris* 'Mont Blanc').

A

B

In its third year, *Cordyline australis* Purpurea Group will just overtop the matching dark foliage and scarlet flowers of *Dahlia* 'Bishop of Llandaff', making a strong focal point in a border. Cordylines in their second year could be used effectively with shorter dahlias, such as *D.* 'Bednall Beauty', 'Preston Park' or 'Moonfire'.

## *Cosmos bipinnatus*

This versatile annual daisy has feathery foliage and single or semi-double flowers in all shades from white to vinous red, and a great height range. Sensation Series, 36 in. (90 cm), has single flowers in pink, carmine and white; white 'Purity' is 36 in. (90 cm); and Sonata Series ♀, in white, carmine and pink, is 24 in. (60 cm). All variants are best planted behind shorter cushion-forming plants. The taller cultivars belong in the second or third rank of a border. They make good bedding, and mingle easily with annuals such as *Verbena bonariensis*, and larkspurs. Sonata Series and other shorter kinds work well with plants of contrasting floral form, including spiky plants such as salvias and pennisetums.

**Perfect partners:** *Cleome hassleriana* p.416 **B**, *Consolida regalis* 'Snow Cloud', *Dianthus barbatus* p.424 **A**, *Pennisetum villosum*, *Salvia farinacea* 'White Victory'

**H: 24–48 in.** (60–120 cm) **S: 18–24 in.** (45–60 cm)
❀ **Midsummer to mid-autumn**
 ◊◊ □-■ Z9 pH5–8

## *Cordyline australis*
**Purpurea Group**

New Zealand cabbage palm (*C. australis* ♀) is a small tree, usually single-stemmed and branching only after flowering. It is very useful for temporary summer display because of its emphatic effect and tropical looks. The leaves of Purpurea Group vary from reddish bronze to purple and ½–2 in. (1–5 cm) in width (as a general rule, deeper color and broader foliage indicate reduced hardiness). The group as a whole is effective with hot colors such as scarlet and orange, warm shades like peach and apricot, and in contrasts with lime green and yellow-green. Good companions include dahlias, nicotianas, cannas, reddish-leaved castor-oil plants and true palms. Variegated 'Albertii' ♀, with broad creamy yellow stripes, makes a striking accent in a border.

**Perfect partners:** *Canna* 'Wyoming', *Chamaerops humilis* 'Vulcano', *Dahlia* 'Alva's Doris' p.418 **A**, *Nicotiana* 'Lime Green', *Pelargonium* 'Orangesonne', *Ricinus communis* 'Impala'

**H: 20 ft.** (6 m) **S: 10 ft.** (3 m)
❀ **Early to late summer**
■ ◊◊ □-■ Z9 pH5.5–7.5

C

A relatively short cosmos such as *Cosmos bipinnatus* (Sonata Series) 'Sonata White' interplanted with a relatively tall scarlet salvia such as *Salvia splendens* 'Rambo' together provide a striking, dramatic contrast of color and form.

# Dahlias

DAHLIAS, especially the dinner-plate dahlias beloved of exhibitors, are among the boldest of garden flowers. Their color range is unequaled by any other plant except perhaps the tulip, lacking only clear blue, green and black. Unlike the tulip, they flower continuously and increasingly freely from early summer until the first frosts. In height they range from miniatures of 10 in. (25 cm) to 8 ft. (2.5 m) giants, and flowerhead size varies from 4 in. (10 cm) to a massive 10 in. (25 cm) or more.

The other main source of variation in the dahlia is flower form. Those classified as Decorative dahlias have fully double blooms with broad, generally flat petals (strictly, ray florets). In Waterlily dahlias the petals are fewer and broader, while in the elegant Cactus or Semi-cactus cultivars they are rolled back into narrow quills. At the other end of the spectrum the Ball and Pompon dahlias have petals rolled into cones arranged in tight spheres. Single-flowered and Collerette dahlias have a single ring of petals around a yellow eye or an inner ruff of shorter petals.

The one weak point of the dahlia is its coarse, potatolike foliage. In 'Bishop of Llandaff' and a few of its modern offspring the foliage is more dissected and an attractive deep bronze-maroon. Some of the species are also more refined, but the majority of dahlias are best surrounded by other plants, in a herbaceous border for example where they will reinforce color schemes with their abundance of flower.

Dahlias are tender tuberous perennials, but in light soil and warm sites most will overwinter successfully in the ground, especially if protected with a thick straw mulch. It is safer, however, to lift the tubers in late autumn, overwinter them in frost-free conditions, and replant in spring. Many of the smaller dahlias are easily raised from seed. They make excellent bedding or front-of-border plants and are ideal for pots and other containers.

## *Dahlia* 'Alva's Doris' ♛

This is a small Semi-cactus Group dahlia, with blood-red flowers, fully double and with petals rolled back to form a quill. Its rich coloring suits combinations with orange, gold and other red flowers, and dark red or purple foliage, and it is a traditional plant of red borders, with its spiky shape echoed by a dark-leaved cordyline and its color emphasized by a background of dark-leaved shrubs. In hot color schemes, it goes well with heleniums, rudbeckias, zinnias, daylilies, euphorbias, Mexican sunflowers and common sunflowers. It contrasts particularly well with yellow-green, magenta, pure blue and green flowers such as nicotianas.

**Perfect partners:** *Cotinus coggygria* 'Royal Purple', *Crocosmia* 'Late Lucifer', *Helianthus* 'Velvet Queen', *Nicotiana langsdorffii*, *Tithonia rotundifolia* 'Goldfinger'

**H: 4 ft. (1.2 m)  S: 24 in. (60 cm)**
❀ **Midsummer to mid-autumn**

 ◊◊ ▢-◼ ◼ **Z9  pH5–7.5**

**Top:** In a border of red flowers and both green and dark foliage, *Dahlia* 'Alva's Doris' and *Lobelia cardinalis* 'Queen Victoria' match perfectly in color, while the grass *Miscanthus sinensis* 'Gracillimus' and spiky *Cordyline australis* Purpurea Group are backlit dramatically by the sun.

**Above:** *Dahlia* 'Alva's Doris' is here joined by the exotic foliage of *Canna indica* 'Purpurea' and contrasting glaucous-leaved cider gum (*Eucalyptus gunnii*), grown from seed sown under glass and used as a bedding plant.

The rounded, sumptuous blood-red blooms and dark foliage of *Dahlia* 'Arabian Night' contrast strikingly in form with those of its neighbor, the sword-leaved, vermilion-flowered *Crocosmia* 'Lucifer'.

## *Dahlia* 'Arabian Night'

This dahlia has exceptionally deep blood-red flowers, fully double with broad flat petals and the rounded outline typical of the Small Decorative Group. Although similar in color to 'Alva's Doris' (facing page), its darker centre are better suited to mellow, sumptuous schemes than to bright or vivacious plantings. However, it combines with many of the partners suggested for 'Alva's Doris', as well as with purple orach, cannas, amaranthus, pelargoniums and tender salvias, and can look opulent with dark-leaved shrubs such as purple smoke bush, berberis or ornamental cherries. It also interacts well with yellow-green to enliven its deeper tones.

**Perfect partners:** *Amaranthus caudatus* 'Viridis', *Atriplex hortensis* var. *rubra*, *Berberis* × *ottawensis* f. *purpurea* 'Superba', *Canna* 'Roi Humbert', *Choisya ternata* Sundance

**H: 40 in.** (1 m) **S: 18 in.** (45 cm)
❀ **Midsummer to mid-autumn**
◊◊ ☐-◼ ◼ Z9 pH5–7.5

## *Dahlia* 'Bednall Beauty' ♔

A typical example of a Dwarf Bedding Group dahlia, 'Bednall Beauty' is useful for bedding or positions toward the front of a mixed or herbaceous border. The colors of its dainty dark leaves and semi-double, rich scarlet flowers suit the same kinds of combinations as 'Alva's Doris' (facing page) and 'Arabian Night' (left), but its shorter stature allows it also to partner smaller companions such as nasturtiums, scarlet verbenas and dark-leaved antirrhinums, heucheras, sedums and beets. As a bedding plant, it may be grown among Patio and Ground Cover roses, and looks effective edged with a yellow-green or variegated grass. It is also excellent in pots.

**Perfect partners:** *Antirrhinum majus* 'Black Prince', *Hakonechloa macra* 'Alboaurea', *Iresine lindenii*, *Rosa* 'Europeana', *Tagetes patula* 'Spanish Brocade', *Verbena* Temari Scarlet

**H & S: 16 in.** (40 cm)
❀ **Midsummer to mid-autumn**
◊◊ ☐-◼ ◼ Z9 pH5–7.5

In this border consisting of a variety of red flowers, and with a warm-colored brick wall behind, *Dahlia* 'Bednall Beauty' is echoed further back by *D.* 'Bishop of Llandaff', with *Rosa* 'Frensham' beyond. The dark blue-green leaved nasturtium *Tropaeolum majus* 'Empress of India' and *Geum* 'Mrs. J. Bradshaw' furnish the border's edge.

Red flowers and dusky foliage are backed by a dark yew hedge and castor-oil plants (*Ricinus communis*) to dramatic effect. *Dahlia* 'Bishop of Llandaff' grows between Small Decorative Group dahlias 'Blaisdon Red' and 'Anchorite', behind the large-leaved *Beta vulgaris* 'Rhubarb Chard', *B.v.* 'Mr. McGregor's Favourite' and verbenas. In the second rank are nicotianas, beefsteak plants (*Iresine herbstii* 'Brilliantissima') and the pink-flowered *Sedum telephium* subsp. *maximum* 'Atropurpureum'.

## *Dahlia* 'Bishop of Llandaff' ♔

Although classed as a Miscellaneous dahlia, this is in effect a tall version of 'Bednall Beauty' (above), with similar finely divided dark foliage and semi-double, rich scarlet flowers. It can be used to echo 'Bednall Beauty' further back in a border, and succeeds in the same associations, as well as in those of 'Alva's Doris' (facing page) and 'Arabian Night' (left). It contrasts effectively with green-flowered nicotianas.

**Perfect partners:** *Cordyline australis* Purpurea Group p.417 **B**, *Dahlia* 'Bednall Beauty' p.419 **B**, *Lobelia cardinalis* 'Queen Victoria' p.307 **C**, *Nicotiana* 'Lime Green' p.438 **A**, *Pelargonium* 'Paul Crampel' p.442 **A**

**H: 4 ft.** (1.2 m) **S: 24 in.** (60 cm)
❀ **Midsummer to mid-autumn**
◊◊ ☐-◼ ◼ Z9 pH5–7.5

## *Dahlia* 'David Howard' ♔

The bronze foliage and soft orange flowers, deeper at the center, of this Miniature Decorative Group dahlia are indispensable for richly colored schemes and autumn combinations with plants such as agastaches, hedychiums and kirengeshomas. It looks very attractive with hot colors such as gold and scarlet, with soft yellow, peach and apricot, with yellow-green (particularly later-flowering euphorbias), and with contrasting purple and blue. Crocosmias, chrysanthemums, yellow daisies and fruiting roses such as *Rosa moyesii* cultivars and hybrids are all excellent autumn companions. Earlier in the season it is good with cannas, achilleas, plume poppies, perennial lobelias, tiger lilies, daylilies and recurrent-flowering Shrub roses.

**Perfect partners:** *Cautleya spicata* 'Robusta' p.249 **B**, *Euphorbia schillingii*, *Hedychium coccineum*, *Kniphofia uvaria* 'Nobilis', *Rosa* 'Geranium', *Spartium junceum* p.141 **B**

**H: 5 ft. (1.5 m) S: 30 in. (75 cm)**
❀ **Midsummer to mid-autumn**

▬▭▭▭▭ ◊◊ ▢-▆ ▆ Z9 pH5–7.5

*Verbena bonariensis* is able to thread itself through the heart of a large plant of *Dahlia* 'David Howard', its lavender florets, emerging from purple calyces, forming a gentle contrast with the warm orange, formal blooms of the dahlia. *Canna* 'Wyoming', with dark leaves and orange blooms that perfectly match the dahlia, just overtops the ensemble, which by autumn has reached almost 6 ft. (1.8 m).

## *Dahlia* 'Gerrie Hoek'

This is a Small Waterlily Group dahlia, very free-flowering with rather informal, fully double, silvery pink blooms. It is suitable for the middle ranks of a border, where it works particularly well with purple, glaucous and dark foliage plants, such as red orach, dark-leaved castor-oil plants and purple-leaved shrubs. It is also good with cool-colored flowers or plants with contrasting floral forms, such as salvias, aconites, actaeas and later-flowering achilleas. Other partners include campanulas, asters, agapanthus, taller verbenas and grasses, such as miscanthus.

The superlative blooms of *Dahlia* 'Gerrie Hoek' form the focal point of this scheme. In the front, *Lobelia × speciosa* 'Vedrariensis' provides contrast in floral form, with the taller *Lavatera × clementii* 'Barnsley' and *Onopordum nervosum* behind.

**Perfect partners:** *Anemone × hybrida* 'Honorine Jobert', *Cosmos bipinnatus* 'Sonata White', *Phlox paniculata* 'Mount Fuji', *Pittosporum tenuifolium* 'Purpureum'

**H: 4 ft. (1.2 m) S: 24 in. (60 cm)**
❀ **Midsummer to mid-autumn**

 ◊◊ ▢-▆ ▆ Z9 pH5–7.5

The luminous blooms of *Dahlia* 'Glorie van Heemstede' shine beneath a cloud of biscuit-colored florets of a plume poppy (*Macleaya microcarpa*), beside the lacy yellow-green flowers of common fennel (*Foeniculum vulgare*).

# *Dahlia* 'Glorie van Heemstede' ♔

Flowering prolifically over a long season, this Small Waterlily Group dahlia can be relied on to provide an eye-catching display of soft yellow blooms on strong stems. Its clear shade of yellow is definite enough to be combined with hot colors, yet not too harsh to complement warm tints such as apricot, and it makes effective contrasts with blue flowers such as perovskias, and caryopteris. It is attractive with glaucous or gold-variegated shrubs, yellow-green foliage, larger grasses and green or yellow-green flowers, including nicotianas and later-flowering euphorbias. Pleasing combinations are also with larger tender salvias, hedychiums and recurrent-flowering Shrub roses in warmer tints.

**Perfect partners:** *Agapanthus* 'Blue Moon', *Elaeagnus pungens* 'Maculata', *Melianthus major*, *Miscanthus sinensis* 'Zebrinus', *Nicotiana langsdorffii*, *Rosa* 'Buff Beauty'

**H: 4½ ft.** (1.4 m)  **S: 24 in.** (60 cm)
✿ **Midsummer to mid-autumn**

◖◗ □-■  ■ Z9  pH5–7.5

# *Dahlia* 'Grenadier'

This is a Small Waterlily Group dahlia, typical of the group in having fully double blooms more than twice as wide as they are deep and with fewer petals than other double dahlias. 'Grenadier' is a rich red cultivar, traditionally used in a similar way to 'Arabian Night' (see p.419) as a key component of red or hot-colored borders. Although differing in flower shape from 'Arabian Night', it succeeds with the same partners, especially in schemes with yellow-green flowers and foliage, and dark or purple foliage plants such as smoke bush, berberis and ornamental cherries. It also combines well with cannas and crocosmias.

**Perfect partners:** *Hemerocallis fulva* 'Flore Pleno', *Prunus* × *cistena*, *Ricinus communis* 'Impala', *Rosa rugosa*, *Verbena bonariensis* p.452 **A**, *Zinnia elegans* 'Envy' ❑ p.307 **B**

**H: 40 in.** (1 m)  **S: 18 in.** (45 cm)
✿ **Midsummer to mid-autumn**

◖◗ □-■  ■ Z9  pH5–7.5

Dark-leaved, shining scarlet *Dahlia* 'Grenadier' makes a dramatic contrast with the cream-edged leaves of the variegated dogwood *Cornus alba* 'Elegantissima'. This relatively steeply banked grouping could be used in a comparatively narrow border.

## *Dahlia* 'Laciniata Atropurpurea'

Probably the parent of modern dark-leaved cultivars such as 'Bishop of Llandaff', this is a single-flowered dahlia with doubly pinnate leaves that bear tiny, deep purple leaflets. It has open-centered blooms with one or two complete outer rows of petals that vary in color according to climate and situation – generally, the flowers are a deep and resonant plummy purple, although in some positions they can appear deep purplish red, even occasionally zoned with blood-red. It is useful for blending into hot color schemes and can also be used in sumptuous combinations with deep purplish blue flowers such as aconites. Steeply banked borders are ideal, allowing its intricate foliage to be seen at close range.

**Perfect partners:** *Aconitum napellus*, *A.* 'Spark's Variety', *Aster amellus* 'Veilchenkönigin', *A. novae-angliae* 'Barr's Violet', *Fuchsia* 'Thalia', *Helianthus* 'Prado Red'

**H: 30 in.** (75 cm) **S: 18 in.** (45 cm)
❀ Midsummer to mid-autumn
▰▰▰ ◊◊ ▢-▨ ▇ Z9 pH5–7.5

A neat plant suited to the second rank of a border, the dark-leaved *Dahlia* 'Laciniata Atropurpurea' here creates a pleasing combination with gentian-blue *Salvia patens* behind a dwarf box hedge.

The shape of the soft yellow blooms of *Dahlia* 'Moonfire' is emphasized by the striking scarlet zone, while the dark purple foliage acts as a perfect foil to the flowers. Its warm-colored companions include a carpet of feathery-leaved *Bidens ferulifolia*, which furnish the stems, and a background of yellow-green *Euphorbia sikkimensis*.

## *Dahlia* 'Moonfire' ♛

This is a fairly compact Dwarf Bedding Group dahlia, with dark foliage and single blooms of amber-yellow with a clear red zone in the centre. Its size and habit suit it for use in summer containers, bedding schemes and positions toward the front of a border, where it can be blended with hot or warm colors. It goes well with purple or bronze foliage, as in bronze sedges, dark-leaved cannas and coleus, and with yellow-green or yellow-variegated foliage or flowers, such as euphorbias and larger grasses. It can be put with bedding plants such as bidens, arctotis and gazanias, as well as perennials such as smaller kniphofias and larger scarlet lobelias.

**Perfect partners:** *Begonia semperflorens* Cocktail Series, *Heuchera villosa* 'Palace Purple', *Solenostemon* 'Crimson Ruffles'

**H & S: 16 in.** (40 cm)
❀ Midsummer to mid-autumn
▰▰▰ ◊◊ ▢-▨ ▇ Z9 pH5–7.5

## *Dahlia* 'Pink Michigan'

A Dwarf Bedding Group dahlia, 'Pink Michigan' has magenta blooms, shading to light carmine-pink. It is well suited to the second or third rank of a border, where it blends with cool colors and glaucous or silver foliage, including argyranthemums, artemisias and osteospermums in white or pink, seedling or stooled eucalyptus, and white-variegated or glaucous grasses. It will partner purple or dark foliage plants, such as red orach, purple smoke bush and black or purple curly kale. Companion flowers include cosmos, asters, verbenas, nicotianas, salvias, clarkias, lavateras, larkspurs, Japanese anemones, aconites, phlox, thalictrums, caryopteris, perovskias, and indigoferas.

**Perfect partners:** *Argyranthemum foeniculaceum* hort., *Brassica oleracea* (Acephala Group) 'Nero di Toscana', *Helictotrichon sempervirens*, *Osteospermum* 'White Pim'

**H: 28 in.** (70 cm) **S: 18 in.** (45 cm)
❀ Midsummer to mid-autumn
▰▰▰ ◊◊ ▢-▨ ▇ Z9 pH5–7.5

*Dahlia* 'Pink Michigan' is grown here towards the front of a purple border behind the rich purple *Aster novi-belgii* 'Cliff Lewis'. By mid-autumn it has reached a substantial size, just overtopped by the magenta *D.* 'Requiem' and pale violet *Aster turbinellus* hort. (beyond). The distant scarlet hips of *Rosa* 'Geranium' provide a touch of contrast and save the scheme from blandness.

## *Dahlia* 'Requiem'

This is a Small Decorative Group dahlia with magenta flowers that become a little paler at the tips of the petals as blooms age. Although taller than 'Pink Michigan' (facing page), its similar coloring suits the same kinds of combinations in the second or third rank of a border. It is particularly good with perennials such as silver artemisias, stooled or seedling eucalyptus, Japanese anemones and later-flowering thalictrums, and it complements taller plants, for example taller asters and aconites. Its rich magenta looks good in dusky and sumptuous schemes with crimsons and purple or dark foliage, such as red orach, purple smoke bush, black kale and red or purple curly kales.

**Perfect partners:** *Amaranthus caudatus*, *Anemone* × *hybrida* 'Max Vogel', *Buddleja davidii* 'Royal Red', *Cleome hassleriana* Color Fountain Series, *Cordyline australis* Purpurea Group, *Dahlia* 'Pink Michigan' p.422 **C**, *Eucalyptus gunnii* (stooled), *Sambucus nigra* 'Guincho Purple', *Thalictrum delavayi* 'Hewitt's Double'

**H: 31 in. (80 cm)  S: 18 in. (45 cm)**
✿ **Midsummer to mid-autumn**
▬ ▬▬▬ ◊◊ ☐-■ ■ Z9  pH5–7.5

Asters are often suited in height and color to autumn combinations with dahlias, providing a significant contrast of flower shape and size. Here, *Aster turbinellus* hort. makes a perfect foil for the richly colored blooms of *D.* 'Requiem' behind the glaucous-leaved *Baptisia australis*. The herbaceous baptisia starts this display in early summer with airy spikes of lavender-blue flowers.

## *Dahlia* 'Yelno Harmony' ♟

Classed as both a Small Decorative and a Dwarf Bedding cultivar, this is a relatively small-growing dahlia, with soft orange petals, deeper at the center of the bloom. Although similar to 'David Howard' (see p.420), the flowers are paler in color and less double. 'Yelno Harmony' harmonizes with warm-colored flowers and bronze foliage, and makes effective contrasts with yellow-green leaves and flowers and with purple or blue. It can be used toward the front of a border, where it combines well with nicotianas, crocosmias, smaller grasses and smaller later-flowering euphorbias, and is especially useful for bedding with verbenas, pelargoniums, salvias, perillas and zinnias.

**Perfect partners:** *Beta vulgaris* 'Bull's Blood', *B.v.* 'Mr. McGregor's Favourite', *Cerinthe major* 'Purpurascens', *Festuca glauca* 'Blaufuchs', *Lysimachia congestiflora* 'Outback Sunset', *Nicotiana* 'Domino Red', *Pelargonium* 'Paul Crampel', *Perilla frutescens* var. *crispa*, *Salvia coccinea* 'Lady in Red', *Zinnia* 'Chippendale'

In this bedding combination, the squirrel tail grass (*Hordeum jubatum*) has been interplanted with *Dahlia* 'Yelno Harmony'. When the grass (18 in./45 cm high) starts to flower and set seed in early to midsummer, its silky seedheads just overtop the dahlia, creating a subtly charming mix.

**H: 24 in. (60 cm)  S: 18 in. (45 cm)**
✿ **Midsummer to mid-autumn**
 Z9  pH5–7.5

A

## Diascia 'Dark Eyes' ♛

This diascia is a tender perennial, popular for
its long and lavish flowering, and normally
grown as an annual from cuttings rooted in
late summer and overwintered under glass. Its
sprawling habit makes it useful for interweaving
with other lax plants such as verbena cultivars
and *Helichrysum petiolare* cultivars. It is good
for the front of a border, and for pots and
hanging baskets, its coral-pink color
harmonizing with peach, apricot, scarlet
and cream, and with bronze or red foliage.
Pleasing contrasts can be made with purple
or mid-blue flowers, and with yellow-green
foliage and flowers. If trimmed back after the
first flush of flowers, it will bloom again.

**Perfect partners:** *Alonsoa warscewiczii,
Isotoma axillaris, Lobelia erinus* 'Sapphire',
*Petunia* 'Frenzy Buttercup', *P.* Million Bells
Trailing Blue, *Scaevola* Purple Fan

**H: 9 in. (23 cm) S: 20 in. (50 cm)**
✿ Early summer to mid-autumn
▬▬▭▬ ◊◊ ▢-▮ Z9 pH5.5–7.5

In this piquant color combination of contrasting plants
in a container, *Diascia* 'Dark Eyes', *Verbena* Tapien Violet
and *Helichrysum petiolare* 'Limelight' intermingle and
trail gracefully over the edge. An alternative in harmonious
cool colors would be to use a mauve diascia such as
*D.* 'Lilac Belle' with the same verbena and the gray-green
leaved *Helichrysum petiolare* itself.

B

## Dianthus barbatus
SWEET WILLIAM

These traditional cottage garden biennials
provide invaluable color after most spring
flowers and before many summer ones open.
Some kinds have dark leaves and flowers –
Nigrescens Group ♛ and 'Sooty', for example
– while others, such as Auricula-eyed
mixtures, have attractive markings. A few are
available as single colors, including Beauty
Series, Hollandia Series and Standard Series.
Dwarf types can be grown as annuals from a
spring sowing under glass, but many have a
dumpy, inelegant habit and a relatively short
flowering season. 'Roundabout', (6 in./15 cm),
has spreading plants flowering from early

A restful effect is achieved by combining harmonious, cool-
colored flowers with glaucous and gray-green foliage in this
grouping consisting of mixed *Dianthus barbatus*, opium
poppies (*Papaver somniferum*), a mixture of short *Cosmos
bipinnatus* and shrubby *Artemisia* 'Powis Castle'.

summer to early autumn. All associate well
with early summer flowers such as shorter
foxgloves, columbines, lupins and early roses.

**Perfect partners:** *Antirrhinum majus* 'Black
Prince' p.411 **B**, *Aquilegia vulgaris* (mixed),
*Digitalis purpurea* Foxy Group, *Lupinus*
'Gallery White', *Rosa* 'Fantin-Latour'

**H: 4–28 in. (10–70 cm) S: 8–12 in. (20–30 cm)**
✿ Late spring to early summer
▬▬▭▬ ◊◊ ▢-▮ Z4 pH5.5–8

## *Diascia rigescens* ♟

This plant has salmon-pink flowers on dense, clearly defined spikes. It is good at the front of a border and very useful for hanging baskets and containers, mixed with trailing verbenas and *Helichrysum petiolare* cultivars. Its coloring suits the same combinations as *D.* 'Dark Eyes' (facing page), but it is a slightly beefier plant and so mixes better with other sprawlers that have larger blooms and leaves. In frost-prone areas, this diascia is not reliably hardy, but even where plants will survive winters outdoors it performs best if raised from cuttings taken in late summer.

**Perfect partners:** *Convolvulus cneorum* (foliage), *Helianthemum* 'Wisley White', *Petunia* 'Scarlet Ice', *Rehmannia elata* p.328 **A**, *Verbena* Temari Blue, *V.* Temari Scarlet

**H: 12 in.** (30 cm) **S: 20 in.** (50 cm)
❀ **Early summer to early autumn**
◊◊ ■-■ **Z9 pH5.5–7.5**

The rich pink blooms of *Diascia rigescens* harmonize with the red centers of their companion pinks and provide contrast of floral form. Both are ideal for the front of a sunny border, backed by mound-forming plants such as catmints.

**Above:** The narrow, one-sided spikes of *Digitalis purpurea* f. *albiflora* provide bold vertical accents in this relatively informal scheme with old roses, *Thalictrum aquilegiifolium* and white sweet rocket (*Hesperis matronalis* var. *albiflora*).

**Left:** The spikes of *Digitalis purpurea* 'Sutton's Apricot', perhaps more accurately described as flesh-pink, match the flat flowerheads of an elderberry (*Sambucus nigra* 'Guincho Purple') behind, while offering an intriguing contrast in form; the white foxgloves (*D.p.* f. *albiflora*) serve to leaven the effect. The large foxglove plants are later replaced by summer bedding as their flowering passes its peak.

## *Digitalis purpurea*
COMMON FOXGLOVE

This biennial or short-lived perennial has magenta or white flowers in a slim, elegant, one-sided spike. 'Sutton's Apricot' ♟ bears soft pale peach color combining attractively with bronze foliage and white or pure blue flowers, for example Tibetan poppies. However, the florets hang towards the sun, unlike showier selections such as Excelsior Group ♟ and Foxy Group, which bear their flowers all round the stem. All common foxgloves are good in a sunny or partially shaded border, or in a lightly shaded woodland garden as drifts of sentinel spikes. Late-flowering azaleas and rhododendrons, as well as elders, make perfect woodland partners. The shorter Foxy Group is also very successful with Shrub roses such as some of the smaller Gallicas. Most foxgloves go well with pink, mauve, crimson and purple, and contrast with yellow-green.

**Perfect partners:** *Abutilon vitifolium* var. *album* p.76 **C**, *Euphorbia polychroma* 'Major' p.268 **B**, *Heuchera villosa* 'Palace Purple', *Meconopsis betonicifolia* p.312 **A**, *Rosa* 'Complicata' p.202 **A**, *R.* 'Fantin-Latour' p.195 **B**, *R.* 'Gruss an Aachen' p.213 **A**, *R. multiflora* p.190 **C**, *R.* 'Penelope' p.207 **B**

**H: 4–6½ ft.** (1.2–2 m) **S: 20 in.** (50 cm)
❀ **Early summer**
◊◊ ■-■ **Z5 pH4.5–8**

The handsome flowerheads of Miss Willmott's ghost (*Eryngium giganteum*), their striking silvery bracts with a hint of blue, benefit from the plain background of contrasting foliage provided by *Berberis thunbergii* 'Aurea'.

## *Eryngium giganteum* ♖
MISS WILLMOTT'S GHOST

In its usual cultivated form, this easy-to-grow biennial bears heads of flowers surrounded by jagged, pale silvery gray-green bracts, at times containing a hint of blue. Each plant makes an imposing candelabra of stems and is particularly effective when surrounded by lower planting and repeated as loosely scattered drifts. The ripening seedheads assume parchment tints, although dead and dying leaves can mar the effect unless screened. The coloring looks outstanding in a white garden or with silver or glaucous foliage; it is worth seeking out strains with more blue in the flowers to combine with cream, soft yellow or blue flowers. Whiter, frillier 'Silver Ghost' ♖ is excellent but should be kept apart from the more usual form if either is to breed true from seed.

**Perfect partners:** *Campanula* 'Burghaltii' p.247 **B**, *Eschscholzia californica* Thai Silk Series, *Glaucium corniculatum*, *Helianthemum* cultivars p.105 **B**, *Helictotrichon sempervirens*, *Lilium regale* p.377 **A**, *Salvia sclarea* 'Vatican White', *Stachys byzantina* p.336 **A**

H: **36 in.** (90 cm)  S: **12 in.** (30 cm)
✿ **Early to midsummer**

 ◊-◊◊ ▫-▪ **Z6 pH5–8**

## *Erysimum* × *marshallii* ♖
SIBERIAN WALLFLOWER

Later and neater than the common wallflower (below), the biennial Siberian wallflower, also known as *E.* × *alliozii*, forms a spreading mound of flowers in a vibrant orange, even richer in 'Orange Queen'; cultivars in other colors such as light orange, golden yellow and pale yellow are occasionally available. The flowers have a delicious scent; since plants prefer good drainage and full sun, they are also suitable for gravel gardens. They blend with peach, apricot, pale yellow, scarlet, yellow-green and bronze, and contrast with blue, purple and magenta. Good companions are forget-me-nots, late tulips and fritillaries.

**Perfect partners:** *Euphorbia polychroma* 'Major', *Iris* 'Curlew' p.297 **B**, *Muscari armeniacum*, *Tulipa* 'Elegant Lady', *T.* 'Queen of Night', *T.* 'Sweet Harmony' ❏ p.394 **A**

H: **20–24 in.** (50–60 cm)  S: **12 in.** (30 cm)
✿ **Late spring**

◊-◊◊ ▫-▪ **Z3 pH5.5–8**

The rich orange flowers and mahogany buds of the Siberian wallflower (*Erysimum* × *marshallii*) contrast effectively with blue alpine forget-me-nots (*Myosotis alpestris*). Bulbs could be planted through both of these, for example fritillaries, or tulips in cream, soft yellow or purple-black.

## *Erysimum cheiri*
COMMON WALLFLOWER

This biennial is indispensable for spring bedding in beds and borders, and as an underplanting for tulips or crown imperials. Single colors are best. The tallest kinds, 16 in. (40 cm) high, are good with taller tulips and come in a range of colors, including 'Blood Red', 'Cloth of Gold', vermilion 'Fire King', 'Purple Queen' and 'Vulcan', in deep crimson. Compact varieties are more limited: Bedder Series, 10–12 in. (25–30 cm) high, is gold, golden orange, primrose, or scarlet.

A mixture of the common wallflower (*Erysimum cheiri*) in warm colors combines beautifully with the bronze foliage of *Euphorbia dulcis* 'Chameleon'. This scheme could be used on a larger scale, perhaps together with bulbs such as crown imperials or cream or red tulips, with a backing of bronze-leaved shrubs such as *Berberis thunbergii* f. *atropurpurea* or *Acer palmatum* cultivars.

**Perfect partners:** *Brunnera macrophylla*, *Erysimum* 'Bowles Mauve' p.96 **A**, *Euphorbia griffithii* 'Dixter' p.267 **B**, *Heuchera* 'Plum Pudding' p.289 **A**, *Rosa* 'Helen Knight' p.205 **A**, *Tulipa* 'Abu Hassan' p.391 **A**, *T.* 'Apeldoorn' p.391 **C**, *T.* 'Burgundy' p.393 **B**, *T.* 'Greuze' p.396 **B**, *T.* 'Negrita' p.398 **C**, *T.* 'Queen of Night' p.401 **A**

H: **10–31 in.** (25–80 cm)  S: **12 in.** (30 cm)
✿ **Mid- to late spring**

◊-◊◊ ▫-▪ **Z7 pH5.5–8**

## *Eschscholzia californica* ♔
### CALIFORNIA POPPY

This colorful hardy annual, easily grown as a biennial in sheltered, warmer areas, ranges widely in size. Tall cultivars, about 18 in. (45 cm) high, include 'Alba', 'Purple Gleam' and 'Red Chief', while shorter kinds (12 in./30 cm) include Thai Silk Series, with fluted flowers in mixed or single colors. Single-colored cultivars with good silver foliage include 'Apricot Chiffon' and 'Rose Chiffon', and there are several fine orange and yellow kinds, such as 'Orange King'. All revel in a well-drained border or gravel garden, combined with scarlet poppies, sprawling anthemis and glaucous, yellow-green or bronze foliage. Shorter types are useful for covering the unattractive bases of Dwarf or Intermediate Bearded irises.

**Perfect partners:** *Anthemis punctata* subsp. *cupaniana*, *Cerinthe major* 'Purpurascens', *Glaucium corniculatum*, *Hordeum jubatum*, *Papaver somniferum* 'Danebrog'

**H: 12–18 in. (30–45 cm) S: 12 in. (30 cm)**
❀ **Early to late summer**
◌◌ ▢-■ Z9 pH5.5–7.5

In California, *Eschscholzia californica* grows as a biennial and flowers in spring, providing a decorative infill between young plants of the chaparral prickly pear cactus (*Opuntia oricola*), which requires the same climatic conditions.

## *Felicia petiolata*

Although often grown as an annual for summer, this plant is actually a sub-shrubby perennial. If given a sheltered microclimate such as within the skirts of a prostrate shrub (a cistus or ceanothus, for example), it can overwinter, even in some frost-prone areas, without protection and will scramble through the supporting shrub. Its flower color varies from a grubby blush-white to a good rose-pink, therefore if combining it with a cistus it is best to choose one in a contrasting color, either in pure white or rich magenta. This felicia is good for the front of a border.

**Perfect partners:** *Argyranthemum foeniculaceum* hort., *Cistus monspeliensis*, *C.* × *purpureus*, *Lavandula stoechas* subsp. *pedunculata*, *Osteospermum* 'Whirlygig'

**H: 18 in. (45 cm) S: 40 in. (1 m)**
❀ **Late spring to late summer**
◌◌ ▢-■ Z9 pH5.5–7.5

This attractive combination of the scrambling *Felicia petiolata* with the slightly hardier *Ceanothus thyrsiflorus* var. *repens* in a frost-prone area is made possible by a sunny microclimate and the protection given by the ceanothus to the felicia. Both plants flower profusely in late spring.

## *Fuchsia* 'Genii' ♔

An upright perennial of borderline hardiness, often grown for summer display, this fuchsia has yellow-green leaves that contrast with the red stems, and cherry-red flowers with a violet corolla that ages to purple-red. It is much more successful outdoors than under glass, where it often drops its buds and flowers, and the bushy growth may be difficult to control. Full sun is needed for maximum flowering, but it may be grown in moderate shade as a foliage plant. It is very effective with hot colors such as yellow, orange and, above all, scarlet, and is useful in pots with scarlet trailing verbenas. Like all fuchsias, it is prone to capsid damage. Yellow-green 'Cloth of Gold', and 'Mr. West', with cream and pale green variegated leaves, are other good foliage plants, but are less hardy.

In autumn, the contrasting flower and foliage colors of *Fuchsia* 'Genii' combine beautifully with other autumn-coloring foliage and fruits, such as those of the dwarf guelder rose (*Viburnum opulus* 'Compactum'). A backing of taller autumn-coloring shrubs could be added, with shorter flowers such as Charm chrysanthemums in front.

**Perfect partners:** *Canna* 'Striata', *Dahlia* 'Arabian Night', *Impatiens walleriana* 'Mega Orange Star', *Pelargonium* 'Orangesonne', *Petunia* Million Bells Lemon, *Salvia coccinea* 'Lady in Red', *Verbena* Temari Scarlet

**H & S: 31 in. (80 cm)**
❀ **Early summer to late autumn**

◌◌ ▢-■ Z9 pH4.5–7

A

The upright *Fuchsia* 'Thalia' adds height to this bold container planting, in which silver-leaved *Senecio viravira* is used to contrast with the fuchsia's dark foliage and bright flowers, as well as filling in around its stalky base. The Ivy-leaved, red-flowered *Pelargonium* 'Yale' scrambles through the senecio and tumbles over the side of the pot.

## Fuchsia 'Thalia' ♔

This vigorous tender perennial is typical of *F. triphylla* hybrids, which have a more erect habit and definite form than most fuchsia hybrids, useful for adding height to container plantings and as dot plants in bedding or in the second rank of a border. It bears red-flushed leaves with a purple-red underside, and bunches of coral-red hanging flowers, often confused with those of the very similar 'Gartenmeister Bonstedt' ♔, in which the flowers have a more bulging tube. 'Thalia' is best suited to subtle schemes in salmon-pink, peach, apricot and deep blood-red. It blends with deep-red foliage and contrasts well with silver, glaucous or yellow-green foliage, and also lime green flowers. Other excellent *F. triphylla* hybrids include 'Coralle', in salmon-pink, and 'Mary' ♔, in cherry-red.

**Perfect partners:** *Beta vulgaris* 'Bull's Blood', *B.v.* 'Mr. McGregor's Favourite', *Canna* 'Erebus', *Dahlia* 'Bishop of Llandaff', *Diascia rigescens*, *Nicotiana* 'Lime Green'

H: 31 in. (80 cm) S: 18 in. (45 cm)
❀ Early summer to late autumn
⬛⬛⬛ ◌◌ ⬜-⬛ Z10 pH5–7

C

By late spring, the winter rosettes of *Galactites tomentosa* have produced elongating shoots clad with elegant, pale and spiky leaves. Here, they conceal the dying foliage of *Allium hollandicum* and provide an infill between its flower stems in front of the contrasting yellow-green inflorescences of *Euphorbia characias* subsp. *wulfenii*.

## Gaillardia pulchella 'Red Plume'

Plume Series, perhaps the most reliable and uniform of the annual gaillardias, includes 'Red Plume' and 'Yellow Plume', whose even color, upright growth habit and fully double flowers make them invaluable for mixing with other annuals of similar habit and flowering season. 'Red Plume' has a distinct richness that adds depth and resonance to jazzier shades of scarlet and orange, and also contrasts effectively with mid-blue or yellow-green. *G.p.* var. *lorenziana*, with petals turned into elegant long trumpets, is usually offered in a double mixture, as is *G.p.* 'Lollipops', which blends bicolors with cream, yellow and blood-red.

**Perfect partners:** *Dimorphotheca pluvialis*, *Eschscholzia californica* 'Orange King', *Nicotiana langsdorffii*, *Osteospermum* 'White Pim', *Scabiosa atropurpurea* 'Blue Cockade'

H: 14 in. (35 cm) S: 6 in. (15 cm)
❀ Mid- to late summer
 ◌◌ ⬜-⬛ Z3–11 pH5.5–7.5

B

The warm, rich color of *Gaillardia pulchella* 'Red Plume' is here contrasted with the cool delicacy of blue lace flower (*Trachymene coerulea*), which was started under glass from a spring sowing. The domed flowerheads of both match perfectly in shape and size.

## Galactites tomentosa

The main attraction of this ornamental thistle is its spiky filigree leaves, heavily veined and netted with white. They are followed by light-mauve flowers, but plants become a little untidy soon after blooming starts. It is perhaps most useful grown as a biennial from a late summer or early autumn sowing, for planting between spring bulbs to help hide their dying leaves with the fresh rosettes of thistle foliage. The delicate leaf markings look best at close range, while the plant's outline can be emphasized by a dark background such as purple bugle or other low ground cover. It is an excellent subject for a white or silver garden, and can tolerate some drought.

**Perfect partners:** *Acaena microphylla* 'Kupferteppich', *Ajuga reptans* 'Atropurpurea', *Muscari latifolium*, *Narcissus* 'February Silver', *Tulipa* 'Ballerina', *T.* 'Elegant Lady'

H: 40 in. (1 m) S: 16 in. (40 cm)
❀ (Early to midsummer)
⬛⬛⬛ ◌◌ ⬜-⬛ Z8 pH5.5–7.5

## *Glaucium corniculatum*
RED HORNED POPPY

This sprawling, short-lived perennial, often grown as an annual or biennial, is a native of sea shores and so thrives in gravel gardens, although it also succeeds at the front of a dry, sunny border, in groups close to contrasting plants such as nasturtiums, teucriums and corydalis species. Its chief glory is its lobed, curled and sculptured glaucous foliage – its flowers usually appearing rather sparsely, especially in moist or rich soils. Its relatives the yellow-horned poppy (*Glaucium flavum*), orange-flowered *G.f.* f. *fulvum* and *G. leiocarpum* (deep-yellow to apricot flowers) are all used in the same way. They blend well with the shorter California poppy cultivars, whose habit and colorings are similar.

**Perfect partners:** *Atriplex hortensis* var. *rubra*, *Crambe maritima*, *Eryngium giganteum*, *Eschscholzia californica* Thai Silk Series, *Limnanthes douglasii*, *Papaver somniferum*

**H: 12 in.** (30 cm) **S: 16 in.** (40 cm)
❀ Early summer to early autumn
◊-◊◊ ▢-■ Z7 pH5.5–7.5

The red-horned poppy (*Glaucium corniculatum*) provides contrasting glaucous foliage and harmonious red flowers in front of *Helenium* 'Moerheim Beauty', whose rusty red blooms are borne just above the poppy.

## *Helianthus*
ANNUAL SUNFLOWER

Tall *H. annuus* scarcely interacts with other plants, but the less ungainly, branching hybrids produce bold effects in sunny borders. 'Velvet Queen', 6 ft. (1.8 m), is mahogany-red and a good foil for warm and hot colors; 'Prado Red' (syn. 'Ruby Sunset') is more uniform. Hybrids with pale creamy yellow flowers and a dark disk include 'Moonwalker', 'Valentine' ♀, and 'Vanilla Ice', all 5 ft. (1.5 m). Short types – such as gold *H.a.* 'Teddy Bear', 24 in. (60 cm), and clear yellow *H.a.* 'Pacino', 14 in. (35 cm) – look striking at the front of a border. Yellow and light orange sunflowers contrast well with blue or purple, and with bold glaucous foliage. The more subdued colors are good in autumnal schemes with buffs, bronzes and burnt oranges. All combine dramatically with heleniums and heliopsis.

**Perfect partners:** Yellow/light orange: *Arundo donax*, *Echinops bannaticus* 'Taplow Blue', *Macleaya cordata*
**Bright colors:** *Berberis* × *ottawensis* f. *purpurea* 'Superba', *Canna* 'Roi Humbert', *Dahlia* 'Alva's Doris'
**Subdued colors:** *Achillea filipendulina* 'Gold Plate' p.227 **A**, *Tithonia rotundifolia* 'Goldfinger' p.450 **C**

**H: 2–16 ft.** (60 cm–5 m) **S: 1–4 ft.** (30–120 cm)
❀ Midsummer to early autumn
◊◊ ▢-■ Z7–9 pH5–7

The sunflower *Helianthus* 'Moonwalker', a 5 ft. (1.5 m) tall hybrid derived from *H. annuus* and *H. debilis* subsp. *cucumerifolius*, branches to provide a succession of flowers, contrasting here with *Verbena hastata* and the spring-sown, short-growing sweet pea *Lathyrus odoratus* 'Chatsworth'.

The small-leaved *Helichrysum petiolare* 'Roundabout', its white-felted foliage edged with cream, intermingles with the sprawling tender perennial *Verbena* 'Kemerton', contrasting well with its magenta-purple flowers. This is a combination that could be used equally successfully in a container or at the front of a border.

## Helichrysum petiolare ♀

Grown for its gray-woolly leaves, this tender, sprawling shrub is very useful for containers, hanging baskets, and the front of borders. It is highly vigorous, but pale yellow-green 'Limelight' ♀ and 'Variegatum' ♀ have more restrained growth. All combine well with other sprawling plants of comparable vigour such as trailing petunias and verbenas, and all scramble freely into and over small shrubs. The species and its variegated sports combine with any colors. 'Limelight' contrasts well with blue flowers and glaucous foliage.

**Perfect partners:** *Agapanthus* 'Loch Hope' p.229 **A**, *Colchicum speciosum* 'Album' p.357 **C**, *Diascia* 'Dark Eyes' p.424 **B**, *Impatiens walleriana* p.430 **C**, *Lysimachia nummularia* 'Aurea', *Pelargonium* 'Hederinum', *Petunia* 'Buttercream' p.444 **B**, *P.* Million Bells Pink, *Rosa* 'American Pillar' p.187 **A**, *Scaevola aemula* p.449 **A**

H: 20 in. (50 cm)  S: 6½ ft. (2 m)
❀ Late summer to mid-autumn
◊◊ ☐-■ Z9 pH5–7.5

Busy Lizzies (*Impatiens walleriana*), seen here in a mixture, can be solid in outline, especially in the case of some compact modern cultivars, and almost too densely covered in bloom. Here, the mass of flowers on rounded plants is broken up by trails of silvery *Helichrysum petiolare*.

## Impatiens walleriana
BUSY LIZZIE

Unlike most bedding plants, this tender sub-shrubby perennial thrives in shade, with its flowers facing in all directions, so it is very useful for window boxes and other plantings to be viewed from the shady side. The colors range from white through salmon-pink, mauve-pink, vermilion, and red to magenta-purple; Starbright Mixed and some of Accent Series have white-striped petals, and there are also picotee cultivars such as Swirl Series. Modern cultivars tend to be short, typically 10–15 cm (4–6 in) high, and make useful carpets for other flowers to grow through, but taller kinds, such as Blitz Series (18 in./ 45 cm), are more generally garden-worthy. All are effective with bronze, silver or yellow-green foliage plants, and associate easily with diascias and pelargoniums. Many busy Lizzie colors contrast well with lime green flowers.

**Perfect partners:** *Antirrhinum majus* Coronet Series, *Begonia* (Semperflorens Cultorum Group) Cocktail Series, *Lobelia × speciosa* 'Fan Orchidrosa' p.433 **A**, *Scaevola aemula* p.449 **A**

H: 4–24 in. (10–60 cm)  S: 8–24 in. (20–60 cm)
❀ Early summer to mid-autumn
◊◊ ☐-■ Z10 pH5–7

## Heliotropium arborescens 'Princess Marina' ♀

The rich purple flowers and dark foliage of this compact, tender sub-shrub provide an excellent base accompaniment for brighter flowers and bolder shapes; its seductive and pervasive scent is an added bonus. Harmonies with pale to mid-lavender blue, mauve, or magenta flowers are effective, as are contrasts with soft orange, apricot, pale yellow, and lime green; stark contrasts are possible with silver-leaved plants such as *Helichrysum petiolare* cultivars. This heliotrope combines successfully with taller ageratums, mauve or carmine busy Lizzies, and sprawling and more upright verbenas.

**Perfect partners:** *Ageratum houstonianum* 'Old Gray', *Argyranthemum foeniculaceum* hort., *Dahlia* 'Yelno Harmony', *Impatiens walleriana* 'Mosaic Lilac', *Verbena* Temari Scarlet

H & S: 12 in. (30 cm)
❀ Early summer to mid-autumn
◊◊ ☐-■ Z10 pH5.5–8

The rich purple blooms and dark leaves of *Heliotropium arborescens* 'Princess Marina' tend to be recessive, not showing up well from a distance unless lifted by paler flowers or foliage, such as the brightly edged *Plectranthus madagascariensis* 'Variegated Mintleaf'. Both of these plants are suited to bedding, the front of borders or containers.

## *Ipomoea tricolor* 'Mini Sky-blue'

This restrained morning glory (a tender perennial usually grown as an annual) is excellent in the second rank of a sunny border or in containers in a sunlit spot. Here it will scramble over neighboring plants, introducing a natural grace that other annuals and bedding plants often lack. Its flowers, which tend to close at about midday, are sky-blue, in some cases with a hint of mauve, and very effective with yellow-green or glaucous foliage, or with blue, white or cream flowers, and in contrasts with yellow flowers. Companion plants need to be sturdy enough to support its meandering stems, so small to medium-sized shrubs or sub-shrubs make the best hosts. Suitable partners are some smaller deutzias, forsythias, fuchsias, hypericums, philadelphus, rosemaries and weigelas.

**Perfect partners:** *Argyranthemum* 'Jamaica Primrose', *Berberis thunbergii* 'Aurea', *Ceanothus* × *delileanus* 'Gloire de Versailles', *Coronilla valentina* subsp. *glauca*, *Fuchsia magellanica* var. *gracilis*, *Salvia guaranitica*

**H: 4 ft.** (1.2 m)   **S: 10–18 in.** (25–45 cm)
❀ **Midsummer to early autumn**

▨▨▨▨▨  ◌◌  ▨  **Z10  pH6–8**

*Ipomoea tricolor* 'Mini Sky-blue' here weaves over and through two tender sub-shrubby perennials used as summer bedding plants: harmonious rich lavender *Salvia farinacea* 'Blue Victory' and gently contrasting creamy yellow variegated, white-flowered *Osteospermum* 'Silver Sparkler'.

A carpet of *Lantana camara* 'Orange Beauty' provides a foil for the spectacular and extravagant purple-flushed, variegated foliage of *Canna* 'Durban'. The canna will soon bear orange flowers matching those of the lantana.

## Lantana camara 'Orange Beauty'

A tender scrambling sub-shrub, 'Orange Beauty' is an adaptable plant that may be used in summer containers and in bedding schemes, or as temporary ground cover. The florets open golden yellow from orange buds and age to vermilion, giving gradations of color within the same flowerhead, blending well with hot colors, yellow-green, and bronze or red foliage, and contrasting with blue flowers. When used as bedding, it can be massed beneath accent plants, including canna. In a border it is successful used with rich blue or white agapanthus, coreopsis, heleniums, crocosmias, larger gold-variegated grasses, and bronze sedges or bronze-flowered pennisetums.

**Perfect partners:** *Agapanthus* 'Lilliput', *Carex comans* (bronze), *Cordyline australis* Purpurea Group, *Miscanthus sinensis* 'Strictus', *Ricinus communis* 'Impala'

H: 12 in. (30 cm) S: 5 ft. (1.5 m)
Late spring to late autumn
Z10 pH5.5–7

If grown as a biennial, the poached egg plant (*Limnanthes douglasii*) blooms in late spring, when the foliage of purple sage (*Salvia officinalis* 'Purpurascens') is most colorful. It will flower again in autumn from self-sown seedlings.

## Lavatera trimestris

This loosely informal hardy annual suits mixed or herbaceous borders and cottage garden schemes. It has rounded flowers in white to deep pink, the latter often with pretty veining and deeper centers. It mixes well with cool colors and purple or silver foliage, including artemisias and heucheras, while the richer, deeper pinks contrast with yellow-green or lime green. Flowers of contrasting form make good companions, especially clarkias and spiky panicles of salvias; further back in the border hollyhocks can echo its shape. Other partners include opium poppies, argyranthemums, verbenas, antirrhinums, larkspurs and asters. Plants sown in autumn flower in early to late summer; those sown in spring bloom in midsummer to early autumn.

**Perfect partners:** *Alcea rosea* Chater's Double Group, *Consolida ajacis* (blue) p.417 **A**, *Gypsophila paniculata* 'Bristol Fairy', *Nicotiana* 'Lime Green', *Veronica spicata*

H: 20–48 in. (50–120 cm) S: 12–18 in. (30–45 cm)
Early summer to early autumn
Z7 pH5.5–7.5

Pairing *Lavatera trimestris* 'Rose Beauty', its flowers just to the blue side of primary pink, with scarlet *Salvia coccinea* 'Lady in Red' gives the frisson of a near clash and contrast of form. The salvia furnishes the lavatera's bare base.

## Limnanthes douglasii
POACHED EGG PLANT

The five-petaled flowers of the poached egg plant are almost round in outline, each petal usually having a yellow base and a white tip; all-white and all-yellow variants are also available. It is useful for the front of a border, for rock gardens and walls, and beside paths. It combines well with warm or hot colors, blue and yellow-green, and looks good with silver carpeting plants such as blue or orange nemesias, shorter artemisias, shorter glaucous or yellow-green grasses, sea kale and some delphinium cultivars. Other partners include anthemis, nemophilas, alchemillas, echiums, marigolds and nasturtiums. It is an annual, but in sheltered and warmer areas it can be grown as a biennial from autumn sowings.

**Perfect partners:** *Crambe maritima*, *Echium vulgare* 'Blue Bedder', *Festuca glauca* 'Blaufuchs', *Iris* 'Nightfall' p.296 **B**, *Nemesia strumosa* 'Blue Gem', *Nigella damascena* 'Miss Jekyll', *Tagetes tenuifolia* 'Tangerine Gem'

H & S: 6 in. (15 cm) Late spring to late autumn
Z8 pH5.5–7.5

In this semi-formal bedding scheme, magenta *Lobelia ×
speciosa* 'Fan Orchidrosa' is planted close to the edge of the
bed, its bold vertical spikes emphasizing the bed's curve.
Gently clashing busy Lizzies (*Impatiens walleriana* 'Accent
Salmon'), on the opposite side of primary deep pink to the
lobelia, furnishes below and between.

## *Lobelia* 'Fan Orchidrosa' ♛

This is a short-lived hardy herbaceous
perennial with a narrow habit, useful for
bedding in drifts or as a dot plant, for
waterside planting, and for massing in moist
mixed or herbaceous borders. Its magenta
flowers, borne in erect spikes, combine well
with dark foliage such as red orach and
purple-leaved heucheras, and cool-colored
flowers and yellow-green or gold variegated
grasses. It contrasts gently with sulfur-yellow
flowers and yellow-green foliage and flowers
or, more vibrantly, with orange or vermilion
flowers. In bedding schemes, it can be
combined with lavateras and cleomes, and in
borders with phlox and late astilbes.

**Perfect partners:** *Atriplex hortensis* var. *rubra*,
*Euphorbia schillingii*, *Hakonechloa macra*
'Aureola', *Nicotiana* 'Lime Green', *Tithonia
rotundifolia* 'Sundance', *Verbena rigida*

**H: 28 in.** (70 cm)  **S: 12 in.** (30 cm)
✿ **Midsummer to mid-autumn**

 ◊◊-◊◊◊ ▪ Z6 pH5.5–7.5

## *Lobelia richardsonii* ♛

Usually raised as an annual from cuttings,
this is a tender evergreen perennial, similar to
*Lobelia erinus* cultivars, from which it differs
mainly in its larger size. It is a good pot and
hanging basket plant that can also be used in
bedding and at the front of a border. Its pale
sky-blue flowers blend with cool colors and
silver and glaucous foliage, and contrast well
with yellow-green foliage or flowers and soft
yellow blooms. It looks very effective with
*Helichrysum petiolare* cultivars, petunias,
especially smaller-flowered cultivars, and
achimenes. When grown on its own, it has
a prostrate habit, but next to a plant of
modest height, such as *Hebe* 'Quicksilver',
it will scramble through its companion.

**Perfect partners:** *Argyranthemum
foeniculaceum* hort., *Bidens ferulifolia*
'Shining Star', *Festuca glauca* 'Blaufuchs',
*Petunia* Million Bells Lemon, *Tagetes tenuifolia*
'Lemon Gem'

**H: 4 in.** (10 cm)  **S: 12 in.** (30 cm)
 ✿ **Early summer to mid-autumn**

▬▬▬▭ ◊◊ ▪ Z10 pH5.5–7.5

In a partially shaded bed beneath trees, there is sufficient
light for *Lobelia richardsonii* to flower freely and for Bowles
golden sedge (*Carex elata* 'Aurea') to color well. This site
also suits the handsomely goffered hart's tongue fern
(*Asplenium scolopendrium* 'Crispum Bolton's Nobile'),
which thrives in shade and becomes scorched by the sun.

*Lunaria annua* 'Variegata' contrasts effectively with tulips in this spring border. The variegated honesty makes a suitable companion for many other late-flowering bulbs, including blue Dutch irises such as 'Wedgwood'.

## *Lunaria annua* 'Variegata'
VARIEGATED BIENNIAL HONESTY

An easy biennial with white, lilac or reddish purple flowers, this is noted for its variegated leaves, entirely green at first but developing a creamy marginal mottling that matures to a pure, creamy white edge as plants flower. At this time, it combines well with other late spring flowers such as bluebells, camassias, comfreys and columbines, together with most cool-colored flowers and purple foliage plants. It can be contrasted with orange and soft yellow or yellow-green. Because it grows mainly when deciduous shrubs and most herbaceous plants are out of leaf, it can be used between these, toward the back of a mixed border, together with pale yellow, cream or pink brooms, and early peonies.

**Perfect partners:** *Camassia cusickii* 'Zwanenburg', *Gladiolus tristis* var. *concolor* p.367 **A**, *Hyacinthoides non-scripta*, *Iris* 'Grapesicle', *Narcissus* 'Actaea'

**H: 36 in.** (90 cm)  **S: 12 in.** (30 cm)
❀ **Late spring to early summer**
⬛⬛⬛⬜ ◊◊ ⬜-⬛ **Z4–8 pH5.5–8**

After being cut to the ground by winter cold, *Melianthus major* makes an imposing mound of magnificent foliage by the following autumn, in color matching exactly that of the lyme grass (*Leymus arenarius*) in front, although contrasting markedly in form. Beside it, the tiny leaflets of a double white form of the Scotch rose (*Rosa spinosissima*) take on fiery tints before being shed.

## *Melianthus major* ♔

This tender shrub has vast glaucous, pinnate leaves and spikelike racemes of mahogany flowers that are perhaps more fascinating than beautiful. It is excellent for helping to create a tropical effect and provide a unifying theme with flowers or foliage of similar color in borders and big containers. Its leaves blend particularly well with white, blue or yellow-green flowers, silver or glaucous foliage and white-variegated plants. It is especially good with foliage of contrasting form, including grasses such as variegated arundo and miscanthus cultivars, and eucalyptus that has been stooled or grown from seed as a bedding plant. Other suitable partners include wigandias, argyranthemums, agapanthus, eryngiums, glaucous cannas and palms (either young plants or those that are naturally low-growing and suckering).

**Perfect partners:** *Canna* 'Erebus', *Chamaerops humilis*, *Cosmos bipinnatus* 'Sonata White', *Eucalyptus gunnii* (stooled), *Miscanthus sinensis* 'Variegatus', *Tetrapanax papyrifer*

**H: 6½–10 ft.** (2–3 m)  **S: 3¼–6½ ft.** (1–2 m)
❀ **Late spring to midsummer**
⬛⬛⬛⬜ ◊◊ ⬜-⬛ **Z9 pH5.5–7.5**

## *Malva sylvestris*
COMMON MALLOW

This highly variable species is a short-lived perennial but variants often behave as biennials, and all forms may be grown as annuals. The typical species is floriferous, blooming mainly in early to midsummer, and is suitable for a wild garden. Forms include white *M.s.* f. *alba*; lavender-blue 'Primley Blue'; 'Brave Heart' (magenta with purple-black veins and base); and *M.s.* subsp. *mauritanica* (magenta flowers marked in deep purple-black with a purple base). Mauve 'Zebrina', vigorous lavender Marina ('Dema') and lilac 'Highnam' are all good with cool colors; the more richly hued variants can be contrasted with soft yellow, yellow-green or orange.

**Perfect partners:** *Achillea* 'Moonshine', *Briza maxima*, *Calendula officinalis* 'Orange King', *Crocosmia* 'Lucifer' p.255 **C**, *Euphorbia cyparissias*, *Nicotiana* 'Lime Green'

**H: 8–48 in.** (20–120 cm)  **S: 12–24 in.** (30–60 cm)
❀ **Late spring to mid-autumn**
 ◊◊ ⬜-⬛ **Z5–9 pH5.5–8**

In this harmony of crimson flowers of similar outline, *Malva sylvestris* 'Brave Heart' mingles with *Knautia macedonica* and *Lychnis coronaria* Atrosanguinea Group, whose gray-green stems and foliage leaven the scheme.

# *Musa* and *Ensete*

BANANA

Despite being regarded widely as trees, these are tender herbaceous perennials with stems that can survive for several years, especially if wrapped up with insulation to protect it from frost in cool areas. As an alternative in cold gardens, they can be overwintered under cover and planted out as a bedding plant, to create a tropical impact or contribute to the boldest, large-scale foliage effects. Their impressive bright green leaves arch out languidly from a stem composed of the furled leaf bases, and can reach 10 ft. (3 m) long in humid positions and moist, fertile soils, although 6 ft. (1.8 m) is more usual. These stems and their leaves die after flowering, and are replaced by suckers from the surviving rootstock.

Good large-leaved partners include stooled paulownias, tetrapanax, gunneras and large grasses such as arundos and bamboos, as well as palms, colocasias, wigandias and castor-oil plants. In favored areas, plants can produce dramatic brown inflorescences, in large, pendent spikes with the buds enclosed in conspicuous bracts, followed by small greenish banana fruits. Although usually used for planting on a grand scale, it is useful for smaller gardens where a dramatically over-scale effect is wanted. It benefits from a sheltered situation because strong winds can shred the leaves, making them look unsightly.

Other bananas for the same conditions and uses include *M. velutina*, 6 ft. (1.8 m) high, with leaves 3–4 ft. (90–120 cm) long and upright spikes of yellow flowers and red bracts. 'Dwarf Cavendish' ♀ is a hardier, more compact cultivar of *M. acuminata*, the main parent of most edible bananas, and in a warm summer can ripen hands of sweet fruits on plants that grow to 10 ft. (3 m) high. Most other banana species are too tender for outdoor cultivation in climates cooler than Zone 10.

**Perfect partners:** *Arundo donax, Canna indica* 'Purpurea', *Catalpa bignonioides* (stooled), *Rheum palmatum, Ricinus communis* 'Carmencita' p.445 **B**

**H: 9 ft. (2.7 m) S: 6½ ft. (2 m)**
✿ **Mid- to late summer**
◾▭ ◌◌ ▭-◼ ◼ Z9 pH5.5–7

Even where summers are barely warm, *Ensete ventricosum* can supply luxuriant tropical effect, provided its growing point and rootstock do not freeze in winter. In this scheme of green foliage, it makes a bold focus behind the curious *Amicia zygomeris*, with its maroon-shaded stipules, and the handsome palmate house lime, *Sparrmannia africana*.

A

## *Myosotis sylvatica*
WOOD FORGET-ME-NOT

Often grown as a biennial, this short-lived perennial, with saucer-shaped, yellow-eyed, blue or white flowers, has a loose, airy habit suitable for informal parts of the garden. It harmonizes well with ipheions, muscari, narcissi, tulips, primroses, yellow or cream wallflowers, white rock cress and *Aurinia saxatilis* cultivars.

**Perfect partners:** *Allium hollandicum* p.349 **B**, *Artemisia ludoviciana* p.237 **B**, *Geranium albanum* p.273 **A**, *Gymnocarpium dryopteris* p.281 **A**, *Iris* 'Grapesicle' p.297 **C**, *I.* 'Wedgwood' p.371 **A**, *Narcissus* 'Actaea' p.378 **C**, *N.* 'Hawera' p.382 **B**, *Polemonium caeruleum* p.323 **B**, *Primula veris* p.327 **A**, *Stachys byzantina* p.336 **A**, *Tulipa* 'Burgundy' p.393 **B**, *T.* 'China Pink' p.393 **C**, *T.* 'Cordell Hull' p.394 **C**, *T.* 'Elegant Lady' p.395 **A**, *T.* 'Palestrina' p.400 **B** ❏ p.162 **B**

H: 8–12 in. (20–30 cm) S: 6 in. (15 cm)
✿ Mid-spring to early summer

 Z5 pH4.5–7.5

The self-sown sky-blue *Myosotis sylvatica* forms a striking contrast with the swordlike foliage of *Libertia peregrinans*, which adopts an orange-brown hue, especially bright along the midribs of the leaves, in winter through to late spring.

## *Nemesia* 'Innocence' ♛

The yellow-lipped white flowers of this tender sub-shrub are charming at close range, but its rather amorphous growth habit suits it to a supporting role with plants of more definite structure. It is attractive in pots and hanging baskets, and at the front of a border, where it combines successfully with silver foliage and most flower colors, especially blue. Like all nemesias, it resents prolonged drought and enjoys similar conditions to diascias, with which it can be grown to create a froth of pale colors as a background for plants that have a more solid shape. Deadheading can help to prolong flowering. Cuttings may be taken in late summer for overwintering under glass.

**Perfect partners:** *Alonsoa warscewiczii*, *Antirrhinum majus* 'Black Prince', *Artemisia schmidtiana*, *Diascia rigescens*, *Pericallis* × *hybrida* 'Royalty Sky Blue', *Salvia farinacea* 'Strata', *Verbena* 'Lawrence Johnston'

H: 18 in. (45 cm) S: 24 in. (60 cm)
✿ Late spring to mid-autumn

 Z9 pH5–7

Sparkling white, yellow-lipped blooms of *Nemesia* 'Innocence' contrast dramatically against the mahogany-red flowers and foliage of *Sedum telephium* 'Arthur Branch'.

## *Nemophila menziesii*
BABY BLUE EYES

This is a pretty annual for the front of a border, where it can sprawl over the edge of adjacent paving or scramble into nearby plants. The bright blue flowers, with lighter blue centers often stained white or yellow, are particularly effective combined with white, cream or yellow flowers, and yellow-green, glaucous and white- or gold-variegated foliage. Attractive color variants include var. *atomaria* (pure white flowers) and var. *discoidalis* (purple-black, edged with white), sometimes sold as 'Penny Black'. All may be grown as annuals if sown in early to late spring, or as biennials from sowings in late summer or early autumn. This plant cannot survive drought but will tolerate a little shade, especially in sunnier climates.

**Perfect partners:** *Argyranthemum* 'Jamaica Primrose', *Euphorbia rigida* (foliage), *Hakonechloa macra* 'Alboaurea', *Limnanthes douglasii*, *Spiraea japonica* 'Goldflame'

H: 8 in. (20 cm) S: 12 in. (30 cm)
✿ Early to late summer

 Z7 pH5.5–7.5

In early summer, the blue flowers of baby blue eyes (*Nemophila menziesii*) are joined in this flat area of planting by the white flowers of *Osteospermum* 'Gold Sparkler', with their slaty reverses, contrasting yellow *Viola aetolica*, and the five-spot (*Nemophila maculata*), to produce a charming millefleurs tapestry of flowers.

## *Nicotiana* **Domino Series** ♔

Upturned, brightly colored flowers adorn these popular plants, which are perennials usually grown as annuals. Being among the taller bedding nicotianas, they can be used toward the front of a herbaceous or mixed border. They are available in crimson, red, purple, white and salmon-pink; some have white eyes or petals edged with a different color. Lime green 'Domino Lime Green' is paler and less acid than *N.* 'Lime Green' (see p.438) and is very effective mixed with white or salmon-pink. 'Domino Red' combines well with hot colors and purple, bronze or red foliage. Unlike with some nicotianas, the florets of all Domino Series stay open during the day, but lack fragrance.

In recent years, many flowering nicotianas planted in Europe have been killed by tobacco blue mold. The risks are decreased by growing a few widely spaced plants, and spraying with fungicide. Old plants should be removed at the end of the flowering season.

**Perfect partners:** *Canna indica* 'Purpurea', *Cosmos bipinnatus, Helichrysum petiolare, Heuchera* 'Plum Pudding', *Perilla frutescens* var.

**Top:** In this richly colored scheme, *Nicotiana* 'Domino Red' is joined by the flat yellow flowerheads of *Achillea filipendulina* 'Gold Plate', the yellow daisy flowers of *Rudbeckia laciniata* 'Herbstsonne', bright red *Dahlia* 'Bishop of Llandaff', the orange spikes of *Kniphofia uvaria* 'Nobilis', orange *Crocosmia paniculata* and *C.* 'Vulcan', the puckered leaves of the beets *Beta vulgaris* 'Mr. McGregor's Favourite' and *B.v.* 'Rhubarb Chard', pelargoniums and verbenas.

**Above:** This is a charming combination of two gently contrasting tobacco plants, *Nicotiana* 'Domino Salmon Pink' and 'Domino Lime Green'.

*crispa, Plectranthus argentatus, Rosa* 'Frensham', *R.* Iceberg, *Salvia farinacea* 'Cirrus', *Verbena* 'Lawrence Johnston'

**H: 16 in. (40 cm)  S: 8 in. (20 cm)**
❀ **Early summer to mid-autumn**
▬▬▬ ◌◌ ⬜-⬛ ⬛ Z9 pH5–7.5

## *Nicotiana langsdorffii* ♔

This annual nicotiana has nodding, rich apple-green flowers, which are rounded at the mouth and borne on slender stems. The flowers are best viewed at close range or, if planted some distance away, they benefit from a background of very dark foliage. Plants combine well with yellow-green, silver, purple or reddish foliage, and with white or pure blue flowers; satisfying contrasts can be made with scarlet, salmon-pink, or rich deep pink. Other nicotianas such as *N.* 'Lime Green' and 'Domino Lime Green' also make excellent partners. While *N. langsdorffii* can reach 5 ft. (1.5 m), it is often much shorter. It is fairly resistant to tobacco blue mold.

**Perfect partners:** *Consolida* 'Frosted Skies', *Cotinus coggygria* 'Royal Purple', *Delphinium* 'Sungleam', *Hydrangea paniculata* 'Greenspire' p.108 **B**, *Onopordum nervosum*

**H: 4 ft. (1.2 m)  S: 16 in. (40 cm)**
❀ **Early summer to mid-autumn**
▬▬▬ ◌◌ ⬜-⬛ ⬛ Z10 pH5 7.5

In this blend of flowers and foliage in subdued colorings, two species tobaccos are used, not for their "flower power," but for their elegant form. In the foreground, *Nicotiana langsdorffii* casts a veil of nodding apple-green bells in front of the handsome foliage of *N. sylvestris*, whose extraordinary, long-tubed flowers cascade in front of a backdrop of the feathery cut-leaved elder, *Sambucus racemosa* 'Plumosa Aurea'.

The elegant, slightly nodding flowers of *Nicotiana* 'Lime Green' are never more effectively contrasted than when combined with scarlet flowers and dark foliage, as here with *Dahlia* 'Bishop of Llandaff', a good partnership for containers or towards the front of a border.

## *Nicotiana* 'Lime Green' ♀

The striking yellowish green of this annual nicotiana's flowers is a sharper, more definite color than that of 'Domino Lime Green' (see p.437), and better suited to creating contrasts with scarlet, coral and pure blue flowers, as well as with reddish, purple or bronze foliage. Like the yellow-green of *Alchemilla mollis*, it is a color that blends easily with most others, whether in gentle contrasts or to make pleasing harmonies such as may be achieved with yellow, white, or cream flowers, and glaucous or yellow-variegated foliage. The slightly airy, open growth habit helps plants withstand cool, wet weather; it also enables them to resist tobacco blue mould more successfully than some of the more congested modern cultivars.

**Perfect partners:** *Alstroemeria psittacina* p.232 **C**, *Ipomoea tricolor* 'Mini Sky-blue', *Lobelia richardsonii*, *Pelargonium* 'Paul Crampel' p.442 **A**, *Penstemon* 'Chester Scarlet'

**H:** 24 in. (60 cm)  **S:** 10 in. (25 cm)
❀ **Early summer to mid-autumn**
◊◊ ▢-▦ ▇ **Z9  pH5–7.5**

## *Nigella damascena*
LOVE-IN-A-MIST

Cultivars of this annual are usually blue, but may be white or pink. The most popular is 'Miss Jekyll' ♀, 18 in. (45 cm), with double sky-blue flowers, together with 'Miss Jekyll Dark Blue', 'Miss Jekyll Rose' and 'Miss Jekyll Alba' ♀. 'Oxford Blue', 30 in. (75 cm), is similar in color to 'Miss Jekyll Dark Blue'; Persian Jewel Series, 16 in. (40 cm), is usually sold as a mixture of blues, pinks and white. All look especially fine in gravel. They bear distinctive, inflated seedpods and feathery foliage that is a useful filigree infill between more solid plants such as Bearded irises, and helps hide the dying foliage of bulbs.

**Perfect partners:** *Achillea* 'Moonshine', *Allium cristophii* p.348 **B**, *Geranium* × *oxonianum* f. *thurstonianum* p.275 **B**, *Rosa gallica* 'Versicolor' p.196 **B**, *R.* 'Raubritter' p.217 **A**, *R.* 'Tuscany Superb' p.198 **B**

**H:** 8–30 in. (20–75 cm)  **S:** 6–9 in. (15–23 cm)
❀ **Early to late summer**
◊◊ ▢-▦ ▇ **Z6  pH5–7.5**

This charmingly simple, single variant of love-in-a mist (*Nigella damascena*) exactly matches exotic-looking *Rehmannia elata* in height, mingling attractively with it.

## *Oenothera biennis*
COMMON EVENING PRIMROSE

The large, sweetly scented, lemon-yellow flowers of this biennial open in the evening and close the following morning. Its relatively undistinguished foliage and growth habit are best screened by shorter plants such as lavenders, catmints, and white-flowered cistus or halimiocistus growing in front. It revels in sharply drained soils, even those low in nutrients, and self-seeds freely. Other comparable species include *O. stricta* and its pale cultivar 'Sulphurea', 31 in. (80 cm) tall, and *O. glazioviana* (syns *O. erythrosepala*, *O. lamarckiana*), 6½ ft. (2 m) high, with soft yellow flowers and mahogany-colored sepals.

*Watsonia meriania*, a tender corm whose flowers range from pink to red or purple, is an unusual companion for the fully hardy evening primrose (*Oenothera biennis*). Both need the same conditions of well-drained soil in a sunny position. Here, the combination is enhanced by bold clumps of ornamental grasses.

**Perfect partners:** *Buphthalmum salicifolium* p.246 **C**, *Deschampsia cespitosa* 'Bronzeschleier', *Lavandula angustifolia* 'Hidcote', *Nepeta* 'Six Hills Giant'

**H:** 5 ft. (1.5 m)  **S:** 24 in. (60 cm)
❀ **Early summer to early autumn**
◊◊ ▢-▦ ▇ **Z4  pH5–7.5**

## *Onopordum nervosum* 🏆

Plenty of space is essential for this biennial cotton thistle to develop its huge candelabra of silvery stems with jagged leaves. It is an imposing architectural plant, especially effective against a dark background or in planting schemes based on white flowers and silver foliage. The mauve thistle flowers add little to the impact of what is primarily a foliage plant, invaluable for use as bold punctuation or as a unifying theme if planted at intervals along a border. It prefers sharply drained soils. Young leaf rosettes should not be crowded by neighbors, and larger specimens may need support to prevent the whole plant from keeling over prematurely.

**Perfect partners:** *Acanthus spinosus, Artemisia ludoviciana* 'Silver Queen', *Cotinus coggygria* 'Royal Purple', *Crambe cordifolia, Lavatera* × *clementii* 'Barnsley', *Miscanthus sacchariflorus, M. sinensis* 'Variegatus', *Rosa* 'Highdownensis', *R.* 'Pink Perpétué' p.192 **A**, *Salix exigua, Sambucus nigra* 'Guincho Purple' ❑ p.420 **B**

**H: 10 ft.** (3 m) **S: 3¼ ft.** (1 m)
**Mid- to late summer**
**Z6 pH5.5–7.5**

The dramatic pale leaves of *Onopordum nervosum* transform this subtly colored scheme, which blends pink blooms of *Pimpinella major* 'Rosea' and *Rosa glauca* with glaucous foliage from the rose and *Thalictrum flavum* subsp. *glaucum*, which also contributes yellow-green buds.

## *Orlaya grandiflora*

This annual umbellifer, with lacy white flowers set off by rich green, feathery leaves, may be used in the same way as *Nigella damascena* (opposite page), as a filigree foil to plants of more definite architectural form. It blends well with other annuals, such as common poppies, cornflowers and corn marigolds, to produce a tapestry of color. A sunny position is essential, together with a soil that is rich enough to encourage the plant to develop a well-branched structure and so continue longer in flower.

**Perfect partners:** *Allium hollandicum* 'Purple Sensation', *Aquilegia vulgaris* (mixed), *Centaurea cyanus* 'Blue Diadem', *C. montana, Iris sibirica* 'Cambridge', *Paeonia officinalis, Papaver rhoeas* (Shirley Group) 'Cedric Morris', *Rosa* Avalanche p.211 **A**, *Tulipa* 'Ballerina', *T.* 'Elegant Lady', *Glebionis segeta* 'Prado'

**H: 24 in.** (60 cm) **S: 18 in.** (45 cm)
**Late spring to midsummer**
**Z6 pH5.5–7.5**

The filigree foliage and lacy flowers of *Orlaya grandiflora* furnish the base of *Phormium* 'Maori Sunrise', softening the plant's rather bold form and strong coloring.

The carpeting habit of *Osteospermum* 'White Pim'(syn. *O. ecklonis* var. *prostratum*) allows it to be used at the front of a shallowly banked border, in a bed of fairly flat planting or in a large rock garden, with other plants of similar low and spreading habit, such as *Veronica austriaca* subsp. *teucrium* 'Kapitän', seen here.

## *Osteospermum* 'White Pim' 🏆

A tender evergreen sub-shrub usually grown, like many osteospermums, as a half-hardy annual, 'White Pim' has shining white ray petals, often slightly mauve-flushed, arranged round a glistening marcasite center. It is an excellent mat-forming plant for the front of beds and borders, and for pots, especially combined with cool colors and glaucous, silver or purple foliage. Other more shrubby, upright osteospermums are ideal for adding height to bedding and container planting. There are long-flowering varieties in colors from rich yellow to white, mauve-pink and purple; some, such as 'Whirlygig' 🏆 and Nasinga Series, have spoon-shaped petals. Similar in many ways to argyranthemums, they generally have less appealing foliage and cannot tolerate long periods of drought; their range includes unrivalled rich purple shades.

**Perfect partners:** *Aeonium* 'Zwartkop', *Argyranthemum* 'Jamaica Primrose', *Brachyscome iberidifolia, Felicia petiolata, Nemophila menziesii, Plectranthus argentatus*

**H: 6 in.** (15 cm) **S: 24 in.** (60 cm)
**Late spring to mid-autumn**
**Z8 pH5.5–7.5**

## Papaver rhoeas

COMMON POPPY

Sometimes called Flanders poppy or field poppy, this annual can be used in its wild, scarlet-flowered state or as cultivars to create flowery meads on sunny sites with well-drained, even rather poor soil. In this role they may be combined with other annuals or biennials such as corn cockles, *Ammi majus* and *Phacelia tanacetifolia*. The most famous variant, Shirley poppy, includes white and pink shades and varied picotees. Selections from these include Cedric Morris Group, Fairy

Wings Group and Mother of Pearl Group. The double Angels' Choir Group mixture is longer-flowering. Selections in which scarlet and salmon predominate may be used for harmonies with peach, apricot and white, or for contrasts with pure blue, and also blend well with glaucous, bronze or reddish foliage. Those with smoky tints work well with carmine, lilac, mauve and magenta flowers, and silver foliage.

**Perfect partners:** *Agrostemma githago, Briza maxima, Centaurea cyanus, Leucanthemum vulgare, Malva sylvestris, Papaver somniferum, Rosa* 'De Rescht' p.195 **A**

**Above left:** If given space to make large, vigorous plants, double *Papaver rhoeas* Angels' Choir Group will bloom into late summer, the red flowers it contains harmonizing with *Crocosmia masoniorum* 'Dixter Flame'.

**Above:** Although once containing only pastel colors, double Shirley poppies now often comprise mostly richer tints, allowing warm-colored combinations with *Calendula officinalis* Fiesta Gitana Series.

**H: 10–16 in.** (25–40 cm) **S: 12 in.** (30 cm)
❀ **Early to late summer**

Z5 pH5.5–7.5

## Papaver somniferum ♀

OPIUM POPPY

The color range of this annual poppy is extensive – white, pink, mauve, scarlet and crimson, to nearly black – and there are both single and double selections. Very double ones ("peony-flowered") include 'Pink Chiffon' and 'White Cloud', while 'Crimson Feathers', 'Fluffy Ruffles' and 'Rose Feathers' all have cut petals. 'Danebrog' (syn. 'Danish Flag') is a single, with frilled scarlet petals marked at the base with a white blotch. All colors except salmon and scarlet blend with cool shades, and make attractive loose groups or drifts in a border. The glaucous foliage is striking, as are the seedpods. Opium poppy self-seeds readily.

**Perfect partners:** *Allium sphaerocephalon, Aquilegia vulgaris* (mixed), *Artemisia ludoviciana* 'Silver Queen', *Briza maxima,*

*Dianthus barbatus* p.424 **A**, *Helictotrichon sempervirens, Iris* 'Kent Pride', *Lavatera trimestris, Nigella damascena* 'Miss Jekyll', *Rosa glauca* ❏ p.215 **A**

**H: 24–48 in.** (60–120 cm) **S: 12 in.** (30 cm)
❀ **Early to late summer**

Z8–10 pH5–7.5

**Above left:** The scarlet flowers of this *Papaver somniferum* selection contrast with its glaucous pods and harmonize with *Lychnis chalcedonica* and *Rosa* Westerland.

**Above:** After flowering, the glaucous pods of opium poppy (*Papaver somniferum*) remain attractive, combined here with *Salvia sclarea* var. *turkestanica, Phlox paniculata* and alliums.

## *Pelargonium* 'Hederinum'

Also known as 'Balcon Rose' or 'Ville de Paris', this is the oldest Ivy-leaved pelargonium cultivar, dating back to 1786. Its numerous sports include 'Hederinum Variegatum' (syn. 'Duke of Edinburgh', 'Madame Margot'), with white variegation; red-flowered 'Roi des Balcons Impérial' (syn. 'Balcon Rouge'); and mauve-pink 'Roi des Balcons Lilas' (syn. 'Balcon Lilas'). These make spectacular cascades from hanging baskets and window boxes, combined with trailing plants of similar vigor such as black-eyed Susans, helichrysums, lophospermums, morning glories and plectranthus. Plants in the shorter-jointed Mini-cascade Series are also useful for containers, mixed with less energetic sprawlers such as ivies.

**Perfect partners:** *Helichrysum petiolare, Ipomoea tricolor* 'Mini Sky-blue', *Lobelia erinus* 'Sapphire', *Lophospermum erubescens, Plectranthus argentatus, Thunbergia alata*

**H: 12 in.** (30 cm) **S: 5 ft.** (1.5 m)
✿ **Late spring to mid-autumn**
◼️◻️◼️ ◊·◊◊ ◻️-◼️ ◼️ Z9 pH5–7.5

The long-jointed stems of pink-flowered *Pelargonium* 'Hederinum' and red *P.* 'Roi des Balcons Impérial' look glorious cascading from balconies and window boxes, lacking the congestion of more compact sorts.

## *Pelargonium* Multibloom Series 🏆

This is one of the most successful series of F1 hybrid pelargoniums that can be raised from seed. Tender perennials usually grown as half-hardy annuals, they are compact and flower very early, having up to 15 flowerheads at one time, each 3½–4 in. (8–10 cm) wide. The series is available as a mixture or in separate shades of red, scarlet, salmon, bright rose, pink, lavender, white and scarlet with a white eye. Plants have a high tolerance of cool, wet summers, and are excellent for carpet bedding and window boxes, although large, older specimens raised from cuttings are better for groups in borders.

Seed-raised pelargoniums are one of the most important advances in bedding plant breeding in recent decades. Because of their low and even habit, they are well suited to extended plantings, mixed with flowers of a contrasting shape such as *Verbena rigida*, which can be used above pelargoniums in carmine or contrasting bright or rich salmon. 'Cherie' has delicately shaded, pale salmon-pink flowers and a dark leaf zone. Very early flowering Orbit Series has large heads, about 5 in. (13 cm) across, in a range of 16 colors;

*Pelargonium* 'Multibloom Salmon' and *Zinnia* 'Dreamland Coral' make good companions, with flowers of harmonious colors but contrasting form on plants of the same height.

the Pulsar (syn. Pinto) Series has strongly zoned leaves and brilliantly colored heads in 11 shades that shine in massed bedding.

Varieties raised specifically for strong performance in cool, wet summers include the dark-leaved Video Series; the strongly branching, free-flowering Sensation Series, in a range of colors that includes blush-pink, coral-pink, rose, cherry-red and scarlet; and the rather spreading Breakaway Series, which has strong semi-trailing branches that make it a particularly good candidate for window boxes and hanging baskets.

**Perfect partners:** *Abutilon pictum* 'Thompsonii', *Canna* 'Lucifer', *Cordyline australis* Purpurea Group, *Heliotropium arborescens* 'Princess Marina', *Lobularia maritima* 'Snow Crystals', *Nicotiana langsdorffii*, *Petunia* Surfinia Blue, *Phormium* 'Bronze Baby', *Senecio cineraria* 'Silver Dust', *Verbena* Tapien Violet

**H & S: 12 in.** (30 cm)
✿ **Late spring to mid-autumn**
◼️◻️◼️ ◊·◊◊ ◻️-◼️ ◼️ Z9 pH5–7.5

## *Pelargonium* 'Paul Crampel'

This is regarded as the archetypal Victorian scarlet pelargonium. A tender perennial propagated only by cuttings, it is much less compact than seed-raised varieties and bears fewer flowerheads than modern kinds, although each contains hundreds of florets so that an individual head can remain in flower for several months. The intense scarlet color combines well with bronze, red, yellow-green, silver and gold-variegated foliage, harmonizes with salmon and hot colors such as golden yellow and orange, and makes good contrasts with lime green or yellow-green. Plants are tall enough to grade into a border effectively, and look impressive in large containers; they can also be trained on a cool conservatory wall, mixed with other climbers.

**Perfect partners:** *Abutilon* 'Savitzii', *Canna* 'Erebus', *Iresine herbstii* 'Aureoreticulata', *Lobelia richardsonii*, *Perilla frutescens* var. *crispa*, *Thunbergia alata*, *Zinnia elegans* 'Envy'

**H:** 18 in. (45 cm)  **S:** 15 in. (38 cm)
❁ Late spring to mid-autumn
◊-◊◊  □-■  Z9 pH5–7.5

This steeply banked planting at the foot of a sunny wall is based on rich scarlet and contrasting pale green flowers with dark foliage. It comprises *Pelargonium* 'Paul Crampel', *Dahlia* 'Bishop of Llandaff', *Nicotiana* 'Lime Green' and *Heuchera villosa* 'Palace Purple', with the castor-oil plant *Ricinus communis* 'Carmencita' behind and *Cordyline australis* providing a spiky focal point.

## *Penstemon* 'Andenken an Friedrich Hahn' ♆

Although one of the hardiest hybrid penstemons, this perennial sub-shrub is best treated as a bedding plant by raising it from cuttings taken in late summer and overwintered under glass. Also known as 'Garnet', it has flowers that are slightly to the blue side of primary red, borne in fairly loose spikes. It benefits from association with plants of more substance, such as grasses and phormiums, or may be grown in the second rank of a herbaceous or mixed border, behind smaller plants such as lavenders or catmints; it is also very appealing planted in front of old roses. Its color combines well with purple, harmonizes pleasantly with pink, and contrasts with lime green flowers and silver, yellow-green, and gold-variegated foliage.

**Perfect partners:** *Alstroemeria ligtu* hybrids p.232 B, *Dianthus* 'Doris', *Lavandula angustifolia* 'Hidcote', *Miscanthus sinensis* 'Variegatus', *Nicotiana* 'Lime Green', *Rosa* 'Geranium' p.203 A, *Verbena* 'Silver Anne' p.453 C

**H:** 24 in. (60 cm)  **S:** 18 in. (45 cm)
❁ Midsummer to mid-autumn
◊◊  ■  Z6 pH5–7.5

*Penstemon* 'Andenken an Friedrich Hahn' furnishes the base of the gold-variegated *Phormium tenax* 'Veitchianum', supplying rich color to complement the phormium's long, dramatic leaves.

## *Penstemon* 'Chester Scarlet' ♆

In spite of its name, the flowers of this cultivar are a rich cherry-red. It is a perennial sub-shrub, like 'Andenken an Friedrich Hahn' (above) but not as hardy, and it tends to produce rather taller plants. It belongs in the second rank of a border, although its higher, longer flower stems qualify it admirably for more steeply banked planting schemes. Its sumptuous color mixes well with purple, rose-pink, coral-pink and salmon, and with hot colors such as scarlet and vermilion. The red flowers form dramatic contrasts with lime green flowers and silver, yellow-green and gold-variegated foliage.

**Perfect partners:** *Pelargonium* 'Paul Crampel', *Perilla frutescens* var. *crispa*, *Phygelius* × *rectus* 'Pink Elf', *Verbena* Tapien Violet, *Zinnia elegans* 'Envy'

**H:** 26 in. (65 cm)  **S:** 16 in. (40 cm)
❁ Midsummer to mid-autumn
◊◊  ■  Z8 pH5–7.5

The relatively upright stems of *Penstemon* 'Chester Scarlet', furnished along most of their length with flowers, are ideal for a steeply banked border behind mound-forming plants, as here with lady's mantle (*Alchemilla mollis*) and contrasting silver-leaved *Artemisia ludoviciana*.

The sheer gorgeousness of the blooms of *Penstemon* 'King George V' lends it to richly colored planting schemes, as seen here with orange kniphofias and the dark-leaved *Actaea simplex* Atropurpurea Group.

## Penstemon 'King George V'

This eye-catching, sub-shrubby penstemon is one of the more tender, large-flowered × *gloxinioides* types, with individual florets that are large enough to create an impression of a fairly solid spike of flowers. Each floret also has a conspicuous white eye, giving the flowering plant a distinct sparkle. It is a showy cultivar, more so than either 'Chester Scarlet' or 'Andenken an Friedrich Hahn' (both facing page), and is well suited to use with hot colors, bronze or purple foliage and yellow-green or gold-variegated leaves. It fits comfortably into the second rank of a bed or border, combined with more exotic-looking plants such as cannas, cordylines, phormiums and dark-leaved dahlias.

**Perfect partners:** *Canna indica* 'Purpurea', *Cordyline australis* Purpurea Group, *Dahlia* 'Bishop of Llandaff', *Diascia rigescens*, *Phormium tenax* Purpureum Group

**H: 26 in.** (65 cm) **S: 18 in.** (45 cm)
✿ **Midsummer to mid-autumn**
◖◗ ◊◊ ▢ Z9 pH5–7.5

## Pericallis × hybrida
CINERARIA

Cinerarias are tender sub-shrubs, grown from cuttings or sown as biennials, in white, pink, crimson, blue or purple. Modern sorts such as Brilliant Group, Jester Series, and Star Wars Series are squat and difficult to combine well, while older clones and species generally have a looser habit, with grayish leaves and almost continuous flowers. Most common of these are 'Purple Picotee', often grown mistakenly as *P. heritieri*, with crimson discs and magenta-tipped white ray petals, and violet-blue 'Webberiana'. Both growing 16 in. (40 cm) tall, they literally shine in pots or at the front of a border in areas with warm summers. They combine well with silver.

**Perfect partners:** *Helichrysum petiolare*, *Heuchera villosa* 'Palace Purple', *Salvia farinacea* 'Victoria', *Senecio cineraria* 'Silver Dust'

**H: 6–18 in.** (15–45 cm) **S: 8–16 in.** (20–40 cm)
✿ **Midsummer to late autumn**
◖◗ ◊◊ ▢ Z9 pH5.5–7.5

From a sowing under glass in late winter to early spring, cinerarias can be used for midsummer to autumn display outdoors. Here, *Pericallis* 'Royalty Sky Blue' forms a striking contrast with the striped grass *Hakonechloa macra* 'Aureola'.

This is a sumptuous combination with *Perilla frutescens* var. *crispa* and *Salvia coccinea* 'Lady in Red' in midsummer. The perilla will grow taller as the season advances and will overtop the salvia, allowing it to be used as a formal accent or dot plant.

## Perilla frutescens var. crispa 🏆

A tender perennial usually grown as a half-hardy annual, this perilla (also known as var. *nankinensis*) is used in carpet bedding as a dot plant with a rich color. The frilliness of its leaves masks the form of the plant, and it is only at close range that their intricacy and iridescent metallic sheen can be appreciated. It is a good container plant, blending equally with hot and cool colors, and may also be used toward the front of a summer border. The purple shiso (var. *purpurascens*) has leaves that are not indented or curled, and can be used in a similar way, although not all selections have the same deep coloring and metallic quality as var. *crispa*.

**Perfect partners:** *Begonia semperflorens* Cocktail Series, *Dahlia* 'Bednall Beauty', *Pelargonium* Multibloom Series, *Salvia splendens* 'Vanguard', *Verbena* 'Kemerton'

**H: 40 in.** (1 m) **S: 12 in.** (30 cm)
✿ **(Midsummer to mid-autumn)**
◖◗ ◊◊ ▢ Z9 pH5.5–7.5

**Above:** In a scheme that would be equally effective in a hanging basket or window box, the soft lavender-blue *Petunia* (Frenzy Series) 'Frenzy Light Blue' is contrasted with sulfur-yellow *P.* 'Buttercream'. *Helichrysum petiolare* 'Limelight', which is able to drape itself gracefully over the edges of any container, adds a contrast of form.

**Left:** Petunias, lobelias and pelargoniums can be combined to provide cheerful color with a variety of floral form. In this window box, the shape of *Petunia* (Ice Series) 'Scarlet Ice' is emphasized by its white edging; it is joined by other petunias in white, pink and purple, *Pelargonium* 'Decora Rouge' and *Lobelia erinus* 'Sapphire'.

## *Petunia* seed-raised cultivars

Tender perennials usually grown as annuals, petunias have showy, saucer- or trumpet-shaped flowers in colors including pink, red, yellow, violet and white. Grandiflora petunias are sprawling plants with very wide, shallow flowers that are often vulnerable to rain damage. The blooms of Multiflora petunias are generally veined, and are smaller but more numerous than those of Grandifloras, as well as being more weather resistant. The many series of Multiflora cultivars include Carpet Series ♡, short, spreading plants in strong colors; Mirage Series ♡, with delicately veined blooms; and Primetime Series, in 24 colors, some with contrasting veins, picotee edges and star-shaped centers. Frenzy Series has one of the largest color ranges, including an exceptional soft yellow, 'Frenzy Buttercup'. It is good at the front of a border, where it mixes well with smaller agapanthus, glaucous fescues, and parsley.

With their flamboyant but barely weather-proof flowers, Grandiflora cultivars are best reserved for hanging baskets, containers and sunny sheltered corners. Celebrity Series is compact, with a wide range of bright shades as well as pastels; Picotee Series has ruffled, white-edged blooms; and Ice Series comprises five outstanding cultivars: 'Blue Ice' (ground color is deep purplish blue), 'Burgundy Ice', 'Rose Ice' (cherry-red ground), deep purple 'Velvet Ice' and 'Scarlet Ice' (white-edged flowers). With this coloring, 'Scarlet Ice' is effective even when used in an all-red scheme, with red or bronze foliage, pelargoniums, impatiens and small-flowered petunias.

**Perfect partners:** Mixed: *Helichrysum petiolare* 'Roundabout', *Perilla frutescens* var. *crispa*, *Senecio cineraria* 'Silver Dust'
Yellow: *Agapanthus* 'Lilliput', *Ageratum houstonianum* 'Old Gray' p.410 **B**, *Brachyscome iberidifolia*

**H: 4–16 in.** (10–40 cm) **S: 4 in.–4 ft.** (10 cm–1.2 m)
**Early summer to mid-autumn**
Z9–10 pH5–7.5

## *Plectranthus argentatus* 🏆

This tender sub-shrub, usually grown as an annual from cuttings, is valued most for its silvery gray-green, silky foliage, although it also has purplish stems and pale lilac flowers emerging from purple calyces. It is useful for a white garden, for beds and borders and for large containers, and by the end of the season can make an imposing plant, especially if grown in relative isolation as a dot plant. It is good with silver foliage plants of contrasting form, including senecios and glaucous or white-variegated grasses, and with purple- or red-leaved plants such as perillas, red orach, sedums, coleus, ornamental cabbages and black, red or purple kale. Although effective with cool colors, it is perhaps most imposing combined with China asters, salvias such as *S. farinacea* cultivars, *Cosmos bipinnatus* cultivars and stooled or seedling eucalyptus. Other good partners include taller verbenas, heliotropes, brachyscomes and eryngiums.

**Perfect partners:** *Callistephus chinensis* Milady Series, *Fuchsia* 'Thalia', *Helictotrichon sempervirens*, *Senecio cineraria* 'Silver Dust', *Solenostemon* 'Crimson Ruffles'

**H & S: 40 in.** (1 m) **Midsummer to mid-autumn**
**Z10 pH5–7.5**

In a scheme that combines varied leaf textures and shapes as well as different flower colors and forms, the silvers, grays, and steely lavenders of *Plectranthus argentatus*, *Anaphalis margaritacea* var. *yedoensis*, and *Aster* 'Little Carlow' are enlivened by the brilliant, black-centered, yellow daisy-like flowerheads of *Rudbeckia fulgida* var. *deamii*, with coral *Agastache* 'Firebird' and grasses in front.

A

B

Just two plants of exotic appearance, *Ricinus communis* 'Carmencita' and the Japanese banana (*Musa basjoo*), contrasting in leaf color and shape, are sufficient to suggest an almost tropical environment.

## *Ricinus communis* 'Carmencita' 🏆

This castor-oil plant is a tender shrub, usually grown as an annual from cuttings, with red-flushed palmate leaves and insignificant flowers that later produce bright red seedpods. Although useful as a dot plant or focal point in the middle of a border, set forward of other plants of its own height, it is grown principally for the bold impact of its foliage in tropical bedding schemes. Here, it can be go with other fine foliage plants such as bananas, palms, cannas, melianthus, wigandias, fatsias, tetrapanax and large brugmansias. Further back in the border, it can be echoed by a larger castor-oil plant such as *R.c.* var. *zanzibarensis*, at 8 ft. (2.5 m), with green white-veined leaves, or *R.c.* 'Red Spire', also 8 ft. (2.5 m), with bronze-flushed leaves and red stems; 'Impala', at 4 ft. (1.2 m), with reddish purple leaves, is good for planting in front. Elsewhere it is effective with dark plants such as purple smoke bush and dark-flowered sunflowers.

**Perfect partners:** *Brugmansia* × *candida* 'Grand Marnier', *Dahlia* 'Bishop of Llandaff', *Melianthus major*, *Nicotiana* 'Lime Green', *Pelargonium* 'Paul Crampel' p.442 **A**

**H: 6 ft.** (1.8 m) **S: 3 ft.** (90 cm)
**Midsummer to early autumn**
**Z10 pH5.5–7.5**

## *Rudbeckia hirta*

These daisies may be treated as biennials from summer sowings planted out in autumn, or as annuals from a late winter sowing under glass. 'Toto' ♀, one of the most compact cultivars at 10 in. (25 cm), has single golden-yellow blooms with a chocolate brown eye; 'Goldilocks', 16 in. (40 cm), is golden yellow with a double row of petals; and 'Kelvedon Glory' (syn. 'Sonora'), also 16 in. (40 cm), is yellow with an almost black disk and yellow-veined black bases to the petals. Taller kinds include golden yellow 'Irish Eyes', 28 in.

(70 cm), with a green eye; 'Indian Summer' ♀, 40 in. (1 m), has single rich gold flowers with a deep brown eye. They all go well with bronze, purple, yellow-green and gold-variegated foliage, while pure yellow cultivars make good contrasts with pure blue. Early-flowering Charm chrysanthemums, yellow or cream argyranthemums, yellow-variegated grasses and coleus are all superlative companions.

**Perfect partners:** *Berberis thunbergii* f. *atropurpurea, Cortaderia selloana* 'Aureolineata', *Solenostemon* 'Lemon Dash', *Tagetes patula* 'Striped Marvel'

**Above left:** Rich golden-yellow *Rudbeckia hirta* 'Marmalade', 20 in. (50 cm) high but here flopping forward to the front of the border, mingles and contrasts with the violet-blue variant of annual clary (*Salvia viridis*).

**Above:** *Rudbeckia hirta* Rustic Dwarfs Group, 18 in. (45 cm) tall, supplies richness and varied flower size to its fellow daisies, *Bidens ferulifolia* and *Argyranthemum* 'Jamaica Primrose'.

**H: 12–36 in. (30–90 cm) S: 12–18 in. (30–45 cm)**
✿ **Midsummer to mid-autumn**
 Z3 pH5.5–7.5

## *Salpiglossis* Royale Series

Salpiglossis flowers deserve to be planted in containers or toward the front of a border, where their deeply embossed texture and intricate veining and lacing can be enjoyed at close range. They are annuals or short-lived perennials, and most resent cool, wet summers, but the Royale Series has been raised specifically to tolerate such climates. Although Royale Series mixed ♀ has shades that do not flatter each other, good combinations can be created from individual colors, such as 'Royale Orange Bicolor' and 'Royale Yellow'. 'Kew Blue' is sumptuous, but with deep purplish blue flowers.

**Perfect partners:** *Aeonium* 'Zwartkop', *Cosmos atrosanguineus, Dahlia* 'Bishop of Llandaff', *Perilla frutescens* var. *crispa, Plectranthus argentatus, Salvia farinacea* 'Victoria'

The rich mahogany, black-veined flowers of *Salpiglossis* 'Royale Chocolate' have a perfect background provided by the dusky foliage of *Heuchera* 'Stormy Seas', with its patchwork of pewter netted with bronzed green veins and its clouds of tiny whitish blooms. The piquant bright yellow-green, red-splashed leaves of the coleus *Solenostemon* 'Pineapplette' lift the combination.

**H: 12–18 in. (30–45 cm) S: 9 in. (23 cm)**
✿ **Midsummer to early autumn**
 Z9 pH5.5–7.5

## *Salvia coccinea* 'Lady in Red' ♛

This shrubby tender sage, usually grown as an annual, is daintier and more elegant in apperance than the familiar *S. splendens* varieties that are used widely in summer bedding schemes. Its scarlet flower spikes have an airy, open arrangement that makes the most impact when plants are grown in fairly generous groups, placed to be seen from a distance. Its brilliant coloring mixes well with hot colors or warm shades such as coral, peach and rich salmon, and with bronze or red foliage. Dramatic contrasts can be made with lime green and yellow-green. 'Coral Nymph' is a mid- and pale salmon bicolor and 'Snow Nymph' is pure white.

**Perfect partners:** *Lavatera trimestris* p.432 **B**, *Nicotiana* 'Lime Green', *Pelargonium* 'Queen of Denmark', *Perilla frutescens* var. *crispa* p.443 **C**, *Salvia splendens* p.448 **C**

**H: 16 in.** (40 cm) **S: 10 in.** (25 cm)
❀ **Midsummer to mid-autumn**
Z10 pH5–7.5

In a sumptuous scheme for early autumn, the scarlet spikes of *Salvia coccinea* 'Lady in Red' clash gently with the purple blooms of interplanted *Verbena rigida* and, behind, skillfully staked with hidden brushwood, lilac *Aster sedifolius*.

The vertical racemes of the sage *Salvia farinacea* 'Victoria' emphasize the swirling lines of this semi-formal bedding, backed by *Ageratum houstonianum* 'Blue Horizon', interplanted with pale lilac *Verbena rigida* 'Polaris', and overtopped by a cloud of purple *V. bonariensis*. In the foreground, the gently discordant kingfisher-blue *Felicia amoena*, with its contrasting yellow centres, saves the scheme from blandness.

## Salvia farinacea

MEALY SAGE

This slightly tender perennial is usually grown from seed as an annual. 'Victoria' ♀, once the best lavender-blue cultivar, now lacks uniformity, making it more useful as a border plant than for bedding. Other, slightly shorter cultivars, 14 in. (35 cm) high, include 'Blue Victory' ♀ and 'Rhea', both in lavender-blue, and 'White Victory' ♀ and 'Cirrus' in white. 'Strata', 18 in. (45 cm), bears lavender-blue flowers emerging from white calyces. All are good in large groups, seen at a distance, with their vertical spikes contrasted with flowers of a different shape, such as airy clouds or horizontal plates. The blue kinds go well with mauve, lilac, purple and silver.

**Perfect partners:** *Argyranthemum* 'Jamaica Primrose', *Brachyscome iberidifolia*, *Ipomoea tricolor* 'Mini Sky-blue' p.431 **A**, *Papaver rhoeas* Cedric Morris Group, *Pelargonium* 'Galilee', *Petunia* 'Frenzy Buttercup'

**H: 18 in. (45 cm)  S: 12 in. (30 cm)**
※ **Midsummer to mid-autumn**
◌◌ ◌◌ ◻-◼ ◼  Z10  pH5–7.5

In this hot-colored border, *Salvia splendens* forms a vibrant foreground in front of *S. coccinea* 'Lady in Red', the lax racemes of *Alonsoa warscewiczii*, the daisy *Helenium* 'Moerheim Beauty', African marigolds (*Tagetes erecta*), dahlias and the arching spikes of *Crocosmia* 'Lucifer'.

## Salvia sclarea 'Vatican White'

The biennial clary, *S. sclarea*, is a variable species, with mauve to lavender-blue flowers (more rarely, white) and, within the flower spike, bracts that are flushed pink or lilac. 'Vatican White' has pure white florets, borne on upright flowering stems like densely branched candelabra; these create soft vertical accents, while the green calyces and flower stems produce an overall impression of pale greenish white rather than pure white, making plants highly effective in contrasts with yellow and blue. It is excellent in white gardens or for weaving through an early summer border, and looks attractive with old Shrub roses or flowers of contrasting form, such as achilleas.

**Perfect partners:** *Achillea* 'Coronation Gold', *Campanula persicifolia* 'Telham Beauty', *Delphinium* 'Alice Artindale', *Hemerocallis* 'Corky', *Iris* 'Curlew', *Papaver orientale* 'Black and White', *Rosa* 'Tuscany Superb'

**H: 36 in. (90 cm)  S: 18 in. (45 cm)**
※ **Early to midsummer**
◌◌ ◌◌ ◻-◼ ◼  Z6  pH5–7.5

The white candelabra of *Salvia sclarea* 'Vatican White' form a backdrop for the bright blooms of an early yellow kniphofia and the contrasting blue flowers of viper's bugloss (*Echium vulgare*) in early summer.

## Salvia splendens

This sage, the archetypal scarlet bedding plant, is a tender perennial usually grown as a half-hardy annual. Its fine cultivars, include 'Red Riches', 'Red River' and 'Scarlet King', 11 in. (28 cm) high, and 'Vanguard' ♀, 10 in. (25 cm), all suitable for carpet bedding, window boxes, and the front of borders. Vista Series, 11 in. (28 cm), and Salsa Series, 10 in. (25 cm), also include lilac, purple, salmon and white. Scarlet cultivars associate well with bold, red or bronze foliage or contrasting texture, such as grasses and phormiums. Late, elegant, cuttings-raised 'Van-Houttei' ♀, 5 ft. (1.5 m), has nodding panicles of scarlet flowers and maroon calyces, good for hot schemes or contrasts with lime green.

**Perfect partners:** *Abutilon* 'Savitzii', *Briza maxima*, *Canna* 'Black Knight', *Cosmos bipinnatus* 'Sonata White' p.417 **C**, *Senecio cineraria* 'Silver Dust'

**H: 8–60 in. (20–150 cm)  S: 8–18 in. (20–45 cm)**
※ **Midsummer to mid-autumn**
◌◌ ◌◌ ◻-◼ ◼  Z10  pH5–7.5

## *Scaevola aemula*

A tender perennial usually grown as an annual, this fan-flower is an immensely useful and vigorous sprawling plant for containers and hanging baskets, or the front of a border, weaving among neighbors of comparable vigor; it also looks impressive cascading from a dwarf or retaining wall. It combines well with silver foliage and white-variegated plectranthus or Ivy-leaved pelargoniums, and with flowers in pink, mauve, purple, blue, magenta or crimson; pale sulfur-yellow makes a good contrast. Blue kinds include 'Saphira' (Blaue Fächer), 'Petite Wonder', 'New Wonder', 'Blue Fandango', 'Blaue Fächer' and 'Sunfan'. 'White Champ' and 'Moon White' are white, and 'Burgundi Gemini' is purple.

**Perfect partners:** *Diascia* 'Lilac Belle', *Leucophyta brownii*, *Lobelia erinus* Cascade Series, *Lysimachia congestiflora* 'Outback Sunset', *Osteospermum* 'White Pim', *Pelargonium* Rose Evka, *Petunia* Million Bells Lemon, *Plectranthus forsteri* 'Marginatus', *Torenia* Pink Moon

**H: 8–12 in.** (20–30 cm) **S: 12–24 in.** (30–60 cm)
**Early summer to mid-autumn**
**Z10 pH5.5–7.5**

In this cool-colored carpet of plants, a compact, rich lavender cultivar of the fanflower *Scaevola aemula* is combined with magenta busy Lizzies (*Impatiens walleriana* 'Accent Violet') and a short *Ageratum houstonianum* cultivar, leavened by the silvery trails of *Helichrysum petiolare*.

A

B

In late spring, the yellow flowers and yellow-green bracts of perfoliate alexanders (*Smyrnium perfoliatum*) mingle with the emerging bronze-tinged fronds of the sensitive fern (*Onoclea sensibilis*) to create an intricate and pleasing pattern. The alexanders turn green after flowering and are removed, leaving just one or two plants to shed seed for the following year's display.

## *Smyrnium perfoliatum*

PERFOLIATE ALEXANDERS

This upright biennial can be used to great effect to echo the bright yellow-green of many euphorbias. It may also be woven among other plants, leaving only a small gap after dying back. Its greenish yellow umbels are particularly effective with contrasting blue plants such as brunneras, larger forget-me-nots, pentaglottis or Tibetan poppies, and in harmonies with pale sulfur-yellow, apple-green or cream flowers, and with yellow-green spring foliage. Dramatic combinations can be made with hot colors such as orange and scarlet, and with bronze leaves. Crown imperials and columbines in contrasting colors are excellent partners. Plants can be raised from fresh seed or left to self-seed.

**Perfect partners:** *Aquilegia* 'Hensol Harebell', *Brunnera macrophylla*, *Euphorbia amygdaloides* var. *robbiae*, *Pentaglottis sempervirens*, *Tulipa* 'Orange Wonder' p.400 **A**

**H: 4 ft.** (1.2 m) **S: 18 in.** (45 cm)
**Late spring to early summer**
**Z6 pH5.5–7.5**

## *Solenostemon*

COLEUS

Coleus are popular for their colorful foliage, varying from yellow-green through orange to scarlet and purple; in many the leaves are attractively margined, veined, ruffled, or divided. Tender sub-shrubs grown from cuttings or as half-hardy annuals from seed, they are shade-tolerant plants, useful for bedding or for the front of a border. Here they go well with French marigolds, scarlet or soft yellow petunias, or contrasting foliage such as cannas and grasses. Among the best cultivars are 'Crimson Ruffles' 🏆, in beetroot-red with a frilled, faint green edge; 'Glory of Luxembourg' 🏆, velvety red edged in yellow; and gold and maroon 'Pineapple Beauty' 🏆.

**Perfect partners:** *Canna* 'Erebus', *Impatiens walleriana* 'Impact Scarlet', *Nerine* 'Zeal Giant' p.386 **B**, *Petunia* 'Frenzy Buttercup', *Salpiglossis* Royale Series p.446 **C**

**H & S: 12–24 in.** (30–60 cm)
**(Midsummer to mid-autumn)**
**Z10 pH5.5–7.5**

C

Coleus (*Solenostemon*) mixed seedlings form a rich tapestry at the front of a narrow border. Feathery *Eupatorium capillifolium* 'Elegant Feather' acts as a foil and separates the coleus visually from the ivy (*Hedera helix* 'Buttercup') behind.

A

The prettily striped flowers of *Tagetes patula* 'Dwarf Harlequin' form an excellent edging to this predominantly orange-flowered border. Its companions include the larger blooms of the dwarf triploid Afro-French marigold *Tagetes* 'Seven Star Red', the bronze-green foliage of *Haloragis erecta* 'Wellington Bronze' and the mixed nasturtiums *Tropaeolum majus* Alaska Series.

## *Tagetes patula*
FRENCH MARIGOLD

This half-hardy annual come in a range of colors from lemon-yellow to orange and mahogany-red; there are striped variants and picotees with blotched petals, and single, double, and anemone-centered cultivars. Dwarf cultivars are useful as carpet bedding or at the front of a border. Medium-sized varieties include 'Spanish Brocade' (double mahogany-red flowers with a gold edge) and 'Naughty Marietta' (single gold flowers with a maroon blotch); both are 12 in. (30 cm) high. Their colors blend with hot shades, bronze or purple foliage, and yellow-green flowers and foliage, while their small flowers and fine texture suit contrasts with grasses.

**Perfect partners:** *Aira elegantissima*, *Canna indica* 'Purpurea', *Nicotiana* 'Lime Green', *Solenostemon* 'Glory of Luxembourg', *Zinnia elegans* 'Envy'

**H: 6–20 in.** (15–50 cm) **S: 6–12 in.** (15–30 cm)
✿ Early summer to mid-autumn
◖◗◗ ▣-▨ Z10 pH5.5–7.5

## *Tagetes patula* 'Striped Marvel'

This half-hardy annual derived from the Victorian 'Legion of Honour' grows high enough to be graded into tall planting in beds and borders. Its flowers blend especially well with orange, vermilion, scarlet or mahogany, with bronze or yellow-variegated foliage, and with yellow-green foliage and flowers. The foliage of cannas, coleus and bolder grasses make effective contrasts. Among other taller French marigolds, at 24 in. (60 cm) high, are Favourite Series and Mischief Series, the latter including single-colored cultivars such as 'Mischief Gold' ♀, 'Mischief Mahogany' ♀, and 'Mischief Orange/Red' ♀. These are all excellent plants for larger containers.

**Perfect partners:** *Argyranthemum* 'Jamaica Primrose', *Rudbeckia hirta* Rustic Dwarfs Group, *Salvia splendens* 'Vanguard', *Tithonia rotundifolia* 'Sundance', *Zinnia* 'Chippendale'

**H: 18 in.** (45 cm) **S: 12 in.** (30 cm)
✿ Early summer to mid-autumn
◖◗◗ ▣-▨ Z10 pH5.5–7.5

B

The relatively tall, elegant French marigold *Tagetes patula* 'Striped Marvel' is a charming plant for close-range inspection and is effective in the second rank of a border. Here, it is seen behind the rich rusty red 'Cinnabar', whose dwarf habit makes it good for use as an edging plant.

C

## *Tithonia rotundifolia*
MEXICAN SUNFLOWER

Cultivars of the Mexican sunflower, a slightly tender annual, range in height from 1–6 ft. (30 cm to 1.8 m). Perhaps the most useful are the kinds from 3 ft. (90 cm) high, with intense orange flowers borne stiffly above handsome foliage. These include 'Goldfinger' and the orange-vermilion 'Sundance', both 3 ft. (90 cm) high, and bright reddish orange 'Torch', at 5 ft. (1.5 m). 'Sunset', 'Aztec Gold', and 'Yellow Torch' are all yellow-flowered cultivars also growing to 5 ft. (1.5 m). 'Fiesta del Sol' is a dwarf cultivar, at 12 in. (30 cm), in rich vivid orange. All Mexican sunflowers

*Tithonia rotundifolia* 'Goldfinger' is a valuable and imposing plant for the second or third rank of a bed or border. Here, it associates easily with the taller reddish brown sunflower *Helianthus* 'Velvet Queen', gently clashing mauve *Lavatera thuringiaca*, and osteospermums.

combine well with hot colors and bronze foliage, and contrast effectively with yellow-green foliage and flowers. They can be used with sunflowers, kniphofias, dahlias and the taller, spikier salvias. They may also be combined with climbers such as *Ipomoea lobata* growing on other supports nearby.

**Perfect partners:** *Crocosmia* 'Late Lucifer', *Haloragis erecta* 'Wellington Bronze', *Kniphofia uvaria* 'Nobilis', *Lobelia × speciosa* 'Fan Scharlach', *Nicotiana* 'Lime Green'

**H: 1–6 ft.** (30 cm–1.8 m) **S: 1–2 ft.** (30–60 cm)
✿ Late summer to mid-autumn
◖◗◗ ▣-▨ Z10 pH5.5–7.5

*Tolpis barbata*, here flopping gracefully across the gravel in which it has seeded itself, might seem thin-textured and insubstantial if grown alone, but it can mingle well with the foliage or flowers of another plant – as here with the golden hop (*Humulus lupulus* 'Aureus').

## *Tolpis barbata*

The flowers of this hardy annual daisy are bright lemon-yellow, set off by a dark central disk. They look very effective planted with cream, gold, orange or mahogany, and with coleus, perillas and similar bronze-leaved plants to echo the chocolate-brown of the flower centre. Plants relate well to gold- or cream-variegated foliage, and also to the yellow-green foliage of a *Helichrysum petiolare* cultivar such as 'Limelight'. Good contrasts include blue flowers and blue-green foliage. For best results, tolpis should be grown in a sunny position towards the front of a border. As a native of Mediterranean regions, it thrives in well-drained sites such as gravel beds and paths.

**Perfect partners:** *Cerinthe major* 'Purpurascens', *Felicia amelloides* (variegated), *Molinia caerulea* 'Variegata', *Perilla frutescens* var. *crispa*, *Pilosella aurantiaca*, *Solenostemon scutellarioides* Wizard Series

**H: 20 in.** (50 cm)  **S: 12 in.** (30 cm)
✼ **Early to late summer**
  ◊◊  ☐-■  **Z7  pH5.5–7.5**

## *Tropaeolum majus*
## Alaska Series ♔

This bushy, hardy nasturtium is usually found in a mixture of yellow, orange, mahogany, scarlet, peach, coral and salmon color forms that are rarely available singly. The leaf variegation is striking at close range, but from a distance it may camouflage the distinctive leaf shape. It tends to sprawl informally over the sides of pots or edge of a border. Plants combine well with yellow-green *Helichrysum petiolare* cultivars and coleus, *Nicotiana* 'Lime Green' and some of the larger French marigolds. For greatest impact it is best with bold, contrasting foliage such as cannas, bronze castor-oil plants or cordylines. To flower prolifically it needs full sun and soil that is neither too rich nor too damp.

**Perfect partners:** *Calendula officinalis* p.415 **A**, *Cordyline australis* Purpurea Group, *Solenostemon* 'Lemon Dash', *Tagetes patula* 'Dwarf Harlequin' p.450 **A**

**H: 12 in.** (30 cm)  **S: 18 in.** (45 cm)
✼ **Midsummer to mid-autumn**
◊◊  ☐-■  **Z10  pH5–7.5**

The striking variegated foliage of the nasturtium *Tropaeolum majus* Alaska Series here provides a unifying theme with the boldly striped leaves of *Iris japonica* 'Variegata'. The warm-colored nasturtium flowers are borne well above the leaves.

Blue *Tweedia caerulea* harmonizes perfectly with this verdigrised laundry copper. Large plants of the tweedia are used in their second season after being raised from spring-sown seed, producing vigorous stems that can mingle with other flowers (here, the profuse daisies of *Argyranthemum* 'Petite Pink'), trail forward, or be trained to the wall behind.

## *Tweedia caerulea* ♔

This twining sub-shrub flowers best in areas with warm summers. However, it can also be grown from seed as an annual, producing in its first year flowers of an extraordinary shade of blue, slightly greener than primary blue, but not quite turquoise. The oldest flowers assume lavender tints before they fade. Its height suits container planting, but it can look charming scrambling over low-growing shrubs, perhaps with a dwarf morning glory or another fairly short twining plant of contrasting floral form. This tweedia is very effective with felicias and other deeper blue flowers, and with pink, white, yellow-green or lime green flowers, such as nicotianas, and glaucous, silver or yellow-green foliage. It also makes an arresting contrast with pale lemon-yellow. Marguerites and pelargoniums make good companions in containers.

**Perfect partners:** *Argyranthemum* 'Jamaica Primrose', *Felicia bergeriana*, *Ipomoea tricolor* 'Mini Sky-blue', *Nicotiana* 'Lime Green', *Pelargonium* Rose Evka, *Thunbergia alata*

**H & S: 36 in.** (90 cm)
✼ **Midsummer to early autumn**
  ◊◊  ☐-■  **Z9  pH5.5–7.5**

## *Verbena bonariensis* ♔

This upright, wiry herbaceous perennial, with heads of tiny lavender florets emerging from reddish purple calyces, is often grown as an annual in areas where it is not hardy. Its slender habit and tall height make it a useful plant for weaving through other plants in a border or gravel garden, and its flower color blends agreeably with other cool colors, yet is strong enough to contrast with hot colors such as yellow or orange and with acid yellow-green. Plants that combine effectively include repeat-flowering Shrub roses, taller bush roses, taller nicotianas, tithonias, annual sunflowers, cosmos, seedling eucalyptus and larkspurs. Taller plants such as Japanese anemones, echinops, daylilies, crocosmias and *Ceanothus* × *delileanus* and *C.* × *pallidus* cultivars are also successful partners.

Companions with similar small, subdivided inflorescences and close color harmonics are best avoided, since they can be visually confusing and flatter neither plant.

**Perfect partners:** *Cleome hassleriana* p.416 **B**, *Dahlia* 'David Howard' p.420 **A**, *Echinacea purpurea* 'Magnus' p.261 **C**, *Patrinia scabiosifolia* p.319 **C**, *Phlox paniculata* 'Orange Perfection', *Salvia farinacea* 'Victoria' p.448 **A**

**H: 6 ft. (1.8 m) S: 18 in. (45 cm)**
❋ Midsummer to mid-autumn
⬛⬜ ◌◌ ⬜-⬛ Z9 pH5.5–7.5

The thin, upright habit of lavender-colored and reddish purple *Verbena bonariensis* allows it to mingle thoroughly with its neighboring plants. Here, the verbena contrasts gently with a rich red Small Waterlily Group dahlia (*D.* 'Grenadier') and a single pale peach Hybrid Tea rose (*R.* 'Mrs. Oakley Fisher').

In this bed of fairly low, gently undulating planting, the magenta blooms of *Verbena* 'Kemerton' perfectly match the vertical inflorescences of purple-leaved lobelia, leavened by silvery *Plecostachys serpyllifolia* (foreground) and *Artemisia arborescens* (behind), as well as *Osteospermum* 'White Pim'.

## *Verbena* 'Kemerton'

A good performer in damp climates and areas with cool summers, this sub-shrub, grown as an annual from cuttings, is a useful, sprawling plant for the front of a border and for pots and hanging baskets. Its rich burgundy flowers go well with cool colors and purple foliage and contrast effectively with silver foliage, orange, soft yellow or yellow-green. Suitable partners include annuals such as mauve or purple alyssums and impatiens, perennials like shorter orange and soft yellow crocosmias and shorter *Aster amellus* cultivars, and later bulbs including earlier colchicums, late alliums and purple-leaved eucomis. It may also be interplanted with cordylines and other plants of definite and contrasting form.

**Perfect partners:** *Agapanthus* 'Lilliput', *Crocosmia* × *crocosmiiflora* 'Lady Hamilton', *Helichrysum petiolare* 'Roundabout' p.430 **A**, *Lobularia maritima* 'Oriental Night'

**H: 14 in. (35 cm) S: 24 in. (60 cm)**
❋ Midsummer to early autumn

⬛⬜ ◌◌ ⬜-⬛ Z9 pH5.5–7.5

## *Verbena* 'Lawrence Johnston' ♔

Unlike many verbenas, this lax, tender perennial, usually grown from overwintered cuttings, is relatively weather-resistant and tolerant of cool, damp summers. The scarlet flowers blend well with hot colors and red or bronze foliage – coleus, salvias, zinnias, scarlet pelargoniums and red curly kales, for example – and contrast memorably with yellow-green or variegated foliage, as well as with yellow-green flowers. Especially good partners include bidens, coreopsis, California poppies and gazanias. It also suits the combinations suggested for *V.* 'Kemerton' (facing page), together with annuals such as ageratums, antirrhinums, lobelias, clarkias, lavateras, petunias, brachyscomes and orange French marigolds, as well as perennials such as penstemons and shorter cranesbills.

**Perfect partners:** *Begonia semperflorens* Cocktail Series, *Brassica oleracea* (Acephala Group) 'Redbor', *Diascia barberae* 'Blackthorn Apricot', *Hakonechloa macra* 'Alboaurea'

**H: 12 in. (30 cm)  S: 24 in. (60 cm)**
❀ **Midsummer to early autumn**
◌◌ ◌◌ ◻-◼ ◼ **Z9  pH5.5–7.5**

The scarlet *Verbena* 'Lawrence Johnston', an ideal carpeting plant for the front of beds and borders, is seen here with the purplish pink flowerheads of *Sedum telephium* subsp. *maximum* 'Atropurpureum' and the crimson-leaved tender perennial beefsteak plant (*Iresine herbstii* 'Brilliantissima').

The fragrant *Verbena rigida* is used here to produce bold swathes of color in a relatively low planting across a broad bed. The bright purple color of its flowers is juxtaposed with the vibrant scarlet of a dwarf cultivar of *Salvia splendens* to create a dazzling effect.

## *Verbena rigida* ♔

Although strictly perennial, this upright verbena (syn. *V. venosa*) is usually grown as an annual. Its purple flowers are carried on wiry stems, the central ones borne stiffly upright while the outer ones force their way diagonally through neighboring plants, so that by late summer its companions are decorated with a haze of purple flowerheads. This phenomenon, which Victorian gardeners called the "shot silk effect," was commonly used with pelargoniums in bright scarlet, but it is also effective with other color contrasts such as soft yellow, yellow-green or orange. *V. rigida* goes well with cool colors, purple or red-leaved plants and glaucous grasses.

**Perfect partners:** *Festuca glauca*, *Pelargonium* 'Orangesonne', *Perilla frutescens* var. *crispa*, *Petunia* 'Frenzy Buttercup', *Salvia coccinea* 'Lady in Red' p.447 **A**

**H: 20 in. (50 cm)  S: 16 in. (40 cm)**
❀ **Midsummer to mid-autumn**
◌◌ ◌◌ ◻-◼ ◼ **Z9  pH5.5–7.5**

## *Verbena* 'Silver Anne' ♔

This tender perennial, usually grown as an annual, makes an upright plant at first, later sprawling outward, and has strongly fragrant flowers that open carmine-pink and become paler with age. It is useful for weaving among other plants, especially in pots around sitting areas, and also at the front of a border, where it can sprawl onto the path. Although not really strong enough to be used for contrasts, its color works well with purple or silver foliage and cool-colored flowers – purple-leaved sedums and heucheras, silver plants such as helichrysums and shorter artemisias, senecios, centaureas, pinks and glaucous grasses such as fescues. Most of the combinations for *V.* 'Kemerton' (facing page) are equally suitable for 'Silver Anne'.

**Perfect partners:** *Helichrysum petiolare*, *Salvia farinacea* 'Strata', *Sedum telephium* 'Arthur Branch', *Senecio cineraria* 'Silver Dust', *Silene coeli-rosa* Angel Series

**H: 12 in. (30 cm)  S: 24 in. (60 cm)**
❀ **Midsummer to mid-autumn**
◌◌ ◌◌ ◻-◼ ◼ **Z9  pH5.5–7.5**

Harmonious colors and contrasting floral form are seen in this striking combination of *Verbena* 'Silver Anne' and *Penstemon* 'Andenken an Friedrich Hahn'.

## *Verbena* 'Sissinghurst' ♟

This tender sub-shrubby perennial, usually grown as an annual in cooler climates, has deep carmine flowers, and a sprawling habit that suits it to containers or the front of a border. It is particularly effective threading through fairly short, silver-leaved sub-shrubs. This verbena goes well with silver, purple or yellow-green foliage, and pink, lime green, yellow-green or deep crimson flowers. Free-flowering, clear white 'Sissinghurst White' is good with the deep pink form. Several recent series combine long flowering, frilly foliage, and horizontal growth, suiting them for the same uses as 'Sissinghurst'. Among them are Tapien Series, 8 in. (20 cm) high and to 18 in. (45 cm) wide, which includes ivory-white, rich violet, salmon-pink and clear pink cultivars, and Temari Series, of similar size, in rich blue, coral-pink, scarlet, violet-purple and white.

**Perfect partners:** *Antirrhinum majus* 'Black Prince', *Leucophyta brownii*, *Osteospermum* 'Pink Whirls', *Salvia officinalis* 'Purpurascens', *Tigridia pavonia* p.389 **C**

**H: 6–8 in.** (15–20 cm)  **S: 36 in.** (90 cm)
❁ **Early summer to early autumn**
⬛ ◊◊ ⬜-⬛ ⬛ **Z9  pH5.5–7.5**

**Right:** Deep carmine *Verbena* 'Sissinghurst' and clear pink *Diascia vigilis*, seen here with the tubular-flowered *Penstemon* 'Evelyn', are both sprawling plants that can interweave and mix with each other and their neighbors to make delightful harmonies in beds, borders, or containers.

**Below:** Threading through the stems of the compact, gray-green leaved sub-shrub *Argyranthemum* 'Vancouver' are *Verbena* 'Sissinghurst', *Diascia vigilis* and lavender *Nemesia caerulea*, all of which are useful plants that mingle together easily, providing an abundant display of flowers.

## *Viola tricolor*

HEARTSEASE, JOHNNY JUMP UP

Best grown as a biennial for late spring and early summer display, *V. tricolor* is a charming perennial with very variable flowers, usually in a combination of lavender-blue, yellow, and white. From this, several more distinct cultivars have been developed. They include *V.* 'Bowles Black', nearly black with a tiny yellow eye; 'Helen Mount' (syn. 'Johnny Jump Up'), in lavender and yellow; 'Prince Henry', in rich purple; and 'Prince John', in golden yellow. Hot, dry summers curtail flowering, but where summers are cool and moist, plants will flower until midsummer and, if then cut back, again in autumn.

**Perfect partners:** *Aquilegia vulgaris* (mixed), *Erysimum* 'Bowles Mauve', *Muscari armeniacum*, *Rosa elegantula* 'Persetosa', *Tulipa* 'Queen of Night', *T.* 'Spring Green'

H: **3–5 in.** (8–13 cm) S: **4–6 in.** (10–15 cm)
✿ **Mid-spring to mid-autumn**

Z4 pH5.5–7.5

In a charming cottage garden mix that has no pretensions to color scheming, compact *Viola tricolor* 'Helen Mount', the pink *Dianthus deltoides* 'Leuchtfunk', and the low-growing cransbill *Geranium* (Cinereum Group) 'Ballerina' fill a narrow border at the foot of a garden wall.

## *Zinnia elegans* cultivars

Zinnias are showy half-hardy annuals that perform best in countries with warm or hot summers. They can be difficult to grow well in regions with cool summers, so in these areas they should be sown no earlier than mid-spring for planting out in late spring or early summer. Sumptuous double or dahlia-flowered kinds such as 'Dasher', 'Parasol' and 'Peppermint Stick' are popular, and good single-flowered cultivars include easy-to-grow 'Chippendale', which is bushy and has deep brownish red flowers with a yellow margin. All suit the front ranks of a border, where they combine with hot colors and bronze foliage, or with yellow-green foliage and flowers. Good plants for contrast include bronze sedges, coleus and purple beets.

**Perfect partners:** *Beta vulgaris* 'Bull's Blood', *Carex comans* (bronze), *Nicotiana* 'Lime Green', *Rudbeckia hirta* 'Marmalade', *Solenostemon scutellarioides* Wizard Series

H: **12–36 in.** (30–90 cm) S: **6–16 in.** (15–40 cm)
✿ **Midsummer to mid-autumn**

Z10 pH5.5–7.5

*Zinnia* 'Chippendale' furnishes the front of a border, backed by *Z.* Giant Double Mixed, the dogwood *Cornus alba* 'Elegantissima' and the shrubby *Bupleurum fruticosum*.

The intricate blooms of *Zinnia* Persian Carpet Group here provide richness to a warm-colored combination with the single-flowered Signet marigold *Tagetes tenuifolia* 'Lulu' and button-flowered *Lonas annua*.

## *Zinnia* Persian Carpet Group

This compact half-hardy annual is suitable for the front of a border or for growing behind a short carpeting plant. The mixture includes a range of colors from deep scarlet to darkest mahogany, with the petals tipped in yellow or cream. The colors are well suited to mixing with cream, rich peach and the richest blood-red or mahogany flowers. It makes good combinations with lime green nicotianas and red-leaved beets, and with the contrasting foliage of coleus, perillas, dark-leaved dahlias and grasses or sedges. Other compact cultivars for similar use include the graceful Star Series, 14 in. (35 cm), with loose and informal single blooms in clear yellows and white; and the Profusion Series, 12 in. (30 cm), with small, shapely, white, orange and cherry-red single blooms that have a fresh, clean appearance all season.

**Perfect partners:** *Carex buchananii*, *Chrysanthemum* Charm Group, *Dahlia* 'Bednall Beauty', *Perilla frutescens* var. *crispa*, *Rudbeckia hirta* Rustic Dwarfs Group

H: **16 in.** (40 cm) S: **8 in.** (20 cm)
✿ **Midsummer to mid-autumn**

Z10 pH5.5–7.5

# COMMON PLANT NAMES

The following list comprises the common plant names used in this book.

Aconite – *Aconitum*
African marigold – *Tagetes erecta*
Algerian iris – *Iris unguicularis*
Alpine forget-me-not – *Myosotis alpestris*
Añu – *Tropaeolum tuberosum*
Annual clary – *Salvia viridis*
Annual sunflower – *Helianthus annuus*
Apothecary's rose – *Rosa gallica*
  var. *officinalis*
Apple mint – *Mentha suaveolens*
Armenian cranesbill – *Geranium psilostemon*
Arum lily – *Zantedeschia aethiopica*
Atamasco lily – *Zephyranthes atamasca*
Azalea – part of *Rhododendron*
Baby blue eyes – *Nemophila menziesii*
Baby's breath – *Gypsophila paniculata*
Banana – *Musa*
Beech – *Fagus*
Beefsteak plant – *Iresine herbstii*
Beet – *Beta*
Bellflower – *Campanula*
Bergamot – *Monarda*
Birch – *Betula*
Black mondo grass – *Ophiopogon planiscapus*
  'Nigrescens'
Black-eyed Susan – *Thunbergia alata*
Bleeding heart – *Dicentra spectabilis*
Blue fescue – *Festuca glauca*
Blue lace flower – *Trachymene coerulea*
Blue oat grass – *Helictotrichon sempervirens*
Blue wheatgrass – *Elymus hispidus*
Bluebell – *Hyacinthoides*
Bog arum – *Lysichiton americanus*
Boston ivy – *Parthenocissus tricuspidata*
Bowles' golden grass – *Milium effusum*
  'Aureum'
Bowles' golden sedge – *Carex elata* 'Aurea'
Box – *Buxus*
Broad-leaved bellflower – *Campanula*
  *latifolia*
Bronze fennel – *Foeniculum vulgare*
  'Purpureum'
Broom – *Cytisus, Genista*
Buddleia – *Buddleja*
Busy Lizzie – *Impatiens walleriana*
Butterfly bush – *Buddleja davidii*
Butterfly weed – *Asclepias tuberosa*
Cabbage – *Brassica oleracea*
  Capitata Group
California poppy – *Eschscholzia californica*
Camomile – *Anthemis*
Campion – *Lychnis, Silene*
Canadian columbine – *Aquilegia canadensis*
Canary creeper – *Tropaeolum peregrinum*
Candytuft – *Iberis*
Canterbury bells – *Campanula medium*
Cardoon – *Cynara cardunculus*
Carnation – *Dianthus*
Carrot – *Daucus carota*
Castor-oil plant – *Ricinus communis*
Catmint – *Nepeta*
Celandine – *Ranunculus ficaria*

Chaparral prickly pear cactus – *Opuntia*
  *oricola*
Cherry – *Prunus*
Cherry plum – *Prunus cerasifera*
Chilean bellflower – *Lapageria rosea*
Chilean glory flower – *Eccremocarpus scaber*
Chilean potato tree – *Solanum crispum*
China aster – *Callistephus*
Chinese lantern – *Physalis alkekengi*
Chinese pink – *Dianthus chinensis*
Chinese wisteria – *Wisteria sinensis*
Chives – *Allium schoenoprasum*
Chocolate cosmos – *Cosmos atrosanguineus*
Cider gum – *Eucalyptus gunnii*
Cineraria – *Pericallis × hybrida*
Cinquefoil – *Potentilla*
Claret vine – *Vitis vinifera* 'Purpurea'
Clary – *Salvia sclarea*
Coleus – *Solenostemon*
Columbine – *Aquilegia*
Comfrey – *Symphytum*
Common box – *Buxus sempervirens*
Common buddleia – *Buddleja davidii*
Common bugle – *Ajuga reptans*
Common camellia – *Camellia japonica*
Common columbine – *Aquilegia vulgaris*
Common daisy – *Bellis perennis*
Common elder – *Sambucus nigra*
Common evening primrose – *Oenothera*
  *biennis*
Common fennel – *Foeniculum vulgare*
Common foxglove – *Digitalis purpurea*
Common holly – *Ilex aquifolium*
Common honeysuckle – *Lonicera*
  *periclymenum*
Common ivy – *Hedera helix*
Common lilac – *Syringa vulgaris*
Common mallow – *Malva sylvestris*
Common montbretia – *Crocosmia*
  × *crocosmiiflora*
Common poppy – *Papaver rhoeas*
Common primrose – *Primula vulgaris*
Common rosemary – *Rosmarinus officinalis*
Common sage – *Salvia officinalis*
Common snowdrop – *Galanthus nivalis*
Common sunflower – *Helianthus annuus*
Common wallflower – *Erysimum cheiri*
Common yew – *Taxus baccata*
Corn cockle – *Agrostemma*
Corn marigold – *Xanthophthalmum segetum*
Cornflower – *Centaurea cyanus*
Cotton thistle – *Onopordum nervosum*
Cow parsley – *Anthriscus sylvestris*
Cowslip – *Primula veris*
Crab apple – *Malus*
Cranesbill – *Geranium*
Crimson glory vine – *Vitis coignetiae*
Crown imperial – *Fritillaria imperialis*
Curry plant – *Helichrysum italicum*
Cypress – *Chamaecyparis*
Cypress spurge – *Euphorbia cyparissias*
Daffodil – Large-trumpeted *Narcissus*
  (Divisions 1 and 2)
Daisy – *Bellis*
Darley Dale heath – *Erica × darleyensis*

Dill – *Anethum graveolens*
Daylily – *Hemerocallis*
Deadnettle – *Lamium*
Dickson's golden elm – *Ulmus minor*
  'Dicksonii'
Dog's-tooth violet – *Erythronium dens-canis*
Dogwood – *Cornus*
Double yellow Banksian rose – *Rosa banksiae*
  'Lutea'
Dutch yellow crocus – *Crocus × luteus*
  'Golden Yellow'
Dutchman's breeches – *Dicentra spectabilis*
Dwarf box – *Buxus sempervirens*
  'Suffruticosa'
Eglantine rose – *Rosa eglanteria*
Elder – *Sambucus*
Elm – *Ulmus*
Eryngo – *Eryngium*
European spindle – *Euonymus europaeus*
Evening primrose – *Oenothera*
False acacia – *Robinia pseudoacacia*
False spikenard – *Smilacina racemosa*
Fan-flower – *Scaevola aemula*
Farrer's threepenny bit rose – *Rosa elegantula*
  'Persetosa'
Feather reed grass – *Calamagrostis*
  × *acutiflora*
Fennel – *Foeniculum, Ferula*
Fescue – *Festuca*
Feverfew – *Tanacetum parthenium*
Five-spot – *Nemophila maculata*
Flaky juniper – *Juniperus squamata*
Flame flower – *Tropaeolum speciosum*
Flax – *Linum. L. narbonense*
Fleabane – *Erigeron*
Florist's chrysanthemum – *Chrysanthemum*
Flowering currant – *Ribes sanguineum*
Flowering dogwood – *Cornus florida*
Flowering quince – *Chaenomeles*
Foamflower – *Tiarella cordifolia*
Forget-me-not – *Myosotis*
Foxglove – *Digitalis*
French lavender – *Lavandula stoechas*
French marigold – *Tagetes patula*
Fringe cups – *Tellima grandiflora*
Fritillary – *Fritillaria*
Gardener's garters – *Phalaris arundinacea*
  var. *picta*
Geranium – *Geranium*
Giant feather grass – *Stipa gigantea*
Giant fennel – *Ferula communis*
Giant reed – *Arundo donax*
Giant scabious – *Cephalaria gigantea*
Giant wake robin – *Trillium chloropetalum*
Ginger lily – *Hedychium*
Globe thistle – *Echinops*
Glory rose – *Rosa* 'Gloire de Dijon'
Goat's beard – *Aruncus dioicus*
Goat's rue – *Galega*
Gold-banded pampas grass – *Cortaderia*
  *selloana* 'Aureolineata'
Golden creeping Jenny – *Lysimachia*
  *nummularia* 'Aurea'
Golden feverfew – *Tanacetum parthenium*
  'Aureum'

Golden hop – *Humulus lupulus* 'Aureus'
Golden male fern – *Dryopteris affinis*
Golden marjoram – *Origanum vulgare*
  'Aureum'
Golden meadowsweet – *Filipendula ulmaria*
  'Aurea'
Golden mock orange – *Philadelphus coronarius*
  'Aureus'
Golden privet – *Ligustrum ovalifolium*
  'Aureum'
Golden rain – *Laburnum*
Golden willow – *Salix alba* subsp. *vitellina*
Goldenrod – *Solidago*
Granny's bonnet – *Aquilegia vulgaris*
  var. *flore-pleno*
Grape hyacinth – *Muscari*
Greater celandine – *Chelidonium majus*
Greater quaking grass – *Briza maxima*
Guelder rose – *Viburnum opulus*
Hart's tongue fern – *Asplenium scolopendrium*
Hawthorn – *Crataegus*
Hazel – *Corylus*
Heartsease – *Viola tricolor*
Heath – *Erica*
Heather – *Calluna vulgaris*
Heliotrope – *Heliotropium*
Hellebore – *Helleborus*
Holly – *Ilex*
Hollyhock – *Alcea*
Honesty – *Lunaria*
Honey locust – *Gleditsia triacanthos*
Honeysuckle – *Lonicera*
Hoop-petticoat daffodil – *Narcissus*
  *bulbocodium*
Hop – *Humulus lupulus*
Horned poppy – *Glaucium*
Horned violet – *Viola cornuta*
House lime – *Sparrmannia africana*
Hyacinth – *Hyacinthus*
Hybrid crack willow – *Salix × rubens*
Hyssop – *Hyssopus, H. officinalis*
Irish yew – *Taxus baccata* 'Fastigiata'
Italian honeysuckle – *Lonicera caprifolium*
Ivy – *Hedera*
Jack-in-the-pulpit – *Arisaema triphyllum*
Jacob's ladder – *Polemonium caeruleum*
Japanese anemone – *Anemone × hybrida*
Japanese banana – *Musa basjoo*
Japanese flowering cherry – *Prunus*
  Sato-zakura Group
Japanese irises – *Iris ensata, I. laevigata*
  and hybrids
Japanese maples – *Acer japonicum,*
  *Acer* Section *Palmata*
Japanese shield fern – *Dryopteris erythrosora*
Jasmine – *Jasminum*
Jerusalem cross – *Lychnis chalcedonica*
Jerusalem sage – *Phlomis fruticosa, Pulmonaria*
  *saccharata*
Johnny jump up – *Viola tricolor*
June berry – *Amelanchier*
Juniper – *Juniperus*
Kale – *Brassica oleracea* Acephala Group
Kingcup – *Caltha palustris*
Lady fern – *Athyrium filix-femina*

Lady tulip – *Tulipa clusiana*
Lady's mantle – *Alchemilla mollis*
Lady's smock – *Cardamine pratensis*
Lamb's ears – *Stachys byzantina*
Larkspur – *Consolida*
Lavender – *Lavandula*
Lavender cotton – *Santolina chamaecyparissus*
Lawson cypress – *Chamaecyparis lawsoniana*
Lent lily – *Narcissus pseudonarcissus*
Lenten rose – *Helleborus × hybridus*
Leopard lily – *Lilium pardalinum*
Lesser celandine – *Ranunculus ficaria*
Lilac – *Syringa*
Lily – *Lilium*
Lily-of-the-valley – *Convallaria majalis*
Lilyturf – *Liriope, Ophiogon*
Lime – *Tilia*
Ling – *Calluna vulgaris*
London pride – *Saxifraga × urbium*
Loosestrife – *Lysimachia, Lythrum*
Love-in-a-mist – *Nigella*
Lungwort – *Pulmonaria*
Lupin – *Lupinus*
Lyme grass – *Leymus arenarius*
Madonna lily – *Lilium candidum*
Maiden grass – *Miscanthus sinensis*
  'Gracillimus'
Maidenhair fern – *Adiantum*
Mallow – *Lavatera, Malva*
Maple – *Acer*
Marguerite – *Argyranthemum*
Marigold – *Calendula*
Marjoram – *Origanum*
Marsh marigold – *Caltha palustris*
Meadow buttercup – *Ranunculus acris*
Meadow clary – *Salvia pratensis*
Meadow cranesbill – *Geranium pratense*
Meadow phlox – *Phlox maculata*
Meadow rue – *Thalictrum*
Meadow saffron – *Colchicum autumnale*
Mealy sage – *Salvia farinacea*
Mexican orange blossom – *Choisya ternata*
Mexican sunflower – *Tithonia rotundifolia*
Mezereon – *Daphne mezereum*
Michaelmas daisy – *Aster novi-belgii*
Miss Willmott's ghost – *Eryngium giganteum*
Mock orange – *Philadephus*
Molly the witch – *Paeonia mlokosewitschii*
Monkshood – *Aconitum napellus*
Montbretia – *Crocosmia × crocosmiiflora*
Morning glory – *Ipomoea tricolor*
Mountain knapweed – *Centaurea montana*
Mountain pine – *Pinus mugo*
Mourning widow cranesbill – *Geranium
  phaeum*
Mrs. Robb's bonnet – *Euphorbia amygdaloides
  var. robbiae*
Musk mallow – *Malva moschata*
Myrtle spurge – *Euphorbia myrsinites*
Nasturtium – *Tropaeolum majus*
New York aster – *Aster novi-belgii*
New Zealand cabbage palm – *Cordyline
  australis*
New Zealand flax – *Phormium*
Oak – *Quercus*

Oak fern – *Gymnocarpium dryopteris*
Onion – *Allium*
Opium poppy – *Papaver somniferum*
Oregon grape – *Mahonia aquifolium*
Oriental poppy – *Papaver orientale*
Ornamental cherry – *Prunus*
Ornamental kale – *Brassica oleracea
  Acephala Group*
Ornamental quince – *Chaenomeles*
Orpine – *Sedum telephium*
Ostrich-plume fern – *Matteuccia struthiopteris*
Oxeye daisy – *Leucanthemum vulgare*
Oxlip – *Primula elatior*
Pampas grass – *Cortaderia selloana*
Pansy – *Viola*
Paperbark maple – *Acer griseum*
Papyrus – *Cyperus papyrus*
Pasque flower – *Pulsatilla vulgaris*
Peach-leaved bellflower – *Campanula
  persicifolia*
Peacock flower – *Tigridia pavonia*
Pear – *Pyrus*
Pencil cedar – *Juniperus virginiana*
Peony – *Paeonia*
Perennial candytuft – *Iberis sempervirens*
Perfoliate alexanders – *Smyrnium perfoliatum*
Periwinkle – *Vinca*
Persian everlasting pea – *Lathyrus rotundifolius*
Persian ivy – *Hedera colchica*
Peruvian lily – *Alstroemeria*
Pheasant's-eye narcissus – *Narcissus poeticus
  var. recurvus*
Pimpernel – *Anagallis*
Pine – *Pinus*
Pineapple broom – *Cytisus battandieri*
Pineapple flower – *Eucomis bicolor*
Pink – *Dianthus*
Pink purslane – *Claytonia sibirica*
Plantain lily – *Hosta*
Plume poppy – *Macleaya*
Poached egg plant – *Limnanthes douglasii*
Poplar – *Populus*
Poppy – *Papaver*
Poppy anemone – *Anemone pavonina*
Porcupine grass – *Miscanthus sinensis* 'Strictus'
Pot marigold – *Calendula officinalis*
Primrose – *Primula vulgaris*
Privet – *Ligustrum*
Prostrate speedwell – *Veronica prostrata*
Purple coneflower – *Echinacea purpurea*
Purple filbert – *Corylus maxima* 'Purpurea'
Purple loosestrife – *Lythrum salicaria*
Purple sage – *Salvia officinalis* 'Purpurascens'
Purple shiso – *Perilla frutescens var.
  purpurascens*
Purple sloe – *Prunus spinosa* 'Purpurea'
Purple toadflax – *Linaria purpurea*
Queen Anne's double daffodil – *Narcissus*
  'Eystettensis'
Purslane – *Claytonia sibirica*
Red ginger lily – *Hedychium coccineum*
Red hot poker – *Kniphofia*
Red orach – *Atriplex hortensis var. rubra*
Red valerian – *Centranthus ruber*
Red horned poppy – *Glaucium corniculatum*

Rhubarb – *Rheum*
Rock cress – *Arabis*
Rock rose – *Cistus*
Rosa Mundi – *Rosa gallica* 'Versicolor'
Rose – *Rosa*
Rose campion – *Lychnis coronaria*
Rosemary – *Rosmarinus, R. officinalis*
Roseroot – *Rhodiola rosea*
Round-headed leek – *Allium sphaerocephalon*
Rowan – *Sorbus aucuparia*
Rue – *Ruta*
Sacred bamboo – *Nandina domestica*
Sage – *Salvia*
Saxifrage – *Saxifraga*
Scarlet ginger lily – *Hedychium coccineum*
Scotch rose – *Rosa pimpinellifolia*
Sea buckthorn – *Hippophae rhamnoides*
Sea holly – *Eryngium maritimum*
Sea kale – *Crambe maritima*
Sea lavender – *Limonium, L. latifolium*
Sedge – *Carex*
Sensitive fern – *Onoclea sensibilis*
Shasta daisy – *Leucanthemum × superbum*
Shield fern – *Polystichum*
Shirley poppy – *Papaver rhoeas
  Shirley Group*
Shrubby cinquefoil – *Potentilla fruticosa*
Shuttlecock fern – *Matteuccia struthiopteris*
Siberian iris – *Iris sibirica,
  I. Sibirica Group*
Siberian squill – *Scilla siberica*
Siberian wallflower – *Erysimum × allionii*
Silver willow – *Salix alba var. sericea*
Silverweed – *Potentilla anserina*
Smoke bush – *Cotinus coggygria*
Snake's head fritillary – *Fritillaria meleagris*
Snapdragon – *Antirrhinum majus*
Sneezeweed – *Helenium*
Snowball tree – *Viburnum opulus* 'Roseum'
Snowdrop – *Galanthus*
Snow gum – *Eucalyptus pauciflora subsp.
  niphophila*
Snow-in-summer – *Cerastium tomentosum*
Snowy mespilus – *Amelanchier*
Soft shield fern – *Polystichum setiferum*
Solomon's seal – *Polygonatum*
Spanish bluebell – *Hyacinthoides hispanica*
Spanish broom – *Spartium junceum*
Spanish dagger – *Yucca gloriosa*
Spanish flag – *Ipomoea lobata*
Spanish gorse – *Genista hispanica*
Speedwell – *Veronica*
Spider flower – *Cleome hassleriana*
Spindle – *Euonymus*
Spotted deadnettle – *Lamium maculatum*
Spruce – *Picea*
Squirrel tail grass – *Hordeum jubatum*
Squirting cucumber – *Ecballium elaterium*
Stinking gladwyn – *Iris foetidissima*
Stinking hellebore – *Helleborus foetidus*
Straw foxglove – *Digitalis lutea*
Sumac – *Rhus*
Summer snowflake – *Leucojum aestivum*
Sun rose – *Helianthemum*
Swan river daisy – *Brachyscome iberidifolia*

Sweet alyssum – *Lobularia maritima*
Sweet pea – *Lathyrus odoratus*
Sweet rocket – *Hesperis matronalis*
Sweet William – *Dianthus barbatus*
Tamarisk – *Tamarix*
Teasel – *Dipsacus*
Thrift – *Armeria*
Tibetan blue poppy – *Meconopsis betonicifolia,
  M. grandis*
Tiger lily – *Lilium lancifolium*
Toadflax – *Linaria*
Toetoe grass – *Cortaderia richardii*
Tree lupin – *Lupinus arboreus*
Tree of heaven – *Ailanthus altissima*
Tree poppy – *Romneya*
Trumpet vine – *Campsis radicans*
Tufted hair-grass – *Deschampsia cespitosa*
Tulip – *Tulipa*
Variegated bulbous oat grass – *Arrhenatherum
  elatius subsp. bulbosum* 'Variegatum'
Variegated biennial honesty – *Lunaria annua*
  'Variegata'
Variegated purple moor grass – *Molinia
  caerulea* 'Variegata'
Variegated yellow flag – *Iris pseudacorus*
  'Variegata'
Vine – *Vitis*
Violet – *Viola*
Viper's bugloss – *Echium vulgare*
Virginia bluebell – *Mertensia virginica*
Virginia creeper – *Parthenocissus quinquefolia*
Wallflower – *Erysimum*
Warminster broom – *Cytisus × praecox*
  'Warminster'
Weeping Colorado spruce – *Picea pungens
  Pendula Group*
Weeping silver pear – *Pyrus salicifolia*
  'Pendula'
Welsh poppy – *Meconopsis cambrica*
White wake robin – *Trillium grandiflorum*
Widow cranesbill – *Geranium phaeum*
Wild strawberry – *Fragaria vesca*
Willow – *Salix*
Willow gentian – *Gentiana asclepiadea*
Winter aconite – *Eranthis hyemalis*
Winter heath – *Erica carnea*
Winter jasmine – *Jasminum nudiflorum*
Witch hazel – *Hamamelis*
Wood anemone – *Anemone nemorosa*
Wood cranesbill – *Geranium sylvaticum*
Wood forget-me-not – *Myosotis sylvatica*
Wood spurge – *Euphorbia amygdaloides*
Woodbine – *Lonicera periclymenum*
Woodrush – *Luzula*
Wormwood – *Artemisia*
Yarrow – *Achillea*
Yellow archangel – *Lamium galeobdolon*
Yellow asphodel – *Asphodeline lutea*
Yellow camomile – *Anthemis tinctoria*
Yellow foxglove – *Digitalis grandiflora*
Yellow skunk cabbage – *Lysichiton americanus*
Yellow horned poppy – *Glaucium flavum*
Yew – *Taxus*
Zephyr lily – *Zephyranthes*

# INDEX

All plants featured in this book are fully indexed below. Other cultivars referred to may not be listed by name, but are indexed by page number. Page numbers in **bold** indicate a main plant entry. Page numbers in *italic* indicate pictures.

## PHOTOGRAPHIC ACKNOWLEDGMENTS

All photographs have been taken by Andrew Lawson, with the exception of the following:
**Jacket** front, clockwise from top left: Gap Photos (Mark Bolton), Photolibrary Group, Andrew Lawson, Andrew Lawson, Andrew Lawson, Gap Photos (Richard Bloom); back, (top to bottom): Andrew Lawson, Jonathan Buckley, Andrew Lawson, Jonathan Buckley, Gap Photos (Clive Nichols/Chenies Manor, Buckinghamshire), John Fielding; spine, Andrew Lawson
**Alamy Photo** John Glover 32-3; **Adrian Bloom** 143br, 257br, 270bl, 282ar; **Jonathan Buckley** 104b, 238, 266a, 271br, 291r, 313b, 319b, 326a, 327br, 336b, 341, 357a & br, 383bl, 392r, 418b, 421br, 445bl, 449br; **Eric Crichton** 183b, 284bl, 378a; **John Fielding** 119al, 197a, 229l, 236b, 249br, 253b, 262b, 276b, 291b, 293, 320ar, 321l, 366r, 368a, 376bl, 378br, 380a, 386ar, 404al, 413br, 428al & r, 430ar, planting design John Fielding 84al, 88a, 95a, 96l & r, 97ar, 100b, 102b, 107b, 120al & r, 134a, 147al & r, 154b, 162br, 172a, 173b, 174b, 175al, 178al, 186, 190b, 207al, 218, 223, 226bl, 228b, 230b, 233b, 243ar, 2480ar, 259bl, 263bl, 267a, 281al, 285b, 287l, 288, 289al, 298a, 300a, 301br, 308, 315br, 317br, 322al & r, 329b, 337b, 344, 354ar, 355b, 357bl, 358al & r, 360b, 366r, 367b, 369al & r, 373r, 377r, 382l, 383ar, 385, 386b, 392l, 393a, 413br, 426b, 430b, 446b, 450b, Blackthorn Nursery 325al, The Garden House 263a, Hadspen Gardens 213ar, 328b, 366bl, B & H Hiley 268bl, Mr & Mrs Phillips 255bl, planting Graham Rice 171b, 410b, 431, 437a, 450a, 451al, RHS Rosemoor 124ar, 138bl, RHS Wisley 83b, 236a, 253a, 424br, 444r; **GAP Photos** photo Richard Bloom 15, 16, 38b, 39, Mark Bolton 48l, 54, Elke Borkowski 29, Jonathan Buckley/design John Massey/Ashwood Nurseries 43, /design Christopher Lloyd 50, /design Sarah Raven 57r, /design Carol & Malcolm Skinner 59, Claire Davies 53, John Glover 40, 41, 47, 58, John Glover/design Piet Oudolf 55, /design Penelope Hobhouse 60, 61, /design Tom Stuart-Smith 68, Jerry Harpur 38a, 45l, 56b, 65a, 66l, /design Ulf Nordfjell 45r, /design Steve Martino 69l, Marcus Harpur/Beth Chatto Garden, Essex 66r, Neil Holmes/design Piet Oudolf 62, Dianna Jazwinski 51, Andrea Jones 36-7, /design Christopher Bradley-Hole 69r, S & O Mathews 56a, Zara Napier 31, Clive Nichols/Chenies Manor 22, /Parsonage, Ombersley, Worcs 48r, /Pettifers, Oxfordshire 57l, /Marchants Harvey Plants 63, Howard Rice/Jonathan Buckland 28, J S Sira 44a, Friedrich Strauss 42, Graham Srong 18, Jo

Whitworth/design Nana Habet 65b, Rob Whitworth/Beth Chatto Gardens, Essex 44b, 46; **John Glover** 12, 17r, 35r, 52, 193al, 211b, 335ar; **Harpur Garden Library** photos Jerry Harpur 224, Marcus Harpur 318bl; **W Anthony Lord** 112b, 120b, 125ar, 127ar, 128l, 134bl & r, 139b, 141ar, 142a, 144r, 146a, 150, 153r, 156br, 157a & b, 158l & br, 160a, 164a & br, 166l, 167a, 171al, 178ar, 179l, 180–181, 182, 185, 198b, 202b, 203b, 206l, 216, 222, 226a, 228ar, 230ar, 232b, 233al, 237b, 239al, 241al, 242al & b, 243al & b, 246a, 247r, 248al & b, 249a & bl, 256b, 257bl, 259a, 264a, b & bl, 265bl, 266bl & r, 267br, 268br, 269ar, 272a & b, 273a & br, 275b, 276ar, 277br, 278al & b, 282al, 283l, 290, 292bl, 296b, 297b, 300 bl & r, 302bl & r, 303ar, 304a & bl, 305b, 307al & r, 308ar, 310ar, 311al & b, 314ar & b, 316a, 318ar, 319ar, 320b, 321r, 330a & b, 331br, 332al, 335b, 336l, 338l, 345, 346, 347, 355ar, 362l & r, 363b, 365br, 367a, 376r, 386al, 387b, 397b, 398al, 400a, bl & r, 402, 403a, 405a, 406–7, 409, 411al, 412ar, b, & l, 413bl, 414b, 415r, 416r, 418a, 420bl, 422br, 423a, 425bl, 426al, 427a, 428b, 429a, 433l & r, 434al & r, 437bl & r, 439bl & r, 440al & r, 441l & r, 444l, 446ar, 447, 448al & b, 449a & bl, 450ar, 451ar, 453a & br, 455ar & b; **S & O Mathews** 97b, 183, 202al, 405br; **Mise au Point** photo Arnaud Descat 75; **Clive Nichols Garden Pictures** 131, 244al, designer Helen Dillon 225, Mrs Glaisher, Kent 190ar, Hadspen Gardens, Somerset 215a, Lakemount, Cork, Eire 74, The Priory, Kemerton 420br, Wollerton Old Hall, Shropshire 199, 257a, designer Elisabeth Woodhouse 296a; **Jerry Pavia** 140bl, 239b, 404bl; **Photolibrary Group** photos David Askham 209, 219ar, Lynne Brotchie 318al, 205al, Christi Carter 202ar, 427bl, 432b, Ron Evans 370, John Glover 91ar, 168b, 258ar, 289b, Sunniva Harte 227ar, 339a, Mayer/LeScanff 30, Clive Nichols 184, Joanne Pavia 271bl, Howard Rice 24–25, 190al, 254r, J S Sira 13r, 188a, 235a, 430al, Juliette Wade 442br, Mel Watson 425ar, Didier Willery 427br; **Photos Horticultural** 83ar, 113l & r, 168a, 188b, 192b, 193b, 219b, 258b, 281b; **Howard Rice** 84ar & b, 93al, 99br, 101ar, 102al, 103r, 110al & b, 118, 119b, 122bl, 125b, 129r, 137ar, 142b, 176b, 207ar, 220–1, 246bl, 279, 283r, 298l, 304ar, 313al, 316br, 317a, 331a, 333al & b, 338ar, 376bl, 383al, 384al & r, 389al; **Harry Smith Collection** 73b, 87b, 100ar, 353br.
Additional credits for photographs taken by Andrew Lawson: Ash Tree Cottage, Kilmington, Wilts 195b, 332ar, Barnsley House, Glos 159b, Bourton House, Glos 372, 412a, Denmans Garden 438b, Hadspen Gardens, Somerset 195ar, 401b, planting Wendy Lauderdale 375, Sticky Wicket, Dorchester, Dorset 337ar.

## PUBLISHER'S ACKNOWLEDGMENTS

The publishers would like to thank the following for their specialist advice and contributions to the text: Richard Bisgrove, Andi Clevely, Geoff Stebbins, and Alan Toogood.